ARISTOTLE'S FIRST PRINCIPLES

ARISTOTLE'S FIRST PRINCIPLES

Terence Irwin

CLARENDON PRESS · OXFORD

*This book has been printed digitally and produced in a standard specification
in order to ensure its continuing availability*

OXFORD
UNIVERSITY PRESS

Great Clarendon Street, Oxford OX2 6DP

Oxford University Press is a department of the University of Oxford.
It furthers the University's objective of excellence in research, scholarship,
and education by publishing worldwide in

Oxford New York

Auckland Bangkok Buenos Aires Cape Town Chennai
Dar es Salaam Delhi Hong Kong Istanbul Karachi Kolkata
Kuala Lumpur Madrid Melbourne Mexico City Mumbai Nairobi
São Paulo Shanghai Singapore Taipei Tokyo Toronto

with an associated company in Berlin

Oxford is a registered trade mark of Oxford University Press
in the UK and in certain other countries

Published in the United States
by Oxford University Press Inc., New York

© Terence Irwin 1988

The moral rights of the author have been asserted
Database right Oxford University Press (maker)

Reprinted 2002

ISBN 0-19-824290-5

TO GAIL

PREFACE

On 5 October 1971, I wrote a short paper on *Metaphysics* 1004b25–6, for a tutorial with G. E. L. Owen at Harvard. Since then I have intermittently pursued some lines of inquiry connected with that passage; the current result of them is this book. The first chapter gives a survey of its contents, and some idea of the main argument. I try to explore some connexions between different areas of Aristotle's philosophy, and to suggest how issues and doctrines in one area may affect his views in another. Whether or not the main thesis of this book is found convincing, I hope it will seem profitable to examine some of the connexions I discuss, and to see how they affect our views about the coherence and plausibility of Aristotle's doctrines.

While I would like to have formed original and convincing views on all the questions I discuss, I cannot claim to have done this. On many points I rely on views that other people have made quite familiar (though hardly standard, given the extent of healthy disagreement in the study of Aristotle). On the other hand, though I cover more topics than are usually covered in a single book on Aristotle, this book is not a general survey; it is quite selective, and it does not attempt to give a balanced impression of Aristotle as a whole. Still, I hope I have provided enough detail to give the uninitiated reader some idea of the main questions, and of some of the main approaches to them, and also to give both the less advanced and the more advanced student some idea of the reasons for my conclusions. While this is not an introductory book, I hope it will be accessible to reasonably persistent readers who have not read much about Aristotle, but are willing to read Aristotle fairly closely; in the main text I try not to presuppose familiarity with the present state of scholarly and philosophical discussion.

The notes discuss some points of detail, and indicate some of my views on issues that have been discussed by other writers on Aristotle. They come after the main text, on the assumption that many readers will find it easier to read the main text before tackling the issues that are raised in the notes. The general excellence of the 'secondary literature' on Aristotle, extending from the Greek commentators to the present, is unrivalled (as far as I know) by what has been written on any other philosopher; and therefore I would like to have done more justice to it than I have. The reader should not anticipate the systematic and judicious selection that would certainly be desirable. I especially regret the brevity of my discussion of some complex issues and of the views that have been expressed about them. It will be even clearer to many readers that my account of Aristotle's views raises many large philosophical questions that I have not pursued very far, and that the positions I do take often leave many objections unanswered.

I am pleased to be able to acknowledge the award of fellowships from the Society for the Humanities at Cornell University, the National Endowment for the Humanities, and the American Council of Learned Societies. The generosity of the Warden and Fellows of All Souls College (in 1982–3), and of the President and Fellows of Magdalen College (in 1987), allowed me to spend a year and a half in Oxford under highly favourable conditions. It was both beneficial and pleasant to discuss Aristotle with Oxford Aristotelians, especially Michael Woods, Christopher Taylor, and David Charles.

I have already mentioned Gwil Owen; and readers who know his work (especially Owen [1965]) will see its influence throughout this book. Ever since I began to think about Aristotle I have benefited from John Ackrill's candid and challenging papers and lectures, and from his incisive and encouraging criticisms. I have had the good fortune to teach in the humane, friendly, and stimulating environment of Cornell philosophy, and hence to learn from other people who have been here, especially from David Brink, Eric Wefald, Alan Sidelle, Sydney Shoemaker, Henry Newell, Nicholas Sturgeon, John Fischer, and Richard Boyd. Helpful written suggestions and corrections by David Brink, Jennifer Whiting, and Susan Sauvé have considerably improved earlier drafts of this book. I have been especially influenced by four recent studies of issues in Aristotle: Ide [1987], Whiting [1984], Shields [1986], and Sauvé [1987]. I have been even more influenced by the authors of these studies; they have invariably offered acute, constructive, and friendly criticism and discussion, and they have improved my views on many more points than I could readily identify. Above all, I have received thorough and relentless criticism, numerous corrections and suggestions, and unwavering help and encouragement, from Gail Fine.

The Delegates, staff, and readers of the Press have treated this book in the tolerant, efficient, and helpful way that I have found to be characteristic of them.

T.H.I

Cornell University,
Ithaca, New York
5 October 1987

CONTENTS

ABBREVIATIONS

Works of Aristotle and other ancient authors are cited by abbreviated titles; full titles are given in the Index Locorum. Aristotle is cited by the standard pages and lines of Bekker [1831]. I have used the editions in the Oxford Classical Texts, or, when these are not available, in the Teubner series. The Greek commentators on Aristotle are cited by page and line from the relevant volume of *Commentaria in Aristotelem Graeca* (fuller reference in Index Locorum).

Other works are cited in the Notes by author's name and date. The date is normally that of the original publication; but the pagination is taken from the source cited first after the author's name. Works by two or more authors (or with two or more editors) are usually cited by the name of the alphabetically first author. Standard works (e.g. commentaries) cited frequently in a particular chapter are often cited by author's name alone, without a date. Well-known philosophical texts (e.g. Hume, Kant) are cited by author and abbreviated title, and the edition used is listed in the Bibliography.

Abbreviations used in the Notes and Bibliography are as follows:

AA	*Articles on Aristotle* (see Barnes [1975a]
AGP	*Archiv für Geschichte der Philosophie*
CJP	*Canadian Journal of Philosophy*
CQ	*Classical Quarterly*
CR	*Classical Review*
DK	Diels [1952]
EAE	*Essays on Aristotle's Ethics* (see Rorty [1980])
HPQ	*History of Philosophy Quarterly*
IA	*Index Aristotelicus* (see Bonitz [1870])
JHI	*Journal of the History of Ideas*
JHP	*Journal of the History of Philosophy*
JHS	*Journal of Hellenic Studies*
JP	*Journal of Philosophy*
KS	*Kant Studien*
OCT	Oxford Classical Texts
OSAP	*Oxford Studies in Ancient Philosophy*
OT	Oxford Translation (see Smith [1910])
PAS	*Proceedings of the Aristotelian Society*
PBA	*Proceedings of the British Academy*
Phil.	*Philosophy*
Phr.	*Phronesis*

PAS	*Proceedings of the Aristotelian Society*
PBA	*Proceedings of the British Academy*
Phil.	*Philosophy*
Phr.	*Phronesis*
PQ	*Philosophical Quarterly*
PR	*Philosophical Review*
PS	*Philosophical Studies*
RM	*Review of Metaphysics*
ROT	Revised Oxford Translation (see Barnes [1984])
SPAS	*Aristotelian Society Supplementary Volume*
SVF	*Stoicorum Veterum Fragmenta* (see Von Arnim [1905])

I
THE EMERGENCE OF
THE PROBLEM

1

THE PROBLEM OF FIRST PRINCIPLES

1. FIRST PRINCIPLES

When Aristotle explains in general terms what he tries to do in his philosophical works, he says he is looking for 'first principles' (or 'origins'; *archai*):

In every systematic inquiry (*methodos*) where there are first principles, or causes, or elements, knowledge and science result from acquiring knowledge of these; for we think we know something just in case we acquire knowledge of the primary causes, the primary first principles, all the way to the elements. It is clear, then, that in the science of nature as elsewhere, we should try first to determine questions about the first principles. The naturally proper direction of our road is from things better known and clearer to us, to things that are clearer and better known by nature; for the things known to us are not the same as the things known unconditionally (*haplôs*). Hence it is necessary for us to progress, following this procedure, from the things that are less clear by nature, but clearer to us, towards things that are clearer and better known by nature. (*Phys.* 184a10–21)[1]

The connexion between knowledge and first principles is expressed in Aristotle's account of a first principle (in one sense) as 'the first basis from which a thing is known' (*Met.* 1013a14–15). The search for first principles is not peculiar to philosophy; philosophy shares this aim with biological, meteorological, and historical inquiries, among others. But Aristotle's references to first principles in this opening passage of the *Physics* and at the start of other philosophical inquiries imply that it is a primary task of philosophy.[2]

It is easy to see why Aristotle says we should begin with what is better known and more familiar to us (*EN* 1095a2–4); we have to begin with the beliefs we initially accept. But his account of the goal of inquiry is more puzzling. He suggests that the first principles are known and clearer 'by nature' or 'unconditionally', even if they are less well-known and less clear to us. Aristotle explains the point by analogy. Someone may be a 'natural musician', because he is naturally suited for it, even if he never learns music, and so never becomes a musician: 'And presumably what is known unconditionally is not what is known to everyone, but what is known to those in a good intellectual condition, just as what is unconditionally healthy is what is healthy for those in a good bodily condition' (*Top.* 142a9–11; cf. *EE* 1235b30–1236a6, 1237a16–18).[3] First principles are known unconditionally because they are naturally appropriate for being known.[4] The beliefs we begin with are 'prior to us' (i.e. 'prior from our point of view'), since they are what we begin from; but the principles we find will be 'prior by nature', and when we have found them they will also be 'prior to us'; for then we will recognize that they are more basic and primary than the principles we began from.[5]

The first principles we find will include beliefs and propositions. But Aristotle also regards things—non-linguistic, non-psychological, non-propositional entities—as first principles. We come to know, e.g., that there are four elements, and this proposition that we know is a first principle; but the four elements themselves are also first principles and are prior and better known by nature. Actually existing things are first principles because they explain other things, and our knowledge of the world requires us to know the explanatory relations in it. To have scientific knowledge (*epistêmê*) about birds is to be able to explain why birds are as they are and behave as they do. The things and processes that explain others are basic and fundamental; when we have found them, we have found the first principles of birds. What is prior and better known by nature is both the propositional principle about, e.g., atoms, and the real principle mentioned in the proposition—the atoms themselves. We grasp both sorts of principles at the same time and in the same way.[6]

It is intelligible that when Aristotle speaks of first principles, he speaks indifferently of propositions and of the things they refer to. For the relations between non-propositional things in the world, not the relations between our beliefs, make one rather than another proposition a first principle. We grasp propositional first principles, and they become 'known to us', when our beliefs match the appropriate propositional principles that match the appropriate non-propositional principles. Once we believe a propositional first principle, we certainly connect it to our other beliefs in specific ways; but the beliefs and the connexions do not make it a first principle. It is a first principle because of the facts external to our beliefs, and we have the correct beliefs in the correct connexions only in so far as we describe the relations between facts independent of our beliefs. Let us say that in so far as we do this, we grasp 'objective' (propositional) first principles describing the (non-propositional) first principles of an objective reality.[7]

2. REALISM

In so far as Aristotle claims that objective first principles must be known by nature, he commits himself to a metaphysical realist conception of knowledge and reality. For he claims that the truth and primacy of a propositional first principle is determined by its correspondence to non-propositional first principles. What is 'known by nature' is not something that happens to be adapted to our cognitive capacities, or to play a special role in our theories or beliefs. It is known by nature because it is a primary feature of the world, and it is known to us only if we are in the right cognitive condition to discover what is really there. The belief we hold when we are in the right sort of cognitive condition does not itself constitute our grasp of an objective first principle; for it is logically possible for us to have coherent, simple, powerful, well-tested theories, meeting all the canons of proper inquiry, without having found objective principles. The primacy of the objective principle makes our belief the grasp of a principle, not the other way round.

Aristotle's remarks about truth show his commitment to metaphysical realism. If you were sitting, and now stand, the statement 'You are sitting' was true, and became false; but he denies that the statement itself has undergone change (of the ordinary sort); he prefers to say that a statement or belief remains unchanged, but receives a different truth-value (the respect in which it is said to change) because the things themselves change (*Catg.* 4a21–37).

This might be construed as a commonsense remark with no great theoretical significance. But in fact it rests on Aristotle's more general conviction that the facts about the world determine the truth of statements, but the converse is not true.

In the cases where two things reciprocate in implication of being, still, if one is in some way the cause of the being of the other, it would reasonably be said to be naturally prior. And clearly there are some cases of this sort. For that there is a man reciprocates in implication of being with the true statement about it; for if there is a man, the statement by which we say there is a man is true, and this reciprocates—for if the statement by which we say there is a man is true, there is a man. Nonetheless, the true statement is in no way the cause of the thing's being ‹i.e. of its being the case that there is a man›, whereas the thing appears in a way the cause of the statement's being true—for it is by the thing's being or not being that the statement is said to be true or false. (*Catg.* 14b11–23)

The asymmetry in explanation described here is taken to be a defining feature of truth about objective reality.[8] In claiming that truth is correspondence to the facts, Aristotle accepts a biconditional; it is true that p if and only if p. But he finds the mere biconditional inadequate for the asymmetry and natural priority he finds in the relation of correspondence; this asymmetry is to be captured in causal or explanatory terms (cf. *Met.* 1051b6–9).

Aristotle does not say much to clarify the explanatory asymmetry he has in mind here; he takes it to be readily understood and accepted. In *Metaphysics* iv he defends some aspects of the realist assumption, against Protagoras and against radical sceptics. But even then it is difficult to say how much he still takes for granted. He assumes that not everything is relative to appearances or beliefs (*Met.* 1011a17–20), and that facts about the world must explain facts about perception, not the other way round (1010b30–1011a2).[9] His assumptions about the natural priority and explanatory asymmetry involved in truth are pervasive, but not fully explained.

Aristotle speaks as though anyone with the normal beliefs about truth is committed to his realist assumptions. He assumes that truth is the appropriate sort of correspondence to the facts, and that the only appropriate sort of correspondence is the one that involves explanatory asymmetry and natural priority. We think p's being true is a different property from p's being believed by someone; and, in Aristotle's view, we do not find an appropriately different property unless we assume the particular sort of correspondence that he has in mind.

He answers only the fairly crude Protagorean attempt to show that a property that is recognizably truth can be understood and explained without a realist assumption. Many more subtle successors of Protagoras have thought they could succeed where he failed. An alternative strategy might concede that Aristotle is right about the ordinary concept of truth and the property it ostensibly picks out, and might then try to show that this concept can safely be abandoned in favour of some substitute that avoids commitment to any realist assumptions.

One reason for rejecting realist assumptions about truth results from their epistemological difficulties. For Protagoras, as for his subtler successors, metaphysical realism seems both to leave room for scepticism and to leave no escape from scepticism; it often seems difficult to see how we could be justified in believing anything of the sort that could meet metaphysical realist conditions. Aristotle's views on truth and natural priority impose a stringent test on anyone, including Aristotle himself, who claims to find objective first principles. We need to give some reason for believing that we have described a state of affairs with properties that explain, and are not explained by, the properties of our beliefs, theories, assumptions, or habits of mind.[10]

We must, therefore, if Aristotle is right, show that our first principles cannot be explained in the way Hume offers to explain some alleged principles, as results of the tendency of the mind to spread itself on objects.[11] In Hume's view, we tend to attribute features to objects because of facts about ourselves and our mental habits; and if we can show this about a putative first principle, then it does not meet Aristotle's conditions for being an objective first principle. To have good reason for believing we have found a first principle, we must have good reason for believing that the Aristotelian rather than the Humean direction of explanation is the right one in this case.

For these reasons, Aristotle is not stating a platitude or a triviality when he claims that philosophy proceeds from things known to us to things known by nature. His claim, as he interprets it, implies that inquiry must reach objective first principles satisfying metaphysical realist conditions. In claiming that progress is required, he assumes that we lack a natural intuition of the objective principles at the beginning of our inquiry, and that a reasonable question arises about whether any of our initial beliefs is an objective first principle or not. And since the (non-propositional) things known by nature must be naturally prior to our beliefs, and must explain their truth, philosophical inquiry must eventually give us good reason for believing we have found (propositional) principles describing such things, if it is indeed a road towards first principles.

3. DIALECTIC AND PHILOSOPHY

In speaking of Aristotle's philosophical works and arguments, I have been referring fairly loosely to those that we would normally count as philosophical, as opposed to his more detailed empirical inquiries. Aristotle himself takes 'dialectical' argument to be the characteristic and distinctive feature of the works that strike us as philosophical; and in describing them this way, he expresses his view of the nature and status of these arguments.

'Dialectic' (*dialektikê*) is Plato's name for the sort of systematic discussion (*dialegesthai*) that is practised in Plato's Socratic dialogues (*dialogoi*). Socrates discusses common beliefs about ethical questions through a conversation that involves the systematic cross-examination of an interlocutor and his intuitive beliefs, exposure of the puzzles they raise, and several attempts to solve the puzzles by modifying the initial beliefs.[12] In the Socratic dialogues the discussion often ends in puzzlement and apparent confusion. But in the *Protagoras* and *Gorgias*, and in many later dialogues, Plato does explicitly what he does implicitly in the earlier dialogues, using the Socratic method to argue for positive philosophical positions; he regards dialectic as the primary method of philosophical inquiry.[13]

For Aristotle as well as Plato, dialectic remains closely connected with the Socratic conversation. The *Topics* is a handbook for the conduct of such conversation—both its procedural rules and the philosophical doctrines that are most generally appropriate in arguments on a wide variety of issues. A Socratic conversation need not aim at positive philosophical progress; we might undertake it simply to see how many reasonable difficulties can be raised for a particular position, or for a particular speaker's defence of it. But Aristotle retains Plato's belief that dialectic is also a method for reaching positive conclusions; this is why he claims that it has a road towards first principles (*Top.* 101b3–4).[14]

The constructive role of dialectic is not as obvious in Aristotle as it is in Plato, because the surviving works do not present his argument in the form of Socratic dialogue. They are not conversations with several speakers, but continuous treatises in which the author appears, as Plato never does in the dialogues, in his own person. Still, this difference in presentation does not reflect a basic difference in method. Aristotle's works show their dialectical character by their conformity to the rules of the *Topics*, and ultimately to the pattern of the Platonic dialogues.[15] Aristotle intends such works as the *De Anima*, the *Physics*, and the *Ethics* to fulfil the claims made in the *Topics* for the constructive uses of dialectic.

4. PUZZLES ABOUT DIALECTIC

If dialectic has a road to objective first principles, then Aristotle's dialectical arguments should give us some reasonable grounds for confidence that they lead us to objective principles that are prior and better known by nature. But at this point a serious difficulty arises. Aristotle's description of dialectical method seems to offer no grounds for believing that it systematically reaches objective first principles. It examines commonly held beliefs (*endoxa*), and if it is successful, it reaches a more coherent version of the beliefs we began with, solving the puzzles revealed by our examination of the initial beliefs. But coherence within common beliefs does not seem to be a ground for claiming to have found objective principles.

This difficulty leads into the central issues that I discuss in this book. The basic issue is quite simple, and arises about any philosopher; we have to compare the philosopher's method with the ostensible conclusion of the arguments, and see if the method is powerful enough to justify belief in the conclusion. Two specific versions of this basic issue apply especially to Aristotle.

First, metaphysical realism has often seemed hard to accept because it seems hard to combine with any reasonable epistemological position.

Realists must allow the logical possibility of the truth of scepticism, since they take truth to consist in the correspondence of beliefs to some reality that is logically independent of them; this logical independence implies the logical possibility that all our beliefs are false, and therefore leaves logical room for the sceptical doubt to be correct. Any justification appealing to coherence between beliefs seems to leave room for sceptical doubt; and it has sometimes seemed that only beliefs immune to doubt could be reasonable foundations for realist claims. The search for beliefs immune to doubt leads naturally to a foundationalist conception of justification, according to which all inferential justification depends on beliefs that are non-inferentially justified and self-evident.[16] It is by no means obvious that this is a satisfactory epistemological position, either in itself or as a companion to metaphysical realism. But it is easy to suppose that a conception of justification as coherence suits a conception of truth as coherence among beliefs, and that a conception of truth as correspondence (interpreted in realist terms) requires a foundationalist conception of justification.

Second, any dialectical method of philosophical argument seems to raise questions about the status of its conclusions. Philosophers have often thought it reasonable to appeal to 'what we intuitively believe' or 'what we find it natural to say', and they think the philosopher's task is to give the most coherent account of these intuitive beliefs. Critics of this method often ask why our intuitive beliefs should be taken as norms of reasonable belief, and why we should be especially concerned to find a coherent account of intuitive beliefs. Perhaps the results of scientific inquiry will challenge our initial intuitive beliefs, and will lead us to say things we initially found unnatural; but why should that lead us to prefer our initial beliefs over the conclusions of science? The use of dialectical philosophy seems to be severely limited; we seem to have no reason to claim that it leads us to the truth. Even if we agree that some sort of coherence among beliefs is a reasonable basis for claims to knowledge, dialectical philosophy seems to overestimate intuitive beliefs.

Each of these two specific issues about methods and conclusions might arise without the other. But they are especially acute in Aristotle, since he seems to face the worst of both worlds. Since he is a realist in metaphysics, but practises dialectical philosophy, the apparent gap between his method and his conclusions should be quite striking, and should raise some questions for us, whether or not Aristotle sees them himself.

In fact he does see some of the questions. Indeed he insists on the limits of dialectic, in order to contrast it with demonstrative science. Science, as opposed to dialectic, is supposed to rely on objective first principles, and to expound their consequences; it claims the sort of objectivity that (in his view) dialectic cannot justifiably claim.

We might suppose, then, that even if Aristotle is wrong about dialectic, that does not matter much, because the task of finding objective first principles and showing that we have found them really belongs to demonstrative science. But this solution fails: for it is not clear how Aristotle can show that any discipline meets the conditions he imposes on scientific knowledge. Each Aristotelian science must assume, but cannot prove, the objective truth of its own first principles, and apparently no scientific argument can show that the principles themselves are objectively true.[17]

These different claims about dialectic and science add up to a puzzle about dialectic, and a more general puzzle about first principles. Aristotle claims that dialectic has a road to first principles, but seems to imply that, because it depends on common beliefs, it cannot reach first principles. Further, he claims that a science must rest on objective first principles; but he cannot explain how we are justified in believing that it has found them.

Aristotle believes, however, that he can argue for the objective truth of first principles; and in *Metaphysics* iv he introduces a science that claims to argue for the first principles of the other sciences; and this science differs from dialectic in so far as dialectic relies on common beliefs, and this science relies on objective truths. This universal science, called 'the science of being' or 'first philosophy', seems to remove the difficulties that we raised about dialectic.

On the other hand, further difficulties now arise: (1) In his earlier works Aristotle seemed to reject the possibility of the sort of universal science that he accepts in the *Metaphysics*. (2) The method of the universal science looks suspiciously similar to the method of dialectic, which seemed unable to reach the objective first principles that universal science is supposed to reach.

These difficulties about the *Metaphysics* raise my main questions. Has Aristotle really found a reasonable conception of a universal science that answers his own objections? Does he show that the objections against dialectic do not affect the universal science? Most of this book is devoted to showing how these questions arise, to defending an affirmative answer to each of them, and to exploring the implications of the answers. These are initially questions about Aristotle's method; but they raise wider issues about his philosophical development, and about the structure and plausibility of his doctrines. I will therefore pause to explain the connexion between the questions about method and these wider issues.

5. ARISTOTLE'S DEVELOPMENT

Ancient and mediaeval students of Aristotle read his works as though the order of composition did not matter, assuming that they all expound the same system. Commentators freely illustrate remarks in one work by appeal to another work, on the assumption that the second work will always express the general view that Aristotle had in mind in writing the first. In the particular case that concerns us, commentators readily expound Aristotle's remarks about dialectic, science, and first principles in the light of his doctrines about universal science in the *Metaphysics*. They do not even raise the possibility that Aristotle might hold different views in different works.[18]

In the nineteenth and twentieth centuries, by contrast, the study of Aristotle has been heavily influenced by questions about Aristotle's development; students normally regard it as a possibility to be taken seriously, even though they disagree about how much difference it makes. It has generally been thought useful to trace the development of Plato's thought; and some students of Aristotle have wanted to do the same thing for him. So far, however, these efforts have not resulted in even the limited degree of fairly widespread (but by no means universal) agreement that has been reached for Plato. Most students (going back at least to Aristotle) at least distinguish Plato's early 'Socratic' dialogues from his middle and later dialogues; but there is no similar agreed division in Aristotle's works.

Some have suggested that since Aristotle spent the first twenty years of his philosophical career in Plato's Academy, he is likely to have agreed with Plato, and likely to have moved away gradually from Platonic views.[19] I will not discuss this view of Aristotle's development, since I think it has been refuted. There is no evidence that Aristotle was ever a disciple of Plato (in the sense of accepting all the main philosophical doctrines discoverable from Plato's dialogues), or that his later works are less Platonic than his earlier.[20]

A more plausible picture of Aristotle's development suggests that his earlier philosophical views are the product of his criticisms of Plato, resulting from actual debate in the Academy; further reflexion on Plato led him, in later works, to form a more sympathetic view of some of Plato's views and doctrines.[21] Like the first picture, this picture presents a philosopher dominated by his teacher; whereas the first picture presents a young disciple gradually bringing himself to differ with his teacher, the second portrays the fierce young critic gradually reaching a more balanced view of the views he initially criticized.

Each picture has parallels in the careers of other philosophers; and we lack the biographical evidence to decide between them. But I think the second picture is much nearer the truth. There are no Platonizing early works (as the first picture would suggest), but in works that are plausibly (on different grounds) regarded as earlier, Aristotle's position is further from Plato's on some important points than it is in some probably later works.

My objection to this second picture is not exactly that it attributes to Aristotle, as the first picture does, specific views that he does not hold, but that it probably exaggerates the extent to which Aristotle consciously reacts against Plato. To this extent, the suggestion that he formed his views in dialectical debate in the Academy seems to me to overlook the probable independence of Aristotle's own reflexion on philosophical problems.[22] I see no good reason to believe that he spent most of his time deciding whether to agree or disagree with Plato, and hence I doubt if attention to debates with Plato or Platonism is likely to explain his philosophical development. I am inclined to think the comments on Plato are an incidental result of Aristotle's reflexion on problems that arise for him apart from any Platonic context. Indeed, it is useful to examine Aristotle's reaction to Plato precisely because Aristotle is aware of questions about Plato that he would probably never have noticed if he had confined himself to thinking about Plato.

Though I do not intend to discuss Aristotle's development in full, the question arises for me, as it does not for some other recent writers on Aristotle, because I think some attention to his probable development throws some light on the doctrine of different treatises. This is not everyone's view. The developmental schemes that have been proposed have been applied to particular Aristotelian works in ways that have not been wholly convincing; and attempts to discover chronological layers have often rested on appeals to alleged contradictions that turn out not to be contradictions at all once we understand the argument better.[23] Justified scepticism about the results of developmental schemes has moved some contemporary students to set aside questions of development, and to return to a more traditional 'static' view of Aristotle. Such a static view is no less probable a priori than either of the developmental pictures; and if we accept it as a working hypothesis, it has some useful results.

If we assume a static view, we will try to see how two allegedly inconsistent doctrines are really consistent, instead of giving up prematurely and assigning them to different stages in Aristotle's development. Equally, different treatises may have different aims that make it reasonable to expound a doctrine in more or less detail, and with greater or less precision; and this explanation of an apparent disagreement is often more reasonable than an assumption about development. In any case, philosophers sometimes hold inconsistent views, since not all inconsistencies are obvious; even if we cannot dissolve the appearance of contradiction, we should not necessarily explain it by development.

I agree that these warnings against premature appeals to development are salutary correctives to some tendencies in Aristotelian studies; and for these reasons I think the static view is prima facie plausible. Still, in some cases the presumption in its favour can be overcome; and I would like to show that Aristotle's views on some issues suggest a hypothesis about development. I discuss two major issues where I think Aristotle changes his mind: (1) As I suggested above, Aristotle's earlier works seem to reject the possibility of a universal science, and the *Metaphysics* accepts such a science. (2) The account of substance in the central books of the *Metaphysics* seems to differ from the account in the *Organon* and in some of the treatises on natural philosophy.

If we reject a developmental account of these differences, we must try one of two static solutions. We may either (*a*) show that the 'earlier' and 'later' accounts are really consistent, and that it is not surprising that they should be expressed in different terms in different works; or (*b*) agree that the two accounts are inconsistent, and argue that Aristotle might well have left the inconsistency unresolved. I will be satisfied if I can give reasons for rejecting the first static solution. It is far harder to decide between the second static solution and a developmental solution. But it is also far less important; for the second static solution agrees with the developmental solution about the philosophical significance of the arguments, and differs only about Aristotle's attitude to them. I will simply try to suggest why a developmental explanation is reasonable, and why it is at least not simply the result of error about Aristotle's views and arguments.

I mention these two particular issues about development because I think they are connected. I want to show that the major difficulties in Aristotle's earlier doctrine of substance result from specific features of his dialectical method; that the conception of universal science in the *Metaphysics* differs from dialectic on these specific features; and that this difference in method suggests revisions that remove the difficulties in the doctrine of substance. It is not a coincidence, in my view, that *Metaphysics* iv introduces a new account of universal science and Books vii–ix introduce a new account of substance; I would like to show that the two accounts are part of a fairly continuous argument. On these central issues of method and doctrine, I hope to show that Aristotle's changes of mind are both intelligible and reasonable.

6. ARISTOTLE'S CONCEPTION OF PHILOSOPHY

I suggested earlier that in the works we naturally regard as philosophical Aristotle regards his method as dialectical. If, then, he introduces the universal science of first philosophy to correct the apparent limitations of dialectic, he should revise his conception of philosophical argument. The issue about dialectic and first philosophy should tell us something about Aristotle's view of philosophy.

Aristotle's 'purely dialectical' conception of philosophy has two striking features that he later reconsiders. First, philosophy is not a rival to the empirical sciences, and is not, as Plato conceived dialectic, the queen of the sciences. Aristotle wants to avoid any suggestion that dialectic can settle scientific questions non-empirically. It prevents errors that might result from confused thinking, on scientific or non-scientific questions; and to this extent Aristotle's view might seem similar to the view of those who regard philosophy as primarily a means of avoiding conceptual confusions. If we are tempted to overlook the fact that a word is being used in different senses, or that someone has affirmed the consequent of a conditional on the strength of the truth of the whole conditional, experience in dialectic will help us to detect these errors.

Secondly, the contrast between dialectic and science might suggest that Aristotle accepts the fairly common view that philosophy is less objective than science. If we are willing to claim that the sciences tell us about an objective world, we may still be unwilling to say the same for philosophy. Perhaps philosophy can clarify our beliefs, remove confusions, alter our point of view, and so on; but all these results seem distinct in principle from discoveries about the nature of an objective reality.

On these two points Aristotle's view is recognizably similar to some familiar conceptions of philosophy. He responds in understandable ways to some rather striking and obvious features of philosophical argument. For all that, his views ought not to satisfy him, in so far as they conflict with his claim (on a reasonable interpretation) that dialectic has a road to objective first principles.

In the *Metaphysics*, therefore, Aristotle changes his mind on these aspects of dialectical argument. He still believes they are true of 'pure dialectic', which argues indiscriminately from common beliefs. But he now believes in a universal science that uses dialectical arguments on an appropriately selected subset of common beliefs; and he claims that this science reaches objectively true conclusions about first principles of the other sciences. In his earlier works he follows the tendency of much of modern philosophy to reduce the objective element in philosophical claims; but in his later works he accepts the sort of view that many modern philosophers have taken to be open to fatal objections, some of which Aristotle himself seems to recognize.

If Aristotle's views on first philosophy express this change of mind about the nature and limits of philosophy, they raise persistent and difficult questions that have concerned philosophers with any reasonable degree of self-consciousness about their discipline.

The claims of universal science are surprising, because they seem to conflict both with Aristotle's doctrines and with the apparent character of the treatises. Aristotle insists on the importance of 'proper principles', those special and appropriate to each area of inquiry.[24] This is indeed one of the reasons for his earlier doubts about the possibility of a universal science. The doubts seem to be reflected in the treatises themselves. Most of these seem to be separate inquiries, not presented as parts of a single system; and Aristotle never appeals directly to a large body of doctrine derived from a universal science to provide him with the premisses of his arguments in a distinct discipline. Just as distinct empirical disciplines have their different proper ranges of empirical evidence and their proper principles, each area of philosophical inquiry has its proper arguments and principles, and Aristotle rejects any attempt at a highly unified deductive structure.

On the other hand, not every system has to be the sort that Spinoza (e.g.) hoped to find. While it is clear that Aristotle insists on the distinctness of different disciplines and their principles, it is equally clear that he sometimes relies on the conclusions of one inquiry in the course of another. If he recognizes a universal science, then the connexions should be important and pervasive.

At this point an inquiry into Aristotle's methods has to face questions about his substantive doctrines. For if we want to know whether his views on a universal science are reasonable, we need to know what such a science claims, what these claims imply for other areas of inquiry, and whether the claims and implications are reasonable. We need to see whether the principles discovered by first philosophy actually improve the rest of Aristotle's philosophical position. I hope to show that Aristotle has a reasonable view of what first philosophy ought to do, and that he actually uses it to do what he says it ought to do.

7. THE EMERGENCE OF THE PROBLEM

The previous sections should have given some idea of the scope and connexions of the following chapters. I will now introduce them a little more fully, to indicate the argument that the reader should expect.

The rest of Part I (Chapters 2–7) is really an introduction to *Metaphysics* iii. There Aristotle prefaces his description of the universal science of first philosophy with a lengthy statement of puzzles and difficulties. The relevant puzzles cover four main areas: (1) Dialectic seems to be the only available method for the discussion of Aristotle's questions, but it seems not to yield the right sorts of results. (2) We seem to be looking for a universal science, but we have reasons for believing there can be no such thing. (3) We want the universal science to discuss substance, but we cannot make up our minds about the appropriate criteria for assessing the claims of different alleged substances. (4) Since we cannot decide on the right criteria, we cannot decide on the claims of form and matter, which sometimes seem to be rival candidates for substance.

I intend to follow Aristotle's advice, and to examine the puzzles before attempting to solve them. Aristotle does not bring up these four puzzles simply as an expository device, or as a list of other people's puzzles and difficulties. They concern him because they arise from his own previous views on the questions. I will argue that readers of Aristotle's earlier works should feel exactly the sorts of puzzles that Aristotle sets out in *Metaphysics* iii.

The order I have followed above divides two puzzles about method from two that are primarily about substantive doctrine. But I want to show that the doctrinal puzzles arise partly because the doctrines are formulated and defended from a purely dialectical point of view; the weaknesses in Aristotle's method are reflected in the limitations of his doctrines. To bring out this connexion, I discuss the two substantive puzzles (about substance (Chapters 3–4), and about form and matter (5)) immediately after the discussion of dialectic (2), before examining the contrast between dialectic and science (6–7).

To raise the puzzles about dialectic, I compare and contrast it with empirical inquiry. Dialectic is similar to empirical inquiry in so far as it involves progress from things known to us to things known by nature; but it differs from ordinary empirical inquiry in ways that reveal its attachment to common beliefs and to the puzzles they raise. This attachment to common beliefs raises some doubts about the capacity of dialectic to reach the objective first principles that are demanded by its constructive functions.

Such doubts about dialectic emerge from a survey of the alleged results of constructive dialectical argument. I therefore examine Aristotle's general views on substance in the *Categories*, and his development of these views in *Physics* i–ii. He appeals to ordinary dialectical forms of argument, but these seem to betray two weaknesses: (1) They seem too indefinite to support his specific conclusions. (2)

Even if they were more definite, they would show how things seem to common sense, not how they really are.

The account of substance betrays the first weakness, since Aristotle argues from intuitive distinctions that do not support his candidates for substance. Though he appeals to a workable distinction between subjects and things predicated of them, this distinction does not seem to show that his favoured substances are the only genuine substances. Aristotle believes that particular men and horses are substances, and that particular musicians are not substances, in so far as they are composites of a substance (man) and a non–substance (musicality); but it is not clear that the dialectical distinctions he appeals to really support his discrimination. This difficulty becomes important when he maintains, as he does in the *Physics*, that form, as opposed to matter, is the primary sort of substance. The distinctions he relies on seem to make matter at least as good a candidate as form.

This first weakness in dialectic would not defeat Aristotle's purpose, if he could give some further reason for advancing beyond the very general conclusions supported by pure dialectic to the more specific conclusions about substance that he actually accepts. He gives no further reason, however, for reaching the more specific conclusions; and to this extent he leaves a gap between his dialectical argument and the conclusion he seems to draw from it.

The second weakness in dialectic affects Aristotle's use of his dialectical arguments in the *Physics*. He speaks as though dialectic can show that form is substance, that formal and final causes are irreducible to purely material causes, and that therefore a purely materialist approach to natural substances is mistaken. He presents his own views on substance and cause as successful rivals to the views of Democritus and Plato. But we may well wonder if Aristotle is entitled to do this. For his opponents claim to describe objective principles and causes, but his dialectical arguments seem to show at most that his opponents' views conflict with common sense. Since his opponents claim to expose the errors of common sense, they might well be unmoved by being told that their views conflict with common sense.

Aristotle speaks as though his claims about formal and final causes are true of the world, not just of common beliefs about the world. But he does not explain how his dialectical argument could give us reason to draw such a conclusion, or how some other argument fills the gap left by dialectic.

It is important to see that the apparent gap between dialectic and objective principles is clear to Aristotle himself; and this point emerges from his account of demonstrative science. For here he shows that he is well aware of the conditions for knowledge that can claim to grasp objective principles; and he clearly believes that pure dialectic itself cannot reach principles meeting these conditions. He insists that the first principles of demonstrative science must be grasped in some way that guarantees their objective truth. Since Aristotle holds a foundationalist conception of knowledge and justification, rejecting infinite regresses and circles as possible sources of justification, he concludes that first principles must be grasped by some form of intuition guaranteeing their objective truth. Since dialectic can only achieve coherence among common beliefs, it cannot give us reason to believe we have found objective first principles.

Aristotle makes first principles seem hard to reach; for no reasonable method of inquiry seems to support the sort of claim that would be needed to meet his conditions. Still, the questions he raises are quite reasonable. It seems quite doubtful that mere coherence between common beliefs could support a claim to have found objective first principles; and if this will not do, we need some answer that avoids the impossible conditions imposed by the doctrine of intuition.

This problem about objective principles makes it reasonable for Aristotle to place the puzzles about universal science in their prominent position in *Metaphysics* iii. For in the *Metaphysics* he sets out to find a scientific argument for first principles; but his own reflexions on science and dialectic seem to assure him that no scientific argument is available for first principles. This puzzle, like the others, emerges directly out of Aristotle's own arguments; and the arguments in the earlier works give no hint that Aristotle has any solution up his sleeve when he presents them.

8. SOLUTIONS TO THE PROBLEM

After setting out the puzzles, I turn to Aristotle's solution in the *Metaphysics*. I do not cover all of this work; and I do not consider all the arguments that have been given for finding doctrinal conflicts or different chronological layers in it. But I take seriously the possibility that at least some parts of it present a connected argument that is controlled by the conception of first philosophy set out in Book iv. It must be admitted that Aristotle does not emphasize any continuity between his arguments about first philosophy in Book iv and his arguments about substance in Books vii–ix. But Books iii–iv regard the discussion of substance as a central task of first philosophy, and it is worth asking if the discussion of substance follows the rules for an argument within first philosophy. What, then, are the rules?

In *Metaphysics* iv Aristotle describes a universal science, called 'the science of being qua being' or 'first philosophy', whose methods are neither purely dialectical nor demonstrative, and for which Aristotle's earlier works leave no room. First philosophy violates Aristotle's earlier prohibition of any scientific defence of ultimate first principles. The only sort of argument that he allowed for first principles was dialectical; and since dialectic is confined to finding coherence among beliefs, it could not, in Aristotle's earlier view, offer scientific arguments.

If Aristotle is to convince us that his second thoughts on philosophy represent an advance rather than a retreat, he needs to show how his alleged universal science works. It must have some plausible method for selecting the 'appropriate' subset of common beliefs for the right sort of dialectical argument. (I will say that such argument belongs to 'strong dialectic'.)[25] A proper account of first philosophy should show why its conclusions meet metaphysical realist conditions. And if we are convinced on these points, we need to see why they do not conflict with the reasonable degree of empiricism that turns Aristotle against any philosophical pretension to legislate for empirical sciences.

In my view, the method of first philosophy is dialectical in so far as it begins from common beliefs and cross-examines them. But 'first philosophy' is not just another name for dialectic addressed to a special sort of question. It uses dialectical arguments with appropriately selected premisses; and the main task in giving an account of first philosophy is to give some idea of how these premisses are to be selected. I argue that the science of being is a universal science in so far as it describes the features of reality that are necessary for it to be an object of scientific study at all. In *Metaphysics* iv Aristotle describes the two elementary features, arguing that an object of scientific study must be a substance with an essence. His arguments against opponents of the Principle of Non-Contradiction, and against subjectivists who deny the independence of reality from our beliefs about it, explore the necessary features of subjects with essences.

If some dialectical arguments argue from the assumption that there are objects of scientific study, they do not begin from common beliefs indiscriminately, and the consequences of this assumption are not just the consequences of any old set of common beliefs. The consequences of denying this assumption are difficult to accept—so difficult, indeed, that they make it hard for opponents of the assumption even to formulate their opposition to it coherently. Aristotle can fairly claim that arguments based on this sort of assumption are both dialectical and not merely dialectical. If first philosophy can offer arguments of this sort, it can defend its claim to be a scientific discipline distinct from demonstrative science and from pure dialectic; and it can show why there is scientific, not merely dialectical, argument for first principles—argument that gives us a reason to believe we have found objectively true principles. First philosophy, then, seems to offer a method that leads us from things known to us to things known by nature; and so its conclusions meet the conditions imposed by Aristotle's metaphysical realist demands.

In these ways Book iv offers a general idea of what an argument in first philosophy should be like; and the scope of first philosophy will depend on how far this general idea can be applied. I consider in particular whether it can be applied to Aristotle's arguments about substance in Books vii–ix, and I suggest some points on which we understand these arguments better if we regard them as arguments in first philosophy.

First philosophy allows Aristotle to formulate the puzzles about substance more exactly than he does in earlier works. In Book iv he argues that science requires subjects with essences; and in vii he argues that the initially confusing variety of candidates for substance reflects our appeals to each of these presuppositions of science. An inquiry into substance shows what subjects and essences must be like if they are to be objects of scientific knowledge—what sorts of basic subject we must recognize, and what their essential properties must be.

I examine Aristotle's inquiry into substance in some detail (though not in enough detail to deal properly with all the controversies about it), because the details of his argument matter for our account of his method. As I understand him, Aristotle thinks his early view—that the subject-criterion is correct, and that such things as particular men and trees satisfy it—is roughly right. But he thinks strong dialectic can both modify his early view and explain the extent to which it is right. First philosophy explains why the subject-criterion is important, and why we cannot do justice to it without also doing justice to substance as essence.

On this view, Aristotle uses strong dialectic to support and correct the conclusions of pure dialectic. Other views of the argument make it harder to attribute such a role to strong dialectic. If we think Aristotle in the *Metaphysics* regards species rather than individuals as primary substances, we ascribe to him a much sharper divergence from his earlier view; the conclusion that God is the only genuine substance departs widely from common beliefs; and if we think Aristotle's treatment remains aporetic throughout, we must conclude that Aristotle's practice of strong dialectic fails to solve the puzzles it confronts. I do not say that my view of Aristotle's doctrine is the only one that fits my view of the role of strong dialectic in *Metaphysics* vii–ix; but views on these two issues must affect each other, and the task of comparing different interpretations is correspondingly complicated.

Aristotle eventually reaches the conclusion that substance is form and that the primary substances are particular forms, as opposed to the matter constituting them. At first sight, his conclusion seems to conflict with my efforts to regard his argument as part of first philosophy. For his actual conclusion—that goal-directed natural organisms are the primary substances—seems to rest on empirical considerations, especially about causation and explanation, that seem distinct from the very general arguments about being qua being that seemed to belong to first philosophy. To see the point of the argument about substance, we have to see how and why these considerations about explanation are relevant. I mentioned that in the *Physics* Aristotle fails to fit these considerations into his dialectical argument; and it is useful to see if he fits them any better into his conception of first philosophy.

To answer these questions, I consider Aristotle's arguments for identifying the essence of some things with their first actuality, a combination of actuality and potentiality, and for identifying this with form. The proper conception of essence for first philosophy identifies something's essential properties with those that explain the rest of its properties and behaviour; such properties are rightly identified with a subject's persistent potentialities; and these persistent potentialities turn out to belong to its form rather than its matter. Hence it is reasonable to identify a basic subject with a pattern of functional, goal-directed organization, rather than with its constituent material.

If this argument can be shown to be reasonable, then first philosophy shows us how to reach a plausible conception of substance. It does not tell us the answer to some empirical questions we need to answer in order to know what the substances are, but it tells us what empirical questions are relevant and what we should conclude from the answers to them. If we have the right conception of first philosophy, and the right conception of the argument in the central books of the *Metaphysics*, then the argument is a reasonable construction following the rules of first philosophy. The solution can reasonably claim not just to resolve the puzzles about substance, but to resolve the puzzles about how dialectical conclusions about substance could describe objective first principles.

9. APPLICATIONS OF THE SOLUTION

To investigate the degree of system in Aristotle's philosophy, I begin from the account of substance, form, and matter in the *Metaphysics*, and see what conclusions Aristotle draws from it for his other philosophical inquiries. If the *Metaphysics* offers us the possibility of strong dialectic and applies it to general metaphysical questions, how far can it be applied in Aristotle's dialectical arguments? How many of these arguments are strongly dialectical, or can be defended by appeal to strong dialectic? I examine this question by considering the role of strong dialectic in the *De Anima, Ethics,* and *Politics.* These works contain a more or less continuous argument, depending on the conclusions of the *Metaphysics,* and defending their principles by strong dialectic. Ethics and politics are two areas where dialectical method seems suitable both to Aristotle and to us, and at the same time where sceptical objections to dialectic seem well-founded. Strong dialectic allows Aristotle to defend his moral and political theory against these sceptical objections.

To investigate the influence of his metaphysics would be a large task, and I have omitted many topics that would be relevant to that investigation. I do not discuss, for instance, the rest of the *Physics,* or the details of the biological works. Nor do I discuss his theology, despite its obvious connexions both with his doctrine of substance and with his ethical theory—though in fact I do not think these connexions should make very much difference to our view of the nature of first philosophy or ethics.[26] I have chosen to discuss the *De Anima, Ethics,* and *Politics,* because they share two features of interest: (1) Their predominant method of argument is dialectical, rather than empirical. (On this point they differ from the biological works.) (2) They seem to appeal at some points fairly directly to the conclusions of the *Metaphysics* about substance, form, and essence. (On this point they differ from the later books of the *Physics.*) These two common features allow us to test Aristotle's use of first philosophy.

So far I have discussed only the possibility of strong dialectic as a universal, non–departmental science. But this role suggests further roles for strong dialectic outside the *Metaphysics.* (1) To defend a dialectical universal science, Aristotle has to defend strong dialectic; and this defence applies to dialectic even in its more departmental inquiries in physics, psychology, or ethics. Here also it is worth seeing whether Aristotle relies on premisses that have some claim on our acceptance apart from common beliefs. (2) One basis for such a claim might be an appeal to first philosophy; if it supports a premiss of our psychological or ethical doctrine, then we have the sort of defence that makes it suitable for strong dialectic.

The first of these possible implications of first philosophy is separable from the second; it is logically possible that the premisses appropriate for departmental strong dialectic are quite unconnected to first philosophy. But in fact Aristotle explores the two implications together, and he is right to think the second is a reasonable way to specify the first.

The use of first philosophy is most obvious in the *De Anima,* where Aristotle offers to answer puzzles about the soul by appeal to his doctrine of substance. He seeks to show that the claims we can reasonably make about the soul and the body are all captured and explained by his views about form and matter; if we identify the soul with substance as form, we find a reasonable account of the different states, conditions, and events that are plausibly attributed to the soul. Dialectic helps us to find and to explore the puzzles about the soul; but the conclusion is not a conclusion of *pure* dialectic. To identify the soul with substance as form is to identify it with something that we have distinct metaphysical reasons to recognize.

The puzzles that demand a solution from Aristotle are general puzzles about the soul and its relation to the body, and more specific puzzles about states of the soul—especially perception, imagination, thought, desire, and action. If his identification of soul with form is a reasonable account of the soul, it should answer both the general and the specific puzzles. If we find faults in Aristotle's account of different states of the soul, we ought to be able to show that his theory of the soul is not responsible for these faults; and it would be a further point in its favour if we could show that a more thorough application of it would avoid these faults. I will examine some faults in Aristotle's views on perception and thought, and try to explain how they might be avoided by closer attention to the theory that is derived from first philosophy.

Aristotle does not conceal his view that some aspects of his moral and political theory are derived from his account of the essence of human beings; and he identifies the human essence with the human soul. Both the *Ethics* and the *Politics* begin with general claims about human nature, and seek to derive specific normative conclusions from these claims. If Aristotle's account of the soul is itself derived from first philosophy, then his moral and political theory rests on metaphysical foundations. It should be worth our while to see how sound these foundations are, how much Aristotle tries to build on them, and how much they can reasonably be expected to bear.

These questions are important for our evaluation of the *Ethics* and its place in Aristotle's philosophical system, because the *Ethics* is often regarded as a clear instance of pure dialectic. Here more than elsewhere, Aristotle seems to rely explicitly on common beliefs, and to seek coherence among them. Those who accept such a method often do so because they think ethical theory should not try to satisfy metaphysical realist conditions; our aim, on this view, should not be to describe any independent reality, but simply to reorganize our initial beliefs.[27] If Aristotle ought to believe this, then he is wrong to claim that moral theory describes objective principles.

This issue makes the connexions between ethical theory and first philosophy quite important; for they offer Aristotle the best prospect of a convincing argument to show why ethical theory can reach objective first principles. If common beliefs can be explained, and partly revised, by appeal to an account of human nature and the human soul, and this account in turn is defensible from first philosophy, then the conclusions of dialectical argument about ethics may claim some support outside the particular ethical common beliefs that are the starting-points of the argument.

Discussion of the questions about method and argument in the *Ethics* ought not to neglect the *Politics*. It throws further light on the *Ethics* from several points of view: (1) Aristotle claims that his ethical works are a part of political science, and he presents the *Politics* as a continuation of the *Nicomachean Ethics*. We should at least see if the two works display any continuous line of argument. (2) The *Politics* appeals more frequently and more explicitly to Aristotle's conception of human nature; it confirms our view that this is meant to support important ethical conclusions. (3) The use of dialectical argument in the *Politics* raises some general questions about this method of argument.

The questions raised under the third head can in fact be raised as a general complaint about Aristotle's dialectical arguments. If we confine ourselves to what seems reasonable to the many or the wise, it may seem unlikely that our conclusions will be startling or radical. A conservative method seems likely to lead to conservative conclusions. This suspicion about Aristotle seems to be amply confirmed by the character of the *Politics*, where both dialectical arguments and metaphysical appeals to human nature seem to support politically conservative conclusions. Aristotle's rather self-assured arguments for the justice of slavery, the inferior political status of women, and the desirability of rule by the middle class seem to show that there is something wrong with his method of argument.

I examine the *Ethics* and *Politics* together in the hope of showing that strong dialectic of the sort practised in *Metaphysics* iv offers a reasonable reply to these charges of inherent conservative bias in Aristotle's methods. Appeal to the conclusions of first philosophy allows us to correct some ethical common beliefs, and to vindicate those we decide to accept; it offers us a partly independent point of view from which we can avoid the biases present in prevailing opinions. If Aristotle consistently follows this method, he ought not to be open to the objection that he simply refines and presents the prejudices of his more conservative contemporaries. But if Aristotle's less plausible conclusions are not to turn us against his method, or against his metaphysical principles, we ought to be able to show that the correct use of his method, and the correct interpretation of his metaphysical principles, do not justify the implausible conclusions that he claims to derive from them. To defend Aristotle's theory against his conclusions, we need to show that his conclusions rest on errors that cannot be justly held against his theory.

For these reasons, the chapters on the *Ethics* and *Politics* are intended to draw together the methodological and the substantive issues in the previous chapters. I hope to show that it makes a difference to our view of Aristotle's moral and political argument if we take it to be strong dialectic, not pure dialectic, and that an appeal to first philosophy makes his moral and political theory more plausible than it would be otherwise. In this case our discovery of the unity in Aristotle's philosophy should encourage us to take his particular theories more seriously.

Indeed, I hope this will be a reasonable conclusion to draw from my argument as a whole. While I cannot hope to argue fully for each point of interpretation, or to defend Aristotle's philosophical position against all possible, or even all important, objections, I hope that the cumulative result will seem plausible and interesting enough, both as an account of Aristotle's position and as a philosophical position, to encourage further discussion of the many issues that will arise both for the reader of Aristotle and for the philosopher.

INQUIRY AND DIALECTIC

10. AIMS OF INQUIRY

Aristotle's metaphysical realism implies that a genuine first principle is 'known by nature', in that it has the right nature and character to be an appropriate object of knowledge; and it has this character, not because of some fact about us, but because of the facts about an objective world whose characteristics do not wholly depend on what we believe about it.[1] If Aristotle thinks we can form beliefs that grasp genuine first principles, he should describe some method for forming them, and give us some reason for thinking that the beliefs we have formed by this method really pass the test.

In fact he describes two methods of inquiry that begin from our initial beliefs and the things we intuitively recognize, the 'things known to us', and claim to reach principles 'known by nature'. Empirical inquiry begins from perception, proceeds by induction and generalization, and tests theories by appeal to experience. Dialectical inquiry begins from common beliefs, proceeds by raising and solving puzzles, and tests theories against common beliefs.

It is useful to distinguish Aristotle's two methods, because they suggest two different ways of passing the metaphysical realist test for genuine first principles. In empirical inquiry, Aristotle relies on naïve realism, in assuming that perception accurately grasps features of an objective world, and on naïve empiricism, in assuming that empirical inquiry preserves objectivity in so far as it simply extends, generalizes, and appeals to the data of perception.[2] We might fairly criticize Aristotle for overlooking several questions about the relation between perception, belief, and theory. But at least we can see how the results of empirical inquiry will count as objective principles if he has the right conception of empirical inquiry.

Aristotle's view of dialectical methods is less naïve than his view of empirical methods. He does not assume that the common beliefs that dialectic begins from must be correct, or that we can identify some correct subset of them in advance of any theoretical assumptions. He recognizes that initial beliefs and proposed principles have to be examined against each other; and he relies on nothing analogous to his appeal to the data of perception. To this extent his view of dialectical inquiry is not open to the criticisms that are justifiably raised against his naïvely realist account of empirical inquiry.

Aristotle recognizes that dialectical inquiry is to an important degree non-empirical; and while this contrast is especially clear if we accept his own over-simplified view of empirical inquiry, it remains even if our view of empirical inquiry is less naïve. But once we appreciate the character of dialectical inquiry, it becomes less easy to see how it can reach objective principles; the naïve realism that supports the objective status of empirical conclusions is not available for dialectic. Since the characteristic method of Aristotle's philosophical works is dialectical, doubts about dialectic imply doubts about his philosophical arguments.

In describing some of Aristotle's remarks as 'naïve' or 'over-simplified', I am to some extent being unfair. Most of them are relatively informal and intuitive; they are not meant to discuss or to resolve the more general questions that we have raised, and it is unfair to criticize them as though they were meant to constitute a philosophical theory. But their informality does not mean that they have no influence on him; and it is worth seeing what he takes for granted as well as what he says about methods of inquiry.

11. THE STUDY OF METHOD

Aristotle recognizes, following Plato, the importance of understanding methods of inquiry and argument (*EN* 1095a30–b1; cf. *Rep.* 511a3–c2, *Phd.* 101c9–102a1). He remarks that his predecessors have gone astray partly because they have not fully understood their methods and aims (e.g. *GC* 316a10–14, *Met.* 992a29–b1). To this extent the discussions of method are meant to be practically useful.

Aristotle is not simply concerned, however, with the practising inquirer. He also wants us to evaluate different methods, so that we know what to expect from different branches of inquiry (*Pol.* 1282a3–7). Competence in such evaluation is a product of education (*paideia*), rather than of professional expertise in any special science:

For it is characteristic of the educated person to be able to judge suitably by a good estimate (*eustochôs*) what is right or wrong in an exposition. For this is what we take to be characteristic of the generally educated person, and we think that being educated consists in the ability to do this sort of thing. In this case, however, we regard the same individual as competent to judge on just about any area, whereas we take ⟨the expert in a science⟩ to be confined to some definite area. . . . Hence it is clear that, in the inquiry into nature as elsewhere, there must be suitable principles (*horoi*) by reference to which we will accept the method of proof, apart from whether ⟨the conclusion⟩ is true or not. (*PA* 639a4–15)[3]

From these methodological studies we learn to distinguish appropriate arguments in literary criticism and historical study from those in mathematics. We learn, for instance, what degree of exactness (*akribeia*) we should demand from one or another area of study (*EE* 1216b40–1217a9, *EN* 1094b22–1095a2; cf. *Met.* 995a12–16). In mathematics we ought not to be satisfied with anything less than demonstration, displaying necessary truths as necessary consequences of first principles that are self-evident and naturally prior; but ethics is less exact, and we must not demand demonstrations there. The educated person is expected to notice this difference.

Since he knows what to expect from a particular branch of study, the educated person also knows what it should prove, and what it should take for granted. We display lack of education if we appeal to considerations foreign to the inquiry being undertaken (*EE* 1217a7–10); Plato's Theory of Forms, even if it were true, would not settle a question about the difference between two species of fish. The educated person knows when it is fair to demand a proof and when it is not (*Met.* 1006a5–11, 1005b2–5; cf. 1011a6–13), and what type of argument can fairly be asked for (cf. *DC* 287b28–288a2). He will therefore be able to estimate the performance of a particular branch of inquiry or of an inquirer.[4]

The educated person does not simply learn the differences between methods of inquiry. He also learns that some are better than others, and tries to find out if an alleged science meets the right standards for a genuine science. He must therefore begin with some conception of the right standards.

For the educated person, then, questions about first principles will be especially appropriate. A proper science must rest on first principles that are prior by nature to their conclusions. To know if this standard is met, the educated person must know what sort of judgment might meet it; he must, therefore, be convinced that the conditions for natural priority are reasonable; for if they are not, there will be no satisfactory account of genuine first principles.

Plato regards the evaluation of different theories and their methods of argument as a task for dialectic. The dialectician understands the different methods of argument appropriate to different questions and disciplines.[5] She realizes, as the mathematicians themselves do not, that they treat their first principles as assumptions, and do not raise the further questions about them that a dialectician ought to raise. Aristotle does not say explicitly that the discipline forming an educated person's view of other disciplines is dialectic; but this seems the most likely candidate.[6]

He says that some people ask for demonstrations in the wrong places because they are uneducated in analytics (*Met.* 1005b2–5). But what they lack is not the capacity to formulate or (in one way) to understand deductive arguments of the sort set out in the *Analytics*, but appreciation of their function and limits. Such appreciation results from understanding of the kinds of arguments, proofs, and objections that are appropriate for different sorts of claims; and this understanding is part of competence in dialectic. At any rate, Aristotle's instructions on dialectical argument include rules about the proper way to challenge, or to leave unchallenged, first principles and the propositions derived from them (*Top.* 158a31–b8). To this extent, the educated person relies on principles secured by dialectical argument; and these principles themselves will be open to any questions that can be raised about dialectical argument in general.

Aristotle's educated person is the intended beneficiary of most of his philosophical work. Such works as the *Physics, Generation and Corruption, De Anima,* and *Posterior Analytics* are not addressed primarily to the natural scientist, but to someone reflecting on the nature and assumptions of a natural science. These reflexions are pursued to the most basic level in the *Metaphysics,* where first philosophy pursues systematically the sorts of questions that concern the educated person reflecting on the sciences. Someone who faces the educated person's questions can appropriately begin with the practice and theory of Aristotle's methods of discovery.[7]

12. WAYS TO FIRST PRINCIPLES

Aristotle's inquiries, described in very general terms, should be ways to reach what is known by nature from what is known to us. He claims, equally generally, that an inquiry should begin from 'appearances', *phainomena.* But his different comments on appearances indicate the differences of method.

Sometimes appearances are the empirical evidence collected for a theory:

Most principles of a science are special to it. Hence it is a task for experience to ⟨supply the principles⟩ about a given area. I mean, e.g., that it is the task of astronomical experience to supply the principles of astronomical science; for once the appearances had been adequately grasped, that was the way to find astronomical demonstrations. And the same is true for any other craft or science. Hence, if the facts (*huparchonta*) about a given area are grasped, our next task will be to set out the demonstrations readily. For if our inquiry (*historia*) leaves out none of the facts that truly hold of things, we will be able to find and produce a demonstration of whatever admits of demonstration, and if something does not admit of demonstration, to make this evident also. (*APr* 46a17–27)

Here the appearances are grasped by empirical inquiry, and form the basis for empirical science. The accumulation of particular appearances results in the discovery of generalizations, and then in demonstrations stating general laws.

Elsewhere, however, the appearances seem to be different, and to play a different role, because they belong to a different type of inquiry. In discussing incontinence Aristotle says:

We must, as in the other cases, set out the appearances, and first go through the puzzles. In that way we must prove, ideally, the truth of all the common beliefs about these affections of the soul, or, if not of all, of most of them and the most authoritative (or 'important', *kuriôtata*). For if the difficulties are resolved and the common beliefs are left standing, that is an adequate proof. (*EN* 1145b2–7; cf. *Phys.* 211a7)

In this case the appearances are commonly-accepted beliefs (*endoxa*). Aristotle does not refer to empirical inquiry, or to the results of experience, or to generalization and demonstration. He speaks of puzzles, and claims that a resolution of the puzzles is an adequate proof; such a standard of adequate proof was not mentioned in the account of astronomical appearances and discovery.

These passages suggest some distinction between empirical inquiry and the relatively non-empirical method of dialectic, two methods of inquiry dealing with two different sorts of appearances. Aristotle claims that dialectic leads to first principles (*Top.* 101b3–4), but he does not claim to practise dialectic in every inquiry that leads to first principles. In empirical inquiries, especially in the biological works, the path from appearances to principles (cf. *PA* 646a8–12) does not seem to rely primarily on dialectical argument. This distinction between dialectical and empirical argument is admittedly rough, and does not imply that the same work cannot include both types of argument. But it looks plausible and significant enough to guide our discussion.

13. EMPIRICAL STARTING-POINTS

Empirical inquiry (*historia*) begins with the appearances (*APr* 46a20–1).[8] To call something an appearance is to contrast it, in a particular context at least, with the conclusion of an argument; what appears to us is what we take to be the case immediately and without reflexion.[9] By this test all sorts of widely shared common beliefs (*endoxa*) will count as appearances; and Aristotle certainly draws on them at the beginning of his inquiry.[10] But he also recognizes a subset of appearances that are especially close to perception; these are immediate and non-inferential because they are the direct result of perception, not because most people find them obvious without argument.[11]

A further subset of perceptual appearances consists of 'what in each case appears authoritatively in accordance with perception' (*DC* 306a16–17).[12] But Aristotle does not say that we can distinguish these authoritative sensory appearances in advance of inquiry. The rule 'Begin from authoritative appearances' cannot be a practical guide for the initial conduct of inquiry, and we cannot assume that we have eliminated false sensory appearances at the start of inquiry.

But though Aristotle must allow that some of the appearances we begin from are false or misleading, he does not draw attention to this possibility as often as we might expect.[13] Indeed, he appeals quite confidently to appearances, on the assumption that they are plainly true; he even counts as perceptual some appearances that seem to have a rather indirect connexion with perception.[14]

All the appearances relevant to inquiry reflect someone's fairly immediate belief. Some are true, some false; some perceptual, some not; some commonly believed, some not. Aristotle uses them all as starting-points for inquiry, as long as they are not seen at the outset to be manifestly false. He speaks as though an appeal to appearances were the same as an appeal to the observed facts; but that is careless of him, since he agrees that the initial appearances include false ones. If he is entitled to assume that a given subset of appearances record the observed facts, he must have some way to isolate these veridical appearances before the formation of a theory explaining them.

14. THE ACCUMULATION OF DATA

In fact he tries to isolate the true appearances; for the appearances forming the basis of a theory are not the ones that we initially accept, but the ones we form as a result of experience (*empeiria*) and inquiry (*historia*).[15] The inquirer looks above all for observational evidence, fuller and more accurate than any that has been compiled previously; and the result of inquiry will be a better grasp of the perceptual appearances, not necessarily of the common beliefs.[16] Experience should isolate the appearances that are 'proper' or 'appropriate' (*oikeia*) to the subject-matter, so that we avoid introducing irrelevant considerations.[17]

A well-conceived inquiry that accumulates experience and discovers the appearances should also advance far enough beyond common beliefs to find the puzzles (*aporiai*) proper to a particular area of study.[18] We find some puzzles by attending to common beliefs and to the opinions of predecessors (e.g. *Metr.* 342b25–7). But we must not confine ourselves to these. The careful inquirer is to find the puzzles inherent in the subject itself, not simply those that other people have found (*DC* 294b6–13; cf. *Phys.* 263a15–18). A mere survey of what people find puzzling may not disclose what is really puzzling.

The source of our puzzles is empirical ignorance leaving us at a loss to say what happens or why it happens. Some of these puzzles are easily removed by collection of fairly accessible observations; others are more recalcitrant, and we need either a theory to explain something, or further appearances to fill the gap in our information. Only experience can tell us which of the puzzles we feel are genuine puzzles, and which initially non-puzzling things are genuine puzzles and therefore should puzzle us (*GA* 755b22–3, 770b28–35, 771b15–19).[19]

The role of experience and inquiry in the discovery of the appearances shows that 'appearances' is to some extent a misleading term for what Aristotle actually wants. Though the term does not mean 'observations' or 'observed facts', these glosses suggest what he wants. The appearances from which a theory should be formed are primarily those that appear to a trained and experienced observer as the result of systematic inquiry.

15. INDUCTION

Finding the appearances, inquiry, the accumulation of experience, and the discovery of the genuine puzzles do not seem to be temporally discrete stages of discovery. They all seem to be the same process, whose product is the possession of the relevant appearances and the awareness of the genuine puzzles. This product, however, is the precondition of a stage that does seem discrete from the ones we have discussed. Induction (*epagôgê*) is the method that Aristotle describes for the approach to first principles. It is the right method because induction proceeds from particulars to universals (*APr* 68b15–29, *APo* 92a37–8, *Top.* 105a13–14); since the things known to us are particulars, induction can lead us from these to the things known by nature (*APr* 68b35–7, *APo* 72b27–30).[20] If the things initially known to us were as universal as the things known by nature, then induction would not be the method that leads us from one to the other; we would have to argue 'syllogistically' (i.e. deductively) (*APr* 42a3–4, 68b13–14, *APo* 71a5–9, *EN* 1139b26–8).[21]

If induction is the primary method of discovery, leading from the appearances to their causes, the appearances must be perceptual, in a fairly narrow sense. For strictly perceptual judgments might well seem to be particular ('This is white', 'This deer has antlers', etc.), but the broader class of appearances includes universal no less than particular judgments, and if Aristotle were concerned with these, he could not so readily assume that induction, rather than syllogism, leads us from the appearances to their causes. By focusing on perceptual appearances, he makes it seem that generalization is the main task in the formation of a theory; and that is why induction is the method of discovery. The task is to consolidate our particular judgment that this F is G, that F is G and so on, into a universal judgment that Fs are Gs.[22]

Induction presupposes that experience has sorted out the true appearances from the false. But even correct perceptual appearances may not be focused on the right properties. A correct view about natural kinds requires revision of intuitive views (*APo* 97b7–39, *PA* 643b9–26, 644b1–8), since it is sometimes difficult to pick out the right similarities and common features (*Top.* 157a25–33, 157b3–8, 156b10–17, 160a37–9). To focus on the wrong kinds is to miss the properties that divide things into genuine kinds by explaining their other properties and behaviour.[23] Inductive generalization must therefore presuppose some explanatory hypothesis about kinds.

Aristotle's suggestion that induction is primarily generalization would be more reasonable if he could justifiably assume that inquiry and experience have already produced perceptual judgments involving the right kinds, and so incorporate the right explanatory hypotheses. But his description of inquiry and experience justifies no such assumption; these are preliminary to the formation of a theory, whereas a plausible explanatory hypothesis is likely to be the product of theoretical assumptions. Aristotle's remarks about induction, and about discovery in general, leave out many of the most important and most difficult questions.

16. THE EVALUATION OF THEORIES

A tentative theory should be tested, in Aristotle's view, by comparison with other possible accounts of the appearances. The simplest test, requiring a theory not to conflict with appearances (e.g. *Metr.* 357b15–23, *GC* 315a3–4), is reasonable only if we have sufficient reason to believe that the relevant appearances are true.[24] In criticizing people who hold on to their theories in the face of recalcitrant appearances, Aristotle insists that the appropriate test for a theory is not its agreement with all appearances, but its agreement with authoritative perceptual appearances:

The result is that though they speak about appearances, they say things that do not agree with appearances. And the reason for this is that they do not acquire the first principles correctly, but want to derive everything from some predetermined beliefs. For presumably the principles of perceptible things should be perceptible, of eternal things eternal, or perishable things perishable, and in general the principles should be of the same kind as the subject-matter. Because of their love of these ⟨beliefs⟩ they would seem to do something similar to those who maintain their ⟨paradoxical⟩ theses; for they are unmoved by any consequences, on the assumption that they have the true principles. They behave as though it were not right to judge some things by their consequences, and especially by their end; and whereas the end of productive science is the product, the end of natural ⟨science⟩ is what in each case appears authoritatively (*kuriôs*) in accordance with perception. (*DC* 306a7–17 ; cf. *GA* 760b28–33.)[25]

In saying that the end or goal of natural science is the appearance, Aristotle presumably means that it is a theory fitting the appearance.[26] The test will give the wrong results unless it is confined to authoritative perceptual appearances.

   Though conflict with authoritative appearances is sufficient reason for rejecting a theory, avoidance of conflict is not sufficient reason for accepting it. For a theory may be consistent with the actual appearances simply because it says very little about appearances at all (*GA* 748a7–11, *GC* 316a6–10), and so does not evidently conflict with them (*DC* 309a21–7). Aristotle, therefore, requires a theory to 'yield' the appearances.[27] It should explain them, and show that they are reasonable or plausible, *eulogon*.[28] A good theory should remove puzzles, by finding an explanation that makes the appearances seem more reasonable than others would be in these conditions.

   A theory should also fit any new appearances that may be discovered.[29] We do the best we can with the appearances we have available, but it is corrigible in the light of further appearances (*GA* 767b28–30; cf. 776a9–10).[30] Evidently, these new appearances are not common beliefs; indeed, the very fact that they are not commonly believed makes it necessary to inquire for them and makes them a useful test of a theory that accommodates the presently available appearances.[31]

   These tests of a theory rely on our capacity to identify the authoritative perceptual appearances, to recognize a bad explanation (if we are testing someone else's theory), and to find a good one (if we are defending our own theory). Aristotle does not claim to begin his inquiries from authoritative perceptual appearances, but at the stage of testing a theory, he assumes he has found them. Either he has no account of how we find them, or he assumes that inquiry and experience sort them out from the false and non-authoritative appearances.

   He speaks as though a theory could safely be constructed by

generalization from repeated observations, and as though the result of such generalization were a sufficient basis for evaluating theories. In giving this impression he fails to notice the importance of initial theoretical assumptions and causal hypotheses, and their influence on our conception of the data from which we generalize. His views about the testing of theories rely on the same assumptions that control his account of inquiry and induction.

17. CONCLUSIONS ON ARISTOTLE'S EMPIRICAL METHOD

Aristotle claims that inquiry leads us from what is known to us to objective principles known by nature, naturally prior, and informing us of an independent reality. His account of inquiry expresses these convictions; for he has no doubt of the accuracy of our authoritative perceptual appearances, and if we use these to form and to test theories, we will reach theories that correspond to the objective reality revealed by our perceptual appearances.

Aristotle does not justify his convictions. His account of inquiry and discovery leaves out those very aspects of them that raise difficulties for realism. (1) He assumes that we can find true perceptual appearances to serve as the basis for our induction and as an independent test of the truth of a theory; but some theoretical beliefs are needed to identify these appearances. (2) Aristotle speaks as though we could perform induction by generalization from surveys of the particular observations; but correct generalization needs some idea of the right kinds. Aristotle does not mention the role of theoretical conceptions in forming our beliefs about kinds. (3) To reject theories that conflict with appearances, we must have found the authoritative perceptual appearances; and to find those that explain appearances, we must be able to find explanations. In each case we need some theory.

Each of these unnoticed complications raises a difficulty for the assumption that we discover objective principles. For if we take account of what Aristotle overlooks at each stage, we must admit that our appearances do not provide a test that is completely independent of theory. If, as Aristotle suggests, we could identify authoritative appearances independently of all theory, then we would have some access to an independent reality against which we could test the theories. If, on the other hand, we recognize the role of theoretical assumptions, we challenge Aristotle's grounds for confidence in the possibility of objectivity, since we challenge the independence of authoritative appearances.[32]

A defence of realism through empiricism is closely connected with epistemological foundationalism.[33] If Aristotle can argue that knowledge of first principles requires grounds that do not themselves depend on further grounds for their support, and that perceptual appearances provide these grounds, then he can claim to have described a way to approach knowledge of genuine first principles. But in fact his own appearances do not seem to constitute completely independent grounds; for in accepting some appearances as authoritative, we seem to rely on further grounds and assumptions that are not themselves simply statements about appearances. Either we have to reject foundationalism or we must reject Aristotle's appearances as a suitable foundation. In either case, we challenge Aristotle's particular defence of realism.

Aristotle sometimes seems somewhat inclined to accept a foundationalist assumption, in so far as he sometimes treats appearances as though they were self-evidently true.[34] But this does not seem a plausible solution. Even if he has some reason for ascribing self-evidence to some appearances, he can hardly ascribe it to all the appearances we need to trust if we are to reach the right conclusion of inquiry. If, then, we doubt Aristotle's naïve realism, his description of empirical inquiry will strengthen, rather than remove, our doubts about the prospects of reaching objectively true first principles.

Some doubts might be removed if Aristotle could give us reasons for confidence in some of the non-perceptual appearances that guide our interpretation and evaluation of perceptual appearances. Since the discussion of these appearances belongs to dialectic, it is reasonable to turn to his account of dialectical inquiry.

18. THE FUNCTIONS OF DIALECTIC

Dialectic is 'a method from which we will be able to syllogize from common beliefs (*endoxa*) about every topic proposed to us, and will say nothing conflicting when we give an account ourselves' (*Top.* 100a18–21). He refers to common beliefs again, in his definition of a dialectical syllogism as the one that syllogizes from common beliefs (100a29–30). Dialectic has different tasks.

It is useful for three purposes: for gymnastic exercise, for encounters, and for the philosophical sciences. (1) It is evident from the facts themselves that it is useful for gymnastic exercise; for if we have a methodical procedure of inquiry, we will more easily be able to undertake the subject proposed to us. (2) It is useful for encounters; for if we have catalogued the beliefs of the many, we will meet them, not from other people's, but from their own views, and redirect whatever remarks of theirs appear to us to be incorrect. (3) It is useful for the philosophical sciences, because if we fully examine the puzzles on each side (*diaporêsai*), we will more easily see what is true or false. And it is also useful for ⟨finding⟩ the first principles of each science. For we cannot say anything about them from the proper first principles of the science in question, since the first principles are prior to everything else. Hence it is necessary to discuss them through the common beliefs on each subject. And this is proper to dialectic alone, or to it more than to anything else; for since it examines, it has a road towards the first principles of all disciplines. (*Top.* 101a26–b4)[35]

These different tasks are connected, and the third function of dialectic relies on the first two.[36]

Gymnastic techniques show us how to argue for different positions, and the ways in which different arguments can be misleading; and if we know this, we can both raise and solve puzzles.[37] Further, we need to know how to conduct 'encounters'; for we have to proceed through the common beliefs on each topic, and we must 'examine' (*exetazein*) the prevalent views.[38] And if our examination is to make progress, we must 'redirect' (or 'modify', *metabibazein*) beliefs in the right direction, and so we must know both what the right direction is and how to make someone else see that it is the right direction.[39]

Aristotle's statement of the third function of dialectic is quite limited. He does not say whether a dialectical discussion of a given proposition will ever supply sufficient reasons for believing that the proposition is a principle of some science. The first principles of a science are supposed to be 'known by nature', and naturally prior, describing objective reality. Aristotle assumes that the discussion of first principles through common beliefs is a way to approach objective principles; and our examination of dialectic has to see how it is to perform this task.[40]

Moreover, in claiming that dialectic has a road towards first principles Aristotle describes an approach that is different from the method of empirical inquiry. For his remarks on empirical method do not accord to dialectic the prominent role claimed for it in the *Topics*. Either (1) dialectic is a very subordinate part of empirical inquiry and (contrary to the suggestion of the *Topics*) has no further constructive role; or (2) empirical inquiry is really dialectic; or (3) they are two distinct methods. A fuller description of dialectic will support the third answer.[41]

19. THE STARTING-POINT OF DIALECTIC

Aristotle says dialectic is argument from common beliefs (*endoxa*); and these are the things prior and better known to us from which inquiry begins.[42] They are beliefs of the many or the wise or both; they are also called 'appearances' (*EN* 1123b22–4, 1145b2–3, *Top.* 105b1, 159b21, *APr* 24b11, *EE* 1216b26–8), since what someone believes is something that appears to him (though the converse does not follow). As usual, appearances are contrasted with arguments (*EE* 1216b26–8), indicating that the appearance is relatively immediate, in comparison with an explicit argument.

The relevant common beliefs, however, are only a subset of appearances. Admittedly, they should be apparent:

> but apparent not to just anyone, but to people of a certain sort; for it is an indefinitely long task to examine the things that make something apparent to just anyone. (*Top.* 170b6–8)

Not everyone's opinions count equally:

> To examine all the beliefs that some people hold about happiness is a waste of time. For many things appear to children, or sick or deranged people, about which no one with any sense would raise puzzles. . . . Nor should we examine the beliefs of the many, any more than of these other people, since they speak haphazardly about practically everything, and especially about happiness. (*EE* 1214b28–1215a2)[43]

The relevant beliefs, then, are those held by fairly reflective people after some reflexion.

In rejecting plainly foolish or 'haphazard' and ill-considered beliefs, Aristotle shows that he does not expect the relevant appearances to be the immediate reactions of the sort that might be reported by a survey of public opinion. While the appearances are not the product of dialectical inquiry, and still contain puzzles and possible conflicts, they should have been formed by people who are fairly careful to form beliefs that seem reasonable in the light of their other beliefs, and whose beliefs as a whole seem initially plausible.

Though dialectic relies on common beliefs, it does not confine itself to discussion of them, and does not exclude the possibility of proving something that sharply conflicts with many of them. Dialecticians also consider 'theses', positions maintained by a philosopher in opposition to common views (*Top.* 105a3, 159b30, viii 5). The falsity of a philosopher's thesis is not assumed at the outset of the discussion, and the dialectician's task is to see how far we must go from the common beliefs if we defend the counterintuitive view. We may find that the counterintuitive position is more consistent than its denial with the bulk of the common beliefs (cf. 173a25–7).

Since dialectical appearances must be common beliefs, and therefore must be commonly accepted, they differ in principle from the appearances from which empirical inquiry proceeds. New empirical information discovered by a single investigator acquiring experience certainly counts as a new empirical appearance, but since it need not be commonly believed, it need not be a new dialectical appearance. While Aristotle claims that empirical inquiry and experience improve our grasp of the appearances, he does not claim, and has no reason to claim, that they improve our grasp of the common beliefs.

Empirical inquiry discriminates in favour of perceptual appearances, and concentrates especially on these in forming and in testing theories. Dialecticians, however, cannot isolate a core of true appearances by picking out the strictly perceptual appearances.[44] Aristotle never suggests that dialectic is especially concerned with perception. We ought to expect, then, that a problem needs dialectical treatment if perception seems inadequate for it.

It follows that the task of surveying and setting out the appearances will be different in the two types of inquiry. A description of the empirical appearances will not confine itself to common beliefs; the inquirer will compile further observations resting on wider experience of the relevant area. There is no parallel in dialectic. Admittedly, it must take some care in the presentation of common beliefs; it must begin with a critical and discriminating survey, and some Socratic examination may be needed to elicit people's real beliefs. Still, the dialectician wants to discover what people really believe, not—at this stage—to replace their present beliefs with others. The sort of information that is collected in the *Historia Animalium* is not particularly useful for dialectic, since perception and observation do not seem especially helpful for solving the problems treated by dialectic.

The distinction between empirical and dialectical appearances is not completely sharp. An empirical inquiry may well begin from, among other things, the very sorts of non-perceptual common beliefs that are the staple of dialectical argument.[45] Similarly, some dialectical questions may be raised by a particular range of empirical appearances.[46] Still, the dialectician does not characteristically rely on the appearances that are discovered by empirical inquiry.[47] Even if they raise some of her problems, they do not solve them for her.[48] For the dialectician as well as the empirical inquirer, experience of the empirical facts is useful; but it is useful for a different reason. The dialectician uses empirical information as a source of dialectical problems, so that she can see what cases the common beliefs need to be applied to; and the information is subsidiary to the examination of common beliefs. For the empirical inquirer new information replaces the common beliefs that were his initial starting-point; he is not bound by them, as the dialectician is bound, for a statement of the appearances.[49]

20. DIALECTICAL PUZZLES

In dialectical argument the next step after setting out the appearances is the examination of puzzles, *aporiai*. Here, as opposed to empirical inquiry, consideration of puzzles seems to be clearly distinguished from the setting out of the appearances, and seems to follow it. This is the order Aristotle regularly observes in his dialectical inquiries (e.g. *Met.* i, iii, *EN* vii 2). Though puzzles are important in empirical inquiry, they are not exceptionally important; the inquirer mentions them in the course of acquiring experience and compiling a list of the appearances. In dialectic, on the other hand, the formulation of the puzzles sets the dialectician her task, and shapes the character of her answer:

For if we want to progress freely (*euporêsai*), it is relevant to have surveyed the puzzles well; for (1) subsequent progress is the resolving of the previous puzzles, and we cannot free ourselves from bonds we do not know.[50] But puzzlement of the mind reveals this about the subject-matter; in so far as we are puzzled, our condition is similar to that of prisoners in bonds, since it is impossible to go forward in either direction ⟨i.e. by choosing either one of the apparently contradictory beliefs causing the puzzle⟩. Hence we should have finished our survey of the difficulties before ⟨trying to resolve them⟩, both for this reason and because (2) those who inquire without first surveying the puzzles are similar to those who do not know which direction they ought to walk in, and besides that do not even know if they have or have not found the thing they are looking for; for the goal is not clear to these people, but it is clear to those who have previously raised the puzzles. Further (3) we must necessarily be better placed for reaching a verdict if we have first heard all the arguments carrying on the dispute, as though they were opponents in a legal case. (*Met.* 995a27–b4)[51]

Here Aristotle distinguishes three functions for the puzzles: (1) They show us that these are the difficulties to be resolved, so that we have more than a vague impression of something wrong. (2) We see more clearly the necessary conditions for an appropriate solution, so that we do not hastily accept a solution that collapses on closer study of the difficulties it was supposed to solve. (3) Our solution will be better balanced if we have listened to both the arguments leading to apparently contradictory conclusions, so that we do not dismiss or ignore a line of argument that deserves to be wholly or partly accepted in the solution.

Since Aristotle attaches such importance to the statement of the puzzles, they are prominent in his description of dialectic. He cites the dialectician's capacity to examine the puzzles as the primary reason for thinking she can contribute to the discovery of first principles (*Top.* 101a35). He even claims that the solution of a puzzle will be adequate if it solves the puzzle and difficulties and leaves the common beliefs standing (*EN* 1145b6–7; cf. 1146b7–8, *EE* 1235b13–18; cf. *Met.* 995a28–9).

In dialectic we are puzzled if we are in the condition produced by arguments that seem equally cogent but reach contradictory conclusions:

> . . . the equality of contrary reasonings would seem to be productive of a puzzle. For whenever we reason on both sides, and everything appears to follow by each of the contrary arguments, we are puzzled about which one we should act on. (*Top.* 145b17–20)[52]

We seem to be able to reason equally plausibly from the common beliefs to contradictory conclusions; we are puzzled and do not know which conclusion to affirm, though we seem forced to affirm one. We need dialectic to help us decide whether we must give up a common belief, or reject at least one argument as invalid, or deny that the conclusions are really contradictory.

Every dialectical inquiry should begin from a puzzle. The dialectician should not pick questions (*problêmata*) from matters that are evident to everyone or most people, since these matters raise no puzzle, or from claims that no one believes, since no one would put these forward (*Top.* 104a3–8; cf. 104b22–4, 105a3–9, *Rhet.* 1356b33–1357a1). These remarks suggest that a dialectician is not concerned with questions that do not puzzle anyone. On the other hand, some dialectical problems (e.g. whether the universe is eternal or not) find the many or the wise or both with no belief (*Top.* 104b1–5), and do not seem to raise puzzles (104b12–17).[53]

'Raising a puzzle', however, can be understood in different ways. Just as empirical inquiry identifies genuine puzzles, not simply questions that we initially find puzzling, so also dialectic, by its different methods, looks for genuine or 'objective' puzzles. We will not actually be puzzled by a question that we have never thought of; but it might be a puzzling question in so far as it will puzzle anyone who thinks about it carefully. If dialectic is concerned with questions that are puzzling even if they do not actually puzzle, the dialectician looks for puzzling questions that do not yet puzzle anyone. But if actual subjective puzzlement is required, then the dialectician is severely hampered; for our views may be systematically mistaken in a way that prevents us from being subjectively puzzled when we ought to be. To discover this we may need to find the 'objective' puzzles that are not yet subjective puzzles for anyone.

Aristotle's own surveys of puzzles make it clear that he seeks objective puzzles. The puzzles he raises concern the common beliefs, and their consistency with each other and with evident facts. But they are Aristotle's own puzzles, not simply transcribed from his predecessors, or from actual questions asked by common sense. Reflexion on common sense may show that we are not puzzled by all the objectively puzzling consequences of our beliefs that ought to puzzle us; and the dialectician's task is partly to show that sometimes common sense is too easily satisfied.[54]

The nature of a dialectical puzzle suggests that it must be wrong or misleading to claim that nothing that is evident to all could be a dialectical problem. For something might be evident to all, but turn out, on further inquiry, to raise severe problems.[55] Perhaps Aristotle will reply that when we think about the question it will turn out not to be evident to us, and hence not to everyone, after all. But then it will not be obvious at the start what is really evident, and we will be unwise to exempt from dialectical scrutiny the propositions that seem evident.

21. DIALECTICAL PUZZLES AND THE AIMS OF DIALECTIC

The nature and role of puzzles reflects the difference between dialectical and empirical inquiry. In dialectic we find ourselves accepting apparently cogent arguments for apparently contradictory conclusions, and we see that some revision and adjustment are needed. Dialectic encourages us to reflect further on the beliefs we already hold; and the puzzles show us where the revision is needed. Aristotle has no formal account of the sort of question that raises a dialectical rather than an empirical puzzle; but he rightly picks for dialectical examination the questions that do not seem to be settled by his methods of empirical inquiry.

Empirical puzzles are different. Most of them are simply the result of ignorance or unfamiliarity; we have no belief at all, or we are surprised at the actual appearances. In his empirical inquiries—those in which he surveys empirical appearances—Aristotle characteristically raises these empirical puzzles. In his dialectical inquiries—those that begin from common beliefs—he characteristically raises the dialectical puzzles that depend on conflicting arguments. Though he uses the same terms for the stages in the two methods, his selection of appearances and of puzzles shows that he thinks they are distinct methods.[56]

The dialectician's response to scepticism results from the special character of dialectical appearances and puzzles. The appearance of cogent arguments for contradictory conclusions is a serious threat to common beliefs. For if common beliefs force us into contradictory conclusions, they conflict among themselves, and we must either give some of them up, or admit that we do not know what to believe. The sceptical argument from conflicting appearances is intended to force us into just this conflict, and to lead us to suspension of judgment, inability to choose between the conflicting views.[57] Since Aristotle wants to show, against the sceptic, that common beliefs are reliable, he wants to show that they do not force us into conflicts and suspension of judgment. He therefore has good reason to anticipate the sceptic, by identifying the puzzles, and showing that we have the resources within common beliefs to solve them; and so he looks for dialectical puzzles.

Certainly a philosopher might be sceptical about the veracity of sensory appearances, and Aristotle replies to such scepticism.[58] But he does not characteristically believe that the truth of the authoritative sensory appearances is open to serious dispute; and so he takes the task of empirical inquiry to be discovery of a theory that fits the appearances, not the vindication of the appearances themselves. Scepticism about dialectical appearances is far more attractive; and Aristotle correspondingly regards it as a more serious challenge to be answered. If the puzzles are insoluble, we may find we have no good reason to accept the common beliefs we began with; and so the search for a theory is not merely a search for an explanation, but also a search for a defence. A counter-intuitive theory such as the Socratic view of incontinence is not dismissed out of hand simply because it conflicts with 'things that appear plainly' (*EN* 1145b27–31). Though Aristotle thinks it is desirable to defend the common beliefs, some argument for their truth needs to be given in each particular case to show that acceptance of the common beliefs is the right response to the puzzles they raise.[59] This demand imposed on dialectical argument distinguishes it from empirical argument.[60]

22. THE CONSTRUCTION OF A THEORY

Once the dialectician has expounded the objective puzzles, her next task is to find some general theory or principle that will solve them. Empirical inquiry begins from the particulars grasped in perception, and proceeds to the universal grasped by reason; but in dialectic the contrast between particular and universal is less prominent. Indeed Aristotle even says that we must proceed from the universal to the particulars, since the inarticulate whole is better known to perception (*Phys.* 184a16–26). We begin with what is confused (184a18–23), and look for a result that is clear.[61] The progress from the confused to the clear is far more prominent than the progress from the particular to the universal.[62]

This difference reflects the difference in the appearances. Some of our empirical data may be confused or inarticulate, but this is not their main fault. Experience helps us to discover new perceptual appearances, and to use them to correct some of our initial beliefs; and it would be quite misleading and distorting to suggest that its main task is the clarification and articulation of our initial beliefs. But the suggestion is not at all misleading for dialectical appearances. The puzzles they generate are a sign of confusion; for if we have arguments for contradictory conclusions, we are unsure about the implications of our beliefs, and therefore about their content. In deciding if they really imply what they seem to imply, we clarify them.

The primary method of empirical discovery is induction. An inquiry begins with perception and tries to add enough perceptions to provide the basis for inductive argument to a universal. Aristotle assumes that the perceptions inform us of particulars, and that our main task in forming a theory is to generalize these pieces of accurate information about particulars. For dialectic, on the other hand, induction, though relevant and useful, is not the primary method.[63] The common beliefs are often already universal in form, and the dialectician's task is not to generalize them. They are unsuitable as first principles because they raise puzzles that the dialectician seeks to solve; and for this purpose it will often be unhelpful to appeal to the generalizing function of induction.

Aristotle's view of dialectical discovery fits the dialectician's professional concern with the puzzles. A full preliminary exposition of the puzzles is the right preparation for an answer, but it would be unwise to try to answer them directly. If we simply claim that one side of a puzzle is true and one false, or if we interpret some other belief in a way that avoids a puzzle, we simply add another conflicting belief to those that we have already found. We need some further principle from which we can derive the distinctions and claims that will solve the puzzles; and if this principle is not itself to generate puzzles and disputes, it should be agreed by the different parties to a dispute.

Aristotle, therefore, characteristically begins his constructive argument by trying to 'make a new start' (*DA* 412a3–6, *Met.* 1041a6–7, *EN* 1174a13–14, *EE* 1218b31–2; cf. *EN* 1097a24). A suitable new start should emerge from appearances, or modified versions of them, that have not been challenged by any of the puzzles that have been raised.[64] These are the beliefs that all sides hold in common (*Phys.* 213a19–22) or those that after examination still seem to be correct (210b32–4); they allow the dialectician to begin with a point that is not in dispute.[65]

Aristotle's advice about making a new start shows how far the character of the puzzles controls the conduct of a dialectical argument; the dialectician's method is different from the empirical inquirer's because the solution of the puzzles is the dialectician's main concern, and he needs to argue from premises that are unaffected by puzzles. Moreover, the advice assumes crucially that we have surveyed the puzzles carefully, and especially that we have raised the objective puzzles. If we make a fresh start from beliefs that are undisputed because no one has thought of disputing them, they may turn out to be highly disputable, and puzzles may arise as soon as we appeal to them. A starting-point that relies on our failure to raise puzzles that ought to be raised is not a reliable basis for claims about truth. Equally, we should not be deterred from relying on a premiss, if puzzles have been raised about it foolishly and are easily answered. In each case we should be guided more by the objective puzzles than by what people have found puzzling. Having used the objective puzzles to find a new start, we can formulate our answer.

Constructive dialectic should profit from the gymnastic and peirastic functions of dialectic.[66] The practice of these functions often requires a defence of false views and an attack on true ones (*Top.* 141a24–37, 159b25–35); but the tactics are also relevant to constructive dialectic.[67] They are legitimate ways of challenging the defender of a thesis; and so resourceful defenders should be sure that they are not open to such challenges.[68] The dialectician becomes aware of reasonable lines of objection, and will be careful, as far as possible, to avoid them.[69]

23. THE EVALUATION OF DIALECTICAL THEORIES

In dialectic as in empirical inquiry, Aristotle rejects theories that conflict with appearances.[70] He urges us not to accept a counterintuitive thesis with absurd or repugnant consequences (*Top.* 160b17–22) just because we are too dense to solve the puzzles that arise from denial of the thesis (*Met.* 1012a17–20, *EN* 1146a21–7). He is reluctant to give up widely or universally shared beliefs:

As for those who object that what all things seek is not good, surely there is nothing in what they say. For things that seem ⟨good⟩ to all things we say are ⟨good⟩; and those who undermine this conviction are not altogether likely to say anything more convincing ⟨in place of it⟩. (*EN* 1172b35–1173a2)[71]

He claims that sometimes the critics of a common belief will undermine their own case against it, since any grounds we might have for believing the critics are much weaker than our grounds for accepting the common belief that the critics challenge.

Still, since the appearances are common beliefs, not initially certified as true, he must and does allow that it is sometimes right to reject them; sometimes we have good reason to support a theory with counterintuit-ive consequences. This is true about some of Aristotle's conclusions in the *Physics*, e.g. his rejection of a separate infinite and of a real void, and about some of his ethical conclusions (e.g. *Top.* 173a19–30).

Aristotle rightly allows that we may be able to defend not all, but only the most and the most important or authoritative (*kuria*; cf. *EN* 1145b5–6), of the common beliefs. This condition corresponds to the claim that in empirical inquiry the ultimate test is the authoritative perceptual appearance. But it is still less likely than in empirical inquiry that we can rely, in advance of any theory, on any firmly established appearances against which we can test the theory. We do need some undisputed beliefs to serve as 'new starts' for our theory; but these need not be accepted as authoritative. They are accepted provisionally, to see if they offer a reasonable basis for solving the puzzles.

Aristotle does not appeal explicitly to the alleged authoritative status of any dialectical appearances as a reason for rejecting a theory that conflicts with them. He does assume readily that some things are clear or self-evident (*Phys.* 193a3–9), and that it is foolish to doubt them (*GC* 325a18–23).[72] But the mere fact that an assumption seems obvious does not assure us that it is authoritative; Aristotle entertains even a theory that conflicts with beliefs that seem obviously true (*EN* 1145b27–9).[73]

Apparently, then, the test of conflict with appearances cannot be autonomous or decisive by itself. Perhaps only dialectical argument itself shows us that some common beliefs are more authoritative than others, because rejection of them would cause the collapse of too many other beliefs that we take to be more trustworthy than our grounds for doubt. In allowing the possibility of a true theory that violates apparently obvious appearances, Aristotle recognizes a complication in the appeal to authoritative appearances that he does not recognize in the case of empirical appearances.

In dialectic, as in empirical inquiry, the appearances should positively support a correct theory, even though they may be consistent with several incorrect theories. Once again, the positive support depends on the theory's ability to explain the appearances and make them seem reasonable.[74] But the type of explanation required of the dialectician, in contrast to the empirical inquirer, corresponds to the special aims of dialectic. An empirical theory should solve the puzzles by removing our ignorance and explaining a puzzling fact; its primary aim is not to give us reasons for accepting the beliefs that raised the puzzle. In dialectic, however, the puzzles arise from apparently conflicting beliefs; and so a theory should show that both the apparently conflicting beliefs are reasonable:

We should find an account that will yield, better than any other, the things that seem true on these questions, and will resolve the puzzles and the contrarieties. It will do this if it appears reasonable that the contrary things seem true; for this sort of account, more than any other, will agree with the appearances. And it turns out that the contrarieties are left standing if what is said is true in one way, and not true in another. (*EE* 1235b13–18)[75]

The resolution of the initial conflict, and the defence or modification of the beliefs that seemed to generate it, are characteristic of the dialectical, rather than the empirical, attempt to yield the appearances.

In dialectic, then, our plausible and undisputed 'new start' should show how far the beliefs that appeared to generate the puzzles are credible, and how far they can avoid generating puzzles. Sometimes our new start allows us to see that at least one of the arguments for the two sides of the puzzle adds some false premises to the appearance that seemed to cause the trouble; sometimes it shows us that when we articulate the appearance more carefully, we should not interpret it in the way that causes the puzzle.[76] On the other hand, a theory will reject some appearances, if a puzzle shows that doubt about them is well founded, and if their rejection allows us to solve the puzzle. Hence the success of the theory must be considered from these two points of view at once.[77]

A correct theory must not only yield, explain, and support the true appearances; it must also explain why the false appearances might have seemed true even though they are false (*Phys.* 211a9–11, *EN* 1136a23–b14, 1144b32–1145a2). Often it will do this in the course of solving the puzzles, by showing what is wrong, though plausible, about one side of a puzzle. An explanation of the false beliefs is part of the dialectician's task since he wants a theory that accounts for all the appearances. It is also part of his task in relation to his audience. Dialectical argument is meant to convince us if we begin by believing the appearances. We are more readily and more fully convinced if our false beliefs can be explained rather than ignored; if they were not explained they might still appear to be sources of objections to dialectical arguments (cf. *EN* 1154a22–6, *EE* 1246a13).

A degree of imprecision in Aristotle's account is really one of its virtues. To solve the puzzles and to give a reasonable interpretation of the appearances, we must reconcile the initial beliefs and the other claims that come to seem reasonable in the course of inquiry. The survey of puzzles shows us that something has to give way, since we cannot be content with the suspension of belief that results from the recognition of unsolved puzzles. We must show either that we have misunderstood our initial belief, or that we must reject part of an argument that seemed plausible. Our choice of solution depends on the consequences for our other beliefs, both about particular cases and about general principles. No particular subset of beliefs is in principle beyond revision; and the theorist's task is to achieve fairly broad coherence.

24. THE SPECIAL ROLE OF DIALECTIC

Aristotle recognizes important differences between empirical and dialectical method; and these differences all begin from the different tasks set for the two methods. Empirical inquiry tries to remove our ignorance and lack of beliefs; it seeks to accumulate perceptual data by experience, and to generalize from them by induction. Dialectic is not concerned with our lack of beliefs, but with conflicts and difficulties in the beliefs we already have. For dialectic, the study of puzzles is central, and induction and generalization are secondary, reversing the order of importance in empirical inquiry. Similarly, the puzzles constrain the form of an acceptable dialectical solution, to a degree without parallel in empirical inquiry.

These differences reflect the relatively non–empirical character of dialectic. It is non–empirical in so far as it is concerned with questions that are relatively recalcitrant to empirical solution. This claim does not imply that empirical discoveries are always irrelevant to dialectical puzzles. We are free to agree that a certain level of empirical information is needed for us to discover certain puzzles, and that further information may make other puzzles seem less compelling, or may make their solution less urgent; Aristotle's views about elemental change, for instance, might raise dialectical puzzles about matter that will no longer bother us if we reject the empirical theory. But such cases do not challenge the general description of dialectic.

Dialectical puzzles concern concepts and assumptions that we use to interpret and understand experience as a whole; they will therefore not be easily modified by experience, since they will control our interpretation of any experience that might seem likely to modify them.[78] If, for instance, we believe firmly and fundamentally that our senses deceive us, we will not be ready to change any beliefs, especially this fundamental one, through sense–experience. Disbelief in the reality of change or in the Principle of Non-Contradiction will make us immune to the normal effects of empirical information; and so it is not surprising that Aristotle treats these as dialectical rather than empirical puzzles.

This description extends Aristotle's claim that dialectic is about first principles, and therefore about questions that are not readily answered by arguments and evidence relying on the truth of those principles. He claims, for this reason, that a science cannot defend its own principles to someone who wants an argument that does not assume their truth. He can fairly claim, for similar reasons, that appeals to experience presuppose principles that need some defence apart from an appeal to the experience that presupposes them.

This account of the non–empirical character of dialectic may sound too Kantian to express anything that is likely to have occurred to Aristotle. But if he had tried to face the general question about dialectic, his views about its appropriateness for first principles might reasonably suggest this answer to him.

25. QUESTIONS ABOUT DIALECTIC

Aristotle claims that his methods lead to the discovery of objective principles that are 'known by nature', because they describe an independent objective reality. How far does he make the necessary realist claims about the results of his methods, and how far does he justify them in his account of the method? We need to ask these questions separately for empirical and for dialectical inquiry, since the answers are different.

Aristotle's attitude to empirical inquiry is a rather naïve form of realism. He tends to assume without question that we can isolate a reliable body of hard perceptual data informing us about an independent reality, and that these firmly determine the shape of an acceptable theory. His assumptions rest on an account of empirical inquiry that is over-simplified at the crucial points.

His account of dialectic removes some of the over-simplification; and if he had recognized more analogies between the two methods his account of empirical inquiry would have been better. He recognizes that we cannot isolate a set of firm data in advance of a theory, and that the demands of the theory may cause us to modify some appearances that at first seemed firm. Dialectic seeks coherence and mutual adjustment; and if Aristotle had recognized the same requirements in empirical inquiry, his account of it would have been less naïve.

If, however, the account of dialectic seems less naïve, it also seems less realist. For though Aristotle must assume that dialectic leads to objective first principles, he does not assert this conviction in his description of dialectical method, and it is hard to see how the method can support any such conviction.[79] If a dialectical inquiry succeeds, we will have achieved coherence among our beliefs, by revision of the appearances we began with. Such coherence may be worth having; but Aristotle seems to give us no reason for believing that it has led us nearer to a description of any objective reality. It seems quite possible to achieve coherence without moving any closer to the truth, and Aristotle does not say why this sort of coherence is not the most that we can expect from dialectical inquiry.[80]

If Aristotle is less realist about dialectical than about empirical inquiry because he is less naïve, then the questions we have raised about the results of dialectic should be raised about the results of empirical inquiry too. The difficulties seem less severe only because Aristotle's description does not expose them as clearly.

Aristotle's educated person ought, therefore, to be unsatisfied by Aristotle's answers. These difficulties will matter to us in two ways. First, we must bear in mind our doubts about dialectic as we examine some of the particular philosophical claims that seem to be defended by dialectical argument. Second, we must see if Aristotle has any better account of how he can achieve the objectivity he claims for the results of inquiry. We will explore the first question by discussing some of the dialectical doctrines of the *Categories* and *Physics*, and return to the second question in examining the theory of science in the *Posterior Analytics*.

In the *Metaphysics* the two questions come together. Aristotle argues that a dialectical justification of appropriate principles can be found. In the most fundamental case, some principles are needed for us to recognize regularity and objectivity in our experience at all; this claim is defended in *Metaphysics* iv. In less fundamental cases the Aristotelian principles are needed to find regularities and explicable tendencies in nature that would otherwise be unavailable to us. This claim is defended in *Metaphysics* vii–ix. A defence of these claims shows how a selective attitude to appearances in dialectical argument can be justified. The sorts of distinctions that Aristotle argues for in the *Categories* and *Physics* are defensible by appeal to something more than shared beliefs.

The kind of argument Aristotle offers in the *Metaphysics* is dialectical in so far as it appeals to some common beliefs; but it is not merely dialectical, since it is systematically selective in its attitude to common beliefs; it is strong dialectic, as opposed to pure dialectic. At this stage I have not tried to say how Aristotle conceives strong dialectic, or how viable his conception of it might be. But we have seen why he needs something like it, if he is to argue for the objective truth of the results achieved by dialectical inquiry.

3

CONSTRUCTIVE DIALECTIC

26. POSITIVE FUNCTIONS FOR DIALECTIC

We have examined some of the difficulties raised by Aristotle's explicit description of dialectic. But to understand the description better, and to see how far the practice of dialectic strengthens or weakens our doubts, we should discuss some of the central Aristotelian doctrines founded on dialectical argument. It is best to begin with the *Topics* and *Categories*, which deal at length with some of the central problems that are classified as 'logical', as opposed to physical or ethical.

Much of the *Topics* consists of rules for attacking or defending theses that involve reference to some central Aristotelian concepts; Aristotle shows how to argue about the four predicables—coincident, proprium, genus, and definition. The categories or 'kinds of predicates' are introduced as a tenfold division of each of the four predicables, the four possible types of properties predicated in a dialectical proposition or discussed in a dialectical problem (103b2–19).[1] The propositions are said to signify one or other of the categories. The distinctions underlying this tenfold division are presented at greater length in the *Categories*.

Aristotle claims that the basic realities are spatio-temporal particulars, e.g. individual men or trees; these are first substances because other realities depend on them in some way in which they do not depend on other realities. The other realities include the natural kinds (second substances) to which the first substances belong (e.g. man, tree), and the items (e.g. colour, height, or shape) that belong in non-substance categories. The treatment of the predicables, the categories, and of other dialectical concepts rests on these ontological views.

An account of these dialectical concepts is useful for gymnastic and peirastic, since it may allow us to identify errors in the opponent's argument; it is useful to point out that he asks questions about relatives that are suitable only for substances. But these concepts are especially important for the constructive function that makes dialectic a road towards first principles (*Top.* 101a34–b4).

Dialectic advances towards first principles through dialectical puzzles. Once we find the conflicting beliefs that cause a puzzle, we try to resolve the puzzle by making a 'new start' (e.g. *DA* 412a3–6).[2] The new start relies on undisputed and authoritative beliefs that have not been

challenged by the puzzles. Since the main dialectical concepts incorporate such beliefs, they should show what Aristotle takes for granted in
dialectical argument.

Aristotle appeals to what we say about (e.g.) the individual man, the
species man, white, double, and half, to support his claims about
substances, qualities, and relatives; often he relies on grammatical and
syntactical features of words and sentences. Throughout he alludes to
standard dialectical tactics, and has in mind the dialectical context, even
though he is not actually conducting a dialectical debate.[3]

But his appeal to common beliefs is selective; for he relies on further
assumptions to justify his acceptance of some common beliefs over
others. Evidently these assumptions determining the choice among
common beliefs need some defence; if they are just common beliefs,
they reintroduce the original problem, but if they have some other
status, it still needs to be explained. The four predicables, the ten
categories, and homonymy, are introduced in *Topics* i. The *Categories*
discusses the categories, and especially substance, at some length; and if
we follow its discussion, we also raise the main difficulties about the
concepts introduced in the *Topics*.

The character of Aristotle's defence of the dialectical concepts helps to
explain his use of them in arguments about first principles. At the end of
this chapter I turn from the *Categories* to *Physics* i, where Aristotle's
exposition of the first principles of natural philosophy relies on the
dialectical concepts examined in the *Categories*. Aristotle's use of these
concepts shows that he takes them to express common beliefs; and in
defending his own views about first principles, he is content to cite the
agreement of his views with common beliefs. But such a dialectical
defence of first principles does not show that they are objective
principles.

27. THE NATURE OF THE CATEGORIES

Aristotle introduces the categories:

Of the things said according to no combination each signifies either substance
or quantity or quality or relative or where or when or being in a position or
having or doing or being affected. (1b25–7)[4]

The items in the categories are beings (*onta*, 1a20), classified according
to their relation to a non–linguistic subject (1a20–b9).[5]

Aristotle draws distinctions between words, but they do not reflect
ordinary grammatical distinctions. For grammatically similar words

may have different functions; some signify an item in just one category, but other grammatically similar words signify items in more than one category. 'Man' and 'musician' are grammatically similar, but 'man' signifies an item in one category, and 'musician' signifies items in two categories—both a substance, a human being, and one of his qualities, musicality.[6]

The different categories correspond to different answers to the 'What is it?' question asked about different things.[7] Aristotle pursues this Socratic question to a more general level than it is pursued in any Platonic dialogue (*Top.* 103b27–35). He suggests that the categories provide the most general informative answers to the Socratic demand for definitions.

In pursuing the Socratic demand Aristotle also restricts it. The most general Socratic question is 'What is a being?', or 'What is it to be something?', and Aristotle refuses to give a single answer to this question, since he thinks there is no one property to be identified. He therefore connects his doctrine of the categories with the homonymy or multivocity (*pollachôs legesthai*) of being. He begins the *Categories* by defining homonymy and synonymy, as different relations between things with the same name. Then he at once asserts that beings are spoken of in four ways; it is reasonable to infer (though he does not say so) that these four ways reflect the homonymy of beings; he has given good reason to suppose that beings are homonymous, and he offers no counterargument or definition to show that beings are synonymous.[8]

In appealing to homonymy Aristotle resorts to a characteristic form of dialectical argument. He thinks we should ask, at the beginning of a Socratic inquiry into F, whether the name 'F' is homonymous, or (equivalently) whether the things signified by 'F' are homonymous or spoken of in many ways (*pollachôs legomena*; cf. *Phys.* 185a21). If we show that Fs are homonymous, we show that no single answer to 'What is F?' applies to all genuine Fs. Sometimes a single answer is ruled out because 'F' has different senses; and some of the tests for homonymy look like reasonable tests for distinguishing different senses of a word.[9]

Further tests for homonymy need not imply difference of sense, but still rule out a single definition stating the essential features of all Fs. If Fs are found in very different subjects (106a23–35, 106b21–5), or are incomparable (107b13–18), they are homonymous, and a different definition is needed for each kind. The different kinds of subjects provide the reason for seeing homonymy in being, one, and good (106a1–8, 107a3–12, 169a22–5, 170b19–25). Here Aristotle seems to be concerned with the correspondence of the names to important distinctions in reality.[10] These tests for homonymy imply that dialectic is more than a technique for the conduct of arguments; for it has to reflect our views about the real distinctions between kinds of things. The correct practice of dialectic requires awareness of the real distinctions.

For these reasons, however, appeals to multivocity have a strictly limited force in settling disputes. If, for instance, the claim that goods are multivocal rests on an account of goods that is challenged by a rival account, the appearance of multivocity is not a firm datum that can fairly be used against the rival account; for the appearance rests on the account that is being challenged. It follows that some of Aristotle's more philosophically interesting and useful appeals to multivocity will require us to examine the controversial assumptions that may underlie them.[11]

The homonymy of being, therefore, implies not primarily a difference of sense in the verb 'to be', but a real distinction among beings. Aristotle argues that predication does not always express the same relation, and that the items it introduces are of different types. We might agree that 'The dog is tall' introduces two different things signified by 'dog' and 'tall', without seeing the importance of the difference; for we might think 'dog' is a name for a certain kind of animal in the way 'Rover' is a name for this animal, and that 'tall' is a name for some other sort of object. But we would be wrong; for whereas Rover has dimensions and is in a particular place, we apparently cannot say the same about the objects named by 'dog' and 'tall'.

To see the importance of these issues is to see the point of the doctrine of the categories. Aristotle agrees that 'tall' names an object of some sort—there is something in extra-linguistic reality corresponding to it— but he denies that it names a further object of the same sort as Rover. In describing substances, qualities, relatives, and the items in other categories, he tries to say more precisely what is implied in speaking of different 'sorts' of objects at this most general level.[12]

Aristotle's method of argument for the categories is dialectical. He remarks, for example, that it seems most special to substance that the same and numerically one thing can receive contraries (*Catg.* 4a10–11). He points out that we can say of some things that they used to be pale before they became dark, but we cannot say anything similar about, e.g., qualities or quantities. Similarly, we can ask of a quantity what it is equal to, but cannot ask this of other things. Aristotle relies on our intuitive views about the sorts of things we introduce in making our assertions. The *Categories* provides an argument for the list of categories, and not merely a description of it, in so far as it appeals to these sorts of common beliefs as grounds for distinguishing categories.[13]

The homonymy of being reveals the differences between the types of beings, and study of these differences reveals the special status of one type of being. Here Aristotle still follows common sense. For we may agree that there is something for 'tall' as well as 'dog' to name, but still assume that somehow tallness is dependent on things like dogs. Aristotle accepts this intuitive assumption. In calling one of the categories 'substance' (*ousia*), he does not just distinguish some beings from the rest, but also implies that some are primary and basic. Though he wants to defend the reality of all ten categories, he especially wants to defend the superior status of substance.

28. SUBSTANCE AND THE CATEGORIES

Aristotle does not introduce 'substance', *ousia*, as a technical term to be defined as he pleases; his own criteria and candidates for substance should capture some common beliefs.[14] Sometimes *ousiai* are supposed to be basic and ineliminable subjects.

We call substance the simple bodies, e.g. air, fire, water and all of that sort, and in general bodies and the animals, deities and parts of them constituted out of bodies. And we call all these substance because they are not said of a subject, but the other things are said of them. (*Met.* 1017b10–14)[15]

Aristotle assumes that everything other than a substance is composed of a substance or is some property of a substance (1001b29–32). In Plato, on the other hand, the question 'What is it?' is usually asked about universals, e.g. piety, and the answer tells us the *ousia* of piety, what piety is (e.g. *Eu.* 11a6–b1, *Phd.* 65d12–e1). Aristotle suggests, similarly, that we refer to the *ousia* of x when we say what x is and find its essence (*Met.* 1017b21–2).[16]

Apparently, then, Aristotle recognizes two criteria for substance— basic subject and essence. In some cases the two criteria seem to produce different results. When we know what white is, we will know its *ousia* (essence), and in this sense non-substances have an *ousia* (cf. *Top.* 140a34, b5, 146b3); but we will not yet know anything about an *ousia* (basic subject).

These two criteria seem to influence Aristotle's treatment of the first category, and especially his tendency to use two different names for it. In the *Categories* it is called substance. In the *Topics* the list of categories is introduced twice with 'what it is' as the first item, followed by the other items on the list in the *Categories* (103b21–7). Aristotle adds:

It is clear from them ⟨sc. the ten categories⟩ that one who signifies the what-it-is sometimes signifies substance, sometimes quantity, sometimes quality, sometimes one of the other categories. (103b27–9)

Then he explains how each of the categories provides an answer to the 'What is it?' question asked about each different type of item; substance is the first category, and what-it-is seems to range over all the categories. The 'essence-criterion' for substance seems to underlie the first list, and the 'subject-criterion' the second.[17]

In the *Categories*, however, Aristotle diverges from common beliefs, since he appeals exclusively to the subject-criterion. He presents a fourfold division of beings—those said of a subject and not in a subject, those said of and in, those in but not said of, and those neither said of nor in. He identifies the things neither said of nor in with first substances, and identifies the species and genera said of first substances with second substances (2a11–19). A substance is not in any subject, and a second substance is said of first substances but not in any subject.[18]

These comments about strong predication ('said of a subject') and inherence ('in a subject') introduce us to the distinction between particulars and universals.[19] Particulars are not said of anything else; and Aristotle takes it to be obvious that his candidates meet this condition. Whatever is numerically one is spatio-temporally unified, not existing in many discontinuous places at the same time (*Top.* 103a14–23).[20] Aristotle claims that this condition is satisfied by particular non-substances (e.g. the particular white that belongs only to Socrates) as well as particular first substances (*Catg.* 1b6–9).[21] Universals are the species and genera of the items they are strongly predicated of.[22]

Among universals those strongly predicated of particular substances are 'second' substances, which are substances to a secondary and lesser degree than first substances.

Among second substances, the species is more a substance than the genus; for it is nearer to the first substance . . . Further, the first substances are subjects for all the other things, and all the other things are predicated of them or are in them; and this is why they are called substances most of all. (2b7–8, 15–17)

First substances are the best substances because they are the basic subjects, and second substances are substances in so far as they are the next-best subjects. Species are subjects for genera, and substantial species and genera are subjects for non-substances; hence substantial species are substances more than substantial genera are, and both are substances more than non-substantial species and genera are (2b15–22, 2b37–3a6).

These divisions diverge from common beliefs, in so far as they assume that the primary criterion for being a substance is the subject-criterion. Aristotle assesses candidates for substance by the degree to which they are subjects. We might suppose that he also recognizes the essence-criterion, since he remarks that second substances count as substances partly because they reveal what first substances are (2b7–14, 30–7). But he does not mean that the essence-criterion is a distinct criterion. It shows that second substances are substances only because it shows how closely related they are to the first substances; hence the subject-criterion is still primary.

In claiming that some substances must be subjects Aristotle can appeal to common sense; but in assuming that all substances must be subjects he seems to overlook the essence-criterion. He relies selectively on common beliefs, apparently ignoring those that would make the essence-criterion a distinct criterion for substance; he has not justified his selective attitude.

29. INHERENCE AND STRONG PREDICATION

Strong predication distinguishes universals from particulars, and therefore distinguishes second from first substances. Inherence distinguishes non-substances from substances, both universals and particulars. It is defined as follows: 'By in a subject I mean what belongs in something, not as a part, and is incapable of being separately from what it is in' (1a24–5).[23] The last clause of the definition simply asserts existential dependence, but the rest needs to be explained.

Aristotle offers some examples to illustrate the distinction between strong predication and inherence. Man is said of the individual man if and only if the individual man is a man, and the individual white is in the individual man if and only if the individual man is white. When adjectives such as 'white' are predicated of a subject-term, they are cognate with abstract nouns ('white' with 'whiteness', 'skilful' with 'skill', etc.) that cannot be predicated of the subject-term (we cannot say 'The individual man is a skill'). The abstract noun signifies an inherent item, and predicating the adjective of the subject-term introduces the inherent item.

In these cases Aristotle says the man is a paronym of whiteness, in so far as he is called white paronymously from the whiteness inherent in him (1a12–15). It follows that F is inherent in x if and only if the adjective 'F-ish' is applied paronymously to x from F.[24] Paronymy indicates the fact that x cannot be called *an* F.[25] Correspondingly, the individual F will be a first substance if and only if we cannot say 'x is a the individual F' (it is not said of anything), and there is no further subject that we can call F-ish paronymously from F (it is not inherent in anything).[26] Aristotle's examples of first substances—the individual man, horse, etc.—all satisfy these conditions.[27]

The distinction between strong predication and inherence indicates one reason for recognizing first substances. To say that x is white or that whiteness inheres in x is not yet to say what it is that is white. We can answer trivially, 'a white thing', but white things are not just white. We still want to ask 'x is a white what?' and we will answer the question by providing a noun 'F' that allows us to say 'x is an F'. The answer finds the first and the second substance. Second substances are the species and genera of first substances, because strong predication places the first substance in its kind and makes it fit for further characterization by its inherent properties.

If we attach an indefinite article to an adjective we still leave a gap: 'a white . . .' still needs to be completed. In using the indefinite article we try to pick out one subject, but 'white' fails to do that, since it imposes no conditions for counting its instances. Applied to a book with a white cover and white pages, 'one white . . .' may refer to the book or to the cover or to one of the pages. The concepts 'book', 'cover', 'page', however, fix conditions for something's being one book etc.; these concepts include their own arithmetic, and 'white' does not.[28] Though Aristotle does not mention this difference between strong predication and inherence, it helps to explain how non-substantial predications depend on some initial substantial predication.[29]

The grammatical tests that distinguish strong predication from inherence rely mainly on the suitability or unsuitability of the indefinite article (more exactly, of the equivalent Aristotelian devices). Aristotle supposes that these tests sort things into the appropriate classes that make them countable subjects. To this extent he seems to pick out a significant class of basic subjects, and we can see some point in the claim that these subjects belong to the category of substance.

30. SUBSTANCE AND QUALITY

So far we have tried to distinguish substantial from non-substantial properties by appeal to the difference between count-nouns that classify subjects and adjectives that merely characterize them. But Aristotle cannot rely on this distinction alone. For if every count-noun applicable to a first substance implies a strong predication of it, there will be more second substances than Aristotle wants. 'White' and 'intelligent' introduce items inherent in a man, and no count-noun corresponds to either of them; but 'musician' and 'painter' are count-nouns, and so (if count-nouns correspond to second substances) musician and painter should be second substances attributable to a man. But Aristotle cannot accept this result.

He may reply that a substantial predication is supposed to say what the subject is, and that mere characterizing adjectives fail to do this. But it is difficult to explain the sense of 'What is it?' in which 'It's a musician' does not answer the question. In exploring Aristotle's efforts to explain this, we must follow some of his views on qualities, change, propria, coincidents, and essence. These will not yield a clear explanation; indeed, they will show how heavily he relies on a rather complex and incompletely explained interpretation of the 'What is it?' question.

Some of the difficulties appear in Aristotle's treatment of the category of quality. Quality is connected with the question 'What sort?' (*poios*, *qualis*); but Aristotle wants the category to collect only a subset of the answers to the question. For he remarks that the question may reflect either the contrast between essential and coincidental properties or the contrast between particulars and universals. All second substances are *poia*, but they all answer the 'What is it?' question about first substances, and hence are not in the category of quality.[30]

In the discussion of the category Aristotle simply enumerates the different types of qualities, with no account of a common feature that would distinguish them from substantial *poia*.[31] Among qualities he mentions shape (*schêma*), figure (*morphê*), condition, state, and capacity as different types of qualities. But it seems easy to think of second substances or differentiae that can be understood this way; being a rational animal is having a capacity, even a tendency, to reason, and naturally having two feet seems to be a state.

The category of quality, then, seems too broad for Aristotle's purposes. The category gets its name because it seems initially plausible to group together all the items mentioned in answering the question '*poion estin* x?', 'what is x like?', but this question reflects a homonymy in '*poion*'.[32] The basic difference between second substances and qualities prevents Aristotle from grouping all *poia* together; but the intuitions that underlie the initial account do not mark or explain the distinctions that he needs.[33]

This conclusion is relevant to our questions about strong predication and inherence; for it shows that we cannot hope to explain that distinction by appeal to any antecedent grasp of the category of quality. We collect the right *poia* in the category of quality only if we already know how to exclude substantial properties; and to do this we have to appeal over again to the distinction between strong predication and inherence. No simple answer to the question 'What is x?' or 'What is x like?' provides the necessary distinctions.

31. SUBSTANCE AND CHANGE

The connexion between substance and change allows some further distinction between different properties of a first substance. For

Aristotle takes it to be a special property (proprium) of substance that a particular can remain in existence while receiving contraries.

> What seems especially special to substance is that what is numerically one and the same is able to receive contraries; in no other case would one be able to bring forward anything which is numerically one and able to receive contraries. The colour, e.g., which is numerically one and the same, will not be pale and dark; nor will the action which is numerically one and the same be bad and good; and similarly with everything else that is not substance. But a substance which is numerically one and the same is able to receive contraries. The individual man, e.g., being one and the same, becomes at one time pale, at another time dark, and hot and cold, and bad and good; this sort of thing does not appear in any other case . . . (4a10–22; cf. b17–18)[34]

First substances are, therefore, subjects of change; and Aristotle claims that this feature distinguishes substances from inherent items. The inherent items are not subjects of change in their own category; this yellow is what it is by being the quality it is, and if it loses its quality it ceases to exist, and hence is not a persisting subject of change at all.

If we still suggest that a quality, for instance, can become more or less interesting or dangerous, Aristotle will argue that in these cases the genuine subject of the change is the substance in which the allegedly changing non-substance inheres. His claim that receiving contraries is peculiar to substance is a corollary of his claim that substance is the basic subject. If non-substances could also receive contraries, then they would also be the basic subjects of these properties. In fact, however, the basic subjects are those in which the properties are inherent.

Questions about change show why there is some reason to recognize substances. Change, as opposed to mere replacement, requires something to persist through it, to be the subject that changes; and if a subject cannot exist without having the property (e.g. whiteness) that it loses in the change, then it is not the subject of the change. There must be some further subject and it must have some further property making it one and the same subject before and after the change.

If a proposed subject of change were inherent in a further subject, then, Aristotle assumes, the further subject would be the real subject of change; hence nothing inherent can be the subject of change. We might appeal to the non-arithmetic character of concepts indicating inherence. If we want to say 'The white became tall from being short', we need to answer 'The white what?' and the answer will identify the relevant subject. We might say 'This individual whiteness became less interesting'; but this is the same individual whiteness at two different times only because it inheres in the same individual man or horse, which must therefore be the real subject of the change.[35]

These facts about persistence and change show why some count-nouns do not refer to second substances. If they correspond to properties that the subject can lose without ceasing to exist, then they cannot indicate what the subject is, and so they cannot indicate substantial predication. If we follow this clue, we will identify the strong predications with those that signify the necessary properties of the subject—those properties that the subject must retain if it is to remain in existence.

32. SUBSTANCE AND ESSENTIAL PROPERTIES

We come still closer to finding substantial properties, however, and we see why they are not simply those that persist through change, if we examine Aristotle's use of the 'What is it?' question. He claims that the genus and the species

. . . alone among the things predicated reveal the first substance. For if you supply what the individual man is, you will supply it appropriately by supplying the species or the genus. (2b30–3)

If, however, you mention some inherent item, you will give an inappropriate answer to the question (2b34–7). The connexion between substance and 'What is it?' is so close that in the *Topics* Aristotle actually uses this name for the category of substance; he implies that a predication in the category of substance answers only this question, and never states any property that fails to answer the question.[36] The *Topics* connects 'What is it?' with the essence; and if we examine Aristotle's treatment of this and related concepts, we will see what is presupposed in a claim that a property is strongly predicated.

The *Topics* discusses essential, special (*idia*), intrinsic (*kath'hauto*), and coincidental (*sumbebêkota*) properties; and the relations between these properties show us some of the difficulties about strong predication. Though Aristotle sometimes seems to promise some understanding of these other properties that is independent of understanding essence, in the end he is committed to explaining them by reference to essence.

The treatment of the proprium, or special property, is rather instructively confused; but it is clear enough to show why not all necessary properties can be strongly predicated.[37] The proprium excludes the essence (102a18); but a subject's own proprium must be intrinsic to the subject (128b34–6).[38] The definition states the essence of the subject, and the statement of the proprium informs us of an intrinsic property derived from the essence.[39] Since the proprium is necessary and non-essential, not all necessary properties are essential, and therefore not all can be said of their substance.

Moreover, since the proprium must be intrinsic to the subject, it cannot be simply a necessary property. The difference between the intrinsic and the necessary emerges from Aristotle's discussion of the category of quantity. Members of this category (quanta) are subjects of quantitative properties; and to this extent first substances might seem to be quanta, since Socrates is six feet tall, and surely must have some height or other. However, Aristotle restricts quanta to subjects that intrinsically have quantitative properties (e.g., lengths, bodies, times, distances), and excludes anything that coincidentally has a quantitative property (*Catg.* 5a38–b10). In his example, an action is long not in its own right but because of the length of time it takes, and it is the length of time that intrinsically has the property of being a year long (5b4–6).[40]

Aristotle does not deny that quantitative properties are necessary to Socrates, but only that they are intrinsic to him. But the rules are not clear. If intrinsic properties are transitive, and if Socrates intrinsically has a body, then he intrinsically has some quantity, since bodies intrinsically have it. Aristotle does not accept this consequent of this conditional, and so he must reject one part of the antecedent. Probably he denies that Socrates intrinsically has the relevant sort of body; the body that is an intrinsic quantum is a geometrical solid, and perhaps Socrates' body simply coincides, though necessarily, with the geometrical solid.[41]

If some necessary properties are coincidental, we cannot identify the distinction between coincidental and intrinsic (non-coincidental) properties with the distinction between necessary and contingent (non-necessary) properties; and Aristotle therefore needs some further account of a coincident. He defines a coincident both (1) by exclusion, as neither genus nor definition nor proprium; and (2) positively, as what admits both of belonging and not belonging (*Top.* 102b4–14). The two definitions do not seem equivalent; for a necessary, non-essential, non-convertible property will be coincidental according to the first definition, non-coincidental according to the second.

This non-equivalence counts against the second definition rather than the first, since the first corresponds with Aristotle's more usual view that intrinsic coincidents are distinct from essence and proprium (e.g. *Met.* 1025a30–4). These are the properties to be demonstrated in demonstrative science and the ones we should be able to infer from a good definition (*DA* 402b16–403a2). In the *Analytics* Aristotle assumes that these coincidents are necessary, and therefore assumes that some coincidents are necessary.

Even some non-intrinsic coincidents seem to be necessary; while a triangle intrinsically has angles equal to 180 degrees, an equilateral triangle has this property only coincidentally, because it is coincidentally a triangle (*Top.* 110b21–5). He surely thinks it is necessary for an equilateral triangle to have angles equal to 180 degrees; he must mean simply that this is true of it qua triangle and not qua equilateral triangle. Though the property is coincidental it is necessary. This assumption conflicts with the second definition, which implies that no coincident is necessary. Aristotle is therefore wrong to offer the simplified second definition, since it suggests, contrary to his usual view, that being necessary is sufficient for being non-coincidental.[42]

Since the second definition conflicts severely with Aristotle's claims about coincidents even within the *Topics*, it would be better if he gave it up. The relation between essential, intrinsic, necessary, and coincidental properties is complex, because it reflects some points on which Aristotle has not clearly made up his mind. But the second definition of coincident blurs some of the important points, and does not deserve Aristotle's support.[43]

Once we see the difficulties in Aristotle's remarks about coincidents, we cannot appeal directly to any antecedently understood conception of the non-coincidental to explain strong predication; for coincidental and intrinsic properties are explained by reference to essence and definition, and these still need to be clarified.

A definition should refer to what is prior and better known (*Top.* 141a26–31). It is also intended to inform interlocutors (139b13–15); and if they are ignorant, a definition through what is prior will not be informative to them (141b15–21). But we must recognize that the substitute we offer as a concession to their ignorance will not be a genuine definition. The genuine definition must state the real essence.[44] It must not misrepresent the real structure and relation of genus, differentia, and species (142b22–9, 143a29–b10, 144a5–22); nor should it pick out inappropriate spatio-temporal properties that are inessential to the subject (144b31–145a2). The definition of a whole should not treat it as the sum of a number of parts (150a15–21, b22–6, 151a1–13, 20–31); for the essence must include the proper arrangement of the parts.[45]

All these requirements imply that a formula with the same meaning as the name still may not capture the essence. Though the *Topics* does not give a complete account of the essence, it shows that if we are to find it we need to rely on more than common beliefs; for the constraints on a proper definition cannot normally be satisfied from the inspection of common beliefs. The sort of definition that concerns Aristotle is not an intuitively familiar sort. The strict conditions he imposes are reasonable only if he is testing claims to say how things are, and trying to find out how things are. And if this conclusion is true about essence, it is true about coincidents, propria, and intrinsic properties as well, since our understanding of them depends on our understanding of essence.

33. THE ANOMALY OF DIFFERENTIAE

We have now found reasons to believe that the distinction between strong predication and inherence is the distinction between essential and non-essential properties. But this solution does not identify second substances.

⟨Not being inherent⟩ is not special to substance; the differentia is not in a subject either. For footed and biped are said of a subject—man—but are not in a subject, since neither footed nor biped is in man. Again, the account of the differentia is predicated of whatever subject the differentia is said of; if footed is said of man, e.g., the account of footed will also be predicated of man, since man is footed. (*Catg.* 3a21–8)

Though the differentia of a substance is strongly predicated of the substance, Aristotle denies that it is a second substance. Is he right?

We initially distinguished strong predication from inherence by distinguishing predication of count-nouns from predication of characterizing adjectives. At first sight 'the individual man is biped' seems to be an alleged case of strong predication that violates this rule. The violation, however, is only apparent. For though the differentia-term is an adjective, its gender agrees with the gender of the understood genus-term, not with that of the subject-term. Thus in 'man is biped' (3a28) 'man' is masculine, but 'biped' is neuter because 'animal' is neuter. In 'prudence is practical science', 'practical' is feminine, agreeing with 'science' (*Top.* 145a13–18).[46] 'Man is biped' is analysed as 'Man is a biped . . .', where the blank is to be filled by the appropriate genus-term.

The preferred analysis shows why Aristotle can still maintain that strong predication is nominal and inherence is adjectival. Though 'the man is biped' looks like adjectival predication, it is really nominal, because it should be analysed as 'the man is a biped animal'. This analysis allows Aristotle to maintain that differentiae are said of their subjects. But then the differentia-term must be 'biped . . .', not just 'biped'; and a biped . . ., e.g. a biped animal, is a second substance. Hence the differentia is a second substance, and so is no exception to the rule that only second substances are said of first substances.

Aristotle, then, has no good reason for claiming that differentiae are strongly-predicated non-substances. Perhaps he is misled into his claim by attending to some features of differentia-terms, and then drawing false conclusions about differentiae themselves. Admittedly, differentia-terms are not predicated in the same way as terms indicating paronymy and inherence; the gender of the adjective marks the distinction. Moreover, they are not second-substance terms; for in predicating the differentia-term ('biped . . .') we do not mention any second substance.

These facts might suggest the conclusion that differentiae are said of first substances, but are not second substances. But the conclusion is not justified. For the differentia-term refers to (without mentioning) the combination of the genus and the differentiating property; this combination is the species; and the species is a second substance. To predicate the differentia is just to predicate the species, by mentioning something else about it.

If differentiae are not second substances, they must fail to answer the 'What is it?' question. And indeed Aristotle argues that while genera say what the subject is, differentiae say only what it is like, or what sort it is (*poion*, *Top*. 122b12–17, 128a20–9, 139a28–31, 142b25–9). This might lead us to think that differentiae are qualities, since *poion* picks out that category; but Aristotle cannot agree, since qualities are inherent and differentiae are not.

And yet, once we see why differentiae are not qualities, we cannot easily deny that they answer the 'What is it?' question. If we just say 'Man is a biped', it is natural to ask 'Biped what?'; indeed the neuter gender of the differentia-term invites this further question. But though the genus-term is not used in the predication, the genus is referred to, and hence the differentia is said of the species. If we keep this in mind, the differentia, since it includes the genus, will answer the 'What is it?' question, even though we will not be able to say what the answer is if we simply mention the differentia-term.[47]

The treatment of differentiae in the *Categories* makes them thoroughly anomalous. Since they are not said of substance, they cannot be in the category of substance. But they cannot be in any non-substance category either; for members of these categories are inherent in substances, and differentiae are not. But if differentiae are not in any category, they falsify Aristotle's initial claim that things said without combination always signify items in categories.

These anomalies are unnecessary, since Aristotle could give good reasons for taking differentiae to be second substances. The fact that he rejects this view of them is significant because it exposes the limitations of his method in the *Categories*. In distinguishing differentiae from inherent properties he follows a useful grammatical clue, the gender of the differentia-term. But he does not attend to the ontological fact explaining this grammatical point. If he had attended to this fact, he

could not reasonably have refused to count differentiae as second
substances. The grounds for refusal are fairly superficial, reflecting
grammatical distinctions that turn out not to justify any distinction
between substantial species and non-substantial differentiae.

We should conclude, then, that Aristotle's conditions for finding
second substances are quite complicated. He must rely on the rather
stringent, non-linguistic, non-intuitive conditions for identifying essential properties; these conditions identify cases of strong predication. But
he must also rely on the intuitive, indeed rather superficial, linguistic
tests that distinguish nominal from adjectival predication, count-nouns
from characterizing adjectives, and the question 'What sort is x?' from
the question 'What is x?'. For he needs these tests to distinguish second
substances from differentiae. The resulting conception of second
substance is an unsatisfactory blend of considerations of quite different
types. Though we must go far beyond the initial intuitive tests that
Aristotle supplies, he cannot completely do without them.

34. THE DIALECTICAL SEARCH FOR FIRST PRINCIPLES

Discussion of the *Categories* has shown how far Aristotle's doctrine of
substance and non-substance appeals simply to common beliefs. He
begins from intuitive distinctions, and speaks as though he articulates
them, even when (as in the account of essence and strong predication)
they turn out not to explain his assumptions adequately. I turn now to
his use of that doctrine in the 'road to the first principles' that is said to
be characteristic of dialectic. In *Physics* i the appeal to common beliefs
pervades and limits his attempt to find first principles.

Aristotle begins the *Physics* by describing the aims and methods of
dialectical inquiry. It will proceed from things known to us to things
known by nature, and from things clear to us to things clear by nature;
and it should lead to the origins or first principles (*archai*) and causes
(*aitia*).[48] Aristotle looks for two sorts of origins and causes. (1) He seeks
the 'endoxic' principles underlying common beliefs (*endoxa*). (2) He also
seeks 'objective' principles that are aspects of reality, beings that are
origins and causes of other beings. The items that are prior, clearer, and
better known by nature are external realities.

It is not surprising that Aristotle wants to find objective origins and
causes, since scientific knowledge includes grasp of the causes. It is more
surprising that this is his aim for dialectical inquiry. Dialectic seems
suitable for clarifying and explaining common beliefs, and for finding
the endoxic principles that they support and presuppose; but it seems
less suitable for finding objective principles. Clarification of our beliefs

will not lead to objective first principles unless our starting-points are fairly near the truth. To be convinced by Aristotle's conclusions, we apparently should be convinced about his starting-points.

The first chapter of the *Physics* forces on us very sharply the questions that arise when we compare Aristotle's view of science with his view of dialectic. Science is knowledge of how things are; but it rests on principles that are reached by dialectic. Aristotle claims that dialectic has a way towards the objective first principles of all the sciences (*Top.* 101b3–4); but he also admits that it argues according to belief (100a25–30), with apparently no further reason for accepting the truth of its starting-points.[49]

But if dialectic is actually to argue for objective first principles, the initial ontological assumptions should apparently not just be taken for granted; for unless the starting-points of the dialectical argument are defensible, it is not clear how the argument can actually support the principles that it reaches, or how they are shown to be objective, not merely endoxic, principles. The *Categories* and *Topics* do not explain why we should pick one set of initial assumptions rather than another.[50] But the question becomes quite pressing once we take seriously the claim of dialectic to find objective first principles.

35. THE ROLE OF DIALECTIC

Aristotle begins with the Eleatics, who claim that what is is one and unchanging. They challenge the first principles of natural science, and no science answers challenges to its own principles.

To examine whether everything is one and unchanging is not to examine about nature. For a geometer has no further account (*logos*) to give to those who have done away with his first principles; giving such an account is a task either for another science or for one common to all the sciences. The same is true in the discussion of first principles. (*Phys.* 184b25–185a3)[51]

In this case Aristotle does not appeal to 'another science', a specialized science superordinate to the one whose principles are challenged. Instead he turns to logical dialectic, a discipline 'common to all the sciences', to examine the Eleatic thesis.[52]

He approaches the Eleatic thesis as a paradox to be dissolved, without setting out to prove its negation.

Examining whether things are one in this way is similar to arguing dialectically against any other thesis that is stated for the sake of argument (e.g. Heracleitus' thesis, or if someone were to say that being is one man), or dissolving an eristic argument—which is the sort that both Parmenides and Melissus offer. (185a5–9)

A philosopher's paradoxical thesis and an eristic puzzle may be presented simply for the sake of argument or to cause confusion, but they are worth studying for gymnastic purposes.[53]

Aristotle allows dialectic only a gymnastic approach to the Eleatic paradoxes, because his claims about first principles seem to him to exclude any other function. He assumes that the first principles are evident and that it would be madness to doubt them, and he infers that dialectic neither can nor should supply a further proof of the principles.[54] Dialectic is useful, not for unsuccessful and unnecessary efforts to find evident first principles, but for arguments against those who argue against these principles. Aristotle does not want to prove to the Eleatics themselves that they are wrong; he wants to prove to believers in common sense that they need not be taken in by the Eleatics.

The functions allowed to dialectic here are rather restricted. Aristotle looks for objective principles; his aim is not just to explain our beliefs, but to describe the external reality that they correspond to when they are true. The only form of argument that he offers for this purpose is dialectical argument, since he claims that dialectic has a way towards principles, and makes no such claim for anything else. But dialectic can claim this role only in so far as it helps us to spot the flaws, as they appear to common sense, in an argument against our first principles. Such a role for dialectic does not show how it can justify the principles themselves.[55]

Perhaps Aristotle thinks this does not matter, because the principles challenged by Eleatics are certain and evident without proof, so that we need no proof of them. This defence will make proofs unnecessary only for the principles that we can convince ourselves are certain and evident. But even for these principles, Aristotle's claim is doubtful. If the only point of a proof were to make something certain and evident for us, Aristotle would be right, since there would be nothing to prove about a claim that is already certain and evident. But this is not the only possible function of a proof. We might want to know what other principles are related to belief in change; how they are related to it; what we would have to give up if we ceased to believe in change. If we find that there is something seriously wrong with our belief in change, measured against our other beliefs, we may decide that though this belief seems evident and certain, it cannot be true, but must be a convenient fiction. This is the conclusion Eleatics might reach, and Aristotle's appeal to self-evidence is no answer to them.

If this is a reason for believing that we might need a proof of first principles, we should also reconsider Aristotle's claim that we cannot have a proof of them. If a proof has to prove a conclusion that is initially uncertain, from premises that are more certain, then we could not expect to prove first principles. But this may be the wrong conception of proof. We may also defend a principle by seeing how it fits our other beliefs, and it is not clear why such an appeal to coherence could not count as a proof.

Aristotle's attitude to these questions will be clearer from a discussion of the *Analytics* and *Metaphysics*.[56] His assumptions in *Physics* i indicate some of the difficulties that he raises for his views on dialectic and first principles.

36. THE DEFENCE OF FIRST PRINCIPLES

Aristotle's argument against the Eleatics follows the rules for dialectic, in so far as it relies on the Aristotelian views that provide the 'common places' (*topoi*) for the dialectician. If the arguments are valid, their force against the Eleatics depends on the reasonableness of these Aristotelian views. He appeals to his own doctrine of the multivocity of unity and being. The Eleatics speak of one being, but do not explain how 'being' and 'one' are to be understood. Aristotle shows that if we accept the doctrine of the categories, and we agree that there can be neither substances lacking non-substantial properties nor non-substances without substances, then the Eleatic conception of one being will seem incoherent.

He does not show, however, why Eleatics must accept the Aristotelian doctrines that convict them of incoherence.[57] Eleatics might agree with Aristotle that their conclusions conflict with common beliefs, and may even seem incoherent to common sense. They argue, however, that their premises are rationally inescapable, and that the arguments from them are valid. Aristotle rejects these Eleatic claims (185a9–12). But to show that the Eleatic premises are false, he simply appeals to common beliefs, and does not face the arguments that an Eleatic might offer for departing from common beliefs. Some of Aristotle's arguments could perhaps be used to dislodge the Eleatic, apart from a mere appeal to common beliefs; but Aristotle does not use them for this purpose.[58]

The discussion of the Eleatics reflects the self-denying attitude of the dialectician who sticks to gymnastic practice and the removal of puzzlement. Aristotle simply argues against those who deny it. He simply argues that if we accept some Aristotelian assumptions about the multivocity of being and unity and about the nature of signification, we will not be tempted to be Eleatics. He offers no further argument that might show the Eleatics, from premises they have to accept, that they are wrong.

It is not at all surprising that Aristotle offers no such argument; his views on dialectic and proof give him no reason to offer it. Since the first principles are evident in themselves, and the only function of a proof is to make something evident that was not previously evident, dialectic should not try to prove the first principles it examines. It does not matter that dialectic seems incapable of arguing reliably for objective principles, since Aristotle does not think they admit argument.

The attitude to first principles that is expressed in this passage of the *Physics* requires an account of their evident and certain character; and the *Analytics* offers an account.[59] Still, the rest of the *Physics* offers dialectical arguments for first principles; and these will seem all the more important the more we doubt Aristotle's doctrine of first principles. For if we do not find the principles self-evident, we will have to turn to the dialectical arguments that Aristotle offers to remove objections to them.

Though Aristotle himself does not intend these arguments to show that his principles are objectively correct, it is still worth seeing how close they come to showing this; for then we will see how they would have to be different if they were to constitute arguments for objective principles. The difference between purely dialectical arguments and the sorts of arguments that might support first principles will be important if we find that Aristotle offers apparently dialectical arguments that seem none the less to be intended to support objective principles. For if he offers such arguments, as he does in *Metaphysics* iv, we will have reason to believe his views on dialectic and proof have changed.[60]

37. GENERAL FEATURES OF CHANGE

Aristotle now looks for some general account of change (*kinêsis*) and becoming (*genesis*), and notices first the consensus that the origins are contraries (*Phys.* 188a19–30). Since his predecessors have reached the true conclusion without any argument to give them a good reason for it (188b26–30; cf. *PA* 642a18–19, *Met.* 986b31), Aristotle offers an argument (*logos*, 188a31) for it.[61] He appeals to the general principle that random things do not act on (*poiein*), and are not acted on by, random things (188a31–4). His appeal is justified only if every becoming is also an action of one thing on another. If it is, and if random action is impossible, random becoming is impossible. Aristotle assumes that every becoming is the causal influence of one thing on another, and that every case of causation involves something non-random; if x causes y, there is some general law relating types of which x and y are tokens.[62]

To avoid random transitions Aristotle wants the termini of becoming to be contraries or intermediates (e.g. black or grey things changing to white) rather than mere contradictories (188a36–b8). To say that all change is a transition from not-F to F or from F to not-F is not to imply a significant regularity; if eggs changed randomly into hens, rocks, and computers, these are changes from eggs to non-eggs, but they imply no significant regularity. Aristotle intends his restriction to contraries to rule out such cases. He argues that apparent exceptions to his rules, such as 'Musical came to be from white' (i.e. the white thing became musical) and 'The statue came to be from bronze' can be paraphrased in his terms as 'Musical came to be from unmusical (which was coincidentally white)' and 'The statue-shape came to be from shapelessness (in the bronze)' (188a31–b2).[63]

Aristotle argues inadequately for his proposals. To show that we can redescribe the termini of becoming in his preferred ways is not to show that we should or must. He will convince us on this further point if he shows that his description of the termini displays properties with regular law-like connexions. But he does not show it. If someone is unmusical, that explains why a change is *needed* for him to be musical; but it does not explain why the change *happens*, since someone could be unmusical and tone-deaf, and incapable of becoming musical. Similarly, all sorts of things lack the shape of a statue; but this lack is insufficient to explain the coming to be of a statue.[64]

Aristotle does not appeal to any consensus among his predecessors to support his claim that a subject as well as two contraries must be present in every change; he merely suggests that it is reasonable (*echei tina logon*, 189a21–2) to admit the third element. His reasons for admitting it rely on acceptance of the general outlook of the *Categories*.[65] He assumes he can fairly rely on the *Categories* to describe what seems reasonable to common sense.

If Aristotle is right about the *Categories*, he has found a dialectical defence for the belief in a subject and two contraries. He has not explained why we should accept this belief as a true account of actual changes in the world. But he has not set out to explain this; in this respect he has observed the restrictions imposed by his initial account of dialectical argument. In another respect, though, he has exceeded the limits of pure dialectic. His initial determinist assumption, ruling out random processes, does not seem warranted by common beliefs. Ordinary descriptions of the termini do not exclude random transitions of the sort that he wants to avoid. Here, as in the *Categories*, Aristotle selects and interprets common beliefs in the light of further assumptions that control his dialectical argument.

It would be exaggerated to claim that Aristotle appeals only to common beliefs, or that he uses dialectic simply to show that common sense is consistent. But this claim represents an important part of the truth about his exposition of the categories, and about his anti–Eleatic argument; and it ascribes a consistent position to him. His actual position is less clear; for sometimes he takes a more ambitious line. In his treatment of essence, and in his appeal to a determinist assumption, he does not seem to appeal simply to common beliefs; and sometimes he claims to find objective principles. But pure dialectic does not seem to justify this more ambitious line.

4

PUZZLES ABOUT SUBSTANCE

38. SUBSTANCES AND SUBJECTS

In the previous chapter I examined Aristotle's exposition and use of the doctrine of substance, to show that he defends it by appeal to common beliefs, and that this sort of defence limits the capacity of dialectic to defend first principles. In this chapter I turn to a further difficulty in the dialectical account of substance. The difficulties I have described so far mostly arise even if Aristotle is right to claim that common beliefs support his doctrine of substance; for even if they support it, they do not show that it describes any objective principles. But his difficulties are still more severe if in fact common beliefs do not uniquely support Aristotle's doctrine any more than they support other views incompatible with his.

I will show that this difficulty actually arises for Aristotle's doctrine of first substance. First I will examine the conditions assumed in the *Categories* for being a basic subject; then I will turn again to *Physics* i, to argue that the indeterminacy of common beliefs implies a fatal weakness in Aristotle's defence of his own conception of basic subjects against the rival views that make only matter a basic subject. First we need to see how the question about basic subjects arises.

We have discussed strong predication and inherence to see how to distinguish substances from non-substances. But even if we grasp strong predication and inherence, this is not enough; for the results we get by applying this distinction depend on our initial choice of subjects. We can rule out all those subjects that are either inherent in or strongly predicated of further subjects; but we are still left with too many subjects for Aristotle's purposes.

Aristotle can defend his claim that 'The individual man is a musician' expresses inherence rather than strong predication, by arguing that musicality is not essential to a man. But to show that musicality is not strongly predicated of a man is not to show that musicians are not substances. For 'the individual musician is a musician' expresses strong predication; and an individual musician (as opposed to his musicality) is not inherent in a man; musicians therefore seem to be first substances. If they are not, then some apparent subjects are not substances. For if we just use the intuitive notion of a subject as a bearer of essential properties that can persist through change, musicians seem to be as reasonable subjects as men, and Aristotle will have to recognize more first and second substances than he wants to.

The extent of Aristotle's difficulties is especially clear in his discussion of relatives; for here he commits himself to reliance on grammatical and linguistic arguments that imply the existence of too many substances. A relative is essentially 'of' something else that is its correlative (e.g., double and half, big and small, master and slave).[1] In finding the correlatives we must use exactly the right term. It will not do to say that a rudder is of a boat or that a wing is of a bird; we must say that the correlatives are the ruddered and the winged (*Catg.* 6b36–7a22). This correlativity applies to descriptions, not to the existence of the things described. Knowledge and the knowable, perception and the perceptible, are correlatives, but the knowable and the perceptible can exist without being known or perceived (7b15–8a12).

The dependence of relatives on descriptions is clearest from Aristotle's efforts to show that no substances are relatives. He remarks that we do not call a particular hand 'someone's some individual hand' but 'someone's hand' (8a15–21). This argument proves only that 'some individual hand' does not combine with a genitive in the way that other relatives do; it hardly follows that the referent of the expression, the individual hand, does not essentially belong to something. Worse still, the argument seems to apply equally to particular relatives; we will not call a particular equal 'some equal to something', but 'equal to something', and so on for the other examples. The argument seems to prove too much, because it concentrates too narrowly on relative expressions.[2]

In trying to prove that no substance is a relative, Aristotle assumes that we know what the substances are, and that they do not include any relatives. But his assumptions are dubious. For many acknowledged relatives seem to be substances, in so far as they admit classifying nouns and characterizing adjectives, and have essential and coincidental properties. We can apparently say that this slave is a man, and that hence he is an animal and a substance. Similarly, he can apparently undergo change and receive contraries; and hence he has the proprium of first substance.

The slave is a man only coincidentally (7a25–b14), and so man is not strongly predicated of him; if he is a first substance, man cannot be a second substance. 'The slave is a man' must apparently express inherence, and if an inherent item cannot be a substance, then apparently man cannot be a substance. If, on the other hand, we say that man is a second substance, because it is strongly predicated of the individual man, we seem to have equally good reason to claim that musician and slave are second substances because they are strongly predicated of the individual musician and the individual slave.

Aristotle wants to claim that, on the contrary, man and horse are second substances, while musicians and slaves are not, because man and horse say what the first substances are. But the truth of this claim seems to depend on the descriptions we choose to use. 'Slave' picks out a subject that is not essentially a man; 'man' picks out a subject that is essentially a man. Different choices of descriptions seem to pick out different subjects and different substances.[3]

But if 'slave' picks out something that is both a first substance and a relative, then one and the same item belongs in two categories.[4] Sometimes, indeed, Aristotle allows this, but with bad results. He argues that some specific states, e.g. grammatical knowledge or virtue, are qualities, but their genus, state, is a relative, because it must be a state 'of' something (of virtue, knowledge, etc.) (6b2–6).[5] For similar reasons the genus knowledge is a relative, because it is knowledge 'of' something (grammar etc.), but the species of knowledge are not relatives because grammatical knowledge is not called 'grammatical knowledge of grammar' (11a20–38). The reasons for assigning these genera and species to different categories rely wholly on features of the genus-words and the species-words. Aristotle relies on grammatical tests for placing things into categories, and in defining the class of relatives he pushes this method to extremes.

The extremes seem to be disastrous. Since the category is said of the genus, and strong predication is transitive, the category of the genus will also be said of the species and of their individual instances, just as substance is said of animal, man, and the individual man. Hence specific types of knowledge, e.g., will also be relatives. But since different categories have different propria, specific states must both have and lack the propria of their different categories. Aristotle's appeal to grammatical tests for relatives has forced him into a serious conflict with his general conception of categories. The arguments about relatives make it especially clear that he must choose between his grammatical arguments and his ontological doctrines. In the *Categories* he tries to maintain both; but the combination results in incoherence.

Aristotle therefore damages his doctrine of categories by uncritically following the grammatical tests that support his claims about relatives. He needs to limit his appeal to grammatical tests. But then he needs some further, not purely grammatical, test to distinguish genuine from merely apparent subjects.[6]

39. BASIC SUBJECTS

We have suggested that for each statement about inherence we can find
or coin a count-noun to yield a strong predication (so that we transform
'The man is musical' into 'The musician is a musician'). But Aristotle
might reply that the subject of the strong predication is itself no more
than a compound of a first substance and one of its inherent properties
(man plus musicality), and that therefore it is not a distinct subject in its
own right, beyond the man and his musicality. We see that being a
musician is not essential to being a man; and if we are willing to trust
our judgments about essential properties that far, we can say that the
man is a more basic subject than the musician.

In the *Categories* Aristotle does not mention more and less basic
subjects. But in the *De Interpretatione* he argues that if G and H are
simply coincidents of the F, and so inherent in the F, there is no one
subject consisting of the F plus G and H.

However many things are said coincidentally, either both of the same thing or
one of them of the other, these will not be one. A man, e.g., is musical and
white, but the white and the musical are not one thing; for they are both
coincidents to the same thing. And even if it is true to say that the white is
musical, still the musical white will not be one thing; for it is coincidentally that
the musical is white, so that the white will not be musical. (*De Int.* 21a8–14)[7]

Whether or not we describe the subject with a single word is irrelevant;
'biped animal' picks out a single subject, but a single word meaning
'white musical thing' would not (20b15–19). Aristotle has equally good
reason for denying that 'musician' picks out a single subject; the genuine
subject picked out is the man (not the musician), and musician is not said
of him. He can therefore deny that the individual musician is a first
substance.

The apparent subjects that Aristotle rejects are not genuine subjects in
their own right, but mere combinations; and only genuine subjects in
their own right are first substances. We might say that the musician is a
mere combination because every musician is a man in whom musicality
is inherent, and that in general any combination of a subject and an
inherent item is not itself a basic subject, and therefore not a substance.
Though this notion of a basic subject does not appear in the *Categories*, it
seems necessary to support Aristotle's choice of men and horses, rather
than musicians or white things, as first substances.

This test for being a basic subject will lead us back to where we started
if we try to identify inherence by the existence or non-existence of the
appropriate abstract noun. This is simply a question about a particular
language, and it might turn out that one language recognizes first

substances that another language counts as merely inherent items. Aristotle, however, does not intend this. He believes, for example, that the ontological relation underlying paronymy may be present even if the non-substantial property has no name at all, or if it is not the right name for paronymy.[8] Outside the *Categories* his view is still clearer; in the passage cited from the *De Interpretatione* he does not think his conclusion is affected at all by the existence or non-existence of a name in a language. We will have to identify inherence by appeal to our beliefs about which properties are or are not essential to a subject; and this means we need some beliefs about genuine subjects and their essential properties.

On this point the *Categories* seems to let us down. The intuitive tests it applies seem to rely on a previous grasp of some non-intuitive conditions that control the intuitive judgments. If the dialectical arguments and conditions are applied without preconceptions, they seem to yield rather superficial conclusions about common beliefs, indeed about the common beliefs and assumptions embodied in a particular language. But it is not clear how we reach the right judgments about subjects and essences, or how we are to combine them with common beliefs.

We are readily inclined to believe that men and horses differ from colours and sizes, in being more like subjects; and we may agree that they seem to be more basic than white things and musicians. But we have no assurance that they are really basic subjects, if we do not know that the same judgments that make them more basic than musicians will not make some other subjects more basic still. The *Categories* gives us no assurance that its candidates are really genuine first substances.

40. MATTER

This difficulty is sharpened by some less prominent examples of substances in the *Categories*. Evidently, Aristotle's standard examples of first substances are individual organisms, members of natural kinds. But he also allows parts of substances, e.g. heads and hands (3a29–32, 8a13–28), bodies (2b1–2), bits of matter, e.g. logs (8a23), and stuffs, e.g. honey (9a33). These last four examples of substance challenge the more usual examples.[9]

We denied that musicians are first substances, by arguing that they are just paronyms, reflecting the inherence of a coincident, musicality, in a genuine subject, a man. But if a statue is made of bronze, why should we not say that it is also simply a paronym? Apparently, the bronze is the subject and the statue-shape is the quality inherent in it. Similarly, on this view, the flesh and bones of an animal are the subject, and the capacities of the animal are inherent qualities. Since Aristotle recognizes both shapes and capacities as qualities (9a14–27, 10a11–16), this paronymous analysis seems natural for him; but then the test that explains why musicians are not substances seems to imply that organisms are not substances either.

This difficulty is most vivid if we remember that the capacity to persist and receive contraries seems most special to first substance. When a musician comes into being, this is simply an alteration in his subject, the man, from one inherent quality to its contrary. But when a statue comes into being, the bronze undergoes a change from lacking a shape to having it, and when an organism comes into being, its constituents undergo a change between contraries. If a man or horse comes into being, then, why is this not simply a change from one contrary to another?[10]

These puzzles are not mentioned in the *Categories*. They become very important in other works, and especially in the *Metaphysics*. But they are worth remarking here, since they unavoidably arise for the conception of substance presented in the *Categories*.

The puzzles expose limitations of dialectic. Dialectic uses both the intuitive, grammatical tests that are prominent in the *Categories*, and the concepts of essence, proprium, and coincident; and these concepts, especially essence, restrict the range of substance, by excluding some candidates that seem to pass the more intuitive tests. Once we fix our subjects, dialectic answers further questions, but it does not fix the range of subjects. Aristotle mentions only the intuitive tests used in the *Categories*, because his use of them is guided by a view about what the subjects are. He is convinced that individual men and horses are obvious and paradigmatic subjects. But he does not defend this conviction.

41. UNIVERSALS

First substances in the *Categories* are important because they are subjects both for non-substances and for second substances. We have seen some ways Aristotle takes substances to be prior to items in non-substance categories and to combinations of subjects and inherent properties. To appreciate the full importance of first substances, though, we must see how they are related to universals, especially to second substances. Some of Aristotle's claims depend on his own rather controversial views about the nature of universals.

Universals appear in the initial division of beings (1a20), and Aristotle never retracts the claim that they are beings. He therefore accepts metaphysical realism, and rejects nominalism, since he believes that universals are genuine beings distinct from particulars and from the names or concepts applying to particulars.[11] Since second substances are subjects, and subjects are beings, second substances must be beings; and since non-substantial specific universals are subjects for generic ones, they must also be beings. Moreover, Aristotle insists that some substances do not signify a this.

Every substance seems to signify a this. With first substances, it is indisputably true that each of them signifies a this; for what is revealed is an individual and numerically one. In the case of second substances, it appears from the character of the name—whenever one speaks of man or animal—that a second substance also signifies a this; but this is not true. Rather, it signifies a such (*poion ti*); for the subject is not one, as the primary substance is, but man and animal are said of many things. But it does not signify a such unconditionally, as pale does; for pale signifies nothing other than such, whereas the species and the genus demarcate such about substance, since they signify substance of such a sort. (3b10–21).[12]

If he did not believe in the reality of universals, he could have claimed that all substances are thises (since they would all be particulars).[13]

When Aristotle calls second substances species and genera, and says first substances 'belong in' them (*huparchein en*, 2a14–15), we might take him to mean that second substances are classes of which first substances are members. Classes, however, are defined extensionally, so that two classes with the same members are the same class; and if Aristotle thinks second substances are classes, he cannot plausibly claim that they reveal what first substances are (2b29–37). Since the class of men is coextensive with the class of grammarians (i.e. things capable of grammatical knowledge), it follows that if man reveals what particular men are, grammarian must reveal it also. But grammarian is a proprium of man, and though the proprium is necessarily coextensive with the species (*Top.* 102a18–23), it is not identical to the species, since it does not reveal the essence (102a18). Aristotle must assume that 'F reveals the essence of G' does not allow the substitution of coreferential terms for 'F', and that the species man cannot be defined extensionally; hence it cannot be a class.

If the species man (e.g.) is not a class, might it be the essential property shared by all the members of the class? Aristotle's definition of a universal does not make clear the relation between universals and properties. He says:

By universal I mean what is of a nature to be predicated (*pephuke katêgoreisthai*) in the case of a plurality of things, and by particular I mean what is not. (*De Int.* 17a39–40)

Since 'of a nature to be predicated' is ambiguous between 'must by its nature' and 'can by its nature', it is not clear if Aristotle takes the existence of a universal to require actual plural instantiation. If plural instantiation is required, universals cannot be properties, since the existence of the property of being a man does not need plural instances.

Aristotle takes actual instantiation to be necessary for the existence of a universal. For he remarks that if everyone is healthy health exists and sickness does not, and if everything is pale-coloured dark colour does not exist (*Catg.* 14a6–10). Since the situations imagined here seem perfectly possible within the laws of nature recognized by Aristotle, it seems possible for some universals to come into and go out of existence.[14]

This remark about actual instantiation, together with the definition of a universal, supports a further demand for plural instantiation. For the definition either requires possible plural instantiation or requires actual plural instantiation; but if it supports the claim about actual instantiation, it cannot merely require possible plural instantiation, but must be taken to require actual plural instantiation.[15]

Moreover, Aristotle assumes that a second substance is not one in number, because it is said of many subjects (3b16–18); it is not a single individual existing in one place at one time, but will be one in species, as water is (*Top.* 103a14–23). If there is more than one individual man, then the universal man (Aristotle seems to argue) cannot be numerically one, since it exists in the many places where the individuals exist. But if only one man exists, the property of being a man exists just where he exists, and therefore seems to be no less a this than he is. Since Aristotle believes universals are not thises, he seems to assume that they necessarily have plural instances, and therefore that they are not simply properties.[16] The universal, therefore, seems to be a non-unit class, intensionally conceived (e.g., in so far as it is the class of men rather than of grammarians).[17]

42. THE DEPENDENT STATUS OF UNIVERSALS

In claiming that particulars are first substances, Aristotle means to claim not only that they are first in some order (e.g. ascending from particular to universal, or looking for subjects with no further subjects), but also that they are the best substances. For he says the particular non-inherent subject is called substance 'most fully and primarily and more than anything else' (*kuriôtata kai prôtôs kai malista*, 2a11–12). To defend this claim he must especially explain why 'second', universal substances are not substance to as high a degree as particular substances are.

He seems to rely heavily on the claim that first substances are subjects more than other things are. He says: 'First substances are called substances most fully because they are subjects for all the other things' (2b36–3a1). This would be a good reason if the subject-criterion were the primary criterion for being a substance. But Aristotle has not explained why we should prefer the subject-criterion to the essence-criterion. If particulars meet the subject-criterion better, universals seem to meet the essence-criterion better; and so even if they are secondary as subjects, they may be primary as essences.

In his introduction of universals Aristotle does not explicitly rely on any previous grasp of the notion of a universal; he speaks of individuals, thises, and particulars, and introduces universals as the things said of them. Apparently he relies on our intuitive grasp of predication to show us what a universal is. By introducing universals this way, he suggests that they are secondary to particulars; but we will accept this suggestion only if we begin with the subject-criterion. If we begin with the essence-criterion and ask what things are, our first substances will be man, horse, red, square, etc., and the subjects of these properties will be second substances.

Aristotle's claim is justified if he can show that substance as subject is prior in some relevant way to substance as essence. The most relevant types of priority that he recognizes are (1) asymmetrical existential dependence (the existence of B requires the existence of A, but the converse does not hold, 14a29–35); and (2) asymmetrical explanation (neither A nor B can exist without the other, but the existence of A explains the existence of B, and the converse does not hold, 14b10–13).[18] But Aristotle does not argue adequately in the *Categories* for the claim that particulars are prior in either way.

Aristotle claims that other things besides first substances are either said of or inherent in first substances.

All other things are either said of the first substances as subjects, or are in them as subjects. This is evident if we examine particular cases. Animal, e.g., is predicated of man, and so also of the individual man; for if it is not predicated of any individual man, neither is it predicated of man at all. Again, colour is in body, and so also in some individual body; for if it is not in some one of the individual bodies, neither is it in body at all. Hence all the other things are either said of the primary substances as subjects, or are in them as subjects. If, then, the first substances do not exist, then neither can anything else exist. (2a34–b6c)[19]

The conclusion shows that he takes the previous claim to mean that universals exist only in so far as they are said of, or inherent in, particular substances.

If a universal is inherent in a particular substance, then clearly it depends on that substance, since inherence implies existential dependence. But it is not clear why we should concede that colour (e.g.) is inherent in a body. If we believe in separated Platonic universals, existing independently of particulars instantiating them, we will reject Aristotle's claim about inherence. His case is even weaker for strong predication. Aristotle needs some further reason to show that second substances exist only if they are said of some first substance or other.[20]

It turns out that a principal claim in the *Categories*, the dependence of other beings on first substances, rests on no explicit argument. Aristotle's claim is not surprising, in the light of his other claims about universals. For we have seen that he takes instantiation, and probably takes plural instantiation, to be necessary for the existence of universals. Since instantiation requires strong predication or inherence, Aristotle's conception of universals does indeed require them to be strongly predicated of particulars. But he gives no argument in the *Categories* for the correctness of his conception of universals.

43. THE INDEPENDENCE OF FIRST SUBSTANCES

Though Aristotle does not argue for the dependence of universals on first substances, it is at least clear that he believes it. It is probable, but less clear, that he believes in the independence of first substances from universals. First substances are supposed to be substances more than anything else because they are subjects for everything else (2b36–3a1). If, however, first substances are equally dependent on other things (even though the other things are not their subjects), then those other beings will be equally basic for the existence of anything else; and mutual dependence seems to challenge the claim of first substances to be substances most of all.[21] Apparently, then, Aristotle ought to argue for the independence of first substances.

If the existence of an individual man is sufficient for the existence of the universal man, it is self-contradictory to claim that the individual is independent of the universal.[22] But if universals require plural instantiation, Socrates' existence does not require the existence of the universal man, pale, etc. Socrates, therefore, is independent of the universals. The demand for plural instantiation leads directly to the independence of first substance; and it might even explain why Aristotle does not bother to argue for the dependence of universals and the independence of particulars.

This conception of universals, however, does not support a very interesting sort of priority for first substances. Even if a particular man does not require the existence of the universal, he requires one instantiation of man. This one instantiation implies the existence of the property of being a man, so that the particular man seems to be dependent on the property. The property does not seem to be the same as the individual man, since the spatio-temporal properties that are essential to him are not essential to it (it would exist if Callias existed and Socrates did not). Aristotle does not recognize such a thing as being a man, distinct from the particular and the universal; but he seems to need it, and it raises further questions about any claim of independence for first substances.

Further difficulties arise in explaining how first substances are independent of particular non-substances. For though the individual man is not necessarily pale, must he not have an instance of some colour or other? In any case, not every inherent property is a non-necessary property; the special property of the species (e.g. capacity for knowledge, in the case of man) is inherent, but necessary. Necessary inherent properties seem to depend on their first substance no more than it depends on them. The argument about asymmetrical dependence seems to show that, e.g., the individual capacity for grammar is as much a first substance as the individual man is; for each of them depends on another particular that also depends on it.[23]

If Aristotle maintains the independence of first substances, he can defend his view that they are primary. He may not have seen the difficulties in showing that first substances are independent; for we have raised difficulties by appealing to two sorts of items (substantial properties with only one instance; necessary inherent particulars) that are not mentioned in the *Categories*. His assumptions about universals and about non-substances need defence.

The primacy of first substances need not depend on their independence of other things. Aristotle could claim that they are primarily and most of all substances because they are prior in explanation to other things, just as the facts are prior to the true propositions that correspond to them, even though both must exist at the same time (14b10–22). But he does not exploit this possibility. He fails to face the crucial issues that arise for his claims about first substances. We saw that his views about first substances depend on controversial assumptions about essences and basic subjects; and our present discussion shows that his belief in the primacy of particular substances depends on controversial assumptions about the nature of universals.

44. WEAKNESSES OF DIALECTIC

The *Categories* practises 'logical' dialectic, in so far as it argues from common sense about questions that are not confined to the scope of any specific science, for conclusions that are presupposed equally by each specific science. Does it advance from what is prior and better-known to us to what is prior and better-known by nature?

We might think that Aristotle only tries to make explicit the ontological distinctions implied in ordinary beliefs and in their reflexion in grammar. Indeed, we have seen that some arguments in the *Categories*, and some of the conclusions (e.g. those on differentiae) display the influence of common sense and of attention to grammatical distinctions. Excessive attention to these distinctions (e.g. on relatives and qualities) leads to anomalies.

And yet the main aim of the *Categories* is not to describe even an idealized version of common sense. Aristotle's conception of substance and non-substance cannot be adequately defended from common sense; it requires a fuller account of genuine subjects and genuine essences than we can find in the *Categories*. The distinction between strong predication and inherence, for instance, is not adequately explained; and it must be applied to the right sorts of subjects, which we must already identify, apart from the distinctions drawn in the *Categories*.

It is easy to overlook the weakness of arguments based on intuitive distinctions, because many of Aristotle's candidates for substance—particular men, horses, and other members of natural kinds—are not unfamiliar or surprising, as Platonic Forms or Democritean atoms would be. Commonsense distinctions might seem to support the familiar candidates against other candidates for substance. But an examination of the *Categories* suggests that this is not so. Principles not immediately accessible to common sense are needed to take us from commonsense dialectical arguments to the commonsense ontological conclusions that Aristotle accepts.

The *Categories*, then, does not succeed in its apparent purpose of arguing for the sort of ontological scheme that is presupposed in logical dialectic, and therefore in all areas of inquiry. The conclusions of common sense and intuition are too ambiguous and too imprecise to support the doctrines that Aristotle wants to rest on them. The support he needs must come from the doctrines that interpret and modify intuition and common sense; but these doctrines themselves must be justified, not simply taken for granted. The *Categories* is a partial introduction to some of Aristotle's views, but not an adequate exposition or defence of them.

45. PRINCIPLES OF CHANGE

In *Physics* i 7 Aristotle applies his doctrine of subject and substance to the understanding of natural change. He believes that his doctrine removes the paradoxes and puzzles resulting from the view of his predecessors, and supports his belief that natural organisms, as well as their matter, are genuine subjects of change. A discussion of his argument will show that the objections raised against the dialectical argument of the *Categories* still apply; for the commonsense distinctions that Aristotle appeals to do not uniquely support his conclusion over rival views.

Aristotle argues that changes, as they are ordinarily understood, can be recognized and described without self-contradiction or paradox. His predecessors argued:

Nothing that is comes to be or perishes, since whatever comes to be must come to be either from what is or from what is not, and it is impossible to come to be from either. For what is does not come to be, since it already is; and nothing comes to be from what is not, since something must be a subject. (191a27–31)

Aristotle wants to show that each of these alternatives is in a way true of what comes to be, and in a way false; and the way each is true and false allows becoming to be coherently described. The tripartite analysis, including the two contraries and the subject, shows us how to describe the termini consistently. We dissolve the puzzle about becoming by showing that its premises are true, but in a sense that makes them consistent with each other and with the possibility of becoming.

The puzzle arises because things seem to come to be either from what is or from what is not, in the senses that suggest the impossibility of becoming. We may say 'The unmusical man became musical' (e.g. 190a4–5); and since unmusical man has passed away, there seems to be becoming from what is not—there would be no becoming if the unmusical man remained the whole time. Similarly, when we say 'It became musical from unmusical', nothing unmusical survives when the musical has come to be, and so there seems to be becoming from what is not.[24] If the only two items involved are the musical and the unmusical, they seem to imply a succession of things—the perishing of the unmusical and the coming to be of the musical—with no account of how the items are related.

Aristotle argues, however, that there is always both a persisting subject and a non-persisting contrary. A full description says that the man who was unmusical becomes musical because he had the quality unmusicality and has lost it, acquiring its contrary, musicality. Other descriptions are true, but less informative, because they do not refer to the items involved in the change under the appropriate full descriptions. We can say 'The unmusical man became musical', and 'The unmusicality (*to amouson*) became musicality', because we refer coincidentally to the appropriate items. The subject has different property-instances that are one in number, since they belong to the same particular subject, but different in 'being' (191a1–3) or 'form' (190a13–17), allowing us to refer to that subject in different ways.[25]

So far Aristotle has considered cases of becoming where, as we ordinarily conceive subjects, the same particular subject (e.g. the man) remains in being and no new subject comes into being. He calls this 'becoming this' (e.g. musical), and contrasts it with 'unconditional' or 'unqualified' becoming, in which a subject comes to be, and does not merely come to be something.

> Things are said to come to be in many ways. Some are said not to come to be but to become this; only substances are said to come to be unconditionally. In the other cases it is evident that there must be some subject that comes to be. For in fact, when ⟨something⟩ becomes of some quantity, or quality, or relative to another, or somewhere, something is subject, since it is only substance that is never said of any other subject, while all the other things are said of substance. However, substances—the things that are unconditionally—also come to be from some subject; this will become evident if we examine it. In every case there is something that is a subject, from which the thing coming to be proceeds—as plants and animals come to be from seed. Some things that come to be unconditionally do so by change of figure (e.g. a statue); some by addition (e.g. growing things); some by subtraction (e.g. Hermes from the stone); some by composition (e.g. a house); some by alteration (e.g. things changing according to their matter). And it is evident that everything that comes to be in this way comes to be from a subject. (190a31–b10).

The puzzles of becoming reappear for unconditional becoming. For if a new subject comes into being, it did not exist previously, and so must have come into being from what is not; if, on the other hand, the same subject persists, no new subject seems to come into being.

In reply, Aristotle returns to his tripartite analysis. Qualified becoming requires a persisting subject because the non-substances are all said of substance (190a33–b1). Substance, unlike non-substances, is not said of a subject, but, like them, it comes to be from a subject (190b1–3), and the tripartite analysis will work for unqualified becoming also. When a statue comes to be, the subject is bronze, the privation shapelessness, and the contrary that is gained is statue-shape (190b10–17).

Some variation is allowed in the analysis. We say that the man becomes musical from the contrary, not from the subject; but we can say that the statue came to be from the bronze, which, unlike the contrary, persists (190a24–6).[26] This is intelligible; for the original subject of qualified becoming (the unmusical man) is the same substance as the substance that results from the process (the musical man), but in unqualified becoming the resultant substance (the statue) is not the same substance as the original subject (the bronze). Something new emerges from the unmusical (in qualified becoming) and from the bronze (in unqualified becoming). When this allowance is made for the explicable differences, we need not doubt that the tripartite analysis applies to these cases as well as to qualified becoming.

Since the analysis works for both types of becoming, Aristotle thinks he has solved the paradoxes that seemed to cast doubt on the possibility of change. We need not suppose that change is from what is, or from what is not, in any objectionable sense. It is from both, in a coherent and intelligible sense.

46. PUZZLES ABOUT UNQUALIFIED BECOMING

The analysis relies on the doctrine of the *Categories*. Aristotle shows how the puzzles of becoming are solved if we recognize that the persisting subject of change is a first substance, and that a substance has no contrary. Since the successive items (e.g. unmusical and musical) are contraries, they are not substances, and hence are not the subjects of the change; their succession is an alteration in the more basic subject (e.g. the man) that is the first substance. Having dissolved this puzzle through the doctrine of the categories, we appeal to the same doctrine to describe the difference between unqualified becoming and alteration; if we know what sort of thing a first substance is, we can say that unqualified becoming occurs when one of these comes into being. The principles of logical dialectic seem to remove puzzles surrounding the first principles of natural science, and so seem to support Aristotle's claim that dialectic has a road to first principles.

We have argued, however, that in fact purely dialectical argument does not secure conclusions as specific as the ones Aristotle actually affirms; though he seems to rely on intuitive distinctions, he cannot justifiably rely on these alone. A similar question arises about his use of his doctrines in explaining becoming. He speaks as though they support his claim, but in fact he needs some further defence.

Aristotle claims both (i) that unqualified becoming can be coherently described, and (ii) that it is exemplified when his familiar first substances come to be and perish. Both claims raise questions.

Questions about the first claim arise from a comparison of the account of unqualified becoming with the definition of first substance. Unqualified becoming requires a substance (e.g. a statue) to come into being; but Aristotle insists that it must have a subject (e.g. the bronze) preceding it. In the *Categories*, however, he defines a first substance as a basic subject, neither said of nor inherent in any further subject. This definition seems to make the bronze a first substance, since it is the subject of becoming. But the statue seems not to be a basic subject, since it has a more basic subject, the bronze; hence it seems not to be a first substance at all. The description of unqualified becoming seems to be incoherent.

To answer this objection Aristotle must show either that the bronze is not a first substance or that it is one, but does not threaten the claim of the statue to be a first substance. The first answer would be hard to defend, since the criteria for substance seem to leave no room for objections. To defend the second answer, he must show that the statue is neither said of nor inherent in the bronze. It is not said of the bronze; but why is it not inherent? Since the nature and persistence of a bit of bronze do not require it to be statue-shaped, the statue-shape is clearly not an essential property of the bronze; why then is it not merely a quality of it, and therefore inherent?

The analysis in the *Physics* does not answer this question. We might say that the statue is a first substance, because 'statue' is the name of a subject, not of one of the contrary properties. But 'musician' also looks like the name of a subject, not of a property; and yet Aristotle regards the coming to be of a musician as a qualified becoming, since the musician is analysable into a genuine subject with an inherent property. If we redescribe the alleged unqualified becoming of the statue as a qualified becoming in which the bronze acquires a new quality, why is this not the correct description?[27]

Aristotle can fairly appeal to common beliefs for (1) the belief in the unqualified becoming of statues, horses, etc.; (2) the subject-criterion for substance; (3) the characteristic expressions that distinguish qualified from unqualified becoming. But in this case common beliefs do not seem coherent; the subject-criterion seems to imply that the bronze is a substance, that the coming to be of a statue is merely a qualified becoming, and therefore that the statue is not a first substance. Moreover, appeals to the ordinary expressions in (3) do not support the candidates for substance that are recognized both by Aristotle and by common sense; for ordinary descriptions show no relevant difference between the becoming of a musician and of a statue. Aristotle's discussion suggests that mere dialectic cannot adequately defend common beliefs, since the common beliefs themselves raise difficulties that merely endoxic principles do not resolve.

47. MATTER AS SUBSTANCE

Aristotle has introduced the subject of unqualified becoming—the bronze, wood, etc. from which the statue or the box comes to be; and his analysis suggests that this formless subject has the best claim to be the first substance. He generalizes from these examples and describes the subject of unqualified becoming as 'matter'.[28] Clearly matter has a strong claim to be substance, since it is a subject; and it seems to undermine the claim of the 'ordinary' substance to be a first substance, since a first substance cannot be said of a subject, and the ordinary substance seems to be said of its matter.[29]

Once Aristotle admits this much, he may seem to be committed to further surprising claims about first substance. Bronze is the matter and subject of the statue; but bronze is itself composed of further matter, which must be its subject, and this matter is composed of further matter. If no first substance can be said of a subject, then apparently the only first substance is the most basic or 'prime' matter that we reach by this process of analysis.[30]

Aristotle need not, however, accept this argument. He does not concede that x's matter is the subject of which x is said; he distinguishes being said of a subject from being 'from' or 'out of' a subject (190a31–b3), and allows only that x's matter is the subject out of which x is made. He leaves open the possibility that x is out of a further subject y, but not said of y, so that x satisfies the subject-criterion for substance.

This possibility might vindicate the account of first substance in the *Categories*. While *Physics* i shows that matter satisfies the subject-criterion, the *Categories* allows this also, and the *Physics* seems to develop rather than reject the position of the *Categories*. The *Physics* has not yet been shown to undermine the assumption in the *Categories* that men and horses are first substances because they are basic subjects.

But though this possibility is open, it remains to be seen whether anything satisfies it. So far no reason has appeared for treating statues differently from musicians. To defend his assumption in the *Categories* that horses are substances and musicians are not, Aristotle must claim that a substance is a basic subject, not a mere combination of a subject and an inherent non-essential property. But any conception of a basic subject that favours horses over musicians seems to favour the bronze over the statue, and hence the matter of horses over horses. Though Aristotle must assume that a first substance is a basic subject, one reasonable conception of a basic subject seems to threaten his own candidates for substance.

48. FORM AS SUBSTANCE

Aristotle himself is not completely satisfied with the results for his view of substance. He says: 'Whether the form or the subject is substance is not yet clear' (*Phys.* 191a19–20). If the answer is not clear, why might the subject seem not to be substance, and why might the form seem a better candidate? If Aristotle accepts the subject-criterion, as he seems to (190a35–b1), then it should apparently be clear that the subject, and hence the matter rather than the form, is substance.[31]

Aristotle, however, contrasts matter with a this, claiming that matter is not one or a being in the way a this is (191a12–13). The claim that thisness and numerical unity are necessary for being a first substance is familiar from the *Categories*; there, indeed, numerical unity seems to be indistinguishable from thisness (3b10–13), and the two conditions seem to be more or less equivalent accounts of a particular.[32] These necessary conditions for being a first substance do not seem to rule out matter. For bits of matter seem to be particulars no less than particular statues or horses are; for if they are not, they can hardly be basic subjects, and Aristotle does not deny that they are basic subjects. In suggesting that matter might not be numerically one or a this in the way a substance should be, he implies that something could be a subject without satisfying these other conditions; but he does not explain how this could be so.

If Aristotle thinks that matter fails to be one, what condition for unity does he assume? A lump of bronze differs from a statue in being homoeomerous; it is divisible into lumps of bronze, whereas the statue is not divisible into statues.[33] If the unity and indivisibility of a first substance (*Catg.* 3b12) excludes the divisibility of homoeomerous things, then a lump of bronze is not a first substance.[34] But then it is not clear why the divisibility of homoeomerous things is relevant to the subject-criterion. Being numerically one and undivided (i.e. being one rather than two or more) seems necessary for being a particular, but being a particular seems to be consistent with being homoeomerous; a 10 kg. lump divisible into two 5 kg. lumps is one 10 kg. lump rather than two, and therefore still seems to be a particular. The claim that nothing homoeomerous is a subject and first substance seems to be unsupported by the *Categories*.

But even if matter is a questionable substance, it is not clear why form is the rival. Instead we might want to consider the statue, which is the example used in the analogical explanation of 'subject': 'As bronze is to statue . . . so the subject nature is to substance, this, and being' (*Phys.* 191a8–12). The statue seems to have the form that the bronze initially lacked, but does not seem to be the form.

Since the statue has the bronze as well as the statue-form, it seems to consist of the bronze and the form. Indeed, Aristotle says that everything that comes to be comes from subject and form, and that the musical man is composed of subject and form, since his account is analysable into theirs (190b19–23). It is reasonable to extend the analysis to the statue, and to take it to be composed of matter and form. Hence we might say that the substance to be contrasted with matter is the compound of matter and form.

This is not, however, Aristotle's own view of the question, since he assumes that the subject and the form are the most plausible, though not evidently successful, candidates. Perhaps he thinks that since the statue is composed of form and matter, it seems to depend on both form and matter, and therefore seems to be a less basic subject than each of them is. Even so, the form does not seem a plausible candidate for substance. Though the compound does not seem to be a basic subject, it at least looks like a subject rather than a property, and therefore seems closer to being a first substance. Measured by this test, the form seems a poor candidate; and if it is not a subject, how can it be a first substance? Matter may lack the appropriate unity and thisness for a substance; but the form seems to lack them even more clearly, since it does not seem to be a particular subject at all.

While it is surprising that Aristotle regards form as a serious candidate for being a first substance, it seems to be a more plausible second substance; for the statue-shape makes the second substance statue predicable of this statue. We might infer that Aristotle confusedly introduces questions about second substance into his discussion of first substance.

49. RESULTING DIFFICULTIES

It is useful to dwell on the puzzling and tentative character of the claims about substance, because our conclusion is very close to Aristotle's starting-point in *Metaphysics* vii. After his preliminary remarks on matter, compound, and form he says:

We should dismiss the substance composed of both—I mean the one composed of matter and form—since it is posterior and clear. And matter is also evident in a way. But we should examine the third ⟨type of substance⟩, since this raises the most puzzles. (*Met.* 1029a30–3)

We have seen why the compound seems to be posterior, and also fairly clear; for statues seem to be clear examples of compounds, and also to be posterior to their components. Bronze and wood seem to be clear examples of matter, and matter seems to be a clear subject. Of all the three candidates for substance the form seems the least promising, and so the most puzzling.

If Aristotle already had in mind the theory of *Metaphysics* vii when he wrote *Physics* i, he could easily have presented the puzzles as sharply as he does in *Metaphysics* vii. Since he does not present them sharply, it is likely that he is looking tentatively for some resolution of the difficulties that he partly discerns, with no definite solution in mind. The passage in *Metaphysics* vii suggests that we are right to be puzzled on reading *Physics* i.

The arguments in *Physics* i show how Aristotle's views lack the support they need for the work they are required to do. In i 6 Aristotle appeals to his own conception of substance and the other categories, and in i 7 he argues that this general schema yields a distinction between qualified and unqualified becoming. He assumes that unqualified becoming happens when we are inclined to say a new substance comes into being. To accept Aristotle's examples of unqualified becomings, we must accept his examples of substances; and these face legitimate objections once we see that the alleged unqualified becomings may be described as qualified becomings. Though common sense treats statues and trees as substances, they seem no more substantial than musicians and white men are; if we are to be guided by reality, we should apparently count only matter as substance, and regard other alleged substances as merely combinations of matter and coincidental properties.

The account of change suggests that reasonable criteria for substance might recognize non-Aristotelian substances and might disqualify Aristotelian candidates. When Aristotle appeals to common sense and the appearances, he appeals, though selectively, both to the accepted criteria and to the accepted candidates, without saying which count for more. When the accepted criteria seem to tell against the accepted candidates, Aristotle must decide what to modify, and on what grounds. If dialectical argument simply seeks a consistent description of common sense, then he is free to modify commonsense views of the criteria or of the candidates as he pleases. But if he intends to reach objective principles from common sense, he must show that the commonsense beliefs he chooses to retain are true. This task is not seriously undertaken in *Physics* i any more than in the *Categories*. But the *Physics* shows us more clearly that the task is important, because it shows how common sense might be challenged.

Aristotle takes it for granted that we need subjects, and that we need those that common sense recognizes. He needs to ask more persistently why and when we need to recognize what sorts of subjects. He can then define a clear issue about whether commonsense subjects are genuine subjects or not, and we will be able to see what he or his opponent might be right or wrong about.

In this discussion I have tried to show that difficulties in Aristotle's conclusions result from more basic difficulties in his method. He speaks as though commonsense distinctions actually support his own candidates for substance. But his appeal to common sense and pure dialectic does not succeed. Even if his candidates for substance (artifacts and natural organisms) are also recognized by common sense, it does not follow that commonsense criteria for substance actually support these candidates; and in fact the criteria seem to support non-Aristotelian candidates at least as well. This is exactly the difficulty that we noticed in Aristotle's treatment of subjects in the *Categories*.

On these points dialectic seems to offer less definite answers than Aristotle wants. In any case, even if its answers were definite enough, they would support claims about endoxic principles summarizing common sense, but not about objective principles. The questions raised by dialectical arguments for first principles are not answered by the arguments we have examined so far.

5

THE FORMAL CAUSE

50. NATURE AND CAUSE

In *Physics* ii Aristotle reopens the questions about matter, form, and substance that he discussed in Book i. He now discusses them with reference to his views about causation. I want to explain why his argument fails to avoid the limitations of pure dialectic, but also shows how these limitations might be avoided.

So far Aristotle has argued that change requires a subject and the contraries; and that substantial change requires matter as the subject, and form as one of the contraries. He has found it to be unclear whether matter or form is substance. In ii 1 he starts again with a subset of changes, those that have an internal origin in a natural organism; and he wants to know what the origin is. The answer is relevant to the questions left over from Book i, in ways that will be clear later.

Things have natures in so far as they have an internal origin of change and stability, and in this way they differ from artifacts such as beds or tables (192b13–27). Aristotle explains 'origin of change' only in ii 3, when he introduces the doctrine of the four causes. These correspond to the four ways we can state a cause or explanation of something, and hence can answer the question 'Why?' (194b17–23). One of these, commonly called the 'efficient cause', is described in terms very similar to those applied to nature, in ii 1; it is 'that from which ⟨there is⟩ the first origin of change or rest' (194b29–30; cf. 195a22–3), or 'that from which the change is' (195a8), or simply 'the origin of change' (195a11). The examples of this cause seem to fit our conception of causes fairly easily; the adviser is the cause of an action, the father of the child, 'and in general the producer of the thing produced, and the initiator of change of the thing changed' (194b29–32).

The account of the four causes raises a difficulty for Aristotle's initial claims about form, matter, and nature. For he seems to imply both that form and matter are efficient causes, since they are origins of change, and that they are not, since they are formal and material causes, not efficient causes.[1] To resolve this apparent inconsistency we need to examine the four causes more carefully; and in examining them we will understand better the dialectical foundation of Aristotle's doctrine. Surprisingly, his exposition of the doctrine of the four causes does not fully explain his use of the doctrine to defend his claim about form and matter; and this is because his exposition stays too close to the common beliefs that it ought to explain.

51. THE FOUR CAUSES

Since different answers to the question 'Why?' pick out the four causes, we might think Aristotle intends the four to be coordinate and mutually irreducible answers to this question. But closer study raises doubts. The different why-questions ask for explanations of different types of things. We may want the cause of a substance (e.g. a statue, 194b25, 195a5–6) or a state of a substance (e.g. health, 195a9, 30) or of an event (e.g. the sinking of the ship, 195a14).[2] One of the four causes may be more suitable for answering the question about substances, another for events, and so on; in that case they will really answer different questions. We do not even seem to be asking the same kind of question about these different things. For sometimes we seem to be asking why something comes to be, sometimes why it exists, sometimes why it is as it is. The types of things we mention in our answers are equally diverse. Sometimes the causes are substances (e.g. the doctor, 195a30), sometimes states of substances (e.g. the statue-maker's craft, 195a6), sometimes events (e.g. slimming, 194b36; the pilot's absence, 195a12–14).[3]

The diversity of questions and answers is not surprising; Aristotle takes them from ordinary questions and explanations, which range easily over events and substances.[4] The doctrine of the four causes is dialectical, in so far as it rests on common beliefs and ordinary questions about causes and explanations. But it reflects the diversity of these questions to a degree that obscures the facts they describe. For some of the questions seem to be reducible to, or abbreviations of, others. If we ask for the cause of the statue, we probably want the cause of its coming into being; and if we say the doctor is the cause of my health, we can say more exactly that her practising her medical science is the cause of my recovering my health. Aristotle himself says that the 'most exact' cause is the actual, not merely potential, cause, e.g. the builder exercising his building craft (195b21–8).[5]

If a cause of one type (e.g. a substance) is reducible to a cause of another type (e.g. an event), it is worth considering whether some of the four causes may not be reducible to others. We may say that the matter and the form are causes of the statue; but 'the statue' seems to be an inexact description of what is to be explained. A more exact description asks for the explanation of the statue's being made, or of its being as it is, or of its remaining in existence. Once we have specified the effect more fully, we also want a fuller specification of the cause. Simply citing the form or the matter does not seem to provide the proper explanation; 'the form is the cause of the statue' seems a mere abbreviation. The cause of the fully specified effect is properly and fully described as 'the sculptor exercising her craft' or 'the customer giving her order'. But now we have stated the efficient cause and not simply the form or the matter.

The appearance of four causes rather than one seems to result from incomplete specification of the causes and the effects. If nothing more can be said for Aristotle's doctrine of four causes, then it does not describe four objectively different causes, but only four ways to describe the cause; and three of these ways are mere abbreviations of the fourth way.

But if Aristotle cannot defend his claim as it stands, that the formal and material causes are different types of causes from the efficient cause, he can still reasonably argue that they are different types of efficient cause, differing from each other, though not from all types of efficient cause. The 'most exact' and fully specified cause of the events we have mentioned is apparently the efficient cause; but different sorts of efficient cause cause different events. The cause of the bed's being burnt is the action of the fire on the matter of the bed; the bed's form is not mentioned in the explanation. But the cause of the bed's being made is the craftsman's exercising his craft to make a bed; both the form and the goal are referred to in the explanation. To mention the formal, material, final, and efficient causes of the statue is not really to maintain four distinct causes of the same thing. When the effect is specified more clearly, reference to the first three causes turns out to be attribution of formal, final, or material properties to the efficient cause.

If this is right, then Aristotle's initial suggestion that form and matter are internal origins of change, and therefore efficient causes, is more nearly correct than his claim that formal and material causes are not efficient causes. He would be well advised to claim that formal and material causes are really efficient causes that have, respectively, formal and material properties as their essential constituents. In claiming that form and matter are nature, therefore, he will claim that the internal efficient causes of an organism's characteristics have formal or material properties as essential constituents.

This is a restatement, rather than a statement, of Aristotle's doctrine. His actual doctrine of the four causes is too purely dialectical, and stays too close to common beliefs, to make clear the centrality of the efficient cause; and his failure to make this clear seriously affects some of the argument in Book ii. Still, the remarks about the actual cause and about the most exact cause show that he is committed to the centrality of the efficient cause; and this centrality makes his claim about form and matter more reasonable than it would otherwise be. It is therefore worth exploring the consequences of Aristotle's restated position for his other doctrines.

52. CAUSES AND FIRST PRINCIPLES

Aristotle's views on causation and explanation affect still wider issues about the extent of his realism about first principles. For he claims that first principles are naturally, not conventionally, prior to other things, and that they are prior because they are explanatory and state the causes. (Indeed, they *are* the causes, since he uses 'first principle' for non-propositional principles as well as for the propositional principles that describe them.)[6] But the claim about explanation may seem to conflict with the realist claim. How, we might ask, does one thing explain another unless it explains to us, relatively to what we already know, to the questions we ask, and to the different theories we apply? And may not different things turn out to be explanatory within different theories? Though Aristotle might appear to demand correspondence between true statements of first principles and independently prior things, the reference to explanation suggests that the structure and context of theories will determine what is prior by nature.

Aristotle need not admit any conflict in his views, if he can plausibly deny that reference to explanation introduces a subjective or pragmatic notion of explanation that makes natural priority depend on our questions and theories. He can distinguish explanation 'for us' from natural or unqualified explanation. In our ignorance we may ask the wrong questions and be satisfied with the wrong answers and dissatisfied with the right ones. If President McKinley was shot on a Tuesday and President Kennedy on a Wednesday, we may ask why Kennedy was shot on the day of the week after the day on which McKinley was shot. If our otherwise reasonable explanation of each shooting says nothing about the importance of the day of the week, we may be foolish enough to be dissatisfied. Only a better understanding of how things are will show us which explanatory accounts ought to satisfy us. These are the accounts that provide the genuine explanations. A reference to explanation does not reintroduce a subjective element into Aristotle's account of first principles; on the contrary, the notion of explanation itself needs to be understood through Aristotle's distinctions.

The conception of explanation assumed by the doctrine of the four causes might initially seem too pragmatic to be an account of objective principles. For the kind of answer we get seems to be determined by the way we put our question; 'What is the cause of the statue?' may be answered by reference to the formal or material cause, whereas 'Why did the statue come into being?' requires us to cite the efficient cause. But this appearance of pragmatic relativity to questions does not really express Aristotle's doctrine. The actual causes and most exact causes are not relative to particular questions; the different questions we ask are different ways, more or less fully specified, of looking for the most exact causes. When we see this, we also see the centrality of the efficient cause more clearly than Aristotle sees it in expounding his own doctrine. Though his explicit account does not make this clear, he implicitly assumes that in looking for causes, we are looking for objective principles and explanations.

But if we allow Aristotle a conception of explanation that is not purely pragmatic and subjective, we can raise a further question for him. Different types of explanations may correspond to different theories; physics, psychology, economics, and history may all explain the same events, and each theory recognizes some things as naturally prior to others. If natural priority is not to be relative to a particular theory, then apparently the theories must themselves be ordered, so that we must regard the things recognized by one theory as prior to those recognized by another. We may think that unless some theories and the entities they recognize are prior to others, we are forced back to a pragmatic conception of explanation.

Though Aristotle does not discuss the questions about priority between different theories, he recognizes four causes, four different types of explanations. Though he does not relate his belief in four causes to his views on first principles, the relation should surely be important. Even if the material, formal, and final causes are really types of efficient cause, not non–efficient causes, Aristotle still claims that they specify irreducibly different explanations. If he is right, there should be different types of things that are naturally prior to other things without being prior or posterior to each other; and if Aristotle believes this, he will have to show that different theories are true, recognizing different entities, but not allowing us to say that one theory is prior to another.

The discussion of causes in *Physics* ii does not state a completely clear or satisfactory view on these issues. The loose and inexplicit character of ordinary questions and judgments about causation infects Aristotle's doctrine; and his claims about form and matter as causes are not all consistent. Book ii, no less than Book i, reflects the limitations of dialectic. But if we can see how to modify Aristotle's claims so as to make a consistent and defensible doctrine of causes, we might also be able to defend some modified version of his claims about the material and the formal cause; they might be part of an account of first principles satisfying the constraints of Aristotle's metaphysical realism.

53. FORM AND MATTER AS CAUSES

In *Physics* ii 1 Aristotle defends his claim, gradually anticipated in Book i, that form is nature and substance. His use of the doctrine of the four causes allows him to offer new arguments, but it also raises new difficulties for his claims.

He presents an argument, ascribed to Antiphon, to show that matter is the nature of things. He endorses the implied conception of nature, and accepts, with important reservations, the conclusion of the argument. Matter is

. . . the first thing present in each thing, being in itself unordered—e.g., the wood is the nature of a bed and the bronze of a statue. (193a10–12)

. . . the first matter that is subject for each thing that has in itself an origin of change and variation. (193a29–30)

Antiphon argues that if you buried a bed and the rotted mass acquired the capacity to put out a shoot, what would grow from it would not be a bed, but wood (193a13–14); he infers that being a bed is simply a coincident of the subject, a temporary arrangement of the wood, and that the nature and substance is the wood, or whatever further matter underlies the wood in the way the wood underlies a bed (193a14–21).

Antiphon argues that the matter is the internal origin of change, and therefore the nature, by showing that the changes happening to the bed are explained by its being wood, not by its having been a bed. He might equally have remarked that if we set it alight or take an axe to it, it will burn or break in so far as it is wood, not in so far as it is a bed. Aristotle said this himself about artifacts (192b16–32); and Antiphon adds that all the changes in the bed happen to it simply as wood. No further subject needs to be assumed, in so far as these changes can be understood by reference to facts about the wood.

Antiphon's argument shows the role of the material cause in relation to the efficient cause. The matter of the bed is not the 'actual' and 'most exact' efficient cause of what happens to the wood; to find that we need to mention some event that is a change in the wood. Still, if we say that a change happens to it because it is wood, we claim that the properties of the wood explain why the change happens as it does. If we mention the matter, we do not necessarily mention the event that is the actual and most exact efficient cause of the change, but we mention an important property of that event. The nature of an organism explains something about the efficient-causal processes it undergoes, and in so far as matter does this, it is the nature of the organism.

Aristotle's arguments to show that form is nature reflect his usual dialectical strategy and expose its weakness (193a31–b18).[7] He appeals to ways we speak of form, when we ascribe a nature to something, and when we mention the origin and conclusion of its coming to be. We imply that an organism has not reached its nature until it has acquired its form; and so we commit ourselves, given Aristotle's account of nature, to further claims about the causal relevance of form as an internal origin of change. But the fact that common beliefs and common ways of speaking commit us to these claims does not show that the claims are true; and Antiphon challenges their truth, not the fact of our commitment to them.

In pointing out that common beliefs, including the conception of nature as internal origin, commit us to claims about causal relevance, Aristotle answers Antiphon in the sense in which he answers the Eleatics in Book i; he shows that some assumptions accepted by common sense require us to disagree with the critic. But this answer does not meet Antiphon's further claim that the assumptions of common sense are false or unjustified. To show that we have good reason to believe form is nature Aristotle needs to answer Antiphon's further claim; and the purely dialectical arguments offered in ii 1 do not even try to answer it.

54. FURTHER DIFFICULTIES ABOUT FORM

It is difficult for Aristotle to show that form is a cause, partly because he has not found quite the right conception of form. In Book i he introduces form as shape; and it might seem all right to say that a statue is what it is by having the physical shape it acquires when it is made from the bronze.[8] But even in this case the identification of shape with form will lead to odd results. A statue could change its shape without ceasing to be the particular statue of Pericles that it is; and a rock that happened to be worn by weather to the very same shape would still not be a statue of Pericles. If the shape is the form, then the form is not essential to the statue, since the statue can survive with a different shape; if so, Aristotle ought not to treat form as the essence of an artifact or organism (cf. *PA* 640a34, 641a25). If the form of the statue is essential to it, then other features besides shape must constitute the form, and the reference to shape can at most give us a very rough first conception of form.

If we turn from artifacts to organisms, it is even clearer that form cannot be just the same as shape. For the same organism can change its shape many times in its life; if Aristotle thinks loss of the form is destruction of the organism, he cannot allow it to change its form as often as it changes its shape. The form must be the right sort of thing to persist throughout the organism's life and to be the internal origin of change.[9]

A further difficulty in Aristotle's conception of form creates difficulties in his conception of substance. In identifying form with nature he identifies it with essence (193a30–1, 193b1–2). We expect this claim to support the claim that form is substance. But the support is dubious. It is easy to argue that if form is the nature and essence of x, it is the substance of x; but the substance of x seems to be a second, not a first, substance. As Aristotle has described it so far, the nature of one tree will be the same as the nature of another. If form is a universal, it is a second substance. If form is only second substance, then apparently bits of matter are the only first substances, because they will be the only subjects.[10]

But the view that form is only a second, not a first, substance is not clearly coherent; for a second substance must correspond to the essence of some first substance, and it is not clear what first substances have form as their essence. The form of a statue is not essential to a bit of bronze. It is certainly essential to a statue; but if a statue is a mere compound analogous to a musician, the form of statue is no more a second substance than the form of musician is. Similarly, the form of a tree cannot be the second substance of anything, if a particular tree is simply a piece of wood with some coincidental properties. Once again Antiphon's argument seems to intensify the objections that Aristotle himself raised in Book i against his ordinary candidates for substance; and his arguments to show that form is nature do not seem to disarm the objections. He does not show why we must believe that there are essentially formal first substances.

For these reasons the claims about form in ii 1 show that Aristotle's conception of it is in some disorder. Antiphon's claims about matter imply that if form is nature, it must have the appropriate causal role. Aristotle's explicit dialectical arguments do not show that form has this role; he does not even explicitly recognize that he ought to show this. Nor does he show how the conception of form as nature fits the claims about substance and subject in Book i.

Most of these questions are left unsettled in Book ii. Nonetheless Aristotle sometimes suggests some of the argument he needs. In ii 2 he alludes to the causal role of the form. In appealing to the analogy of craft and nature he says that a supervisory craft must know the form that is the goal of production by a subordinate craft (194b2–7). Since the goal introduces the final cause, Aristotle's remark suggests how the form of an artifact is causally relevant. To justify the analogy with crafts he must show that the form of natural organisms is also a final cause and therefore an internal origin of change, as a nature should be.

Aristotle does not say that his claims about form must be defended by an argument for final causation in nature. The claims rest on purely dialectical arguments, showing how belief in form as nature is entrenched in common beliefs; he does not say that entrenched beliefs are false unless final causation can be defended. None the less he argues for final causation in nature; and since these arguments are even more important for his claims about form and matter than he explicitly recognizes, we should examine them.

55. DISPUTES ABOUT TELEOLOGY

Aristotle normally assumes the truth of teleological explanations as confidently as he assumes the truth of other common beliefs. He suggests that we should begin with the appearances, and then look for the causes (*PA* 639b8–10, 640a13–15). But among the appearances, the things we 'see', are the four causes among which the final cause 'appears' primary (639b12–16). The claim that the goal is prior to the process in craft and nature, and that the process is for the sake of the goal, is included among the appearances from which we set out to construct our theory (640a10–19). Once this claim is granted, it is used against Empedocles' account of reproduction (640a19–b4; cf. *Phys.* 193b8–12).

The status of Aristotle's belief in teleology suggests some constraints on interpretation. He evidently thinks it is an appearance that should guide further inquiry, not a conclusion of detailed empirical study, resulting from the examination and elimination of rival explanations. The teleological assumption should not, then, rely on the sort of detailed empirical evidence that requires us to go beyond widely accessible appearances. Certainly Aristotle might be wrong about the proper evidential basis for a belief in teleology; but if we are to see what he thinks its evidential basis is, we should begin from the fact that he thinks it counts as itself an appearance, rather than a conclusion from appearances.

He is not justified, however, in taking final causation for granted without showing why it is preferable to other views. In *Physics* ii 8 he recognizes what he fails to recognize in ii 1 and in *PA* i, that the belief in teleology deserves some defence against rival views. He may not think teleology *needs* this defence; he may think it is really quite obvious and simply does not appear obvious to those who are misled by the Presocratics. But at least he suggests the type of argument he would need if he thought, correctly, that an argument was needed.

He faces opponents who claim that (1) everything in nature happens of necessity, according to deterministic non-teleological causal laws referring to purely material properties of natural organisms; (2) a complete efficient-causal explanation of natural processes can be given in such terms; and so (3) there are no final causes in nature (198b10–27). Aristotle clearly rejects the third claim; and if he thinks final causation has implications for efficient causation, he should also reject the second.

His attitude to the first claim is less clear. For now it is enough to notice that if our previous account of the four causes is right, rejection of the second and third claims does not require rejection of the first. Even if every natural event has a material cause whose material properties explain the material properties of the effect, some of these events might still have final causes whose formal properties explain the formal properties of the effect. First we should see if Aristotle has an argument for the positive claim about final causation, and then see what it implies about the extent of material causation.

At once Aristotle sees a serious difficulty for his view. He asks why we should not say that apparently teleological processes have their results only coincidentally. If some process or condition is good for an animal, in promoting its survival and flourishing, we might infer that its function in achieving that good result explains why it happens. Aristotle rejects the inference; the rain does not fall to make the crops grow, even though this is a reliable result of it, any more than it falls to destroy the crops on the threshing-floor, even though this is sometimes the result (198b16–23).[11]

Once we reject the inference from conjunction to explanation, we may wonder if we are equally wrong in believing that any natural processes have final causes. Empedocles argues that the beneficial results of having teeth are merely coincidental, and have nothing to do with why creatures have the teeth they have; creatures have useful teeth only because the creatures without them have died.

Why not suppose, then, that the same is true of the parts of organisms in nature? It will be from necessity, e.g., that the front teeth come up sharp and suitable for biting, and the back ones broad and useful for chewing food— since this result was coincidental, not what they came about for. And the same will be true of all the other parts that seem to be for something. On this view, then, whenever all the parts came about coincidentally as though for something, these animals survived, since their chance constitution made them suitable for survival. Other animals, however, were differently constituted, and so were destroyed—indeed they are still being destroyed—as Empedocles says of the man-headed calves. (198b23–32)

Aristotle seems to admit clearly that regular benefit is insufficient for teleology.

56. THE DIFFERENCE BETWEEN FINAL CAUSATION
AND COINCIDENCE

Before we consider how Aristotle replies to the Empedoclean argument, we should pause at a prior question. What does he take to be necessary and sufficient for real teleology, as opposed to regular but coincidental benefit? We must interrupt discussion of ii 8 and return to the discussion of luck (*tuchê*) and chance (*automaton*) earlier in book ii; for here he explains the standards that a genuine teleological explanation must meet.

The lucky event involves X, who is collecting subscriptions for a club, and Y, who owes X a subscription. X happens by luck to be in the market-place when Y is there, and so X collects the subscription from Y (196b33–6).[12] The lucky event is the sort of thing X would have decided to do; if he had known Y would be in the market then, X would have come to meet him and collect the money (196b33–4). Moreover, it is caused by a decision, hence 'done from thought' (196b22).[13] X's decision to sell his goods causes him to be in the market at 9 a.m.; 9 a.m. is the time when Y is in the market; hence X's decision to sell his goods causes him to be in the market when Y is, and hence causes X to meet Y (196a1–11).

Aristotle does not deny this account of the cause, but wants to show that none the less it is a matter of luck. He appeals to the distinction between intrinsic and coincidental causation. We can truly say that the builder, or the pale thing, or the musical thing, caused the house, if the builder is both pale and musical (196b24–9); but only 'the builder' describes what intrinsically causes the house. The pale, musical builder builds the house because he is a builder, not because he is pale or musical.

This general conception of coincidental causation explains how lucky events are caused. A lucky event, as such, is the coincidental result of thought, and therefore is only coincidentally for the sake of some end, which is different from the result that is actually reached (196b20–1, 29–30). For X came into the market with quite a different purpose (196b34–6).[14] The cause of X's being in the market when Y is there is X's decision to sell his goods; but this is only the coincidental cause. X's decision to sell his goods explains his being in the market at 9 a.m., and hence is the intrinsic cause of that property of the event; but it does not explain his being there when Y was there, since this was no part of X's decision. What explains X's being there when Y is there is the fact that the time when X has arrived is the time when Y has arrived. Though X would have planned this had he known, he did not plan it. The event is a matter of luck, because the contribution of the event to X's debt-collecting plans is not linked to X's plans by the right causal connexion; he did not decide on the event because he thought it would fulfil these plans.[15]

Aristotle's discussion of lucky and random events shows that the difference between an event with a genuine final cause and an event without it is a difference in efficient causation. When there is no final cause, the beneficial result secured does not explain anything about the efficient causation of the event.[16] Aristotle's argument confirms our previous claim, that if something is the final cause of an event it must be relevant to the efficient causation of the event.

Aristotle's doctrine of the causes implies that material, formal, and final causation are really types of efficient causation; the most exact and actual cause will be the efficient cause of which the formal or material properties are essential constituents. The discussion of luck shows that he accepts the centrality of the efficient cause, even though he does not state it in his account of the four causes; for the difference between matters of luck and properties of an event that have genuine final causes turns on the absence or presence of the right sort of efficient causation. If final causation were not a type of efficient causation, this condition would not be reasonable; but if the condition is reasonable, and expresses the right view of final causation, it must also be a reasonable condition for natural teleology.

57. THE ARGUMENTS FOR TELEOLOGY

To answer Empedocles' attempts to explain apparent natural teleology as mere coincidence, Aristotle ought to show that the benefits in natural processes really explain the processes. His actual answer, however, is rather curt and obscure.

⟨Empedocles'⟩ argument, then, and others like it, might puzzle someone. In fact, however, it is impossible for things to be like this. For these ⟨teeth and other useful parts⟩, and all natural things, come to be as they do either always or usually, whereas no result of luck or chance does. (For we do not regard frequent winter rain or a summer heatwave, but only summer rain or a winter heatwave, as a result of luck or coincidence.) If, then, these ⟨teeth etc.⟩ seem to be either coincidental results or for something, and they cannot be coincidental or chance results, it follows that they are for something. Now surely all such things are natural, as even those making these claims ⟨about necessity⟩ would agree. We find, then, that things are for something when they come into being and remain in being naturally. (198b32–199a8)[17]

The most obscure and important claim says that some natural processes happen 'always or usually'. It is important to know what Aristotle means by this claim; what grounds he has for believing it; and what it contributes to the argument for natural teleology.

If 'always or usually' just implies uniformity, then surely Aristotle is unjustified in assuming final causation.[18] Final causation requires the right sort of efficient causation, not mere uniformity. If surviving animals uniformly or frequently have beneficial teeth, it does not follow that the benefit of the teeth has anything to do with their efficient causation. Empedocles accounts for the uniformity by saying that some animals were coincidentally born with beneficial teeth, and the animals without them died; this account avoids all final causation. If Aristotle simply takes uniformity to be sufficient for teleology, he entirely misses the point of Empedocles' argument; such obtuseness is surprising when Aristotle has himself shown how Empedocles can account for uniformity, and has shown us in the account of luck and the random that some appropriate causal connexion is needed for final causation.

Aristotle might be more prone to obtuseness here if he did not quite see that his account of luck made uniformity insufficient for final causation. For in his discussion of luck he seems to think that what happens always (necessarily) or usually cannot be a matter of luck (196b36–197a5; cf. 199b24–5). Perhaps, then, he means that if X uniformly or frequently meets Y in the market, this cannot be a matter of luck. If this is what he means, then here also he illegitimately infers final causation from uniformity.

Probably, however, he avoids this illegitimate inference. He says that if X met Y always or usually as a result of hanging around the market to meet Y, then his meeting Y would not, on these occasions, be a matter of luck.[19] Aristotle wants to say that X's decision to meet Y explains his meeting Y even if it is only usually followed by meeting Y. In saying this he does not imply that mere uniformity or frequency of X's being in the market when Y is shows that the meeting is non-coincidental; he implies only that he does not think a cause must be sufficient for its effect. X's decision to meet Y is only usually followed by meeting Y, because other conditions besides the decision are needed for the meeting, and these may not always obtain. None the less the salient causal influence we want to pick out is the relevant mental state of X; and we correctly believe his decision has this salient influence.[20]

If he applies the same conception of 'always or usually' to the argument against Empedocles, Aristotle does not confuse uniformity with causal connexion, and does not move without defence from one to the other. Rather, the 'always or usually' claim itself means that there is an invariable or usual causal connexion between the benefit secured by the natural process and the process itself, explaining why the process comes about.[21] In speaking of a usual connexion Aristotle already means that the beneficial result has the right sort of explanatory relevance to the process; and then he is entitled to infer that the process happens for the sake of the result.

Now, however, Aristotle seems to beg the question. His claim about the always-or-usual connexion is not a purely statistical claim about uniformity that an opponent must already accept. It is already a causal claim, from which the step to teleology is very short. But if it is a causal claim, it is not clear why an opponent must accept it. Aristotle seems simply to claim without defence the sort of causal relevance he needs. He is certainly at fault for failing to defend his claim; but the fault is remediable, if we can see some defence.

Aristotle and Empedocles disagree about why beneficial teeth tend to arise, as a present and stable tendency in nature. Empedocles claims that in every single generation it is a matter of chance that they arise; the benefit of teeth is not causally relevant for explaining why the dog born today has beneficial teeth. On Empedocles' view, many animals are born with beneficial teeth, and many are born with useless teeth; no final cause explains the condition of the teeth in either case, but the animals with bad teeth die and those with good teeth survive. The character of the teeth helps to explain why some die and others survive, but not why they have good or bad teeth.

Aristotle replies that things do not happen as they would if Empedocles were right. We see that animals needing teeth are uniformly or frequently born with beneficial teeth or acquire them in the process of growth; we do not see large numbers of toothless or blunt-toothed creatures perish for the want of good teeth. Aristotle assumes that a reasonable explanation of this pattern involves reference to the benefit of teeth; and indeed Empedocles' own account shows why this is a reasonable explanation.

To show why it is not a matter of coincidence that animals have beneficial teeth, we may appeal to the fact that members of the previous generation with bad teeth have perished, and hence presumably have been unable to reproduce in large numbers. While Empedocles agrees that bad teeth explain perishing (198b29–32), he does not see that his admission undermines his claim that the beneficial teeth in later generations are a coincidence. In later generations they have a final cause, since their benefit explains their presence. If Empedocles had taken this further step he fails to take, he would have applied his claims about perishing to reproduction; and then he would have had to admit final causation.[22]

58. THE BASIS OF THE ARGUMENT FOR TELEOLOGY

Aristotle suggests an appropriately ad hominem argument against
Empedocles. He does not himself accept Empedocles' view of the non-
teleological origins of beneficial teeth. But for present purposes, he does
not challenge it; he does not say that the past could never have been as
Empedocles says it was. In failing to challenge Empedocles' version of
natural history, he suggests that this version itself supports the view that
the uniform or frequent occurrence of beneficial teeth has a final cause.
He does not explain why Empedocles must admit the final cause; but the
description of Empedocles' view suggests the explanation that Aristotle
omits.

Elsewhere Aristotle discusses Empedocles' claim that plants grow
upwards and downwards because fire tends to rise and earth tends to
sink (*DA* 415b28–416a2). In Aristotle's view, we also need to know
what prevents the earth and fire from being pulled apart when they
move in these contrary directions (416a6–9). Similarly, those who think
the nature of fire is, without qualification or addition, the cause of
growth and nutrition must explain why the growth does not go on
indefinitely, but only to a certain limit (416a9–18). Reference to the
formal, and hence to the final, cause explains why the material and
efficient causes cited by Empedocles operate as they do. Aristotle
implies that the benefit of growth and nutrition explains why they
happen as they do, and why the efficient-causal processes vary as they
do (416a7–9, 15–18).[23]

This passage suggests more clearly than *Physics* ii 8 does why we
should appeal to a final cause. If we appeal to it we can explain a striking
regularity (the tendency of organisms to hold together and grow in
certain ways) that we cannot explain without appeal to it. Even if we can
explain everything about the addition and subtraction of the matter of
each individual body, we will not have explained this regularity about
some types of material body. A similar point applies to Empedocles'
account in *Physics* ii 8; Empedocles cannot explain, without reference to
the benefit of teeth, why later generations mostly have the sort of teeth
they have. Aristotle correctly implies that we need not accept his own
belief in the fixity of species and in the teleological structure of the
universe, in order to recognize final causes among the appearances.
Even the false Empedoclean explanation of the appearances does not
undermine final causation.[24]

The argument stays too close to pure dialectic to show its theoretical
commitments clearly, and so it displays a fault that we have previously
noticed in the first two books of the *Physics*. Aristotle assumes the truth
of the common belief in final causes, and defends it by citing the sorts of

examples in which common sense sees final causes. He does not, however, openly recognize the claims about efficient causation that follow from common beliefs but are not certified by them. Common sense does not assume the truth of any one particular efficient-causal account of a given natural process; but it requires some account involving formal and teleological properties to be true, and hence is not compatible with all logically possible empirical accounts. [25]

Aristotle sees that the belief in teleology is fairly flexible about its empirical basis; for he defends it without challenging Empedocles' account of the empirical basis. To some extent he also sees that belief in final causation is inflexible in assuming the sort of efficient-causal connexion that excludes mere coincidence; for he recognizes this condition in distinguishing luck and chance from final causation, and he alludes to it in insisting on an always-or-usual connexion that is not purely statistical. Still, he neither clearly identifies nor clearly defends the efficient-causal component of the common belief in natural teleology.

Aristotle's failure is understandable, both because of his conception of dialectical argument and because of his account of the causes, a particular product of his dialectical method. The account of the causes does not display the central place of the efficient cause, and so does not make clear the implications of a claim about final causation; hence these implications are not as prominent as they should be in the argument for teleology. In both cases Aristotle's approach is dialectical. He wants to articulate the appearances and common beliefs, and to remove objections and puzzles, by referring to other beliefs and recognized examples. Dialectical method does not try to do any more; but if it does no more, it can offer only a limited 'road towards first principles'.

Aristotle does not examine the common beliefs far enough to expose the causal assumptions they rest on, and the further claims that he would have to defend if he wanted to show that the endoxic principles underlying common beliefs are also objective principles. Nothing in *Physics* i–ii suggests that he sets himself this particular task; to the extent that he does not try such a defence of common beliefs, he offers no explicit answer to important questions about his principles. Doubts about natural teleology do not seem to be doubts about something self-evident; and if Aristotle thinks some objective principles justify the belief in natural teleology, he can fairly be asked for a further defence. [26]

59. TELEOLOGY AND NECESSITY

Aristotle clarifies to some extent the causal commitments of common-sense teleological assumptions, in his discussion of conditional and unconditional necessity. He rejects the view that only non-teleological explanations are appropriate; but we still need to see if he rejects the view that every natural event conforms to deterministic non-teleological causal laws referring to purely material properties of natural organisms.

Belief in this non-teleological necessity threatens belief in teleology, if we take teleological claims about an event to be superseded by a non-teleological causal explanation of it. If we do not know much about a thermostat, we may get a rough idea by supposing it has a little man in it who knows when it reaches 68 degrees and then turns it off. But when we really understand it, we see that these intentional notions are false; if we keep on using them it is only because they are convenient and familiar, as we speak of the sun rising even though we know it does not rise. On this view, once we find a non-teleological explanation for an event that we explained teleologically, the teleological explanation becomes superfluous; necessity undermines teleology.[27]

Aristotle might try any of three possible answers to this objection:

1. Teleological claims do not conflict with non-teleological explanations, because they imply nothing about efficient-causal explanations at all. If the relevant cases display, uniformly or frequently, the order that we see in artifacts and natural organisms, our teleological claim is justified, no matter what the efficient-causal explanation may be.[28]

2. Teleological claims are causal, and they are ineliminable because they explain events that have no non-teleological explanation.[29]

3. Teleological claims are causal, and are ineliminable because they refer to explanatory properties of events that may also have non-teleological explanations.[30]

The first answer is in some ways easiest for Aristotle if he relies on pure dialectic; it appeals to the sorts of facts that might reasonably appear to be evident to common sense. But such a defence undermines the right of teleological claims to supply final causes, on Aristotle's own conception of final causes. His account of luck and chance shows that true teleological claims require the truth of some efficient-causal claims. To distinguish final causation from coincidence Aristotle must apparently go beyond what pure dialectic can give him, and must make causal claims that rule out the first answer to the necessitarian challenge.

The second answer commits teleological judgments to a very strong causal claim about the absence of non-teleological explanations. Aristotle can hardly claim to know that this claim is true, much less that common sense knows it is true. If he accepts this claim, it is hard to see how he could even suggest that the truth of teleology is one of the appearances; far from being an appearance, it would require knowledge of the guaranteed failure of numerous conceivable attempts to find non-teleological causal explanations.

Moreover, it is hard to see how the second answer is consistent with the efficient-causal claims implied by a teleological claim. For a claim about a final cause invites us to look for a certain sort of efficient cause. If, for instance, we say that an axe is made to chop wood, we justify our claim by showing that it is in fact made by an efficient-causal process to which the chopping capacity of an axe is relevant; reference to the intentions of a designer would show the sort of relevance we want. But this efficient-causal explanation is no longer a teleological explanation; if we find it, and if Aristotle accepts the second answer, we will have eliminated any reason for accepting the final cause.[31] On this view, claims about final causation, understood in Aristotle's way, will be peculiarly self-destructive, undermined by their own success.

If we are right about the relation between teleological explanation and the search for non-teleological efficient causes, then Aristotle's view ought to be the exact reverse—that if a teleological explanation is true, some sort of non-teleological explanation is also true, and our knowledge of its truth is part of our grounds for claiming to know the truth of the teleological explanation. Unless he believes that the truth of a non-teleological causal explanation implies the falsity of a teleological account of the same event, Aristotle has no good reason to accept the second answer; and the efficient-causal implications of teleology give him very good reason to reject it. The third answer is the most reasonable, if he can show that the non-teleological explanation does not allow us to eliminate the teleological explanation.

Aristotle's discussion in *Physics* ii 9 does not make his view clear. He recognizes two kinds of necessity—the conditional necessity that depends on teleology, and the unconditional that does not (199b34–5). What is conditionally necessary is needed to obtain the goal; we need a hammer, for example, because it is necessary if we want to drive nails into wood. Such conditional necessity soon relies on unconditional necessity.[32] For a hammer must be made of iron; and hence for driving nails into wood we need something made of iron (200a11–13). Iron is conditionally necessary for hammering; but the necessity of hammers to be made of iron reflects the unconditionally necessary nature of iron (200a8–9). It is unconditionally necessary that iron is, and other things are not, hard enough for hammering; and statements of conditional necessity must assume this sort of unconditional necessity.

This discussion shows that Aristotle thinks there is both conditional and unconditional necessity, and hence both teleological and non-teleological explanation, in nature. It does not show whether he denies, affirms, or allows that teleologically explained events may also be explained non-teleologically by unconditional necessity. A passage in *Parts of Animals* i, however, is more helpful (642a32–b4). There Aristotle argues that we can explain respiration by saying that it happens for the sake of some end, but we can also say that 'this happens because of this from necessity' (642a32). He then distinguishes the usual two types of necessity; and in describing parts of the process of respiration he appeals to unconditional necessities (642a35–b3).

It follows that at least some parts of a process are non-teleologically explained even if the whole process is teleologically explained. In that case, some events are explained both teleologically and non-teleologically, since each of these parts of breathing will have both types of explanation.[33] We take in cool air to breathe and to secure the benefits of breathing; at the same time we take it in because of the unconditional necessities about hot and cold. Here, then, Aristotle seems to allow, indeed to require, two types of explanation for the same event.[34]

The evidence we have considered is not clear enough to show that Aristotle thinks everything explained teleologically must also be explained non-teleologically. But he nowhere affirms the incompatibility of the two types of explanation; and if he did, he would be in open conflict with the particular cases we have discussed. Nor does he suggest why the double explanation he describes should not be equally discoverable in all events that are explained teleologically. These are good reasons for supposing that he admits the general possibility of double explanations.[35]

We have some reason, therefore, to believe that Aristotle ought to hold the third of the three answers we distinguished earlier, that teleological claims refer to causally explanatory properties of events that may also have non-teleological causal explanations. To believe in double explanations would be consistent with the first answer, that teleological claims are not ordinary efficient-causal explanations at all; but this answer conflicts with Aristotle's basis for distinguishing coincidences from final causes. The second answer conflicts with the apparent possibility of double explanations. We make most sense of Aristotle's different claims if we suppose he is committed to the third answer.

Still, he does not clearly present the third answer in the *Physics*; and if he had, he would have needed to revise some of his argument. For we have seen that his account of teleology does not make its efficient-causal assumptions clear, and that if these were clear, the argument against Empedocles would need to be strengthened. His silence about the third answer marks his failure to explore the implications of his different views and their effects on each other.

60. TELEOLOGY AND SUBSTANCE

Some of Aristotle's views on teleology and necessity are relevant to his claim in ii 1 that form as well as matter is the nature of living organisms.

To defend the claim, he ought to show that form is an internal origin of change for living organisms; he shows this if he shows that the form is the final cause. Final causation in natural organisms needs the right kind of efficient causation. Aristotle implicitly defends himself through (i) the definition of nature as an internal origin of change; (ii) the implied primacy of the efficient cause; (iii) the difference between final causation and coincidence; and (iv) the claims about teleology and necessity. But he does not use this implicit defence in his account of the formal and final causes.

This conclusion about Book ii supports our view of the argument in Book i. There Aristotle accepts the commonsense view that particular men and horses are substances, and that their constituent matter is not the only sort of substance. But he seems to have no good defence of common sense against the view that since ordinary substances can be reduced to matter and its coincidents, only mater is substance. In Book ii he defends common sense by claiming that form is the nature and essence of natural organisms; but this claim is itself a commonsense assumption needing further defence, and Aristotle does not offer the further defence.

These facts about Book i and Book ii have a common explanation, in Aristotle's conception of dialectical method. As he uses and explains it in his reply to the Eleatics, it is not meant to defend common sense against a doubter, but to show that common sense has no reason within itself to take the doubts seriously. If the accounts of matter, form, and teleology are measured by this standard, then to some extent they succeed. For they show that the relevant beliefs are entrenched in common sense; and they point out paradigmatic cases where we make confident judgments using the concepts in question. Such arguments help to show that we need not doubt, from within the outlook of common sense, the application of these concepts to reality.

Both in the *Categories* and in the *Physics*, however, Aristotle expects too much of his dialectical arguments. He does not believe they are merely consistent; he thinks that if the Eleatic position conflicts with the *Categories*, the Eleatic position is wrong. He assumes that the dialectical argument of the *Categories* has found objective principles, but he does not defend his assumption.

Apart from this general question about the results of dialectic, it remains doubtful whether dialectic supports principles as specific as those Aristotle accepts. Pure dialectic, relying on intuitive judgments, recognizes distinctions between subjects and properties, and between classification and characterization. In the *Categories* Aristotle relies on these to support his claims about form as substance. But the dialectical arguments by themselves do not seem to support Aristotle against Antiphon; though they recognize a distinction between substance and its coincidents, they do not show that men and trees must be substances.

The direction of the argument in *Physics* ii suggests what Aristotle has to add to the pure dialectic practised in the *Categories* and in *Physics* i. He connects form and matter with causation, and implies, without explicitly stating, that the efficient cause is central. By marking these connexions, he commits himself to the truth of causal claims whose truth is not assured by common beliefs themselves. His defence of form and teleology would be reasonable if the application of these concepts to reality depended only on the sorts of conditions that are accessible to common sense; but the causal components of these concepts assure us that common sense cannot settle the issue.

The causal aspect of claims about form produces internal tension within Book ii. It also emphasizes the difficulty of reconciling the different remarks about form, matter, and substance in Books i and ii. Form has to be shape, nature, substance, essence, and internal origin of change; but it is not clear how one thing can fill all these roles.[36] To be a first substance it apparently has to be a particular basic subject; but only matter seems to be the right sort of subject. To be a second substance form has to be the essence of some first substance; but if only matter is first substance, the right sort of first substance seems to be lacking. To be an internal origin of change form must be properly related to an efficient cause; but Aristotle has not argued that form, as he conceives it, meets this condition. Though these are distinct difficulties in the conception of form as substance, they have a common source; they are all results of the method of pure dialectic.

61. FURTHER DEVELOPMENTS

Aristotle does not leave us without resources for possible solutions for some of the difficulties. The connexion between formal and final causes shows why he thinks something's form corresponds to significant laws and regularities. And we can see reasons for being guided by the existence of these laws in our judgments about which things are basic subjects and first substances. Once we are convinced of the truth of teleological laws, we have reasons for recognizing first substances defined with reference to them.

If this is true, then closer attention to the causal role of form will actually throw light on the problems of Book i, and explain to us why form can be a particular subject. We saw that a critic might challenge Aristotle's conception of the subjects and first substances there are by urging that the commonsense and Aristotelian conception rests on an arbitrary preference; it treats some combinations of matter and coincidents as subjects and substances and dismisses others (e.g. musicians and white men) as merely coincidental beings. Aristotle can show why the preference is not arbitrary, and why form is a genuine substance and subject, if he can show that the formal cause is a genuine cause, properly related to the efficient cause.

Such a defence of form would not require Aristotle to abandon dialectical for empirical argument. If he held that teleological and non-teleological explanations of the same event are incompatible, then his belief in teleological explanations would commit him to very specific and detailed empirical predictions. If he claims that some events with non-teleological explanations also have ineliminable teleological explanations, his claim is empirically falsifiable, but much less specific and much less easily falsified. Our evidence of goal-direction in particular systems or processes, artificial or natural, might justify us in believing that a teleological explanation is correct, even if we did not know the precise non-teleological efficient-causal explanation that would assure us that there is the right causal connexion. Even though we might be proved wrong, we may sometimes have good reason for not taking the possibility very seriously.[37]

Aristotle's argument suggests how he might reach a fuller statement and defence of his position. But he does not show that he intends such a defence; and to reach it he would have to revise his dialectical approach to the questions. It is important neither to underestimate nor to exaggerate the limitations of the argument. We should not assume that Aristotle must have seen the implications of the causal claims that he commits himself to; had he seen them he would have seen that the rest of his argument needs revision. Equally we must not pretend that he is a long way from seeing the consequences of his own assumptions. If we see how far he has gone and how far he has still to go, we can see some of the important differences between the *Physics* and the *Metaphysics*.

The *Physics* follows the purely dialectical method of the *Topics* and *Categories*, and applies it to one of the tasks assigned to dialectic by the *Topics*—finding a way towards the first principles of the sciences. A minimal interpretation of this task makes it seem quite modest; Aristotle sometimes suggests that dialectic confines itself to removing puzzles and misunderstandings that might lead us to think common sense is inconsistent. A more ambitious interpretation of the dialectical task would suggest that dialectic offers a positive argument for first principles that does not merely appeal to consistency with common sense.

Aristotle's explicit view of dialectic in the *Physics* is closer to the first view; his comments on the Eleatics express a fairly modest claim for dialectic. Some of his arguments and their limitations are intelligible if his ambitions for them are modest. But he does not clearly stick to such a modest outlook. Some of his arguments and suggestions might well lead us to think he intends to carry out the more ambitious task of offering positive arguments for objective first principles; and it is worth asking, irrespective of Aristotle's intentions, how well his arguments carry out this task. In the *Physics* he suggests that the commonsense scheme of substance and the categories, supplemented with the concepts of form and matter, will provide some of the first principles of natural science; but his exposition of the commonsense scheme itself assures us that it raises questions it cannot answer. If we are to find objective, not purely endoxic, first principles, we apparently cannot simply rely on pure dialectic.

6

CONDITIONS FOR SCIENCE

62. SCIENCE AND JUSTIFICATION

A comparison of Aristotle's methods with his goal raises doubts about whether they reach it. The goal is defined by his metaphysics, and especially by his views about truth and natural priority. Objective principles are prior to, and logically independent of, our beliefs; a belief is true because it fits how things are, not the other way round. Hence the truth of our beliefs must be logically independent of any of their internal properties—consistency, coherence, simplicity. Aristotle's methods of inquiry, however, do not seem to justify belief in the objective truth of their conclusions. They seem to fail for two reasons.

1. Metaphysical realism about truth might seem to imply that the coherence of one belief with another cannot be a source of justification. Since coherence is an internal property of beliefs, logically independent of their truth, why should we think the coherent beliefs are true? Aristotle's methods, however, seem to be methods for reaching coherent beliefs, and hence seem to do little to justify those beliefs.

2. Even apart from this general objection to coherence, we might doubt if Aristotle's particular arguments lead us towards his goal. For dialectical inquiry seems to proceed from widely held beliefs, common sense, and ordinary forms of speech, and to seek conclusions that are coherent with these. Even if we accept some appeals to coherence, we need not suppose that every starting-point for seeking coherent beliefs is equally good; and we may doubt if Aristotle picks the right starting-point, since the one he picks seems likely to include errors infecting the conclusions.

Aristotle notices this weakness in his methods. In his theoretical comments about dialectic he is quite reserved about its prospects of reaching the truth. He does not openly express such doubts about empirical inquiry; but they would be quite appropriate, and it is only Aristotle's over-simplified account of empirical method that conceals the difficulty from him. He regularly contrasts the dialectician, who argues 'according to belief', with the scientist, who argues 'according to truth'.[1]

Understood one way, this contrast is indisputable. For the dialectician begins with beliefs that include true and false ones. The scientist begins with premisses that are true, and it is none of his business to convince an interlocutor of their truth. Scientific argument assumes the truth of the first principles of the relevant science; and dialectic would lose its point if it went in for scientific argument of this sort.

Aristotle, however, seems to intend a further limit on dialectic. He suggests that the conclusion is also a matter of belief rather than truth, so that it is not justifiably asserted as true. On this view, dialectic cannot itself claim to discover the truth. Indeed, he never claims that dialectic reaches the first principles, but only that it has a way towards them; and this does not require success in reaching them. In the *Physics*, Aristotle does not say that dialectic should prove the first principles, since he takes at least some first principles to be self-evident, and only requires dialectic to remove puzzles and confusions.[2] If he limits dialectic in this way, he should defend his claim that the principles are self-evident.

We might reasonably expect an account of scientific knowledge to display the crucial difference from dialectic. Aristotle needs to say what features of a discipline show that it argues according to truth and not just according to belief, how we can tell if a discipline has these features, and how we can reach such a discipline. If he describes a science, but offers no prospect of our reaching one, then he does not explain how his own inquiries reach their goal.

The *Posterior Analytics* describes the structure of a science and of the content of scientific propositions.[3] Aristotle sees the weaknesses we have noticed in his methods, and his views on justification support and explain some of his demands on scientific knowledge. These same views, however, seem to imply demands that he cannot meet within any plausible conception of justification.

63. SCIENCE AND UNIVERSALS

Aristotle's description of what the propositions of a science say, and what they say it about, conforms to the demands of his metaphysical realism. Scientific propositions must be true, and known to be true; they must therefore correspond to some objective reality (a reality that is logically independent of our beliefs about it). Since a science purports to state truths about universals, not about particulars, universals are the primary subjects of which a science predicates properties (*APo* 77a5–9, 83a30–5, 85b15–18, *Met.* 1003a14–15, 1059b24–7). If truths about universals correspond to some objective reality, universals must exist. Aristotelian universals are not Platonic Forms existing independently of particulars (rejected at 77a5–9, 83a22–5); but statements about them are not just about the particulars that exemplify them. A science is intended to describe a natural, objective kind, not to distinguish kinds whose existence depends on being spoken of or thought.[4]

In claiming that a science offers explanations, Aristotle assumes the reality of universals. Explanations state laws that refer to properties of particulars, and if the laws are true the properties must really exist. The laws do not simply say that certain linguistic predicates or thought-dependent concepts are applied to particulars. A nominalist view would undermine the claim of scientific propositions to meet metaphysical realist conditions for truth. Aristotle claims that universals are better known by nature than particulars are, and he is justified in so far as propositions referring to universals explain facts about particulars; but he would be completely unjustified if he took a nominalist view of universals or scientific laws.

Since Aristotle requires scientific propositions to be about universals, he refuses to allow singular statements about particulars to be part of science. The explanatory function of a science makes his restriction intelligible. The explananda include facts about particular subjects, but the explanation of these facts will refer to a subject's essential properties and to the properties derived from them, and will therefore refer to the appropriate universals. Since scientific statements explain, they must be about universals.[5] Facts about the nature of a subject explain some facts about it; but in any individual case we will need perception to estimate the many different conditions that may affect this case. Aristotle wants to distinguish the techniques needed to apply general laws from the knowledge that is embodied in the statement of the laws. Hence he confines 'scientific knowledge' to the statement of these laws.

Aristotle's demand that scientific knowledge should grasp necessary states of affairs, those that 'cannot be otherwise' (71b9–16), is a further result of his concern for explanations referring to universals. What holds universally of a subject must hold of it intrinsically.

> By universal I mean what belongs to its subject in every case and in itself and as such; universals, then, evidently belong from necessity. What belongs to the subject in itself is the same as what belongs to it as such. Point and straight, e.g., belong to line in itself, since they belong to it as line; and two right angles belong to triangle as triangle, since triangle is in itself equal to two right angles. (73b26–32)

An intrinsic property must be either an essential property or derived from the essence.[6] Such a universal property is not merely one that always happens to be true of the subject; for such an invariant property is distinguished from a proper universal (73a32–74a3), and necessity is ascribed only to a proper universal.[7] To find universals and necessary truths we must find the essential properties and intrinsic concomitants

of the subjects. These reflect the concern of science with explanation; for
the intrinsic non-essential properties are those that belong to the subject
because it has the essential properties it has. An account of what holds
necessarily of a universal subject will derive some of the properties of
the subject from others that explain them. Aristotle's demand for
necessity reflects his demand for explanatory laws.[8]

64. EXPLANATORY PROPERTIES AND BASIC SUBJECTS

If there is scientific knowledge, then, Aristotle assumes, there must be
real natural kinds; and belief in these affects his doctrine of substance. In
the *Categories*, Aristotle's primary criterion requires a first substance to
be a basic subject, neither said of nor inherent in a further subject. But to
identify basic subjects and to distinguish them from non-substances
(e.g. musicality) and combinations of substance and non-substance (e.g.
musicians) he relies on rather simple and intuitive tests. These tests are
not reliable, since they seem to depend on the presence or absence of
abstract nouns in a particular language.

An argument in the *Analytics*, however, shows how Aristotle means
to avoid inferences from apparently obvious facts about predication to
mistaken conclusions about subjects and substances. We say 'The large
thing is a log' or 'The white thing is moving' (83a1–4), as though white
things were subjects.[9] But Aristotle denies that they are subjects:

For whenever I say that the white thing is a log, then I say that the thing which
has the coincident of being white is a log, but not that the white thing is the
subject for the log. For neither by being essentially white nor by being
essentially some white thing did it come to be a log, and hence ⟨the white thing⟩
is not ⟨a log⟩ except coincidentally. (83a4–9)[10]

In some cases the apparent subject is really just a combination of subject
and coincident, and hence not a genuine single subject.

In this remark Aristotle tries to prevent abuse of the tests offered in
the *Categories*. We might argue that white things or musicians are
subjects with predicates ascribed to them, and that they endure through
change. But Aristotle answers that these can be treated as subjects only
because they belong to some more basic subject; it is because the white
thing is a log that it is long or short, and in saying that the white thing is
a log we are identifying the more basic subject (the log), not predicating
some coincidental property of it (as when we say that the log is white).[11]

To apply Aristotle's tests, we must be able to decide when something
is F by being G rather than by being F; and to do this, we must
distinguish the essential properties from the coincidents that they
explain.[12] If something's being F explains its being G and the converse is

not true, then the F is the basic subject, and therefore the substance, and the G is a combination of a substance with a coincident. The appropriate description of a substance must identify the essential properties; that is why men are basic subjects and musicians are not.[13]

Aristotle, therefore, accepts the demand in the *Categories* for a basic subject of predication, but shows more clearly than the *Categories* showed that intuitive tests may not pick out basic subjects, and that commonsense subjects may not be substances. He now claims that a substance must belong to a natural kind defined by explanatory properties. If common sense is very far wrong about these properties, Aristotle's views about substance and explanation will commit him to the radical rejection of commonsense candidates for substance.

65. EXPLANATORY PROPERTIES AND THE ARGUMENTS ABOUT SUBSTANCE

Aristotle's tests for a genuine basic subject raise questions about his defence of his own candidates for substance. In *Physics* ii he considers Antiphon's materialist attack on common sense; and in the *Generation and Corruption* he considers Atomism. The tests in the *Analytics*, however, prevent him from simply appealing, as he does in the *Physics*, to well-entrenched common beliefs supporting ordinary views about substance and form. If the substantial properties are those that explain other properties, commonsense candidates for substance must meet this condition. In the *Physics* Aristotle does not clearly set out to meet this condition; but in the *Analytics* he clearly imposes it.

It is just the sort of test he needs to sharpen the issues about form and matter as substance. In *Physics* ii Aristotle identifies form with nature, an internal origin of change; if he is right, then something's formal properties will explain its behaviour and movements. The *Analytics* shows how these claims affect the subject–criterion for substance; the basic subjects must be defined by the explanatory properties from which the other properties are to be derived.

If, then, Aristotle wants to reject Atomist views on substance, he cannot argue that the results of scientific inquiry are irrelevant to decisions about the substances there are. He must argue, on the contrary, that scientific inquiry largely confirms and explains the common views about the substances there are. In his view, the explanatory properties will not be very far from some intuitive classifications; for since he recognizes natural teleology, he thinks ordinary terms for species and genera correspond to important explanatory properties.

Nonetheless, he recognizes that ordinary classifications may contain homonymies that are to be eliminated in a scientific classification (97b7–39). Common-sense kinds will be homonymous, not because of any semantic feature of the kind-terms, detectable by common sense, but because common sense has not found the right explanatory properties.[14] We will remove the homonymy only by scientific inquiry that finds the explanatory properties. Aristotle thinks it is sensible to begin from the kinds recognized by common sense; but he does not stop there.

These claims about science and substance are not surprising for a metaphysical realist. In accepting them Aristotle shows that he intends a demonstrative science to meet metaphysical realist conditions. Our conclusion about which things are substances, which properties are essential and which accidental, depends on the conclusions of science.

These conditions for being a substance do not conflict with those in the *Categories* and *Physics*; in fact the *Physics* refers to the distinction between essential properties and intrinsic coincidents (193b25–8). But we have not so far found that Aristotle tries to connect his views about explanatory properties with his criteria for substance. The *Analytics* marks the connexions far more precisely; it still leaves Aristotle the task of showing how his criteria and candidates for substance meet his conditions about explanation.[15] These conditions support the claim of a putative substance to be a genuine substance, an ineliminable constituent of an objective world; and so Aristotle should show that his favoured substances meet this condition.

Aristotle tends to regard the results of dialectic as truths about an objective reality, not simply about the structure and presuppositions of common sense. Still, it has not been clear that the dialectical argument of his earlier works entitles him to ascribe to his conclusions the status he apparently intends for them. The *Analytics* states more sharply the conditions that Aristotle's fuller discussions of substance, form, and matter have failed to meet.

66. NATURAL PRIORITY IN DEMONSTRATION

In discussing the ontology of a science we have already made some assumptions about its structure. Since essential properties explain the others, and since this relation is to be mirrored in the structure of the science, statements about the coincidents must be derived from those about the essence.

The proper way to transmit truth, necessity, and explanation is demonstration. In a demonstrative syllogism, as in an ordinary syllogism, the premisses and conclusion are universal, and the conclusion follows necessarily from the premises; but the premises of a demonstration must also be true, necessary, and explanatory of the conclusion. The demonstrative syllogism is intended to satisfy the demand for explanation, and to display the appropriate relations between essential properties and coincidents.

The premises of a demonstrative syllogism must also be prior to their conclusion, since a science is supposed to state the first principles and to derive other truths from them. Since the syllogism is scientific, the priority cannot just be priority to us.

> They must be explanatory, better known, and prior. They must be explanatory, because we know just when we know the explanation; they must be prior if they are indeed explanatory; and they must be previously known not only in the sense that we comprehend them, but also by our knowing that they are true. (71b29–33)

The premises must be prior and better known by nature; demonstrative science makes them also better known to us.

Natural priority cannot simply be the result of our choice to put some propositions before others in our favourite presentation of the science. In defining the logical constants we can define 'if . . . then' and 'and' through 'or' and 'not', or take 'and' as primitive and define 'or' through 'and' and 'not'. If we choose one of these procedures we do not make 'or' naturally prior or posterior to 'and'. Rather, the fact that we can do it equally correctly either way shows that neither constant is naturally prior to the other. When the relation is natural priority, it cannot be equally correct to define it either way.

Hence Aristotle insists that a proper definition must be through things 'prior and better known' (*Top.* 141a26–7), and for the purposes of a science should be through things that are naturally prior and better known (141b3–34). Since there is only one objective order of priority and knowledge, there cannot be several genuine definitions of the same thing (141a31–b2, 141b34–142a9).[16] Similarly, if the priority of one proposition to another is natural, it must correspond to some fact about independent reality; and if it corresponds to such a fact, no other arrangement of the propositions will correspond equally well to the fact.

Claims about natural priority and real first principles express Aristotle's realist assumptions. We reach a correct grasp of first principles in so far as we grasp principles that are already, independently of our beliefs and theories, naturally prior; and propositional principles are prior and better known by nature in so far as they mention the things that are prior and better known. The propositional principles are not prior and better known because of some attitude we take to them, or because we decide they will be the first principles.

Aristotle's realism about first principles is a special case of his general views about truth. The truth of a proposition consists in its correspondence to how things are independently of anyone's belief in the proposition (*Met.* 1051a34–b9, 1027b18–28).[17] First principles are genuinely first in so far as they correspond to things that are genuinely first. They provide true explanations in so far as they correspond to independent things that genuinely explain.

67. NATURAL PRIORITY COMPARED WITH EPISTEMIC PRIORITY

Aristotle has some metaphysical realist grounds for believing that an order or priority in the objective world should be reflected in the order of scientific knowledge. But it is important to see how his particular version of the demand for priority relies on epistemological claims distinct from this realist assumption.

The demand for natural priority might be interpreted as a claim about the structure of explanation. Aristotle believes that the explanans is naturally prior to the explanandum even if the existence of one implies the existence of the other; hence, for instance, the fact that p is prior to the truth of the statement that p, because the fact explains the truth of the statement and the converse is not true (*Catg.* 14b11–23).[18] Given this condition for natural priority, the essential properties that explain, and are not explained by, the intrinsic coincidents of a kind, are naturally prior to intrinsic coincidents, and the premisses mentioning the explanatory properties are naturally prior to the conclusions drawn from them. Since explanations reflect objective facts, not merely the interests or beliefs of the explainer, Aristotle reasonably insists that the order in an explanatory demonstration is not a matter of choice, but must reflect the objective relations between explanans and explanandum.[19]

Appeal to explanation, however, cannot justify all of Aristotle's demand for natural priority. He recognizes that explanation justifies a demand for priority (71b31), but he also demands priority in knowledge; if p is prior in knowledge to q, then we can know p without knowing q but cannot know q without knowing p (71b31–3).[20] Since he demands natural epistemic priority, not just priority to us, Aristotle must mean, not that we can believe p without believing q, but that we can have the right objective grounds for knowledge of p without knowing q. We must come to know that x is F independently of knowing what it explains, and then find that it explains x's being G. Aristotle can admit that we come to *believe* that x is F partly as a result of believing that x's being F explains x's being G, but he must claim that once we have reached the knowledge that x is F it is independent of the *knowledge* that x is G.

This strong demand for epistemic priority by no means follows from acceptance of explanatory priority. On the contrary, epistemic priority conflicts with one view of how explanations increase our knowledge. We may have reason to believe that x is G and then find that x's being F is the best explanation of x's being G; hence we might infer that x is F. If we have sufficient grounds for claiming to know that x is G, then we may be ready to claim knowledge that x is F also. No doubt such a claim must also rely on connexions with other reasonable beliefs; but it remains true that part of our warrant for claiming to know that x is F is our claim to know that x is G, and that this claim to knowledge itself partly rests on the way that our belief in x's being G fits into a good explanatory theory.

If we rely on inference to the best explanation to increase our knowledge, then we cannot claim that 'x is F' is epistemically prior to 'x is G'. Though the explanatory relation is asymmetrical, the knowledge of each proposition is reciprocal; they will be simultaneous in our knowledge, with neither prior or posterior to the other. Aristotle cannot rely, then, on the asymmetry of explanatory priority to justify his claim about epistemic priority.

68. THE CASE FOR CIRCULAR DEMONSTRATION

His argument for epistemic priority is easiest to see in *Analytics* i 3, where he considers alternatives to his conception of demonstration.

Some think that because we must know the primary things, there is no knowledge; while others think that there is knowledge, and that everything ⟨knowable⟩ is demonstrable. Neither of these views is either true or necessary. For the first party, those who assume there is no knowledge at all, claim that we face an infinite regress. They assume that we cannot know the posterior things because of the prior things, since these lead to no primary things; and their assumption is correct, since it is impossible to go through an infinite series. If, on the other hand, the regress stops, and there are principles, these are, in their view, unknowable, since they are indemonstrable, and demonstration is the only way of knowing that they recognize. But if we cannot know the primary things, then neither can we know the things derived from them unconditionally or fully; we can only know them on the assumption that we know the primary things. The other party agree that knowledge results only from demonstration, but they claim that demonstration of everything is quite possible, since they think demonstration can be circular and reciprocal. (72b5–18)

Aristotle rejects both an infinite regress and a circle.

Defenders of a circle claim that every scientific proposition can be demonstrated, because demonstration may be circular; we can claim to know p1 by appeal to p2, and in finding the ultimate premisses of p2 we will return to p1, so that p1 and p2 will be demonstrated both through themselves and through each other (72b15–18).

Aristotle replies that this circular argument results in no proper demonstration.

And clearly, unconditional demonstration cannot be circular, since it must be derived from what is prior and better known. For the same things cannot be both prior and posterior to the same things at the same time, except in different ways, so that, e.g., some things are prior relative to us, others prior unconditionally—this is the way induction makes something known. If this is so, our definition of unconditional knowledge will be faulty, since there will be two sorts of knowledge; or perhaps the second sort of demonstration is not unconditional demonstration, since it is derived from what is better known to us. (72b25–32)

If we demonstrate p1 by p2, p2 by p3, and so on, and eventually reach p1 again, then p2, p3, etc. will be both prior to p1, since they are among the grounds for p1, and posterior to p1, since p1 is among their grounds. We can allow the same thing to be both prior and posterior only if on one occasion we mean 'prior to us' and on the other 'prior by nature'; but this distinction will not help to defend a claim about demonstration, which must refer univocally to what is prior by nature.

Defenders of circularity can reply that they allow a type of natural priority. Each proposition that we know is demonstrated, in their view, by a 'local demonstration'; D1 demonstrates p1 with reference to its immediate ground p2, D2 demonstrates p2 by p3, and so on, until Dn demonstrates pn by p1. Within each local demonstration the grounds are prior to the conclusion; since p1 is not part of the finite demonstration of p1, p1 will not be prior to itself. Though in D1 p2 is prior to p1, and in Dn p1 is prior to pn, we must not infer that p1 is prior to p2 and therefore prior to p1.

This defence claims to accept Aristotle's demand for natural epistemic priority, if it is confined to 'local priority' (within a given local demonstration), but must reject the demand if it is applied to 'global priority' (in the relation of one local demonstration to another). For since local demonstrations form a circle rather than a hierarchy, they do not display the sort of epistemic priority that is found in local demonstrations, and therefore demonstrations as a whole cannot display global priority. From this point of view, Aristotle's criticism seems to combine the justified demand for non-conventional priority—satisfied by local demonstrations—with the unjustified demand for global priority—unsatisfiable in circular demonstration.

Aristotle is entitled to demand global, not just local, epistemic priority, if he shows that circular argument does not confer justification; but he cannot fairly use the fact that circular demonstration allows only local priority as a reason for rejecting circular demonstration. His argument here seems to assume what it is supposed to prove; for we will be convinced that there is something wrong with a system that prevents global priority only if we are already convinced that there is necessarily something wrong with circular arguments. If Aristotle's argument is stated fully, it seems to display the vice of circularity that he attacks in his opponents' position; for the circle in his own argument seems too small to count as justification for either of the disputable claims it includes.

Still, if Aristotle rejects circular justification, his demand for global epistemic priority is intelligible. Though the fact that circularity precludes global priority is not an independent reason for rejecting circularity, he might have other grounds for rejecting it. Unless we have some independent reason to believe the premisses from which we derive p1, it is not clear how they really give us reason to believe p1; without some independent reason, they seem to prove consistency and to provide conditional support, but not actual justification. We need some ground for believing the premisses that is independent of the conclusion; but if it is no better than our ground for believing the conclusion, belief in the premisses seems not to justify belief in the conclusion. If we express these doubts, we challenge coherence between propositions as a source of justification; and then Aristotle's demand for global epistemic priority may well attract us.

69. THE REJECTION OF COHERENCE AS A SOURCE OF JUSTIFICATION

The next argument (72b36–73a6) raises more explicitly this issue about the independent grounds for believing the premisses of a demonstration. He argues that if the demonstration of p1 eventually reintroduces p1, it amounts to saying 'If p1, then p1'; 'and if that is all it takes, it is easy to prove anything' (72b34–5). Aristotle assumes that we offer a series of conditionals: 'if p1, then p2; if p2 then p3, . . .' until we come to 'if pn, then p1', and claims that if we believe in circular demonstration we ought to be able to leave out all the intermediate steps and still have a demonstration, 'if p1, then p1'.

He must assume that demonstrations are transitive in the way that conditionals are; for he supports his claim by remarking that from 'Nec (if p1, then p2) & Nec (if p2, then p3)' we can infer 'Nec (if p1, then p3)'. But in assuming that a series of demonstrations will behave like a series of conditionals, he seems to leave out the important features of demonstration that he has pointed out himself. The premisses of a demonstration must explain the conclusion; and it is by no means clear that the explanatory relation is transitive in the way the conditional or (on some views) necessity is.[21] If the explanatory relation is not transitive, then the opponent need not concede that he should have a perfectly good demonstration left even when he has dropped the intermediate steps.

Aristotle might argue, however, that he is entitled to drop the intermediate steps from the alleged demonstration. For they form a series of genuine, rather than merely possible, explanations only if they are known to be true; and apparently we must know this before we can say whether they form an explanatory series; if we do not know this already, we can fairly treat them as simply a series of conditionals. If this argument convinces us, we will also agree with Aristotle in stating the putative demonstration in the form 'If p, then p', rather than 'Since p, then p'. For simple coherence without initial and independent credibility seems to offer us nothing more than a series of conditionals.

If Aristotle relies on this defence, his argument proves the impossibility of circular demonstration only on the assumption that coherence provides no justification. This more basic epistemological assumption, underlying his explicit argument against circularity, supports the demand for global epistemic priority. The argument we have stated is still rather rough; to estimate its force we need to consider more exactly what is implied in 'coherence' and in 'initial credibility' and 'independent grounds'. So far we have interpreted these conditions in ways that favour Aristotle's objections; but we should not assume that we have interpreted them correctly.[22] But so far it is reasonable to find Aristotle's demands attractive; though he does not clearly state his basic objections to circularity, they are clear enough to allow a defence of his position.

His objections to circularity, and his more basic objections to coherence, are even easier to understand if he requires justification to give us reason for believing the truth of a proposition, and interprets truth in metaphysical realist terms, so that it requires correspondence to an objective reality, not wholly determined by anyone's beliefs or possible beliefs. We have already noticed that this metaphysical realist assumption underlies his contrast between science and other disciplines or forms of inquiry. If we have coherent beliefs and can answer any challenge to them, it still does not follow that we have found the truth, and hence it does not follow that we have found knowledge. Since coherence informs us only about relations between propositions themselves, it may well seem to give us no reason to believe that they are true of an objective reality.

This further objection to coherence makes it reasonable for Aristotle to demand epistemic priority. He will argue that we can transmit justification, of the sort required by metaphysical realism, from premisses to conclusions only if we are sufficiently justified in claiming to know the premisses apart from our belief in the conclusions. If we attribute some argument of this sort to Aristotle, we can understand his objection to circular demonstration, and the underlying objection to coherence as a source of justification; and in the light of this argument we can understand the demand for epistemic priority.

70. THE REJECTION OF AN INFINITE REGRESS

Once Aristotle demands epistemic priority for the premisses of a demonstration, he has to claim that the most ultimate premisses, the first principles of a particular demonstrative science, are unprovable. His commitment is clear in his rejection of an infinite regress of demonstration (72b5–15).

The opponent suggests that since all knowledge is demonstrative, we must always derive every proposition known from some further proposition. Once we rule out circular demonstration, we have only two unattractive options. (a) If we never come to a first and underived principle, we can never stop deriving principles from higher principles. Knowledge therefore requires us to perform an infinite task, and since we cannot do that, knowledge turns out to be impossible; 'we will not know the posterior things because of the prior if there are no primary things among them' (72b9–10). (b) Suppose, then, that the regress is not infinite, and that we eventually come to primary underived propositions with none prior to them. Since all knowledge requires derivation from something prior, these primary propositions will not be known, and so the posterior ones will not be known either (72b11–15).[23]

Aristotle agrees with his opponent's view that the first option prevents knowledge because it implies an infinite regress, and therefore an infinite task (72b10–11). He assumes that knowledge of p requires an actual demonstration of p from some higher premiss q that we also know. Since we claim to know q, we must also demonstrate q from a still higher premiss r, and so on; and since we claim to know each premiss, we must complete an infinite task of demonstration before we can claim to know anything. Since we cannot complete an infinite task, we cannot, on these assumptions, know anything.

Both Aristotle and his opponent, however, make a disputable assumption in supposing that if there is an infinite regress of propositions providing grounds for a claim to knowledge, anyone claiming knowledge faces the infinite task of demonstrating all these propositions. We might concede that there is an infinite series of propositions, but claim simply that at each stage we must be able to find a demonstration from a higher premiss; since there is an infinite series of propositions about which we must claim to know, we must agree that there is no upper limit on the stages at which we may be asked for a demonstration, but it does not follow that to justify anything we must actually produce an infinite series of demonstrations.

On this view, the infinite regress of knowledge might not impose an infinite task on us if we want to justify claims to knowledge. At each point we can offer a 'local demonstration', rather similar to what we might offer if we accept circular demonstration; in each case we reject the demand for a justification that displays all the justifying principles at once and includes only principles that are prior to the proposition justified.

Aristotle ought to have considered this approach to the regress, which is parallel to the defence of circles by appeal to local demonstrations. Defenders of each position might claim to accept the Aristotelian demand (for epistemic priority in the one case, for a finite regress in the other), if it is narrowly interpreted (so that it applies only to local demonstrations); perhaps Aristotle confuses this narrow and reasonable interpretation with the unreasonably broad interpretation (demanding global epistemic priority in the one case, a finite regress of actual demonstration in the other) that is needed to secure his conclusion.

71. FOUNDATIONALISM

Aristotle rejects the narrow interpretation of his demands that allows infinite regresses and circles of demonstration. He assumes the wider interpretation, because he thinks nothing less will provide an adequate justification. To justify the conclusion, in his view, we must show conclusively, with no further question to be raised, that it is derived from premisses that are prior and better known. We have not shown this if we can only offer a local demonstration, since that leaves open a further question about the status of the premisses, and to settle this further question we need first principles that are prior and better known.

Since, in Aristotle's view, circular argument cannot show that first principles have the appropriate status, we must demand epistemic priority; and once we demand this, we cannot allow an infinite regress. The demand for a conclusive display of grounds leads us to demand first principles that are grasped as true independently of the further propositions they justify.

Aristotle therefore recognizes first principles with no further justification; but he denies that his view makes knowledge impossible, because he denies that demonstration requires demonstrable first principles. In denying this, he implies that in some cases complete justification is non-inferential, since it does not require derivation from other propositions. Non-inferentially justified first principles allow us to claim knowledge without facing an infinite regress or a circle.[24]

Aristotle's conclusion implies a foundationalist doctrine, requiring true and non-inferentially justified beliefs as the basis of knowledge and justification.[25] His treatment of the circle and the regress exposes his different reasons for reaching such a conclusion. One reason results from his metaphysical realist conception of truth and the conviction that coherence cannot provide justification for believing a proposition to be true if truth is understood in metaphysical realist terms. But this argument by itself does not show what would be wrong with an infinite regress. Aristotle's rejection of the regress relies on his demand for the complete removal of possible grounds for challenge. This demand requires justifications to stop with principles that are non-inferentially justified; and the same demand will also explain why circular demonstration must be rejected.

The demand for removal of grounds for challenge reflects another aspect of Aristotle's belief in the objectivity of scientific knowledge. A scientific argument is not addressed, as a dialectical argument is, to a particular interlocutor, and does not count as scientific by convincing particular interlocutors. A scientific argument for p should show not merely that if you begin with appropriate beliefs you will have to accept p, but that p is rationally compelling irrespective of anyone's initial beliefs. We find such a defence of p if we show that it is a necessary consequence of some principle that is rationally compelling in itself; this is the non-inferentially justified first principle that Aristotle demands as the basis of scientific knowledge.[26]

72. THE STATUS OF FIRST PRINCIPLES

Aristotle sees that he demands this of first principles, since he requires them to be known through themselves:

The true and primary things are those that have their credence (*pistis*) not through other things, but through themselves. For in the case of principles of a science, a further reason must not be sought; rather, each principle must be credible (*piston*) itself in its own right. (*Top.* 100a30–b21)

. . . the rest are proved through the principles, but these cannot be proved through any other things, but it is necessary to come to know each of them by a definition. (*Top.* 158b2–4)

No proof should be given of a principle, because 'it must necessarily be true because of itself and seem true' (*APo* 76b23–4). The principles are 'evident' (*phaneron*) and known because of themselves; Aristotle compares an attempt to prove them with a deductive argument about colours offered by someone blind from birth (*Phys.* 193a4–9).[27] A sound deductive argument could be constructed, but it would not be a demonstration, and it would be a waste of time for someone with sight; to the sighted person it will simply be evident that there are colours, and this further argument will not increase his confidence in the conclusion.

This comparison with what is self-evident to the senses makes it clear how strong a claim Aristotle intends for our grasp of first principles. Demonstration must be from what is prior and more credible (*pistotera*), and since nothing is prior to the first principles they must be known (*gnôrizein*) through themselves. The demonstrative scientist should rely on these principles and should not attempt to demonstrate them.

> About these ⟨sc. the demonstrated propositions⟩ the geometer should give an account from geometrical principles and conclusions; but the geometer qua geometer should not give an account of the principles. (*APo* 77b3–6)

An attempt to prove them would be a form of begging the question (*APr* 64b28–38).[28]

In claiming that the principles are known through themselves, Aristotle cannot simply mean that nothing else is needed to justify them within the demonstrative system; he must also mean that nothing else is needed to justify them at all. If the principles are primary within the demonstrative system, the reason cannot be that this is how we have chosen to set up the system; such merely conventional priority falls short of Aristotle's demands. Even the non-conventional priority in the explanatory relation falls short of epistemic priority. Neither conventional nor merely explanatory priority can justify the primacy of the first principles in a demonstration.

For the same reason, Aristotle cannot concede that someone other than the geometer gives a genuine proof of the geometer's first principles of demonstration; for a genuine proof requires principles that are naturally prior to the geometer's principles, implying that the geometer's supposed principles would not be first principles after all. On the other hand, a merely dialectical argument could not show that the geometer's principles are naturally primary, and so could not justify their place in the demonstrative system. Aristotle's demands for epistemic priority rule out all types of non-inferential justification, not merely demonstration. The principles are not entitled to their primacy unless they are non-inferentially justified altogether.

Aristotle's demand for self-evident first principles is not an anomaly, and does not result from some superficial aspects of his views about science and knowledge. He can defend it from some of his central views on first principles—his demand that they satisfy a metaphysical realist conception of truth and his demand that they satisfy objective conditions for knowledge.

PUZZLES ABOUT SCIENCE

73. INTUITION

We have seen how Aristotle's account of scientific knowledge develops from his metaphysical realism and his epistemological foundationalism. His account implies that dialectic cannot itself give us sufficient reason, for claiming to have found first principles of science. Aristotle therefore owes some different account of our grasp of first principles; and he needs to show that it does not raise puzzles worse than those it avoids. In this chapter I will argue that he sketches the appropriate sort of account, and that the puzzles it raises are serious enough to justify us in reexamining the assumptions that lead him to it.

If Aristotle claims that we are not inferentially justified in accepting first principles, we should infer that we grasp them by some sort of non-inferential intuition. The knower must grasp self-evident principles as such; for if they are grasped non-inferentially, without any further justification, they must be grasped as true and necessary when considered in themselves, with no reference to anything else. If first principles are to meet all Aristotle's conditions, they must be grasped by intuition that certifies that they have the relevant properties.

Intuition is needed, then, to secure the epistemic priority that Aristotle demands. This priority implies that our knowledge of the lower principles depends on our knowledge of the higher, but our knowledge of the higher is independent of our knowledge of the lower. If we reject intuition, we cannot guarantee the appropriate asymmetry in knowledge, and can no longer claim that the highest principles are prior in knowledge. If we deprive Aristotle of any belief in intuition, we deprive him of his grounds for claiming that his principles satisfy his demand for epistemic asymmetry, and therefore leave him to face his own objection to coherence as a source of justification.[1]

These claims of Aristotle's make it clear that he needs a doctrine of intuitive cognition, and the doctrine will not be an isolated error, but will result from central epistemological assumptions of the *Analytics*. His conception of demonstration embodies a foundationalist conception of justification. The right sort of foundation must avoid both infinite regress and vicious circle; and Aristotle can meet this requirement only if he recognizes self-evident first principles grasped by intuition.

74. THE DOCTRINE OF INTUITION

Aristotle says the first principles are grasped by 'intellect' or 'understanding', *nous* (100b5–17).[2] *Nous* of first principles must be aware of the principles as true, primary, and best known. We must be justified in believing them apart from our belief in anything else; this epistemic priority makes them cognitively prior. And we must be aware of being better justified in believing them than in believing anything else; that is what makes them best known, and removes any objective ground for challenging them.[3]

His remarks about *nous* and about the cognitive status of first principles show that he sees what he is committed to, and thinks he can accept the consequences. In *Analytics* ii 19 he undertakes to discuss 'about the first principles, how they come to be known (*gnôrimoi*), and what is the state that knows them (*gnôrizousa*)' (99b12–18). The first question seems to consider the operations that result in the grasp of first principles; the second question seems to consider the state we are in when we possess them ('what is the state that knows (*gnôrizousa*) them') (99b17–19).[4] Not surprisingly, both induction and *nous* are mentioned in the answer; the claim that 'we must come to know the first principles by induction' (100b3–5) suggests the process, and *nous* is perhaps understood as the product, though not necessarily excluded from the process.[5]

The product, however, cannot depend for its warrant on the induction that has produced it; for such warrant would not explain how a proposition grasped by *nous* could be naturally prior to the demonstrated propositions derived from it.[6] Aristotle insists strongly on the natural priority of the propositions grasped by *nous*.

Since (1) among the states of mind that yield truth some are always true . . .; (2) these are scientific knowledge and understanding (*nous*); (3) no kind ⟨of state⟩ except understanding is more exact than scientific knowledge; (4) the principles of demonstrations are better known ⟨than the conclusions⟩; (5) and all scientific knowledge requires an account (*logos*); it follows that (6) there can be no scientific knowledge of the principles; and since (7) there can be nothing except understanding that grasps the truth more than scientific knowledge does, (8) it follows that understanding ⟨is the state that⟩ grasps the principles. (100b5–12)

In steps (3) and (4) of this argument Aristotle reaffirms his demand for natural epistemic priority in the premises of demonstration. In (5) he infers that they cannot be objects of scientific knowledge, since it requires inferential justification ('requires an account'), and the arguments against the regress and circle rule out inferential justification.

Nothing other than scientific knowledge and understanding is even a candidate for grasping principles, because of steps (1) and (2); these are the only cognitive conditions that are defined so as to certify the truth of what they grasp. Once we accept (5), we must accept (6); and then either we must agree that we have no appropriate grasp of the principles, so that demonstration is impossible, or we must accept (7) and (8), recognizing non-inferential intuitive cognition of the principles. Without a doctrine of intuition Aristotle would leave a striking gap in his account of scientific knowledge.[7]

75. INTUITION AND INQUIRY

We may be reluctant to agree that Aristotle demands an intuitive, non-inferential grasp of first principles, if we think it conflicts with his views on method. He is invariably hostile to any who think they can find appropriate first principles by simply trying to intuit them; he insists on a careful survey of the relevant appearances and puzzles before we try to form any theory. But if he thinks first principles can after all be intuited, does he not take the sort of illegitimate short-cut he criticizes?[8]

Aristotle can fairly reply that this allegation mistakes the appropriate place and time for intuition. Not just anyone's untrained and inexperienced judgment about self-evidence is proof of self-evidence. Discovery of the appropriate first principles demands the right experience; and when we have this we will be able to see what is self-evident. Aristotle does not claim, indeed he denies, that what is self-evident in itself will always seem so to us before we inquire.

The demand for preliminary inquiry does not, however, trivialize the demand for intuition. Experience and familiarity with appearances are useful to us as a way of approaching the first principles; they may be psychologically indispensable as ways to form the right intuitions. But they form no part of the justification of first principles.[9] When we come to have the right intuition we are aware of the principle as self-evident, with no external justification. That is its real nature, and that is what we grasp after we have used ordinary methods of inquiry. The acquisition of *nous* is not meant to be magical, entirely independent of inquiry. Nor, however, is it simply a summary of the inquiry, or a conclusion that depends on the inquiry for its warrant.

Hence a demand for intuition does not conflict with Aristotle's claim that empirical inquiry, induction, or dialectic is a way towards first principles. Their heuristic role does not, in his view, imply any justifying role. These methods of inquiry do not certify for us that we have found a first principle, and we are no longer engaged in them when we are aware that a principle is self-evident.

To this extent dialectic and empirical inquiry have the same function and the same limitations. But the difference (as Aristotle conceives it) between them may still affect their respective claims to be a suitable basis for reaching self-evident and objectively correct intuitions. In the *Analytics* Aristotle mentions perceptual appearances and induction as the methods for forming a scientific theory, but never attributes this role to dialectic, though he does not expressly exclude it; and some differences between empirical and dialectical inquiry may explain his silence.

The two forms of inquiry deal with different ranges of appearances; empirical inquiry begins from perceptual appearances, and dialectic begins from common beliefs. Aristotle is confident, though without sufficient reason, that in empirical inquiry we can isolate the true appearances, without relying on any further theory, before we form the theory we are looking for; and these perceptual appearances might seem to offer a firm objective basis for intuition of first principles. Disciplines that rely on perceptual appearances will, to this extent, be entitled to claim the truth and objectivity that are needed for a science. In dialectical argument, however, he does not claim to have found a completely firm pre-theoretical basis for first principles; it is more obvious here that the first principles and the appearances are adapted to each other.[10]

Dialectic, then, has two limitations: (1) Like empirical inquiry, it provides at most the basis for intuition, and does not itself contain or produce the proper grasp of first principles. (2) Unlike empirical inquiry, it does not even provide a suitable basis for intuition, since we lack sufficient assurance about the objective correctness of the appearances that are its starting-point. Aristotle should have seen that this second objection to dialectic works equally well against empirical inquiry; but since he does not see this, he normally contrasts demonstrative science, based on intuition of first principles, with dialectic rather than with the results of empirical inquiry. It will be useful to explore the contrast with dialectic a little further, always remembering that in fact the problems raised by dialectic spread further than Aristotle realizes.

76. DIALECTIC AND JUSTIFICATION

Aristotle's reservations about dialectic help to explain why he thinks demonstrative science requires first principles grasped by intuition. Dialectic argues according to belief; its solutions are shaped by the common beliefs it starts from, and are always open to challenge by anyone who rejects the starting-point. Scientific knowledge, on the other hand, is supposed to be beyond any challenge based in the objective facts; and such knowledge cannot, for Aristotle, rest on dialectical argument alone. Since dialectic seems to yield coherence, not truth, it is not clear why we should believe that its results are first principles of the sciences. In exposing this weakness in dialectic, Aristotle claims to expose a serious weakness in Plato's account of the foundation of the sciences; and in appealing to intuition he claims to remove this weakness.

For Plato dialectic is the systematic practice of the Socratic cross-examination that is displayed in the early dialogues. It has the gymnastic and peirastic functions recognized by Aristotle; but it also has the constructive task of approaching first principles. Indeed this is a crucial difference between dialectical thought (*noêsis*) and the hypothetical thought (*dianoia*) that relies on assumptions without asking for any account further of them.

⟨At the stage of *dianoia*⟩ the soul is compelled to use assumptions . . ., not proceeding as far as a first principle, since it is not capable of reaching higher than assumptions. (*Rep.* 511a3–6)

⟨Dialectic⟩ treats the assumptions not as first principles, but as being in reality assumptions, as places to set out and advance from, until it advances to what is not an assumption, reaching the first principles of everything. (511b4–7)[11]

⟨Dialectic⟩ must assemble the disciplines they learnt in isolation in their previous education, so that they see as a whole (*sunopsin*) the connexions between disciplines, and in the nature of what there is . . . And this is the most important test of whether someone's nature is apt for dialectic or not, since the person who can see things as a whole (*sunoptikos*) is a dialectician, and the one who cannot is not. (537c1–7)[12]

Plato assumes that the 'synoptic' outlook of dialecticians allows them to justify the special principles of different sciences.

This synoptic outlook requires us to appeal to coherence; for it will make us aware of the relation between different principles, and the effects of accepting or rejecting one putative principle on our other principles. If dialectic uses these synoptic methods to justify the principles of the special sciences, then Plato must assume that the coherence displayed by dialectical argument is a source of justification.

Aristotle agrees with Plato that since the special disciplines are deductive, and assume the truth of their first principles, dialectic is needed as a way towards first principles. Plato, however, also believes that dialectic reaches first principles, and hence the dialectician has the best claim to genuine scientific knowledge (*epistêmê*; *Rep.* 533d4–e2). Aristotle, by contrast, denies that dialectical method actually reaches the first principles of the special disciplines; these special disciplines are the genuine sciences, and dialectic is not a science at all.[13]

77. CRITICISMS OF DIALECTIC

In Aristotle's view, the pretensions of dialectic to reach a supreme science above the special disciplines rest on assumptions that are exactly the reverse of the truth. Metaphysical realism about truth, combined with foundationalism about justification, excludes any Platonic justification of the first principles of a special science. The particular sciences must be shown to make justified claims to objectivity; but dialectic can never justify such claims, since all it can reach is coherence. Plato's conception of the supervisory role of Platonic dialectic assumes that coherence is a source of justification; but Aristotle's attitude to the regress of justification is foundationalist. Since he cannot accept Plato's view of justification, he cannot appeal to dialectic for justification, but must show that first principles meet his foundationalist conditions.

Aristotle's dispute with Plato about the powers of dialectic rests on a question about Plato's whole philosophical method. Dialectic proceeds by Socratic inquiry, beginning from the interlocutor's beliefs, but Plato thinks this method can transcend these beliefs and tell us how things really are. Aristotle is not convinced; he refuses to recognize the conclusions of dialectic as scientific knowledge of first principles.[14]

Since a science can claim objectivity, but dialectic cannot justify the claim, another source of justification is needed. Aristotle finds it in perceptual appearances. A special science can claim objective truth because it explains a specific range of appearances; and since different ranges of experience seem appropriate for treatment by different theories, the different special sciences will be autonomous. Aristotle claims autonomy for the special sciences, by demanding principles that are 'proper' (*oikeiai*) to their conclusions; and he insists on this condition even though it is sometimes hard to apply (76a26–30).

The proper principles are those that are special to a particular discipline, and not derivable from the principles of a more general science.[15]

It is evident that the special principles of a particular area cannot be demonstrated; for those principles ⟨from which the special principles would be demonstrated⟩ will be the first principles of everything, and the science of them will be in charge of everything (*kuria pantôn*). For if one has knowledge from higher causes, one has scientific knowledge to a higher degree; for one has knowledge from prior causes whenever one has it from causes that have no causes . . . But demonstration does not extend to another genus . . . (76a16–23)

Aristotle assumes that the ultimate principles of a special science are ultimate without qualification. An alleged universal science 'in charge of everything' would have to find more ultimate principles; but Aristotle thinks it cannot succeed. Dialectical argument cannot yield more ultimate principles than the intuitively grasped principles of the special sciences, since dialectical conclusions cannot be naturally prior to the principles grasped by intuition. It is both pointless and hopeless to look for external principles that will justify the special principles of a science.

Aristotle's foundationalist assumptions about justification explain why he disagrees with Plato both about the role of dialectic and about the possibility of a universal science. The second disagreement is really a product of the first; for since mere coherence does not yield the sort of justification that satisfies a metaphysical realist's demands on a science, dialectic cannot produce the right sort of justification, and can neither be a universal science itself nor vindicate the claims of any other discipline to be a science.

Moreover, no non-dialectical conception of a universal science is at all plausible. No range of appearances beyond those underlying the special sciences is available to support a more general science; and once the claims of dialectic are rejected, the prospect of displaying coherence will not seem to support the claims of a universal science. Aristotle has no reason to value Plato's synoptic method of justification. He has no reason to try to connect the principles of different sciences; connexions would result in a more coherent range of theories, but, in Aristotle's foundationalist view, it would add nothing to their justification.

Aristotle agrees with Plato that the premisses of a demonstrative science must be in some way prior to, and better known than, the conclusions. The assumptions must be shown to be non-arbitrary, and some further source of justification must be found. Unlike Plato, however, Aristotle rejects coherence as a source of justification; he therefore demands epistemic priority, and this demand leads him to claim that the principles are self-evident.

The doctrine of intuition supports the autonomy of different sciences. Intuition shows us that a principle is true and primary in itself, not because it is derived from anything else; and no further appeal to coherence is necessary or relevant. Hence no higher science provides the metaphysical basis for a special science. Plato thought dialectic should do this for a special science because the special science could not give an account of its own principles, and so could not justify them. Aristotle agrees that a special science cannot give an account of its principles, and denies Plato's inference that it cannot justify them. For intuition confers justification with no account; it allows Aristotle to reject the pretensions of Platonic dialectic and to defend the autonomy of the special sciences. Conversely, if he gives up the doctrine of intuition, he will find it harder to answer the Platonic claims about dialectic.

Aristotle's dispute with Plato, then, highlights his own views about knowledge, truth, and justification, and shows why he needs a doctrine of intuition. Dialectic and empirical inquiry are stimuli and occasions for intuition, but do not justify belief in an intuitive principle once we have reached it. Dialectic argues according to belief, but intuition takes the first principles beyond the infirmities of belief.

For these reasons, even apart from the more direct evidence, it is reasonable to ascribe to Aristotle a doctrine of intuitive *nous* that grasps first principles. If we refuse to ascribe this to him, we leave him with unanswered questions; his foundationalist views about justification and his objections to Plato will create demands that he does not try to satisfy. It is more reasonable to accept the evidence for a doctrine of intuitive *nous*, and to allow Aristotle some answer to the problems that he evidently raises and very probably sees that he raises.

78. OBJECTIONS TO ARISTOTLE'S SOLUTION

Reluctance to ascribe a doctrine of intuitive *nous* to Aristotle partly rests on doubts about the truth of such a doctrine. These well-founded doubts raise problems needing Aristotle's further attention.

After sufficient experience we might well treat a principle as self-evident to some degree, so that we ask for no grounds for it, entertain no doubt or question, regard any conflict with another proposition as a reason for rejecting the other one, and refer to it in proof of others. We could defend our unquestioning attitude by pointing out that this principle explains the appearances and yields the other principles of the science. But an appeal to these features of the principle is an inferential justification; hence, though our unquestioning attitude may seem like *nous*, it cannot be *nous*, since it rests on this inferential justification. If, on the other hand, we can offer no such defence of the principle, we will justifiably doubt whether we are right to take it for granted. In either case we do not satisfy Aristotle's conditions for *nous*.

Aristotle agrees that we lack the right intuitions if we are inexperienced in the appearances; but he argues that dialectic and empirical inquiry are simply means of discovery, not essential for justification. If he denies any justifying role to the inferential connexions of a principle with other beliefs, he must explain the privileged heuristic role of dialectical and empirical inquiry. He might say that they are just psychologically useful for reaching stable convictions about principles; if we are already familiar with the appearances, we are less likely to encounter unfamiliar appearances that undermine our confidence in the principle.[16]

But if inquiry has only this role, it seems to be dispensable; for we could make our convictions stable without inquiry, if we were dogmatic enough, and protected our convictions from exposure to possibly recalcitrant appearances. If we admit this, we cannot explain why our preferred methods of inquiry should be preferred as ways to discover principles to be grasped by intuition. We might want to say that these methods are preferable because they give us better reasons for believing the principles we reach; but that is the very argument Aristotle cannot use if he wants to show that principles are grasped by *nous* in such a way that they need no inferential justification.

Apparently, then, Aristotle cannot plausibly combine the claims he wants to make about first principles, how we are aware of them, and how we reach them. His own view of what the principles are makes it especially clear that he cannot say all he wants to say about them. For the principles are not merely basic and obvious truths, such as the Principle of Non-Contradiction, that might seem to be self-evident to everyone; obviousness is not a condition for being grasped by *nous*. Nor are they simply the elementary perceptions that might seem necessary as a basis for any inquiry.

Aristotle accepts neither the rationalist nor the empiricist conception of the principles that are appropriate objects of intuition.[17] He correctly believes that to justify the claims of science within foundationalist constraints he must recognize intuitively grasped principles that do not seem self-evident to everyone. The principles include those that he thinks must be the product of rational inquiry. But he cannot explain why they must be the product of such inquiry without conceding to inferential connexions a justificatory role that he rejects.

These objections to Aristotle's doctrine of intuition suggest that his foundationalist assumptions, applied to the first principles of scientific knowledge, force him into an indefensible position. But to reach this conclusion is not to find a reasonable alternative; even if foundationalism leaves us with a mystery, appeals to coherence may preclude even a prospect of proper justification. Philosophers resort to foundationalism or to coherence from a keen sense of the inadequacies of the opposite position. We might agree that each side relies on unattractive assumptions, but still insist that the third option, scepticism about justification, is even less attractive. Aristotle's objections to coherence lead him to believe, correctly, that only a doctrine of intuition will satisfy his demands; but he has not made his doctrine plausible, except by suggesting that it is the only alternative to coherence.

Our objections ought to suggest that foundationalism may be worse off than an appeal to coherence would be. For it requires a cognitive state that we have good reason to think is impossible; alleged non-inferential justifications are either inferential or not justifications. A justifiably unquestioning attitude to first principles must appeal to the relation of the principles to other beliefs, and so eventually relies on coherence after all.

If our efforts at justification force us back to coherence, we should reconsider the objections to coherence as a source of justification. A coherence theory of justification requires something whose possibility is at first difficult to see—some ground for proceeding beyond claims about coherence to claims about truth, construed in metaphysical realist terms. Unless this difficulty is really an impossibility, coherence is better off than intuition, since the doctrine of intuition demands a cognitive state that is apparently impossible. So far, then, we must incline to coherence.

79. INTUITION AND THE COMMON PRINCIPLES

It is especially difficult for Aristotle to account for the general principles that a special science takes over from outside its proper range. His foundationalism and empiricism lead him to reject the claim of any discipline, and especially Platonic dialectic, to be a universal science; but he still must explain how we can claim knowledge or intuition of these general principles.

The relevant general principles include the 'axioms' or 'common principles' (76a38), those 'which someone must grasp if he is to learn anything' (72a16–18). Because they are necessary for all the special sciences in common, they are not proprietary to any one special science.

The sciences have in common the common ⟨principles⟩—by 'common' I mean those that a science uses in so far as it demonstrates *from* them, not those the science demonstrates *about*, nor *what* it demonstrates. Dialectic is also common to all the sciences, and so ⟨would be⟩ any ⟨science⟩ that tried to prove the common ⟨principles⟩ universally, e.g. that everything must be affirmed or denied, or that equals result if equals are removed, or others of that sort. Dialectic is not assigned to any definite genus in this way ⟨sc. in the way a science is⟩. For if it were, it would not ask questions; for in the course of demonstrating we cannot ask questions, since if contraries are ⟨assumed⟩, the same thing is not proved. (77a26–34)

A genuine science, Aristotle assumes, must deal with some definite genus; but since beings as a whole do not constitute a definite genus, and they would be the only genus appropriate to a science that demonstrated the axioms, there is no such science. Nor can dialecticians hope that their interrogative techniques applied to the axioms will lead to the principles of any science.

No range of appearances could support a universal science. And even if there were such a science, it could not demonstrate the axioms, since there are no prior and better-known principles from which the axioms could be demonstrated.[18] Nor can we grasp an axiom by intuition. Intuition grasps the first principles of demonstration, and since each axiom is perfectly general, intuition would have to grasp it as a first principle of a general science; since there is no general science, no such intuition is possible. The universal science of the axioms is purely counterfactual.[19]

The axioms would raise no difficulty for Aristotle's account of science if he were willing to treat them as mere matters of belief, resting on dialectical argument.[20] But he apparently cannot treat them this way; for every demonstrative science must rely on them, and if they are mere matters of belief, demonstrative science essentially contains these ineliminably non-scientific components, threatening its scientific status.[21]

But though Aristotle speaks of the axioms as common principles, he thinks this is a misleading way to speak of them.

They are common by analogy, because ⟨each⟩ is useful to the extent that it falls within the genus studied by the science. A common principle is, e.g., that if equals are taken from equals, equals are left. Each of these is adequate to the extent that it falls within the genus; for it will have the same effect ⟨for the geometer⟩ if he assumes it only for magnitudes, not for everything, and it will have the same effect for the arithmetician if he assumes it ⟨only⟩ for numbers. (76a38-b2)

The principle that is assumed is defined by its use and effects in the special science that assumes it:

. . . and this is not needed universally, but to the extent that it is adequate, and it is adequate as applied to this genus. By 'as applied to the genus' I mean the genus about which one adduces the demonstration. (77a23-5)

Strictly speaking, then, there are no common principles assumed both in geometry and arithmetic; and so there is no subject-matter for a universal science. We will intuit a version of an axiom as a principle of our special science; we need not assume the sort of general intuition that would have to belong to a general science of all reality.[22]

This device of dividing the axioms shows how they can be fitted or forced into the structure of autonomous demonstrative sciences. But Aristotle must extend it beyond the axioms. Each science takes over conclusions of the 'logical' branch of dialectic. In this area Aristotle does not entirely reject Platonic ambitions. Though the study of predication in general does not reveal Platonic Forms, he thinks it shows something about the nature and structure of reality. The study of relations between particulars and Forms is replaced by the study of relations between substances and non–substances.

Aristotle thinks logical dialectic is different from a Platonic science; and admittedly it does not reveal non–sensible Forms, entities that are beyond the range of common beliefs. Nor does it constitute a science; it does not claim knowledge that entitles it to prescribe to the special sciences. Still, Aristotle's beings are not just what common sense recognizes; if Plato requires us to revise or go beyond common sense, Aristotle may require us to do the same. Moreover, Aristotle certainly thinks all inquiry must presuppose the doctrine of the categories; and we may wonder why the doctrine should not be part of a general science.

Each special science must therefore presuppose, for instance, the dialectical doctrine of the categories (96b15–21), and the dialectical distinctions between essence and coincident, species and genus, particular and universal. The science, however, cannot attribute to them simply the status that is warranted by dialectic; for the conclusions of dialectic are only matters of belief, and before they can be taken over into a special science they must be grasped by intuition, and therefore must be divided, as the axioms are. Each special science must rely on its own special version of the doctrine of the categories; and this special version will be only analogous to the doctrine assumed by another special science.

The conclusions of dialectic play still another crucial role. The argument in the *Analytics* about demonstrative science is not demonstrative, but dialectical, relying on common beliefs about knowledge, definition, essence, explanation, and so on.[23] This dialectical argument is part of what the educated person must understand to see the special status of a demonstrative science; the grounds for admitting the special status of demonstrative science are not themselves demonstrative or scientific, but dialectical.[24] Aristotle frustrates the whole aim of his account of science if he must admit that the whole structure of demonstrative science rests at a crucial point on nothing but belief. To avoid admitting this he must divide the conclusions of the *Analytics*, just as he divided the axioms, among the special sciences.

80. DIFFICULTIES IN ARISTOTLE'S POSITION

Aristotle divides ostensibly general principles so that he can make each special version of a general principle a suitable object of intuition within a science, not simply a conclusion of dialectic, which is a mere matter of belief. But if he splits the dialectical conclusion into special versions for the different sciences, he adduces no new consideration in its favour, and can hardly prescribe any new cognitive attitude to it; why should it suddenly become an object of intuition rather than belief? If we say that it is an object of intuition simply because we have declared the special version of the dialectical conclusion to be a principle of the science, we make it a matter of convention and choice that something is an object of intuition; and that is the very thing Aristotle wants to avoid. He cannot reasonably claim that the mere act of splitting a dialectical conclusion makes a limited version of the conclusion an object of intuition.

He might suggest, then, that a special version of a dialectical conclusion becomes an appropriate object of *nous* in so far as we see that it is fundamental and necessary within a special demonstrative science. But to see this, we must see how the special version is related to the other propositions of the science; and then we seem to return to an inferential justification. Moreover, it is hard to see how the appearances underlying, say, a biological theory give us some special reason for asserting a special version of the doctrine of the categories; our reasons are the general reasons that underlie the dialectical conclusion about the categories in general.

Any attempt to explain how special versions of dialectical conclusions become appropriate objects of *nous* seems to fail, and Aristotle seems to have no plausible account of how they could fit into demonstrative science. The questions raised by dialectical conclusions only highlight our previous difficulties about intuition. The difficulties are not quite so clear with special principles that do not have to be split; but the source of the trouble is the same. To show why something is an appropriate object of intuition Aristotle must appeal to the inferential justification he rejects.

And yet, Aristotle cannot simply admit that demonstrative science rests partly on dialectical argument. All objective scientific knowledge, in his view, rests on principles that are better known than the conclusions; but if common principles are simply conclusions of dialectic, they are simply matters of belief. If putative scientific knowledge rests partly on belief, there is no genuine scientific knowledge.

This unwelcome result emerges directly from Aristotle's requirements for science, his views on justification, and his conception of dialectic. Scientific knowledge must be justified in claiming access to an objective reality; but coherence between beliefs cannot yield this sort of justification; and dialectic secures only coherence between beliefs. He has good reasons for accepting each one of the three assumptions that together prohibit him from making dialectic the foundation of science; and so if he also seems to be forced to rest science on dialectic, something is badly wrong in his basic principles.

81. CONSEQUENCES OF ARISTOTLE'S POSITION

Aristotle's attack on Platonic dialectic may usefully be compared with the attempt by twentieth-century positivists to free science from metaphysics. Like the positivists, Aristotle rejects the pretensions of a non-empirical discipline claiming to be a science and to prescribe to the genuine empirical sciences; the alleged universal science has no claim to objectivity, since any such claim can be justified only by appeal to definite items of experience. Just as Aristotle rejects Platonic dialectic, positivists reject any a priori metaphysical foundation for empirical science.[25] They allow philosophy to be an account of the conceptual structure of ordinary language or of the language of science. Similarly, though Aristotle abandons Platonic ambitions for dialectic, he accepts dialectic for the study of common beliefs, and especially for understanding the claims made by a science.

Positivists have found it difficult, however, to interpret philosophical claims as claims about the nature of language rather than the world, and have found it difficult to interpret science itself without some metaphysical assumptions; even the ontology assumed by science seems to involve empirically unverifiable metaphysical claims. To avoid such claims, some positivists resort to the claim that adoption of an ontology is a matter of choice and convention rather than correspondence to reality. But this device for avoiding metaphysics rests on a misconstrual of the difference between convention and discovery; it fails to show that the ontological assumptions of a science are merely conventional in any sense that prevents them from being genuine questions about the non-linguistic facts.[26]

In any case, the positivist must interpret not only the statements within a science, but the arguments of positivist philosophy itself; and since these do not seem to be arguments within any science, they seem to be non-scientific, metaphysical, and therefore, in a positivist's view, meaningless. For this reason, the positivist attempt to distinguish science from metaphysics has often seemed self-defeating. Philosophical arguments have to be treated as accounts of conventions, as linguistic proposals and stipulations; and such a treatment raises the same doubts about the force of appeals to convention.

Aristotle's position is not as clearly self-defeating as the positivist position has often seemed to be, since he is not forced to agree that dialectical statements are meaningless. He does claim, though, that they constitute belief rather than knowledge, and he therefore faces an analogue to the positivist's problem; for he must explain why we should admit that the common principles presupposed but not proved by the sciences are objectively true. We must have good reason to believe this if we are to retain our confidence that the sciences are genuine sciences, true accounts of an objective reality; but dialectical arguments for the principles yield only coherence with common beliefs. For Aristotle as for the positivist, the non-scientific status of philosophical argument seems to undermine the whole project of explaining why scientific argument is superior to non-scientific argument. Science presupposes conclusions of non-scientific philosophy; it therefore seems to be infected by the non-scientific status of its presuppositions.

Aristotle's difficulties suggest that he should reject some of his assumptions about truth, knowledge, and justification. Still, the assumptions themselves seem reasonable. The objections to coherence as a source of justification legitimately force the defender of coherence to show how Aristotle has underestimated it. The doubts about coherence are especially reasonable for Aristotelian dialectic. Coherent common beliefs seem to fall short of knowledge, in so far as we seem to lack reasonable grounds for being confident that they are not all false, or that we have not modified them in a direction that leads us further from the truth. Even if we accept some sort of coherence as a source of justification, we may not think dialectic provides the sort of coherence that ought to satisfy us.

82. THE UNSOLVED PUZZLES

In the *Analytics* Aristotle tries to show how scientific knowledge both escapes the limitations of Aristotelian dialectic and renounces the baseless ambitions of Platonic dialectic. But his conception of justification imposes on him an unacceptable doctrine about intuition of first principles. To resolve the difficulties he raises, he might give up his assumption that knowledge must rest on principles with at least the cognitive status of knowledge.[27] But if he does, he cannot allow that just any old belief is a sufficient basis for a claim to knowledge; he must still distinguish the sort of belief that is a proper foundation from the sort that is not.

Alternatively, Aristotle might allow that some sort of coherence justifies claims to knowledge. He must then describe the right sort of coherence, and say whether dialectic can provide it. If dialectic provides it, then a general dialectical science may be possible. Plato will be proved right, and Aristotle will have to restate his views on the autonomy of the special sciences and their relation to dialectic.

A defence of justification without intuition should answer the different claims and assumptions that lead Aristotle to foundationalism: (1) If coherence is taken simply to be a relation between propositions, it does not seem to yield justification; some of the propositions must be initially credible, and a mere relation between propositions does not ensure this. (2) If justification justifies us in believing that something is true, and truth requires correspondence to objective reality, then a mere relation among beliefs does not guarantee the appropriate relation between beliefs and objective reality, and hence does not yield justification. (3) If justification requires conclusive removal of all grounds for challenging a belief, then circular or infinitely regressive arguments will not confer justification; no form of coherence will make any belief beyond challenge in principle.

The combination of these three objections to coherence supports Aristotle's version of foundationalism. But together they seem to impose unsatisfiable demands. For the third objection requires intuition for first principles; but when we try to explain why some propositions are more appropriate than others for being grasped by intuition, we seem to reintroduce the inferential justifications that an appeal to intuition was supposed to avoid. Aristotle's assumptions about knowledge and justification do not seem to yield a solution to the problems he has raised for himself; either the sort of intuition he advocates is indefensible or (if the right defence is found) it is superfluous.

If Aristotle's third objection results in an unsatisfiable demand, we might consider the consequences of giving it up. We answer the first objection if we ascribe initial credibility to the appearances and common beliefs; we can certainly be asked to give reasons for doing this, and presumably our answers will appeal to still further common beliefs (e.g. about the reliability of the processes by which common beliefs seem to have been formed). The second objection requires us to show why we should regard one reconstruction of common beliefs, as opposed to other logically possible reconstructions, as most probably true. We will see how Aristotle faces this requirement in other works.

We tried to distinguish objections to intuition within a science from objections to intuition applied to general principles that a science takes over from outside. The two sorts of objections are connected; for once we see that intuition is not appropriate for the general principles, we may find similar objections to it for special principles. However, the connexion between the objections may not be obvious; and this is important for our expectations about Aristotle. If he comes to admit that dialectical argument can yield scientific conclusions, we need not expect him to abandon entirely his doctrine of intuition of special principles. Concessions to dialectic are certainly a reason for reconsideration of intuition; but we cannot assume that Aristotle will reconsider everything he should.

If Aristotle sees any of the difficulties in the project of the *Analytics*, then we ought to expect him to reconsider his views on dialectic, and with them his views on coherence as a source of justification and knowledge. And if he is more favourable to dialectic, we should see whether he can find the sort of argument he favours for the sort of general principle that special sciences must assume but cannot justify. In describing what we ought to expect we have described the programme of the *Metaphysics*.

II
SOLUTIONS TO THE PROBLEM

8

THE UNIVERSAL SCIENCE

83. THE AIMS OF METAPHYSICS

We have found that if Aristotle is to defend his first principles as objectively true, not merely the products of common sense, he needs to show how they can be defended by scientific argument. But his conception of science seems to make scientific argument unsuitable for the defence of first principles. In his view, a science must demonstrate its theorems from self-evident first principles, and these principles must be grasped by self-certifying intuition; we cannot, then, justify the first principles by any argument. Outside the special sciences we can use dialectic; but since dialectic concerns belief, not truth, it cannot justify any of our principles.

The *Metaphysics* should help us with these difficulties, because it announces, describes, and uses a new science. In Book i Aristotle calls it 'wisdom' (*sophia*) and 'philosophy' (*philosophia*), the science of the ultimate causes and principles. He assumes that a science is about causes and principles of some sort; and in looking for the causes studied by philosophy, he relies on a dialectical survey of the common beliefs about the wise person (982a4–19). He accepts the common view that the wise person knows about everything, but not because he has encyclopaedic knowledge:

We suppose, first, that the wise person knows everything, as far as possible, but not by having knowledge of each thing individually. (982a8–10)

. . . This feature of knowing everything belongs necessarily to the one who, more than anyone else, has the universal science, since he knows, in a way, all the things falling under it. (982a21–3)[1]

Aristotle seems to recognize the possibility of a completely universal science.

In describing his inquiry as the task of 'wisdom' and 'philosophy', he already claims scientific status for it. For in the *Organon* he normally applies the terms 'philosophy' and 'philosopher' to the demonstrative scientist, in contrast to the dialectician.[2] In doing this the *Organon* rejects Plato's claim that dialectic has the right to be called philosophy because it is a universal science, and asserts that only a demonstrative, departmental, discipline has the right to be called science and philosophy.

But whereas the *Organon* rejects the universal science as a Platonic fantasy, *Metaphysics* i expresses no caution or doubt.[3]

In Book iii, however, Aristotle acknowledges that we face severe puzzles in explaining how it is possible and what it is like; and indeed the conception of science in the *Organon* raises severe difficulties for the possibility of a universal science. In Book iv, therefore, he begins to explain how a universal science is possible, and, in particular, what method it will follow; he now calls the universal science 'the science of being qua being' or 'first philosophy'.

These names show how the science is universal. Since it treats beings in so far as they are beings, and not in so far as they are numerable or changeable, its conclusions apply to all beings alike; and since these are the most general features of beings, they are the ultimate and first principles, and the science studying them is properly called first philosophy. After describing first philosophy, Aristotle tries to show that it is an actual and useful discipline, not a mere logical possibility. He turns to some of the questions that have the appropriate universal relevance to be studied by a universal science; and he practises first philosophy, first in Book iv, in arguing for the Principle of Non-Contradiction, and then in Books vii–ix, in an extended argument about the nature of substance.[4]

The first questions arise about Aristotle's view of first philosophy. For if the *Organon* prohibits any genuine science with the scope of first philosophy, Aristotle must revise his conception of a science. He needs to revise it in any case, since the *Analytics* solves some epistemological problems about science only by raising worse ones. If Aristotle denies that either a universal science or dialectic can prove first principles, he leaves them with no justification; but first philosophy offers further possibilities.

It is equally important to continue the investigation of first philosophy beyond Book iv, and in particular to examine Aristotle's discussion of substance, to see if it is influenced by his conception of first philosophy. He returns to questions about first and second substance, matter and form, particular and universal, that he discussed in his earlier works. We found reasons for dissatisfaction with Aristotle's conclusions in those earlier works, and our reasons were closely connected with limitations in his methods of argument. The discussion was purely dialectical, and we found no reason to claim objective truth for the conclusions. In so far as Aristotle seems to claim to have found objective principles, his conclusion seems unjustified.

The *Metaphysics*, in contrast to earlier works, represents the discussion of substance as part of the science of being. Though Aristotle presents some 'logical' argument (1029b13), he claims to go beyond it: 'Certainly we ought to examine how one ought to speak on a particular question, but we ought no less to examine how things are' (1030a27–8).[5] If the discussion is genuinely scientific, Aristotle should be able to claim objective truth for its conclusion. In doing so, he should be able to answer some of our still more general questions about the apparent conflict between dialectical methods and realist conclusions. In the *Metaphysics* he defends his claim to have found objective, not merely endoxic, principles. He has seen that he cannot adequately defend his principles by purely dialectical argument limited to common beliefs. We must see how far the allegedly scientific arguments of the *Metaphysics* really differ from the confessedly dialectical arguments of the earlier works, and whether they are arguments for the same conclusions.

84. WISDOM AND SCEPTICISM

Since philosophy, as Aristotle conceives it in *Metaphysics* i, aims at knowledge of the highest causes and principles, it faces sceptical doubts about the possibility of any route to objective first principles. The inquirer has to begin from common beliefs, perceptions, and the beliefs of previous inquirers. The sceptic tries to show that each of these starting-points is so unreliable that it casts doubt on all our conclusions. Both common beliefs and the views of previous theorists seem to disagree with each other; we find that equally convincing-looking arguments can be found for contradictory conclusions. This argument from disagreement becomes a standard sceptical weapon, providing the motive for sceptical surveys of the history of philosophy.[6]

The sceptical conclusion rests on a realist assumption—that genuine knowledge of the world would have to be knowledge of an objective world, and so of properties that it has independently of our beliefs and appearances. Protagoras rejects the sceptical conclusion by rejecting the realist assumption. In his view, the apparently conflicting appearances correspond to many different ways the world is—for the different people who have these different appearances. If Protagoras is right, then Aristotle's belief in things being as they are by nature, and especially in things that are naturally or intrinsically prior to others, must be rejected.

Though Protagoras offers a way out of scepticism, he demands a higher price than Aristotle wants to pay. Aristotle's metaphysical realism must allow a possible gap between the conclusions of our inquiry and the way things really are; and this gap must leave logical room for sceptical argument. Non-realists leave the sceptic no room when they close the gap between our conclusions and the world in itself; but Aristotle cannot close this gap without rejecting his account of the aims and point of inquiry. He will be better off if he can show that his metaphysical position leaves room for sceptical doubts that his methods can answer.

Protagoras' solution, however, is a natural conclusion from some Aristotelian premises. For though Aristotle wants to find objective principles, his methods seem to justify us only in believing that we have found a plausible and consistent account of the appearances; and they suggest that someone else might have begun from the same appearances and reached different, equally plausible, conclusions. Protagoras has won part of what he sought, if Aristotelian conclusions have only a Protagorean status, not the status Aristotle wants to claim.

The danger of reaching a sceptical conclusion from surveying the history of philosophy encourages some non-sceptics, including Descartes, to turn away from historical study.

Concerning objects proposed for study, we ought to investigate what we can clearly and evidently intuit or deduce with certainty, and not what other people have thought, or what we ourselves conjecture. ⟨In reading past philosophers,⟩ . . . we would always be uncertain which of them to believe, for hardly anything is said by one writer the contrary of which is not asserted by some other. It would be of no use to count heads, so as to follow the view which many authorities hold. For if the question at issue is a difficult one, it is more likely that few, rather than many, should have been able to discover the truth about it.[7]

Descartes thinks only an intuitive grasp of first principles can free us from the endless controversy leading to scepticism.[8]

Aristotle believes that the study of past philosophers is productive and useful because it is a special case of dialectical inquiry. His methods suggest his implicit answer to both Protagoras' and Descartes's use of arguments from conflicting opinions. He maintains that common beliefs and perceptions are not the hopeless confusion of conflicting appearances that sceptics make them seem to be. He argues that when we apply normal and accepted tests to discriminate among common beliefs, they are widely agreed, and we can isolate a body of them that are not open to serious challenge. They still raise serious puzzles, and leave some questions unanswered—that is why inquiry is worth while; but they support enough agreement to begin the inquiry.

A more explicit answer to scepticism emerges from *Metaphysics* i. To a Protagorean the history of Greek speculation might well appear to be a sequence of equally arbitrary claims about objective reality, resulting in a series of insoluble disputes. Aristotle wants to show that the different claims are not arbitrary; the right approach to past philosophers shows why some of their claims seemed reasonable, and why it was hard to avoid some of their errors. He also wants to show that the disputes are not insoluble; once we see why different theorists went wrong, we can also see the solution that they could not have seen.[9]

Aristotle's aims are expressed in the distinctive structure and argument of the historical survey in *Metaphysics* i. He does not simply test the views of his predecessors dialectically, against common beliefs; he tests them against some very general assumptions that are themselves tested against the questions raised by his predecessors. Since wisdom is the science of the highest causes, we need to know what these are. Aristotle suggests that there are four types of causes—his usual four— and then begins to examine his predecessors, to see how many of the four they have found (983a24–b6). He expects to show that 'either we will find some other kind of cause or we will have more confidence in the causes that we are speaking of now' (983b5–6).

Aristotle shows that he does not intend to take the doctrine of the four causes for granted. He expects us to find either that it is reasonable or that it needs to be changed. Its status as a statement of common sense and appearances does not protect it against revision; and if Aristotle is willing to revise it, he does not assume that his argument is adequate if it is merely based on common beliefs. He expects the examination of past philosophers and of the belief in four causes to lead closer to the truth on both questions. A historical inquiry is nothing new for Aristotle, but his conduct of it in the *Metaphysics* indicates the distinctive outlook of this work; and the organizing principle sets *Metaphysics* i apart from Aristotle's other historical surveys.[10]

85. UNIVERSAL SCIENCE AND THE FOUR CAUSES

Aristotle argues that because his predecessors failed to recognize all the causes, or failed to understand them properly, they could not explain everything that needs explanation. They found or nearly found the four causes, because the appearances (986b31) and 'the truth itself' led them and compelled them to search (984a18–19, b9–11; cf. *PA* 642a14–28, *Phys.* 188b28–30). The initial questions should lead a reasonable inquirer into further questions that are answered only by appeal to the four causes.

The materialists recognize only a material cause, and regard the whole universe as a single stable material subject that changes its non-essential properties (983b6–18). These theorists have to explain the variation of non–essential properties at different times; and they cannot simply mention the permanent subject and its composition, since these alone do not explain why the changes happen at some times and places rather than others. The further cause that is needed is the efficient cause, essentially referring to the change that explains the different behaviour of different bits of the original subject. It follows that we cannot answer the materialists' own questions if we agree with them in recognizing only the material cause.[11] Even though they do not initially recognize the efficient cause, their own questions, not some questions raised by another theorist from within quite a different theory, require the recognition of an efficient cause. Aristotle therefore confirms his claim that the efficient cause is one of the causes; and his argument is not purely dialectical.

He suggests that we must also recognize a formal cause, to say what something is, and so to state the definition that describes the thing's substance (987a19–22, 988a8–11, 988a34–b6). For we admit an efficient cause when we want to explain the change that happens to one bit of the material subject and not to another, and so we distinguish different bits of the subject and the different ways they change. Since the definition and essence are supposed to include those properties of the subject that explain its other properties and behaviour, explanation of the changes in different bits of the subject will refer to definitions. To recognize distinct, relatively constant, definable bits of the original material subject is to concede part of what Aristotle conceives as the formal cause.

These definable bits of matter cannot be defined simply by their material composition. The Presocratic materialists assume that such a definition need only list the thing's material composition, since they identify the substance of things (*ousia*, 983b10) with a material stuff. If they are wrong about definitions, we must recognize a formal cause distinct from the material.[12] And we can see they are wrong, once we recognize an efficient cause. Both porridge and oatcake contain oats, water, and salt; but they react differently with other things, partly because their ingredients are combined in different proportions. The definition must refer, not simply to the ingredients, but also (as the Pythagoreans saw) to the proportion, and so must introduce a minimal degree of form. This is certainly far less than Aristotle normally includes in form; and in Book i he does not say how far beyond such a minimally formal property we must go in explaining change. He is not to be faulted for his silence. The whole task of Books vii–ix is to argue for a more definite view of the formal cause; and in Book i Aristotle confines himself to introducing a formal cause of the most minimal sort, showing why the questions about form must arise for a self-conscious inquirer.[13]

Aristotle thinks his predecessors never quite managed to distinguish the final cause. To explain goodness they appealed to whichever of the other causes they more or less recognized; but they overlooked the distinctive features of the final cause:

For those who speak of mind or love treat these causes as good, but do not speak of anything that is either being or coming to be for the sake of these, but rather speak of change as coming from these. (988b8–11)

Those who appeal to the Platonic Forms fail in the same way to see the distinctive features of the final cause (988b11–16). The distinctive logical features of explanation referring to some goal are lost in the attempt to identify final causation with the ordinary sort of efficient causation. Aristotle's predecessors assume that the good that is in fact the end of action must be its efficient cause, and Aristotle agrees that final and efficient causation are connected; but he thinks the connexion is less simple than such an account makes it appear. His predecessors' view confines final causation to the pattern that Aristotle sees in the design production of artifacts; but he believes that a proper understanding of design shows why there may be final causation without design.[14]

In *Metaphysics* i as elsewhere, Aristotle offers no a priori argument, and no exhaustive empirical argument, to show that all and only the four causes must be recognized. But still his method is different from, say, the introduction of the four causes in *Physics* ii or *Parts of Animals* i. In those other works Aristotle speaks as though he can read off the four causes from the appearances and from ordinary ways of speaking about causes. In *Metaphysics* i he suggests a further defence of his view. He stands outside his own view of the appearances, and shows why his predecessors could have answered their own questions better by recognizing the four causes.

The argument is still ad hominem, in so far as it assumes that the Presocratics were asking reasonable initial questions. They could avoid the force of Aristotle's argument by simply giving up their initial search for an explanation, once they see that this search forces them to recognize more causes than they initially recognized. But this does not seem a reasonable response to Aristotle's argument; his initial assumptions about explanation are quite weak and minimally controversial, and it is difficult to see how we could still be interested in explanation if we gave them up. In its choice of starting-points Book i differs from pure dialectic, and in the aim and scope of its argument it anticipates Book iv. Both books claim to conduct a scientific, not a merely dialectical, inquiry.

86. THE CHARACTER OF UNIVERSAL SCIENCE

Aristotle argues that his predecessors have found the causes to some degree, but only 'dimly' (985a13, 988a23, 993a13). They have been 'mumbling' (985a5, 993a15).[15] They are like unpractised boxers, who can strike lucky blows, but are not acting from knowledge (985a10–18).

In explaining his complaint Aristotle also clarifies his conception of wisdom.

We might suppose that wisdom is an encyclopaedic first-order science, including the principles of all the departmental sciences. This was the aim of Aristotle's predecessors. But his criticism shows that they were conducting first-order inquiry relying on erroneous second-order assumptions about the proper conduct of the first-order inquiry; and the errors in their assumptions show that we need a second-order universal science.

Aristotle thinks his predecessors have been looking for answers to questions that they have not properly understood, and have overlooked questions that they ought to have asked. They have not realized what causes they ought to look for, and they have not formed the right conception of the causes they have looked for. The aim of a universal science is to answer these questions that are preliminary to the conduct of first-order inquiry, not to offer another theory in competition with first-order theories. A second-order science may be universal even if first-order sciences must be departmental. Though no single set of principles implies the truths of both arithmetic and physics, a single set of principles may show that arithmetic and physics should investigate two different sorts of causes. In *Metaphysics* i Aristotle argues that we need this sort of second-order science.

On this point he accepts Plato's claim that dialectic not only finds first principles, but also defends its view of the right principles to look for. The practitioners of the sciences resting on assumptions cannot see the limits of their knowledge until the dialectician points out that there is a type of first principle that they have not found (*Rep.* 511a3–c2).[16] In the *Organon* Aristotle allows some of this role to dialectic, in so far as he assigns it a critical function; but he does not assign this function to any science, since he does not count dialectic as a science. In the *Metaphysics*, however, he thinks the four causes should not be taken for granted on the strength of common beliefs, and that some further scientific argument is needed.[17]

To this extent Book i justifies us in taking the *Metaphysics* to be a metaphysical inquiry; as Kant says, '. . . in dealing with reason it treats of those elements and highest maxims which must form the basis of the very *possibility* of some sciences, and of the *use* of all'.[18] Kant suggests that metaphysics is second-order, in so far as it examines, not the questions about the world that directly concern inquirers into nature, but the questions raised by the assumptions made by these inquirers. Aristotle's universal science is second-order in this sense. His questions arise in the course of reflexion on the successes and failures, agreements and disputes, of those who inquired into nature and tried to explain changes in the physical world. The second-order questions come after (*meta*) physical inquiry, because comparison of different attempts to find the causes of change suggests that something is wrong with the prevalent conceptions of causes, and that therefore the first-order theories will be significantly misguided. Aristotle claims that the second-order questions admit of scientific, not merely dialectical, argument, and that the result will be a universal science.

87. PUZZLES ABOUT UNIVERSAL SCIENCE

Book iii discusses puzzles about the science that is assumed in Book i:

> In the search for the science we are looking for we must first treat the issues that ought to raise the first puzzles; these issues are those raised by other people's views on them, and also any apart from these that may turn out to have been overlooked. (995a24–7)[19]

'The science we are looking for', marks two features of the universal science. First, we do not have it yet, since we are still looking for it. Second, we would like to have it, since otherwise we would not be looking for it; Book i has shown that other inquirers have made mistakes because they have not answered questions that this science would answer. In the puzzles Aristotle explores these two features of the projected science.[20] The puzzles form two main groups, each group concerned with one of the two features of the 'science we are looking for'.

The first four puzzles are methodological, or, more exactly, puzzles about the nature and possibility of universal science itself, suggesting that we cannot say clearly what it will study or how it will conduct its study (995b4–27). These puzzles show that we are still looking for the universal science and have not yet found it.

The other puzzles discuss substantive questions, about form and matter, universal and particular, and the range of substances (995b27–996a15).[21] The substantive puzzles refer to the second feature of the projected universal science. They are puzzles *for* rather than *about* a universal science. They show that we would like to find such a science, because we can raise difficult puzzles that seem insoluble within any of the recognized sciences. The substantive puzzles encourage us by their very existence to try to solve the methodological puzzles; and any acceptable solution of the methodological puzzles must describe a science that can solve the substantive puzzles.

88. METHODOLOGICAL PUZZLES

The methodological puzzles arise naturally out of Aristotle's own claims about universal science. A puzzle arises from apparently cogent arguments for apparently conflicting conclusions; and the apparent conflict emerges from a comparison of Book i with Aristotle's earlier works. On the one hand, Book i suggests that we can describe a universal science, and that it has useful work to do. On the other hand, the *Organon* suggests that there can be no such science. We raise the negative side of the puzzle in so far as we treat the alleged universal science as a demonstrative science of the sort described in the *Posterior Analytics*, and show that a universal science cannot match this demonstrative model.[22] To resolve the puzzle we must either deny the possibility of a universal science or reject the demonstrative model.

Aristotle raises the methodological puzzles by suggesting that a universal science is impossible, because we can give no satisfactory account of what it will study. If it studies the causes, it seems to conflict with the different special sciences studying different causes (996a18–b1).[23] If it studies substance, it can hardly be the science of the axioms as well; for it should take the truth of the axioms for granted, as other sciences do, and should have no proprietary concern with them (996b33–997a5).

It is hard to see how there can be a science of all substances as such.[24] Such a science would have to discuss both the essence and the coincidents of substance; 'the science of substance will also be some sort of demonstrative science, but there seems to be no demonstration of the essence' (997a30–2). Scientific knowledge concerns only the intrinsic coincidents, and has to take for granted the substance and essence.[25]

If, on the other hand, universal science studies the axioms rather than substance, it must study them as the principles of the genus it studies. But since the axioms are completely universal principles, the genus must consist of everything, and the universal science must be the science of everything. In that case, there must be a universal genus consisting of all beings, and the universal science must describe their coincidents (997a5–11).[26] But we have good reasons for denying that there is any such universal genus.

Though these puzzles most directly concern the object of the projected science, they indirectly concern its methods too. For the difficulties arise if we think a universal science should meet Aristotle's criteria for a first-order, demonstrative science. These criteria, presented in the *Analytics*, require distinct demonstrative sciences, each with its own proper area of appearances and its own undemonstrated assumptions. A universal, first-order, demonstrative science violates these criteria. As a first-order science studying substances or causes in general, it preempts the special sciences studying subsets of substances or causes. As a demonstrative science studying the axioms and the essence, it must seek to demonstrate truths that we know to be indemonstrable within a science, since every demonstration must assume them.

Still, the result that the topics of universal science are not topics for scientific argument at all is unsatisfactory. Aristotle asks: 'If it is not the philosopher's task to study what is true and false about the axioms, who else has this task?' (997a14–15). We are inclined to think these are questions deserving scientific study; and our inclination is more reasonable if we can see why scientific argument need not be demonstrative.

Since the acceptance of the demonstrative model forced us into the difficulties, rejection of the model should release us from them. But to raise this logical possibility of a non-demonstrative science is not to find a solution to the puzzle; a solution requires a convincing account of a type of argument that satisfies reasonable conditions for being scientific without being demonstrative.

The extent of this difficulty is clearer if we consider an initially attractive answer to the puzzle about who studies the axioms. The general, non-specialist character of the questions suggests that it might be the dialectician's task to study them (cf. 1004b1–4). Aristotle agrees that dialectic studies the questions, but insists that it gives the wrong sorts of answers. Universal science examines substance, same and different, like and unlike, contrary, prior and posterior, 'and all other things of this sort, all those about which the dialecticians try to examine, examining from the common beliefs alone' (995b22–4). Admittedly, dialectic seeks to argue that some claims are true and others false; its function is not purely gymnastic or critical. But since it relies on the common beliefs alone, it cannot, in Aristotle's view, claim to know the truth of its conclusions.

An appeal to dialectic neither removes doubts about a universal science nor shows that we can do without it. On the one hand, dialectical method is a constructive, non-demonstrative form of argument for first principles, and therefore seems to be a plausible candidate for being the method of a universal science; on the other hand, it is confined to beliefs, and therefore seems an unlikely source of scientific argument.

89. SUBSTANTIVE PUZZLES

The substantive puzzles raise specific questions about the nature of the first principles, and about the claims of different entities to be first principles. Aristotle returns to the first-order questions discussed in

Book i, and now states them in more abstract terms, looking for the general assumptions underlying particular theories.

Book i surveyed different views about the principles and causes of things. Some theorists think the principles are the highest genera, the most general kinds; others prefer the primary constituents (998a20–b14).[27] Some affirm, and some deny, that perishable substances have perishable causes (1000b20–1001a3).[28] Some argue that the principles must be universals that exist 'beyond' (*para*) particulars, since otherwise knowledge will be impossible (999a26–9); others claim that knowledge requires principles to be numerically one (999b26–7). If we allow universals beyond particulars, we must also allow genera beyond species, and this seems to be impossible (999a29–32; cf. a6–14). We seem to need universals that are 'beyond', and therefore (so the puzzles assume) separated from, particulars, and from each other; but we do not seem able to conceive them satisfactorily (999a14–22).[29]

Book i recognized form and matter as principles and causes, and the puzzles about universals and particulars seem to apply to them also, since matter tends to be identified with the particular, and form with the universal (998b4–8). If we believe in forms, apparently we must believe in the sorts of universals that raise the difficulties urged against Platonic Forms. Aristotle asks if there is anything 'beyond the compound' (999a32–3), analysing the compound as matter with something predicated (999a33–4). What is 'beyond the compound' seems to be a universal.

The puzzles about principles imply puzzles about substance, since substance is intended to be some sort of principle.[30] The previous puzzles force us to ask how substance can be particular or universal, and how it can be form or matter. We see some reason to identify substance with the particular, material, and perceptible, but also some reason to identify it with the universal, formal, and intelligible. But now further puzzles arise. For we cannot see how universals can be principles if they are not substances; we cannot see how universals are substances; we cannot see how anything except universals is knowable; and we cannot see how principles are unknowable.

The different puzzles ask questions about principles, universals, particulars, form, matter, and substance, and take for granted a conception of the thing they are asking about. Aristotle's survey of the substantive puzzles is meant to show that the conception we take for granted may be wrong, and its wrongness may explain the puzzles. We have been warned in Book i that 'first principle' and 'cause' can be understood in different ways; there are four causes, and the claims of matter and form to be causes are consistent if different types of causes are intended. But further inquiry shows that we should not take for granted our initial beliefs about the nature of form and matter or universal and particular, any more than we should take for granted our initial beliefs about causes. In asking which of these things are causes, we have to reckon with possible errors in each of our initial conceptions.

The puzzles about universals show how different errors may be connected. The eighth thesis claims that if only particulars exist, and there is nothing beyond them, there is no universal, and hence no knowledge (999a26–9); but we cannot evaluate this claim until we know what it means to say that only particulars exist and there is nothing beyond them. If the existence of particulars requires the existence of universals, then, in one sense, nothing 'beyond' particulars is required for the existence of universals—we need not assume anything whose existence is not assumed in assuming the existence of particulars. In another sense, however, we may say that the existence of particulars already ensures the existence of something 'beyond' them—we cannot consistently assume that there are just particulars, and no universals, once we see what particulars have to be (any more than we could assume that there are just slaves with no masters). To evaluate the puzzle, we need to know the sense of 'beyond' that applies to the claim that things beyond particulars are necessary for knowledge.[31]

The claim of form and matter to be principles depends on their relations to particular and universal and to substance.[32] If forms must be universals, then questions about the reality of the formal cause must depend on the possibility of universals that are substances (if principles and causes must be substances); but the issues will be quite different if all or some forms are particulars.

Puzzles about substance arise in connexion with puzzles about first principles, because we assume that first principles must be substances. But this assumption may be false or at least misleading. We assume that if universals are primary in our knowledge, and therefore are first principles, they must be substances. But perhaps only those things that are prior in being need to be substances, and what is prior in knowledge need not be prior in being. In speaking of first principles Aristotle assumes some order; but he may not be speaking of the same order each time, and he may not need the same things to come first in each order. On the other hand, perhaps there is something wrong with the conclusion that what is prior in being is not prior in knowledge. If knowledge is meant to grasp the objective order as it really is, how can it involve a different order from the order of being?

If we are unsure about the exact significance of these questions, let alone about the right answer to them, we are foolish to accept the terms in which the puzzles are stated, and we only frustrate ourselves by premature attempts to answer the puzzles. We are foolish if we rush to answer the questions raised *in* the puzzles without first examining the more basic questions raised *by* the puzzles themselves and by the terms in which they are formulated.

90. PUZZLES AND PRELIMINARY QUESTIONS

These reflexions on the puzzles should modify our expectations about the structure of the *Metaphysics*. The puzzles raise serious preliminary questions about the nature of principles, particulars, universals, form, matter, and substance; and we would be wrong to try to answer the puzzles directly, without having first answered the preliminary questions. The rest of the *Metaphysics* may be an appropriate sequel to Book iii even if it does not explicitly answer all the puzzles; we ought not to be surprised if Aristotle occupies himself at least as much with the preliminary questions as with the puzzles that raise them.

The importance of the preliminary questions explains an initially surprising feature of the later books. The puzzles seem to emphasize Platonic questions and questions about the super-sensible; but this emphasis is not present in all the following books.[33] Kant remarks that the problems about super-sensible reality, formulated in the Antinomies, stimulated his interest in metaphysics, and shaped the formulation of his own doctrines.[34] But his doctrines are not concerned exclusively, or even primarily, with claims to knowledge of super-sensible reality. Rather, such claims to knowledge suggest to Kant the more general preliminary questions that need further discussion; and the answers to these preliminary questions show us the right approach to the problems about super-sensible knowledge.

The similar structure of Aristotle's puzzles and of Kant's Antinomies is striking; and the similarity between their views is still deeper. Aristotle sees, as Kant sees, that some first-order questions rest on preliminary assumptions needing more scrutiny than they usually receive. And he agrees with Kant in thinking that failure to understand the preliminary questions, as they apply to ordinary, familiar, sensible reality, is the source of errors in claims about non-sensible reality. Much of the *Metaphysics* is devoted, as is much of Kant's *Critique*, to the discussion of preliminary questions that over-eager theorists have neglected in their premature efforts to defend the thesis or the antithesis of each puzzle. Attention to sensible substance does not imply that Aristotle forgets the puzzles, or that he changes the plan of the *Metaphysics*. On the contrary, the difficulty and importance of the preliminary questions shows why it would be wrong to approach the puzzles directly.

By identifying and examining the preliminary questions, Aristotle hopes to challenge the sceptical version of the history of philosophy. The exposition of the puzzles seems to present evidence in favour of scepticism. The sceptical historian of philosophy might well offer these numerous unsolved puzzles as reasons for thinking that scientific and philosophical inquiry is nothing more than a sequence of undecidable disputes. Indeed we noticed that Descartes takes the existence of unsettled disagreements to be a reason for thinking we cannot make philosophical progress by studying the views and arguments of previous philosophers.[35]

Aristotle acknowledges this argument for scepticism, as Kant acknowledges the apparently interminable and insoluble character of disputes in metaphysics. But Kant sees a way out, in a different approach to the preliminary questions:

Thus the critique of reason, in the end, necessarily leads to scientific knowledge; while its dogmatic employment, on the other hand, lands us in dogmatic assertions to which other assertions, equally specious, can always be opposed— that is in *scepticism*.[36]

Aristotle, similarly, thinks the case for scepticism can be answered. He intends to show that the disputes seem insoluble only because we have not studied the preliminary questions they raise, or because we have not realized that these questions can be answered by scientific argument. To expose the preliminary questions is only to confirm sceptical doubts, if we cannot see how to answer the questions scientifically; but Aristotle projects a universal science that will answer them.

The substantive puzzles, therefore, suggest why we need the second-order science that raised the methodological puzzles, and why we ought to keep looking for such a science. For the preliminary questions raised by the substantive puzzles seem to need Aristotle's universal science, 'the science we are looking for', to answer them. The universal science is supposed to discuss first principles; since substance is a first principle, it will discuss substance; since there are questions about the nature of particulars and universals and of matter and form, and about their relations to substance, it will discuss all these questions.

We are not likely to find the sort of answer we want in a demonstrative, departmental science. For every such science begins by assuming an account of principles, causes, and so on, and it is not the task of the science itself to defend such assumptions. And yet the puzzles show us that our assumptions on these questions may need to be reexamined. This task of reexamination would rightly be assigned to dialectic, which is expected precisely to examine the assumptions that a departmental science has to take for granted (*Top.* 101a36–b4)—if dialectic could be expected to yield knowledge. Since dialectic cannot yield knowledge, we are still looking for the science we need.[37]

91. THE POSSIBILITY OF A UNIVERSAL SCIENCE

Aristotle often begins his solution of dialectical puzzles, not by a frontal attack on the conflicting arguments, but by 'making a new start', appealing to some assumption that has not been called into question even by the most thorough survey of the puzzles.[38] The choice of a new start determines the status of the solution. If the new start is an assumption that is generally accepted, but could easily be rejected, then the solution is purely dialectical; it relies essentially on the actual agreement of particular interlocutors. But if the new start is also difficult to reject, then it depends less on the fact of agreement. What makes an assumption easy or difficult to reject must still be discussed.

If Aristotle makes the right sort of new start in Book iv, he should describe a conception of the universal science that is not undermined by the objections raised in Book iii. The objections challenge the possibility of a first-order demonstrative universal science of first principles; and within Aristotle's conception of a science, they are quite powerful. He needs a conception of a science that both avoids the objections and is clearly a plausible conception of a science rather than of some other discipline.

In the first chapter of Book iv Aristotle sketches his answer to these questions:

(*a*) There is a science that studies being qua being and its intrinsic properties. (*b*) This is not the same as any of the sciences called departmental (or 'special', *en merei*). For none of the other sciences examines universally about being qua being, but each cuts off a part of it ⟨sc. being⟩, and about this part studies what coincides, as the mathematical sciences do. (*c*) Since we are seeking the origins and the highest causes, clearly they must be ⟨the causes⟩ of some nature in itself. (*d*) If, then, those who were seeking the elements of beings were also seeking these ⟨highest⟩ origins, it is necessary also for ⟨the elements⟩ to be the elements of being not coincidentally but qua being. Hence we too should find the first causes of being qua being. (1003a21–32)

In (*a*) Aristotle describes the subject-matter of the science, in terms not used in Book iii. Since he avoids any of the descriptions that raised the first puzzles in iii, the projected science does not evidently collapse in the face of objections to a universal science.

Still, it is clearly meant to fall within the intended scope of these objections, since it is meant to be a universal science. It is 'the science we are looking for', the same one that was sought in Book i and raised the puzzles in Book iii. In (c) Aristotle affirms that he still wants a universal science that will study the most ultimate causes (1003a26–8).[39] In (d) he agrees with those who were seeking the elements of beings (986a2, 992b18; cf. 1071a29), and assumes they were right in looking for something as general as the elements of being; he simply adds that the inquiry must be about being in itself, in so far as it is being.[40] A science that claims to study the elements of being raises puzzles about its subject-matter; but Aristotle implies that when we add 'qua being' to the description, we can avoid the puzzles.

To see why the addition of 'qua being' solves the puzzles, we need to see what Aristotle means by claiming that the special sciences do not study being qua being, that none the less they study being, and that the universal science studies being qua being.

A special science, according to (b), cuts off a bit of being and studies its coincidents (cf. 1025b3–13). This 'cutting off' is not simply isolating a class of things to study. Someone who studies diseases of animals with hearts must consider all and only the animals with livers, if the two classes have the same members; but the properties she studies are those explained by having a heart, not by having a liver. The cardiologist, therefore, 'cuts off' creatures with hearts, not creatures with livers (which are cut off by a hepatologist), and studies them qua having hearts, not qua having livers.

As usual, Aristotle uses the 'qua' to distinguish the referentially transparent place preceding it from the referentially opaque place following it. The science of being studies not primarily a distinct class of objects, but a distinct property of objects. Just as nothing prevents the cardiologist and the hepatologist from studying the same animals, nothing prevents the student of being from studying different properties of the very things that the mathematician or astronomer or natural scientist studies (1004b5–8).[41]

This explanation of 'being qua being' answers those puzzles that seemed to make the universal science a rival to the special sciences. No rivalry results even if it studies the same beings that are studied by a special science, unless it also studies them qua the same things—unless, in other words, it studies the same properties of the same beings. But it does not study the same properties; the universal science is the science of being qua being, mathematics is the science of some beings qua mathematical objects and physics is the science of some beings qua changeable.[42] The science of being studies the same things that are studied by other sciences, but studies different properties of them, discovering these properties by a different level of abstraction. But it does not create the properties by abstraction; it discovers properties for scientific study that others have not explicitly recognized, even if they have implicitly discussed them (1005a23–b2).[43]

92. THE OBJECT OF UNIVERSAL SCIENCE

So far we see why 'qua being' prevents competition between the universal science and special sciences; but we still want to see why it marks off a legitimate area of study for the universal science. The answer depends on the claim that a special science cuts off a part of being.

A special science assumes that it begins with a subject that has properties; for it has to distinguish the essential properties, which it takes for granted, from the intrinsic coincidents, which it studies. It does not ask what something must be like to be a subject with essential and coincidental properties, or why we should believe there are any such subjects. Equally, a science must assume that we have some grasp of how things objectively are, not just of how they seem. For it assumes we have intuitive understanding of first principles, and this intuition is the basis of claims to demonstrate the derived truths about the intrinsic coincidents.

A particular discipline counts as a science only if these assumptions are true; if they are true, it has successfully cut off a part of being. But no demonstrative science demonstrates that it has itself cut off a part of being. It does not ask how things must be if objective truths about them are to be possible, or whether any things satisfy the appropriate conditions.[44]

The universal science, by contrast, studies being qua being, because it studies those properties of the objects of special sciences that the special sciences themselves must assume. It asks how something must be if it is really and objectively a subject with essential and coincidental properties, and asks whether anything meets the conditions that we discover. The special sciences do not seek, but assume, answers to these questions; a science of being is needed to find and to justify the answers. The science of being qua being is equally the science of the object of science qua object of science.

Aristotle asks the Kantian question, 'How is science possible?', by asking how things must be if there is scientific knowledge of them. He asks the question about the necessary features of the object known, not primarily of the knowing subject, and so does not express the question in Kant's primarily epistemological terms: 'What must we believe, and on what grounds, if we have scientific knowledge?' But the parallels are suggestive, and the differences may be less deep than they seem.

The right conception of being qua being explains why the science that studies being qua being must study substance; contrary to the suggestion in the puzzles, these are not two different areas of study for the universal science.

It is clear, then, that it is also a task for one science to study beings qua beings. And in every case a science is strictly and properly (*kuriôs*) concerned with what is primary ⟨in its genus⟩—the thing on which the others depend and because of which they are called what they are. If, then, this ⟨primary thing⟩ is substance, the philosopher ought to grasp the principles and causes of substance. (1003b15–19)

The universal science is the science of being because it studies the sort of being that is presupposed by the possibility of the other sciences; and it is primarily the science of substance because substance is the primary sort of being, and all other beings are focally connected to it.[45] Each being is to be defined either as a substance or as something dependent on a substance as its first principle (*pros mian archên*, 1003b6).[46]

The study of being qua being, the sort of being presupposed by the special sciences, requires the study of substance, since the sciences assume that they are studying a subject with essential properties.[47] The science of being asks both what sort of subject is required, and whether there are any such subjects. The discussion of the Presocratics suggests, and Books iv and vii show in detail, that this inquiry into subjects and essences is precisely an inquiry into substance. In studying the nature of substance and the beings dependent on it, the science of being should both explain and justify the assumption made by a special science.

The primacy of substance is actually supposed to explain the special way in which the science of being is a universal science. Aristotle claims for the philosopher the task of studying general 'logical' questions about whether Socrates is the same as Socrates seated, whether one thing has only one contrary, and so on. The concern of first philosophy with these questions is its ground for claiming to study everything (1004a31–b4).[48] But it studies them in their connexion with substance: 'Those who examine these questions are not in error in the sense of not doing philosophy, but because substance is prior, and they have not heard of it' (1004b8–10). To fail to study beings in their connexion with substance is to fail to study being qua being; and in studying the connexion with substance we discover the sort of being that is presupposed by the special sciences.

This relation between the science of being and the special sciences justifies Aristotle in calling the universal science '*first* philosophy', since it examines basic principles that are presupposed by special sciences.[49] It equally deserves its other name 'metaphysics', since it is the product of second-order reflexion on the study of nature. In connecting the study of substance with the study of being qua being, Aristotle dispels the suspicion that a science of substance will rival special sciences of different kinds of substances. It is a second-order inquiry into sub-stance, asking what substance must be like if there is to be a subject for any first-order science; it examines the conception of substance that a first-order science must assume if it seeks to tell us anything about the substances it recognizes. To say that the science of being qua being is a second-order science is not to imply that it is concerned more with what is said about the world than about the world itself; it is concerned with the world in a particular abstract way, asking what things have to be like to be subjects for sciences.[50]

93. THE UNIVERSAL SCIENCE CONTRASTED WITH DEMONSTRATIVE SCIENCE

Aristotle has now answered the puzzles about the subject-matter of the universal science; by arguing that the universal science studies being qua being, he has shown why it does not compete with the special sciences. He has still not explained, though, how it can be a science, since he has not yet answered the puzzles that cast doubt on the possibility of a universal demonstrative science of the most ultimate principles. He must show either that the science of being will, despite appearances, be demonstrative, or that it will somehow be both non-demonstrative and scientific.

Aristotle denies himself the first answer, since he implies that the science of being cannot be demonstrative. He has pointed out in Book iii that a demonstrative science must define a distinct genus for itself. The science must assume its first principles, without proving them within the science; in particular it must 'assume the essence' taking for granted a conception of the subject whose coincidents are demonstrated. If a universal and second-order science, with the scope we have assigned to the science of being, had to rely on such assumptions, its method would be self-defeating. It has no distinct genus of the right sort.[51] Nor can it assume the essence. In trying to demonstrate from assumptions it would be taking for granted a conception of the first principles; but what a science is 'of' is not the essence it assumes, but the intrinsic coincidents it demonstrates; and so if the science of being has to assume some first principles, it will be the science of the properties demonstrated from these principles, not the science of the principles themselves.

Aristotle, therefore, contrasts the method of the science of being with the method of the special sciences.

They do not concern themselves with being unconditionally or in so far as it is being. Nor do they give any argument about the essence; but some make it clear by perception, others take it as an assumption, and from this demonstrate with more or less necessity the intrinsic attributes of the genus that concern them. Hence it is clear from this survey of examples that there is no demonstration of substance or of essence, but some other way of making it clear. (1025b9–16)[52]

The whole point of the science of being is to be the science *of* the absolutely first principles, and therefore to study their nature; it must justify, not take for granted, a conception of the first principles. The method of demonstration seems just the wrong one for the tasks assigned to this science.

This objection to a demonstrative science of being does not rest on any doubts about Aristotle's conception of a demonstrative science. We have argued that in fact such doubts are perfectly justified, and that Aristotle's appeal to intuitive *nous* to explain how we grasp first principles is a bad solution to the difficulties raised by his own view on demonstration. We will be justifiably pleased, then, if the conception of first philosophy as a science does not rely on the doctrine of *nous* to explain how this science grasps the first principles. But even if we completely accepted the doctrine of *nous*, we could not invoke it to understand first philosophy. For any science that relies on intuition of first principles is not the science of those principles, and does not argue for them; the principles must be prior to the arguments of the science. If we knew that a science relied on intuition of such principles, we would know that this science could not be first philosophy; for the principles assumed would be prior to the truths that the science is of, and so the science would not be the science of the ultimately first principles.

First philosophy is the science of the ultimately first principles, including the axioms, which cannot be demonstrated from prior principles.[53] It is concerned with the axioms, just as it is concerned with substance and essence, because it is concerned with being qua being. The special sciences differ from the science of being in taking the essence for granted, and in taking the axioms for granted (1005a23–9). The science of being, therefore, must argue that the axioms are true (1005a29–b2), and not simply take them for granted; and since they are first principles, it cannot demonstrate them. If, then, first philosophy is to fulfil its task, it cannot be demonstrative.[54]

It does not follow, however, that some other method is the right one for first philosophy; for the tasks assigned to it may be impossible. If it is required to argue for first principles without assuming first principles, what can it argue from?

This question does not simply reflect a peculiarity of Aristotle's conception of demonstrative knowledge; it arises from a more general question about justification of first principles. Aristotle claimed in the *Analytics* that first principles of demonstration had to be grasped by intuition, because he rejected both infinite regresses and circular arguments as sources of justification. In putting forward a science of the *ultimate* principles, with the task of justifying the principles that cannot be derived from a higher science, he seems to ignore his own views about justification.

94. THE UNIVERSAL SCIENCE CONTRASTED WITH DIALECTIC

Aristotle's only method of argument about the principles taken for granted in demonstrative science is dialectical; and so it is reasonable to expect that the method of universal science will be in some way dialectical. We have further reason for thinking so when we see that the second-order questions about substance, particulars, universals, and so on are the topics of Aristotle's dialectical works, both logical and physical.[55]

On the other hand, Aristotle has warned against attempting to solve the puzzles by identifying the universal science with dialectic; for he insisted in Book iii that the dialectician examines questions from the common beliefs alone (995b22–4), and therefore cannot make the claim to objective truth that we expect from scientific argument. Book iv still accepts this contrast between dialectic and science on the crucial point: 'dialectic tests in the area where philosophy comes to know' (1004b25–6).[56]

This contrast suggests that philosophy studies being in so far as it is being, and dialectic studies being in so far as it is commonly believed to be.[57] To reach conclusions about being in so far as it is being, we must be justified in believing conclusions saying that this is how things really and objectively are. A science assumes that we are justified in believing this, since it assumes that it has 'cut off a part of being' as its object of study. Since the universal science takes being qua being to be its object of study, it must equally claim objective truth for its conclusions; and if we think there is a science of being, we must think we are justified in believing conclusions claiming objective truth.

Ordinary dialectic makes no such claim for its conclusions; it seeks to give a coherent account of the common beliefs, but makes no further claim about the status of its conclusions. The fact that we have reached a conclusion by ordinary dialectical argument gives us no sufficient reason for claiming objective truth for the conclusion. This weakness of ordinary dialectic requires the view of its role that Aristotle suggests in *Physics* i. On that view, dialectical argument does not seek to prove the truth of a principle, since it only argues from common beliefs, and need not prove the truth of principles that are certain and self-evident. Dialectic need only remove the puzzles and confusions that prevent us from seeing that the principle is self-evident.[58] This limitation on dialectic, if consistently observed, requires very dubious claims about intuition; we must be able, for instance, to see that the particular part of the doctrine of the categories needed for mathematics or natural science is self-evidently true, not simply the result of logical dialectic.

Aristotle does not in fact regularly advert to this limitation on his dialectical conclusions. He speaks as though his arguments about the categories, substance, form and matter, and causes supported claims to have found objective first principles. But his account of dialectical method suggests that he ought not to suggest this, and the contrast drawn in *Metaphysics* iv between dialectic and philosophy suggests that he sees this very difficulty.[59]

It seems, then, that dialectical method is the only method that Aristotle has to offer for defending first principles, and that dialectic, as he normally conceives it, cannot give the sort of defence he wants.[60] We can resolve this puzzle if we suppose that first philosophy practises some type of dialectical argument, but a type that differs from ordinary dialectic. Let us call this special type of dialectic *strong dialectic*, recognizing that so far it is, as Aristotle says about universal science, a method 'we are looking for', and not assuming that there really is any such thing.

95. THE DIALECTICAL CHARACTER OF UNIVERSAL SCIENCE

To see whether there is such a thing as strong dialectic, we should see how it will have to modify ordinary dialectic if it is to achieve the results that Aristotle expects in first philosophy.

We can see the modification that is needed, if we see the source of the weakness of ordinary dialectical conclusions. The conclusions tell us only about common beliefs, because premisses are admissible as long as they express (or are suitably connected with) common beliefs.[61] Since the dialectician is relatively undemanding in her choice of premisses, she cannot expect the conclusions to meet any more demanding standards. It may now occur to us that we could perhaps find conclusions with a better claim to objective truth if we were more selective about the premisses. Apparently we need to select from the subset of common beliefs that we have reason to regard as suitable premisses for the right sort of conclusion. If we can find the right subset, then the prospects of strong dialectic may be more encouraging.

This argument may seem to get us no further forward. For how can we find suitable premisses for an argument to first principles without relying on some further first principles, so that our original first principles were not first after all, and we face an infinite regress? If, alternatively, we appeal to the principles that we are supposed to be arguing for, we seem to face a vicious circle. We seem unable to select the appropriate subset of common beliefs unless we have already found principles that would make the selection unnecessary.

Such objections should not immediately discourage us. For we may have some views about which of the admitted common beliefs are reliable; and these views do not necessarily depend on our having a definite view about first principles. It is true that these views themselves may be matters of common belief, so that ultimately we are appealing to common beliefs; but we are appealing to a further level of common beliefs that may be more selective than our first-order common beliefs are.

We have not yet given any reason for thinking that any of our views about which common beliefs are especially reliable are themselves especially reliable. But if we can find some reasons for trusting our judgments about the reliability of some common beliefs, and if our dialectical arguments confine themselves to the subset of common beliefs that are judged reliable, then these arguments will give us more reason than we have in ordinary dialectic to believe in the objective truth of our conclusion. If we can give arguments of this sort, we will give the sort of argument needed for strong dialectic. If Aristotle intends to offer arguments of this sort, then he is not evidently wrong to claim that first philosophy can be both dialectical and scientific; for he can at least state a coherent conception of strong dialectic that satisfies the appropriate conditions.

He suggests that dialecticians fail to argue scientifically because 'they have not heard' of substance (1004b8–10), and do not consider being qua being. He cannot mean that they have no concept of substance; he probably means that they have not heard of its role in the study of being qua being. To consider being qua being is to examine the presuppositions of the special sciences; and Aristotle implies that such an examination will result in arguments that are not purely dialectical.

The assumption that there is something for scientific study is not just a common belief. While many widely shared beliefs could be given up without serious damage to our other beliefs, this belief is quite fundamental, and could not be given up without serious loss. Since we have good reason for thinking this belief is true, we have reason for claiming that dialectical arguments founded on it are not purely dialectical. The belief may indeed be challenged; but we may see that the results of challenging it are more incredible than any of the assumptions underlying the challenge could be. In iv 4–5 Aristotle seeks to show this about the first principles and challenges to them.

Strong dialectic follows the normal dialectical policy of 'making a new start', from premises that have not been challenged by the puzzles. But, as we noticed, different types of new start introduce different types of dialectical argument. The arguments of first philosophy belong to strong dialectic, in so far as they rely on a new start that is not simply a matter of general agreement. The assumption that there is such a thing as being qua being is a presupposition of any scientific study of an objective world at all (even if we do not realize that we are committed to recognizing such a thing as being qua being); and if our new start rests on this assumption, it does not simply argue from common beliefs. Aristotle's account of dialectic and of the starting-point of first philosophy makes it reasonable for him to claim that the method of first philosophy is both dialectical and scientific.

96. THE TASK OF THE UNIVERSAL SCIENCE

These arguments are not meant to prove that Aristotle's conception of first philosophy is reasonable. It may indeed be unreasonable, if he has no plausible way of isolating the reliable subset of common beliefs. All I have argued is that it is not *evidently* unreasonable, as we might well have supposed if we examined his views on dialectical and on scientific method. To see whether any arguments meet the conditions Aristotle imposes on the arguments of first philosophy, we should examine some of the arguments he actually offers.

We will perhaps be able to focus the issues more clearly if we examine some of the arguments in the *Metaphysics* for conclusions about substance that are defended by purely dialectical argument in the *Organon* and the physical works. Since these earlier works rely on the sorts of premises that satisfy us in ordinary dialectical argument, their basic ontological scheme claims to reflect common beliefs. We may quite fairly ask why that makes the scheme true, and especially why the Aristotelian scheme is more likely than any less intuitive Platonic or Democritean scheme to be true. Aristotle himself sees this limitation in dialectical argument; that is why he says it proceeds according to belief and not according to truth. This is the unsatisfactory position that he tries to escape in the *Metaphysics*. He wants to show that ontology can rest on a scientific, though not a demonstrative, foundation, because its claims about beings rest on requirements for being, not merely on common beliefs.

From Aristotle's claims about universal science we have found that he recognizes a second-order science whose arguments will be both dialectical and scientific, and which will argue for its first principles. In recognizing such a science he commits himself to acceptance of some important aspects of Plato's account of dialectic.[62] He also changes his mind about philosophy, both in his sense and in the modern sense of the term.

Both in Plato and in Aristotle, the method of dialectic has the best claim to be characteristic of what we call philosophy. But whereas for

Plato dialectic deserves the honorific title of 'philosophy', for Aristotle in the *Organon* it does not. There he agrees with Plato in thinking that 'philosophy' in the honorific sense should be a science—objective, provable truth about a reality independent of the subject's own beliefs or preferences—but he thinks dialectic cannot claim this status for its results.[63] His reasons are plausible and fairly familiar reasons for doubts about the claims of philosophical argument. Philosophy, as we understand it, seems to begin from common sense and to argue from what seems obvious, or what we would all say, or what we intuitively believe, to reach conclusions about the nature of reality. The resources seem inadequate to yield the desired results; and philosophers as well as non-philosophers have been sceptical about the claims.

In the *Organon* Aristotle, as we have seen, admits these limitations on dialectic, but does not face all the consequences. Though he distinguishes the conclusions of dialectic from the results of scientific argument, he accepts them as an account of how things are. He does not suggest that the ontology of the *Categories* simply expresses ordinary beliefs and common sense, or that it may need to be revised or abandoned if we come to know more about the world. Indeed, he rejects rather brusquely the revisions proposed by Platonists and Atomists, as well as the more radical objections urged by Eleatics.

He seems to have more confidence in dialectic than is warranted by his own views about its capacities. We might think it tells us about appearances—how things seem to common sense, rather than how they are; and we will be content with appearances only if we hold the Protagorean position, which Aristotle rejects no less firmly than he rejects extensive revisions of common sense. The status of dialectic expresses most sharply the distance between what Aristotle is entitled to and what he achieves.

The *Metaphysics* suggests that Aristotle sees these difficulties and tries to solve them. He faces Presocratic and Platonic ontologies; he distinguishes the arguments of universal science from those of ordinary dialectic, suggesting that they will rely on strong dialectic; and he attacks Protagoras. Each of these features of the *Metaphysics* reflects a difference from the earlier works; and together they show how Aristotle might remove our doubts about his position.

9

THE SCIENCE OF BEING

97. ARGUMENTS OF UNIVERSAL SCIENCE

One of the puzzles in Book iii asked whether and why the science that studies the axioms will also study substance, and which study will be prior to which (*Met.* 996b26–997a15). The common axioms were not mentioned as the source of any of the substantive puzzles in Book iii. But precisely for this reason they provide a useful test for the science of being. In the case of the substantive puzzles we do not antecedently agree on the conclusion that we expect a science of being to reach (about whether, e.g., particulars or universals are substances); and so we cannot use the conclusions reached by the putative science as a test of its method.

Everyone agrees, however, that the axioms are true, and everyone uses them; and so we agree about what we expect a science of the axioms to prove. We may be doubtful about the prospects of a science of the axioms for a quite different reason; they seem so fundamental that we cannot easily see the premisses from which we could reasonably claim to prove them. It is not initially clear what the universal science will show about the axioms if it expects to argue about them.

Aristotle answers that the universal science must study both substance and the axioms, precisely because it studies being qua being (1005a19–b8). A defence of the axioms should show us what it is like to argue about being qua being, and in particular whether such argument is a scientific way to argue about first principles that are too fundamental to admit demonstration. If we are convinced on this point, we will perhaps see how an argument about being qua being might be applied to the more contentious preliminary questions raised by the substantive puzzles.

In studying being qua being the universal science studies the sort of thing that the special sciences take for granted—a subject with essential properties, whose intrinsic coincidents are studied by the special sciences. In studying substance the universal science explains why a science must presuppose this sort of subject, why the presupposition is justified, and what the subject must be like. The first step in this study is to show that the subject must satisfy the axioms; since these are the most general truths about being qua being, and 'qua being' implies 'qua the sort of subject that a science must presuppose', Aristotle wants to show first philosophy can argue for the truth of the axioms. He concentrates on the Principle of Non-Contradiction (PNC), arguing that the principle must be true for some of the properties of any subject.[1]

The defence of PNC is a test for the method of first philosophy. For Aristotle admits, indeed insists, that PNC cannot be demonstrated (1006a5–11).

Now some people actually demand that we demonstrate this also. They do this from lack of education; for we show our lack of education if we do not know what we should, and what we should not, seek to have demonstrated. For in general it is impossible to have everything demonstrated, since there would be an infinite regress, and so even then there would be no demonstration; there are some things, then, of which we must not seek a demonstration. In that case, they could not say what principle they would think had a better claim than this one ⟨PNC⟩ has to be left undemonstrated. (1006a5–11; cf. 1005b2–5)

He cannot claim, therefore, that the first philosopher's special competence consists in demonstrating PNC. On the other hand he has claimed some special competence for first philosophy, in contrast to the special sciences, none of which 'undertakes to say anything about them ⟨sc. the axioms⟩, whether they are true or not' (1005a29–30). First philosophy should undertake this task that the other sciences avoid. It cannot discharge the task by offering a merely dialectical argument; for, unlike dialectic, it seeks knowledge of the truth, not simply a coherent account of common beliefs.

Aristotle ought, therefore, to offer an argument that is neither demonstrative nor purely dialectical.[2] And in fact he claims to offer a 'demonstration by refutation':

But still, it is possible to demonstrate by refutation even that ⟨the denial of PNC⟩ is impossible, if only the disputant speaks of something. If he speaks of nothing, it is ridiculous to look for a rational discourse (*logos*) with someone who has rational discourse about nothing, in so far as he does not have it; for in so far as he lacks rational discourse, such a person makes himself like a vegetable. (1006a11–15; cf. 1008b10–12)

It is plain that this 'demonstration by refutation' is not demonstrative in the usual way, and fairly plain that its method is to some degree dialectical, since it begins with something conceded by the interlocutor. Still, if it belongs to a science, it ought not to be purely dialectical; for Aristotle claims that philosophy acquires knowledge in the area of being qua being, whereas dialectic is purely peirastic in this area. To see if Aristotle can fairly claim the status that he needs for the argument, we must examine its strategy more closely.

98. THE DEFENCE OF THE PRINCIPLE OF NON-CONTRADICTION

Aristotle considers an opponent (O) who claims that for any subject and for any of its properties it is possible for that subject to have both the property and its negation. Aristotle wants to show that O is committed to the denial of this thesis. This is an argument about being qua being, since Aristotle and O are arguing about something that the special sciences presuppose. To show what a science must presuppose, we should try to reject a given alleged presupposition, and see if we still have an object of scientific study. O and Aristotle agree that scientific study presupposes a subject with properties, but O denies that it presupposes a subject satisfying PNC. To show that O is wrong, Aristotle seeks to show that O has no object of study left if O refuses to presuppose PNC.

Now the starting-point for all such things is not a demand for ⟨the respondent⟩ to say that something either is or is not ⟨and not both⟩—for someone might perhaps suppose that this would be begging the question; it is a demand for him to signify something both to himself and to another. For he must do this if he speaks of something, since otherwise he has no rational discourse either with himself or with another. If he grants this, there will be a demonstration ⟨by refutation⟩, since something will be definite as soon as he grants this. (1006a18–25)

Aristotle argues from what O himself must presuppose. First he leads O to agree that O cannot state his position unless he and we agree on these points:

1. O signifies something, some subject S to which he ascribes the properties F and not-F.
2. F and not-F are contradictory, and therefore non-identical, properties; for if they were the same property, O's thesis would be a trivial truth different from the proposition O means to assert.
3. It is the same subject S that O signifies as the subject of both properties.[3]

Aristotle wants to argue that if O's thesis is true, then its presuppositions are true; if they are true, then O's thesis is false; hence if it is true it is false; hence it is false.[4]

Aristotle assumes that O signifies a subject, man, and he asks O what the name 'man' signifies. We agree that it signifies biped animal, and we will say that this is being a man: 'By "signifying one thing" I mean this; if man is this, then if anything is man, this will be being man' (1006a32–4). The subject that is signified is man, and being man is being the subject it is.[5]

To see the importance of this move we may consider it for

contradictory predicates at different times. If I say, e.g., that a man was fat at t1 and is not fat at t2, I say it about the same subject, the man; though he has lost his property of being fat, he must retain whatever property is necessary for his being the same subject. If this is so, he must have some other property besides being fat and besides being not-fat. We need not commit ourselves to any strong doctrine of essential properties here; we need not say that there is one property that must persist in all change, or that the property can be described in purely qualitative terms; perhaps some primitive ostension or unanalysable temporal continuity is all that is needed. But whatever this property is, the subject must have it throughout the change; hence it cannot have only properties that it loses in the change. If it lost all its properties, it would go out of existence; two different subjects would exist, and no change would be ascribed to a single subject. A single subject undergoing change cannot have simply the property it loses, but must also have the essential property that makes it the same subject.

When O denies the Principle of Non-Contradiction, he wants to ascribe contradictory properties to the same subject at the same time, not at different times. But the point that held for change must hold here too; the subject must have whatever property makes it the same subject when the two contradictory properties are predicated of it. Aristotle properly insists that O must signify a single subject.[6] When O says 'Man is F and not F', his thesis can be expanded into 'Man is F and man is not F'; and if O is to present the thesis he intends to, he must signify the same subject in both occurrences of 'man'.

The subject signified in each occurrence, then, must satisfy the conditions necessary for it to be the same subject as the one signified in the other occurrence; and therefore the subject signified on each occasion must have the same essential properties. In signifying the same subject, therefore, O must signify the same essential property.[7] Let us suppose that the essential property of man is F (in Aristotle's argument it is biped animal), the very property that O both affirms and denies of man. This is a fair assumption, since O's denial of PNC is meant to apply to every property of the subject.

We have so far clarified O's thesis, and seen why it presupposes the same subject with the same essential property. We have therefore defended Aristotle's claim that O's thesis presupposes the first and the third of the presuppositions mentioned above. We now need to understand the second presupposition. O asserts that man is both F and not F, where 'F' refers to the property signified by 'man', the essential property of man; and Aristotle insists that 'F' and 'not F', as they occur in O's thesis, must signify different properties. He claims: 'It is not possible, then, for being man to signify essentially not being man, if "man" signifies not only of one ⟨subject⟩ but also one thing '(1006b13–15).[8] To see Aristotle's point we may suppose that 'man' and 'not man' signify the same things, so that F (signified by 'man') and not F (signified by 'not man') are the same property (1006b22–5). If they are the same, then O's assertion 'Man is F and not F' ascribes the same property twice to the same subject. But this is not what O intended to do. To maintain his original thesis he must maintain that being man is different from not being man.

We have now examined the three presuppositions of O's thesis, and found that it commits him to claiming that he signifies man, that F is what man is, and that F is different from not-F. We can add up O's presuppositions, and see that they cannot be consistently combined. (1) To deny every instance of PNC, O must say it is possible for the *same* subject, man, to have the contradictory of each of its properties. (2) If O is speaking of the same subject, he must acknowledge that he signifies the essence, the property that makes the subject of two predications the same subject. (3) Hence, since the subject man is essentially F, a subject that is not F is not the same subject as the one signified by the first occurrence of 'man'. (4) Hence when O says that man is not F, O is committed to denying that this subject (the one that is not F) is the same subject that as the one that he said is F, since being F is the essential property of man.

Though O wanted both to assert and deny the same property of the same subject, he has failed to do this.[9] He has to deny the presuppositions of his own position. For he has presupposed that he can signify the same subject; but the conditions for doing this turn out to be inconsistent with rejecting PNC for the essential property that must be signified in signifying the same subject. If O cannot signify the same subject, he cannot ascribe contradictory properties to it.

99. FROM NON-CONTRADICTION TO ESSENCE AND SUBSTANCE

Aristotle's argument against O shows the connexion he sees between the defence of the axioms and the discussion of substance, the two concerns of the science of being:

In general our opponents do away with substance and essence, since they must say that everything is a coincident, and that there is no such thing as being essentially man or being essentially animal. For if something is essentially man, this will not be being not man or not being man; but these are the denials of being man ⟨and hence should be true if PNC is false⟩. For there is, as we saw, one thing signified, and this is the substance of something. Now to signify x's substance is to signify that being x is nothing else. But if its being essentially man is being essentially not man or essentially not being man, then being it will be something else ⟨than the substance, which is self-contradictory⟩. Hence they must say that nothing has the sort of account ⟨that signifies substance⟩, but everything is a coincident; for the difference between substance and coincident is just this, that white coincides in man because man is white but not essentially white. Now if everything is said coincidentally, there will be no primary ⟨subject⟩ of which it is said, if ⟨i.e. since⟩ in every case a coincident signifies a predication of some subject. (1007a20–b1)[10]

If we see why O's position is undermined by his failure to recognize essence and substance, we should also be able to see why we need to recognize them.

O must deny any essential properties, because he has to say that for any property of the subject, it is possible for the subject to lack that property. If it is possible for a property not to belong to a subject, the property is not necessary, hence not essential.[11] Hence all the properties of the subject must be merely coincidental. But now O cannot say that the same subject is both F and not F either by being F or by being not F; for if both F and not F are coincidents, the subject could be the same even if it lacked them; and the same is true for every other property of the subject. But if O does not concede that any property makes the subject the same subject, he cannot claim to talk about the same subject when he claims that the subject is both F and not F; he cannot explain why we should not take the subject that is F and the subject that is not F to be different subjects. Hence O's implicit denial of essence leaves him with no single subject for the contradictory properties (1007a33–b1).

Aristotle's defence of PNC has shown why we must recognize subjects and essences. For he has argued that a subject of discourse and predication is a single subject in so far as it has an essence (1007a25–6). A substance, on this view, will be a subject with an essence that makes it the same subject in different predications. The argument for PNC has shown us why we need substances, and something about what substances are like.

Nothing has been said, however, about the sort of subject that Aristotle has in mind.[12] The example he picks is an item in the category of substance—man. But is it a particular man or the universal man? The argument seems to work equally well with either at most points. Nor is it affected if we choose a subject from a non-substance category. When Aristotle discusses essence and coincidents, his examples are Socrates and his coincidents (1007b5–16), but nothing seems to depend on this choice of examples.

Similarly, if O claims to be speaking of a single subject with contradictory properties, he must allow some property without its contradictory to belong to the subject; x cannot be the same subject *simply* by being F and not F. But this conclusion still allows many views about what the essential property might be. It might be a disjunctive property; or it might be a temporally indexed property (e.g. being F from t1 to t2, G from t2 to t3, etc.). Though these are not the sorts of essential properties that Aristotle normally recognizes, they are not ruled out by the argument for PNC.

Aristotle is right not to claim that at this stage he can defend his own conception of subject and essence. We must, indeed, expect a fairly indefinite conclusion from the very general arguments about being qua being. The puzzles about substance in Book iii showed that we ought to settle some preliminary questions about the general conditions for being a substance, before trying to settle disputes between Aristotle, Plato, and the Presocratics, about the types of things that meet these general conditions. In the argument for PNC Aristotle focuses on the basic subject of properties and on the essence of such a subject; both subject and essence are connected with substance, though Aristotle does not yet clearly identify either of them with substance. We still need to know what sort of thing can be a subject and what sort of property can be its essence.

100. THE DIALECTICAL CHARACTER OF THE ARGUMENT

Aristotle admits that he has offered a dialectical argument, and indeed an argument of the sort that might arouse our suspicions about the place of dialectical argument in the science of being.[13] He acknowledges at the outset that an argument in defence of an absolutely first principle such as PNC might seem to be in grave danger of begging the question; we might well suspect that the argument for PNC must assume the truth of PNC.[14] Our suspicion seems justified by the actual course of the argument; for we seem to assume PNC, in assuming that the same subject cannot both have and lack its essential property.

Such begging of the question does not worry Aristotle. For he claimed at the outset that the argument would be quite all right if he could make O seem to beg the question, and thereby avoid any dialectical objection to the refutation:

It should be noticed, though, that demonstration by refutation is not the same as demonstrating. In attempting to demonstrate ⟨PNC⟩ someone might seem to beg the question; but if the respondent is responsible for such a thing, it will be a refutation, not a demonstration. (1006a15–18)[15]

If O finds himself having to assume PNC, he cannot complain that it has been assumed, contrary to dialectical rules, without his agreement.

Indeed, Aristotle makes O beg the question. Aristotle has not insisted in his own right that the same subject cannot both have and lack its essential property. His account of O's position has shown that O must himself presuppose this, or else undermine his claim to be asserting contradictory properties of the same subject. Aristotle must admit that PNC has been assumed, and that to that extent the question has been begged. He can fairly point out, though, that if we reject the assumption about essential properties, we need not agree that O is speaking of the same subject. Since O cannot afford to deny that he speaks of the same subject, he cannot afford to reject PNC.

This argument, then, looks like ordinary dialectic, in so far as it relies on the interlocutor's agreement. And if in fact it begs the question, even though the interlocutor cannot complain, must it not fall short of the standards required for a proof in a scientific argument? Dependence on common beliefs and the agreement of interlocutors seems to be a weakness that prevents dialectical argument from being scientific. If Aristotle admits that his argument is ad hominem in so far as it requires the interlocutor to beg the question against himself, he apparently should not present it as an example of strong dialectic, supporting a claim in the science of being.

The argument follows tactics that are even more reminiscent of the use of dialectic for encounters and contests. If Aristotle set out the logical consequences and presuppositions of each admission before inviting O to make the admission, O would notice that PNC was being assumed, and might refuse to make the admission. The tactic of concealment is needed to prevent O from seeing that he makes a fatal admission.[16] An argument that relies on such debating tricks does not seem a credible route to scientific conclusions.

In fact, however, the argument is crucially different from ordinary dialectic. In ordinary dialectic, the initial agreement may depend on contingent and relatively unstable features of interlocutors; different interlocutors with different ethical views may, for instance, find one or another ethical premiss plausible. Moreover, if the beliefs that lead us to a dialectical conclusion are fairly easily given up, our initial acceptance of the truth of the premisses and our later acceptance of the validity of the argument does not commit us to acceptance of the conclusion; we may prefer to give up one of our initial admissions once we have seen its consequences.

The argument for PNC does not suffer from these objections. To show that it does not assume any particular background of beliefs that some interlocutors might lack, Aristotle deliberately picks an extreme case. O tries to maintain a view sharply opposed to common beliefs; and if O has to accept PNC, everyone will have to recognize it. Similarly, it will not be easy for O to withdraw his initial admissions when he sees their consequences. He cannot refuse the initial concessions without denying that he signifies a subject and ascribes properties to it. If he denies this, he must deny that he is saying anything about how things really are at all.

If O must concede Aristotle's crucial premisses, anyone with more modest claims about how things are must also concede them. The use of concealment does not reduce the argument to a purely ad hominem status. Concealment is possible because we do not at first see the connexion between O's thesis, the belief in a single subject, and the acceptance of PNC. The discovery of the concealment does not show O a way to escape Aristotle's conclusion; it shows how O's thesis has presupposed its own falsity.

Hence the fact that the argument makes O beg the question does not show that it is merely ad hominem in a sense that makes it depend on the beliefs of a particular subset of interlocutors; for no other interlocutor who remains an interlocutor can refuse the concession that O has to make. Aristotle says that anyone who refuses to make O's concessions might as well be a vegetable, no longer attempting to communicate his beliefs about how things are (1006a11–15, b5–9).[17]

101. THE STATUS OF THE CONCLUSION

Aristotle does not mean his argument for PNC to be a demonstration or to cause doubters to believe it is true (since perhaps no one really doubts it). Still, he can justly claim to have given a reason for believing it to be true. If strong dialectic convinces us that PNC is presupposed in any rational inquiry into the sort of subject that is studied by a science, our conviction gives us a reason for believing PNC.[18] We do not need this reason to cause us to believe in PNC, but once we have this reason we see why PNC should be taken for granted without demonstration.

Aristotle has not given an argument that makes it logically impossible for PNC to be false; for we might be wrong in thinking there are any subjects of the sort that are assumed by rational inquiry. But a reason that fails to rule out the logical possibility of error may still be a good reason. Aristotle has argued that PNC is true of being qua being; though his arguments (naturally enough) appeal to the role of PNC in our beliefs about objective reality, they are arguments *for* the conclusion that it is true of objective reality—that reality conforms to PNC whether or not we believe it does. To this extent Aristotle intends his argument to reach a realist conclusion; and though the premisses are not logically inconsistent with the falsity of the realist conclusion, they still constitute a good argument for it.[19]

Aristotle does not make it clear what PNC is necessary for—meaningful thought or speech, discourse about subjects, or discourse about how things are—about the sorts of subjects presupposed by science. But the third focus best suits the place of the argument in the science of being. The subject is introduced as the sort of thing we study in studying objective reality, and O raises no objection to this. He signifies this sort of subject in so far as he signifies the essential property that makes it the same subject; and Aristotle argues that O prevents himself from signifying any single subject. Perhaps we could construct an argument parallel to Aristotle's, in order to show that PNC is necessary for meaningful thought or speech as well; but this is not his main concern.

It follows that O could reject Aristotle's argument by rejecting any belief in subjects, and by confining himself to speaking of property-instances, not combined into subjects with more than one property. Even if subjects have to conform to PNC, perhaps not everything spoken of has to conform to it. Aristotle does not explain why O ought not to give up subjects, though he returns to this question in his discussion of scepticism. But none the less, his argument relies on a presupposition of scientific study; he has 'made a new start' from a premiss about being qua being.

In these ways Aristotle's defence of PNC counts as strong dialectic, not ordinary dialectic. For the premisses are not ordinary common beliefs; they are common beliefs that we cannot give up without ceasing to take part in rational discourse about how things are. The fact that they have this status gives us a good reason for relying on them that we do not have for just any common beliefs.

It does not follow that the premisses of Aristotle's argument are self-evidently true or logically necessary; it is logically possible for us to be wrong in thinking that we take part in rational discourse about how things are, and logically possible for us to give up taking part in it. Still, if this is what it takes for us to reject the premisses of the argument, we have quite strong reasons for accepting them, and they are quite reasonable examples of the sorts of premisses that Aristotle needs if his dialectical arguments are to justify more than ordinary dialectical conclusions. The conclusions are about being qua being; for they show how we must conceive subjects that can be regarded as bearers of coincidental properties. We can see why the argument is dialectical, and why the conclusion is more than a merely dialectical proof about being qua being.

102. PROTAGORAS AND THE SCIENCE OF BEING

In his argument against Protagoras Aristotle defends a further aspect of his views on substance. He believes that the Protagorean doctrine and the denial of PNC follow from each other, and that both result from the same way of thinking (1009a6–7). Having seen why the denial of PNC results in an intolerable conception of how things are, we ought to see that the Protagorean conception is intolerable for the same reason, that it does not admit the sorts of subjects that must be recognized in an account of being qua being. We therefore learn something further about the subjects we must recognize; not only must they have essences, but the essences must be of a sort that is incompatible with Protagoras' view of the world.

Protagoras begins from the problem of conflicting appearances.

Some have come to believe in the truth of appearances from perceptible things. In their view, we should not judge whether something is true by the large or small number ⟨of people who believe it⟩; but the same thing seems sweet to some who taste it, bitter to others, so that if all were sick or all insane except for two or three healthy or sane people, these two or three, not the majority, would seem to be sick or insane. Further, many of the other animals have appearances contrary to ours about the same thing, and even for each one of us in relation to himself things do not always seem the same in perception. It is unclear, then, which appearances are true or false; for these are no more true than those, but all are true or false alike. This is why Democritus says that either nothing is true or what is true is unclear to us. (1009a38–b12)[20]

Protagoras wants to resist Democritus' sceptical conclusion, by arguing that the appearances do not really conflict. Just as Socrates can be both tall and short (in relation to different people), things are hot and cold, white and black, for different perceivers. Different apparent properties of objects reflect different interactions between objects and the sense-organs of perceivers, and nothing has any of its properties except in so far as it enters different relations with perceivers.[21]

In Aristotle's view, Protagoras offers an account of being qua being—of how things really are, and of the sorts of things that can be objects of scientific study. He does not take Protagoras to maintain a subjectivist thesis (there is nothing except states of consciousness) or a sceptical thesis (we are not justified in believing in the existence of anything beyond states of consciousness).[22] He takes Protagoras to offer an account of the world external to the perceiver.

As Aristotle understands him, Protagoras wants to avoid scepticism or subjectivism, while conceding the premises that seem to force us into one of these positions. Aristotle thinks it fair to ask opponents of PNC what account of reality they can give: 'If what he says is true, then

what would it mean to say that such is the nature of things that are?'
(1008b3–5). His question is fair in an argument about being qua being.
He assumes that Protagoras also wants to give an account of the nature
of things, and asks him the same question.

This interpretation explains why Aristotle thinks Protagoras is
committed to a Heracleitean doctrine of radical flux. Protagoras needs
flux if he is to maintain the infallibility of perception against any
possibility of correction:

Further, seeing that all of this nature is changing, and that nothing is truly said
of what is ⟨in the course of⟩ changing, they thought it impossible to say
anything truly of what is ⟨in the course of⟩ changing in every way in all
circumstances. (1010a7–9)

If the qualities of things did not change with different perceivers or
different states of the same perceiver, a perceiver might be wrong. But if
something we speak of is already in the course of changing, we cannot
say that it is still white, if it appeared white to Smith at time t1 and will
appear pink to Jones at t2.

The senses turn out to be right, therefore, not about the changing
things that last for some length of time, but about the purely
momentary things that we perceive in a particular perceptual encounter.
I perceive a momentary quality-instance, or several of them; but none of
these is a persisting subject that changes. Each momentary quality
disappears when we perceive something else. This argument does not
prove that the senses report correctly on momentary qualities, but it
removes any grounds for challenging or doubting their correctness;
appeal to their incorrigibility undermines objections to their infallibility.
Protagoras can therefore remove objections to his doctrine by appealing
to the truth of the Heracleitean doctrine of flux.[23]

103. THE REPLY TO PROTAGORAS

Aristotle examines the subjects of change that are presupposed by
radical flux, and argues that Protagoras, no less than opponents of PNC,
has an unsatisfactory account of these subjects. The relevant subjects of
change are not the momentary objects that we perceive, but the
persistent objects whose interaction produces the momentary perceived
objects.[24] Protagoras claims that the same wind is hot and cold, the same
man pale and dark. He must say the same about substantial properties,
those that allow us to speak of the same subject; for he must treat 'man',
'horse', 'stone', etc. as he treated such predicates as 'hot'. Since

something may appear to you, but not to me, to be a stone, it is both a stone and not a stone; it has these properties only in relation to a particular perceiver at a particular time.

Being a stone and not a stone implies a change in some subject; but it must be a rather minimal subject. Even Aristotelian prime matter always has some actual qualities, as opposed to their negations, and always has definite capacities, as opposed to their negations.[25] But Protagoras must apply his restrictions to these properties too. Since the subject can appear to some perceivers not to have any of these properties, he must say that it can be the same subject even though it lacks them; he cannot say that the subject is the same because it retains some property in undergoing change.

In his reply, therefore, Aristotle appeals to the identity of the subject throughout the change, and argues that Protagoras cannot give an account of it:

Changing according to quantity is not the same as changing according to quality. Let us grant that something does not persist according to quantity; still, it is according to the form that we know all things. (1010a23–5)[26]

The Heracleitean theory has to claim that the same subject can remain in being, but change in all respects. Aristotle replies that the claim turns out to be internally inconsistent, once its presuppositions are made clear.[27] If the same subject persists, it must keep the same essential property (the 'form' he mentions here); but if it changes in every respect, it cannot keep its essential property.[28] Protagoras, no less than the opponent of PNC, has taken for granted some conception of the identical subject to which he attributes properties; in this he conforms to the practice of a special science. But, unlike the special scientist, Protagoras ought not to take such a conception for granted; for once we understand it better, we see that it rules out Protagoras' conception of the world, and that therefore being qua being cannot have the properties that Protagoras ascribes to it.

A similar neglect of the subject explains Protagoras' views about the dependence of external reality on perceivers. Since Protagoras restricts being to what is perceived, he must say that nothing exists independently of animate perceivers; but, for Aristotle, this result is impossible, since the subject that produces the perception must be prior to the perception (1010b30–1011a2). Just as we expect movement to be explained by properties of the mover interacting with properties of what is moved (1010b37–1011a2), we expect perception to be explained partly by properties of the object.[29] The objects must have some stable properties explaining why, when perceivers exist, the objects become perceptible. These stable properties persist when the objects are not perceived; they are the sorts of properties that Aristotle calls potentialities. Protagoras' view must deny the existence of potentialities that explain the occurrence of perception when it occurs.

This argument explains what is lost if we do not allow for persistent subjects. Our account of being qua being should take enough account of change to show how change might be a proper concern of a science that studies a part of being. If we are describing changing things, the point of recognizing a persisting subject with a stable essence is to explain changes by referring to interactions between persistent subjects. Aristotle claims that among the persistent properties of objects we must include stable potentialities; without these, nothing about them would explain the changes in them or their interactions with other objects. Those who deny the existence of non-actualized potentialities lapse into Protagoras' conception of objects; for since they deny the existence of stable potentialities, they prevent the proper explanation of change, as Protagoras does (1047a4–7). It is reasonable for Aristotle to discuss potentialities further in his fuller account of subjects and essences.[30]

104. SCEPTICISM AND THE SCIENCE OF BEING

Aristotle has explained why Protagoras does not give an adequate account of 'the nature of things that are', if such an account is supposed to describe a subject of a science that studies a part of being. We may still, however, not be convinced that the science of being rests on a firm foundation. For the refutation of Protagoras and of the opponent of PNC assumes a subject to which different properties are attributed. Aristotle's normal realist assumption claims that objective features of the world (i.e. those it has independently of our beliefs about it) explain the truth of our beliefs.[31] Protagoras (as Aristotle construes him) wants to regard the world as a subject for scientific study, but does not think it has to be objective; he answers scepticism about an objective world by allowing the world to change with every change in appearances. Aristotle replies that Protagoras cannot dispense with objectivity so easily; for his attempt to describe the changing subject leaves no coherent description of a subject at all. To this extent Aristotle defends against Protagoras the realist assumptions that he normally takes for granted.

Still, the defence of the realist assumptions assumes belief in a world containing subjects that are proper subjects for scientific study; and this belief seems so close to the realist assumption that it may seem open to any doubts that arise about the realist assumption itself. Aristotle's defence of the realist assumption against Protagoras seems to leave room for a consistent and radical form of scepticism. Sceptics appeal to conflicting appearances. We cannot judge, they suggest, by majority opinion; for if only a minority were sane and the majority were mad this criterion would give the wrong answer (1009b2–6). Nor can we judge by how things appear to us, as the particular people we are; they appear differently to other animals, to different human beings, and to ourselves in different conditions.[32]

The sceptics, therefore, see no good reason for accepting one of a pair of conflicting appearances over the other; they find that the conflicting appearances are 'equipollent' (Sextus, *PH* i 8, 10), and their recognition of equipollence leads them to suspension of judgment. These radical sceptics refuse to acknowledge the existence of any subject beyond their own appearances. It is useful to see how far Aristotle recognizes such a possibility, and how he replies to it.

He seems to recognize radical scepticism as a consistent position immune to his arguments against the opponent of PNC.

Some people, including some who are persuaded by these things and some who merely put forward these arguments, are puzzled. They ask who is to judge which people are healthy, and, in general, who is to judge correctly about each thing. These sorts of puzzles are like being puzzled about whether we are now awake or asleep. All such puzzles have the same significance; those posing them expect to be given an argument for everything, since they seek a principle, and seek to reach it through demonstration—for it is evident in their actions that they are not really persuaded. But as we said, this is what happens to them; they seek an argument for things for which there is no argument, since the starting-point of demonstration is not a demonstration. These people might easily be persuaded of this, since it is not hard to grasp. But those who will be satisfied with nothing less than an argument that forces them are asking for the impossible; for they demand ⟨that we refute them by⟩ stating contrary things ⟨to what they say⟩, but then at once they state contrary things ⟨in rejecting PNC⟩. (1011a3–16)

Those who always reject PNC, and always see when it is being assumed against them cannot be refuted; for Aristotle himself points out that the argument for PNC makes the opponents beg the question by relying on an instance of PNC. If they refuse to let PNC be assumed at any stage of the argument, they also prevent themselves from attributing different properties to the same subject; but if they accept this consequence, and are willing (as Aristotle puts it) to be in the condition of vegetables, they cannot be refuted.

For similar reasons Aristotle agrees that the arguments against

Protagoras will not work against a revised Protagorean who gives up Protagoras' claim to be describing the nature of things that are. He sums up his argument against Protagoras:

If not all things are relative to something, but some things are also in themselves, not everything that appears will be true. For what appears appears to someone. Hence whoever says that everything appearing is true makes every being relative to something. (1011a17–20)

Aristotle takes this result to refute Protagoras. For he has asked 'In virtue of what about the same object is it both a man (to me) and a warship (to you)?', and he has found that Protagoras has no convincing answer to the question. But he thinks the revised Protagoreans can avoid the force of his argument, if they refuse to speak of how things are, and confine themselves to saying how things appear to them to be. They must also restrict the Protagorean thesis in the same way; but if they are careful, they cannot be refuted (1011a21–b12).[33]

105. THE REPLY TO SCEPTICISM

While Aristotle recognizes this consistent sceptical position, and agrees that it cannot be refuted from premises a sceptic will accept, he does not infer that it is irrefutable. Instead of trying to find some internal inconsistency in scepticism, he challenges the premises of the sceptical arguments about conflicting appearances; he insists against the sceptic that we have good reasons for preferring one of a pair of contradictory appearances over the other. In defending this reply, he must also challenge the sceptic's conditions for justification.

In Aristotle's view, we have satisfactory ways of deciding that some appearances are correct and some are not.

Further, one may justifiably be amazed if they are puzzled about such questions as: 'Are magnitudes and colours such as appear to be to observers from a distance or to observers close at hand? Are they such as they appear to healthy people, or to sick? Are those things heavier that appear so to feeble people, or to vigorous? Are those things true that appear so to people asleep, or to those awake?' For it is evident at least that they do not really think ⟨the appearances of the dreamer etc. are true⟩—at least, no one who is in Libya and one night supposes ⟨in a dream⟩ that he is in Athens goes off to the Odeion. (1010b3–11)

Since discrimination between appearances is not as difficult as the sceptic suggests it is, the sceptic's problem does not arise.

This reply may seem to miss the force of the sceptical arguments. The sceptic appeals to conflicting appearances, claiming that we cannot say which are true and which false.

We have no agreed criterion through which we will judge what we are going to judge in advance, and we are not supplied with a demonstration that is true and judged ⟨to be true⟩, since we are still seeking the criterion of truth, through which it is also fitting to judge in addition the true demonstrations also. (Sextus, *PH* ii 53)[34]

The sceptic assumes that we are justified in believing that p only if we can prove p by appeal to some further principle q that we are justified in believing independently of believing p, and we can produce the proof of all the predecessors of p (i.e. of q, of the justification of q, . . . etc.). We can stop an infinite regress only if the sceptic agrees to a principle; but he will not agree to one, because at each stage he can demand a further proof.

Aristotle, however, seeing that the sceptics rely on these epistemological claims, rejects them. He answers the claims about conflicting appearances by pointing out that in fact we trust some appearances more than others; and then the sceptics ask who is qualified to settle conflicts between appearances (1011a3–6). Aristotle's impatient reply will not deter the sceptics from raising the same questions over again; and we may think he is unreasonably dogmatic.

His reply, however, rests on a stronger foundation than mere dogmatism. For he argues that his opponents have the wrong conception of the proper sort of justification; they look for demonstrations when they should not (1006a5–11, 1011a3–13). In asking why we believe the doctor, or how we can tell we are awake, the sceptics keep asking for a further principle, so that they will not have to take anything on trust without a demonstration. But this demand will never yield the right sort of justification; 'it would go on to infinity, so that there would be no demonstration that way either' (1006a8–9). Once the sceptics see that the demand for demonstration is the source of their puzzles, and is itself an unreasonable demand, they will give up their challenge (1011a11–16).

Aristotle sees that the sceptics' case will collapse unless they can persuade us, as non-sceptics, to accept their demand as reasonable. We might accept it either because we implicitly accept these standards already, or they might persuade us to adopt them. If Aristotle is right, we do not accept the sceptics' standards already. We do not expect every belief to be justified by some more certain universal principle; and so the sceptics cannot simply take their standards for granted in trying to undermine Aristotle's claim about the waking observer and the doctor.

They must, then, try to persuade us to adopt their standards. But the standards do not seem self-evident. Moreover, the fact that they lead to scepticism does not commend them to us, since we are not sceptics yet. The sceptics need to show *both* that the standards follow from other beliefs about the nature of justification *and* that we have better reason to maintain these other beliefs than to modify them once we see they imply the standards that lead to scepticism. Alternatively, sceptics may show *both* that acceptance of the standards is required, not by our views about justification in particular, but by our other beliefs and practices, *and* that we have better reason to maintain these beliefs and practices than to modify them when we see their sceptical implications. Sceptics have little hope of proving their case by any of these routes.

We should not, then, dismiss or ignore Aristotle's reply to scepticism or accuse him of failure to face the sceptical challenge. He faces it in the right way, not by simply rejecting the consequences of scepticism, but by challenging some of its premisses and presuppositions. He fastens quite appropriately on claims about justification.

106. THE KNOWLEDGE OF FIRST PRINCIPLES

Aristotle is quite right to challenge the sceptical claim that no undemonstrated principles should be accepted as the basis for arguments that reach true conclusions about an objective world. But his challenge to the sceptic brings us back to a basic question about the argument in Book iv. Even if the premisses of our arguments need not be demonstrated, the sceptic will fairly complain if the premisses rest on nothing more than common beliefs. To show that this complaint is unwarranted, Aristotle needs to show that his premisses can claim more than the status of ordinary dialectical premisses.

It is not so easy to say what further status Aristotle claims for his premisses. Either (*a*) his arguments are pure dialectic, or (*b*) they involve essential appeal to intuition, or (*c*) they involve strong dialectic.[35] The first answer is ruled out by Aristotle's contrast between dialectic and philosophy, unless he has entirely misconceived that contrast. We still must choose between the second and the third answers.

When Aristotle says we must not ask for a demonstration of everything, he might be endorsing a foundationalist doctrine, that we must accept some things with no inferential justification at all, and that these basic beliefs warrant all our inferred beliefs. In the *Analytics*, indeed, he thinks a self-evident, non-inferentially justified foundation is the only way to avoid a vicious regress or vicious circle of justification; and the objections to a regress or circle support the doctrine of intuitive understanding. In *Metaphysics* iv, then, he might mean that we must rely on intuition of the truth of principles or of particular judgments or of both, if we are to avoid scepticism.[36]

If Aristotle relies on these foundationalist principles in *Metaphysics* iv, he leaves himself open to the sceptical arguments against 'assumptions' (*hupotheseis*) (Sextus, *PH* i 168). An assumption seems arbitrary if it is not further defended; but any further defence seems to force us back into inferential justification, and into the questions about circles and regresses. Moreover, if Aristotle appeals to a self-evident foundation, he makes it hard to understand the methods of the science of being. This science finds knowledge of first principles, not treating them as assumptions, but offering inferential justification by dialectical argument. The inferential justification introduces some circularity; but Aristotle ought to deny that the circle is vicious.

He has good grounds, then, for rejecting in *Metaphysics* iv the conception of justification accepted in the *Analytics*. There he treated foundationalism as the only alternative to scepticism. He does not say this in *Metaphysics* iv; his arguments never rely on foundationalist doctrine, and indeed, as we have suggested, they are inconsistent with it.[37] Our discrimination among appearances, and our belief that some people are competent judges and others are not, are not casual or arbitrary preferences. Without them we would have no grounds for belief in an objective world open to scientific study. The conclusion that there are persistent subjects with essential properties and stable potentialities is defended, not as a consequence of commonsense assumptions, but as a prerequisite for belief in objects of knowledge at all.

This defence of an aspect of common sense relies on circular argument; but the sceptic has still to show why there is anything wrong with that. Certainly Aristotle cannot safely reject all circular argument himself. In the *Analytics* he rejected relatively small and uninteresting circles, and suggested that all circular reasoning would share their faults.[38] If he is to defend the arguments in *Metaphysics* iv, he cannot afford such a sweeping rejection of circular argument.

The conclusions therefore rest on dialectic, since they involve dialectical procedures; but since they rest on a restricted and basic set of common beliefs, they rest on strong dialectic. The difference that Aristotle sees between dialectic and philosophy is the difference between ordinary or 'mere' dialectic and strong dialectic.[39] If we know only that our opponents reject a premiss of an ordinary dialectical argument, we know only that they have departed to some degree from common sense. If we know that they reject a premiss of a strong dialectical argument, we know that they must reject the possibility of objectivity and knowledge altogether.

Aristotle has now answered the methodological puzzles raised in Book iii. He has described the scope and methods of the science of being, and shown how it argues for first principles. He ought, therefore, to face the substantive puzzles, since these drove us to look for a second-order science. Different conceptions of substance, and of its relation to form and matter, universal and particular, seemed to rest on disputes about more basic principles. If Aristotle has shown how a second-order universal science is possible, he should also show how it can resolve these disputes.

Book iv suggests what the disputants about substance have been arguing about, and what standards an acceptable account of substance should meet. A science must study a part of being, and hence, in Aristotle's view, must study persistent subjects with essential properties. This general demand rules out a Protagorean or Heracleitean conception of reality; it requires us to recognize potentialities explaining change in the subject and in its relation with other beings. These results do not tell us who is right in the disputes about substance—whether it is particular, universal, form, or matter; but they tell us something about what we ought to look for. The best candidate for substance will be the one that best fulfils these conditions; and if we can find it, we will have knowledge about substance—the knowledge sought in Book i.

10

SUBSTANCE AND ESSENCE

---

107. FROM BEING TO SUBSTANCE

At the end of *Metaphysics* vii 1 Aristotle claims that his inquiry into being qua being requires, and indeed can be reduced to, an inquiry into substance: 'Hence the question that for a long time in the past, and still in the present, indeed always, is pursued and always raises puzzles—"what is being?"—this is the question "what is substance?"' (1028b2–4)[1] The old question about being is the question that the Presocratics were asking, without realizing it (1003a28–31, 1004b8–10, 1005a29–b2). In Book iv Aristotle already claimed that substance is prior to other beings, and now he defends that claim, by appeal to the doctrine of categories.[2]

In Book iv Aristotle argued that the sort of being that can be an object of knowledge must be a persistent subject with an essence; if something does not itself satisfy that condition, but is appropriately related to a subject, it is still a being. But he needs to show that this primary subject is a substance. First he argues that the doctrine of the categories assigns the right role to the category of substance; the relation of substance to the other categories indicates the relation of the basic subject to other beings, and therefore the discovery of the genuine substances will be the discovery of the basic subjects.

Though Aristotle did not formulate the doctrine of the categories with the metaphysical demands of Book iv in mind, these demands show that the doctrine is important in the study of being qua being, in so far as it isolates the basic subjects. Book iv did not tell us which Aristotelian category the basic subjects would belong to; but in vii 1 Aristotle argues that they must belong to the category of substance. He is not arguing for a trivial claim; he is asserting that the sorts of basic subjects we need cannot be quantities, qualities, and so on, because none of these meets the proper conditions for being a basic subject.

In Book iv Aristotle demands not only basic subjects, but basic subjects with essences. Either demand could be expressed as a demand for 'substance', *ousia*; for in Book iv, as often elsewhere, he seems to speak indiscriminately of both subject and essence as *ousia*. He should apparently be more careful, however; for though substance as subject and substance as essence are closely connected, they seem to satisfy different criteria for substance. Questions about the two criteria arise immediately from the appeal to the categories, since the category of *ousia* seems to include essences no less than subjects.[3]

In claiming that substance is basic, Aristotle draws attention to these questions. First he appeals to the essence-criterion, remarking that non-substances tell us the quality, quantity, etc. of something, not what it is (1028a15–18). We may argue that this does not exclude qualities etc. from the category of *ousia*, since they are the *ousia* of white etc., no less than man is the *ousia* of men.

In reply, Aristotle examines non-substances further.

Hence someone might actually be puzzled about whether walking, flourishing, or sitting signifies a being; for none of these either is in itself or is capable of being separated from substance. Rather, the walking or seated or flourishing ⟨thing⟩ is a better candidate—if indeed this counts as a being. But these appear better candidates because they have some definite subject—the substance and the particular—which is indicated in such a predication; for this subject is implied in speaking of the good or seated ⟨thing⟩. Clearly, then, it is because of substance that each of those other things is also a being; and so what primarily is, what is not something ⟨else, as the sitting thing is a man⟩, but is unconditionally, is substance. (1028a20–31)

This may not seem to help. Aristotle appeals to the subject-criterion, implying that non-substances are not independent ('capable of being separated') subjects in the way substances are; but he does not explain why substances are not equally inseparable from non-substances. If a man, for instance, is not capable of existing without colour or shape, then on this point substances are no different from non-substances.[4]

108. THE PRIORITY OF SUBSTANCE

Aristotle faces this objection more directly, by introducing such compound things as walkers and musicians, which at first seem to falsify his claims about non-substances. On the one hand they ought to be non-substances, in so far as they essentially have properties in non-substance categories (they are essentially musical etc.), and so differ from Aristotle's favoured substances (as he conceives them). On the other hand, they seem to be quite good substances, by Aristotle's main criterion; for if an individual man exists independently of anything else, so also, apparently, does an individual walker.[5]

In Aristotle's view, however, these compounds actually support his claims. For musicians etc. are not genuine subjects in their own right; since they are compounds, they require a more basic subject (e.g. man) and a non-essential property (e.g. musicality) (1028a24–9). The claim that non-substances do not answer the 'What is it?' question now turns out to be more reasonable, if the question is applied to basic subjects. Hence the fact that 'It's a musician' answers the 'What is it?' question about musicians does not show that musicians are substances.

The relation between the man and the musician suggests an answer to the question about separability. A particular three-foot length lasts through time in so far as it belongs to some surface of some body that is three feet long. Similarly, the persistence of a particular item in some other non-substance category consists partly in the persistence of the very same particular substance. If the substance perishes, then this particular non-substance perishes, even though it may be replaced by another just like it.[6] On the other hand, the persistence of a substance does not consist in the persistence of any one of its particular instances of non-substantial properties. Socrates does not need his particular instance of colour or shape or size to remain in existence, even though he needs some property-instance in these categories.

These points also explain why a compound of a substance and a non-substance—e.g. a walker or a sitter—also depends on a substance. The walker persists only in so far as the man who is the walker persists, but the man's persistence does not consist in the persistence of the walker. As Aristotle says in the *Analytics*, the walker is a walker by being something else, a man, whereas the man is not a man by being something else (cf. *APo* 83a9–14). Non-substances are beings 'by being qualities (etc.)' of substance (1028a18–19); none of them can be separated from substance (a23–4), and the other things are beings because of substance.[7]

These claims about the relation of substance to non-substances (including musicians and similar compounds) imply that substance is prior to non-substance; Aristotle makes this claim explicit by asserting that substance is prior in three ways: in nature, account, and knowledge (1028a31–b2).[8] Each type of priority is intelligible from the previous remarks about substance.

Substance is naturally prior in so far as it is separable from other things and they are not separable from it; the same man can exist without being a musician, but the same musician cannot exist without being the same man. For priority in account 'it is necessary that in the account of each thing the account of substance should be present' (1028a35–6). This priority is illustrated in the claim that non-substances are essentially qualities (etc.) of substance, and also in the claim that ostensible subjects such as musicians are not spoken of without substance.[9]

Priority in knowledge is explained as follows: 'We think we know each thing most, whenever we know what man or fire is, rather than when we know the quality or quantity or place, since we also think we know each of these things whenever we know what the quantity or quality is' (1028a36–b2). It is illustrated especially by the claim that the substantial properties of a subject tell us what it is; for these are the properties that provide knowledge.[10]

Since some of these claims about priority refer to subjects, and others refer to essences, Aristotle will find the substances if he finds the basic subjects and the basic essences. Book iv argued that an account of being qua being must refer to basic subjects and essences; and vii 1 connects that argument with the doctrine of the categories. The claim that substance is the first category, and somehow prior to non-substances, is justified by the demand of first philosophy for subjects and essences. To this extent vii 1 continues the argument of the science of being.

109. CRITERIA FOR SUBSTANCE

The argument now takes a controversial direction. The puzzles in Book iii tended to suggest both that universals must be substances because they are prior in definition and knowledge, and that particulars must be substances because they are prior in being. These suggestions raise a severe difficulty if universals and particulars are competing for a single role that they cannot both occupy. To remove the difficulty it seems plausible to suggest that substances are multivocal—that in one sense of 'substance' (i.e. 'basic subject') particulars are the substances, and in another sense (i.e. 'essence') universals are. Aristotle's doctrine of first and second substance in the *Categories* might suggest this solution, though it is not the solution he actually adopts there.[11]

It is striking that in Book vii Aristotle denies himself any solution that appeals *at the outset* to multivocity. In vii 1 he begins by remarking that the first type of being signifies 'what it is and this' (*ti esti kai tode ti*, 1028a11–12); and so he already combines the criteria that suggest multivocity.[12] He speaks of substance as a 'definite subject' that is 'the substance and the particular' (1028a26–7); but he appeals no less clearly to the connexion between substance and essence. He does not at all suggest that different types of substance might display the different types of priority. It would have been easy for Aristotle to add 'We have distinguished first and second substances elsewhere', if he had wanted to appeal to multivocity; and so his silence about multivocity at this stage is probably the result of deliberate choice.

He remains silent about it in his formulation of the main question. In vii 2 he lists the diverse candidates for substance; but then he begins Chapter 3 with a new list:

Substance is spoken of, if not in several ways, at any rate in four main cases. For in fact the essence, the universal, and the genus seem to be the substance of each thing, and the fourth of these is the subject. (1028b33–6)[13]

He groups the first three ostensible criteria together, in contrast to the fourth, and so offers two main criteria, as though they are clearly criteria for the same thing (cf. 1042a12–16).[14] His formulation of the question is most misleading unless he intends the reader to avoid relying on assumptions about multivocity.

The difference between Aristotle's earlier treatments of substance and the presentation of the issues in vii 1–3 shows how he thinks he should conduct this part of the science of being.[15] He turns away from a merely dialectical solution, by refusing to exclude views simply because they offend common sense; hence he does not argue from agreed examples. Nor does he appeal, as ordinary dialectic might, to multivocity. Substances may still turn out to be multivocal; but such a claim should result from the argument, and it should not be imported at the outset from reflexion on common beliefs.

While Aristotle avoids some moves that belong to ordinary dialectic, he also relies on moves that belong to strong dialectic, and so have a proper place in first philosophy. In Book iv he finds that talk and knowledge of being must be about persistent subjects with essential properties; and he sees that different candidates for substance reflect different attempts to satisfy this demand. The four ostensible criteria for substance turn out to presuppose these two basic demands on being. If we can see what satisfies the demands, we can justly claim to have found genuine substances—not just those recognized by common sense, but those that should be recognized in a science of being.

Aristotle avoids the appeal to multivocity because it conceals apparently genuine questions. If we argue, by appeal to multivocity, that particulars are substances because they are subjects and hence are prior in being, and that universals are substances because they are essences and hence are prior in knowledge and definition, we still have not solved all the puzzles. For the remarks (in vii 1) on priority suggest that the same things should be prior in all the different ways; and if this is true, then there will after all be just one correct account of substance, and we will miss it if we begin by assuming multivocity.

Moreover, by avoiding any initial appeal to multivocity, Aristotle actually stays closer to common beliefs and to the history of metaphysical speculation. There seems to be a significant dispute about whether matter or form, particular or universal, is substance, and we do not seem to dissolve the question if we say that the different candidates satisfy different accounts of what a substance is. It still seems reasonable to ask which of the accounts is the correct or basic account, and which candidate is the genuine substance.[16]

If some one type of substance satisfies all the criteria, we can defend an aspect of common sense that may otherwise seem indefensible. The puzzles about substance puzzle us partly because we have a fairly firm conviction that commonsense objects such as horses, trees, and men— the first substances of the *Categories*—are in some way basic realities; we do not want them reduced to temporary modifications of matter or to temporary instantiations of universals. If, however, we recognize two multivocal types of substance meeting different criteria, we may well find that the commonsense objects fall unsatisfactorily in the middle; they may seem to be neither the clearest subjects nor the clearest essences. But if we insist that the best candidate for substance must satisfy both criteria, then the commonsense objects may do better. Though first philosophy does not confine itself to the common beliefs— or rather, because it does not confine itself to them—its defence of them may be better than any defence that ordinary dialectic can offer.

110. SUBSTANCE AS SUBJECT

At the end of vii 2 Aristotle distinguishes different views about the types of substances there are; and immediately he sketches in outline his own view of what substance is (1028b27–32). The different views are the ones that raised the puzzles in Book iii; and Aristotle does not answer the puzzles immediately. Though his initial sketch takes him a mere fifteen lines, the questions it raises require considerable further discussion before its correctness is clear. As Books iii and iv have suggested, the preliminary questions raised by the puzzles need to be discussed, so that false assumptions about the questions do not lead to misconstrual of the puzzles. In this case the false assumptions concern the interpretation of the subject-criterion and the relation between subject and essence. The task of removing these false assumptions occupies Aristotle for the rest of Book vii.

Far from suggesting that substances are multivocal, Aristotle argues very briefly for one univocal outline account of substance, and for the allegedly successful candidate for substance. He claims that the subject-criterion tells us what substance is, and he suggests that form is the candidate that best meets the subject-criterion. He implies that only one criterion needs to be considered, and that this one criterion leads to only one successful candidate.

It is reasonable to begin by discussing the subject-criterion. The Presocratics conceive substance as the persisting subject, and therefore identify substance with matter (983b6–18). Aristotle himself recognizes the importance of a basic subject (1007a20–b1). In Chapter 1 he suggests that a basic subject is a particular substance such as a particular man (1028a25–8). This suggestion runs ahead of the argument; for since the criterion is still unclear, he cannot justify a decision about the candidates. In Chapter 3 he affirms the correctness of the subject-criterion, and prepares to clarify it.

He presents the outline answer as a consequence of the subject-criterion, suitably interpreted:

Now the subject is that of which the other things are said, but which itself is not said of any other thing; hence we must define it first, since the first subject seems to be substance most of all. Now matter, shape, and the thing composed from them are called ⟨the first subject⟩ in three different ways. (By 'matter' I mean, e.g., bronze; by 'shape' the arrangement of the figure; and by 'thing composed from them' the statue, the compound.) And so if form is prior to matter, and more of a being, it will also, by the same argument, be prior to the thing composed from both. We have now said in outline, then, what substance is: it is what is not ⟨said⟩ of a subject but what has the other things ⟨said⟩ of it. (1028b36–1029a9)

The first sentence of the passage specifies the subject-criterion through the 'predication-formula', describing the subject as the ultimate bearer of predicates.[17] In speaking of substance 'most of all' and of the 'first' or 'primary' subject, Aristotle implies that one substance can be more or less a substance than another.[18] To identify the highest grade of substance, he augments the subject-criterion; and he concludes that substances of the highest grade are the subset of subjects that are primary subjects. If there are primary subjects, they must meet some further condition besides the predication-formula, which simply picks out subjects. Some subjects must be prior to others, in one or more of the three ways distinguished in Chapter 1; these are the primary subjects.

Aristotle now strongly suggests that form is a primary subject, and indeed prior to matter and compound. In claiming that form is the successful candidate, and at the same time accepting the subject-criterion, he implies that the form satisfies the subject-criterion.

Aristotle never rejects this outline answer, or the claims of form to be the successful candidate. But both the answer and the candidate seem highly controversial, and Aristotle realizes this. We will have a better view of the direction of his whole argument about substance if we raise some of the objections to the answer and to the candidate, and see what Aristotle must say to meet the objections.

111. STRATEGY

The major criteria for substance seem to challenge different parts of Aristotle's outline answer. The essence-criterion seems to lead to the universal, and therefore to the genus, which is more universal than the species (cf. 998b14–19); but the subject-criterion seems to lead to the particular. If one criterion requires substance to be a generic universal, and another requires it to be a basic particular, no one candidate seems to satisfy both criteria.

The outline answer is therefore surprising, because it seems to attend exclusively to the subject-criterion, but ought to attend to the essence-criterion. The view that both criteria ought to be considered leads naturally to the conclusion that substances must be multivocal, since it is not clear how the two criteria could be criteria for the same thing.

To reject the resort to multivocity, and to defend the outline answer, Aristotle must argue that (*a*) an essence need not be a universal, or that (*b*) a subject need not be a basic particular. In fact he argues for a version of both claims. First he argues that a subject need not be the sort of basic particular that matter is. Next he argues that the essence need not be a universal. If the two criteria can be reinterpreted in these ways, the outline answer is more plausible than it seemed.

Aristotle's suggestion that form is substance is also controversial. He has given no argument for the suggestion, and his discussion of substance in earlier works does not clearly support it.[19] His earlier works do indeed suggest that form is essence; and hence he might reasonably suggest that form is substance if he were appealing to the essence-criterion. However, he actually defends form by appeal to the subject-criterion, which does not seem to favour it.[20]

The claims of form to be substance will be far more plausible if the two criteria for substance are reinterpreted in the way that favours the outline answer. The right reinterpretation, Aristotle thinks, will show that form is both the right sort of subject, satisfying the essence-criterion, and the right sort of essence, satisfying the subject-criterion. Later in Book vii it turns out that the particular form satisfies both criteria, and therefore is substance.

In these ways the outline answer presented at the beginning of Chapter 3 introduces the whole argumentative strategy of Aristotle's discussion. He sees that his outline is brief and controversial, and he seeks to settle the controversy by further explanation.

His strategy results naturally from his attitude to the puzzles that were raised in Book iii and suggested in vii 2. The puzzles raised preliminary questions about the proper criteria for substance; and Aristotle suggests that a reexamination of the criteria will lead to a new attitude to the different candidates. It is easy to suppose that the subject-criterion must favour particular material subjects, and that the essence-criterion must favour universal essences. Either we decide that the puzzles are insoluble, or we resort to multivocity. Aristotle focuses on the preliminary questions about the nature of subjects and essences, and argues that the criteria, rightly understood, allow us a reasonable solution that avoids the puzzles. We need not resort to multivocity if we see that a single account of substance and a single candidate will solve the puzzles.

The emergence of the preliminary questions from the puzzles in Book iii has prepared us for an approach to the puzzles that is characteristic of dialectic in general, but especially appropriate for strong dialectic. Aristotle advises the dialectician to approach the puzzles by 'making a new start', beginning from some assumption that has not been called into question in the arguments leading to the puzzles.[21] He follows this advice in vii 3. The puzzles raise questions about the different candidates, and even about more general conditions for substance— both particulars and universals seem to violate reasonable conditions. But these puzzles have not shown that we should reject the subject-criterion and the essence-criterion.

Moreover, Book iv has given us a special reason for not rejecting these criteria. For study of being qua being has shown that we should recognize subjects with essences; and further study of these criteria for substance should show us how to combine them satisfactorily. On this point first philosophy guides us in choosing the assumptions to be used for the 'new start' in answering the puzzles. We have some argument, apart from common beliefs, for accepting these assumptions as the basis of the argument about substance.

Though Aristotle does not make the progress of his argument clear at each stage, the stages are discernible, and viii 1 marks them in its summary, emphasizing the importance of the discussion of essence (1042a17–21), claiming that the universal is not substance (1042a21) and that the subject is substance (1042a26).[22] We must try to follow the stages of the argument to this conclusion. Though this conclusion is reached in viii 1, the rest of viii and ix are also important, since they explain some of the major claims in vii.[23]

112. SUBJECT AS MATTER

Aristotle begins his defence of the outline answer as soon as he has stated it. First he acknowledges that it needs further explanation.

However, we must not confine ourselves to this answer. For it is inadequate in two ways: first, the answer itself is unclear, and further, matter turns out to be substance. For if this is not substance, it escapes us what other substance there is. For when the other things are removed, nothing ⟨else besides matter⟩ evidently remains. (1029a9–12)[24]

The outline answer is inadequate by itself because it does not justify the claims of Aristotle's candidate. Instead of making it clear why form satisfies the subject-criterion, and therefore counts as substance, the outline answer by itself allows us to claim that either matter is the only substance or there is no substance.[25]

This complaint, however, does not lead Aristotle to reject the outline answer, or to reject the subject-criterion and the predication-formula that support the answer. He must, therefore, intend some reinterpretation that avoids the unwelcome result about matter. The predication-formula must be open to two interpretations, one implying that either matter is substance or nothing is, and the other supporting the claims of Aristotle's own candidate.

The predication-formula suggests quite readily that matter is the only subject. The 'other things' that we remove are the things said of a subject; and their removal is quite reasonable. For the predication-formula requires us to distinguish them from the subject itself (cf. *Catg.* 7a31–b1) if we are to find what satisfies the subject-criterion for substance.

The removal has two stages. First (1029a12–13) we remove the affections, actions and capacities of a body, leaving a body as the subject. The removal certainly means that the affections etc. are not substances. But it also means that the body, in so far as it has these affections, is not a substance; its having these affections does not make it a substance. For the body qua affected is predicated of the body; to speak of the pale body is already to speak of pallor predicated of the body, and hence the pale body, as such, cannot be the subject.

The second stage of removal (1029a14–16) argues that we cannot stop with the subject we have found at the first stage (cf. 1001b26–1002a8). The body as such is analysable into dimensional properties and the subject that they are predicated of, so that the subject bounded by these dimensional properties is substance: 'so that matter must appear the only substance if we examine it this way' (1029a18–19). If we accept the subject-criterion and the predication-formula, then apparently we make matter identical to substance, the only substance, because nothing predicated of matter seems to meet the test for being a subject.

Aristotle *seems* to have applied to his 'ordinary' substances the sort of argument that he normally applies to 'apparent subjects' to show that they are not genuine subjects. We find that a walker or a musician is not a substance because he is not a genuine subject; he can be analysed into a more basic subject, a man, and some non-essential property. We have often noticed that Aristotle's ordinary substances seem to allow the same sort of analysis, into a more basic subject, their matter, and some non-essential property. In vii 3 he sees this point, and uses it to show why matter appears to be the only basic subject, and hence the only real substance. The argument is powerful because it seems to be the one that Aristotle uses in vii 1 to show that walkers are not substances.

In vii 1 he also insists that substance must be independent of, and prior to, non-substance; and in vii 3 he explains why matter meets this condition:

By 'matter' I mean what in itself is neither said to be something, nor said to be of some quantity, nor said to be any of the other things by which being is defined. For there is something of which each of these is predicated, and its being is different from that of each of the things predicated; for the other things are predicated of substance, and substance of matter. And so the last thing is in itself neither something nor of some quantity nor any other ⟨of the things mentioned⟩; nor is it ⟨in itself⟩ the negations of these, since the negations as well ⟨as the positive properties⟩ will belong to it coincidentally. (1029a20–6)

A piece of matter, e.g. the lump of bronze that now constitutes this statue, has both positive and negative properties coincidentally. Just as Socrates does not need his particular colour or shape if he is to remain in existence, the lump of bronze needs none of its particular categorial properties—it need not be a statue, or have this shape or colour.[26] It remains the same piece of bronze as long as it retains the capacities for affecting and being affected that are essential to bronze; its being, as Aristotle would say, consists in its capacities.[27]

If one thing is naturally prior to another, then the first can exist without the second, but the second cannot exist without it. A piece of matter seems to meet both these conditions. First, it is separable from an 'ordinary' substance (e.g. the particular statue or man) in the way it is separable from its coincidents. Second, an ordinary substance and its property-instances seem to depend on the existence of a piece of matter, and therefore seem to be predicated of it, whereas it is not predicated of them. Since the matter is naturally prior, it alone seems to satisfy the predication-formula, and hence seems to be the only substance. The same argument seems to show why an ordinary substance and its form do not satisfy the predication-formula.

The subject-criterion, therefore, seems to provide strong reasons for believing that either matter is substance or nothing is. Aristotle appeals to his arguments in Chapter 1; suggests that the predication-formula underlies them; and argues that the predication-formula, as he interprets it, allows matter, at most, to be substance. Since the argument is not obviously invalid and he seems to accept the premisses, he needs to explain why he rejects the conclusion. In particular, he should explain why the predication-formula does not require the unwelcome conclusion.

113. FURTHER TESTS FOR SUBSTANCE

Aristotle insists that matter cannot be the only substance:

And so, if we study it from this point of view, the result is that matter is substance; but that is impossible. For being separable and being a this also seem to belong to substance most of all; hence the form and the compound would seem to be substance more than matter is. (1029a26–30)

Attention to separability and thisness is supposed to show that form and compound are substances to a higher degree than matter; and we have seen (1029a1–2) that degrees of substance correspond to more and less primary subjects. Separability and thisness should therefore distinguish primary subjects from other subjects. These tests should not replace the subject-criterion; and they should still imply that something is a substance if and only if it is a subject satisfying the predication-formula. They ought, moreover, to show us what is wrong with the argument that makes matter the only substance; if we simply find other powerful arguments for treating form and compound as substances, we have raised a further puzzle.

At this point Aristotle does not explain how he understands 'this' and 'separable', or how he thinks attention to these features of substance will challenge the argument for matter. Instead, he ends the chapter by reasserting that matter, form, and compound are all substances:

We should dismiss the substance composed of both—I mean the one composed of matter and form—since it is posterior and clear. And matter is also evident in a way. But we should examine the third ⟨type of substance⟩, since this raises the most puzzles. (1029a30–3)

The only reason he has given for treating these three as substances is his previous claim that they satisfy the subject-criterion and the predication-formula (1029a2–7). Since, therefore, he reasserts that they are substances, he cannot suppose that the subject-criterion and the predication-formula really make matter the only possible substance. He ought to show how form meets these tests for substance and turns out to be a more primary subject than matter.

This conclusion of vii 3 needs emphasis, because Aristotle recalls and uses it later in his argument about substance. He accepts the three candidates for substance (1035a1–2; cf. *DA* 412a6–9), and reaffirms that they satisfy the subject-criterion (1042a26–31). Form is a subject, and it is a primary substance because it is a this (1038b4–6, 1042a28–9, 1049a34–5; cf. *DA* 412a7–9). Since it is not obvious how form is a subject, Aristotle is quite right to say that it raises the most puzzles.[28]

To resolve the puzzles he does not explain his claims about thisness and separability, but turns instead to the discussion of essence as a criterion for substance (1029b1–3). He does not forget the point of his argument, however. For he remarks in Chapter 13 that he has now finished his discussion of the subject-criterion and the essence-criterion, and that he has found two types of subjects—the this (i.e. the form) and the matter (1038b5–6).[29] This same distinction between two types of subject is drawn in ix 7 (1049a27–36), where the first kind of subject is again called a this (1049a28), and in the second case the item predicated of matter is called a form and a this (1049a35). In both passages Aristotle implies that the first type of subject is also the second type of item predicated, and that it is a form.[30] Elsewhere too, he claims that the form is a this (1042a28–9); his claim is only to be expected, since in vii 3 he insists that form is the best candidate for being the sort of subject that is substance.

Aristotle's discussion of essence, then, should show how form is subject and substance; and in the course of the argument he should also undermine the argument for matter in Chapter 3, since otherwise he will create a new puzzle.

114. ESSENCE AND SUBJECT

Aristotle justifies his attention to essence by appeal to his normal method of proceeding from what is knowable to us to what is knowable by nature (1029b3–12).[31] The notion of essence is reasonably familiar, and appropriate for the sort of dialectical discussion found in the *Topics*. Aristotle begins with some 'logical' discussion of it, the sort of thing to be expected in pure dialectic (1029b13; cf. 1041a28); he introduces this dialectical discussion by considering the use of a common expression, 'in itself' (1029b13–14).

But he soon turns from purely dialectical discussion to a different sort of argument, asking us to consider both 'how we ought to speak' and 'how things are' (1030a27–8). 'How we ought to speak' is the concern of pure dialectic; and from this point of view, everything that we can define as being a certain way 'in itself' counts as having an essence. 'How things are' is the concern of strong dialectic, practised by first philosophy; and from this point of view, essence belongs in the primary way only to substances and thises (1030a28–32).[32]

This claim explains why clarification of the essence-criterion should clarify the subject-criterion, and therefore explains why discussion of the essence-criterion precedes the clarification of the subject-criterion. A proper grasp of the essence-criterion should lead us to a certain type of basic subject. The essence of x, as Book iv has understood it, is the property of x that makes x the same subject in different predications—the property that x must retain to remain in existence. To find something that has an essence is to find a subject; some subjects will have essences in their own right, and others will not. If, for instance, the persistence of x consists partly in the existence of y, but the persistence of y does not consist partly in the persistence of z (whether or not z = x), y has an essence in its own right, and x has an essence only because of y. If we examine essence according to 'how things are', not simply according to 'how we ought to speak', we ought to find the things that have essences in their own right.

Aristotle approaches this question by beginning from pure dialectic, and asking whether there is such a thing as the essence of pale man and of similar compounds of substance and non-substance (1029b22–7). At first the answer seems to be clearly Yes. If the essence of something is simply what is specified in its definition, it seems obvious that pale man has an essence, since we can say what a pale man is 'in himself'. From the purely dialectical point of view, there is no difficulty; and in the *Topics* Aristotle suggests no reason for discrimination between items in different categories.

In the *Metaphysics*, however, he requires a substance to be a genuine basic subject, not simply a subject recognized by grammar or common sense. In Chapter 1 he contrasts men with walkers, remarking that a walker has something else—the substance and the particular—as its subject, since the walker is not spoken of without this subject (1028a20–8). The fact that the walker is not spoken of without its subject shows that it is not separable in the way a substance is (cf. 1028a22–4, a28–9, a33–4).

This contrast is relevant to essence; for a thing's essence includes properties that it must retain if it is to persist through time and change. Since a walker cannot persist without being (e.g.) a man, he has no genuine essence of his own; his persistence depends on the persistence of some more basic subject independent of him. If the man is not similarly dependent on some more basic subject independent of him, he has a genuine essence.

If we recognize an essence corresponding to every account of what something is, and we allow that something persists just as long as its essence persists, then we must allow a surprisingly large number of things to come to be and to perish. If a pale man ceases to be pale, then the essence of the pale man perishes, and the pale man perishes. We are inclined to say that in fact nothing has really perished; all that has happened is that a man has ceased to be pale. If we say this, however, we must claim that what primarily has the essence is the man, not the pale man as such; pale men, as such, are not the sorts of things that come to be, persist, and perish.[33]

Aristotle claims that walkers are not separable in the way men are; and his argument about essence explains that claim too, since the particular walker depends on the particular man for his survival, but the particular man does not depend on the particular walker. So far, as we expect, the basic subject turns out to be separable. It also turns out to be a this; for Aristotle claims that the basic subject, the primary bearer of an essence and definition, must be a this (1030a2–6).[34]

In vii 1 substance is said to signify the this as well as the what-it-is (1028a11–12); the answer to the 'What is it?' question is supposed to pick out substance (1028a13–20); and the substance is the particular (*to kath'hekaston*, 1028a27) that is the 'definite subject' (a26–7) for such things as walkers and healthy things. A this must be a basic subject, the sort of thing that was described in the *Analytics* as something that is what it is 'not by being something else' (*APo* 83a9–14). The same contrast between different ways something can be what it is is marked in *Metaphysics* vii 1 as the contrast between 'being something' (applying to non-basic subjects) and 'being unconditionally' (applying to substances) (1028a29–31).[35]

In Chapter 4 Aristotle explains that the thises, the basic subjects, are those that have the primary essential properties. The description that picks out a this is the one that correctly answers the 'What is it?' question, and we answer this question by identifying the properties whose persistence is the persistence of the subject. Since the persistence of the musician depends on the persistence of the man, but the persistence of the man is independent of the persistence of the musician, the man has the primary essential properties, and therefore he is (as far as this argument goes) the basic subject and the this.

115. A REVISED CRITERION FOR SUBSTANCE

Aristotle connects his discussion of essence, subject, substance, and thisness with the argument of Chapter 3, by reintroducing the predication-formula.

The essence is what a this is; but whenever one thing is said of another, it is not what a this ⟨is⟩, if being a this belongs only to substances. (1030a3–6)

. . . and such ⟨i.e. primary⟩ are however many things are spoken of not by one thing being said of another. Hence essence will belong to none of the things that are not species of genera, but to these alone, since they seem to be spoken of not in accordance with participation and affection nor as a coincident. (1030a10–14)

Satisfaction of the predication-formula seems to be necessary and sufficient for having an essence and so being a this.

This appeal to the predication-formula may puzzle us. As he says of another dialectical argument, he seems to have taken a different route that has brought him back to the same place (*EN* 1097a24). In Chapter 3 he seems to argue that the search for a basic subject leads to matter. Grammar seems to make walkers and musicians subjects; but common sense recognizes that they are not genuine subjects in the way that men or horses are. The question is whether common sense can defend this distinction without being forced to go further and admit that men are not genuine subjects either.

The argument in Chapter 4 takes one new turn, which at first only increases the puzzle. For Aristotle now seems to insist that a this and a primary subject must satisfy the predication-formula; but in vii 3 the predication-formula seemed to make matter the only substance, and thisness was supposed to show how form and compound would be substances to a higher degree than matter. Moreover, Aristotle implied that form and compound did not satisfy the predication-formula; for he said that substance is predicated of matter (1029a23–4), and even if he had not said so it would seem obvious that 'the bronze is a statue' must express such a predication.[36]

If the predication-formula makes matter the only substance, and thisness requires satisfaction of the predication-formula, appeal to thisness will apparently not reveal any substances other than matter. If, on the other hand, thisness does not imply satisfaction of the predication-formula, being a this seems neither necessary nor sufficient for being a substance; and if it excludes satisfaction of the predication-formula, no this can be a substance.

The predication-formula, however, was said to be insufficient by itself and unclear (1029a9–10), leaving itself open to different interpretations; and we should now be able to say what the unclarity is. If the predication-formula implies that thisness and separability are further conditions beyond satisfaction of the formula, but also implies that they are just the same condition as satisfaction of the formula, it cannot be the same formula that has both implications. Hence the original formula must be ambiguous between two different formulae with different implications.

Aristotle suggests what the different formulae might be, when he says that the primary objects of definition 'are spoken of not by one thing being said of another' (1030a10–11), instead of saying simply that they are not said of another thing. The two different predication-formulae implicitly distinguished here are these:

1. The broad predication-formula: x is a substance if and only if x is not predicated of anything else, as, e.g., the statue is predicated of the bronze in 'The bronze is a statue'.
2. The narrow predication-formula: x is a substance if and only if x is not spoken of by y being predicated of z (whether or not y = x), as, e.g., the musician is spoken of by musicality being predicated of the man.

If something can satisfy the narrow formula without satisfying the broad formula, then the admission that something is predicated of matter does not imply that it is not a substance. The argument for identifying matter with substance is sound, if the broad formula is assumed; but if the narrow formula is assumed, the argument has not been shown to be sound.

This difference between the broad and the narrow formula explains why the argument about essences and basic subjects might not lead to the identification of matter with the basic subject and substance. In finding which things have essences in their own right, and which have essences because of something else, we should rely on the narrow formula, not the broad formula. For the broad formula does not imply that the thing predicated essentially depends on the subject it is predicated of; but in the narrow formula the extra phrase 'spoken of not by one thing being said of another' implies exactly this essential dependence. Pale men are essentially one thing said of another; that is what their being consists in, because they depend on the more basic subject. If the bronze is a statue, however, it does not follow that the statue depends on the bronze; appeal to the narrow formula does not force us to agree that matter is the only substance.

If Aristotle intends the narrow formula, he is entitled to claim that its requirements coincide with those of separability and thisness.[37] The man is separable from, and naturally prior to, the musician, in so far as this man can exist without being this musician but the musician cannot exist without being this man. A man is a this and a musician is not, if a man is not, but a musician is, spoken of by one thing being said of another. The test for thisness expresses the demand that substance should be prior in account and knowledge.[38]

Aristotle has good reason, then, for assuming that thisness and separability pick out the same candidates for substance, and that the subject-criterion makes them reasonable tests for substance.

116. A PRELIMINARY SOLUTION OF THE PUZZLES

If this is right, then Aristotle's discussion of essences and primary subjects in vii helps to solve the puzzle he has raised. In Chapter 3 he suggested that the predication-formula is correct; that it is not equivalent to the requirement for thisness and separability; and that it makes matter the only substance. We now see that the last two claims are true only for the broad formula, and that the first is true for the narrow formula. The narrow formula, introduced in Chapter 4, is equivalent to the requirement for thisness and separability. The introduction of these requirements at the end of Chapter 3 suggests that Aristotle accepts the narrow rather than the broad formula.

This conclusion is important for our estimate of the strategy of Book vii. For if only the broad formula captured the subject-criterion, it would have been quite odd of Aristotle to end Chapter 3 by reaffirming both the subject-criterion and the claims of form and compound to be substance; for the broad formula undermines these claims. We would perhaps have to conclude that Aristotle abandons the subject-criterion, even though he clearly speaks as though he accepts it. If, however, the narrow formula captures the predication-formula, the subject-criterion may not make matter the only substance, and so Aristotle may be right to imply that form and compound satisfy the subject-criterion.

Aristotle still accepts the subject-criterion. We have not been convinced yet that form and compound satisfy the subject-criterion, or that form satisfies it better than matter and compound do. Since the form was his favoured candidate, and since he takes it to be separable and a this, he implies that it satisfies the narrow predication formula. He has not argued for this implicit claim; it may turn out that form depends essentially on some more basic subject in a way that undermines its claim to satisfy the subject-criterion. But it does not seem hopeless for Aristotle to try to convince us of his claims; for the narrow predication-formula offers an interpretation of the subject-criterion that might support his claims.[39]

The discussion of essence in vii 4 defines more exactly what must be proved about form. An essence belongs to whatever has a definition; but only a primary thing, not one thing said of another, has a definition. What has the essence is the primary thing that persists; this is the basic subject, and so it is the substance. Hence the search for the primary bearers of essences leads us back to the primary subjects, which are substances. The secondary things will depend on substances for their essences. This claim supports the assumption of vii 1, that such apparent subjects as walking (a non-substance) and the walker (a coincidental combination) depend for their essence on the primary subject with the primary essence.

The claim about essence is metaphysical, and so cannot be proved by ordinary dialectic, because it rests on views about how things really are. It is reasonable to claim that some things will have essences primarily, other things secondarily. But it is not clear what the primary things with essence are. Aristotle speaks as though they are the items in his category of substance—men, horses, etc. But he has given no adequate reason for treating these as the primary subjects with essences.

117. ESSENCE AS PARTICULAR

In vii 4 Aristotle argues that the primary bearers of essences are the primary subjects, and hence the substances.[40] In vii 6 he argues further that the primary subjects and their essences are really the same, so that in a way it is misleading to distinguish the bearer of the essence from the essence it bears. This claim is introduced in the report of two common beliefs: 'Each thing seems to be nothing other than its own substance, and the essence is said to be the substance of each thing' (1031a17–18).

We may suspect an equivocation here; the first claim seems to refer to substance as subject, but the second to substance as essence. Aristotle's argument, following his strategy in Book vii, seeks to show that no equivocation is involved. In Chapter 1 he speaks as though the same thing would be both a this and an essence. In Chapter 3 he claims that form, the most plausible candidate for meeting the essence–criterion, meets the subject–criterion. In Chapter 6 he supports this claim by arguing that the primary subjects must be identical to their essences.

In Chapter 4, Aristotle prepares for his claim about substance and essence, by distinguishing primary from secondary bearers of essences; and the conclusion of Chapter 6 observes that distinction.

Clearly, then, in the case of the primary things, those spoken of in themselves, a thing and its essence are one and the same. And it is evident that the sophistical refutations aimed against this position are all resolved by the same solution that solves the puzzle of whether Socrates and his essence are the same; for there is no difference in the ⟨assumptions⟩ from which one would ask ⟨the sophistical questions and the questions about Socrates⟩ or in the ⟨premises⟩ from which one would find a solution. (1032a4–10)[41]

The 'primary things' are 'spoken of in themselves', and so not 'by one thing being said of another'. They therefore satisfy the narrow predication-formula, and so satisfy the subject-criterion. These subjects are identical to their essences.

This passage suggests that Socrates, taken to be a 'primary thing', is identical to his essence; but we may find it difficult to identify a particular with its essence. For we may suppose that essences are properties; properties are universals; only universals can be identical to universals; and therefore only universals can be identical to their essences.[42] It follows that, if substances are identical to their essences, only universals can be substances.

If Aristotle means this, however, he damages his argument. For the things that are identical to their essences are primary and intrinsic beings (1031b13–14, 1032a4–6); these primary and intrinsic beings should be the things so described in Chapter 4 (1030a7–14); these are substances (1030a19, 23); and substances are thises (1030a3–7, 19). Moreover, Aristotle has already committed himself to a definite view about the sorts of things that are thises. In Chapter 1 he connects substance, this, and particular. In Chapter 3 thisness and separability imply that the form and the compound are substances, and therefore subjects, more than matter is; and the subjects recognized so far have been particulars.

If Aristotle does not intend the primary and intrinsic beings to be particular subjects, he has misled us; for in Chapter 4 the primary beings seemed to be thises and particulars, and if this is not true in Chapter 6 also, the argument has gone strangely off course. Throughout the argument so far he has assumed both that substance is the particular subject, and that the subject-criterion and the essence-criterion must pick out the same candidate. If Chapter 6 is to advance his argument, he must explain how a particular can be identical to its essence.

He must therefore explain how the essence can be a particular. For, as Aristotle conceives identity, identical things must come to be and perish at the same time (cf. 1003b29–30); but a universal exists in more than one particular, and therefore is not necessarily destroyed when any one particular is destroyed. Aristotle's conception of essence, then, must allow particular as well as universal essences. And indeed he seems to recognize them both, when he says, '. . . the substance of one thing is one, and things whose substance is numerically one are numerically one' (1040b17).[43] Since what is numerically one is a particular, and 'substance of' here means 'essence of', Aristotle implies that there are particular essences.

A particular essence cannot be the same as an essential property. Socrates' essential properties are all those whose instantiation constitutes the continued existence of Socrates—man, animal, and any others that may belong to Socrates in particular. Since these universals exist even if Socrates does not, he cannot be identical to them. But it is easier to say he is identical to the particular instances of these universals that correspond to his essential properties; for his existence consists in the existence of these particular instances.

118. ESSENCE AS SUBJECT

If this is Aristotle's conception of particular essences, then his claim that a particular is identical to its particular essence seems plausible, even unexciting. His arguments for the identity of subject and essence are fairly obscure, but their point is reasonably clear.[44] He argues that if something is an object of knowledge, and to know it is to know its essence, then its essence cannot be different from it (1031b6–7, 20–2). This claim is not simply that knowing the essence is a means to knowing the subject (as knowing about quadrilaterals might be a means to knowing about squares). Aristotle claims that the knowledge of x is just knowledge of what x is, the essence of x, and it is hard to see how knowledge of x could consist wholly in knowledge of something else, y; for x and y will have different properties, and our knowledge of y will leave out some properties of x or include some properties that x lacks.

A further argument shows that some things must be identical to their essences on pain of an infinite regress (1031b28–1032a4). The absurdity of taking the essence to be non-identical to its bearer appears if we give the essence a name—suppose we call the essence of F 'EF'. We then have to ask what the essence of EF is; and when we find this (call it 'EEF') we can ask what the essence of EEF is, and so on (1031b28–30). Once we see the absurdity of the result we may say that EF is really just the same as EEF; but then why should we not admit from the start that F is identical to EF? We have been forced into absurdity by the assumption that the essence of something cannot be identical to its bearer.

The argument so far seems to imply that any knowable subject is the same as its essence. It is rather surprising, then, that Aristotle seems to limit the conclusion to primary and intrinsic things, and to reject it for coincidental things such as musicians and pale men (1031b22–4). Why should a pale man not also be the same as the essence of pale man?

Aristotle does not, however, really deny that the pale man is identical to his essence, if that claim is properly understood; he claims that the pale man is not identical to *his own* essence, in so far as the essence he is identical to is partly the essence of something else (the man).[45] The arguments about primary subjects in Chapter 4 help to elucidate this claim. The pale man's existence and survival consist partly in the existence and survival of something else, the man; and he is different from the pale man in so far as he can exist and survive without remaining pale. In Chapter 4 Aristotle describes this difference by saying that the man has an essence in the primary way. In Chapter 6 he describes the same difference by saying that the man is identical to his essence, whereas the pale man depends for his essence on the essence of the man who is not essentially pale. Both arguments isolate the primary subjects and the primary essences.

Aristotle reasonably concludes that the primary essences belong to 'species of genera' (1030a11–14), because these are the genuine kinds of things that exist, and their members are the genuine instances of coming to be and perishing.[46] We think there is good reason to recognize horses rather than pale horses or pale things as natural kinds. If the pale horse 'perishes' and the horse does not perish, we say that nothing has really perished, and that the alleged perishing is just an alteration in a more basic subject. In saying this we assume that more important laws and regularities are associated with something's being and remaining a horse than with its being and remaining pale or a pale horse. A subject that is identical to its own essence, and does not depend on the essence of anything else, undergoes genuine coming to be and perishing; its coming into existence and going out of existence are not merely an alteration of some more basic subject.

If a subject does not depend on some more basic subject for its coming to be and perishing, then it has an essence, and indeed is an essence, in its own right. Hence it is not spoken of 'by one thing being said of another'; and so it counts as a subject according to the narrow predication-formula, which gives the preferred interpretation of the subject-criterion. Particular essences turn out to be basic subjects.

119. THE PROGRESS OF THE ARGUMENT

Aristotle has argued that the claim of essence to be substance is well founded, and that it supports the claim of the subject to be substance. Essence was introduced with the universal and the genus, in contrast to the subject (1028b34–5); and so we might have thought it would support different candidates for substance. Aristotle claims that in fact it supports the same candidates, since the primary subjects are identical to their essences. If we ask what something really is, what its essence is, the answer may pick out an item in any of the categories—this is why Aristotle allows essences for non-substances. But if we ask what things in general really are, we look for some basic underlying item. The Presocratics were searching inarticulately for this; and Aristotle argues that this search for essence brings us back to basic subjects. The connexion between basic subjects and essences becomes clear when we inquire into either of them.[47]

The strategy suggested by this argument explains how Aristotle goes beyond ordinary dialectic. In *Metaphysics* iv he insisted that we must recognize basic subjects that are the same when different properties are truly predicated of them. In vii 6 he adds that these basic subjects are identical to their essences, and suggests more clearly how the essences are to be identified. He follows common beliefs in choosing putative examples of substances (cf. 1029a33–4), but he does not assume that they are really substances. Equally, he has endorsed form as the successful candidate for substance, and so has implied that it satisfies both the subject-criterion and the essence-criterion. But he has shown neither that the forms he recognizes satisfy these criteria, nor that they coincide with the commonsense examples of substances. They count as substances only if they correspond to natural kinds embodying significant laws and regularities.

Aristotle, then, has not yet justified the claim of one or another candidate to be substance. Still, he has shown what is needed to justify the claim. Metaphysical argument shows that we must look for persisting subjects, and that these must be identical to essences that correspond to natural kinds. The *Analytics* insisted that a genuine subject must have essential properties that explain its other properties.[48] If the *Metaphysics* observes this requirement, it should argue that the favoured subjects have the right explanatory properties. But to say which subjects these are we apparently need more than the abstract metaphysical argument of Book iv.

By the end of vii 6 Aristotle has suggested how first philosophy might solve the puzzles about substance that are raised by his own and other people's views. In looking for the type of being presupposed by the special sciences, we find that we must recognize persistent subjects with essences. In considering the puzzles about substance as subject and as essence, we see that they are really puzzles about the very questions that are raised by the study of being qua being. For our intuitive distinction between men and musicians, and our intuitive belief that substances must be subjects, thises, and essences, are explained on the assumption that we are looking for the basic persistent subjects that first philosophy tells us to look for.

So far, we have not found out what these subjects and essences are. Indeed, we may be inclined to make a typical complaint about the early stages of an argument that 'makes a new start', according to dialectical rules. In his discussion of happiness Aristotle remarks: 'But, presumably, to say that happiness is the best good is apparently something agreed, and we still feel the lack of a clearer statement of what it is' (*EN* 1097b22–4). A parallel complaint applies at the end of vii 6. Aristotle wants to provide the clearer account; but he also thinks the apparently 'agreed' first steps should not be neglected, or dismissed as platitudes, and that they will help us to reach the clearer account.

11

ESSENCE AND FORM

120. SUBSTANCE AND POTENTIALITY

In *Metaphysics* vii 1–6 Aristotle argues for the coincidence of the subject-criterion and the essence-criterion, and for the identification of substances with primary subjects. He does not confine himself, however, to these general arguments about criteria. He also suggests that form is substance; and if the two criteria coincide, form must be both a particular basic subject and a primary essence. To support this suggestion, he must say more about what form is, and about why it meets both criteria. Especially he must show why it is the sort of explanatory property that is the essence of a basic subject.

At the beginning of vii 13 Aristotle thinks he has done this; for he claims to have shown that a form is a this. He assumes some controversial conclusions, however. For he summarizes his argument by saying that in one case the matter is the subject for the actuality (1038b6); he speaks of actuality, without explanation, when we expect him to speak of form. No explanation is given in vii 7–12, which do not connect form with actuality. An explanation is given, however, in viii–ix; Aristotle defends the identification of matter with potentiality and form with actuality. If we examine this defence before we discuss the rest of the argument in vii, we can also see an important part of the argument for identifying form with essence, and hence with substance.

First, Aristotle has good reasons for identifying the essence of a substance, and so the substance itself, with its persistent potentialities. In *Physics* i he assumes that changes are not random, but all involve the action of one thing on another (*Phys.* 188a31–4) according to definite laws and regularities. This determinist assumption suggests that our description of the elements of the change should pick out the properties involved in the laws explaining the change. Aristotle argues that change requires contraries and a subject, but he does not make it clear why the subject is needed, and how it must be described.

The description he offers is inadequate. For he speaks as though the subject's role in the change is explained by its possession of contrary properties at different times; but the contraries do not properly explain the change. It is insufficient to say, for instance, that a man became musical from being unmusical, since his being unmusical does not explain the change to being musical; he might be entirely unmusical because he is tone-deaf and cannot learn music. A man's potentiality for music is the persistent feature of him that explains why he, rather than the tone-deaf man, becomes musical. But though Aristotle should appeal to potentiality, and though he recognizes its relevance to the analysis of change (191b27–9), he does not see its importance for his claims.[1]

What is missing in *Physics* i is more clearly present in *Metaphysics* iv, in Aristotle's discussion of Protagoras.[2] Protagoras wants to accommodate appearances by allowing things to change enough to make all appearances true. In allowing this, though, he still claims to recognize continuing subjects undergoing the changes. Aristotle replies that Protagoras gives us no reason to suppose that the alleged subject of all the changes in a Protagorean world is really a continuing subject. If it is a continuing subject, it must have the same persistent traits, lasting from one change to the next and making it capable of undergoing both changes; and these persistent traits are its essential properties. Since these persistent traits are potentialities (making the subject capable of undergoing the changes), Aristotle's initial concern with persistent subjects and their essences leads him naturally to a concern with potentiality.[3]

If we see the connexion between potentialities and persisting subjects of change, we can also see why some subjects (e.g. men) are more genuine subjects than others (e.g. musical men). A persistent subject needs a persistent potentiality explaining the changes that happen to it. If we find that rather little is explained by reference to permanent potentialities of musical men as such, and more is explained by reference to permanent potentialities of men as such, we have some reason for thinking that men are more genuine subjects than musical men are. Aristotle claims in *Metaphysics* vii 4–6 that some, but not all, apparent subjects are thises and primary subjects, identical to their essences. If the persistence of explanatory potentialities determines the basic subjects and essences, an account of potentialities should help us to see which essences and which subjects satisfy his conditions.

For these reasons we expect the essence of a persistent subject to be at least partly constituted by its persistent potentialities for change. If, then, the primary subjects that are substances are identical to their essences, they should be at least partly identical to their persistent potentialities. Moreover, if form is to be identified with essence and subject, it should be some sort of potentiality.

121. SUBSTANCE AND ACTUALITY

Another part of Aristotle's argument, however, seems to lead in a different direction; for in viii 2 he identifies substance with actuality (1042b9–11). To provide an analogy with substance (1043a5–7), he mentions different non-substances that come to be when a piece of matter is changed in the appropriate way for the resulting product. A threshold results when a block of stone is put in the right place; a breakfast results when a roll of bread is put on the table at the right time of day; a box results when planks are hammered together, and so on. In each instance the product is defined by the modification of the matter (1042b25–31). These cases provide an analogy with substance:

> From what we have said, it evidently follows, then, that if substance is the cause of a thing's being, we should seek the cause of each thing's being in these ⟨differentiae⟩. Though none of them is substance even when combined ⟨with matter⟩, still it is analogous ⟨to substance⟩ in each case; and just as in substances, what is predicated of the matter is the actuality itself, so also in other definitions ⟨what is predicated⟩ is most of all ⟨the actuality⟩. (1043a2–7)

The actuality that results from the modification of stone is stone placed on the ground before a front door; and this is the cause of its being a threshold.

These examples show how the contrast between matter and form corresponds to the contrast between potentiality and actuality. We find something's constituents, and the modification or arrangement that actualizes them in this particular thing; and then we have found the matter and the form. The examples support Aristotle's identification of form with actuality, in vii 13 (1038b6); in contrast to the matter, identified with potentiality (1042b9–10), he identifies the form with the state resulting from the modification of the matter.

But though it is easy to see why form is identified with actuality, it becomes difficult to see how it could be identified with the primary essence or basic subject. Identification of actuality with form, and of form with substance, seems to imply too general a conception of form, and too lax a standard for being a substance. Breakfast is the modification or actuality of a roll that consists in its being served for a morning meal. If this is all I normally have for breakfast, but one day I leave it and it is served again for lunch, it is no longer breakfast. If actuality and form are substance, we must say that one substance, the breakfast, has perished, and another, the lunch, has come into being. Clearly, however, we believe there is only one continuing substance, the roll, that has simply acquired a new temporal property. If, however, the roll had been made into crumbs after breakfast time, and the crumbs put in the stuffing served at lunch, the roll would have been destroyed even though the crumbs still existed.

The introduction of potentiality and actuality revives the questions that arose about such 'coincidental combinations' as musicians. The musician actualizes a potentiality of a man, but Aristotle does not count him as a new substance. On the other hand, he does count a human being as a new substance because he actualizes a potentiality of flesh and bone. In counting such things as human beings as substances Aristotle rejects Democritus' claim (alluded to in 1042b11–15), that the only substances are atoms, and other apparent substances are mere coincidental combinations of atoms. But since Democritus simply applies to men the sort of analysis that Aristotle applies to musicians, Aristotle should explain how the two cases are different.

He should not simply appeal, as we did in discussing the roll, to intuitions and common beliefs about when some new subject has or has not come into being.[4] Such an appeal is characteristic of pure dialectic; but in the *Metaphysics* Aristotle insists that first philosophy must go beyond pure dialectic, and argue scientifically about how things really are. He needs to say, therefore, apart from intuitions about substance and genuine becoming, which actualities indicate substances and which do not.

It is initially difficult, then, to see how Aristotle can identify actuality with form and substance; and even if his argument succeeds, he must still reconcile its conclusion with our apparent reasons for identifying substance with potentiality. He seeks to remove these difficulties by explaining potentiality and actuality more fully, and restricting them in ways that allow the right connexions with matter and form.

122. POTENTIALITY

Aristotle sees that he must restrict the range of potentiality and actuality. In his initial series of examples he assumes, for instance, that breakfast is an actuality of this roll. Putting the roll on the breakfast table certainly realizes a possibility for the roll; and so it clearly actualizes a potentiality of the roll if possibility is sufficient for potentiality. Aristotle, however, denies this account of the connexion between possibility and potentiality, and mentions three cases where he thinks it gives us the wrong result:

1. If it is possible for x to change into y and for y to change into z, then it is possible for x to change into z. And if possibility for change makes one thing the matter of another, it will follow that if x is the matter of y and y of z, then x is the matter of z. But Aristotle disagrees:

'We must state the most proximate causes. For instance, what is the matter ⟨of a man⟩? Not fire or earth, but the special matter' (1044b1–3).

2. If possibility for change to F implies potentiality for F, then if it is possible for x to become F and possible for x to become the contrary of F, x has the two potentialities. But Aristotle denies that a normal body is potentially both healthy and sick:

There is a puzzle about how the matter is related to contraries. If, for instance, a body is potentially healthy, and illness is contrary to health, is the body therefore potentially both? And is water potentially both wine and vinegar? Perhaps it is the matter of one contrary by having its own ⟨proper⟩ state and form, and of the other by being unnaturally deprived and corrupted. (1044b29–34)

3. If possibility implies potentiality, and potentiality and actuality are matter and form, it follows that x is potentially y and y is the form of x even if the coming into being of y involves the destruction of x. Aristotle rejects the conclusion:

And there is also a puzzle about why wine is not the matter of vinegar, or potentially vinegar, even though vinegar comes from wine, and about why a living man is not potentially a corpse. Perhaps the corruptions are coincidental ⟨to being wine or being a man⟩, and the matter of the animal is itself the potentiality and matter of the corpse by being corrupted, and so also in the case of water and vinegar; for in these cases one thing comes from another ⟨only⟩ in the way night comes from day. And when things change into each other in this way, they must revert to matter; if, e.g., an animal comes from a corpse, the corpse must turn into ⟨more elementary⟩ matter, and then into an animal; and the vinegar must first turn into water and then into wine. (1044b34–1045a6)

Since the substance has to revert to matter, Hotspur 'becomes' food for worms (only in the way that day 'becomes night', without persisting) only after first becoming a corpse.[5]

These results all assume that potentiality is just possibility, and that every realization of a possibility also actualizes a potentiality. If Aristotle can show that this is the wrong conception of potentiality, he can perhaps also defend his identification of substance with actuality, if the apparent examples of actuality without substance rest on the wrong conception of potentiality.

123. POTENTIALITY AND POSSIBILITY

Some of Aristotle's reasons for restricting the range of potentiality reflect its role in the explanation of change. This role becomes clear in his criticism of the Megarians in ix 3; for it is the role that their view of potentiality has to deny. The Megarians' doubts advance Aristotle's argument in the same way as his opponents' doubts advanced it in Book iv; and indeed he sees a close connexion between the Megarian and the Protagorean position. He takes the Megarian doctrine to imply that nothing ever has any unactualized potentialities, since everything is incapable of doing anything except what it is actually doing. He accuses the Megarians of accepting a Protagorean conception of things; for on their view things will not be perceptible or have perceptible qualities except when they are actually being perceived (1047a4–6). Neither the Megarians nor Protagoras can say what makes something a persistent subject receiving different changes, or why this subject is capable of some changes and not of others; for to say these things they would have to recognize something with a stable nature of its own apart from its appearances on different occasions.[6]

Since reference to potentiality explains changes by reference to features of the subject itself, we have reason to say that its potentialities have changed only if it has itself changed: on this view, if x is capable of F at t, and nothing changes in x between t and t1, then x is still capable of F at t1. Between t and t1 the external circumstances may have changed so that x will no longer F, but Aristotle insists that these changes should not be treated as a change in potentiality, since they involve no change in the subject (1046b36–1047a4). The Megarians have to say that when we are not actually seeing, we lose the potentiality to see, and therefore become blind; but in treating potentialities this way, they miss the point of ascribing potentialities to subjects.[7]

The reasons for rejecting the Megarian view of potentiality are also reasons for Aristotle to deny the equivalence of possibility and potentiality; for purely external changes can make something impossible for a subject without changing the subject itself, and some possibilities may be open for a subject without corresponding to any appropriate permanent state. The point of Aristotle's conception is clearer when we see why he believes that possibility is neither necessary nor sufficient for potentiality.[8]

The agent has the potentiality to act on the patient when the patient is in the right conditions.

Necessarily, then, when any subject with a rational potentiality desires ⟨to produce an effect⟩ for which it has a potentiality, and in the way it has it, it produces ⟨the effect⟩. It has the potentiality to produce ⟨the effect⟩ when the patient is present and is in a certain state; otherwise it will not be capable of producing it. We need not add the condition 'if nothing external prevents it'; for it has the potentiality in the way in which it is a potentiality of producing, and it is a potentiality for producing not in all conditions, but in certain conditions, which exclude the presence of external hindrances, since these are excluded when some of the conditions mentioned in the definition are present. Hence even if at the same time one has a wish or an appetite to produce two effects or to produce contraries, one will not produce them. For that is not the way in which one has a potentiality for them, nor is it a potentiality of producing them both at the same time; for it will produce ⟨the effects⟩ it is capable of ⟨only⟩ in this way, ⟨which precludes producing them both at the same times⟩. (1048a13–24)

To say that the agent has the potentiality 'to produce the effect when the patient is present and in a certain state' is to describe the potentiality that the agent has all the time (as long as it does not change), even when the patient is not present or not in the right state.

This description of the potentiality does not restrict the times at which the agent has the potentiality to those at which the patient is present and in the right state.[9] If Aristotle did intend to restrict, by reference to these external conditions, the times at which I have my potentiality, then my potentiality would be relatively transient, and I would lose it when the external conditions changed, even if I did not change.[10] Aristotle, however, intends the clause about external conditions to define a permanent state I have even when external conditions prevent its exercise. If I am a builder, but I lose all my tools and cannot replace them for a week, then for a week it is impossible for me to build; but since I do not change, I do not lose my potentiality to build.[11]

Rational potentialities (e.g. the skill of a craftsman) show why possibility is not only unnecessary, but also insufficient, for potentiality; for Aristotle argues that these potentialities must be acquired by having been previously exercised (1047b31–5; cf. *EN* 1103a26–b2, *EE* 1220b2–3). In this previous exercise I perform an action for which I have not yet acquired the potentiality; if I perform the action, it must have been possible for me to perform it. Possibility, therefore, cannot be sufficient for potentiality.

Aristotle's assumption about potentiality is defensible. If I am thrown into the water, and manage a couple of swimming strokes to get to the side, I have the potentiality for self-preservation, and I exercise it by swimming to the side. It was because my action was self-preservation, not because it was swimming, that some persistent state of mine explained why I did it then. No persistent state equipping me to swim is needed to explain my action; and so it does not actualize a potentiality for swimming. Trained swimmers, however, have a potentiality to swim, not just to preserve their lives, because it is the fact that they are swimming that explains why they do it. They have been trained for swimming, not (except coincidentally) for saving their lives or making money. If this is how Aristotle understands potentiality, then he can fairly deny that actual swimming requires a potentiality to swim.[12]

Potentiality requires more than mere possibility, because it requires reference to a permanent state of the subject that explains the actuality in question.

124. DEGREES OF POTENTIALITY

A subject's potentiality for some actuality is a relatively permanent state of the subject explaining the actuality. Potentialities will differ, then, in so far as they explain actualities in different ways and to different degrees. We saw that Aristotle does not think I have a potentiality to swim just because it is possible for me to swim; for in this case the potentiality for swimming is not the state that explains my swimming. The more closely the potentiality is connected with a determinate actuality, the more reasonable it is to offer the potentiality as an explanation of that actuality.

Aristotle clarifies 'closeness' and 'connexion' by introducing degrees of potentiality.

We must also make distinctions about potentiality and actuality, since just now we were speaking of them without ⟨the appropriate⟩ qualifications. One sort of knowledge is what we mean in saying that human beings know because they are the kind of things that know and have knowledge; another is what we mean in saying that the person who has grammatical knowledge knows. These are capable in different ways—the first because they have the right sort of genus and matter, the second because he can attend to something when he wishes, if nothing external prevents it. A third sort is what we have when we are attending to something, actualizing our knowledge and fully knowing (e.g.) this A. In the first and second case we pass from potentially to actually knowing; but in the first case we do so by being altered through learning, and by frequent changes from the contrary state, while in the second case, of passing from having without actualizing arithmetical or geometrical knowledge to actualizing it, we do so in another way. (*DA* 417a21–b2)

Having a suitable genus and matter for knowing French is a fairly *remote* potentiality (something parallel to what we mean in speaking of a 'remote possibility'), since it does not itself explain my competent speaking of French. The speaking is explained by my more *proximate* potentiality, which is present when I have learnt to speak French.

To convert a remote into a proximate potentiality, learning or training or growth is required; but to actualize a proximate potentiality no further learning is needed (417a32–b12). Actualization requires only the right external condition (in the case of seeing) or this together with the agent's desire (in the case of rational potentialities).

These differences show why a proximate potentiality explains more of an actuality than a remote potentiality explains. To explain someone's being a carpenter by appeal to her remote potentialities (cf. 417b31–2) is not completely useless; for being a carpenter involves the realization of some of her natural skills and talents, and if she had not had these, she could not have become a carpenter, or would not have become the sort of carpenter she is. But since these natural capacities could have been left unactualized, or actualized in other skills besides a carpenter's, appeal to her natural talents does not explain why she has actualized them in this particular sort of skill. To this extent my potentiality to be a carpenter is more remote than my potentiality to have some knowledge (of which carpentry is a possible example).

A proximate potentiality, on the other hand, explains much more of the actuality, leaving less to be explained by external conditions. A normal animal has a natural ability to see, needing only an external object in the right conditions if it is to be actualized; to explain why it sees *this object* we need to say why this object rather than some other is present, but to explain why *it sees* we need only refer to the natural ability and the presence of a suitable object. The more proximate the potentiality we appeal to, the more determinate the features of the actuality we can explain by it. Since we investigate potentialities in order to explain actualities by appeal to persistent states of the subject, we have good reason to identify as many proximate potentialities of the subject as we can.

125. PROXIMATE POTENTIALITY

Aristotle refuses to describe the actualization of a proximate potentiality as a mere alteration.

Nor is there just one way of being affected. While the first type is a destruction of contrary by contrary, the other type is preservation, not destruction, of a potential F by an actual F, when the potential F is ⟨not contrary, but⟩ like the actual F, as a potentiality is like its actuality. For the second case, in which the possessor of knowledge comes to attend to his knowledge, is either not alteration at all—since the addition leads to ⟨the knowledge⟩ itself, and to the actuality—or else it is a different kind of alteration. That is why we should not speak of alteration in the intelligent subject whenever it exercises its intelligence, any more than we should speak of it in the builder whenever he is building. Hence, first, if the understanding and intelligent subject is led from being so potentially to being so actually, we should call this something other than teaching. (417b2–12)

The description of the actualization as a mere alteration leaves out an essential feature of it—the fact that the proximate potentiality explains the actualization. Learning, by contrast, involves alteration of the subject; to explain why I know French it is not enough to appeal to my natural linguistic ability, but we must also appeal to other changes that are not themselves explained by that ability (my having been taught French as opposed to Spanish, for instance).

Still, the same principles that distinguish actualization of a proximate potentiality from learning also distinguish learning from mere alteration; and so Aristotle introduces this as a second case:

Again, if a subject with potential knowledge learns and acquires knowledge from a teacher with actual knowledge, then we should either say that this is not a case of being affected, or that there are two ways of being altered—change into a condition of deprivation, and change into possession of a state and into ⟨the fulfilment of the subject's⟩ nature. (417b12–16)[13]

Though I have no proximate potentiality for speaking French, I have a proximate potentiality for learning a language that I can actualize only by learning some particular language, and my learning French (or German or English) actualizes this proximate potentiality. By contrast, my becoming pale or tanned does not actualize a proximate potentiality; I am not naturally organized for acquiring a particular skin colour, though my natural constitution and environment make it possible for me to become pale or tanned. In this case the transition is merely an alteration; for it is not the actualization of a potentiality for becoming pale or tanned, though it is certainly the realization of a possibility.

These distinctions show why Aristotle has good reason to deny that possibility is sufficient for potentiality. A potentiality for seeing is supposed to explain why an animal sees; seeing is one of the activities that the animal is for. Equally, seeing explains the potentiality for seeing, since the animal is constituted as it is so that it can see. Aristotle's teleology shows him how to identify the proximate natural potentialities; and since he is looking for these, he rightly denies that possibility is sufficient for potentiality. A creature's nature leaves many possibilities open to it, but only some of them reflect its natural potentialities. If its seeing is explained by the presence of organs and traits whose presence is in turn explained by the fact that they result in seeing, then it has the potentiality for seeing.[14] It is equally possible for the creature to go blind; but nothing about it is explained by the fact that it results in blindness; it therefore has no potentiality for going blind.

The same grounds for distinguishing potentiality from possibility explain a distinctive feature of rational potentialities.

Every potentiality involving reason is one and the same potentiality for both contraries, whereas every nonrational potentiality is from just one contrary; what is hot, e.g., is only the potentiality to heat, whereas medical science is the potentiality to produce both illness and health. This is because scientific knowledge is a rational account (*logos*), and the same rational account makes clear both the thing and its privation (though not in the same way), so that in a way it is ⟨the science⟩ of both contraries, but in a way it is the science of the ⟨positive⟩ property, rather than of the privation. Every such science therefore must also be of contraries, but must be in itself the science of one contrary ⟨the positive property⟩, and not in itself the science of the ⟨privation⟩. For the rational account is of one thing in itself, and of the other coincidentally, in a way; for it makes clear the contrary by denial and removal, since the contrary is the primary privation, and the privation is the removal of the ⟨positive property⟩. (1046b4–15)

The potentiality is for the actuality that explains its presence; since doctors learn about drugs because they are useful for healing, not because they are useful for poisoning, the potentiality they acquire is for healing, no matter how they use it. As Plato insists, the doctor 'on the exact account' is a healer not a money-maker, even though the doctor makes money (*Rep.* 342d2–7). In Aristotle's terms, doctors become capable only coincidentally of the other things they become able to do in learning to be doctors.[15]

126. CONDITIONS FOR POTENTIALITY

Similar reasons explain Aristotle's denial of the transitivity of potentiality. Possibility seems to be transitive; if at t1 it is possible for x to become F at t2, and if becoming F at t2 makes it possible for x to become G at t3, then at t1 it is possible for x to become G at t3. If, for instance, it is possible for children to grow up and enter a university, and once they enter a university it is possible for them to graduate, then it is possible all along for them to graduate from a university when they grow up. But Aristotle rejects the parallel inference for potentialities.

The point of his denial is clearest in the examples of production by a craft (1049a5–12). He allows that building materials are potentially a house only when they are all complete and nothing needs to be added, removed, or changed, and they are all ready for the building craft to be applied to them. If the materials are at an earlier stage, and still need the brickmaker's, woodcutter's, and glass-maker's crafts applied to them, Aristotle denies that they are potentially a house, even though it is possible for them to be made into a house. At this stage they are potentially bricks, not potentially a house.[16]

Since natural processes and conditions have an internal, not an external, cause, the account of potentiality is different.

We must distinguish when a thing is potentially, and when it is not, since it is not potentially at just any time. For example, is earth potentially a man, or not? Is it so when it has already become seed, or perhaps not even then? (1048b37–1049a3)

⟨When the origin of becoming⟩ is in the subject itself, ⟨it is potentially⟩ whatever it will be of itself if nothing external prevents it. For example, the seed is not yet ⟨potentially a man⟩, since it must ⟨be put⟩ in something else and changed; but whenever through an origin in itself it is such, then it is potentially a man. In its first condition, it needs another origin ⟨outside itself⟩, just as earth is not yet potentially a statue, since it must change to become bronze. (1049a13–18)[17]

The process or condition is to be explained by the result that will come about from an origin in the subject itself, not by some other result.

Earth is not potentially a man before it is changed, because becoming a man is irrelevant to its movements. Becoming a man is relevant only when earth is suitably combined with other things to produce something with a different nature. A seed is closer to being a man, but not close enough. Before it is united with an egg, its tendency to become a man does not explain how it behaves; though a possible causal sequence will result in a man, the result is not relevant to the seed's origin of change. With organisms the only thing that fulfils the conditions for potentiality is the body of the actual organism; nothing else will be of the right sort through itself and through its own origin of change.

Aristotle infers that matter has life potentially only if it is the natural organic body whose actuality is the soul (*DA* 412a19–22). This body belongs to a normal natural organism that is actually alive; and such a body already has actual life, needing no further changes to make it actually alive. If the only thing that is potentially a living organism is the subject whose movements are *for* the activities of a living organism, then only the body of a living organism satisfies this condition. The characteristics and behaviour of the seed and embryo are explained by reference to their development into an organic body; they are therefore potential organic bodies (412b26–7), but they are not potentially the organisms that have these bodies.[18]

By arguing that not every possibility corresponds to a potentiality Aristotle has shown that his claims about potentiality are not arbitrary, but reflect further claims about the proper explanatory states. If these claims support the recognition of potentialities, they also support his attempt to identify matter and form with potentiality and actuality. If every realization of a possibility corresponds to a new substance, a man becomes a new substance when he becomes pale, and a roll becomes a new substance when it is put out for breakfast; but Aristotle need not recognize all these substances, since he identifies form with actualization of potentiality, not with realization of possibility, and the possibilities in these cases are not potentialities. Some changes, e.g. becoming musical, actualize genuine potentialities, but leave enough of the subject's previous potentialities undisturbed so that they do not imply the existence of a new substance. By appealing to his restricted conception of potentiality Aristotle shows he has some systematic, non-arbitrary reason for denying that these are new substances.

The same restrictions on potentiality allow an answer to one difficulty in identifying matter with potentiality. If potentiality is simply possibility, then wine is potentially vinegar and a man is potentially a corpse or food for worms. If, however, we restrict potentialities in the way Aristotle suggests, we need not recognize these odd potentialities. It is certainly possible to make wine sour, to get vinegar. But this happens because the wine is first changed; and it is changed because it has this material constitution, not because it has the form of wine. In the same way it is not the form of a man that explains why he becomes a corpse; he becomes a corpse, and then food for worms, because of his matter, not because of his form. Hence we need not agree that a man is potentially a corpse; and we need not reject the identification of matter with potentiality.

127. POTENTIALITY WITHOUT CHANGE

If the explanatory character of potentialities distinguishes them from possibilities, it is reasonable to identify a continuing subject with its continuing potentialities. Aristotle identifies potentiality with matter, and form with actuality; but if potentialities are potentialities for change, then actuality, and therefore form, will be some sort of change. This is an unwelcome result for Aristotle, since he identifies form with substance, and therefore with some sort of persistent subject. If the account of potentiality and actuality is to support his claims about form and substance, he needs to loosen the connexion between potentiality and change, and to show that an actuality may be a persistent state rather than a change or episode.

To loosen this connexion, he remarks that the potentiality involving change is not the most useful one for his purposes (1045b36–1046a2), and turns to potentialities for static actualities; for these include the relation of matter and substance (1048b6–9). He argues that F is a proximate potentiality of the subject x for the actuality G if (1) F is a permanent trait of x, making G possible for x in the right conditions, and explaining why G happens, and (2) G also explains why x has F, so that x has F *for* G.

This account of potentiality and actuality extends them in the direction Aristotle wants; for these relations are present not only when x has to change to being G, but also when x is F and G at the same time. Perhaps, for instance, x is G because its constitution is F, so that F makes G possible as the material cause makes a result possible. But equally, the fact that G results from being F explains why x is F, so that G is the final cause of F. Since this relation holds in artifacts and in natural organisms, potentiality and actuality apply here also.[19] A block of stone is a (non-proximate) potential statue before it is carved; but even after it has been carved it still has the appropriate relation to the statue, and is a (proximate) potential statue, even though it now constitutes an actual statue.

The extension of potentiality and actuality from change to conditions involving no change implies that they may express simultaneous, not successive, states of the same subject, by describing the same subject in two different aspects. The statue is an actuality of how the bronze previously was, but also of how it now is, as a constituent of the statue; for the bronze is in its present condition in order to constitute a statue. The potentiality and the actuality are two distinct aspects of the same subject. Hence Aristotle suggests that once we understand potentiality and actuality we will see why form and matter are one (1045b17–23; *DA* 412b6–9).

The example of some artifacts shows how it is reasonable to identify an actuality with a stable condition of a subject. The question is more complicated with organisms (and with some machines), since their existence essentially involves change, and many of their vital activities are intermittent. Aristotle therefore identifies substance and form with *first* actuality, the permanent state of the organism, as opposed to the intermittent vital activities.

Actuality is spoken of in two ways—as ⟨the state of⟩ knowing or as ⟨the activity of⟩ studying. Evidently, then, the soul is the sort of actuality that knowing is. For both being asleep and being awake require the presence of the soul, and being awake corresponds to studying, and being asleep to the state of inactive knowing; moreover, in the same subject the state of knowing precedes the activity. Hence the soul is the first actuality of a body that has life potentially. (*DA* 412a22–8)

In relation to matter this permanent state is actuality, but in relation to particular vital activities it is potentiality; hence it is second potentiality as well as first actuality (*DA* 417a21–9). A living organism has a material body, a collection of tissue, limbs, and organs, that is organized for something. We have previously suggested that it is organized for the vital activities of the organism; but this suggestion needs to be modified, and the modification shows why first actuality is needed.[20]

To explain the particular vital activities of the organism, we must explain why they happen just when they do. The structure and potentialities of the body do not explain this. We must refer to other events, and especially, since we are explaining goal-directed actions, to the properties of the organism that explain them teleologically. These properties belong to the organism's form; for its particular activities are teleologically explicable by reference to its goal-directed properties, and especially to the particular states it has by being an appropriately organized body. The body is organized for the permanent states that are the organism's form; hence these permanent states are the final cause of the material body. The particular vital activities are, from one point of view, the final cause of the form—these are the activities it is for. From another point of view, however, the particular activities are for the continuation of the states that are the form; the form is not merely a potentiality for the activities.

Aristotle therefore has reason to recognize a subject, distinct from the organized material body, that has the proximate potentiality for the vital activities. This subject is the form that coexists with the material body. He is justified in identifying the persistent organism both with the actuality of the organized material body that is potentially alive, and with the potentiality for the vital activities that are the episodes of its life.

128. FORM AS ACTUALITY

We have followed Aristotle's account of potentiality and actuality, to see how far they clarify his claims about form, and support his claim that form is substance.

He claims that actuality is prior in substance to potentiality, because potentiality is for the sake of actuality; we have sight for the sake of seeing, not the other way round, and similarly 'the matter is potential because it might reach the form' (1050a15), not the other way round. The traits and activities that explain teleologically the structure and composition of some body are the actuality for which the body has the potentiality, and they are the form for which the body is the matter.

Substances should be basic subjects, the continuants whose coming to be and perishing are substantial changes, not merely coincidental changes in some more basic subject. In identifying substance with form and form with actuality, Aristotle explains his view of the basic subjects. Their continuity is determined by continuity of form, not by continuity of matter; and form is continuous when the organization, structure, and modifications of the matter are explained by the same teleological laws.

This conception of form and substance supports Aristotle's claim that substance is a cause and origin (1041a9–10).[21] The substance of a house should explain why these bricks and mortar constitute a house (1041b4–9); and Aristotle argues that the form and function are the cause, because they explain why the matter is composed and organized as it is. The first actuality is the final cause, and therefore the essence and substance of the material object.

If Aristotle is right in his claim that organisms conform to these teleological laws, he has shown that common sense and the *Categories* are right in recognizing such things as individual men, horses, and trees as substance. He is not content to rely on common sense, however. He appeals to *Metaphysics* iv to set the metaphysical standards that substances must satisfy; they must be basic, continuing subjects. He appeals to his own teleological conception of nature to show that his preferred subjects conform to the sorts of laws that entitle us to regard them as basic subjects.

129. FORM AND MATTER IN DEFINITIONS

The discussion of potentiality and actuality in Book ix should now allow us to understand better the point and presuppositions of the argument in vii 10–11. There Aristotle claims that the essence of natural organisms is their form, not their matter; and this claim is supposed to support his eventual claim that form is a primary subject, and therefore a primary substance. If we have understood from Book ix what the form is supposed to be, we may find Aristotle's claims about it more plausible.

In vii 7–9 Aristotle prefaces his discussion of form and essence with an account of the coming to be of artifacts and natural organisms. This account suggests that the artifact or organism comes to be from preexistent form and matter, and that what results is the compound of form and matter.[22] We might infer that the essence of the artifact or organism will also be a compound of form and matter. But this is the inference Aristotle wants to reject, or to accept only with severe qualifications.

First he asks which parts of a thing are parts of the account, and which are only parts of the compound that consists of the account and the matter; and he illustrates the question with a series of four examples— circle, bronze ball, snub nose, and statue (1034b24–1035a9). Matter is clearly not meant to be part of the account of circle; for a circle is defined as a purely geometrical object whose essence is pure form.[23]

In this respect a circle differs from a snub nose and a bronze ball. For snubness essentially occurs in noses, and hence in flesh, as its subject; and similarly a bronze ball, as such, is essentially made of bronze. These, in contrast to the circle, are both essentially *materiate* universals, in so far as the account of each includes essential reference to some type of matter. But they may not be exactly parallel examples. Snubness requires flesh, and flesh has some particular chemical constitution; but does snubness require just this chemical constitution, or does it only require matter that does what the matter constituting flesh does? Matter may be part of the essence of snubness, and of the essence of bronze ball, but in different ways.

In his fourth example Aristotle speaks of a statue as a form, matter, and compound.

If, then, there is matter, form, and the composite of these, and matter, form, and the composite of them are all substance, then it follows that in one way matter is also called a part of something; but in another way it is not, but only the components of the form are parts. For example, flesh, the matter in which concavity comes to be, is not part of concavity, but it is a part of snubness. Again, bronze is a part of the compound statue, but not a part of the statue spoken of as form. For we should call the form—i.e. ⟨or 'and'; *kai*⟩ the thing in so far as it has form—the thing ⟨e.g. statue⟩, but we should never call a material thing in itself ⟨in so far as it is material⟩ the thing ⟨e.g. statue⟩. This is why the account of a circle does not include that of the segments, while the account of a syllable does include that of the letters; for the letters are not matter, but parts of the account of the form, while the segments are parts ⟨only⟩ as matter in which the form comes to be. (1035a1–12)

Apparently, a statue is properly identified with its form or with itself 'in so far as it has form', but not with its matter, and, by implication, not with the compound of its form and its matter.

130. FORMAL AND MATERIAL ESSENCES

When Aristotle speaks without distinction of the form of the statue and of the statue in so far as it has form, he relies on the conclusion of vii 6, where he identified the basic subjects with their essences. In his view, 'this man's essence' and 'this man in so far as he has his essence' describe exactly the same subject by reference to the same properties. In vii 10 he considers identifying the form with the essence; hence 'the form of the statue' and 'the statue as having form' will be equivalent in the same way.[24]

If the statue is identical to its form, and the form is the essence (cf. 1032b1–2), it ought not to follow that the statue is not essentially material; for statues are essentially material in a way circles are not. A non-material representation of Socrates might or might not be possible, but it surely would not be a statue of him. If the statue is essentially material, but its essence is its form, the form must in some way include matter. The universal statue must be materiate, since it includes essential reference to matter.

Still, if the statue is properly identical to its form, the universal statue must somehow be a form; if the universal were matter (e.g. bronze), or compound (e.g. bronze ball), then the statue would also be identical to the matter or compound. To support his claim that the statue is the form, Aristotle seems to distinguish a formal universal (e.g. statue) from a compound (e.g. bronze ball). He cannot identify the bronze ball with its form, as opposed to the matter or compound; for since it is essentially made of bronze, its essence cannot be simply being a ball, but must be being a bronze ball. Aristotle's remarks about the statue as form imply that in one way the statue, though certainly a material object, is more like the circle than like the bronze ball.[25] He has now distinguished immateriate forms (e.g. circle), materiate forms (e.g. statue), and materiate compounds (e.g. bronze ball).[26]

The statue and the snub are most like the natural substances that Aristotle has promised to discuss (1029a33–4; cf. 1042a24–6, 1043a38–b2). He often uses artifacts to illustrate natural organisms; and he uses the snub to illustrate the appropriate pattern of definition in the study of nature (1025b30–1026a6; cf. *Phys.* 194a1–7, 12–17). In vii 11 he resists the assimilation of artifacts or organisms to such compounds as bronze balls; he remarks that actual embodiment in matter does not justify the assimilation, any more than the mere fact that all observed circles were made of bronze would show that circles are essentially materiate (1036a31–b7).

He equally resists the opposite direction of assimilation that would treat the essences of artifacts or organisms as immateriate forms similar to circles. This is the error of Socrates the Younger, who claimed that the flesh and bones of a human being are simply the matter in which this form happens to be present, as the immateriate form of circle happens to be present in bronze and wood. This comparison 'leads us away from the truth, and makes us suppose that it is possible for a man to exist without his parts as ⟨it is possible⟩ for a circle ⟨to exist⟩ without bronze' (1036b26–8). The universal form of a natural organism cannot be purely immateriate.

Aristotle claims, therefore, both that matter is part of a living organism's form and essence and that it is not. If he is consistent, he appeals to different types of matter. We need to understand the difference, and we need to see if his appeal to it supports his claim that the essence of natural organisms is their form.

131. TYPES OF MATTER

Even apart from his claims about matter and definition, Aristotle's remarks about matter cannot all be true of the same thing.

He recognizes a type of matter that cannot survive the death of the living organism. In vii 10–11 he twice mentions the parts—hands, feet, etc.—that are the matter of an organism (1035b21, 1036b22–8), and that exist only when they fulfil their function: when the organism has perished these material parts are replaced by mere homonyms (1035b14–25, 1037a30–2).[27] Some of an organism's matter, however, survives the death of the organism.

For if a line is divided and destroyed into halves, and a man is destroyed into bones, sinews, and bits of flesh, it does not follow that these compose the whole as parts of the substance, but only that they compose it as its matter. They are parts of the compound, but not of the form, which is what the account is of; that is why they are not included in accounts either. (1035a17–22)

For this reason, the clay statue is destroyed into clay, the ball into bronze, and Callias into flesh and bones. (1035a31–3)

Since the same type of matter cannot both survive and not survive the organism, Aristotle's remarks, if they are consistent, must refer to different types of matter.

In some contexts he explicitly recognizes different types of matter; for he remarks that in stating the matter of a man we should mention his special matter, not fire or earth, and thereby state the most proximate cause (1044b1–3).[28] Let us therefore call this the *proximate* matter, and contrast it with the *remote* matter (e.g. fire, earth) that constitutes it.[29] In discussing potentialities, I have already spoken, without explicit warrant in Aristotle, of proximate and remote potentialities; if it was right to do this, his claims about matter and about potentialities should help to explain each other.

To show why the organic parts, rather than their chemical constituents, are proximate matter, Aristotle must show that they provide the proximate causes; and to show this he must appeal to his doctrine of proximate potentialities. The form is the actuality of the matter that has the potentiality for the functions that together make the form. But the subject of the proximate potentiality is not the hand in so far as it is made of these determinate material constituents, but the hand in so far as its material constituents are suitably combined and organized. The material parts that are parts of the animal are those with the appropriate proximate potentialities; and these are hands in working order, not combinations of chemical constituents (1036b30–2).[30]

Proximate matter, such as an arm or a leg, is always constituted by some kind of remote matter or other, since each type of limb has some definite chemical composition. But the proximate matter has no one definite kind of chemical stuff as its matter. Different arms or legs with different chemical constitutions may be instances of the same proximate matter of an organism.[31] The same bit of stuff will serve both as proximate and as remote matter; but the same properties are not relevant to its being proximate and to its being remote matter. Hence if two stuffs share some properties and differ in others, they may be different types of remote matter but the same type of proximate matter.

The connexion between proximate matter and proximate potentiality is clearest in Aristotle's conception of the body of living creatures. This body is matter, but it is not a mass or heap or lump of remote matter. As Locke remarks, '. . . in these two cases—a mass of matter and a living body—identity is not applied to the same thing' (*Essay*, ii.27.4). A soul is the form and actuality realizing the potentialities of a material body. But the material body that has these potentialities is itself the actuality of further material components. Legs and arms are the subjects of the proximate potentialities for walking, gripping, and so on; and the whole body is the organic whole with the proximate potentialities for the state that is the creature's life (conceived as first actuality).

This is why Aristotle identifies the organic body, not its chemical components, with the matter of the living creature. A plant is a single organism, 'which has such an organization of parts in one coherent body, partaking of one common life'; and it keeps the same coherent body

as long as it partakes of the same life, though that life be communicated to new particles of matter vitally united to the living plant, in a like continued organization, conformable to that sort of plants. (Locke, ii.27.5)[32]

This body does not outlive the creature; and the body that survives the creature's death is not the body that has the potentiality for the creature's life (*DA* 412b25–6). The vital activities of the creature realize the functional properties of its proximate matter, not the physical properties of the remote matter. The soul is the essence of the proximate, not the remote, matter.

The distinction between proximate and remote matter explains why statues and organisms are intermediate between circles and bronze balls. They essentially include some definite type of proximate matter, but do not essentially include any definite type of remote matter.

132. TYPES OF COMPOUNDS

These differences between remote and proximate matter imply parallel differences in compounds. When Aristotle says a certain kind of thing is a compound, he might refer either to a compound of form and proximate matter (a *formal* compound) or to a compound of form and remote matter (a *material* compound). Since these two compounds have different properties, Aristotle's apparently inconsistent claims turn out to be true of different compounds.

Some claims are plausible if and only if they refer to the formal, not the material, compound. Aristotle distinguishes soul as form, body as matter, and the universal man as a compound of the two (1037a5–7; cf. 1035b27–31); and he remarks that it is sometimes not clear whether the name (e.g. 'animal', and presumably also 'man') signifies the compound or the form.

Now we must realize that it is not always obvious whether a name signifies the composite substance, or the actuality and form (*morphê*). Does a house, e.g, signify the composite (that it is a shelter composed from bricks and stone in this position), or does it signify the actuality and form ⟨i.e. shelter⟩? Is a line twoness in length, or twoness? Is an animal a soul in a body, or a soul? For soul is the substance and actuality of a certain body; and 'animal' might be applied to both ⟨form and compound⟩; it will be spoken of with reference to one thing, not in one account. This question makes a difference in other areas, but not in the inquiry into perceptible substance; for the essence belongs to the form and actuality. For soul and being soul are the same; but man and being man are not the same, unless the soul is also to be called the man. Hence ⟨being man is the same⟩ as one thing ⟨soul⟩, but not ⟨the same⟩ as another thing ⟨soul plus body⟩. (1043a29–b4)[33]

The claim about essence shows that the distinction between form and compound is unimportant only if the form and the actuality is the essence of the compound as well as of the form. This is a defensible claim about the formal compound. For Aristotle claims that the subject in potentiality is one and the same as the subject in actuality (1045b17–23); and if they are the same subject, they will have the same essence. If the form is the essence of the formal compound, and also its own essence (as it must be if it is a primary substance), then, since things that have the same essence are identical, form and formal compound must be identical. If, as Aristotle claims, the form is also the essence of the proximate matter (*DA* 412b11), the same argument will show that the form, the formal compound, and the proximate matter are identical.

On the other hand, the form is not identical either to the remote matter or to the material compound, since its life-history (see 1003b29–30) is different.[34] For while the proximate matter (the living, organic body) exists only in so far as the form (the first actuality realizing the body's capacities) exists, the same is not true of the remote matter (the chemical components), which can exist without constituting a living organism. Aristotle's claim that the form and the compound have the same essence must, therefore, be restricted to the formal compound.

For the same reason, some of his remarks about the compound must refer to the material compound. For he contrasts natural organisms and artifacts, on one side, with bronze balls, on the other, and treats the latter, but not the former, as essentially compounds of form and matter; since he agrees that the former are formal compounds, he should mean that the latter are material compounds.

Similarly, the material parts into which a man perishes (bones, flesh, and sinews, 1035a18–19) are not parts of his form and essence, and hence are not mentioned in the account of him, 'unless the account is of the thing taken together with matter' (1035a23).[35] These parts are the material stuffs that survive the organism, and the compound that includes them is the material compound of form and remote matter; as Aristotle says, the essence of the material compound will not be the same as the essence of the organism constituted by the remote matter. In this case it cannot be unimportant whether we think we are talking of the form or of the compound; for the difference between form and material compound is just the difference Aristotle sees between statues and bronze balls.

Aristotle claims that compounds are not identical to their essences (1037a33–b7, 1043b2–4), and in particular that man is not the same as the essence of man, if man is taken to be the compound rather than the form (1043b2–4). We know from vii 6 that whatever is not identical to its essence cannot be a basic subject, and therefore cannot be a substance; and so if natural organisms are not identical to their essence, they will not be substances.

He avoids this conclusion, however, if the claims about compounds refer only to material compounds, and natural organisms are formal rather than material compounds. Things that are not identical to their essences are 'coincidental compounds', such things as musicians, that are composed of a more basic subject and a coincident of it.[36] They are not identical to their essences, since their essence depends on the essence of something else—the more basic subject. The material compound satisfies this condition for being a coincidental compound; for its persistence depends on the persistence of the form and the formal compound, but their persistence does not depend on it.

Aristotle appropriately suggests that the relation of matter to form is parallel to the relation of coincidents to their subject (1049a27–b2); but the parallel holds only for material compounds.[37] The test we have applied makes formal compounds identical to their essences, since their persistence consists in nothing more or less than the persistence of the form that is their essence. If, then, natural organisms are formal compounds, Aristotle's remarks about compounds and their essences do not imply that natural organisms are not identical to their essences, and therefore do not imply that natural organisms cannot be substances.[38]

133. THE ESSENCE OF NATURAL SUBSTANCES

In vii 10 Aristotle identifies the essence of natural organisms with forms, not with compounds of form and matter; on the other hand he refuses to identify them with immateriate forms of the same type as circles. Our discussion of matter and compound should now explain these claims; formal compounds are the same as materiate forms, and natural organisms are essentially forms rather than compounds, in so far as they are essentially formal rather than material compounds.

Aristotle argues that natural organisms are an intermediate case between immateriate forms and material compounds; and to find the right sort of intermediate case we must see the importance of function in the definition of natural organisms (1035b14–25, 1036b28–32). The definition stating the essence states the form rather than the matter, since it describes the organism by its functions rather than by its composition. However, the functional definition does not make man analogous to circle. The functions are functions of something, actualities that actualize some potentiality; and there must be a subject with the appropriate capacities to be actualized. Hence the definition needs to mention the material subject whose capacities are actualized in the functions of the organism.

Aristotle therefore rejects the view of Young Socrates on the definition of natural substances:

For an animal is something that perceives, and cannot be defined without motion, and hence cannot be defined without the parts in a certain condition. For the hand is not in just any condition a part of a man, but ⟨the only one that is a part is⟩ the one that is capable of fulfilling its function, and hence the one that is ensouled; when it is not ensouled it is not a part. (1036b28–32)[39]

Aristotle insists that the definition and essence must include material parts, so that the essence of man is materiate, different from the immateriate essence of the circle, and therefore some sort of compound. Still, the definition includes these parts only in a certain way, as defined by their capacities and functions, so that the essence is a formal compound (or materiate form) rather than a material compound.

Form is the first actuality that explains the structure and organization of the matter. In this case, perception is an actuality of this material body, and part of its form, because it explains why this body is composed and organized as it is. It explains these things teleologically by showing how the activities for which the body is organized are good for the creature. If such an explanation is true, the creature must have other actualities besides perception, and in particular it must be capable of moving itself, since the function of perception is to guide a creature's movements for its benefit. For a creature incapable of motion, perception would not have this function, and therefore would not explain its movements; hence perception would not be part of the essence.

In the *De Anima* Aristotle notices this connexion between perception and the other activities of a living creature (*DA* 414b1–16, 415a6–7), and he relies on it in our present passage, in connecting perception with motion.[40] He infers that the essence of a natural organism is the essence of a material body, since only a material body is capable of the appropriate sort of motion. Since the essence includes matter, it must be different from the essence of circle, which is a pure form; therefore the universal man must be a materiate universal.

This is Aristotle's defence against Socrates the Younger. He has argued that his views on essence and actuality require the essence of natural organisms to be actualities that essentially belong to material bodies.[41] He has therefore given reasons for claiming that natural organisms are essentially compounds of form and matter, rather than pure immateriate forms. The relevant matter, however, is not the four elements, or even stuffs such as blood and tissue, but the organic parts of the organism—heads, hands, etc.—that are capable of fulfilling their functions. These parts must be matter (since otherwise they are irrelevant to the reply to Young Socrates), but they must be parts of the materiate form (the formal compound), not of the (material) compound.

These claims about the essence of natural organisms help to show how form is substance (1029a32–3, recalled 1035a1–4). Aristotle argues that substance is essence, and then that form is essence; the essence of natural organisms is their materiate form, as distinct from the material compound. His argument depends on the distinction between proximate and remote matter, which in turn rests on his conception of potentiality.

Aristotle was right to claim, in vii 3, that form is more obscure and puzzling than matter and compound, and that it is prior to them (1029a5–7, 30–3). A proper understanding of form has changed our initial views about the relation of form to matter and to compound.

When we see that the form is the explanatory actuality realizing the proximate potentiality of the matter, we can see why the form that is the essence of natural organisms must include proximate matter. Aristotle has therefore strengthened his claim that form is essence.

12

FORM AND SUBSTANCE

134. PARTICULARS AS FORMS AND COMPOUNDS

So far we have explained why Aristotle thinks form is the essence of a natural substance, and therefore satisfies the essence-criterion for substance. We still have to show that it satisfies the subject-criterion. Aristotle reminds us at the beginning of *Metaphysics* vii 13 and again in viii 1 that substance is subject, and in viii 1 insists that form is subject, and also a this and separable in account (1038b5–6, 1042a26–9). These remarks assure us that he still intends substance to be a subject, a this, and separable. We must still be convinced that the same thing that satisfies the essence-criterion will satisfy the subject-criterion. We have seen why Aristotle has good reason to identify certain universals—the essential properties of natural organisms—with form rather than matter; but we need to see if he can also argue that the subject is form.[1]

In vii 1 Aristotle assumes that a basic subject is a this and a particular (1028a12, 25–7). The remarks about thises in vii 3–4 do not count against this initial assumption; and it is equally reasonable to assume that the primary subjects identified with their essences in vii 6 are particulars.[2] Aristotle continues to apply 'this' to particulars. He calls the product resulting from production or becoming a this (1033a31–2). He calls Socrates or Callias a this (1033b23–4), and 'this soul and this body' (1037a9), and also calls him a particular (1035b30, 1037a10, 1040b2). He insists that matter is needed for everything that is not an essence and form 'all by itself' (*auto kath'hauto*) but a this, and continues: 'Hence matter does not belong to the universal circle, but these ⟨material parts⟩ are parts of the particular circle' (1037a1–3). Aristotle argues that since thises have matter, particulars have it; he must assume that the thises are particulars.[3]

These remarks suggest that a substance is a particular material subject; and so if form is to be substance, it must be a particular material subject. Aristotle insists that a particular such as Socrates is a compound of form and 'ultimate' (i.e. particular) matter (1035b30–1, 1036a2–3, 1037a32–3, 1039b20–31). Such remarks suggest that the contrast between form and compound is a contrast between universal and particular, between the formal property and the subject that has the property. If that is the only relevant contrast between form and compound, then forms cannot be particular subjects.

We have already seen, however, that Aristotle draws more than one contrast between form and compound, and that being a form and being a compound are not always mutually exclusive. Among universals he distinguishes immateriate forms (circle), materiate forms or formal compounds (statue, horse), and material compounds (bronze circle). A parallel distinction between particulars identifies particular forms that are also formal compounds.[4]

Aristotle's use of different contrasts between form and compound makes his position harder to state. In his view, a particular must include some particular bit of matter, since this is needed for a unique spatio-temporal location. Since it has this location, it is not a universal, which is in many places at once (1040b25–6). There are two instances of the universal circle only because there are two individual bits of matter embodying them (cf. 1035b1–3). Universals, both materiate (such as bronze ball and statue) and immateriate (such as circle), are immaterial, since none of them is a material object; and particulars, whether they exemplify immateriate or materiate universals, are material. Aristotle marks this contrast by saying that universals are forms and particulars are compounds.

It follows that a materiate universal form (e.g. statue, man) is both a compound (in contrast to circle) and a form (in contrast to the particular); and sometimes Aristotle exploits both contrasts at once. He says the universals man, horse, etc. are not substances, but a compound of this form and this matter 'as universal', while Socrates is composed of this particular matter (1035b27–31).[5] In this case both the universal and the particular are compounds. On the other hand, Aristotle comments that the parts of the account are the parts of the form only, and the account is of the universal—being circle is the same as circle and being soul is the same as soul. In contrast to the (universal) form, a (particular) compound, such as this circle and any other particular, has no definition, since that applies only to universals (1035b31–1036a8). In this case the compound is the particular and the form is universal; no distinction is drawn between immateriate universals such as circle and materiate universals such as statue or bronze circle.[6]

By speaking of form and compound to mark two different contrasts Aristotle makes his claims more obscure, but not necessarily inconsistent; each contrast is intelligible in its own right, and if we can combine the two, we can understand his views on particulars. Some particulars will be material but immateriate forms (this particular circle), others material and materiate forms, i.e. formal compounds (this statue), others material compounds (this bronze ball). Aristotle is quite justified in speaking of particular forms that are compounds of form and particular bits of matter.

135. PARTICULAR FORMS AS SUBSTANCES

If the distinction between form and compound allows particular forms that are also formal compounds, it remains to show that Aristotle has good reason to believe in such things, and to believe that they are substances.

The particular substantial forms he recognizes are particular natural organisms such as horses and trees. In contrast to particular circles, these are not pure forms, but formal *compounds*. A particular circle needs some particular bit of matter or other if it is to be a particular, but the circle does not essentially actualize the potentialities of any bit of matter; there is no matter whose natural organization and structure are explained by its circular shape. Particular materiate forms, however, are formal compounds. A particular tree essentially includes not just some particular bit of matter or other, but a bit of matter of the right functional type whose potentiality it actualizes—a bit of proximate matter.

On the other hand, a natural organism is a *formal* compound, a materiate *form*, in contrast to such particular material compounds as bronze balls. A particular bronze ball is a material compound because it essentially includes a bit of matter of just the sort of composition that makes it bronze. A particular natural organism does not essentially include matter of such a definite type, but only the right sort of proximate matter. We can therefore speak of a particular materiate form either as a form or as a compound, if we are clear about what we mean.

Just as Aristotle is unconcerned about whether man is a (materiate) form or a (formal) compound (1043a37–b1), he is unconcerned about the particular man:

If the soul also is Socrates, then he is twofold—some ⟨speak of him⟩ as soul, others as the compound. But if this soul is unconditionally also this body, then the particular is as the universal is. (1037a7–10)[7]

A particular formal compound essentially includes a particular bit of proximate matter; and hence the conditions for its persistence are different from the conditions for the persistence of a particular material compound (e.g. this bronze ball). The same bit of proximate matter persists as long as it retains its functional properties, those that belong to it as part of this particular organism; and it may retain these even if its constituent piece of remote matter perishes. The piece of remote matter perishes if enough bits of it are replaced, even if they are replaced by other bits of the very same kind of stuff; but the proximate matter may survive. The same proximate matter of a crown may persist even if eventually all the original bits of its remote matter are replaced, as long as the crown keeps the same functional properties, and therefore the same proximate matter.[8]

Aristotle is therefore justified in believing both that particulars such as Socrates are compounds, and that they are particular forms. Since Socrates includes a particular bit of proximate matter, he differs from the materiate universal form, and Aristotle is justified in speaking of the universal as 'the account ⟨i.e. form⟩ without qualification'. He contrasts it with the essence of the particular, an essence which is a compound, comes into being and perishes (1039b20–31), because it includes a particular bit of matter. The essence of this house is 'the form in the matter, and one of the particulars' (*DC* 278a9–10). Aristotle refers to the same particular essence as both a compound and a particular form, since it is both a materiate form and a formal compound.[9]

If the same subject is essentially a piece of proximate matter, a particular form, and a formal compound, these three different properties may still explain different sets of further properties. Aristotle recognizes three types of subject—matter, form, and compound—and claims that matter is a this potentially but not actually, form is a this and separable in account, and the compound is separable unconditionally and the proper subject of becoming and destruction (1042a25–31). These three descriptions are probably meant to be true of the same material substance and subject.

The matter that has the potentiality to be a this is the proximate, not the remote matter (cf. *DA* 412a6–10).[10] The form that is the this is the particular formal compound. In so far as it is a compound, it includes a piece of proximate matter that makes it separable from any particular bit of remote matter. In so far as it includes a piece of proximate sensible matter it comes into being and ceases to be.[11] The descriptions 'matter', 'form', 'compound' cannot always be substituted for each other, since they identify different features of the particular substance; and the form is primary, since it explains the substantial status of the proximate matter and formal compound.[12]

A natural but mistaken conception of the difference between form and compound might lead us to suppose that if particular organisms are compounds, as Aristotle says, then they cannot be forms. On the other hand, a correct grasp of the distinction shows that the distinction between materiate form and compound applies both to universals and to particular natural substances, and that particular forms are good candidates for being particular substances. The particular form is the first actuality of its proximate matter; its persistence does not require the persistence of any bit of remote matter, and therefore it counts as a basic subject, something identical to its essence. Aristotle fulfils his aim of showing that form meets the conditions for being a basic particular subject.

136. THE NATURE OF PARTICULAR FORMS

Socrates and Callias share the same specific form, man, and differ because of their matter (1034a5–8).[13] The differences caused by their different matter must imply that their particular forms are different; for since Socrates' form is identical to Socrates and Callias' form to Callias, the identity of the two forms would imply, absurdly, the identity of Socrates and Callias.[14] The differentiating features of particular compounds are coincidental to the specific form (1058b8–12), since the peculiarities of Socrates or Callias are not essential to his being a man; but they cannot be coincidental to the particular forms. Socrates' particular form is identical to Socrates, and Callias' particular form to Callias; hence, if the difference between particular forms is coincidental to them, it must also be coincidental to Socrates that he is different from Callias. But it cannot be coincidental to a particular that it is distinct from another particular; and so this cannot be coincidental to the particular form either. The difference between the particular forms must be essential to them.[15]

But what sort of difference is it, and what sort of differentiating property is essential to each form?[16] It can hardly be a purely numerical difference, distinguishing different particular forms by their different bits of remote matter.[17] For no particular bit of remote matter is essential to Socrates' particular form. Socrates' existence depends on the existence of a bit of proximate, not of remote, matter; and persistence of a bit of proximate matter depends on the persistence of its particular form.[18]

It is easier to see what sorts of properties are essential to a particular form if we appeal to the explanatory role of form and essence. The particular substantial form ensures the persistence of the particular whose form it is, because it is the essence of the particular. Hence a man has a particular substantial form, while a musical man has none, because the essence of a particular man explains more about this particular than the essence of a musical man explains; that is why the perishing of the man is a genuine substantial change and the perishing of the musical man is not. If the form is to explain the character of this bit of proximate matter, it should include the right sorts of qualitative features to distinguish it from other particular forms and to explain the special features of this bit of proximate matter.[19]

137. THE ROLE OF PARTICULAR FORMS

Aristotle's clearest references to particular form, in *Metaphysics* xii and *Generation of Animals* iv, suggest this explanatory role. The causes of substances are particulars, your matter and form and efficient cause or mine.

For the particular is the origin of the particulars; for man is the origin of man universally, but there is no such man ⟨who is no particular man⟩, but Peleus is the cause of Achilles, and your father of you, and this B of this BA. (1071a20–2)

. . . and ⟨the causes⟩ of the things in the same species (*eidos*) are different, not in species (*eidos*), but because different particulars have a different cause—your matter, form (*eidos*), and moving cause, and mine—but these are the same in universal account. (1071a27–9)

The forms that are thises must be particular instances of some universal form, and they will need the right special properties to explain the particular events they are required to explain.[20]

Aristotle argues that the most proper cause of generation is the particular more than the genus. The particular provides what is special to Coriscus, and is more important.

What is special and particular always has a greater influence towards generation; for Coriscus is both a human being and an animal, but human being is closer to what is special to him than animal is. Now both the particular and the genus generate, but the particular does so more; for that ⟨i.e. a particular⟩ is what substance is. For indeed what comes into being certainly comes to be of some kind (*poion ti*), but also a this; and that ⟨i.e. a this⟩ is what substance is. (*GA* 767b29–35)[21]

The species is closer than the genus to the special features of the particular man Coriscus; but in saying that the most special and the most particular is most important Aristotle refers to features special to Coriscus as opposed to Socrates. What is special and particular is identified with a this and a substance. Here as earlier in the *GA*, Aristotle assumes that 'the substance of (or 'among') things that are is found in the particular' (731b34); and by 'particular' he means a spatio-temporal individual such as Coriscus or Socrates (768a1–2, b13–15). A parent provides the cause of becoming by providing the form (729a10); and if this is particular, it must be 'your form and mine', the particular form mentioned in *Metaphysics* xii.

If the form is to explain the peculiar characteristics of the offspring resulting from generation, it must be the particular form of the parent, since the specific form does not explain peculiarities.[22] The particular form of Callias' parent explains the characteristics of Callias and of his particular form at birth, and Callias' particular form explains Callias' behaviour in his lifetime. Since Aristotle intends this explanatory role for particular forms, he must intend them to include the qualities of Callias that provide a teleological explanation of his behaviour.

In the *GC* Aristotle attributes the appropriate explanatory role to a particular form. He claims that the form persists as long as the particular organism is alive, and that it is the proper subject of growth (321b25–8). If the form is to grow it must include some matter, and so must be a compound; and since it replaces its remote matter in growth, it must be a formal, not a material, compound. The form, rather than the remote matter or the material compound, is the proper subject of growth, because the process of growth in organisms is controlled by the functions and relations of the organs—it is not a mere quantitative increase in the matter (cf. *DA* 415b28–416a18).[23]

If a form grows and changes, then it must presumably differ qualitatively from other conspecific particular forms, since not all conspecific organisms grow in the same way. In conceiving the form as a particular subject of growth Aristotle attributes to it the same sort of explanatory role that he attributes to it in the *GA*; it must therefore have the appropriate peculiar qualities.[24]

In describing the change and persistence of a political community, Aristotle relies on something parallel to the particular form that persists through the growth of an organism. He denies that simply being in the same place makes a city the same, as it makes rivers the same (*Pol.* 1276a34–b1).

For since a city is a type of association, and specifically an association of citizens in a political system, it is necessary that if the system becomes other and different in form, it will seem that the city is not the same either, just as we say that a chorus that is now comic and now tragic is a different chorus ⟨on these occasions⟩, even though often the people in it are the same, and likewise we say that any other association or combination is different, if the manner of combination is different, as for instance we say that the same notes produce different scales, if the scale is in one case in the Dorian mode, in another case in the Phrygian. (1276b1–9)

In this case also Aristotle has in mind a particular mode of organization of the constituent matter, and takes this to persist and to change (since, e.g., Athens could clearly modify its democracy without becoming a different city, though it could not change from democracy to oligarchy). The particular form plays the same role in the individual substance.

Since the form of a living creature is its soul (1037a5–10), particular forms should be particular souls. If Socrates' soul is to have the explanatory role that Aristotle intends for particular form, it should differ from Callias' soul in having those features of Socrates' character and personality that distinguish Socrates from other people. For further details on particular souls we must turn to the *De Anima* and the *Ethics*. But we can infer enough from the *Metaphysics* to justify us in expecting Aristotle to develop his view in this way.[25] Some of the evidence we have appealed to is, admittedly, outside *Metaphysics* vii–ix. But that does not make it irrelevant; for the strategy of these books requires particular forms to satisfy Aristotle's demands of substance.

138. PARTICULAR FORMS AND THE CRITERIA FOR SUBSTANCE

If we are now fairly convinced that Aristotle means to identify substance with particular form, we must see if it really satisfies his initial constraints. He claimed in vii 3 that if we attend to separability and thisness, we find that form and compound are substances to a higher degree than matter is (1029a29–30).[26] He should now be able to defend that claim by appeal to his conception of particular form.

The parts of the proximate matter fail some of the conditions for being basic subjects, and Aristotle denies that they are substances.

Further, even among the things that seem to be substances, most are evidently ⟨only⟩ potentialities. These include the parts of animals (for none of them is separated; whenever they are separated, they exist ⟨only⟩ as matter), and also earth, fire, and air. For none of these is one, but each is a sort of heap, until they mature and some one thing comes to be from them. One would be most inclined to suppose that the parts of ensouled things and the corresponding parts of the soul turn out to be beings both in actuality and in potentiality; for they have origins of motion from some ⟨source⟩ in their joints—that is why some animals keep on living when they are divided. But nonetheless, all these things are ⟨only⟩ in potentiality—as long as they are one and continuous by nature, not by force or by growing together (that sort of thing is a deformity). (1040b5–16)

A part is inseparable because its continued existence is essentially the exercise of its function in the whole; if the whole is destroyed and only a hand (as we tend to say) is left, that is not really the same hand, but only a homonym. When the hand has been separated (and therefore has ceased to exist), all that is left is a piece of remote matter. The proximate matter depends on the form, and so cannot claim to be a more basic subject than the form.

Moreover, bits of remote matter, in Aristotle's view, are just heaps, not proper unities. Matter is potentially a this (1042a27–8), but not actually a this, if it is a heap, but not a whole, and therefore not a proper unity.[27] Unity requires some natural continuity of the sort that makes the subject more than a mere collection; and this sort of unity is characteristic of 'a whole that has some shape and form' (1052a22–3), and especially of something that 'has within it the cause of its being continuous' (1052a24–5).[28]

A whole has some further unity beyond the collection of its parts because its identity is distinct from the identity of the collection. A sign of its unity is the impossibility of dividing it into parts of the same sort; a bit of gold is divisible into bits of gold because it is just a collection of bits of gold, whereas a tree is not divisible into trees, because it is not a mere collection. Aristotle might appeal to this feature of wholes to show that they satisfy his demand in the *Categories* for numerical unity, which he takes to require indivisibility.[29]

Since a whole is composed of a particular collection of parts it can be predicated of them; but they need not be prior to it in nature or account. For some wholes (e.g. living organisms) can survive the loss of some of their constituents; and since the persistence of a collection requires the persistence and juxtaposition of all of its components (cf. 1043b35–1044a1), the whole can survive the destruction of this particular collection. Wholes are therefore good examples of thises, and they remain in being because of their forms rather than their matter; hence the form is separable in account and in nature from its matter.

A heap, by contrast, is nothing more than this collection of constituents, and its persistence consists in the mere continued juxta-position of these constituents which do not depend on it in the same way; we cannot, therefore, regard it as a basic subject or a this or separable.[30]

In so far as matter comes in heaps and collections, it is not a subject in its own right; the narrow predication-formula shows that it is not a substance, since its being consists in the collection being predicated of its parts, which are more basic subjects than the collection itself. Once the predication-formula and the subject-criterion are properly understood, they show that matter cannot meet the conditions for being the best type of substance; like the material compound, it turns out to be secondary to form, as Aristotle suggested at the very beginning of his argument (1029a5–7).[31]

Forms, therefore, are thises because they are wholes independent of their constituents; there is no more basic subject whose persistence partly constitutes the persistence of the tree or dog.[32] To say this is not to say that the form requires no matter at all. It always requires some suitable remote matter, but it does not require any particular bit of remote matter. Though it requires a bit of proximate matter, this matter is not independent of the particular form, and therefore does not count against the claim of form to be a basic subject. Since Aristotle thinks the proximate matter and the particular form are one, he could have said that proximate matter turns out to be substance; but he would not be saying in that case that matter *as opposed to* form is substance.

Aristotle, therefore, still believes that substance is subject, and that form is the primary type of subject (1029a2–7). He has shown that the essence-criterion and the subject-criterion lead to particular forms. In vii 3 he mentioned the essence, the universal, and the genus together, as though the essence-criterion pointed to universals as substances, and only the subject-criterion pointed to particulars (1028b33–6). But the summary in vii 13 implies a different relation between the criteria:

> Just as the subject, the essence, and the ⟨compound⟩ from the two are said to be substance, so is the universal. We have discussed the first two—the essence and the subject—and ⟨we have found⟩ that something is a subject in either of two ways, either by being a this, as the animal is the subject for its attributes, or as the matter is the subject for the actuality. (1038b2–6)

The first sentence of this summary suggests that the subject is matter and the essence is the form; but the second sentence rejects any opposition between subject and essence, and insists that the this is also a subject. Since Aristotle has shown that the this is a particular form which is also the essence, he identifies the essence with a type of subject.[33]

139. PARTICULAR FORMS AS PRIMARY SUBSTANCES

If Aristotle has good reason to identify particular forms with basic subjects and primary substances, he has proved only part of his initial claim. For he affirms that form, matter, and compound are all subjects, and therefore substances. His account of form as substance should therefore justify this more generous construal of the range of substance.

Aristotle compares the three successful candidates:

> The subject is substance. In one way matter is a subject. (By 'matter' I mean what is potentially but not actually a this.) In another way, the account and the form (*morphê*) which, being a this, is separable in account ⟨is a subject⟩. The third ⟨type of subject⟩ is the compound of these two; only this comes to be and perishes, and it is unconditionally separable. Some substances specified by the account are unconditionally separable and some are not. (1042a25–31)

Form is the primary candidate, since it is a this in its own right, and a subject is a this in so far as it is a form (*DA* 412a6–9). Hence form is the primary substance (1037a28–9).

Aristotle's admission that matter and compound are substances (e.g. 1035a1–2) extends in the first instance to proximate matter and the formal compound. The 'matter and material substance' that he describes (1049a36) is the proximate matter. For he argues that we can say a box is wooden, but not earthen, because the wood, not the earth, is potentially the box, and therefore its proximate matter.

> Sometimes we call something not *that*, but *that-en*—e.g. a box is not wood, but wooden; nor is wood earth, but earthen; and again, earth, if the same applies, is not that other thing, but that-en. In all these cases ⟨where F is G-en⟩, G is unconditionally potentially F; e.g. a box is neither earthen nor earth, but wooden, since wood is potentially a box, and this is the matter of the box— wood in general of box in general, and this wood of this casket. (1049a18–24)[34]

In general we can say that 'F is G-en' only in cases where G is the proximate matter of F.

The matter that is expressly identified with substance is the proximate matter. This depends on the form for its identity no less than things such as musicians depend on men for their identity; hence the proximate matter, like musicality, fails to identify a definite subject in itself, and so is 'indefinite' (1049a36–b2; cf. 1028a26–7), though (unlike musicality) it is identical to the form that makes it a definite subject.

The proximate matter, therefore, counts as a substance for reasons that are inapplicable to the remote matter. The remote matter and the material compound turn out not be primary substances, because they are not basic subjects. Remote matter is not a basic subject, because its components are more basic subjects on which it depends. The material compound is not a this, because the form and the matter are more basic subjects on which it depends. By contrast, since the form does not depend on the persistence of a particular bit of remote matter, it does not depend on a more basic subject.

Still, it would be reasonable to concede that remote matter and the material compound are subjects and substances to some degree. Though he denies that fire and earth are the proximate matter of a human being, Aristotle allows that they are a human being's matter (1044b1–3). Since a substance is predicated of its matter, the human being should be predicated of his remote matter, and the remote matter should be to that extent a substance; and since the remote matter of a human being is the more proximate matter of his body, it should count as the material substance that is the subject of the proximate matter. It is not as much of a substance, since it is neither a genuine unity in its own right nor identical to a genuine unity (as proximate matter is identical to form), but it is a substance to some degree.

Similarly, a material compound is not a genuine unity in its own right, since it depends on the persistence of the form and the remote matter. But it is a subject of change (the bronze ball, e.g., undergoes changes either in its form or in its matter), and so may be a substance to some degree; every change in a formal compound implies some change in a material compound, just as every change in proximate matter requires some change in remote matter. Though Aristotle does not explicitly concede substantial status to remote matter and the material compound, he probably intends to concede it, and his theory makes the concession reasonable.

Aristotle is not exclusive in his view of what counts as a substance. He argues that form satisfies the criteria for substance, suitably interpreted, better than other candidates. But he concedes that from one point of view the compound is more separable than the form. He does not require the primary type of substance to satisfy all the criteria completely, under every natural interpretation; he allows candidates that satisfy some of the criteria to some extent to count as substances to some degree. By appeal to the conditions for being a this and a basic subject, Aristotle can decide when to be strict and when to be lax about the initial criteria. He has good reasons both for treating form as the primary substance and for allowing matter and compound to be substances to some degree.

Though Aristotle does not sum up his discussion in exactly these terms, it exploits a familiar Aristotelian technique. In iv 2 he claims that beings are focally connected to substance, and in vii 1 he repeats this claim, applying it to the categories. His view about substance suggests that matter and compound are focally connected to form, so that focal connexion appears among substances, not only between substances and other beings. Particular form is the primary type of substance because it is a basic subject; matter and compound are substances to the extent that they are subjects. Aristotle's views about substance can be explained so that they conform to a central guiding principle of the *Metaphysics*.

140. OBJECTIONS TO UNIVERSALS AS SUBSTANCES

If these views about substance constitute a satisfactory theory, however, they must answer the puzzles that were raised in Book iii. The solution summarized at the beginning of vii 13 (quoted above, § 138) removes one reason for thinking that universals must be substances, by showing that particular forms satisfy the essence-criterion. But Aristotle has not yet analysed all the arguments that seemed to show that universals must be the first principles, and therefore must be substances. Unless he can show that the truth in these arguments is consistent with his view of substance, he has left his view exposed to a serious objection. In vii 13–16, therefore, he discusses the claims of universals.

He presents a series of arguments to show that 'it would seem to be impossible for any of the things spoken of universally to be substance' (1038b8–9), and that 'it is evident from these things that none of the things belonging universally is substance' (1038b35).[35] Especially he discusses the claim of the universal to be something's substance, arguing that in fact it does not satisfy the essence-criterion. He still assumes that 'each thing seems to be nothing other than its own substance, and the essence is said to be the substance of each thing' (1031a17–18). It follows that the substance of x will have to be the essence of x and therefore (by the argument of vii 6) identical to x, so that if x and y have the same substance and essence they are identical.

These claims about substance and essence undermine the claims of the universal.

First, each thing's substance is the substance peculiar to it, which does not belong to another thing; the universal, however, is common, since what is called universal is what naturally belongs to more than one thing. Then which thing's substance ⟨among the things it belongs to⟩ will the universal be? It must be the substance either of all or of none of them. It cannot be the substance of all; if it is the substance of one of them, then the others will be this one too, since things that have one substance also have one essence and are themselves one. (1038b9–15)

If the species is the substance of any one of its particulars, every other particular in the species will be identical to that one, since the species is no more the substance of Socrates than of Callias and Coriscus.[36] The species will therefore have only one member, and there will be no plurality for the universal to belong to. To claim that the universal is substance is to abolish both a plurality of conspecific particulars and the universal that is supposed to be common to the plurality; if there are no many, there is no one belonging to the many.[37]

This argument requires a universal substance to be the substance and essence of whatever we count as a basic subject, and therefore to be identical to the basic subject.[38] This was the requirement for essence in vii 6; and to fulfil it an essence had to be particular and identical to its subject. Universals cannot fulfil the condition in this way.

Aristotle also appeals to the subject-criterion: 'Further, substance is what is not ⟨said⟩ of a subject, but a universal is in every case said of a subject' (1038b15–16). The subject-criterion was used to pick out substance in vii 3; but it needed careful interpretation to avoid making matter the only subject. We found that Aristotle interprets the criterion through the narrow, not the broad, predication-formula, and therefore counts form as a subject; for the form is not said of a subject in the narrow sense, that its being consists in one thing being said of another.

Our account of particular form has shown why this is so. A particular form includes a particular bit of proximate matter; but its being does not consist in its being said of any remote matter, even though it cannot exist without some bit of remote matter or other. A universal, by contrast, has its being in being said of a subject. Aristotle assumes that its being a universal is essentially its being a property of a subject; it therefore requires a subject distinct from it, and cannot be the subject that is properly identified with substance.[39]

Aristotle assumes that a substance must be a this; and since he takes a this to be a basic subject, he must deny that universals are thises once he denies that they are basic subjects (1038b34–1039a2). Only particular substances will be thises, and the species-form, since it is in many places at once, is a universal, not a particular, not a this, not a subject, and therefore not a substance. Aristotle concludes:

Nothing that belongs universally is a substance, and nothing predicated in common signifies a this, but a such. Otherwise there are many ⟨unwelcome⟩ consequences, including the Third Man. (1038b35–1039a3)

The Third Man results from treating a species, man, as a this, as a particular substance and subject.[40]

These criticisms support Aristotle's positive arguments for his own view of substance. In vii 10–11 he explains form and essence in a way that shows why particular forms are essences and substances. In vii 13 he continues the argument by explaining why species and genera are not substances.[41]

141. THE CASE FOR UNIVERSAL SUBSTANCES

None the less, Aristotle seems to say that some conditions for being a substance are met only by universals and not by particulars. Universals are the objects of scientific knowledge, which is of general laws; and since these laws apply without spatial or temporal restriction to all the particulars of a given kind, they must be about universals. In the *Analytics* Aristotle affirms the reality of universals (*APo* 85b15–18), and he has no reason to retreat in the *Metaphysics*. We have scientific knowledge about Socrates only when we grasp the universal man; and our knowledge of the universal does not depend on our knowing Socrates. Priority in knowledge is one of the types of priority held to be characteristic of substance; and universals seem to satisfy it. Equally, they seem to be prior in definition; for Socrates is essentially a man, and the definition of the universal man will be part of Socrates' definition, but the converse will not be true.

Each universal natural kind has a definition that is the basis for demonstration of the intrinsic coincidents. The definition tells us the essence of the universal; and since the conditions for identity and persistence of a particular instance are not the same as those for a universal, the definition of the universal cannot be the definition of the particular. Since a particular has matter it is generated and destroyed (1039b27–31), and has a spatio-temporal position and career. Since these features are essential to it, and incompatible with being a universal, its definition cannot be the same as a definition of the universal. Seeing this, Aristotle sometimes says a particular has no definition (1036a2–9, 1039b27–1040a7), but explains himself by saying it has no *scientific* definition (1039b32). It is essentially material and matter makes it indefinable (1036a2–9).

Everlasting particulars that are the only members of their kind, e.g. the sun, are also indefinable, though not because they are perishable. Even if we find the essential properties of the sun, we have not found a definition if the properties are capable of being duplicated by another particular; for the sun is a particular, as Cleon and Socrates are.

As we have said, then, we fail to notice, in the case of everlasting things that are ⟨particulars⟩, especially those—e.g. the sun or moon—that are unique, that they are indefinable. For sometimes people mistakenly add the sorts of things (e.g. going around the earth, or being hidden at night) which can be removed without its ceasing to be the sun. For ⟨this sort of definition implies⟩ that if it stops going around or shows at night, it will no longer be the sun. But that is absurd, since the sun signifies a substance. ⟨Sometimes they mistakenly mention only features⟩ that can all be found in something else. If, e.g., something else of this sort comes to be, then clearly this will also have to be the sun, and in that case, the account will be common ⟨to the two⟩; but in fact, the sun is a particular, as Cleon and Socrates are. (1040a27–b2)

In this objection Aristotle shows that he does not believe two particulars with the same definition are the same particular. If he did believe this, he would say that something else satisfying the definition of the sun would be the sun. He assumes that if the sun were definable, it would be logically repeatable (i.e. capable of more than one instantiation) as a universal is.

Such repeatability would be no objection if Aristotle believed that a proper name is simply an abbreviation for a list of repeatable properties. If he believed this, he would allow the possibility of two Socrateses.[42] On the other hand, he does not allow a definition to include spatiotemporal properties. If he did, he could no longer be sure that any definition of the sun would make the sun logically repeatable. If, then, he insists that particulars are indefinable, he need not mean that they are ineffable or have no essence. He may mean only that their essence cannot be stated in purely qualitative, non–spatio-temporal terms.[43]

Still, his emphatic claim that particulars are indefinable seems to raise a serious doubt about their claim to be substances. For in vii 4 he claimed that substances are the primary things that have essences, and that something has an essence only if its account is a definition (1030a6–7). If a particular cannot have a definition, apparently it cannot have an essence or be a substance. Aristotle seems to suggest this when he contrasts the indefinable particular with the definable universal form:

⟨As a compound⟩ with matter he has no account, since matter is indefinable; but he has an account according to the primary substance, e.g. for man the account of soul; for the substance is the inherent form, from which and the matter the compound substance is spoken of. (1037a27–30)

This remark applies not only to the particular material compound, but also to the particular form; it cannot have a universal account, since it essentially includes a particular bit of matter and essentially has spatio-temporal properties.

142. THE STATUS OF PARTICULAR SUBSTANCES

Part of the case for universals seems to suggest that being a universal is a necessary condition for being a substance (since particulars seem to be indefinable and posterior in knowledge and definition); part of it seems to suggest that it is a sufficient condition (since universals seem to meet the conditions for priority as well as particulars meet them). To see how well Aristotle answers the case for universals, we should see how he answers each part separately. First, he has some replies to the objection that particulars cannot be substances.

Aristotle cannot, for the reasons we have just seen, allow that the particular is in itself an object of definition and scientific knowledge; but he can still fairly insist that scientific knowledge and definition apply to a particular form. A particular man is essentially a particular form that is an instance of the universal species-form, and because of this our scientific knowledge applies to the particular; its particular form places it in its proper natural kind. Aristotle says: 'In every case we speak of and recognize ⟨particulars⟩ by the universal account' (1036a8). He allows that we can apply our scientific knowledge of the universal to the particular; and we can apply it because the particular form is an instance of the specific form.

On this view, particular forms partly satisfy the requirements for being objects of knowledge. Not being universals, they are not the primary objects of knowledge; but they are among the objects that scientific knowledge applies to. We might say they are what science is *about*, though not what it is *of*. Indeed, they are more important than that. If there were no particular forms, there would be no universal forms either, and no scientific knowledge; in this way particular forms are necessary, though no particular one is necessary, for scientific knowledge.

But if this defence shows that particulars are knowable, it does not thereby show that they are prior in knowledge. Indeed, it seems that they are not, if our knowledge is primarily of universals. Knowledge of the universal is necessary for us to distinguish being a man from being Socrates, and for us to apply to Socrates the laws that hold good of him in so far as he is a man, not in so far as he is this man. In so far as they are prior and basic in scientific knowledge, universals have a claim, not yet undermined, to be substances, and for the same reason particulars seem not to be substances.

It is equally difficult to see how particular forms can be prior in account or being to universal forms. For since it is essential to this particular form of this man that it is the form of a man, must it not instantiate the specific form, and must the specific form therefore not exist? In that case, the particular form seems to depend on the universal, and so cannot be separable from it; but separability is necessary for priority, and so for being a substance.

143. THE DIFFERENCE BETWEEN UNIVERSALS AND PROPERTIES

Perhaps, however, particular forms do not depend on universals. For Aristotle describes what is common as being present in many places at once (1040b25–6); and since a universal is common (1038b11), its existence seems to require not just instantiation, but plural instantiation at a time.[44] In that case the particular form that is Socrates could exist even if he were not an instance of the universal man, because no other men existed. His existence requires the instantiation of the property of being a man, but not the existence of the universal.[45] Being a man consists of only some of the features that constitute being this man, since it lacks the determinate properties and spatio-temporal position that makes Socrates the man he is as opposed to some other man; but since it does not require plural instantiation, as the universal man does, it does not make Socrates depend on the universal.

These distinctions raise further questions about priority. The particular form is essentially particular, not logically repeatable and not definable in qualitative terms, whereas being a man allows plural instantiations; and so the property is not identical to the particular form. Moreover, the property is independent of this particular form, even though it depends on some particular form or other. Aristotle, therefore, can maintain that the particular is prior to the universal only if he admits that the property is prior to any given particular.

Moreover, a property distinct from a universal is hard to fit into Aristotle's scheme.[46] He cannot allow that it is essentially a universal, even though plural instances of it are possible; if it has just one particular instance, it will apparently itself be a particular. On the other hand, he cannot claim that it is essentially a particular, since it will have plural instances sometimes (when more than one man exists), and will become a universal. He must apparently claim that the property is sometimes a particular, sometimes a universal.

If Aristotle recognizes properties that are sometimes particulars and sometimes universals (depending on the number of instances), he seems to raise a question about his conception of particularity. For his claims about Socrates and the sun imply that particulars are logically unrepeatable, that they essentially include definite spatio-temporal characteristics. If a property with only one instance is a particular, it does not satisfy this demand for unrepeatability; the demand will be true only for things that are *essentially* particular. But if Aristotle concedes this much, he needs some further argument to show that the particular form of Socrates is essentially particular, and not simply a determinate property that in fact (but not essentially) has only one instance.[47]

It is difficult, then, for Aristotle to defend the independence of particulars without raising further questions about his claims. If he wants to distinguish universals from properties, he can show that particulars are independent of universals, but only if he makes them dependent on properties, and revises his conception of particularity to accommodate properties. Even though he might win a nominal victory against defenders of universal substances, he seems to have conceded one point that they urge—the dependence of particular substances on other things that are not essentially particulars.[48]

144. PARTICULARS AND UNIVERSALS AS SUBSTANCES

These questions about universals challenge the claim of particular forms to be substances, because they seem to show that particular forms are not prior in being, knowledge, or definition, and so do not display the three types of priority that were taken to be necessary for substance. The challenge clearly succeeds, if Aristotle intends a successful candidate for substance to be the only thing that completely satisfies the demand for priority.

His defence of form against matter and compound suggests that he does not intend such a strong claim about priority. He argues that the particular form is the primary substance, not because it alone fully satisfies all the criteria for substance under every natural interpretation, but because it best satisfies the criteria as a whole, interpreted by reference to a reasonable conception of a basic subject. From some points of view, for instance, the material compound is more separable than the form is, and the form does not completely satisfy the demand for separability. Still, Aristotle believes that form is the most plausible basic subject and substance, when all the criteria together are considered.

This defence of form implies that since matter and compound both satisfy some criteria, they also count as substances to some degree. The different substances are focally connected, and matter and compound will be secondary substances. It is reasonable of Aristotle to stick to his initial claim that form, matter, and compound are three types of substance. His argument does not support form to the exclusion of matter and compound, but simply implies that the legitimate claims of matter and compound depend on the prior claims of form.

If this is Aristotle's conclusion about form, matter, and compound, a similar solution removes some of the difficulties about universals. Such a solution concedes that universals satisfy some criteria for substance, even that they satisfy some criteria better than particulars do, but argues that particulars are primary substances, and universals (in the category of substance) are secondary substances.

Sometimes Aristotle seems to agree that his arguments require universals to be substances of some sort.

We have found that the compound and the account are different ⟨types of⟩ substance; I mean that the first is substance by being the account combined with matter, and the second is the account without addition. Now the substances spoken of as being compounds all perish, since they also all come into being. But the account does not perish in such a way that it is ever ⟨in the process of⟩ perishing; for it has no ⟨process of⟩ coming into being either. The essence of this house, not the essence of house, is ⟨in process of⟩ coming to be; but accounts are and are not without ⟨any process of⟩ coming to be and perishing, since we have shown that no one generates or produces them. (1039b20–7)

Since every particular must be a compound of form and matter, so must a particular form; and that is what Aristotle calls the essence of this house. The essence of house must be the universal form of house; and since he calls this a substance, he must recognize universal as well as particular substances.[49]

Aristotle's explicit remarks, then, give us good reason for taking him to believe that universals are secondary substances.[50] Such a view is also his best defence against nominalism.[51] All Aristotle's reasons for believing in the reality of universals apply just as strongly to the *Metaphysics* as to any other work. Book vii does not undermine the arguments given in Book iii for the reality of universals. The view that universals are secondary substances explains why Aristotle says both that they are substances and that they are not, just as a similar account of matter and compound resolves other apparent conflicts.[52]

In the *Organon* Aristotle accepts a doctrine of secondary substances. He retains it in the *Metaphysics*, just as he still believes in the primacy of particular substances. But he gives a different defence of the substantial status of substantial universals. The *Categories* treats universals as second-best subjects; but the *Metaphysics* also appeals to the essence-criterion, and to the place of universals in scientific knowledge; they are no longer merely second-best subjects.

The *Metaphysics* gives up the term 'secondary substances' for universal substances, perhaps because it should not refer only to universals. Aristotle has analysed particulars more carefully than in the *Organon* and *Physics*, and has found that matter and compound are secondary substances; and a parallel argument justifies the claim of universals. The formal character of a particular form makes it a this and a basic subject to which matter and compound are secondary; its particularity makes it a this and a basic subject to which the universal is secondary. Since Aristotle's defence of particular forms as primary substances allows other things to be secondary substances, he can accommodate universals without having to take back any of his arguments for particular forms.

Perhaps this argument would be convincing if the only non-particulars to be considered were universals actually belonging to many particulars. But if Aristotle is committed to belief in properties as well as universals, we might wonder why properties rather than universals should not be secondary substances. If we concede for the moment that particulars are primary substances, and that there are non-particular secondary substances, why are these not properties rather than universals?

Aristotle does not face this question, since he does not see that his conception of particulars and universals requires belief in properties. He must at least agree that properties are no less substances than universals are; but must he also agree that properties rather than universals are the objects of scientific knowledge? If he agrees about this, then belief that universals are substances results from failure to distinguish universals from properties.

Perhaps he can reply that the plural instantiation necessary for universals is also necessary for something to be an object of scientific knowledge. While the qualitative properties we attribute to universals are just the same as those we attribute to the corresponding properties, plural instantiation is necessary if universals are to explain features of the spatio-temporal world. We understand particulars in so far as we *group* them into kinds under universals, and belief in universals shows us features that the many particulars of a given kind have in common. The epistemological and explanatory functions of universals seem to suggest that they still have a claim to be substances even if we also recognize properties. At any rate, this is the direction we should look if we want to see how many of Aristotle's claims about universals might survive the recognition of properties.

145. THE PRIMACY OF PARTICULAR SUBSTANCES

Do Aristotle's concessions to universals leave any reason for believing in the primacy of particulars? He is a realist about universals; he must concede that particulars depend on properties, even if they do not depend on universals; and he seems to agree that universals are prior in account and knowledge. If he sees the force of his arguments, should he not conclude that neither particulars nor universals are prior?[53]

He does not defend his belief in the priority of particulars over universals as well as he defends his belief in the priority of form over matter and compound; and his claim about the priority of particulars is less central and important for his general view of nature and explanation. Still, he might fairly appeal to the sort of priority that is suggested by his concern with basic subjects. The English 'subject' suggests, as Aristotle's Greek does, that the subjects of the sciences are what the sciences are about or apply to. Though we would have no scientific knowledge of particulars without knowledge of universals, the existence of the particulars explains why we have the science, not the other way round. We do not have reason to believe in particulars because we have to explain something about universals; we believe in universals because they allow us to understand facts about particulars.

To this extent particulars are prior in knowledge and theory to universals; to justify belief in a given universal we need to show that it explains facts about particulars, and this is the ultimate test of our belief in universals. The function of our belief in universals is essentially explanatory; our belief in particulars essentially identifies what is to be explained.

This argument suggests that Aristotle's claims about priority have to be quite complicated. He suggests that what explains is more knowable than what is explained (*Phys.* 184a16–26); it will therefore be prior in one way (*APo* 71b29–72a5), and Aristotle acknowledges this in counting universals as substances. But if we ask why universals explain anything, we will have to answer by appeal to the existence of the right sorts of particulars; and this relation, he wants to say, is not symmetrical. To this extent the search for the cause or explanation will actually lead us to the thing to be explained, since its existence explains why we have anything to explain in the first place. Aristotle expresses his realism by insisting that facts about the world explain the truth of statements about them, and are therefore prior to them (*Catg.* 14b10–22).[54] For similar reasons he might plausibly claim that we have reason to believe in the universals we believe in *because* they explain the features and behaviour of actually existing particular forms, and that this 'because' indicates the priority of particulars that he wants to defend.

Aristotle needs a similar argument if he is to show why particular substances are also prior to properties. We have seen that a particular man does not seem to be prior in being to the property of being a man. Perhaps Aristotle ought to agree that the property—rather than the universal or the particular—is the genuine substance, since it seems to satisfy the criteria better than either of the other candidates does. If Aristotle has a way out of this conclusion, he must argue that particulars are prior as explananda to properties in the same way as they are prior to universals. He should claim that we recognize properties such as being a man because we want to explain facts about particular men; in this way the particular is the cause of the property, not the other way round.

If this is Aristotle's claim, it is still open to doubt, but it is not an arbitrary preference for particulars, and it attributes to them a type of priority that is compatible with realism about universals and properties. Aristotle began the *Metaphysics* with an inquiry into the four causes. He has seen that to justify the use of a pattern of causal explanation we need to argue for the existence of something that it applies to. Seeing this, he sees that the basic question is about the existence of the basic subjects. The question about basic subjects leads him through the argument of iv and vii–ix. Our explanations involving formal and final causes will refer to something in the world if there are really particular forms and actualities that actualize the potentialities of matter; and so Aristotle tries to show how we must conceive the subjects that can be identified with these forms and actualities. In finding the right subjects he finds the point and justification of belief in universals as well. For this reason he can still claim that particular forms are the primary substances.

146. RESULTS OF THE *METAPHYSICS*

In *Metaphysics* i Aristotle suggested that his predecessors had been too hasty, since they had looked for the causes without knowing what they should be looking for. Though universal science studies the causes, it should not try to answer all the Presocratics' questions within one science; it should be a second-order science prescribing the method of a first-order science. *Metaphysics* iv explains that this second-order science is dialectical, but not purely dialectical; for it offers to prove conclusions about how things really are, not merely how they seem to be on a coherent account of common beliefs. These claims for the universal science of being are partly justified by Aristotle's defence of the Principle of Non-Contradiction.

The rest of the argument in Books vii–ix may be recapitulated as follows:

1. In iv we find that if we speak of some persisting bearer of properties, it must have an essence. Hence we look for the basic subjects with essences, and for their essences. That is the inquiry begun in Book vii.
2. The basic subjects are identical to their essences, since the subject and its essence come to be and perish together.
3. The essence of something is its cause, or, more exactly, its explanatory property. When we divide the world into persisting subjects, we identify the subjects with the properties that best explain the rest of what happens. (We believe, e.g., that this is the same bench with a new coat of paint, not a new bench created by the new coat of paint.)
4. The relevant cause is the form. Aristotle reaches this conclusion from his discussion of potentiality and actuality, and his identification of form with actuality.
5. Hence substance is form. Since substances are basic subjects identical to their essences, they turn out to be particular forms.

The conclusion of the argument supports the original claim in Book i about the necessity of recognizing the four causes. We identify the basic persistent subjects by reference to the properties that provide efficient-causal explanations of change and stability. Some of these properties are material, but some are formal and final (in natural substances the same properties have both features); and so we must recognize both material and formal substances if we are to investigate all the causes that are the proper concern of science.

147. THE ROLE OF A PRIORI AND EMPIRICAL ARGUMENT

The first two steps of the previous argument are needed if it is to belong to first philosophy, concerning 'how things are' (1030a28). Knowledge of how things are should rest on arguments leading us from the commonsense starting-points, the things 'known to us', to the genuine first principles, the things 'known by nature'. Some things are by their nature proper objects of knowledge because they are basic in the explanations that best explain the appearances. A demonstrative science rests on the discovery of these explanatory entities; and such a science tells us how things are. First philosophy is not itself a demonstrative science, but it is intended to find the first principles of demonstrative science. It is therefore justified in claiming that views about explanation should determine our views about the number and nature of the persisting subjects there are. The third step of Aristotle's argument, like the first two, rests on a priori considerations about the relation between ontology and explanation.

But these a priori considerations themselves suggest that the fourth step of the argument will not rest purely on a priori considerations. For once Aristotle appeals to causes and explanatory properties, he makes it clear, on a priori grounds, that the argument will not be entirely a priori. The empirical considerations enter with the appeal to explanatory properties.

When we look for basic subjects in a spatio–temporal context we look for basic subjects persisting through change. Subjects persist in so far as they retain their essential properties; and so the substances will be the basic persisting subjects of change in so far as they have the basic essential properties. These basic essential properties will be the potentialities for the relevant changes.

If we are to be justified in counting some changes as non–essential changes in a subject, and others as the coming to be or perishing of a subject, we need to make some assumptions about the significant laws and regularities in the world. Aristotle believes that the significant laws and regularities include those that explain the behaviour of a natural organism teleologically. The persisting subject is the natural organism, in so far as it has the formal properties that are both actualities realizing goal-directed potentialities of the proximate matter, and also persistent potentialities for goal-directed activities.

Aristotle needs to show that laws and regularities appear from the recognition of wholes apart from aggregates. He could claim this fairly confidently about organisms, to the extent that, whatever we know or do not know about their origin, they react in fairly constant and predictable ways to their environment despite the material changes that they undergo. This might still be true even in the logically possible conditions where we are quite wrong about the origin of organisms. Suppose, for instance, that an organism's capacity for survival in the environment were quite irrelevant to its reproduction and the survival of its offspring; suppose a malicious demon had chosen quite arbitrarily to destroy one individual and let another survive without reference to its fitness for survival in its natural environment. It would follow that the functions, design, and structure of the organisms familiar to us would be quite irrelevant to how they came into being or reproduce themselves. This would not prove that organisms are not substances or that they are mere aggregates. For we could still see them observing laws, and understand their behaviour in the light of these laws, though we would be quite wrong about how they came to observe them.

Aristotle's actual argument, however, relies on his belief in teleology. This general theory assures him that the formal and functional properties of natural organisms are genuinely explanatory properties. Teleology assures him not only that the behaviour of organisms follows laws that refer to properties of the whole organism, but also that the origin and growth of organisms follow the same laws. It is not just an accident that the mature organism follows laws that involve wholes; that is the predictable result of other laws affecting the growth and maintenance of the organism. Features of the matter in turn are understood by reference to the form and function.

Aristotle assumes that if we recognize material constituents as the basic realities, and insist on mentioning only these in our basic laws, we will find it hard to trace regularities and differences in the behaviour of compounds such as natural organisms. For we will not necessarily be able to find the appropriate terms and laws to replace such simple regularities as 'When an animal has had nothing to drink for a long time, it tends to try to drink any liquid it sees'. If we deny the reality of organisms, we will find it hard to express anything equivalent to this commonsense law. We might suggest that ordinary objects are heaps and aggregates, and that commonsense laws are about these, giving rough approximations to the truth. But then *which* aggregates are the subjects of these laws? Unless we allow ourselves the resources of common sense, we may not be able to say.

These faults in a purely compositional approach to substances are especially obvious in the particular Atomist approach familiar to Aristotle. The Atomists come nowhere near to plausible laws that would explain the behaviour of persisting subjects. Though they are committed to the reduction of commonsense substances to coincidental heaps, they have no prospect of making the reduction seem plausible.

On this point our position must be different from Aristotle's, since we now have a less remote possibility of explaining events in the world without reference to commonsense functionally described substances. But to say we can explain them is to say we can find some sort of explanation, not that we can find the appropriate explanation. If we can find laws about wholes and organisms that resist reduction to laws about more elementary substances, we can accept Aristotle's argument. We can still agree that the main principles of Aristotelian natural philosophy pass the test that Aristotelian first philosophy prescribes for them, since they recognize the right sorts of basic subjects to capture the appropriate laws and regularities. Aristotle can fairly claim that a theory refusing to admit goal-directed organisms as basic subjects will fail to find all the appropriate laws.

Aristotle's defence of the reality of form implies that neither formal nor material causation is really prior to the other.[55] The order of natural priority that he recognizes makes the more basic explanations prior to the less basic; but in this case neither form nor matter is prior, since neither explanation is more basic.[56] In so far as Aristotle has distinguished two reasonable types of explanations, and shown that neither is appropriately reduced to the other, he has defended the irreducibility of form.

To believe in particular forms is simply to be guided by the explanatory role of form and function in our judgments about persistent subjects. The persistent subject that is properly identified with Socrates is not the material compound; if he were one of these, then comparatively trivial and (from the explanatory point of view) insignificant changes would cause him to perish. He must therefore be identified with the particular materiate form. The particular form is a basic subject identical to its essence; this is what we have been looking for in our inquiry into substance; and so Aristotle has good reasons for identifying particular form with substance.

The argument for identifying substance with form rests partly on a priori, partly on empirical, argument. The role of empirical argument implies no retreat from the principles of first philosophy. First philosophy shows us the connexion between substance, essence, and explanation. Once explanation is introduced, a more specific answer to the questions about substances must be expected to rely on some empirical claim. The conclusion will be more secure the more plausible the empirical claim is; and Aristotle is wise enough to rely mostly on fairly general and plausible claims.

148. FIRST PHILOSOPHY AND STRONG DIALECTIC

Aristotle sketches an account of substance that meets the conditions imposed by the methods of first philosophy. The common belief that such things as Socrates, this horse, and so on are substances turns out to be justified in a way, once we consider what is required for being a basic subject. But the common beliefs that are justified also need to be modified. For the basic subject and primary substance turns out to be something that common sense does not initially recognize—the particular form.

Aristotle examines and criticizes common sense by examining the basic subject and the primary essence. His critical attitude actually allows him to accept more of common sense than he could accept if he were less critical. If we simply follow common sense, we may rely on the broad predication-formula to interpret the subject-criterion; and then matter, at most, turns out to be substance. Similarly, if we assume that essences must be universals and that natural organisms must be compounds of form and matter, we may recognize universal forms and particular material compounds, but since we will not recognize particular forms identical to their essences, natural organisms will appear to be coincidental compounds. Moreover, we may think the claims of particulars and universals to be substances are mutually exclusive, and that no single answer to our initial question about substance is defensible.

Aristotle shows how common sense may lead us astray at these stages of the argument, since some of its natural and intuitive assumptions lead to unacceptable and inconsistent conclusions. Left to its own devices common sense, and purely dialectical argument, must conclude that its demands are inconsistent and its initial intuitions unjustifiable. It needs the help of first philosophy to show that most of its demands and intuitions are defensible.

We cannot see exactly how first philosophy works, or how it differs from pure dialectic, without going into some details of the interpretation of Aristotle's views on substance. In my view, he does not depart so far from common sense and the *Categories* as he would if he believed that universals are the primary substances. Nor do I think his treatment is purely or primarily aporetic, and to that extent purely dialectical, pointing out that different plausible candidates for substance conflict with some plausible criteria. If Aristotle simply tried to split the difference between common beliefs, he would be keeping very close to pure dialectic. If, on the other hand, he assumed that only an immaterial substance could be a proper substance, he would be departing quite far from common beliefs. I have tried to show that he defends the central common beliefs, and that his judgment about which ones are central relies on the demand of first philosophy for basic subjects.

First philosophy shows what must be added to common sense. We are right to think Socrates is a substance. But we have not yet identified exactly what it is about Socrates that makes him a substance. We must say that he is a particular form; for this, not the remote matter or the material compound, justifies our normal views about the persistence of Socrates. We are right to think Socrates is a more important continuant than musical Socrates, and that his becoming and perishing are genuine substantial changes; and we cannot justify these views if we identify Socrates with a material compound. We find a basic subject with Socrates' temporal career and essence only if we recognize a particular form, which is also a formal compound.

Metaphysics of the sort described in *Metaphysics* iv defends common beliefs, but not the very same beliefs that we began with. Aristotle acknowledges this in arguing that most of the generally recognized substances turn out not to meet the conditions for substance that are met by particular form (1040b5–16). We may think that Socrates' hands and feet exist when he no longer exists, and we may think a log is a substance in the same way Socrates is; both of these beliefs turn out to be false, in Aristotle's view, once we see why Socrates is a substance.

Hence the eventually successful candidate for substance is not one that common sense recognizes at once; it did not appear at all in the *Categories*, where Aristotle's term for form, '*eidos*', was the name of a universal, not of a particular. In the *Physics* form is introduced by contrast with matter, but nothing suggests that it is meant to be a particular form. The particular form appears in the *Generation and Corruption*, but with no argument to show that it is a substance. In the *Metaphysics* Aristotle argues that the truth in commonsense views about substance requires the recognition of particular forms, and the rejection of some common beliefs about subjects and about parts of substances.

At the crucial points the theory is not supposed to rely, as ordinary dialectical argument relies, simply on the support of common beliefs. We do not simply endorse common candidates for substance. We argue that substances must be the basic continuing subjects; that these must be identified with their essences; and that essences are found by reference to causes. These claims express the importance of continuing subjects and essences. They allow us to apply tests for substance apart from the common beliefs, and the tests do not guarantee in advance that the common beliefs will come out true.

I have often remarked that these claims about substance are not entirely foreign to Aristotle's earlier works; indeed, Aristotle often defends or assumes such views about subjects, essences, and causes. In his early works, however, he fails to explain how views on these questions properly determine our views on substance. He fails to explain this because he regards the doctrine of substance as a product of pure dialectic. I have tried to show how, from the point of view of strong dialectic, these different issues are connected, and why an understanding of the connexion leads to a different doctrine of substance.

Dialectic is useful to Aristotle because it deals with questions that do not seem to be open to the ordinary sort of empirical inquiry. We look to dialectic for answers that we presuppose in empirical inquiry.[57] First philosophy performs the same functions. It is especially clear in Book iv that it inquires into the presuppositions of empirical science; for an empirical science assumes that it deals with an objective world, and with substances and their essential and coincidental properties. First philosophy shows why we should accept these presuppositions, and what happens if we attempt to give them up.

The same is true to some degree of Books vii–ix. They argue for a particular conception of reality that we use to guide empirical inquiry, so that it cannot itself be an ordinary object of empirical inquiry. Aristotle argues for the reality of form by showing the difficulties of a purely compositional account of basic realities. In arguing for a teleological conception of form, he makes some apparently more empirical claims. But even these may be presuppositions rather than simply results of empirical inquiry; for it may turn out that we have to apply teleological and formal conceptions to ourselves as inquirers. That raises a further issue to be considered in the *De Anima*.[58] While it would be quite wrong to claim that arguments in first philosophy are wholly non-empirical, it is still true that, like dialectic in general, they are prior to empirical inquiry, in so far as they defend the assumptions taken for granted in empirical inquiry.

If Aristotle's arguments succeed, their consequences for some of his other inquiries are important. If we find that he relies on common beliefs about substances and their essences, we will not at once conclude that his argument is merely dialectical in the sense that restricts its claim to yield knowledge of objective principles. For his general conception of substance itself relies on a firmer basis than mere dialectic. He can therefore justify an appeal to substance by referring to the defence he has offered in the *Metaphysics*. To see if Aristotle defends himself this way, or presents theories needing this sort of defence, we should turn to two further Aristotelian inquiries. Psychology clearly depends on the theory of substance in ways we will examine. The dependence of ethics is less clear, but we will see that it is no less important.

III
APPLICATIONS OF
THE SOLUTION

13

THE SOUL AS SUBSTANCE

149. ARISTOTLE'S TASK

In the *Metaphysics* Aristotle argues for a theory of substance, form, and matter. The theory is a product of first philosophy, and the method of first philosophy is strong dialectic. He argues for the existence of first substances that are particular forms; these are natural organisms identified by the potentialities that are their functional and teleological properties, and not by the remote matter that is the basis for these properties. In Aristotle's view, the common belief in the reality of substances irreducible to their matter is correct; first philosophy justifies this belief by showing that it rests on more than common sense, because it rests on the defensible view that formal and functional properties are ineliminably and irreducibly explanatory.

Aristotle identifies soul with form, and body with matter. He assumes that to have a soul is to have the functional properties that are the form, and that the relation of soul to body is the relation of form to matter, and of actuality to potentiality. If Aristotle is right to assume that first philosophy answers the main questions in philosophy of mind, we must admit the power and plausibility of his metaphysical theory.

We must, therefore, ask whether Aristotle fairly examines the specific problems and questions about soul and body, and shows that the theory of the *Metaphysics* offers reasonable answers to them.[1] Though soul and body do not coincide exactly with mind and body, Aristotle's theory may contribute something to philosophy of mind. It will pass an important test if it helps to answer reasonable questions that Aristotle himself has not asked.

The *De Anima* not only discusses general questions about the relation of soul and body, but also describes the different states of the soul—perception, imagination, thought, and desire. This aspect of the *De Anima* will concern us in Chapter 14. If we examine it, we should be able to see whether Aristotle uses his general theory, and whether the theory is responsible for the better or the worse aspects of his account.

Aristotle believes that his view of soul and body allows us to understand the nature and essence of different types of living organisms, and that when we understand this, we can discover their good. His account of psychic states is therefore the basis of his ethical argument.

He needs to show that some basic ethical principles themselves rest on principles of first philosophy, and hence can be defended by more than purely dialectical argument. In Chapter 15 we will begin to see how far Aristotle can justify any such claims about ethics.

150. PUZZLES ABOUT THE SOUL

Strong dialectic of the sort practised in first philosophy must justify the common beliefs, or most of them, by appeal to some independently reasonable principles. In *De Anima* i Aristotle presents the common beliefs, and the puzzles they raise. As usual, it is worth examining the puzzles, to see that the questions have not been stated correctly. We agree at the outset that the soul is 'some sort of principle (*archê*) of animals' (402a6–7); but this extent of agreement does not take us far.[2]

Do all souls belong to the same species or not? If not, do they differ ⟨only⟩ in species, or ⟨also⟩ in genus? As things are, those who discuss and investigate the soul would seem to ⟨ignore this question since they⟩ examine only the human soul. Nor should we forget to ask whether there is just one account of soul, as there is of animal, or a different account for each type of soul—e.g. of horse, dog, human being, god. ⟨On this second view⟩, the universal animal is either nothing or else it is posterior to these; and the same will apply to any other common thing predicated. (402b1–9)[3]

Even if the soul is some sort of principle, it may not be worth investigating in its own right; for things with souls may not (as such) have any genuine or important common property.

   To find out whether having a soul is an important common property we turn to its commonly accepted attributes. 'All define the soul by three things, one might say—by movement, by perception, and by being incorporeal' (405b11–12).[4] Such different beliefs about the essential features of soul might well suggest that different theorists are really talking about different things. We cannot simply combine different answers and say that the soul is the cause of both perception and movement; for if the cause of perception and the cause of movement have nothing more in common, our use of the term 'soul' for them will not show that having a soul is an important common property.[5] It will be especially hard to see any common property if we follow the conception of cause that previous theorists have assumed. For they seek material causes, and different material causes seem appropriate for understanding movement and perception.[6]

   Aristotle even suggests, contrary to common beliefs, that the soul is the principle of life, not simply of animal life, and hence that plants as well as animals have souls.[7] If we agree that everything that is alive has a soul, we cannot even assume that the soul is essentially the cause of movement or perception. If its functions must include the nutritive and reproductive functions of plants, it seems even clearer that having a soul is not a genuine common property, but a mere disjunction of properties.

So far we might assume general agreement that the soul is some sort of material stuff. But Aristotle denies even this degree of agreement; for he claims that common beliefs also associate the soul with the incorporeal.[8] We think that in some way an organism is one because it has one soul (410b10–15); and no material stuff seems to explain this role. For if we identify the soul with the stuff that causes movement or perception, we want to know what makes that stuff and the rest of the material components into one organism; and the stuff that causes movement and perception does not answer this question (411b5–14). If the soul were simply a material stuff distributed through parts of the body, then we would expect to be able to split the body into different parts, and to find a part of the soul in each; but we do not think this is possible (411b14–30).[9] We believe the soul is indivisibly present in the whole organism; and this belief is hard to explain if we identify the soul with some type of material constituent.

We connect the soul not only with the unity of organisms at a time, but also with their identity and persistence through time. We think Socrates exists as long as his soul exists, that without the soul he perishes (411b7–9), and that if one soul replaces another one person has perished and been replaced by another. But we find it hard to see how this feature of the soul could be explained by some particular material stuff of the sort that might seem to explain perception and movement.[10]

If a corporeal soul seems not to explain some features of the soul, we might conceive an incorporeal soul in different ways. First, we might argue that if it cannot be a material substance, it must be an immaterial substance, neither identical to nor constituted by a material body. This is the Platonic solution. Aristotle argues that it underestimates the close connexions between the soul and the body whose potentialities it actualizes (407b13–26).[11]

Alternatively, if some functions of the soul seem not to be functions of a material stuff, but we think the soul can be a substance only if it is a sort of material stuff, we infer that the soul is not a substance at all, but some arrangement or 'attunement' (*harmonia*) of material constituents. This theory shows that we can recognize the non-material character of the soul without treating it as an immaterial substance. None the less, Aristotle rejects any such theory, (407b27–408a28), maintaining that the soul is a substance.[12]

The survey of common beliefs about soul shows that a general account of the soul cannot be read off them, and that we cannot even expect to solve the puzzles they raise by a direct attack. For it is not clear that the apparent disagreements (about whether the soul is material or not, and about what kind of material it is) are really disagreements about the answer to one question. If questions about the soul are really just questions about the cause of perception and motion, and about the source of unity in the subject, then different answers need not be contradictory. In this case, as in *Metaphysics* iii, Aristotle's predecessors have overlooked some important preliminary questions; for we can hardly settle their apparent or real disagreements without deciding what we should expect an account of the soul to be like.

151. THE SOLUTION

In the *Metaphysics* Aristotle solves the puzzles by isolating the preliminary questions, and answering them through his own doctrine of substance, form, and matter. The puzzles raised in *De Anima* i seem to him to demand a similar approach.

The Presocratics assume that if the soul is to be the cause of movement or perception, we must find the sort of material that is suitable for these processes; some common material feature of the material processes must be present in all and only perceptions or movements. If we look for this, we may believe that the soul-stuff must itself be highly mobile if it is to cause movement, or that it must be similar to the stuff in the external world that it perceives. If these causes of the two different processes must be material causes, they may not involve the same sort of matter; and therefore the soul may not be an object of study in its own right.

The assumption that causation must be material causation affects even those who accept non-materialist conceptions of the soul. Those who think the soul cannot be a material cause infer that it cannot be a cause at all, and so accept an attunement theory. Correspondingly, those who reject the attunement theory because they think the soul is a cause and a substance, but not a material stuff, infer that it is an immaterial substance; for they assume that if it were material, it could play only the causal role of a material stuff. They conceive an immaterial substance on the pattern of a material stuff, and explain its special characteristics by reference to the special stuff composing it.

Aristotle's metaphysical views imply that these are not the only reasonable ways to conceive the soul. For he has argued that formal as well as material causes are genuinely explanatory, that form as well as matter is a genuine substance, and that form provides the principle of unity; and he believes that none of these arguments need involve immaterial substances. These doctrines may therefore solve the puzzles that arise if we recognize only material causes.

Aristotle seeks to solve the puzzles by arguing that the soul is substance, but substance as form rather than matter, and therefore a formal rather than a material cause. Once we conceive the soul in this way, we can see why having a soul is an important common property of living organisms. He assumes the threefold division of substance as matter, form, and compound, as in *Metaphysics* viii (1042a26–31); the form is a this, and identified with actuality as opposed to matter as potentiality (*DA* 412a6–11).[13] Living bodies are recognized examples of substances, and can be regarded as form, matter, and compound (412a11–16); Aristotle wants to show that the soul is the natural substance in so far as it is form.

It follows that every natural body that has life is a substance as compound. But since it is also *this sort* of body—i.e. the sort that has life—soul cannot be body, since the body ⟨is substance⟩ as subject and matter, not said of a subject. The soul, then, must be substance as the form of a natural body that has life potentially; and since substance is actuality, the soul will be the actuality of this sort of body. (412a15–21)[14]

His argument, however, is not completely clear, and some premisses need to be supplied.

He begins from the assumption that 'the soul is that by which primarily we live and perceive and think, so that it would be some account and form, not matter and the subject' (414a12–14). This assumption is not obviously correct. For the common beliefs described in Book i treat the soul as a principle of animals, not of all living organisms; and though Aristotle has assumed in some places that plants have souls, he has not justified the assumption. Indeed, it might seem to make the problems worse; for if it is hard to find a single account of soul to apply to all animals, it might seem still harder to find one that will apply to plants as well.

Aristotle, however, argues that if we ascribe soul to all living creatures, we can explain what souls have in common. For he understands 'life' in teleological terms: 'By life we mean nourishment, growth, and diminution through oneself' (412a14–15). Teleology is implied in the claim that a creature is nourished, grows, and diminishes through itself—from a causal origin within itself rather than from the action of external agencies; for Aristotle rejects any attempt to describe or explain nourishment without appeal to final causation (415b28–416a18).[15]

This account of life is Aristotle's answer to the suspicion that being alive is really several homonymous properties. He thinks being alive is an important common property because it is a teleological order of the parts and bodily processes of the organism to achieve some constant goals—the survival and flourishing of the organism or of its species. The claim that something is alive implies that it is ordered to achieve these goals, and therefore implies some fairly definite expectations about the subject's structure and behaviour.

In saying that the soul is that by which we live 'primarily', Aristotle denies that the soul is the material stuff or component that something has if and only if it is alive. Even if we found any such stuff, it would not be that by which we live primarily. What we live by primarily is whatever explains our vital activities; and since Aristotle has shown that these are goal-directed activities, their primary explanation must refer to the teleologically organized, goal-directed features of the subject, to the form rather than the matter.

For substance, as we said, is spoken of in three ways, as form, matter, and the compound of both; and of these, matter is capacity, form actuality. Since, therefore, the compound of body and soul is ensouled, body is not the actuality of soul, but the soul is the actuality of some sort of body. (414a14–19)

If the soul is what we live by primarily, it must be the final cause of living, hence a formal, not a material, aspect of the subject, and hence the actuality of the body.

The problems about the soul surveyed in *De Anima* i now turn out to have concerned the explanation and understanding of the vital activities of living organisms. The problems seemed hard to solve because we did not realize that vital activities have to be understood with reference to formal and final causes. We have the clue to this solution when we notice that questions about the soul are questions about vital activities, and that both materialist and immaterialist answers seem unsatisfactory. To complete the solution we only need to agree that the soul is the formal and final cause.

152. THE RELATION OF SOUL TO BODY

Aristotle ought to explain why his account of body and soul as matter and form solves the puzzles that arose about the relation of soul to body. We should be able to see why the soul is not a body or a constituent of a body, why it is a substance in its own right, not a mere attunement or other non-substantial aspect of a body, and why none the less it need not be an immaterial substance independent of a material body.

Aristotle claims that a natural body sharing in life is a compound substance (412a15–16). The body that is subject and matter is potentially alive (412a19–21). The body that survives the loss of the soul, and so is no longer alive, is not potentially alive either (412b25–6); nor, however, is the seed from which the living body grows potentially alive in the relevant sense (412b26–7).[16] Hence the only body that is potentially alive seems to be the one that is actually alive; but that body seems to be the compound rather than the matter. The relation between these different claims about bodies is obscure.

If we have understood the *Metaphysics* correctly, these puzzles ought to disappear. Since the proximate matter, the materiate form, and the formal compound are identical, these are three different ways of describing the same subject.

And so if we must give some account common to every sort of soul, we will say that the soul is the first actuality of a natural organic body. Hence we need not ask whether the soul and body are one, any more than we need to ask this about the wax and the shape or, in general, about the matter and the thing of which it is the matter. For while one and being are spoken of in several ways, the actuality ⟨and what it actualizes⟩ are fully one. (412b4–9)

Soul and body are one in the way that form and matter are one (cf. *Met.* 1045b17–23).[17]

Aristotle identifies the form with the first actuality of the body, and therefore a sort of potentiality (412a22–7; cf. 417a21–b2). The living creature performs its particular goal-directed activities when it does, and in the sequence it does, because it has the functional organization and functional states it has; and these are the states that Aristotle identifies with the soul and first actuality, which is the proximate potentiality for the vital activities.[18] The next sort of proximate potentiality will be the one that explains, and is explained by, the functional organization and states; and this is the sort of potentiality that Aristotle ascribes to the body as matter. To have the proximate potentiality for the right functional states is to be potentially alive; hence the material body is potentially alive, as the proximate matter of the functional states. The sort of body that is potentially alive is a body with organs (412a28–b1), since these are the potentialities explained by the final and formal cause.[19]

It follows that only the body of an actual living organism is potentially alive; for if the organism does not exist, the right potentialities do not exist either. For similar reasons this organic body does not outlive the soul; for a dead body lacks the potentialities of the organic body, and so can no longer be the matter of a living organism. Aristotle clearly and often insists on this point for organs, which are defined by their potentialities (412b20–2); and the same point applies to the whole body (412b22–5).

To show that this is not the only type of matter that is relevant, Aristotle adds the comment that initially surprised us: 'It is not the body that has lost a soul that is potentially such as to be alive, but the body that has a soul' (412b25–6). The comment implies that there is a body that has lost its soul without ceasing to exist; it therefore refers to the difference between proximate and remote matter. The body that is the proximate matter of a living organism is not just a collection of chemical stuffs, not even a collection of compounds of them; and this body does not outlive the soul. The remote matter—the chemical stuffs and the lumps composed of them—survives the body. When Callias perishes into flesh and bone (*Met.* 1035a31–b1), these must be his remote matter; correspondingly, the whole remote body survives the perishing of the soul and the proximate body.

So far the doctrine of the *Metaphysics* explains the claims about soul and the different types of body. It should also explain, however, why the soul is not the proximate body (412a17), even if body and soul are identical.[20] Aristotle should mean that the soul and the body are different 'in being', so that what it is to be a body is not the same as what it is to be a soul.[21] Soul and body are one because they have the same histories and the same modal properties; when a particular organism exists, that is both a particular soul and a particular body, and whatever happens, actually or possibly, to one happens to the other as well. On the other hand, Aristotle can fairly claim that something is a proximate body because it has the right potentialities for functional states, and that the same thing is a soul because it has the functional states that are the right potentialities for vital activities; it will follow that being a proximate body is not the same property as being a soul, but that every subject that is a soul is also a proximate body.[22]

The distinctions drawn in the *Metaphysics* explain Aristotle's claims about body and soul and show how they are consistent. Moreover, if he is right in claiming that the soul is the primary source of life, and in accepting a teleological conception of life, his metaphysical theory supports the account of soul as substance and form.

153. ANSWERS TO PUZZLES

It is still not clear, however, that we should accept Aristotle's claim that the soul is the primary source of life. At the beginning of the *De Anima* he claims only that the soul is a first principle of animal life, and he still needs to give us some reason for recognizing more souls than we were initially inclined to. His view is controversial, in so far as we (and Aristotle's original audience) tend to assume that creatures with souls must have states of consciousness; we must give up this view if we agree with Aristotle on soul and life.

Following his usual practice, Aristotle begins his discussion of the soul with a description of the common beliefs; and if he argues dialectically, he should give an account of the common beliefs, show why they are mostly correct and intelligible when incorrect, and resolve the puzzles that they have raised. We can judge whether his argument is dialectical, and how good a dialectical argument it is, by seeing how it copes with the common beliefs. We have already surveyed the puzzles that arise from the different views of soul that focus on its role as the cause of perception or movement, the source of unity, and as something incorporeal. Each of these views is far more restricted than Aristotle's claim that everything alive, as such, has a soul; and if he is right, he should show how the more restricted views of soul, properly understood and modified, are consistent with each other, and how they reflect different parts of the truth about souls.

First, we understand why the soul is connected with perception and with the initiation of movement, and why some one thing is connected with both. Both are appropriately mentioned in a teleological account of an animal and are parts of the animal's form. If we agree about this, we explain why the cause of movement and the cause of perception have some important feature in common, and why having a soul is not a mere disjunctive property (having a cause of perception or having a cause of movement). But this solution implies that the causes of movement and perception belong to the soul in so far as they belong to the animal's form; and then plants turn out to have psychic states too. For the common feature of the cause of movement and the cause of perception is shared by the goal-directed states of plants without states of consciousness.

If the soul is the form, we can resolve some of the puzzles about its relation to the body, and show that we need not sacrifice the beliefs that seemed initially plausible but not clearly consistent. For we are proved right to some extent in believing that the soul is a substance, and that it is 'incorporeal'. It is a substance irreducible to a material (remote) body, though not an immaterial substance, and not independent of a proximate material body, but identical to it.[23]

Since the soul is a substance, it is not a mere attunement of the bodily parts, but counts as an efficient cause of movement. To regard it as an attunement is to overlook the reasons for regarding it as a substance. For if the soul is simply an attunement, the body and its parts are the basic substances, and the soul is simply a quality of them, not a further substance. Aristotle, however, insists that a form is not simply a coincident of matter (though it is that among other things). The soul does not depend on any particular remote body, though it always requires some remote body. It does depend on its own particular proximate body; but this body also depends on the soul, since it does not outlive the loss of the potentialities derived from soul.[24]

Since the soul is form, it is the source of unity that makes a heap of material constituents into a single organism. We believe that one living organism has one soul, not a collection of many souls (e.g. one for movement, one for perception, and so on), and that it is one organism in so far as it has a single soul; somehow the unity of the soul explains the unity of the organism (411a24–b30). If soul is form, then Aristotle's theory of form and matter explains a belief about the soul that we might otherwise find puzzling. For a collection of flesh and bones constitutes a single living organism in so far as it is teleologically organized; the activities of the single organism are the final cause of the movements of the different parts. Since the organism has a single final cause, it has a single soul and a single body, which are the soul and body of a single organism.

Similarly, since the soul is the form, its identity and persistence determine the identity and persistence of the creature that has it, explaining why Socrates is properly identified with his soul. If something has a soul in so far as it has life, then it is reasonable to say that Socrates ceases to exist whenever his soul ceases to exist. His soul will not simply be his elementary biological vital processes. Since animals have perceptive souls and human beings have rational souls, Socrates' soul will continue to exist as long as Socrates' vital rational activities persist.[25] In the *Metaphysics* we found reasons for believing that Aristotle identifies particular substances with particular forms, and therefore identifies Socrates with his soul. If he assumes this doctrine, he can explain the common belief that a particular person's identity is especially connected with his soul. Aristotle agrees with Plato's assumption in the *Phaedo* that Socrates will survive just as long as his soul survives.[26]

154. THE CONTRIBUTION OF FIRST PHILOSOPHY

To this extent, then, Aristotle's account of the soul is part of a dialectical argument solving dialectical puzzles. For he begins from puzzles in common beliefs, and tries to solve the puzzles by relying on the right principles—those whose truth implies the truth of most of the apparently conflicting common beliefs, and removes the appearance of conflict among them (cf. *EN* 1145b2–7). If Aristotle's account of soul is plausible, it should answer recognizable questions about souls. His assumption that the soul is the primary source of life is not intuitive; but it is justified by its role in the argument for the account of soul as form, and by the role of that account in solving puzzles about the soul.

If this were all we could say about Aristotle's theory, it would be merely dialectical. In fact, however, he tries to justify his solution in stronger terms, by appeal to first philosophy, and therefore to strong dialectic. He identifies the soul with form, not simply because this account solves the puzzles in the common beliefs, but because it gives us reason to believe that there really are such things as souls and that they really explain the states and behaviour of living organisms. We assume at the start that the soul is 'a principle of animals' (402a6–7), something that genuinely explains their behaviour; but to justify this assumption, we need to make claims about nature that cannot be justified simply by appeal to common beliefs. For we could imagine a purely dialectical account of soul that offered a plausible reconstruction of the common beliefs, but gave us no further reason to believe in the existence of the souls in question.

Aristotle's account goes beyond such a purely dialectical solution, in so far as it appeals to the further arguments presented in the *Metaphysics*, for believing in the reality and significance of form. To this extent the *De Anima* is more than purely dialectical. It gives us some reason, apart from consistency with common beliefs, for claiming that soul is form. That claim in turn justifies us in believing that the soul is an explanatory principle, since we have good reason to think that formal properties explain, and hence that formal substances are genuine substances. To identify soul with form is to show why souls are also genuine substances.

By connecting the account of soul with his metaphysics Aristotle allows it to claim the support of first philosophy and strong dialectic. He might still, however, quite reasonably deny that his argument is non-dialectical. Though it is more restrictive than pure dialectic needs to be, it does not rely on premisses that are simply imported from outside into dialectical argument. The crucial claims in the account of soul are those that connect soul with life and appeal to the teleological conception of life and nature. Aristotle does not think a teleological doctrine is inaccessible to dialectical argument. On the contrary, he takes some awareness of teleology to be part of the appearances; he probably underestimates the empirical character of the belief in teleology, and the scope for empirical challenges to it. Still, he might reasonably defend it both as true and as part of any reasonable conception of nature; we cannot easily abandon it without a radical alteration that we have no reason to entertain in our classification of subjects. The argument, therefore, appeals only to those common beliefs that we have some further reason, beyond common beliefs about the soul, to think reliable. The further reason comes from the rest of our beliefs about nature.

In the *Metaphysics* we saw how Aristotle could lead dialectic from mere consistency with common beliefs to some reasonable claim to objective truth; and we began our study of the *De Anima* to see if he offers the same sort of argument for his account of the soul. We have found that he does.

155. DUALISM

Aristotle discusses and rejects both the Presocratic assumption that the soul is some sort of body, and the Platonic claim that it must be something entirely non-bodily. His own hylomorphic account (treating the body as matter and the soul as form) is meant to show that these other views are not the only possible positions, and that hylomorphism is preferable to both. We choose one of these extreme positions when we see the difficulties of the other; but Aristotle suggests we need not choose either.

The two views he rejects seem fairly similar to materialism and dualism, as they appear in later discussions of mind and body. A materialist argues that mental states are simply material states, and that a person (or other subject of mental states) has no components apart from the material components of his body. A dualist argues that mental states must be non-material states, and that therefore the material components of a person's body cannot be all his components. This is a rather rough description of dualism and materialism, and each general position includes several more specific versions that need to be distinguished. But it is useful to begin by looking for Aristotle's attitude to each position.[27]

He briefly expresses his attitude to both positions, in the course of his discussion of Young Socrates, in *Metaphysics* vii 11. Young Socrates allows that any individual soul must exist in some body, but allows no closer relation between soul and body than between circle and the particular bits of matter it is embodied in (*Met.* 1036b24–8). To this extent Young Socrates is a dualist, arguing that the soul is not essentially material, and therefore not a material substance, even if in fact no soul exists without a body. Aristotle argues against him that a soul essentially has a proximate organic body (1036b28–30).[28]

Aristotle challenges dualism on teleological grounds. Something has psychic states to the extent that its behaviour can be teleologically explained. We understand why parts, organs, structure, and other bodily processes of an animal are as they are when we understand them in psychic terms. Equally, however, the soul is essentially the final cause of the body; we have no more fundamental account of the soul's nature than this. If states of the soul provide teleological explanations of the animal's behaviour, they cannot belong to a body that is just coincidentally joined to the soul; hence we must reject one form of dualism. Aristotle's teleological conception supports his objection to the Platonist view that any old soul can be associated with any old body (*DA* 407b20–4).[29]

Dualism identifies the soul with a non-material component of the compound of body and soul. But Aristotle argues that if soul is form, it cannot be simply a non-material component; for the presence of the component cannot be the primary cause of the unity of the whole compound, whereas the form is the primary cause of the unity.

> Now what is composed from something is composed so that the whole thing is one, not as a heap is, but as a syllable is. A syllable is not its letters (*stoicheia*)—B and A are not the same thing as BA—and flesh is not fire and earth; for when the components are dissolved, the flesh or syllable no longer exists, although the letters or the fire and earth still exist. Hence the syllable is something, and it is not only the voiced letter and the voiceless, but some further thing; and similarly, flesh is not only fire and earth, or the hot and cold, but some further thing.
>
> Is this further thing an element (*stoicheion*) or composed from elements? If it is an element, there will be the same argument all over again; for flesh will be composed from this ⟨new element⟩, plus fire and earth, plus some further thing, so that it will go on to infinity. If the further thing is composed from an element, it is clearly not composed from one (since this one would be it), but from more than one; and then we will repeat the argument about it as about flesh or a syllable. It would seem, however, that this further thing is something other than an element, and that it is the cause of one thing's being flesh and another thing's being a syllable, and similarly in the other cases. Now this is the substance of each thing, for this is the primary cause of its being ⟨what it is⟩. (*Met.* 1041b11–28)

If we accept the connexion between soul and unity as a good reason for identifying soul with form, then we cannot identify soul with an immaterial component that would simply raise the problem that soul is meant to solve (cf. *DA* 411b5–14).[30]

Aristotle rejects dualism, then, in so far as he refuses to identify the soul with an immaterial component of the living organism. He recognizes the attraction of dualism, in so far as he sees why we might not want to identify the soul with a material component of the body; but he thinks dualism reaches the wrong answer in adding to the material body an immaterial component. In his view, the reasons for denying that the soul is a material component rest on the connexion between soul and unity; and this connexion makes it equally reasonable to deny that the soul is an immaterial component.[31] The facts apparently supporting dualism, therefore, do not support it. We correctly believe that psychic states are not reducible to purely material states, because psychic states have a teleological role that resists reduction. This hylomorphic, teleological conception of soul, as the primary source of unity in a living body, may seem to require dualism, but actually excludes it.

It does not follow, however, that Aristotle rejects everything that a dualist wants to maintain; in particular he need not deny that a living organism has some immaterial component, or even that the organism has a soul if and only if it has an appropriate immaterial component.[32] This quasi-dualist doctrine is not an account of the soul, since the immaterial component is not itself the form of the living body; quasi-dualism describes the composition that is (supposedly) necessary and sufficient for a body to be ensouled.

The notion of a necessary and sufficient condition for soul that is different from soul is familiar to Aristotle. He suggests that the heart or brain might be the sort of component that is 'crucial (*kuria*), in which the account and the substance belong primarily' (*Met.* 1035b25–7). This sort of primary component is neither prior nor posterior to the (formal) compound living organism, since each depends on the other (*hama*, 1035b25).[33] There is no living body without a heart in working order, and no heart in working order without a body; and there is no heart that is not a heart in working order, since a dead heart is a mere homonym. Now suppose that instead of, or as well as, a material heart a person needs an immaterial component—call it a spirit—to have a soul. We could even claim that when the person dies this component will survive his death. In that condition it will not be a spirit, except homonymously—let us say it is an ex-spirit; and if any psychic functions are independent of bodily organs, it is possible for the ex-spirit to exist with these functions. Hence what survives the compound we call 'Socrates' is not in fact, as Plato thought, Socrates himself, but only Socrates' ex-spirit.

This degree of dualism is consistent with Aristotle's hylomorphism, and it might legitimately appeal to some dualists.[34] For one source of doubt about materialism is doubt about the possibility of explaining all a person's actions by appeal to things or processes with a purely material composition.[35] Aristotle neither endorses this doubt nor claims that it is completely unfounded.[36] He offers no general argument to show that a spirit is not a necessary component of explanatory things or processes.[37]

Such a concession to dualism does not weaken Aristotle's arguments against dualism. He argues that a reasonable conception of the relation between the soul, life, and the unity of a living organism precludes the identification of soul with an immaterial component of the organism. If this point is conceded, the case for quasi-dualism depends on more specific questions about possible explanations for different kinds of psychic states; and Aristotle wisely avoids trying to settle these specific questions through his general claims about the nature of souls.

156. MATERIALISM

Aristotle's dispute with Young Socrates gives his reason for rejecting both dualism and some forms of materialism. We have taken dualism to assert that the material components of a person's body cannot be all his components, and we have seen how someone might wrongly reach a dualist conclusion from the correct belief that the soul cannot be identified with a material component. The extreme, eliminative materialist believes that there are no genuine formal causes, and that therefore there are no formal psychic states. A less extreme, reductive materialist believes there are such things as formal causes and formal states, but argues that these are to be identified with determinate types of material states, so that we could in principle speak only of the material states to which the formal states have been reduced. A still less extreme, non-reductive materialist believes that particular psychic states are identical to, or composed of, particular material states, but are still distinct and irreducible states.[38] It will be useful to keep these different materialist views in mind in examining Aristotle's position.

His position needs to be interpreted carefully because of his views about matter. He agrees that an account of a human being must mention some bodily parts; and we might argue that states of the soul are just states of these bodily parts. But he does not commit himself to reductive materialism. For the relevant bodily parts and processes belong to the proximate, not the remote, material body; they are the ensouled parts, not the parts described without reference to these psychic properties. The parts that have the capacities actualized in the vital activities are the ensouled parts, not their material constituents.

Aristotle, therefore, makes no significant concession to reductive materialism, since the proximate body is itself essentially ensouled. Having a soul is not simply a condition of a body, since it must be a condition of a proximate, ensouled body. Nor can psychic states simply be states of bodily parts, since they must be states of ensouled bodily parts.

Reductive materialists will not easily eliminate this reference to the soul from the account of the bodily parts. To eliminate it they must show that the laws and explanations stated in teleological terms can be reduced to non-teleological laws and explanations; and this may not be easy to show. The kinds of substances, events, and processes recognized in teleological explanations will not be recognized in non-teleological explanations; and it is rather bold to expect that the non-teleological laws will apply to kinds that actually correspond to the kinds conforming to teleological laws. An account of digestion will mention teleologically equivalent organs in different animals and species of animals, but the material composition of these organs may be different, and so the explanations referring to it may be different.

If the soul were identical to a remote body, or to a phase of it, rather than to a proximate body, then a reductive position would be plausible. For in this case there would be reason to recognize souls, but no reason to recognize them as substances distinct from remote bodies. We could then say that Socrates' soul exists just as long as this remote body exists, or else that it is a coincident of the remote body (parallel to the whiteness of a white man), which can perish without causing the body to perish too. Aristotle, however, does not identify the soul with the remote body, but only with the proximate body. The soul outlives several remote bodies; and one remote body outlives the soul. But the soul is an exact contemporary of its proximate body; and this cannot be defined without reference to soul and cannot exist without having soul. Hence the identification of the soul with the proximate body does not imply a reductive materialist conception of the soul; neither the soul nor the proximate body is either identical to or a coincident of a remote body.[39]

If there are irreducible laws about states of soul, then irreducible psychic properties are mentioned in these laws. We may still agree that the subjects of these mental properties are also material, if we reject immaterialism about the soul; but they are no more purely material than they are purely psychic. Moreover, acceptance of Aristotle's argument about souls requires us to recognize subjects that we would not have to recognize otherwise, even though these are not immaterial subjects. A particular organism is a particular form that exists as long as the same set of vital activities continues. It is contemporary with, even identical to, the proximate body that is defined by reference to the soul. It is not contemporary with the remote body that is defined by reference to the material constituents. If a reductive materialist account were correct, we would have no reason to recognize souls and proximate bodies as well as remote bodies.

Aristotle is not a non-reductionist about minds only, but about souls in general, and indeed about forms in general. Human beings with mental states are no more irreducible to their remote matter than animals and plants are; and if artifacts have forms, these too are irreducible to their remote matter. Materialists about the mind may reply that the issue concerning them is not the one illustrated by plants and hammers; surely the sense in which these things are found to be irreducible to matter is not much help to the opponent of any materialism that is worth defending? If Aristotle's argument is sound, the materialists are wrong; the issues that they thought were different turn out to be the same, and if they reject reduction for teleological systems in general, they must reject it for minds too.

Materialism, however, need not be reductive; and if it is not, it is untouched by these arguments. Non-reductive materialism insists that everything must be composed entirely of material components; and such 'compositional materialism' is as clear as 'component' and 'material' are. It is neither inconsistent with nor implied by Aristotle's conception of soul; for we saw that his conception leaves quite open the possibility of spiritual components.[40] Aristotle has further empirical arguments for accepting compositional materialism for some psychic states and rejecting it for others; but we could accept his general conception of soul without accepting these further arguments.

Though Aristotle does not endorse compositional materialism, his account of the soul makes it more attractive, by removing some reasons for thinking it cannot be true. If we identify soul and body with form and matter, we can see why compositional materialism might be true about souls. For some forms realized in matter do not at all tempt us to be immaterialists; we do not think a hammer must have an immaterial component just because it is not reducible to its material components. If the features of the soul inconsistent with eliminative and reductive materialism are explained by the hylomorphic conception of soul, they do not justify rejection of compositional materialism in favour of dualism.

On the other hand, and for similar reasons, the hylomorphic account of soul shows us how quasi-dualism might be true even if dualism is false. Indeed, quasi-dualism is simply the immaterialist analogue of compositional materialism, arguing that the relevant component must be different from the recognized kinds of matter.[41] Aristotle's argument for hylomorphism does not settle this issue between different views of the composition of the soul.

Aristotle wants to show that first philosophy can persuade us to reject both dualism and the eliminative and reductive versions of materialism. But the most important part of his doctrine is his positive account of the soul as formal cause. This positive account can be accepted by those who disagree about materialism and dualism, provided that they qualify the dualist or materialist claims so as to avoid the arguments that Aristotle has challenged.

157. EMPIRICAL ARGUMENT, DIALECTIC, AND
FIRST PHILOSOPHY

Aristotle characteristically distinguishes the sorts of 'appearances' that are the basis of empirical argument from those that are the starting-point of dialectic.[42] The study of the soul offers a useful test of this distinction. For Aristotle argues that the dialectician and the student of nature define psychic states differently, and that the student of nature mentions the matter that the dialectician leaves out (403a24–b19). In the *De Anima* he largely avoids empirical argument about the material basis of psychic states. In doing so, he shows that he thinks empirical argument is not the proper concern of dialectic and first philosophy.

Aristotle's arguments about dualism and materialism support his views about the relation of dialectic to empirical evidence. For these arguments tend to separate the empirical issues that are involved in deciding between compositional materialism and quasi-dualism from the less empirical considerations that support a hylomorphic theory against its dualist and materialist rivals. The arguments for the hylomorphic theory are largely a priori, as we ought to expect if they are drawn from first philosophy. If states of the soul are parts of the formal and final cause, then first philosophy shows that the soul is a substance, and therefore irreducible to remote matter. The arguments from first philosophy are not completely a priori; we have noticed that Aristotle's belief in the reality of formal and final causes depends on some empirically falsifiable assumptions.[43] But it depends on relatively few and uncontroversial assumptions; it does not rely on the more detailed empirical arguments that are needed to decide between quasi-dualism and compositional materialism.

To this extent the method of the *De Anima* is dialectical, and therefore suitable for the philosophical questions discussed here, while the more detailed empirical issues treated in the *Parva Naturalia* are examined through far more obviously empirical arguments. Aristotle shows good judgment about the kinds of questions he can expect to settle by dialectical argument. If he were going to discuss the matter as well as the form, dialectic would not be so suitable. An account of the relevant physiological processes would require empirical detail going beyond common beliefs. For a formal account, however, dialectic seems suitable, since such an account need not rely on detailed information about physiological processes. An account of the formal cause requires knowledge of what an organism does; and though common sense is not fully informed about this, it is less likely to be totally astray. Inquiry into the material cause must be largely empirical, while inquiry into the formal cause may be largely dialectical.

Aristotle does not seek a merely dialectical account of psychic states, since his methods are not merely dialectical. First philosophy does not simply collect the common beliefs, or take them for granted, or simply try to make them consistent; and for its aims the ordinary dialectical account would be insufficient. Dialecticians define states of the soul simply with reference to the associated behaviour.

If this is so, then it is clear that the attributes are accounts involving matter. Hence the ⟨right⟩ sort of defining formula will be: 'Being angry is a certain movement of this sort of body or party or capacity by this agency for the sake of this'. Hence study of the soul—either every sort or the particular sort ⟨that requires a body⟩—turns out to be a task for the student of nature. Now the student of nature and the dialectician would give different definitions of each of these attributes—e.g. of anger. The dialectician would define it as desire for inflicting pain in return for pain; and the student of nature as boiling of the blood and the hot element around the heart. The student of nature describes the matter, and the dialectician describes the form and the account; for this ⟨desire etc.⟩ is the account of the thing, but its existence requires this sort of matter. Similarly, one account of a house says that it is a shelter preventing destruction by wind, rain, or heat; another will say that it is stones, bricks, and timber; another will say that it is the form in these ⟨stones etc.⟩ for the sake of this end ⟨preventing destruction⟩. Then which of these people is the student of nature— the one concerned with the matter in ignorance of the account, or the one concerned only with the account? Or is he more properly the one who mentions both form and matter? Then what is each of the first two? (403a24–b9)

Aristotle describes the dialectical definition as an account of the form alone but this description is somewhat misleading; for if we agree that states of the soul are materiate forms, a definition that fails to mention this fact will not describe the sort of forms that they are.

An accurate description of the form, then, will have to mention the matter. But it need not mention matter in the way that Aristotle's example suggests, referring to the physiological processes assumed to underlie anger. Such an account mentions the remote matter, whereas we give the right account of the materiate form by mentioning the proximate matter. First philosophy shows us that the form is the final cause of the matter; to define states that are part of the form we need to describe them as final causes of the proximate matter, and so the definition must mention proximate matter. On the other hand, it need not mention remote matter, since this is not needed to indicate that the form is a final cause. Our definition must describe a formal compound, or materiate form, not a material compound including remote matter.[44]

Here, no less than in the *Metaphysics*, Aristotle's initial question, 'Should the definition mention the form or the matter?' presents only two sharply contrasted options, but his theory requires us to recognize

more options. In the *De Anima* we must recognize these further options
if we are to see how first philosophy differs both from mere dialectic and
from empirical natural science. First philosophy seeks to show that
common beliefs about the soul are roughly right if a teleological
conception of the soul is right; such a conception requires us to
recognize psychic states as final causes actualizing the proximate
potentialities of the proximate matter. We need not be surprised that the
De Anima does not describe at the outset the possibility that Aristotle
eventually accepts; it begins with a fairly intuitive contrast between
form and matter, but first philosophy shows why the contrast needs to
be more complicated.

The strategy of first philosophy requires a modification of common
beliefs that dialectic does not require. The *Metaphysics* requires us to
deny the status of complete substance to some things—heaps and parts
of animals—that might have seemed to deserve it. The *De Anima*
requires us to be more generous than we are normally inclined to be,
and to allow souls to plants. We must extend our initial belief that the
soul is a principle of animals to allow that it is the principle of life as a
whole. The modifications of common beliefs are defended as the best
way to extract the truth from common beliefs as a whole. We do not
think souls are totally homonymous in the different types of creatures
that have them; and we suppose that the different parts and capacities of
the soul are parts and capacities of the same subject. These views are
reasonable if they are understood with the help of Aristotle's conception
of soul.

If, then, we want to contrast first philosophy and its method both
with dialectic and with empirical science, our answer cannot be
completely tidy. If we accept the broad and not absolutely sharp
distinction between dialectical and empirical appearances, we must add
some further empirical element to the dialectical appearances, in order to
reach the arguments of first philosophy applied to nature. The
teleological assumptions that determine the metaphysical interpretation
of substance, form, and matter, and therefore of soul, are empirically
falsifiable. On the other hand, such assumptions are different from the
empirical information relevant to an inquiry into the material basis of
psychic states. Aristotle's inquiry into the soul is especially useful for
our purposes, since it displays the different contributions of dialectic,
first philosophy, and empirical science. His arguments for his hylomorphic conception, and his implicit attitude to different versions of
dualism and materialism, show that he understands the nature and force
of his arguments.

158. SOUL AND MIND

Aristotle's account of soul avoids the less plausible aspects of dualism and of some versions of materialism. But his solution should satisfy us only if it rests on a reasonable account of psychic states. He must show not only that his account justifies common beliefs about the soul by appeal to first philosophy, but also that if we construe a state of the soul as part of the formal cause, we correctly grasp the nature of that state. To see if he is right on this point, we need to examine his account of different psychic states and types of souls.

Aristotle himself agrees that this is necessary. Souls form a hierarchy, in which the lower type of psychic state is necessary for the higher type and the higher soul is potentially the lower.

Clearly, then, soul will have one single account in the same way that a figure has; for just as figure is nothing besides the triangle and those that follow in order, so equally the soul is nothing besides those ⟨capacities⟩ we have mentioned. Still, we can find a common account of figure that fits all of them, and is special to none; and the same is true for the souls. It is ridiculous, then, in these and other such cases, to search for a common account that is not special to any being, and does not fit the proper and undivided species, if ⟨in our search⟩ we neglect this ⟨special⟩ account. Hence we must ask what the soul of each particular ⟨kind of thing⟩—e.g. a plant, a human being, or a beast—is. What is true of the soul is rather similar to what is true of figure; for in both cases the earlier is potentially present in its successor, e.g. the triangle in the square, and the nutritive in the perceptive. (414b20–33)[45]

To understand each type of soul is to understand the specific way these specific psychic states are the form of this specific sort of creature.

The nutritive soul fits the general account well, since the account supports the rather unintuitive attribution of souls to plants. It is easy to see how the nutritive and reproductive capacities are part of the creature's formal and final cause.[46] At the next stage, however, when Aristotle comes to discuss perception, we might be dissatisfied.

His account should apparently capture the distinctive features of mental states; we might, indeed, assume that it should make psychic states coextensive with the mental states we intuitively recognize. His initial examples of psychic states are recognizable mental states, and in treating the soul as the source of movement and perception, he almost picks out mental states. But to confine psychic states to mental states would conflict with Aristotle's teleological conception of soul; and he claims that the processes of nutrition, digestion, and growth that go on without any mental states—even in creatures that have mental states— will be states of those creatures' souls.

Aristotle must violate intuitions to some degree by treating nutritive states as states of the soul. But he can still isolate mental states among psychic states, if he can show that they characteristically and essentially play some particular sort of teleological role. If he can show this, he will be right to claim that the teleological aspect of psychic states is essential to them and the clue to understanding their nature.

When we say x does F for the sake of G, we imply that G is causally relevant to x's doing F; that is, the fact that F produces G is part of the causal explanation of x's doing F.[47] If x is an artifact, then teleological explanation will sometimes lead us to a causal explanation mentioning a state of the artifact itself, but will always eventually lead us to an intention of the designer. If we say 'Thermostats turn the heat on and off to keep the room at a constant temperature', we refer to some mechanism in the thermostat that has been designed for this purpose by the designer; if it has not, our claim was false. If the instrument maintained itself in this condition for efficient turning on and off, we would have *some* reason for saying it had a soul.

Teleological explanation of a plant does not imply an external designer; it refers to a state of the plant that is what it is because of the goal it promotes. Here the actual past effects of this type of state explain, if we accept a theory of evolution, why the plant has this state now. Since the plant maintains these goal-directed states in itself without the deliberate intervention of some external agency to alter the plant's workings, we are more inclined to attribute life and soul to the plant than to a thermostat.

With an animal the teleological explanation is different. It is true that plants put down roots to get water and that lions approach water to get water. With plants we assume some past causal connexion between putting down roots and getting water. With the lion we assume a causal connexion between the movement and a previous desire and perception that focus on getting water. The 'focussing' is not merely the result of the past behaviour of the lion's ancestors; it is a feature of the state itself. Plants are not organized to do what seems best to them, or what seems to them to promote their survival, but to do what actually tends to promote their survival.[48] A lion, however, is teleologically organized to do what appears desirable to it. The lion acts to get what seems to it to be water, and the apparent, not the real, existence of the water explains the action. Hence it is possible to deceive the lion, though not the plant.

This is the sort of creature to which Aristotle attributes 'appearance', *phantasia*; and these states associated with appearance seem to be coextensive with those we intuitively regard as mental. Perceptions, feelings, thoughts, and desires are all associated with appearance, and a condition that captures all these states is a plausible condition for having mental states.

Aristotle is entitled to a still stronger claim. If we tried to ascribe sensations or thoughts to a being without any way that things appeared to it, we would be puzzled. To have things appear a particular way is to have a particular point of view on things; and that seems to be just a way of describing the subjective point of view that is plausibly regarded as characteristic of mental states. While things are good or bad for a plant, they are not literally good or bad from the plant's point of view, but only from the point of view of someone considering the good of the plant. But things are desirable or undesirable from the lion's point of view, not only from the point of view of someone considering the good of the lion.

Does this account of mental states really explain what they are? Can we understand the notion of appearing or seeming that Aristotle appeals to, without already grasping the sort of thing that a mental state is?

It may be true that to grasp the notion of appearance that Aristotle relies on, we must be able to recognize some mental states. But even so, the explanans is not too unhelpfully close to the explanandum. An appearance expresses a point of view, a selective description of an object. Selective descriptions themselves do not require mental states. An egg-sorting machine that first separates large eggs and then stamps them 'large' is selectively describing them. But it has no mental states, since its selective descriptions are not formed in the right way from previous selective descriptions; no comparison of this egg with previous ones causes its present description, and so it does not look to the sorting machine as though the egg is large. An appearance, by contrast, is a selective description of an object, caused by the appropriate transition from previous selective descriptions.[49]

If the transition is appropriate for appearances, the present descriptions must be affected by the content of previous descriptions. The physical characteristics of a painting affect me if I am knocked over when it falls on me or the fumes from the varnish choke me. But it is a picture of, say, Pericles; the depiction of Pericles is its content, and I am affected by the content if, e.g., Pericles in the picture looks imposing, I suppose the picture is accurate, and I comment that Pericles must have looked imposing. A system that is affected by the content of its previous selective descriptions is to that extent a claimant to appearances and mental states. It is not enough to be affected, as some machines might be, by a physical state of an object that is correlated with some content—if, e.g., a machine could reliably detect statues of Pericles by tracing their shape; the content itself must be part of the explanation of later selective descriptions.[50]

Aristotle does not explicitly raise or answer a question about the nature of mental states. Still, his initial examples of psychic states are familiar mental states; and in connecting them with appearance, he offers a plausible account of what they have in common. In perceptive and rational creatures, final causation works through appearances, since these creatures are teleologically organized to pursue apparent objects of desire in response to their appearances. If Aristotle's conception of soul explains what mental states have in common, that is another point in support of his conception of the soul as form.

We should therefore follow Aristotle's advice and proceed from his general claims about soul and body to his account of different psychic states; for this account will itself be part of the argument for his general claims. If a creature's soul is its form, then each psychic state must be part of the form. Such an approach to psychic states should help us to distinguish the features of mental states, and to see how one mental state differs from another.

14

SOUL AND MIND

---

159. PERCEPTION AS A STATE OF THE SOUL

Aristotle's views on sense-perception offer a test of his account of soul and mind. If sensory states are part of an animal's formal cause, then they should be mentioned in a teleological explanation of its behaviour. Moreover, sensory states are also mental states; they involve appearance, the sort of awareness that distinguishes animals from plants. Aristotle ought to explain why perceptual states have these apparent features.

Aristotle's account of the soul seeks to show the common feature of souls and to remove the suspicion that having a soul might be a merely homonymous property, not a genuine common property of creatures with souls. He has a similar task with perception, since he takes perception to be a single faculty of the soul. He should display the unity of the faculty in the different sorts of animals that have it. There should be something, for instance, about touch that makes it clearly the same capacity in an amoeba, a cow, and a man. The perceptive faculty is shared by rational and non-rational animals; and a common account of perception should show that it is not a mere homonym that is present in non-rational animals. The general account of perception should require no more than can be ascribed to non-rational animals, and in rational animals the account should not be falsified by the distinctive features of rational perception.

Since perception is part of a teleological account of an animal, it should be good for the animal; unless its acting for the sake of some end resulted fairly often in actual benefit to it, we would lose our reason for attributing final causation to it. Aristotle begins from his usual assumption that nature does nothing pointlessly.[1] Sometimes, admittedly, an organism has some particular property because of its matter or because of some side-effect of a process that benefits the organism; and in these cases we have not found part of the form. If perception is part of the form, it should benefit the perceiver.

Aristotle finds it fairly easy to defend this claim for perception. Animals respond more flexibly and effectively to situations if they perceive their environment than if they have to be affected by physical interaction as plants are; a dog can move towards water in different situations when it sees water, but a plant cannot do much if it puts its roots down for water that is not there.[2]

If perception is to benefit animals, we cannot ascribe it to them without making other assumptions as well. Suppose, for instance, that perceptions were always false, or that the animal could not act on them, or that it was always perverse and disregarded its perceptions in its action. In each of these cases the animal's perception would be no good to it, and to rule out such cases Aristotle must insist on ascribing perception only when other states can also be ascribed.

Without some assumptions connecting perceptions with desires and with the actual good of the animal, we will not know what perceptions to ascribe to it at all. If we suppose that an animal wants to kill itself but does not succeed, we can suppose that it systematically misperceives things—that when it drinks it has mistaken the water for poison, or has not seen the water at all, and just blunders into it. Unlimited and variable perversity of desires is even worse, since we can link it with unlimited variety in the perceptions ascribed. And if perception always results in harm, what has the animal perceived? Perhaps its perceptions have been right and its desires perverse or its desires have been sound but the perceptions mistaken; and many varieties of mistaken perceptions can be assumed. We have some systematic way of ascribing perceptions only when we have some connexion with action, and the kind of connexion that fairly regularly secures the animal's benefit. Aristotle's teleological assumptions can be defended without appeal to his doctrines about cosmic order in nature.

Aristotle therefore believes that perception requires desire.

While plants have only the nutritive part, other things have this and the perceptive part also; and if they have the perceptive part, they also have the desiring part. For desire includes appetite, emotion, and wish; and whatever has any perception has pleasure and pain, and finds things pleasant or painful, and therefore has appetite, which is desire for the pleasant. Moreover all animals have perception of food, since touch is perception of food, . . . ⟨and therefore have pleasure and appetite⟩. (*DA* 414a32–b7)

It would not be enough if perception somehow systematically triggered actions, in the way that a loud noise may make me jump even if I am not frightened by it; for the action might be quite unrelated to any good for the animal. Desire links perception with the animal's good. The animal desires pleasure and the avoidance of pain; it is capable of acting on its desires, and Aristotle assumes that the action will in general be beneficial. Hence every animal with perception must also have desire.

The same sort of argument shows why perception requires appearance (*phantasia*). Since perception requires desire, and desire requires

appearance, perception requires appearance (413b22-4).[3] Creatures that
have appearances have a point of view on their environment; they can respond to particular features of it without the normal sort of physical interaction with those features (as, e.g., animals respond to the presence of
water before the water wets them). If such a response contributes to the
creature's good, it requires a fairly accurate sort of contact, different from
ordinary physical interaction, with the environment, and a fairly successful
way of using this contact for the creature's good. 'Contact' and 'using'
indicate vaguely the physic states that should be described more clearly in
an account of perception and desire.

160. PERCEPTION AS PROCESS AND ACTIVITY

Aristotle defines the soul in general as a first actuality, and therefore as a
potentiality for second actuality. Since perception is one part of the soul
it will also be a potentiality for second actuality (417a21-9).

It is easy to assume that actually perceiving is a movement or process
(417a14-17), but Aristotle gradually modifies this assumption (417a30-
b6, 431a4-7). He never denies that actual perception includes or requires
a process, but he claims that it cannot be just a process.[4] Even if 'F' and
'G' are coextensive, it does not follow that a potentiality for F is also a
potentiality for G; for the property of being G may not be the property
of the actuality that stands in the right explanatory relation to the
potentiality. Hence, even if every perceiving is also a process of
alteration, it does not follow that it is a perceiving because it is a process,
or that to perceive is to undergo a process; for we may not find that a
process stands in the right explanatory relation to the potentiality.

Aristotle argues that the actualization of a second potentiality (the
transition from first to second actuality) is not an alteration (417a30-
b2).[5] For being altered or affected is essentially the destruction of one
contrary by another, e.g. of cold by hot.[6] Every change in a subject
actualizes some potentiality in the subject, in so far as only a subject
capable of being heated can cease to be cold and become hot; but it does
not follow that the features of a sequence of events that make it a process
or change (kinêsis) also make it the actualization of another sort of
potentiality. A change in a subject requires a passive potentiality for
being affected by external objects; and Aristotle believes that such a
view of perception does not capture its essence.

A comparison with nutrition explains the point. Nutrition might
seem to be a passive potentiality, since it requires the subject to be
affected in certain ways by the air, water, or soil in its environment. But
the essential feature of nourishment is what it does for the organism, not
how it results from being affected by the environment. For it is

essentially a capacity to maintain the organism with its form, tending towards its final cause; the fact that it can do this only as a result of alteration by the environment is inessential, though causally necessary, to the nutritive character of the potentiality.

A similar argument explains why perception is not merely a process. Goal-directed potentialities essentially tend to advance the subject's ends; they do not essentially tend to replace one of its properties with another as a result of interaction with an external object. For this reason perception cannot be a mere passive potentiality to be affected by external objects. Indeed Aristotle would have made his point clearer if he had shown how it holds for all potentialities of the soul, not simply for perception (cf. *Phys.* 246a10–b2). Since the soul is the form, and since the processes of alteration, coming to be and destruction are not essential to formal states, the actualities of the soul are not processes. A form has to come into existence from some process involving the material compound that constitutes it; but it is not itself the subject whose properties explain the actual process of becoming. Similarly, formal states arise only in the processes that constitute them; but they are not themselves essentially processes, but tendencies towards the final cause, or, as the *Physics* says, 'completions' (246a13).

Aristotle adds that the acquisition of a first potentiality by learning from a teacher should not be called a way of being affected, or else we should recognize a type of alteration that is not the deprivation of a contrary but the acquisition of a state and of something's nature (417b9–16).[7] He means that the acquisition is more than a deprivation, not that it is not a deprivation at all. When a subject learns, the learning is an actualization of his potentiality and the fulfilment of his nature. The subject is the way he is for the sake of having and using some sort of knowledge. If he were trained instead to walk with a limp or to repeat nonsense syllables, he would be trained to do something that is possible for him, but he would not be fulfilling a potentiality or developing towards his own nature.

Aristotle sees some temptation to agree with dualists in denying that perception is any sort of bodily process, but he denies that the truth underlying the temptation really supports dualism. We are right to distinguish perception from its underlying material process, because the essential features of the remote material process are not the essential features of the goal-directed state that perception is. Since organisms are constructed to gain the benefits of perceiving, perceiving is an actualization of their natural potentiality; it is part of an animal's form, the final cause of its structures and organs. Aristotle solves the puzzle about perceptions and processes by appeal to his general views on form.

161. THE ACCOUNTS OF PERCEPTION

Aristotle should also show how perception is part of the formal and final cause. In general, perception benefits an animal by allowing it to react more selectively and successfully to relevant features of the external world than it otherwise would; and it reacts better because in some way and to some extent its own states correspond to states of the external world. But it is more difficult to say what sort of correspondence this is.

The account of perception as a process seemed attractive because we tend to assume that perception involves some sort of causal interaction. But not every sort of interaction implies perception; when plants interact with the soil and are nourished, they do not perceive anything in the soil.

If we assume that perception involves both causal interaction and useful correspondence with the external world, we might at first take it to be a sort of similarity produced by the interaction. A feature of an external object is somehow accessible to perceivers; and we might infer that it, or at least something similar, is somehow actually present in them. Hence some Presocratics assume that perception is to be explained by the literal similarity of the perceiving agent and the perceived object, so that my composition (e.g. the four elements) corresponds to the composition of the external world. Though Aristotle easily shows that mere material similarity explains nothing, he still appeals to correspondence and similarity.[8] Since accurate perceptions are true of the external world, the correspondence that underlies truth must also be present in perception.[9]

Aristotle offers three formulae for the understanding of perception. The first shows that he takes similarity seriously:

F1. The perceiver becomes like the object (417a18, 418a5).

This formula implies that in truly perceiving the actual perceptible qualities (colours, smells, tastes, etc.) of things in the world we become similar to them on the right occasions. But F1 seems to have strange results. I become like white paint if a tin of it is spilt over me; or, if I peel onions, my hands acquire the smell of onions. But this sort of passive affection and this sort of similarity do not imply perception (424b12–18).[10]

Seeing this objection to F1, Aristotle offers a second formula:

F2. The perceiver that was potentially F (e.g. white) becomes actually F when it perceives the actually F object (418a3, 422a7, b15, 423b30, 424a2).

If a tin of white paint is spilt over me, I become white, but I do not realize a natural potentiality of mine. F2, however, insists that genuine perception is the sort of similarity that actualizes a natural potentiality of mine. My being whitened by the paint realizes a passive potentiality to be affected by an external object, which in this case coincidentally makes me similar to it; but the event does not actualize any potentiality to become similar to the object. F2 restricts F1 to actualizations of a potentiality to become similar. On this view, perception is good for the animal in so far as it allows it to respond appropriately to features of the world; hence the becoming similar that is involved in perception will be the actualization of a natural potentiality. Appropriate response is the result of the assimilation; hence we have the potentiality for the assimilation.

It is not clear, though, that F2 restricts F1 to genuine cases of perception. When I drink water, my body gets wetter, but I do not necessarily perceive water; the nutritive part of my soul is involved, but the perceptive part need not be.[11] Aristotle therefore modifies F2.

F3. The perceiver acquires the form, but not the matter, of the object (424a18–24, 425b23, 431b29).

F3 is meant to explain why plants do not count as perceivers:

This is why plants do not perceive, even though they have a part of the soul and are affected in some way by tangible things, since they are heated and cooled; the reason is that they have no intermediate condition and no principle of the sort that can receive the forms of perceptible objects, but they are affected together with the matter. (424a32–b3)

Aristotle does not mean that my matter is quite unchanged when I perceive an object, or that there is no process of material interaction involving me and the object; he means that the similarity between me and the object does not consist in my matter being affected in the way that makes my causal powers similar to those of the object.[12]

In speaking of the form 'in the perceiver', and in the perceiver's soul, Aristotle needs to distinguish a form of F that *realizes* F from a form that *expresses* F.[13] Consider a wooden hammer, a steel hammer, a picture, a sculpture, and a plan of a hammer. The wooden and the steel hammer both realize the same form, since they are both made for the same function. The other things do not realize the same form, since none of them is made for the same function (even if the sculptor happens to sculpt something that would serve as a hammer). But they have something in common with the actual hammers; we may say that they express the form of a hammer, in the sense that we could infer from them what a hammer would have to be like. Expressions need not be very similar to each other or to their realizations—Austria is not very like a painting or aerial photograph or map or written description of

Austria; but all of them have something in common that makes them all expressions of Austria. To this extent all the expressions are similar to the expression that is also the realization.[14]

But if expression simply requires some appropriate correspondence, it will include more than perception. Perhaps my eating causes my digestive states to correspond in some way to the states of the cheese I ate; e.g. if it contains fats and carbohydrates, the fat-digesting and carbohydrate-digesting digestive states correspond to its states. We might even say that my digestive states partially express the cheese, just as the line on the chart of a barograph expresses the changing atmospheric pressure, or in general the states of a measuring instrument express what it measures; in all these cases we might also say that one thing is sensitive to the states of the other.[15]

These cases do not require the presence of the form without the matter. My digestive states corresponding to the states of the cheese may in turn cause me to do other things; but their correspondence to the cheese is causally irrelevant. Digestion affects other bodily processes because of its chemical effects and its teleological role; its correspondence to the cheese is no part of the explanation. If, by contrast, the immaterial form of the house is in the builder's soul, then the state of her soul expresses the house; it causes the realization of the house; and its character as expression is relevant to the stages of the building of the house, since she builds as she does because she wants to build a house with the features that are in her design of the house. In this case we have some reason to say that an immaterial form is actually present.

The points of correspondence between the state and the object constitute the content of the state; and so we can say that it expresses through its content. Hence a state of perceiving red will affect my reaction to red things because of its content. If a dog regularly eats red meat, and then tries to eat red rubber that is roughly similar to meat in size, shape, and smell, but refuses anything with two of these qualities that lacks the other one, we have some reason to infer that it perceives the colour, taste, and smell of meat and other things, and, in particular, that it sees red. It sees red if it reacts to red things in ways that are best explained by this content of its psychic states.

If, then, F3 captures the difference between perceivers and non-perceivers, it shows why Aristotle's account of particular psychic states must depend on his general view of the soul as formal and final cause.[16] We cannot examine the intrinsic features of a creature's particular psychic state in isolation from others, and decide whether it has absorbed the form of an object without the matter. To distinguish the subject that perceives from the instrument that merely records we have to look at the rest of its behaviour, and see if it should be explained by reference to the content of its states. To apply this test we must have some conception of the appropriate sort of explanation to seek; and Aristotle tells us the appropriate sort when he claims that the soul is the formal and final cause.

162. FORM AND MATTER IN PERCEPTION

The three formulae explaining the nature of perception reflect the dialectical character of Aristotle's argument. If the *De Anima* is a largely dialectical account of the soul as form, it should not rely heavily on empirical details about the process of perception, since such empirical details will belong to an account of the matter.[17] On the other hand, the form is the final cause of the matter, realizing its proximate potentiality; and the matter that has the proximate potentiality for the formal activities is the proximate matter, not the remote matter that constitutes it. An account of the form, therefore, should include some account of the proximate matter.[18]

Aristotle applies the three formulae of perception to the sense-organ that is part of the matter, as well as to the faculty of perception that is part of the form of the animal.[19] The sense-organ as proximate matter is distinct from its constituent matter. Qua sense-organ and proximate matter, it must have the properties that allow the faculty and its actualization to belong to it. F1 and F2 imply that the organ becomes like the object, and all along has potentially the qualities of the object that it has actually in perception. We can infer that the organ is potentially hot and becomes actually hot in perception, and so on for all other perceptible qualities.

The sense becomes like the object in so far as it acquires the form without the matter of the object; and this same restriction on likeness must be applied to the sense-organ as well.

On the other hand, tangible ⟨qualities⟩ and flavours do affect bodies; otherwise, what would affect and alter soulless things? Then will the other objects of perception also affect bodies? Perhaps not every body is liable to be affected by smell and sound, and those that are affected are indefinite and impermanent— e.g. air, since it acquires a smell as though affected in some way. Then what is there to smelling, beyond being affected? Perhaps smelling is ⟨not only being affected, but⟩ also perceiving, while air that is affected ⟨by smell⟩, by contrast, soon becomes an object of perception. (424b12–18)

The perceiver who 'acquires' the smell of cheese by perceiving it does not necessarily himself become smelly; nor does his nose. Aristotle seems to think that what happens to the air around the cheese is the sort of 'being affected with the matter' (424b2–3) that is not a necessary feature of perception.[20]

Aristotle's formal and dialectical account of perception confines itself largely to common beliefs.[21] These same beliefs, however, imply further empirical claims. We might claim to know a priori that sense-perception requires a causal process involving features of external objects and features of the perceiver—perhaps even features of the perceiver's body—so that, for example, if we believe we see colours, we must also believe that there is some causal process linking coloured objects and ourselves. We may not know, however, how the process works; we may know only that it fails if some conditions are not normal (cf. e.g. 419a1–15).[22]

Aristotle's formal account is not beyond conceivable empirical refutation. It would be false if at least one of these claims were false: (1) Reception of the form without the matter of the perceptible qualities sometimes results from a causal interaction between one of these qualities and a perceiver. (2) This reception of the form affects the behaviour of the perceivers by its content, in ways that benefit perceivers.

Neither of these claims is true in all logically possible worlds. But they are not as easily refutable as the physiological aspects of Aristotle's account. To reject the formal account we would have to change our conception of the world so that it would no longer include perception. Such a change would be so sweeping that we would find difficulty in conceiving its consequences, and in saying how we could have good reason to make such a change. In particular, if we were to have evidence to justify us in rejecting these claims about perception, would we not need to believe we were getting some of it through perception? If we deny ourselves perception, we seem to deny ourselves some of the evidence to support the theory that denies us perception, and hence we seem to challenge the theory itself.[23]

While it is logically possible for the formal account of perception to be false, it is hard to see how we could have reason to believe that it is false. If Aristotle can safely appeal to this sort of argument, then his formal account of perception is quite resilient in the face of different views about its empirical basis. This is the sort of account he ought to offer if his argument is to be dialectical, rather than empirical, and if it is to rely on assumptions that are more fundamental than mere common beliefs.

163. REALISM ABOUT PERCEPTIBLE QUALITIES

Aristotle accepts a realist view of perception, since he claims that the perceiver absorbs the form of some quality that the object has whether or not it is being perceived. The teleological aspects of his theory equally require realism; absorption of the form of the object allows the perceiver to act in the way appropriate to how the object really is. Aristotle assumes that the colours, sounds, etc. of external bodies exist in the bodies before they are perceived.[24] He wants to know what features of the world perceivers detect when they respond appropriately to their circumstances.[25] The different senses correspond to the different useful properties that an animal can detect (434b9–435a10).

Aristotle's realist and teleological assumptions help to explain an initially puzzling claim. He argues that when I perceive an object, the actuality of the object is one and the same with the actuality of the perceiver, and that it is in the perceiver, not in the object (425b26–426a6; cf. *PN* 439a13–16). More generally, he claims that the actuality of a change is in the patient rather than the agent (*Phys.* 202a13, 224b4, 25–6, *GA* 742a30–2, *Met.* 1050a29). The relevant sort of change is essentially doing something *to a patient*, not simply *doing* something. When the builder builds a house, it is primarily something done to the bricks and mortar, and only secondarily a series of movements by the builder; the primary beneficiary of the change is the patient, not the agent.

The explanatory asymmetry that often concerns Aristotle helps to elucidate his point here. What the builder does counts as a case of (successfully) building because something happens to the bricks; it is not because he makes these movements that the change happening to the house counts as its being built. Ann's acting on Bert counts as (successfully) teaching Bert because Bert actually learns something, not the other way round. If the bricks and the pupil are recalcitrant, the agents might do the very same thing (understood one way), but what they did would not count as successful building or teaching; it is the difference in the patient that makes the difference between failure and success at building and teaching.[26] Aristotle appeals to the same teleological assumptions that guide his claims about potentiality.[27]

The same argument ought to show why the actuality of the perceiver and of the object are in the perceiver. Though we speak of the object 'being perceived', suggesting that it is a patient, the passive verb is misleading, since it is really the object that affects the perceiver. My perceiving the rock is my being affected by the rock; being perceived is not a change in the rock or something that the rock does to exercise one of its proximate potentialities.[28] I have a potentiality to perceive objects, but objects do not have potentialities of the same sort to be perceived by me. The event counts as its being perceived because of the change in me, not the other way round. The object does not become suitable to have its form absorbed when I perceive it; it was suitable all along, and its being perceived by me is no real change in it. When I perceive it, therefore, I must become aware of it as it has been before I perceived it. Aristotle still implies a realist view of the objects of perception.

164. THE REJECTION OF REALISM

So far, then, Aristotle is justified in saying that my perceiving a red object is primarily an event in me, not in the object. But he assumes further that the relevant actuality of the object is its becoming red, and so he concludes that its becoming red consists in its being perceived as red.[29] This conclusion conflicts with the formulae of perception. For F2 says that the perceiver is potentially what the object is actually, and that in perception the perceiver becomes actually what the object has been actually all along. Similarly, F3 says that the perceiver acquires the form that the object had all along. But Aristotle's conclusion implies that the object is only potentially red before it is perceived. The formulae of perception assume the objective existence of real perceptible qualities independent of the perceiver; but Aristotle's conclusion makes their existence depend on their being perceived.

Aristotle is entitled to claim that the perceived object has an actuality corresponding to the state of the perceiver as teaching corresponds to learning—the same event viewed from the other side. This event is the object's being perceived as red; and it no more implies that the object becomes actually red than the identity of the teaching and the learning implies that the teacher learns when the learner learns.[30]

Aristotle sees that his conclusion seems to threaten realism, and he distinguishes himself from subjectivists and relativists, who make the sensible properties of external things depend on how they appear to perceivers. He argues that his opponents are right about actual perceptible qualities, which do indeed depend on perceivers, but not about potential qualities, which are independent of perceivers (426a20–6).[31]

This reply, however, does not defend very much of the realist position. Aristotle's opponents could fairly easily agree that there are external subjects causing our perceptions, but they need not concede that our perceptions reveal to us any truths about the nature of the external subjects. The fact that two objects are capable of appearing white to us, and hence of becoming white, does not show that the two subjects have some property in common, or that they appear to us as they really are. If only the potentiality is allowed to exist unperceived, it is not clear how Aristotle can distinguish sensory qualities such as colours from qualities such as painfulness; we know that objects causing us pain are capable of causing pain, and that they are therefore painful; but it does not follow that this causal tendency of theirs corresponds to any further common property, and that is why we do not think painfulness itself is a real quality of objects in the way we think colours are.

If Aristotle's claim about the real existence of potentially coloured objects amounts only to a weak claim about causal tendencies, it seems to raise grave doubts about how perception can yield any knowledge of external objects. His views would be both more consistent and more plausible if he had not added these aberrant remarks.

165. THE INFALLIBILITY OF THE SENSES

Still, this view about actual sensory qualities is not merely aberrant; for Aristotle's defence of the reliability of the senses shows why he might incline to such a view. He defends the surprisingly strong claim that each sense is infallible about its special objects (427b8–16), apparently because he accepts the sceptical claim that if we can justifiably distrust one of our sensory judgments we can distrust them all.[32] If, for instance, green light shines on a red wall, and I mistakenly see the wall as brown, Aristotle might say that this is not a mistake by sight, but a mistaken inference from correct information given by sight. If he is right, I must be seeing something that is really brown, but still different from the wall and its real colour; it must be a purely phenomenal colour.[33] From this view of special sense-objects, Aristotle can defend the infallibility of the special senses against the more obvious grounds of objection, and therefore he can defend the veridical character of the senses against sceptical objections.[34]

But this anti-sceptical argument is perfectly useless for Aristotle's purposes. He seeks to show that the senses are veridical about external qualities, but his argument abandons realism in its attempt to defeat scepticism.[35] If this is the only viable anti-sceptical strategy, then first philosophy is incoherent. For it offers to answer scepticism about the senses (in *Metaphysics* iv); it defends the general hylomorphic account of substance that is supposed to support a hylomorphic account of the soul; this account of the soul requires perceptual realism, and therefore needs an answer to scepticism; but the answer to scepticism rejects perceptual realism.

The incoherence, however, is present in Aristotle's interpretation of his views, not in the views themselves. For *Metaphysics* iv defends perceptual realism against the sceptic, without requiring the senses to be infallible, and therefore without accepting the anti-realist view that is needed to defend infallibility. Only Aristotle's assumptions about infallibility make first philosophy incoherent; and if he rejects these assumptions, he does not undermine the rest of first philosophy.

The faults in Aristotle's anti-sceptical strategy reflect a more general fault in his views about methods of inquiry.[36] His account of empirical method reflects a rather naïve empiricism, an uncritical confidence in the veridical character of the senses; it does not occur to him that the sensory 'appearances' used in the construction of a theory may themselves be the product of theory and interpretation. He has a special reason for resisting such a thought to the extent that he sometimes holds a foundationalist view of justification; if we must justify a perceptual claim by appeal to some further principle, and we can raise questions about the reliability of that principle, we might seem to face a vicious regress. These views together make it intelligible for Aristotle to claim that some perceptual judgments provide an infallible basis for other justified judgments. The infallible basis described in the *De Anima* is useless, however, for his purposes.

The anomaly in Aristotle's claims about perception deserves attention, therefore, because it reveals the influence of his naïve empiricism and foundationalism. We have previously insisted that these assumptions, prominent as they are in some of his claims about inquiry and knowledge, really conflict with his most fundamental views. Dialectical method requires us to treat coherence as a source of justification, and to begin from data that we recognize as subject to revision. First philosophy attempts to strengthen dialectic; but we will not take its attempts seriously unless we reject foundationalism. The anomalous claims about perception rest on prominent Aristotelian assumptions; but these assumptions conflict with the most plausible and fundamental principles of first philosophy. We can therefore see not only that his claims about perception are anomalous, but also explain why they are anomalous, and why Aristotle, in the light of a proper understanding of his own views, should reject them.

166. COMPLEX PERCEPTION

Aristotle's teleological account of perception requires the absorption of the form of the perceptible object. This seems to involve simply a state of the perceiver's faculty and organ of perception; but in fact it must require more. For we will have no reason to suppose that the perceiver really absorbs the immaterial form unless we have reason to believe that the representative features of its perceptual state help to explain its other psychic states and behaviour. Hence the account must include some description of the process leading from the absorption of the form to action. The intervening stages require reference to how perceivers take the perception, or how the perception appears to them; and in this process 'appearance' (*phantasia*) and inference will be important.

In some cases Aristotle realizes this. In 'coincidental' perception we might say, for example, 'I see that he is a diabetic'. In such cases we see something that we take to indicate the level of blood sugar, and with further thought have taken this to indicate diabetes. 'See that . . .' is to be analysed into what we really see plus inferences to what we believe.[37] We can allow the senses to have a fairly limited and fixed range of objects if we add the appropriate inferences.

Aristotle does not offer this explanation, however, in every case where it might seem suitable. He attributes to a sense some functions that we might ascribe to inference from perception. The common sense has its objects, including size, shape, and number, that are all perceived by motion (425a14–20). These are related to, though not the same as, the properties that Plato calls 'common' because they are grasped by the soul itself, not by the senses (*Tht.* 185b7–9). Aristotle resists Plato's argument that because these are not the objects of any of the normal five senses they must be grasped by inference from the senses, not by the senses themselves.

The Platonic view makes the common sensibles coincidental objects of sense, and Aristotle rejects this view of them (425a24–7), arguing instead for a unified faculty of perception. He uses the same device to explain how one sense can coincidentally grasp the special object of another, so that we say we perceive by sight that something is sweet. He uses it again to explain second-order perception; on his view, we can properly say that we perceive by sight that we are seeing, and need not attribute this awareness to some non-sensory psychic faculty.

In all these cases Aristotle must assume a role for appearance that he does not explicitly recognize. Awareness of motion, the basic common sensible, requires awareness that something is different from the way it was; but this awareness requires awareness of time, which requires memory, to remember the earlier moment when we perceive the later; and memory requires appearance, since our perception of the earlier moment must somehow be represented in our later awareness. The common sense, therefore, requires appearance. If so, the common sensibles seem to be coincidental sensibles parallel to the son of Cleon; in one case as in the other the additional information comes from memory, appearance, and inference.[38]

A parallel objection faces Aristotle's attempt to distinguish coincidental perception by one sense of the object of another sense (e.g. the perception of sweetness by sight) from the coincidental perception of the son of Cleon (425a21–7). In his view the second case is not really a case of seeing at all, since it is not the faculty of sight that informs us that this is the son of Cleon. But in the first case as well as the second we need memory and appearance; for we must notice that this white thing has in the past been associated with a sweet taste, and infer that it will be associated with such a taste this time as well. If so, appearance and inference seem to have no less role in this perception than in the perception of the son of Cleon. In both cases we see a colour and infer, by memory and appearance, some further property of the object. Aristotle seems to exaggerate the role of the senses, and to underestimate the role of appearance.[39]

He seems to do the same in his account of second-order perception, the awareness that we see or hear. He suggests that second-order awareness is a function of the same sense that has first-order awareness; sight, for instance, makes us aware of our seeing.[40] He adds that such second-order awareness requires a unified sense-faculty (426b24–427a14), since our awareness of seeing requires awareness of the difference from hearing and other types of perception. This argument shows that the common sense is also needed; for the unified sense requires awareness of unity, number, sameness, and difference, and this awareness belongs to the common sense (426b12–24). But for the reasons we have already considered, Aristotle cannot go this far without appeal to memory, since that is needed for awareness of time and movement, of the difference between this sweet thing and that earlier loud thing, and of this perception following that one; and memory requires appearance, not merely perception. Aristotle assigns to perception a function that seems to belong properly to appearance.

Aristotle's exaggeration of the role of the senses perhaps reflects his rather over-simplified view of the accuracy of perception. The more we think of perception simply as a transaction between the senses and the external world, the easier it may seem to insist that we perceive what is really there by absorbing features that are already there. Hence, if we can show that some property is absorbed by the senses, we have all the better reason for insisting that it really exists; and this may be part of Aristotle's reason for treating common sensibles as objects of sense.

His rather naïve attitude to observation and induction shows why this view of the senses might appeal to him, and how it might support some of his other views. To the extent that we allow appearance and memory to affect perception, we may seem to increase the role of construction and reduce the role of detection and discovery. Aristotle's formulae of perception show that he wants to avoid conceding too much to construction; and this motive explains why he tries to make perception as self-sufficient as possible.

If this is Aristotle's strategy, however, it is mistaken; and Aristotle himself cannot afford to accept it too far, since he combines realist claims about perception with a teleological conception that must appeal to appearance and memory. If perception is to play the appropriate role in explaining the creature's behaviour, the creature must interpret its perceptions, remember them selectively, associate them, and link them with desire. Aristotle has no reason not to appeal to these same psychic functions to explain the types of complex perception that he ascribes to the senses alone. His teleological view of perception is not responsible for his over-simple claims about perception. On the contrary, the source of these claims is the foundationalist epistemological outlook that conflicts with the conception of strong dialectic underlying the teleological account of the soul.

167. APPEARANCE

If we simply believe that a dog has seen a red object, we cannot infer much about what it will do. We can explain much more if we add facts about how the object appears to the dog. If it looks green, then our expectations about the dog's actions will be different.[41] Appeal to appearance makes actions seem explicable that might otherwise have seemed inexplicable.

But if we suppose that something appears red to a dog, we still may have no expectations about action, since it may not respond in any uniform way to the same appearance. Aristotle suggests that the further state to be assumed is some form of desire. But assumption of a desire affects our view of the appearance, since any plausible desire will usually be selective (an animal is unlikely to want to get everything of the same apparent colour). Aristotle believes animals desire something as pleasant, and hence that its appearance as pleasant helps to explain the action. But this appearance is consistent with inaction if we see no possible action to attain the pleasure; and so the appearance of an action as a possible means must be assumed. We must, then, refer to all these types of appearance, if we are to extend teleological explanation as far as is reasonable.

These different roles for appearance are hard to understand unless we take them to involve some sort of inference. We need to understand the process of transition from one state to another, e.g. from perception to appearance or from appearance to desire. We could try to understand them in purely material terms; but if we seek a teleological explanation and describe them as mental states, we will look for relations between the content of the different states. When we see a dog confronted by water and trying to drink it, we understand his behaviour if we assume that he sees the colour of the water, remembers that this is the same colour as the water that has previously satisfied his thirst, and so infers that this water is desirable; he notices that there is nothing to stop him getting the water, and so infers that it is worth his while to try to get it.

If we think his mental states have their contents related in these ways, we have some conception of the laws observed in the transition from one state to another.

This result shows that a hylomorphic account of perception must include more than perception and behaviour. If we are to find the right links between them we must also ascribe to the subjects the further states of appearance and desire; and we cannot explain the regular transitions between these states without attributing inference to the subject. Creatures with perception need appearance, desire, and inference, if we are to be able to attribute these states to them in a teleological account of psychic states.

168. APPEARANCE AND THOUGHT

At this point, however, we face a difficulty in reconciling the demands of the teleological account with some of Aristotle's explicit claims and with a plausible view of the facts. When we see the general form of a teleological explanation involving perception and appearance, we readily suppose that it will include inference; and once we mention inference we readily mention belief—we are inclined to say that because the dog believes the water is available, and wants the water, it tries to get it. This account of its mental states, however, seems to conflict with Aristotle's claim that non-rational animals have appearance without belief.

But belief implies conviction (*pistis*) (for it is impossible to have a belief without conviction in what one believes); but no beasts have conviction, whereas many have appearances. Further, every belief implies conviction, and conviction implies being persuaded, and persuasion implies reason; but some beasts have appearance, whereas none has reason. (428a19–24)[42]

Since they lack reason and belief, they will be unable to reason from one belief to another, and therefore will lack the capacity for inference. If a teleological account of their psychic states requires us to ascribe to them states they cannot have, it leads us astray.

It will prove helpful to raise a further difficulty at this stage. Aristotle attributes truth and falsity both to perceptions and to appearances, and a teleological account cannot easily avoid this. On the other hand he seems to imply that perception and appearance cannot be true or false. For he insists that no linguistic item is true or false unless it is a sentence making an assertion—mere single words or sequences do not constitute anything true or false (*De Int.* 16a9–18); and in the same way combinations of mental states do not add up to anything true or false unless they are the sort of combination that makes an assertion (432a10–12). The appropriate combination makes a belief; and simply having mental states that can be components of a belief or assertion is not believing or asserting. Since non-rational animals lack beliefs, their mental states cannot be the bearers of truth and falsity.

We must clarify three different contrasts that Aristotle draws between the states of rational and of non-rational subjects:

1. Mere perception and appearance are not sufficient for thought.

2. A mere collection of thoughts does not make the combination that is necessary for belief and assertion. The four thoughts 'to runs man bank' do not make any further thought with further content of its own. We have to combine them in the right way, into 'the man runs to the bank' before we have the sort of thing that can be true or false.

3. The right sort of combination yields something that is capable of truth or falsity; but it is not enough for assertion or belief, an actual bearer of truth. Though Aristotle lacks a special term for the entertaining of a proposition, he needs to distinguish it from belief and supposition (*hupolêpsis*, 427b16–26).[43]

Aristotle therefore needs to distinguish appearance from thought, thought from entertaining a proposition, and entertaining from asserting.

169. THOUGHT

The first distinction to be understood contrasts appearances with thoughts (*noêmata*), apart from any appeal to combination. Aristotle sees that if combination is left out of account some types of thoughts are hard to distinguish from appearances (432a12–14). Still, he tries to draw a distinction; and in fact he draws several distinctions that do not seem obviously connected:

1. Animals lack any grasp of a universal, and have only appearances and memory of particulars (*EN* 1147b4–5).
2. Thought requires us to grasp essences—what flesh is, as opposed to flesh (429b10–18).
3. Intellect is not affected by matter in thinking in the way that perception is affected in perceiving (429a31–2).

The most surprising of these claims is the first. It seems odd to deny that in perception we are aware of universals, since we are aware of things as red or hard. Moreover, memory, repetition, association, and appearance make us aware of mental contents apart from what is presented to us at the moment; why do they not make us aware of universals? The dog that sees the water seems to be aware of it not only as silvery but also as pleasant; and it seems hard to deny that the universal pleasantness is part of the content of the dog's appearance.

Aristotle should claim that an animal's appearances may be explained by their relation to some universal even though the animal itself does not grasp the universal as such. Perhaps grasp of a universal as such requires the capacity to regard different features of an object as giving reasons for attributing the universal to it. If, for instance, I have the concept of a golf ball, I have some beliefs about the shape, size, and behaviour that give grounds and reasons for calling something a golf ball. I need not deploy all these beliefs in an explicit inference whenever I use the term; but if I were incapable of them, and could still pick out golf balls, I would be picking them out by something other than my grasp of the concept and my knowledge of the universal. If one perceiver grasps a universal and the other does not, both may pick out instances of the same universal. But the 'mere' perceiver will not give the right account of relevant features; it may confuse the relevant features with irrelevant but constantly associated features.

Aristotle assumes these conditions for grasp of a universal. In his view, the universal is present in the subject only after the operations of sense, memory, and experience (*APo* 100a3–9, *Met.* 981a5–7). He agrees that in one sense perception is of the universal (*APo* 100a16–b1; cf. *Phys.* 184a23–6); but he does not agree that the universal is present in the subject until more demanding conditions are met. He must, therefore, distinguish the awareness that merely corresponds to a universal from the awareness that includes some grasp of the universal as such; the second sort of awareness is confined to subjects that can recognize some feature of their experience as a ground for attributing the universal to a particular they experience.

This first feature of thought leads naturally to the second, the claim that thought grasps essences and not just their instances. Subjects who are aware of 'being flesh' use a conception of what flesh is in their judgment that this is flesh; subjects who are simply aware of flesh need not recognize flesh as such, and therefore need not use any conception of what flesh is. If I recognize flesh as such, I need not know the account of the real essence of flesh; but I need some roughly correct conception of what it is. Aristotle reasonably supposes that subjects applying a concept of F to their experience are aware of grounds for calling something F; and this is why thought must grasp what it is to be flesh.

The third feature of thought now becomes intelligible from the first two. Aristotle insists that the intellect is unaffected by material objects, in some way that distinguishes it from the senses. The senses themselves are not affected by matter in a straightforward way, since they absorb the sensible form without the matter. But they are affected by matter in a way the intellect is not, in so far as they are essentially related to essentially material spatio-temporal particulars. Perceiving is essentially perceiving some particular that has causally affected us because it is the sort of material object it is. By contrast, the causal interaction required for grasp of the universal F is just perceptual interaction with instances of F; for there are no universals separable from particulars and we must be aware of particulars through perception (432a3–10).[44] The non-perceptual aspects of our grasp of universals consist in thought about the particular object in relation to others of the same sort, not in any further causal interaction with the object.[45]

170. THOUGHT AND INFERENCE

The three features of thought that we have considered help to explain the difference between mental states involving thought and those that lack it. In asserting that belief and assertion require the combination of thoughts and appearance does not (432a10–12), Aristotle does not distinguish them accurately. Merely entertaining a proposition already requires some combination of thoughts, and something more is needed for assertion and belief. Moreover, those appearances that depend on memory seem to involve some combination resulting from the perceptions that form them; and if this is not combination of thoughts, Aristotle needs to say why not.

To entertain a proposition is to grasp its logical structure; to grasp the sense of 'p and q' is to understand that if it is true it makes p true and also makes q true. In grasping the logical syntax and structure of the proposition, we grasp the inferences it requires or permits. To entertain the proposition that dogs are animals is to grasp two concepts, associated with different sets of inferences, and to combine the inferences into new possible inferences. We have no reason to attribute this sort of inferential combination to non-rational perceivers.

This type of combination also distinguishes assertion and belief from appearance. Aristotle claims that belief involves conviction and persuasion, which involve reasoning and are not present in non-rational perceivers (428a19–24). Subjects capable of conviction and persuasion can consider evidence and reasons, and 'make up their minds' by reaching a conclusion from them. To reach a belief is to realize one of the possibilities that we take to be open when we entertain the proposition that we come to believe. These conditions for belief and assertion justify Aristotle's claim that non-rational perceivers cannot have it.

Aristotle denies grasp of universals as such to non-rational perceivers, because grasp of universals involves the capacity to recognize features of objects as reasons for applying a concept to them. But this capacity to recognize reasons cannot be separated from the capacities exercised in combination of thoughts and in belief and assertion. Though it is convenient to distinguish the grasp of a single concept or universal, e.g. the property of being a dog, from combination of this thought with others, and from beliefs about dogs, this distinction should not mislead us into thinking that the grasp of a single concept can precede the capacity to combine and to believe.[46]

Aristotle does not explain the relation between his different conditions for thought in contrast to perception. But they turn out to be closely connected; each of them explains the others, and is satisfied only if the others are satisfied. The central capacity presupposed by all these is the capacity to recognize and make inferences on the basis of reasons; for it explains the different features he ascribes to thought, and the ways it differs from appearance. Aristotle must distinguish the 'synthesis of reproduction in imagination' from the 'synthesis of recognition in a concept'.[47] He does not tell us exactly how to mark this distinction but his conditions tell us enough to show how he ought to mark it.

171. THOUGHT, CONTENT, AND STRUCTURE

Now that we have seen how Aristotle distinguishes thought, belief, and inference from mere appearance, we should return to the question that we raised previously about the role of appearance in the teleological account of a perceiver's psychic states. Aristotle might easily seem to assume that a non-rational perceiver has true and false beliefs and inferences from one belief to another; but his account of thought and appearance assures us that he is not entitled to assume this. We now want to see if we can understand his claims about appearance without forcing him into severe inconsistency.

We may be sceptical about ascribing any definite appearance to a non-rational perceiver at all. If a dog sees a bone, how does the bone appear to it? Does the dog regard it as a bone, or a bone in the corner, or as a long white thing, or as food? If a creature has the relevant thoughts and concepts of bone, white, food, and so on, it is reasonable to ask which way its experience appears to it; but a creature without thoughts apparently cannot find that its experience appears any of these ways.[48] Still, we can hardly explain how its perception is related to desire and action, unless we assume an appearance with some content described in conceptual and propositional terms.

If, for instance, the dog sees the white thing, it may be deceived into regarding the object as red, and may react to it as it would to a red object. (Suppose, e.g., the dog's food has always been red, it is hungry, a red light is shining on the white object, and the dog tries to eat it.) To explain its action we naturally say that the white thing appears red to it, and we assume the propositional content 'that's red'. But we cannot assume a mental state that includes the thought of something's being red, and we cannot assume a belief, since the dog has neither thoughts nor beliefs. To grasp a thought and entertain a proposition, we must have some grasp of the logical structure of the thought and of the inferential possibilities it involves. If a creature is not aware of any of the grounds for belief and inference that belong to the structure of a thought, we ought not to ascribe the thought to it.

A propositional description may capture the character of a non-rational creature's mental states. For even a rational subject may not grasp all the logical structure and inferential possibilities of a thought; and in that case the propositional description will provide a less exact description of his mental state, but it will still capture the state's role in the transition from one mental state to another. If I grasp the inferential function of 'and' so poorly that I accept (p & q), but do not accept p and q if I am asked about them separately, then the attribution to me of a belief in a conjunction may be misleading (if an observer expects me to accept the conjuncts separately); but still my belief that there is bread and butter on the table may explain my going to the table in circumstances where I would not have gone for either without the other. A partial grasp of the proposition explains the beliefs I hold.

Non-rational subjects will not literally grasp any of the grounds for inferring one proposition from another, but something like a partial grasp may explain their other mental states and their behaviour. If a dog seeing a piece of meat has the appearance 'that it's red', the dog need not have the appearance with the structure 'that it's red'; the propositional description may describe the role of the appearance in the transition from the dog's causal interactions with the red object to its attempts to eat the object. We claim only that the dog has the mental state that plays a role similar to the role of the belief that this is red. Though the dog has no concepts at all, in the way a rational subject has them, some are more appropriate than others for describing its appearances. If a dog bites a stranger who is the Prime Minister, the stranger does not appear to the dog to be the Prime Minister but she might appear to the dog to be unfamiliar or unwelcome, since that description might indicate the role of the dog's state in explaining its actions.

This account of non-rational appearances relies on Aristotle's own explanation of abstraction. In abstraction, we treat a triangle as though it existed without the physical object that it is actually embodied in; but no falsity results, since we rely neither on the claim that a triangle can exist separately nor on the features that this particular material triangle happens to have (*Phys.* 193b31–5, *Met.* 1078a14–21).[49] Similarly, in describing non-rational mental states we may seem to attribute too much content, because we identify the state in terms that imply more content than it really has; but we restrict ourselves to explanatory roles warranted by the content we ascribe. We can therefore claim on Aristotle's behalf (though he does not claim this for himself) that his defence of abstraction supports his use of propositional descriptions for the content of appearances.

This account of the content of appearances also explains why Aristotle takes perceptions and appearances to allow truth and falsehood, even though he takes these to be properties of assertions (428a11–12, a16–19, b17–30).[50] Since true and false propositions describe the content of perceptions and appearances, these mental states may themselves be called true or false; but they need not have the structure that properly belongs only to assertions and beliefs.

172. THE COGNITIVE FACULTIES

Aristotle regards perception, appearance, and thought as 'discriminative' (*kritikon*) faculties, allowing us to distinguish one type of external object from another, so that we can react in different and appropriate ways. We have tried to see the implications of Aristotle's hylomorphic theory for his claims about the cognitive faculties. Sometimes the general theory helps to explain and vindicate different aspects of Aristotle's view; but sometimes it requires us to reject some of his claims, or to alter his emphasis.

At first sight the three cognitive states seem clearly separable. We take perception to cover seeing, hearing, and so on, appearance to be a further mental state added to perception, and thought to be a third level added to the first two. But on closer inspection the divisions are less clear. If perception is a cognitive state, including some awareness of features of the external world, then it cannot do without appearance. To have perceptual knowledge I must not only perceive something that is actually red, but must also perceive that it is red; my perception cannot be combined with other states to explain my behaviour unless some propositional content is ascribed to it. If it has a propositional content, it appears to me in some way, and so requires appearance.

Rational perceivers have perceptual appearances involving a further level of complexity; for how the object appears to them is determined by their concepts. The perceptual appearance that leads to action often includes a belief; and a belief results from acceptance of a proposition on the basis of evidence and reasons. The Stoics construe perception as the product of a perceptual affection (*pathos*), appearance, and rational assent (*sunkatathesis*).[51] Analysis of Aristotle's account shows that he is committed to the same view; though he seems to confine perception to the first stage of the process, he cannot do this if he is to attribute truth and falsity to perception.

Aristotle does not actually deny any of these points about the connexion of perception with appearance and thought. But he does not seem to see their importance, since he does not describe the role of judgments in concepts or of concepts in perception. Questions about the conceptual apparatus required for genuinely cognitive perception concern Kant; but they also concern Plato, in his discussion of the 'common properties' (*Tht.* 184–6), and the Stoics, in their views on the role of appearance and thought in perception. Aristotle, however, is silent on these questions.

His general theory does not lead us to expect these silences. Quite the contrary; his hylomorphic, teleological view of the soul requires him to attend to the connexions between perception and other psychic states. His doctrine of the soul rests on his general metaphysical theory of form and matter; and if he had attended more closely to the implications of that theory, his account of the particular psychic faculties would have been closer to the Stoic account.

Aristotle is influenced, however, by the naïve realism that also affects his treatment of perception as a source of evidence for a theory. He suggests that perception, without interpretation or further inference, is in itself a reliable foundation for claims to knowledge; and he suggests this partly because of foundationalist assumptions about justification. These views lead him to claim that perception is infallible; and since appearance is not infallible, he treats perception as a cognitive state separable from appearance.

Here he is misled; for his own theory explains why perception cannot be a cognitive state contributing to the teleological explanation of action unless it includes the propositional content that requires appearance. Aristotle is mistaken in thinking that the appropriate role for perception in knowledge and justification requires it to be non-inferential and infallible; indeed, his attempts to secure infallibility lead him to deny realism about perception. If he faces the implications of his general teleological theory, he must abandon his over-simplified view of the role of perception in knowledge. We have seen that he ought to abandon this view anyhow, since it prevents a proper understanding of the role of dialectic in inquiry and justification. The account of the soul depends on first philosophy, which itself implies a role for dialectic that conflicts with Aristotle's over-simplified views about perception.

Aristotle's over-simplifications support an unavailing defence of realism and objectivism. If we agree that our informative perceptions reflect our appearances and concepts, we may infer that we perceive things only as they appear to us, not as they really are; and then we seem to agree with Protagoras. Aristotle's solution is his appeal to a level of perception that precedes the distorting effects of appearance; but this solution assumes an implausible account of perception that Aristotle himself cannot maintain.

These defects in Aristotle's views on perception explain three more general defects in his method:

1. Aristotle tends to distinguish perceptual appearances from the broader class of common beliefs, and to regard the perceptual appearances as more reliable. His division is intelligible if he regards basic perceptions as a means of direct access to reality.

2. Hence, when he thinks we can perceive something directly, e.g. the presence of teleological sequences, he thinks this perception reflects no interpretation and needs no defence.

3. In appealing to those appearances that are common beliefs less directly derived from appearance Aristotle is more reluctant to claim truth for the premises or conclusions of his arguments. Hence he is reserved about the claims of dialectical arguments to discover the truth.[52]

Aristotle's views on perception, then, encourage over-hasty confidence in 'genuine' perceptual appearances, and over-hasty suspicion of dialectical argument from non-perceptual appearances. In the *Metaphysics*, on the other hand, he is more willing both to defend perceptual appearances as though they needed defence and to claim truth for the premises and conclusions of some dialectical arguments. Both sides of him are reflected in the treatment of the cognitive faculties in the *DA*. The over-simple view is reflected in the division of the faculties. More complex views are reflected in the description of the faculties, showing that they are less separable than Aristotle might lead us to believe.

We should not be surprised, then, to find a conflict between the demands of Aristotle's hylomorphic theory and some of his particular claims about the cognitive faculties. For some of Aristotle's basic metaphysical claims depend on the rejection of the sort of naïve realism that affects some of his epistemological claims. The explanatory role of perception makes it clear that informative perception must involve appearance, since that is the link between perception and desire. The faults in Aristotle's views on perception should help us to notice some broader faults in his views about method; but they should not turn us against the method of the *DA*, which actually shows us how to correct some of his errors.

If, then, we attend to the connexion between the theory of the soul and first philosophy, we can see why Aristotle is committed to views that are more plausible than those he actually presents. Our attention to the metaphysical background of his philosophy of mind shows us how to make a reasonable choice on Aristotle's behalf between conflicting elements in his views about psychic faculties; he has good independent reasons to abandon the assumptions underlying one side of the conflict.

15

ACTION

173. DESIRE AND PERCEPTION

Since Aristotle's account of the cognitive faculties belongs to a teleological account of the soul, he ought to show how perception and appearance help to explain behaviour. By themselves they are not enough to explain it; we need to add some further state to explain how the selective awareness present in the cognitive faculties affects the creature's good. This further state is the one that initiates movement; Aristotle remarks that the soul in animals is defined by two faculties, the discriminative, belonging to sense and thought, and the faculty of initiating movement (*DA* 432a15–17).[1]

In looking for this part that initiates movement (432b7–8) Aristotle insists strongly on two claims; first, this part is not separable from the other parts and faculties of the soul; and second, it is one part, the desiring (*orektikon*) part, and not several different parts sharing this role. Both of these claims express the role of desire in the teleological account of the soul.

Aristotle argues that the desiring part is not separable, because it is closely connected to perception; it is a faculty of the perceptive soul, not marking out another type of soul.[2]

Perceiving is like simply saying and thinking. But whenever ⟨something is⟩ pleasant or painful, after having, so to speak, affirmed or denied, ⟨the animal⟩ pursues or avoids; and having pleasure or pain is actualizing with the perceptive mean in relation to the good or bad as such. And avoidance and desire in actuality are the same thing, and the desiring and the avoiding part are not different, either from each other or from the perceptive part, but their being is other. (431a8–14)

Finding something pleasant is simply perceiving it in a certain way, and finding it pleasant is sufficient for desiring it.

When Aristotle says that the psychic parts are the same but their being is different, he perhaps means that for an animal no further mental process or capacity is required for action once it has recognized an object as pleasant and seen that this is the way to get it. A particular capacity, as the perceptive part, absorbs features of the external object; as the desiring part, it originates movement. We ascribe two roles to the same capacity.

We know what perceptions we should ascribe to a creature when we also know what appearances and desires are reasonably ascribed to it. Equally, we have no reason to attribute a particular desire to a creature unless we suppose it is capable of acting on the desire in particular circumstances; and we have no ground for attributing one desire rather than another in particular circumstances unless we also assume something about the creature's perceptions. If we see a dog moving towards water, we can reasonably assume that it wants water only if we also suppose it has an appearance of water; if we thought that it was hallucinating and that the water appeared to it as meat, we would assume a different desire.[3] We must attribute perceptions, appearances, anticipations of pleasure and pain, and desire all at the same time, and we lack grounds for attributing any one without the others.

Aristotle therefore refuses to treat the desiring part of the soul, or any subdivision of it, as a separable part; to think of it this way is to conceal its essential connexions with other psychic states in a teleological explanation of behaviour. It is reasonable for him to begin his discussion of desire by insisting on its inseparability from the other parts of the soul; his reasons for insisting on this express his guiding assumptions about the nature of psychic states.

174. THE UNITY OF DESIRE

Aristotle now refuses to attribute the origination of motion to more than one part, separable or inseparable. Instead of recognizing two sources of motion, reason and desire, he insists that there is one mover, and that this is the desiring part.

The mover, then, is one, the desiring part. For if the movers were two, thought and desire, they would move according to some common form. But as it is, thought plainly does not move us without desire (for wish is desire, and when we are moved according to reasoning we are also moved according to wish), while desire moves even contrary to reasoning, since appetite is a ⟨kind of⟩ desire. (433a21–6)[4]

If we speak of the conflict this way, we can maintain that there is one mover; and Aristotle assumes that whenever we seem to have found two movers, they will move 'according to some common form' (433a21–2), and this common form will be the one mover we should have been looking for.[5]

We might say that sometimes the thought that an action promotes my health moves me to do the action, though sometimes it does not; it may not move me if I have a strong desire for some conflicting immediate pleasure, or a strong aversion to a pain involved in the action, or if I am convinced of a moral obligation to do something else.[6] But none of these countervailing motives invariably causes a different action; the conflicting desires may be overridden, or I may ignore the moral obligation I recognize. When Aristotle looks for a common form, he refuses to stop with such a list.[7] He thinks he can find the general laws explaining the particular causal claims; for he thinks thought does not move without desire. When we are moved in accordance with reasoning, we are moved in accordance with wish, which is a form of desire (433a23–5). Hence rational motivation is not an exception to the general claim about the necessity of desire for action.

This claim is useful and non-trivial only if the desiring part is genuinely a single part. The perceptive part is a single part, not because Aristotle collects a group of psychic functions with the same effects and calls them all by the same name; rather, the three formulae of perception suggest that perception is unified by its relation to its object. Aristotle offers a similar unifying formula for desire; for he claims that the object of desire (*to orekton*) is either the good or the apparent good achievable in action.

Hence in every case the mover is the object of desire; and the object of desire is either the good or the apparent good—not every sort of good, but the good that is achievable in action—and therefore it admits of being otherwise. (433a27–30)

Understanding or appearance conceives the object of desire (433b11–12), and because we recognize it as something we desire we try to get it.[8]

Desire is the single and unified faculty that originates goal-directed movement, because it rests on a true or false conception of the creature's good. We have already seen why we assume such a conception in ascribing mental states to a creature at all.[9] Desire deserves to count as a single mover because it makes this crucial connexion between perception and action in a teleological explanation.

Aristotle seems to raise a difficulty, however, for his own account of animal desires. If he means that objects appear as goods to animals, he seems to ascribe to their appearances a content that he elsewhere denies. Normally he says an animal is moved to action by the appearance that something is pleasant (431a8–11).[10] He distinguishes the appetite that animals have from the wish that only rational agents have, by saying that appetite is for the pleasant and wish is for the good (414b2–6; cf. 432b5–7). Hence he distinguishes human beings, as the only animals that are aware of good and bad, from those that are aware only of the pleasant and the painful (*Pol.* 1253a15–18).[11]

This issue affects Aristotle's claim about the unity of desire. For if the object of desire is either good or pleasant, desire may appear to split into two parts, rational desire seeking the good and non-rational desire seeking the pleasant. If we say they constitute a single desiring part because they both pursue an object of desire, we still need a better description of the object of desire than 'good or pleasant'.

175. DESIRE AND APPARENT GOOD

Aristotle must answer that 'apparent good' need not refer to something's appearing *as* good, but may instead refer to the good that appears, even if it appears as something other than good—as pleasant, for instance. The teleological conception of psychic faculties supports this appeal to an apparent good. For if an animal is teleologically organized, teleological principles should explain how things appear to the animal, and the fact that things appear to it at all; and so we should see how its action on its appearances is good for it. When the animal acts to get what appears to it, the appearance must be in general an appearance of its good—an appearance of something that is in fact good for the animal, though not necessarily an appearance of it *as* good. To say that animals aim at what appears good is not to describe the content of their mental states, since 'good' is not an intentional object of any of their desires. Their appearances must be suitably connected to their good, even though any individual appearances may fail to aim at a real good.

Desire, therefore, is a single faculty because it focuses on the object of desire that is the apparent good, whether or not it appears as good to the subject; and this connexion with the good of the subject must belong to the subject's desires taken as a whole, not taken individually. The connexion explains Aristotle's claim that thought does not seem to move us to action without desire. For he believes that thought moves us when it aims at an end we desire, because then our action will in some way be suitably related to our good, and so will be teleologically intelligible.

This claim must also apply, despite apparent difficulties, to rational agents. Unlike other animals, they have their own conception of the good, not simply appearances of what is pleasant; and this conception of their good may be wrong. It may none the less be connected with their good. Even if I have a gravely erroneous conception of my good, I may be better off acting on this conception than on no conception at all; however bad it may be, I can at least act on relatively systematic, conscious, and coordinated plans that would not be available to a non-rational agent.

Aristotle, therefore, believes that action requires desire because desire involves the appropriate relation to the agent's good. But it does not seem obvious that all desires belong to some conception of the agent's good. Some appetites for pleasure not only do not belong to my conception of my good, but may even conflict with it and move me to act incontinently (*DA* 433b5–10). Appetite conflicts with reason because it does not foresee the future.

To cope with these cases we must recognize two relations to the agent's good in a rational agent's desires. Rational desires are unified by their relation to the agent's conception of his good. Non-rational desires are unified in the way that an animal's desires are unified, because on the whole the agent benefits from acting on appearances and desires. A rational agent's desires are all related to the agent's good, but in these two different ways; and the different relations make possible the sort of conflict that may result in incontinence. Hence Aristotle thinks he can concede the difference that is implied by conflict without endangering the unity of desire.

The moving part is one in species; it is the desiring part, qua desiring—and first of all the object of desire, since this causes motion, by being thought or by appearing, without being moved; but the movers are more than one in number. (433b10–13)

The unity of the faculty is secured by its relation to the agent's good.

Aristotle thinks he has shown that the desiring part is parallel to the faculties of nutrition, perception, thought, and deliberation. He suggests that someone who recognizes the Platonic parts must recognize that these parts differ from each other more than the Platonic parts differ (433a31–b4); and yet he thinks conflicts between desires do not threaten the sort of unity he sees in the desiring part.

176. REASON AND DESIRE

We might easily identify Aristotle's view with the apparently similar claims of Hume, who also believes desire is necessary for motivation. Hume also believes that the faculty of desire is non-trivially unified; he does not define a desire or passion as whatever moves us to action, but argues that whatever moves us to action must satisfy the conditions that we antecedently know to be satisfied by desire and passion. Hume makes his claim non-trivial by insisting that every desire ultimately depends on a passion; a passion is, among other things, a tendency to pursue a certain type of object irrespective of any reasoning about it. This is part of what he means in calling a passion an 'original existence', and insisting that reason is and ought to be the slave of passion. He means to exclude the possibility that practical reason could move us to pursue some end for which we do not have some desire that is independent of any reasoning; and to this extent he severely restricts the scope of reasoning in motivation and action.[12]

Aristotle also wants to restrict the scope of reason, but not in the same way. He insists that reason moves us only when it reasons for the sake of some end that is desired (433a22–5, *EN* 1139a35–b4); but he refrains from the crucial Humean claim that the desire for this end must be a passion that is independent of reason. Unlike Hume, he can readily agree that motives originate in reason no less than in desire; but he requires them to be appropriate parts of a teleological explanation, and therefore to be suitably connected to the agent's good. This connexion with the agent's good implies the connexion with desire.[13] States that lack this sort of connexion are not appropriate parts of the formal account that describes the soul. These claims about the unity of desire rest ultimately on Aristotle's teleological conception of mental states; and to this extent the argument of the *De Anima* is both coherent and cumulative.

The argument is dialectical, in so far as it begins from common beliefs and tries to find a rational revision of them. But it displays the method of strong dialectic, as we have seen it in the *Metaphysics* and *De Anima*. Aristotle revises common beliefs, to adjust them to the principles of his conception of the soul. He is discontented with the common beliefs as they stand because he is sure there must be some one mover, and that it must be the desiring part, which must be non-trivially unified. He has reasons for being sure on these points; they are derived from his theory of the soul; and they guide his modification of common beliefs. At this point the *De Anima* relies on the view of the *Metaphysics*.[14]

177. RATIONAL DESIRES

Aristotle denies that a rational animal is moved by something other than desire. Still, he has assumed that reason marks out a distinct type of soul coordinate with the perceptive and nutritive soul (*DA* 415a7–11); and he will not have shown this unless he can show that reason makes a difference to action. Aristotle remarks: 'some non-rational creatures do not even have appearance, and others live by this alone' (415a10–11). If reason did not affect how rational creatures live it would not mark out a distinct type of soul; it provides a distinctive type of desire that implies a different soul.

Non-rational creatures lack beliefs and a grasp of universals, and so are confined to appearances and memory of particulars, because they lack the right sorts of capacities for rational assessment and inference.[15] Aristotle must mention universals in his description of animals' appearances, and he must agree that, in one sense, things appear to animals under universal descriptions; for he thinks things appear pleasant to them. He denies, however, that the animal reaches the appearance on the basis of reasons, or by inference from (e.g.) the general belief that sweet things are pleasant and the particular belief that this is sweet.[16]

This rational capacity, however, might make a minimal difference to action. If a rational and a non-rational creature acted the same way, and their appearances and desires had a different structure, but the very same content, the presence of rational beliefs would not mark a different kind of life. Aristotle needs to argue that, on the contrary, the presence and influence of reason is pervasive and important.

The rational agent has a deliberative appearance, and deliberation has a distinctive role.

For whether he will do this or this is now a task for reasoning; and it is necessary to measure by one thing; for he pursues the greater; so that he is capable of making one appearance out of several. (434a7–10)

Aristotle assumes that I answer the question 'Am I to do x or y?' by considering what is to be said for and against them; I consider this with the aim of finding the action with more to be said for it. But if I find that x offers more pleasure than y and y offers a clearer head tomorrow, I still do not know whether x or y has more in its favour; I want to know, then, that there is more of the same sort of thing to be said for x. Hence Aristotle insists that I must measure by some one standard, so that I can find what has more of that to be said for it. I need to be able to make one appearance out of many; when I say that x has A, B, C to be said for it, and y has D, E, F, I must be able to decide whether more is to be said for x or for y.[17]

178. THE SCOPE OF DELIBERATION

Deliberation plays a significant, but still strictly limited, role in a rational agent's life if her only deliberative appearances are those that identify the best instrumental means to the satisfaction of her desires. But if it is strictly limited to this role, deliberation will not result in a life guided by deliberative appearance.[18] If I do not modify a desire when deliberation points out its exorbitant cost to me, in relation to my other desires, I will be grossly irrational, even though reason has completed its instrumental task for me. If we think the task of deliberation is purely instrumental, then we will have to agree with Hume that it is not contrary to reason to prefer the destruction of the world to the scratching of my finger; the deliberation of Hume's rational agents informs them that this will be the cost of satisfying their desire not to have their finger scratched, but they are quite uninfluenced by this information.[19]

Aristotle intends a larger role for deliberation, and assumes that agents guided by it will also deliberate about which of their desires to satisfy, not simply about the means to satisfy a particular desire.

. . . desires become contrary to each other, and this results when reason and appetite are contrary, and this happens in agents that have perception of time; for understanding urges us to resist because of what will happen, while appetite ⟨urges us on⟩ because of what is present. (For what is pleasant now appears both pleasant without qualification and good without qualification because of not seeing what will happen.) (433b5–10)[20]

A rational judgment that might conflict with appetite requires more than perception of time. A lion seeing a deer might spring at the place where—as we might appropriately say—it expects the deer to be; but it still need not have a rational desire.[21] To form a rational desire we must compare the present and future benefits and harms of different actions, and reach a conclusion that will be expressed in a desire.

'Seeing what will happen' is not enough by itself for this sort of desire. I might be able to predict accurately the future results of my actions without being able to direct my desire on the predicted states of affairs at all; and even if I could form a desire that differs from the desire focused on the present object, this would not necessarily be a rational desire. We have a rational desire only when we compare the advantages of the two courses of action. Perhaps our end is F and we find the only means to F is G; but if we consider the relation of F and G to our more ultimate end H, we may find that we promote H better if we avoid G and hence lose F than if we get F at the price of doing G. As long as deliberation does not require us to focus on just one limited end at a time, we can consider the value of achieving one end against our other ends.

179. RATIONAL AGENCY AND THE GOOD

Aristotle connects rational agency with awareness of the good; but not just every conception of one's good implies rational agency. To conceive my good, as opposed to my pleasure, I have to be able to deliberate, and to compare the results of different actions; and I will reach a view about what is best to do as a result of the comparison of present and future that we have described. If I want A, B, and C, and deliberation shows me that x will get me A and B without C, and y will get me C without A and B, it does not follow that I will want to do x rather than y; clearly that depends on how much I want C compared to A and B. Rational deliberation will consider x and y with reference to the strength of my desire for A, B, and C. If I register the strength of desire for A as 5, for B, as 4, and for C as 7, then I will discover that I satisfy my desire more by doing x than by doing y. I measure by one standard and pursue what seems greater.

In such cases I still limit the extent of rational deliberation about my actions. I assume the initial strength of my desires, and confine myself to finding the action that gets me what I most want. I do not criticize or modify the relative strength of my desires, and I recognize no alternative standard of comparison besides strength. Even if I know that the relative strength of my desires will change, so that at a later time I will rank the satisfaction of these present desires differently, that knowledge gives me no reason to change my reaction to my present desires—unless I happen to have a stronger desire for the satisfaction of the desires I will have in the future.

The limits of such rational agency show how it falls short of Aristotle's demands. He says rational agents have decision (*prohairesis*), while non-rational agents have only appetite and emotion (*EN* 1111b11–13, *EE* 1225b26–7, *Phys.* 197b1–8). Decision is deliberative desire (*EN* 1113a9–12); and so it seems to be the sort of desire that will result from a rational appearance. It is a desire formed by deliberation beginning with some more general desire. But not just any general desire can underlie a decision; it must be a wish (*boulêsis*), a rational desire for the good, not an appetite or emotional desire.[22]

We might suppose that a plan based on just any second-order desire (e.g. 'Do what you have the strongest desire for'; 'Act to satisfy the largest number of desires') counts as a desire for the good. But Aristotle demands more.[23] The wise person deliberates with a view not to this or that limited end, but with a view to living well (i.e. happiness, *eudaimonia*) in general (1140a25–8). In this case living well is our end and we deliberate about how to achieve it (1111b28–30). Good deliberation will find what is suitable to the end that is grasped by wisdom (1142b31–3).[24] This deliberation about what promotes living well as a whole will form the wise person's rational wish, the way she conceives happiness; and this conception of happiness will be the rational wish from which she begins the sort of deliberation that results in a decision.

Aristotle thinks deliberation can do more than find the action that will maximize the satisfaction of my current desires. For to ask about what promotes my happiness is not the same as to ask about what maximizes the satisfaction of my current desires. A correct conception of my good requires some conception of the sort of being that I am, some view of my nature, and some thought about the sorts of desires and aims that best suit my nature. This aspect of deliberation implies a fairly extensive possible criticism and rational assessment of current desires.[25]

180. THE TEMPORAL ASPECTS OF RATIONAL AGENCY

A fully rational agent, then, has a conception of herself and her life, and chooses things as goods for herself by reference to her life as a whole. This is not a trivial difference from other agents. I might desire something unreflectively, without considering any other desires at all. Again I might strengthen or weaken a desire by considering the effects of satisfying it on the likely satisfaction of other desires I now have. In either case I am not necessarily thinking about my good. Thought of my good requires thought of my life as a whole; and this requires the thought of myself as existing in past, present, and future.

If I am moved by this thought, I will consider both my present and my possible future desires when I choose what to do now. Consideration of my future desires is not the same as consideration of the future effects of my present desires; and the agent concerned with her good must be concerned with herself as something present and future, not just with the desires she has now. This is still a fairly weak condition. It does not imply that a rational agent sacrifices the present to the future. Nor need she be prudent in the ordinary sense that implies thrift. She needs a more general form of prudence that requires some degree of concern for herself as a temporally extended self.

Aristotle does not often notice this aspect of rational agency; but some of his remarks show that he assumes it and relies on it. One of the types of association peculiar to rational agents is lifelong association between wife and husband. Other animals associate to produce children, but human beings associate 'for what concerns their life' (1162a19–22). 'Life' here refers to the other aspects of one's present life besides child-bearing, but also to the other stages of one's lifetime. Human beings are concerned for their welfare over their lifetimes. The temporal reference of 'life' is clearer in the definition of a household as an association established 'for every day' (*Pol.* 1252b12–14). The most extensive association, the city, is concerned 'not with the present advantage . . . but with the whole of life' (*EN* 1160a21–3), where Aristotle again refers both to the content—the whole of life and not just a part—and to the length of time.

This is one reason why the city is peculiar to human beings, who have a reasoned conception of the good, and not merely awareness of pleasure (*Pol.* 1253a7–18). Animals and slaves are incapable of forming a city 'because they have no share in happiness or in living according to decision' (1280a32–4). The lack of decision makes them incapable of forming designs for themselves and their lives as a whole.[26]

These different remarks suggest that Aristotle believes that rational agents conceive themselves, and hence their good, as extended both in the present and the future. A rational agent is aware of having a 'whole life' at the moment; he considers what to do by reference to his other desires, not just the particular desire excited by this object. And he is aware of himself as having a 'whole life' that extends into past and future, and is not restricted to the desires he is aware of at the moment. The deliberation and decision that rest on this conception of a whole life are characteristic of a rational agent.

The good of such an agent must be a complete good that belongs to a complete life (*EN* 1098a18–20); and a rational agent will consider his particular desires and actions against some view of how they will affect his complete life. A non-rational animal or a child has no conception of his whole life or of how he might shape his desires in the light of this conception; and so he is incapable of forming the states of character that Aristotle takes to be essential to happiness (1099b32–1100a1).[27]

Aristotle's different conditions demand more of a rational agent than he initially suggests. If he is to argue that reason marks out a distinct type of soul, he needs to show that it marks out a distinct type of life in which a creature 'lives by' reason, as opposed to appearance (cf. *DA* 415a8–11). He will not have shown what he needs if he shows only that a rational agent deliberates about the ways to satisfy a particular desire. Even if the creature can deliberate effectively about maximizing his desire-satisfaction, that difference does not clearly imply a different sort of life; it may just indicate greater efficiency in the conduct of the same sort of life. But if Aristotle can show that a rational creature is moved by reasoning about his good, resulting from reflexion on his life as a whole, he has good reason to claim that reason marks out a different sort of life.

A rational creature's life, on this view, will aim at ends that play no part in explaining the non-rational creature's behaviour. A plant's life is a different sort of life from an animal's in so far as appearance plays no role in the end that the plant aims at, but does play a role in the animal's end. Similarly, the rational creature's end is partly determined by his conception of himself and his good as a creature with different capacities and different temporal stages; Aristotle has good reason to claim that such a creature has an essentially rational soul.

181. RATIONAL AGENCY AND RESPONSIBILITY

Aristotle's view of rational agency explains some of the assumptions of his ethical theory, by removing some of the puzzles they raise if they are considered without reference to rational agency. We will see the importance of rational agency if we follow Aristotle's own advice, and begin with some of the puzzles.

It is not immediately clear why he thinks human beings are the only ethical agents. Ethics is about the virtues of character (*êthos*) that are acquired by habituation (*ethismos*); but non-rational animals can have their actions and desires modified by training that involves rewards and deprivations, and hence they seem capable of habituation and of forming a good or bad character.[28]

Aristotle seems to answer this objection by insisting that virtue and vice are objects of praise and blame; since only voluntary (*hekousia*) actions are open to praise or blame, only agents who act voluntarily will be ethical agents. But this answer only raises further puzzles. For he concedes that non-rational animals act voluntarily (*EN* 1111a24–6), and so they should apparently be open to praise and blame.[29] It seems reasonable in any case to claim that we can praise or blame animals and children; in training and habituating them we can communicate our pleasure and pain in their action, and so influence their behaviour. They still seem to count as ethical agents.

This conclusion is warranted only if we assume that mere communication of pleasure and pain is sufficient for praise and blame, and that an agent influenced by such communication is really a proper object of praise and blame. We might instead reject the assumptions. Perhaps such an agent does not really deserve praise and blame, and perhaps the positive and negative reinforcement we offer is not genuine praise and blame. Aristotle might reasonably argue that normal adult human beings are *properly* praised and blamed for their actions, and that animals are not; though we try to modify the behaviour of animals, we do not praise or blame them in the same way.[30]

Perhaps rational agents are morally responsible, and the proper sort of praise recognizes a responsible action. On this view, animals, being incapable of responsibility, are not candidates for praise or blame, hence are incapable of the right sort of habituation, and hence are incapable of virtue or vice. But if Aristotle accepts this answer, he owes some account of responsibility that is distinct from his account of voluntariness; for voluntariness will not make the right distinctions.

We can approach the same puzzles about ethics from another direction. The right sort of habituation results in a virtue, and Aristotle thinks a virtue requires the right decision (*prohairesis*), not simply the right actions (1105a28–33). But his claim should puzzle us. We can see why he should require a permanent state that causes the virtuous agent to do the right thing regularly; but why should this require the right decision? Decision requires the wish and deliberation that are peculiar to rational agents; but both rational and non-rational agents are capable of being habituated to form the right permanent inclination in favour of virtuous action. The question that arose about responsibility seems to arise again; for Aristotle seems in fact to confine his discussion to rational agents, but gives no clear reason for confining it to them.

If I act on my strongest occurrent desire, and my rational desire simply seeks to satisfy my occurrent desires, it is not clear why my rational desire should leave me open to some special sort of blame and praise, or why I should be especially responsible for the actions resulting from rational desire. For the character of the action depends on the character of the occurrent desires, and I am related to these no differently from the way a non-rational agent would be. It is not surprising that a theory such as Hume's, identifying responsible action with action caused by a persistent trait of the agent, gives no reason to confine responsibility to rational agents.[31]

In Aristotle's view, however, a rational agent is influenced by a conception of his life as a whole and the conception of happiness that he wants to belong to this life as a whole. He can modify his particular desires, and vary his satisfaction of them, according to his conception of happiness. His decision will reflect the results of his deliberation about his happiness, and therefore will express the sort of attitude that a non-rational agent cannot take to himself. A virtuous character formed by decision will express the agent's view that the sort of life he chooses for himself should include his valuing the virtuous actions for their own sakes.

If responsible agents act on such a conception of their good, a special sort of praise or blame is especially suitable for them. If we praise the agent *for* doing something good, he should be moved by the property of the action that he is praised for, and not merely by properties that coincide with it. This agent is the virtuous person who decides on the virtuous action for its own sake as part of his happiness.

We have some reason, then, to confine praise and attribution of responsibility to rational agents, if we really praise them for the way they have formed their conception of their good and expressed this conception in their actions. That sort of praise is not appropriate to non-rational agents, since they do not form a conception of their good; they do not conceive themselves as temporally extended agents with a possible good, and they do not modify their particular desires to fit that conception. Similarly, if virtue requires the formation of the right conception of one's good, it is reasonable for Aristotle to believe that it requires the right decision, and therefore is confined to agents capable of decision.

182. ASPECTS OF RESPONSIBILITY

Aristotle, however, seems to suggest that voluntary action is sufficient for responsibility, and that an action not done by force or because of ignorance is voluntary.[32] If we are to show that he connects responsibility more closely with rational agency, we need to show that he takes responsible action to require something more than these minimal conditions.

His conditions for voluntariness are more complex than they seem at first sight. In defining forced action he insists that the origin of the movement must be external and that the agent himself must contribute nothing (1110a2). But he also insists that forced action is always painful, so that what we enjoy cannot be forced (1110b11–13).[33] He implies that if you push me into my enemy and I am pleased, then the cause of my behaviour is not external and I contribute something, even if your push would have had the same result whatever I thought or felt; for if what I do with pleasure is unforced, it cannot have an external cause to which I contribute nothing. Aristotle suggests that in this case the behaviour has an internal cause, and that I contribute to it, even though my contribution is quite unnecessary for the result. He denies that such behaviour is involuntary, even though the actual causal sequence is just the same as it would be in an involuntary action; the process of your pushing me and my bumping into my enemy would have been no different.

Aristotle draws a related distinction in his discussion of ignorance. He argues that if I act because of ignorance, and do not regret my action, I have acted non-voluntarily, but not involuntarily; involuntary action requires regret as well as ignorance (1110b18–24, 1111a19–21).[34] In this case also the causal process leading to the action will be just the same, but the attitude of the agent separates the genuinely involuntary actions from the others.

The distinctions Aristotle draws are curious if he simply wants to identify the agent's actual causal relation to his action; and since this relation concerns us in judgments of legal responsibility, these judgments are probably not his primary concern. His distinctions are more reasonable if his primary concern is the relation of rational agency to the action. Though my pleasure and pain may make no actual difference to what happens, they indicate my attitude to the action, and so reveal my character (1104b3–11) and the decision that has formed it. If I appear to be forced to break a promise, but am pleased by the result of this apparent force, I show that my character and decision are defective. I show the same thing about myself if I act because of ignorance but without regret. Even if I would have avoided striking you so hard if I had known the blow would disable you, my pleasure at the result of the action I did because of ignorance shows a disorder in my character.

If Aristotle wants our judgments about praiseworthiness and blame-worthiness to focus on this aspect of the agent, he is right to argue that the agent's pleasure affects his responsibility, even if it does not affect the action. But to focus on this aspect of the agent is exactly to focus on the distinctive feature of rational agency, as we have described it—the agent's conception of his good and the states of character he has formed to shape his whole life in a particular way. Distinctions that initially seem anomalous turn out to be reasonable in the light of his view of rational agency.

Since Aristotle's discussion of involuntariness includes these elements that betray a more general concern with rational agency, we can more easily understand why he thinks he has found a criterion for responsible action when he seems to have found only a criterion for voluntary action.

He claims that in all voluntary action the origin must be in the agent (1110a17–18, 1111a22–4, 1113b20–1).[35] But if this internal origin ensures only voluntariness, it does not seem to ensure responsibility; Aristotle insists that animals and children act voluntarily, but he never suggests that they are proper candidates for the sort of praise and blame that suits responsible agents. If we act on appetite or emotion in the way an animal or child does, the origin seems to be in us, as it seems to be in them; but if they are not proper candidates for responsibility, it is not clear why we should be, if the causation of our action is the same.

This objection, however, overlooks the difference in the nature of the origin. When Aristotle says the origin is in 'us', we need to ask more carefully what he identifies with 'us'. If we are essentially rational agents, then the origin will be strictly in us only in so far as it is in our rational agency; otherwise it will only be incidentally in us, since one of our non-essential features will be the origin. I have a rational soul in so far as I live by decision and rational planning resting on some conception of my life as a whole. The origin that is internal to an animal 'itself' will not depend on its rational agency, since it is not essentially a rational agent. Since I am essentially different from an animal, the origin in me will support claims about responsibility even though it would not support them for the animal.

This appeal to the origin in the agent does not imply that we are responsible only for the actions that are actually caused by our decision and deliberation.[36] As we have seen, Aristotle's search for the origin of an action leads him beyond the actual causal sequence to the agent's attitude and character. Even if I act without deliberation and premeditation on a sudden impulse of emotion or appetite, the origin may still be in my character and decision; for the presence or strength of my desire may be the result of the character and decisions I have formed. I may have deliberately cultivated this sort of impulse, or I may have failed to do what I could reasonably be expected to do to prevent its growth. If my voluntary actions are related in this way to my decision and character, their origin is in *me* in the relevant sense, and I am fairly held responsible for them, even though an animal would not be held responsible for its voluntary actions.[37]

The conception of rational agency that we have ascribed to Aristotle supports his claims in the *De Anima* and in the *Ethics*. Without this conception he leaves serious gaps and anomalies both in his account of the soul and in his claims about responsibility. The initial appearance of his dialectical argument fails to display his theory, and his eventual conclusions do not seem to follow from the apparent dialectical argument. Neither feature of the discussion will surprise us if we remember that Aristotle's argument is dialectical, but not purely dialectical, and that it legitimately relies on the results of an argument ultimately resting on first philosophy.

183. THE FORM OF HUMAN BEINGS

Our discussion of responsibility has led us beyond the *De Anima* in an effort to understand the distinctive characteristics of the rational soul that Aristotle attributes to human beings. We can now usefully return to the tasks he has set himself in giving an account of the soul, and see if he has fulfilled them. Two main questions need to be raised: (1) Has he described all and only the genuine states of soul? (2) Has he justified his claim that the soul is the essence of the creatures we call men, horses, etc.?

Aristotle has suggested that we can explain what psychic states are if we take them to be the states mentioned in a teleological explanation of the behaviour of a living creature. Mental states are those that involve appearance and that contribute to a teleological explanation of the creature's behaviour that involves reference to desire and appearance of the good. Aristotle claims that psychic properties are the essential properties of logically possible subjects, and also of actual subjects—the trees, dogs, and people familiar to us. These are material as well as formal; but their form is their essence. Their formal properties are permanent traits that explain behaviour and justify us in thinking that some genuine substance persists as long as the individual instance of the specific form persists.

Aristotle identifies the human soul with the type of rational agency that relies on a conception of the agent's good. He must suppose that such a conception explains the behaviour of human beings, and that the persistence of a human being is the persistence of a rational agent with a conception of his good. He can hardly require the very same conception of my good to persist if I persist; in that case I would cease to exist whenever I understand more and improve and whenever I lapse. It is more reasonable to identify the persistence of a human being with the persistence of a conception of his good that is formed by the same thoughts, desires and experiences, and aims at the good of the same self with the same or coherently changing future states and experiences. The states will change coherently in so far as changing beliefs about my future circumstances or future good will cause changes in plans for my future good; and my conception of my good will change coherently with my other states.

If this is Aristotle's view, he supposes that each human being is the human being he is because of his conception of himself and his plans for the good of the self he conceives. If Socrates' plans suddenly changed, not because of previous experience or reflexion causing the change, and he thought of his future self quite differently from the way he had previously thought of it, then Socrates would have ceased to exist. If desires and plans for Callias' future welfare were caused in just the same way as plans for Socrates' welfare, then Socrates and Callias would be the same person. 'Just the same way' excludes the normal case of one person's concern for the good of another; if I am concerned for another's good, I think of his conception of his good as well as my conception of it, but I do not have to do this with myself.

If Aristotle intends this feature of a human being to determine his identity, we might think he attends too much to a type of practical reasoning that is a far less universal feature of human beings than he thinks it is. He will reasonably reply that such an objection underestimates the extent and role of practical reasoning. To have a conception of my good I need not have a conscious or detailed plan for my future welfare; I need to be ready to adjust one desire to another and to think about the effects of my action on my future self, regarded as the same self that now chooses. Continuity in these habits of choice and concern makes me a single self.

To test such a claim about the human essence we might see if it explains common practices and beliefs that rest on assumptions about a person's identity and persistence. Aristotle supposes that his account of the essence of human beings explains why the treatment accorded to them as responsible agents is appropriate for them. In so far as we take normal human beings to be distinctively responsible for their actions, and in so far as we connect responsibility with rational agency reflected in decision, we confirm Aristotle's view that such rational agency is an essential feature of human beings. To this extent Aristotle's account of responsibility shows how his psychology supports one element in the ethical principles prescribing treatment of human beings.

Its relevance to ethics is still broader. The *DA* argues that the essence of human beings is their capacity for rational thought, desire, and action—that these are the properties that mark them out as a distinct kind, from a teleological point of view, and explain their vital activities as·a whole. The *Ethics* is about what is good for creatures of this kind; from understanding that human beings are essentially rational agents we are supposed to be able to form a theory of their good. This theory will identify virtues and virtuous actions—states and actions promoting the good of human beings, and for which they are appropriately praised.

The account of the human essence explains why human beings are the appropriate subjects for ethics. They are open to praise and blame because they have the capacity for decision and for the rational desire that forms a conception of the agent's happiness. It is the same capacity that makes someone a responsible agent and makes him an agent properly concerned with ethics. Hence Aristotle offers his advice to 'everyone who is capable of living in accordance with his own decision' (*EE* 1214b6–7).[38]

If Aristotle means this, he commits himself to quite a strong and initially implausible claim. It is essential to a human being that he guides his action by a rational conception of his good referring to his whole life; and Aristotle seems to claim that from this fact we can derive an account of his actual good that need not be identical with his good as he conceives it. He seems to claim that someone's acting on a conception of his good implies that one conception is the right one.

If this is really Aristotle's claim, and if he can justify it, then the psychology of the *De Anima* is still more important than it has appeared to be so far. For its account of the human essence will determine an account of the human good, and hence, in Aristotle's view of ethics, the foundation of a complete ethical theory. We may find Aristotle's aim interesting, or perversely misguided, or both; but we must consider its execution.

THE GOOD OF RATIONAL AGENTS

184. MORAL AND POLITICAL ARGUMENT

The questions we have raised in previous chapters about the scope and powers of dialectical argument should apply with particular force to the *Ethics*; for there the dialectical character of Aristotle's method is even clearer than in the works on natural philosophy and metaphysics, and the empirical element is far less prominent. In looking for an account of the human good he notices that the many disagree with the more cultivated (*EN* 1095a20–2); and to resolve the disagreement he undertakes to examine (*exetazein*) the beliefs that are widespread or seem to have something to be said for them (1095a28–30; *EE* 1214b28–1215a7).[1]

Aristotle does not confine this dialectical method to the study of what is right and good for individuals. He applies it equally to the structure and design of whole communities. He claims that the discipline undertaken in the *Ethics* is political science (1094a26–b11, *MM* 1181a243–b27), and he continues the same inquiry in the *Politics*.[2] It will be useful to examine Aristotle's methods and doctrines in both works together. Though my exposition will be less orderly and more digressive than a seriatim discussion would be, it should result in a clearer view of the structure and connexion of the arguments and conclusions.

At first sight, it seems clear that the *Ethics* practises pure dialectic. Aristotle insists that he does not practise demonstration in this area.[3] We are to begin from 'the things known to us' (1095b2–3), the common beliefs, and rely on them as tests of any theory (*EE* 1216b26–8). We should attend to the appearances rather than relying completely on theories that are removed from appearances (1217a10–17), and we should be reluctant to accept any theory that conflicts with clear appearances (1145b27–9) or 'forces' the appearances (1236b21–3).

Proper attention to the appearances and to the puzzles they raise also seems to determine the character of our preferred solution. Aristotle wants to dissolve the puzzles that arise from the initial survey of common beliefs and to leave the original common beliefs standing (1145b2–7); and he suggests that a reply to the puzzles is a sufficient solution (1145b6–7, 1146b6–8, 1215a5–7). He assumes that we can take universal consent that certain things are goods to show that they are goods (1172b36–1173a1); and this universal consent seems to constrain the solutions that need to be considered.[4] We assume that the common beliefs are true, and simply need to be clarified (1216b28–35; cf. 1138b25–6).[5]

This is by no means a full and fair account of Aristotle's method in the *Ethics*, as we will shortly see. But it is plausible enough for us to explore its consequences for Aristotle's aims in ethical inquiry. We have seen in general that if Aristotle admits his conclusions rest only on pure dialectic, they have no claim on anyone who does not accept the initial common beliefs that the arguments began from. This may not seem to matter when the initial beliefs are not widely disputed; but even there we have seen that it does matter, if Aristotle wants to defend the objective truth of his conclusion.[6] In ethics, however, it matters more obviously if we take common beliefs for granted, since they are likely to be controversial.

It takes an Eleatic or a Heracleitean or a Protagorean, some fairly radical and pertinacious philosopher, to reject all the common beliefs that Aristotle appeals to in the *Physics* or *Metaphysics*—though even there we saw that, for instance, he relies more heavily than he should on common beliefs about teleology. It does not take a philosopher to challenge the ethical appearances; a radical critic of common ethical beliefs raises a practical, not merely a philosophical, challenge to Aristotle's ethical principles. In Greek philosophy as in later philosophy, moral scepticism and nihilism seem to be practically reasonable and significant options in ways that other forms of scepticism and nihilism do not. It is fairly easy to believe sceptics about the external world if they say they will go on acting like the rest of us and we will not notice the difference; it is much harder to believe a similar assurance from consistent moral sceptics.[7]

It is rather tempting to suppose that Aristotle simply ignores this sceptical challenge, or even that he thinks he cannot meet it. Plato clearly thinks it is both a significant and an answerable challenge. Callicles in the *Gorgias* and Thrasymachus, Glaucon, and Adeimantus in the *Republic* state the case against common morality; and they are not to be answered by being told that their views conflict with evident appearances. Plato tries to answer them by an argument that seeks to go beyond the appeal to appearances. We may well think Aristotle is less ambitious than Plato here.[8] He requires the student at his lectures to have been well brought up, precisely because the argument begins from what is 'known to us' (1095b4–8). Someone who is too young or morally immature will get no benefit from ethical instruction (1095a2–11); early training is all-important (1103b23–5) because bad training makes us impervious to sound moral arguments (1179b23–9).

We might easily (though, as we will see later, wrongly) suppose that in these passages Aristotle admits he cannot answer a radical critic. A purely dialectical method requires him to admit as much, if his ethical conclusions rest on the common beliefs that a radical critic can consistently reject. Aristotle admits that some people have been persuaded that the subject-matter of ethics, the fine and the just, are mere matters of convention (1094b14–16); and pure dialectic gives no answer to their doubts. If he is to answer the radical critics, he must show that they have some further reason, besides an appeal to common beliefs, for accepting his premises.

185. THE CONTENT OF ETHICS

Even if we defend moral arguments by more than pure dialectic, we might still not resolve doubts about morality. For we might show that moral principles rest on objective facts, not just on common beliefs, but the facts might be of the wrong sort to convince critics to take morality seriously. Political science considers the fine and the just; but an account of these might not answer the critic of morality.

Politicians concerned with moral education want to make the citizens 'good people and obedient to the laws' (1102a9–10); in prescribing the laws and requiring obedience to them they form the citizens in the practices and attitudes that constitute general justice (1129b14–29); and these are ones that produce and preserve happiness for the political community (1129b17–19). It is clear why the politician is concerned with general justice, since he is concerned with the good of the community. But it is less clear why submitting to the politician's concern is in my interest, since I have not yet been shown why it is in my interest to be concerned with the good of the community. Aristotle admits that general justice seems to be 'another person's good', as Thrasymachus puts it in his objections to justice (1130a3–5; *Rep.* 343c3–4, 367c2–3).

The same question can be raised about the fine (*kalon*). In the *Rhetoric* Aristotle identifies fine and praiseworthy, in contrast to expedient, action especially with action that reflects concern for others and not for the agent himself.[9] The community, or the dominant group or party or class in it, might reasonably commend and praise fine action; but why should a rational person choose to do, for his own sake, the actions that the community regards as fine and just? Since each of virtue of character is said to aim at the fine (1122b6–7), the same question arises about all of them.

To answer the question, a rational person might try to form a conception of his own interest, so that he can see if fine, just, and virtuous actions, as commonly understood, really benefit him. The *Rhetoric* (i 5) surveys the common beliefs about happiness (*eudaimonia*); and the results of the survey scarcely recommend the virtues to the rationally self-interested critic. Happiness includes as 'parts' the states, conditions, and possessions that seem to be needed to achieve security and self-sufficiency (*autarkeia*) (1360b14–15, 24, 29); these will satisfy the desires and needs of the fairly demanding person. The parts of happiness include health, wealth, good friends, good children, good old age, good fortune, and also virtue and pleasure (1360b14–30), both internal goods—conditions of the person himself—and external goods—conditions of his environment (1360b24–9).

This account of the parts of happiness gives no clear criteria for counting something as a part of happiness. Aristotle offers 'doing well with virtue', 'self-sufficiency of life', 'the pleasantest life with security', and 'prosperity of possessions and bodies with the capacity to keep and achieve them' as alternative general accounts of happiness (1360b14–18). He does not decide between them; he does not show how each of them implies or suggests one or another list of the parts of happiness; and he does not say how we choose when the different accounts lead to different lists of the parts of happiness. But even an improved and systematized general account does not seem likely to support the claims of the virtues of character aiming at the fine. Though Aristotle certainly mentions these as parts of happiness, it is not clear why he should. And if happiness has other parts besides the virtues, why should we not prefer these parts when they conflict with the practice of the virtues?

In leaving these questions vague and unanswered, the *Rhetoric* probably represents common beliefs fairly well. Our conception of happiness seems to rest on rather unsystematic common beliefs; we might well regard it as purely a matter of convention, reflecting no underlying objective truths about the nature of happiness. And in any case, the link between happiness and the virtues is not clear.

These questions make it especially important and hazardous to decide whether ethical theory has to rest on pure dialectic. It is important, because the mere appeal to common beliefs seems to give critics of common morality no reason to take it seriously if they reject common beliefs. It is hazardous, because we cannot be sure in advance that the answer leading us beyond the common beliefs will actually justify the virtues, as common sense conceives them.

If Aristotle is to answer the critic, he need not defend precisely the common conception of each of the virtues; like Plato, he is free to argue that common sense is wrong to some degree.[10] But he needs some theoretical basis for selection among common beliefs if he decides to revise them. In the *Metaphysics* he cannot fairly assume without argument that a correct conception of substance justifies the common view that individual trees and dogs are substances; he has to show why it would be wrong to agree with Platonists or Atomists against common sense. In the course of defending common sense against these rivals he revises common sense; his own favoured candidate, particular form, is not explicitly recognized by common sense, and common sense does not clearly see why the remote matter and the material compound are inferior candidates. His solution involves claims about potentiality that at first seem counterintuitive; he requires us to say what we normally would not say, that the proximate matter of the tree is potentially the tree when it actually constitutes the tree. Still, the account of substance is recognizably a defence of the commonsense view of substance against rival views that depart widely from common sense.[11]

If, then, Aristotle can present a parallel defence of common ethical beliefs, showing that they rest on objective facts independent of common beliefs, and that we are entitled to accept the connexion they assume between virtue and self-interest, he will have answered a critic's reasonable questions about common morality.

186. THE DIRECTION OF MORAL ARGUMENT

In trying to answer a critic of morality, Aristotle considers happiness. For beliefs about happiness seem to raise the most serious doubts about common morality; and if he shows that the doubts rest on a mistaken view of happiness, he answers the critic. Aristotle needs to show that he has found a true account of a human being's happiness, and a true account of the human virtues, and that these true accounts fit together in the right way. The first task is to see what sorts of facts might help us to go beyond common beliefs.

Two directions of argument identify the relevant facts: (1) Aristotle constructs a theory of substance from premises supported by strong dialectic, relying on more than common beliefs. This theory supports an account of souls and animate organisms, including rational agents. In approaching ethical problems Aristotle is entitled to appeal with some confidence to the conclusions he has reached by these other dialectical arguments that do not depend wholly on the ethical common beliefs in dispute. (2) Fairly uncontroversial common beliefs about ethics suggest to Aristotle that his account of substances and souls will be relevant. For it is plausible to assume that answers to the questions 'What is the good for F?' and 'What is a good F?' both depend on the answer to the question 'What is F?'. Both the good for a dog and the goodness of a dog seem to depend on the sort of thing a dog is. An answer to the first of these questions gives us an account of happiness, and an answer to the second gives us an account of virtue.[12]

Aristotle, therefore, has these two independent and mutually supporting reasons for believing that his account of the rational soul in the *De Anima* should help him. It should help to answer questions about method in ethics, by showing how ethical conclusions can rest on more than pure dialectic. Moreover, it might explain why a rational person with a true conception of his own good has reason to accept and to cultivate the moral virtues that are commonly recognized.

The procedure of the *Ethics* is dialectical, without the degree of self-consciousness that we find in *Metaphysics* iv; and Aristotle regularly appeals to common beliefs without saying whether the particular beliefs he appeals to have any further warrant than being commonly accepted. We must look at the premisses of his arguments, and ask ourselves whether in fact he is entitled to claim further warrant for them, and whether he sees that he is entitled to claim it.

187. TASKS FOR THE *POLITICS*

We cannot fairly assess Aristotle's argument in the *Ethics* without seeing how well he extends it to political inquiry. For he describes the *Ethics* as a work of political science, the science that regulates and orders the practice of the other sciences and crafts.

. . . its end will embrace the ends of the other sciences, so that its end will be the human good. For even if the good is the same for an individual and for a city, still it appears greater and more complete to acquire and preserve ⟨the good⟩ of a city; for we must be content ⟨to acquire and preserve it⟩ even for an individual by himself, but it is finer and more divine ⟨to acquire and preserve it⟩ for a nation and cities. Hence our method of inquiry aims at this ⟨good for individuals and cities⟩, being a type of political science. (1094b6–11)

The all-embracing concern of political science makes it the right science to study the human good.

Aristotle does not say that in the *Ethics* he is concerned only with the individual, or that we can find the individual's good without finding the good for the city. He says we would have to be content if we could find the good for 'an individual by himself'; but this is not the same as the good for the individual. The good for 'an individual by himself' will be his good, to the extent that we can grasp it without considering his relations to a state; and Aristotle warns us here that the extent is quite limited, since we find the complete good for an individual only when we consider his relations to the state.

The contrast between the limited good we find by considering the individual in isolation and the more complete good we find by considering his relations to the state is clarified later in Book i. For Aristotle argues that a complete and self-sufficient end cannot be considered for an individual by himself, living a solitary life, but must include the good of family, friends, and fellow-citizens, since a human being is naturally political (1097b8–11). The task of the *Ethics* is to find the complete good for an individual human being, and it cannot fulfil this task by considering only his good in isolation from the good of others. It must, then, be a work of political science.

Later in the *Ethics* Aristotle explains more fully the political character of his account of the good. He supports his claim that a human being is naturally political, by arguing that each person's self-realization requires her intrinsic concern for the interests of others. A friendship formed by this intrinsic concern constitutes a community (or 'association', *koinônia*) regulated by principles of justice aiming at its common interest; and to the extent that someone has reason to form such a community, she has reason to accept the principles of justice for it. The *Ethics* assures us that the state will hold a special place among the communities that realize different forms of friendship; for it is the all-embracing community (1160a8–23), in so far as it regulates the others and nothing further is needed to regulate it; it is the community that is necessary and sufficient for securing the human good.

Aristotle does not explain how the state regulates other communities, or why such regulation is necessary; and in the *Ethics* he fails to show how the state is the all-embracing community. Moreover, general remarks about 'the state' are of limited use; for Aristotle knows as well as his readers do that there are different types of states with different political systems (viii 10–11), and that differences in political systems affect the way a state carries out the roles Aristotle intends for it.

The part of political science that concerns the *Ethics* is the account of an individual's happiness, and in particular of the virtues whose realization is the achievement of happiness. Even if we have some account of the happy life, we have no picture of the community in which it will be achieved; and in so far as the happiness of a community is a necessary part of an individual's good, our account of the good must remain incomplete until the community is described. The *Politics*, therefore, should offer some fuller account of the special role of the state in securing the human good, and of the specific type of state that fulfils this role; it examines states in general, and the ideal state that achieves the human good.

Aristotle urges us to study political theory 'so that as far as possible our philosophy about human matters will be completed' (1181b14–15).

The argument of the *Ethics* would be incomplete without a political sequel; for if its ethical principles imply political demands, we need to see how plausible these demands are. This question about the ethical principles would be inappropriate if they were fundamental principles needing no further justification or were wholly derived from such principles. But Aristotle accepts neither of these foundationalist views about ethical first principles or about their metaphysical and psychological premisses. If his ethical principles or his assumptions about human nature do not support his political views, then he has reason to reconsider all the views concerned. If his principles and assumptions do seem to support his political views, but these views themselves seem to us quite mistaken, we have reason to reconsider any sympathy we might have formed for Aristotle's ethical views. An examination of the *Politics* is important for our view of Aristotle's larger philosophical outlook, not just for our view of his political theory.

188. THE AIMS OF THE *POLITICS*

Some books of the *Politics* discuss questions raised by the *Ethics*; Books i and iii discuss the nature of the state, and Books vii and viii describe the ideal state, while Book ii criticizes previous accounts of it. But Books iv–vi take up the empirical description and analysis, from a historical and sociological point of view, of political systems, and offer practical hints of the sort that might be expected from a technician and consultant; they discuss the variety of actual states, the causes of their instability, and ways of making them more stable.[13] It is not obvious why the project begun in the *Ethics* involves these further inquiries. We might infer that the *Politics* is a composite work, a loosely connected compilation from separable types of inquiry, just as we might suppose that the *Metaphysics* is a collection of essays on more or less similar topics rather than a continuous argument.[14]

We misunderstand the *Politics*, however, no less than we misunderstand the *Metaphysics*, if we do not see its unity. Aristotle argues that the empirical and technical inquiries will help the argument about the best state.

First, then, let us try to review any sound remarks our predecessors have made on particular topics. Then let us study the collected political systems, to see from them what sorts of things preserve or destroy cities, and political systems of different types; and the reasons why some cities conduct politics well, and some badly. For when we have studied these questions, we will perhaps grasp better what sort of political system is best; how each system should be organized so as to be best; and what habits and laws it should follow. (*EN* 1181b15–22; cf. *Pol.* 1260b27–36)

Common beliefs are to be found, not only in the statements of the many and the wise, but in the actual practice of different states and in the judgments that the many and the wise pass on them. The best theory should explain and defend what seems most reasonable in the political systems and our judgments on them.

Moreover, the nature of Aristotelian ethics itself shows why more detailed empirical study is needed. Ethical argument should rest on facts about human nature; when it is extended into political theory it should rest on further facts about human nature, and about human beings in relation to each other and to external circumstances. Appreciation of these circumstances shows us why a community with specific institutions is needed to realize the human good.

The conception of the human good that is outlined in the *Ethics* is to be embodied in the best state described in the *Politics*; and this best state has to assume highly favourable external conditions (1260b27–9, 1288b23–4, 1323a14–19). But Aristotle claims that virtue is always the best policy, even if external conditions become unfavourable; and political theory should guide us if external circumstances prevent full achievement of the human good. Aristotle wants not only to find the ideal state, but also to find how each type of political system should be organized to reach its best condition (1181b22). He argues that if we study the best system we should also study the best for particular external conditions, the best 'given an assumption'—the best version of each type of political system—and the system that best fits most states (1288b21–37).[15]

Ethical theory also guides empirical analysis. Empirical analysis seeks to understand the varieties and structures of cities and their constitutions, and the sources of change and stability; and, in Aristotle's view, we understand these things best from the correct conception of happiness and justice. Different cities pursue happiness and justice in different ways; and they are stable or unstable partly because of their degrees of success and failure in achieving justice and happiness. A correct ethical theory, as Aristotle understands it, will describe the psychological and social effects of the different virtues and vices, and in doing so will allow us to form new causal hypotheses that we can test against the empirical evidence.

In the *Politics* no less than in the *Metaphysics*, once we understand Aristotle's aims and arguments better, we can see the unity and order in the treatise itself. He constructs the ideal state partly by reference to the empirical facts accumulated in describing actual states, and his conception of the ideal state illuminates the structure and behaviour of actual states; he cannot, therefore, offer a tidy linear argument.

189. DIFFICULTIES IN POLITICAL ARGUMENT

The common beliefs used in the *Politics* are similar to those in the *Ethics*, those of the many or the wise, expressed in current opinions and in previous philosophers. In both works Aristotle discusses both points of agreement and points of dispute. But in the *Politics* there is a particular reason for the prominence of disputes. The *Ethics* sometimes refers to disagreements about the interpretation of some general principle (e.g. 1125b8–18); but in the *Politics* such disagreement helps to explain differences in political systems and of contending factions within a single system.[16]

The extent of agreement and dispute about happiness illustrates this general feature of common beliefs. While everyone agrees that the best political system is the one that achieves happiness, and that happiness requires some share in the virtues, people disagree about the role of virtue; many think that virtue is a relatively minor part of happiness, and that external goods are the most important part (*Pol.* 1323a24–38). Even those who think virtue is important disagree about whether the virtue should be political or philosophical (1324a23–35); and some of those who value the political life think it requires us to seek power wherever we can (1324b2–3). Similar disputes arise about justice. The contending parties agree that justice is some sort of equality and fairness, and that it requires equal distribution to equals, but they cannot agree about the relevant standard of equality (1280a7–25).

These political disputes show us, more clearly than any other Aristotelian work shows us, some of the difficulties in practising pure dialectic if we look for an answer with some claim to objective truth. We cannot pretend that we simply record the consensus with minor adjustments. While most people may agree on a rough distinction between substance and quality, or even on the list of the virtues of character, we cannot assume they agree on political principles. The area of agreement seems too schematic to tell us anything clear or useful (as Aristotle suggests about some general features of happiness; *EN* 1097b22–4). If constructive dialecticians want to find anything that the disputing parties have reason to accept, they must not embrace just one partisan view.[17]

Aristotle often argues that each of two conflicting views has something to be said for it, though neither is quite right as it stands. He tries to arbitrate between the disputed beliefs, instead of simply supporting one side in the dispute.[18] Arbitration, we might suppose, seeks a formula that both sides will accept; if they are keen enough to make an agreement they will give up something, as long as they are not required to give up so much that the costs outweigh the benefits of the agreement.

If this is what Aristotle does with beliefs about justice, his view might be no nearer the truth than either of the original views was; indeed, the disputants might think it is further from the truth, though more expedient for present purposes. This is often the attitude of those who compromise over legislation or over a resolution to be put to a vote. Two or more ways of reaching such a compromise might be equally correct; it all depends on what each side wants, and they might reach an equally satisfactory solution with one concession as with another.

Sometimes, and especially in the *Politics*, it is tempting to suppose that the arbitration Aristotle wants is a compromise that each of the contending parties can live with, getting enough of what they want to make the agreement worth their while. It is easy to form this impression about his defence of the middle class, and about his devices for repairing and stabilizing different regimes. And it is easy to suppose that at a more general level the same compromising outlook is the basis of his attempt to reconcile conflicting beliefs in his dialectical solution.

On this view, dialectic itself becomes a device for reducing tension and conflict, and for removing some of the ideological sources of struggle. Philosophically as well as politically, Aristotle may seem to be an advocate of consensus against conflict. In so far as he rejects radical challenges to accepted beliefs and institutions, his philosophy suits his essentially conservative social and political preference.[19] Unlike Socrates, Plato, Diogenes, and Zeno, he advocates no startling deviations from the established moral and political order; and we may think the bias of his philosophical method makes his conclusion predictable.

This cannot be the right picture of Aristotle's philosophical aims and outlook. Dialectic seeks to reach true answers by examination of common beliefs, not simply a compromise that people can put up with if they have to. Aristotle notices that some beliefs are formed in ways that undermine an impartial person's confidence in them; most people are bad judges when their own apparent interest is involved (*Pol.* 1280a14–22, 1287a41–b5; cf. *EN* 1109b1–12). These biased judgments will not count equally with other beliefs. Just as we need impartial laws in a state to protect us against personal biases (*EN* 1134a35–b1, *Pol.* 1287a28–32, 1318b38–1319a1), we need to look at common beliefs from an impartial point of view that will lead us to be suspicious of some of them (*EN* 1113a33–b2). The arbitrator is an officer of justice, whose task is not to find the distribution that the two parties can be persuaded to agree on, but to find the just distribution (1132a19–24; cf. *Met.* 995b2–4).

190. STRONG DIALECTIC IN POLITICAL THEORY

This line of argument shows us once again why Aristotle needs strong dialectic, to make up for the weakness of pure dialectic. He thinks he can evaluate the common beliefs from a sufficiently independent point of view, because he has metaphysical arguments to justify some of his leading principles, and especially those principles that support his view of substance, form, matter, nature and essence. His metaphysical arguments are not non-dialectical, since they do not stay outside common beliefs altogether. But they are not merely dialectical, since they rest on premises that we must believe if we are to believe in an objective world at all, or if we are to understand or explain nature. The arguments of strong dialectic resting on these principles underlie Aristotle's conception of the soul and of human nature, which in turn underlies the main claims of the *Ethics*.

Strong dialectic is used in the *Politics* also.[20] Book i relies frequently and explicitly on claims about human nature, to support claims about the nature of the city and its proper structure and functions. Similar claims are used in Book iii to decide between different conceptions of citizenship and of justice. Since views about citizenship and about justice are held to explain the differences between political systems, Aristotle's claims about human nature determine the structure of both the ethical and the empirical parts of the politics. It is no less true in the *Ethics* that the claims about human nature carry the main weight of the argument. But while these claims are relatively unobtrusive in the *Ethics*, they are unmistakable in the *Politics*; it is clear that we must make up our minds about them if we are to decide about the coherence and plausibility of the whole work.

The *Politics*, however, raises a rather serious question about Aristotle's principles. For he uses claims about human nature, together with auxiliary empirical premises, to support his belief in the justice of slavery, the inferiority of women, and the exclusion of manual workers from full citizenship. If we reject Aristotle's conclusions, we must challenge the validity of his argument or the truth of some of the premises. If the argument seems valid and the auxiliary premises seem true, then perhaps we should reject Aristotle's claims about nature.

In any case, Aristotle's claims about nature easily raise doubts. He sometimes seems to rely on empirical generalizations telling us what human nature is like; but on the other hand he dismisses some general tendencies as 'contrary to nature', suggesting that his appeal to nature depends on something more than empirical generalizations or even natural laws.[21] But does the appeal to nature not rely on ethical principles that are themselves supposed to rely on appeals to nature? The appeal to nature seems to rest on a blend of ethical and empirical claims that are honest specimens of neither.

The *Politics*, then, should make it especially clear to us both why Aristotle needs convincing arguments drawn from strong dialectic and why it is hard to find them. Difficulties in his method that are less obtrusive in other works are evident here. To see if Aristotle can solve them, we must begin with his ethical first principles and the further premises they rely on; and then we should see how far he develops a theory that avoids the objections raised against his methods. Aristotle makes his argument depend on his account of the human good, and that is the place to start.

191. THE FINAL GOOD

The *EN* begins by arguing that a human being has an ultimate good, an end that we wish for for its own sake, and for the sake of which we wish for other things (1094a18–19). This ultimate end is happiness (1095a14–20), for the sake of which all of us do all the other things (1102a2–3). Having shown that we pursue this ultimate good, Aristotle offers to prove that it must meet some formal conditions—conditions that we can agree on before we consider any actual candidates for the good. He argues that it must be complete and self-sufficient (1097a15–b21). We need to examine the character of the actual and possible arguments for these claims.

Aristotle does not simply assume that there is an ultimate good for human beings.[22] He argues that there must be one, because there is a supreme science; since every science and craft aims at some good, the supreme supervisory science must aim at a good that is ultimate in relation to their goods (1094a24–7). This supervisory science is political science; and it is supreme because it prescribes the proper pursuit of all the other sciences. Since it regulates the pursuit of the other sciences, its end 'includes the ends of the others, so that this would be the human good' (1094b6–7). We pursue a final good if we pursue an end with the structure of the end of political science; and we have reason to pursue this final good if we have reason to pursue an end with this structure, including and regulating the pursuit of subordinate ends.

Aristotle addresses agents capable of forming their lives by rational decision.

On these points we must first notice that everyone who is capable of living in accordance with his own decision sets up some goal of living finely—either honour or reputation or wealth or education—with reference to which he will

do all his actions; for not having one's life organized with reference to some end
is a sign of much folly. (*EE* 1214b6–11)[23]   .

Decision and wish, as opposed to non-rational desire, are the mark of a
rational agent, who acts on a deliberative, not a purely perceptual,
appearance (*DA* 434a5–11).[24] A rational choice depends on comparison
of the value of different options to see which is best; and this comparison
depends on some view of the good that each of them is to promote. To
make the right comparisons we need the conception of an inclusive
good.[25]

   An agent who was indifferent to the goals he might have in the future,
and never took account of them in reaching his view about what to do
on this occasion, would have a conception of his final good that might
vary radically from one occasion to another. Aristotle, however, argues
that failure to have one's *life* organized towards some end is a sign of
much folly. He addresses an agent who is concerned about the character
of his life, not simply with his desires at each stage of his life.

   Such an agent might have no explicit conception of the good; one task
of the *Ethics* is to form such a conception. But if he finds that his
proposed action conflicts with his good, measured by considering the
other goods he recognizes in his life as a whole, then he tends to
reconsider the action; and if he finds that an action promotes this good,
he tends to want to do that action. An agent is rational to the extent that
he acts on these tendencies that are guided by his conception of his good.
So far Aristotle's assumptions are not arbitrary, and not mere matters of
common belief. He begins with reasonable assumptions about the
desires of rational agents.

192. THE COMPLETENESS OF THE FINAL GOOD

If we agree that rational agents pursue a final good, we may not think
we have conceded anything of interest for ethics. For we have conceded
nothing about the content of this final good, and we may think the very
general features of rational agency we have mentioned determine
nothing about this further question. Aristotle, however, disagrees. He
believes we can infer enough about the content of the final good to show
that any final good that is a reasonable object of pursuit by a rational
agent is the sort of good that requires the Aristotelian virtues.

   This project readily provokes doubt. We may compare Kant's
attempt to argue from general features of moral agency and from the
necessary features of any moral principle, to definite conclusions about
the character of the only morally acceptable moral principle. We might

say that in a similar way Aristotle tries to argue from the form of rational agency to the character of the virtuous moral agent. 'Form' here is used in the Kantian sense rather than the Aristotelian; but in this case the connexion with the Aristotelian conception of form is rather close.[26]

Aristotle follows the dialectical method that we have examined in the *Metaphysics* and *De Anima*. Consideration of the puzzles identifies the preliminary questions. Aristotle approaches these questions by 'making a new start', appealing to some basic principles not open to reasonable dispute. Though the principles may seem trivial or platitudinous to some, Aristotle thinks they are the key to a proper resolution of the puzzles. In the *Metaphysics* we can agree that a substance must be a subject and an essence, before we decide whether Democritean atoms or Platonic Forms or Aristotelian individual organisms satisfy the criteria. It is important to see that each of the contending parties has reason to accept the criteria, so that they can fairly be used to test the candidates and to rule out the Platonist and Atomist candidates.[27] In the *De Anima* he makes a new start by assuming that the soul is the primary cause of life, and arguing from this to his conception of the soul.[28]

In *EN* i he recognizes disputes about the life that is the successful candidate for being the final good (1095a16–28), but instead of answering them directly, he makes a new start (1097a15–25). He sees that the disputes about the candidate for happiness raise preliminary questions about criteria for happiness; what sort of thing raises the dispute about whether it is wealth, honour, pleasure, and so on? He suggests that the final good must meet two formal criteria, by being complete and self-sufficient. These are formal criteria in so far as we can agree that an acceptable candidate for the final good must satisfy them, even before we agree that any candidate is successful.[29]

Aristotle claims that the final good must be complete (*teleion*) (1097a25–b6); even though we pursue many goods for their own sakes, one complete good is our ultimate end. Aristotle claims that an unconditionally complete end must always be chosen in each of our choices, always for its own sake, and never for the sake of any further end (1097a33–4); and he assumes that a rational agent can pursue only one such end. He therefore rejects the possibility that there are several goods that meet this condition, each pursued for its own sake and none pursued for the sake of anything else.[30]

For Aristotle, anything complete must be a whole, leaving nothing outside (*EE* 1219b7–8, *Phys.* 207a8–10, *Met.* 1021b12–23, 1023b26–34), and a unified whole, in contrast to a mere collection.

In one way we call a thing one if it is a quantity and continuous. But in another way we do not call anything one unless it is some sort of whole—that is to say, unless it has one form. We would not say, for instance, that the parts of a shoe were one thing in such a way, if we saw them combined in any old way, but only that they were one by continuity; we would say they were one thing only if they were combined so as to be a shoe, and thereby had one form. Hence the circle is the line that, more than any other, is one, because it is whole and complete. (*Met.* 1016b11–17; cf. 1024a6–8, *Phys.* 228b11–15)

If we claim to pursue pleasure, honour, and virtue for their own sakes only in all our actions, Aristotle replies that we also pursue them for the sake of happiness, the final good, so that really only one end satisfies the condition for unconditional completeness (1097a34–b6). He assumes that a rational agent wants her life to be a whole, not simply a collection of ends without further structure. If we agree about this, we will agree that only one end is unconditionally complete, and that it must cover the whole of a person's life; any less global end would have to be chosen for the sake of a whole life that includes it as a part.

We already know that Aristotle regards a substance as a whole, and therefore as a unity that is more than a mere heap (*sôros*) of its parts (*Met.* 1040b5–10).[31] He requires the parts of an organism's life to have the same sort of structure, both synchronic and diachronic, and in a rational agent he assumes some awareness of the structure. Since he relies on this assumption about rational agents, he has some justification for the assumption that might otherwise seem arbitrary, that there is only one unconditionally complete end.[32]

193. THE SELF-SUFFICIENCY OF THE FINAL GOOD

If we allow Aristotle to assume that the final good is complete, and we agree that what is unconditionally complete must be some sort of organized whole, we may still find his conception of the good quite indeterminate. The organic whole that I see in my own desires and aims will depend on what I initially desire, and the organic whole you see in your desires will depend on your, perhaps quite different, initial desires, so that lives with quite different aims will satisfy the same formal condition. Since, on this view, one's good will be relative to one's desires and aims, we may call it a *conative* conception of the good.[33]

A conative conception makes the rest of the *Ethics* seem unconvincing. For Aristotle thinks the same fairly specific states are virtues in everyone, and this is why the *Ethics* is about *êthos*, character; but the conative conception of the good cannot justify his account of the virtues.

He might, then, deny that an agent who achieves a complete conative good really achieves a complete good. If some of our desires are mistaken, and there are some goods that we neither desire nor achieve, our rational aims cannot achieve a complete good. On this view, the complete good is determined by objective norms and standards, beyond the agent's desires, for real goods. Let us, then, call this a *normative* conception of the good.[34]

Aristotle's initial exposition of completeness does not show whether his conception of the complete good is normative or conative. But he introduces a second formal condition, self-sufficiency.

> By self-sufficient we do not mean sufficient for a person himself on his own, living a solitary life, but sufficient also for parents, children, and wife and, in general, for friends and fellow-citizens, since a human being is by nature a political ⟨animal⟩ . . . we suppose that what is self-sufficient is what all by itself makes a life choiceworthy and lacking in nothing. (1097b8–15)[35]

Since he claims that the complete good seems to be self-sufficient (1097b7–8), the account of self-sufficiency explains how he understands completeness.

Aristotle must reject a purely conative account of the final good. For we have no reason to suppose that all rational agents want to realize their political nature. Some may apparently be indifferent to many aspects of their nature; and Aristotle will say they have mistaken desires, because they do not determine their conception of their good in the right way. His account of self-sufficiency, and hence of completeness, is normative.[36] We achieve a complete good, according to the normative conception, only if we completely fulfil our nature, not if we simply fulfil our conception of our good.

A purely conative conception would make the final good a weak foundation for Aristotle's theory of virtue. A normative conception avoids this objection; but it seems to face another. A conative account seems to rest fairly firmly on necessary features of a rational agent, and to this extent supports Aristotle's theory from something more than common beliefs. So far we have found no similar support for a normative interpretation of the formal criteria.

194. RATIONAL AGENCY AND THE HUMAN FUNCTION

To support a normative account of the final good Aristotle appeals to the function of a human being.[37] Relying on the *De Anima*, he assumes that the function of an organism will consist in some kind of life, and considers the different kinds of lives. Since these correspond to the different grades of soul listed in *De Anima* ii 3, he passes easily and permissibly from talk of life to talk of souls (1098a7). Each different type of soul is named after its dominant and distinctive potentiality. An animal's soul is perceptive because perception is the feature that distinguishes animals from plants and because an animal's desires and actions are guided by perception. But the function of a perceptive soul is not confined to perceiving; it includes a nutritive part as well as parts for perception, imagination, and desire.[38]

Aristotle's way of distinguishing souls is important when we come to consider the proper function of a human being, which is 'some life of action of the rational part; and part of this is rational as obedient to reason, part as having reason and thinking' (1098a3–5).[39] In confining the human function to a life of action of the rational part, Aristotle does not exclude all animal or vegetative activities. He assumes only that rational activity is the distinctive and essential feature of the human soul, and that this organizes the human being's other activities in the way perception organizes a non-rational animal's other activities. The life of action will include other activities besides the activity of reasoning; but in a human being they are essentially guided by reasoning.[40]

This view of what the human function includes should make it easier to believe Aristotle's claim that there is one. The appeal to function rests on the conception, defended in the *De Anima*, of natural organisms as goal-directed systems; different types of goal-directed action explain the behaviour of different types of organisms, and justify us in ascribing different souls to them. To claim that the human function consists in a life according to reason is to claim that human behaviour is teleologically explicable as the product of practical reason guiding other activities. This is a plausible claim, if the general conception of the soul in the *DA* is plausible, and if Aristotle is right about how the human soul fits into that general account.

Aristotle argues that if the human function is 'actualization of the soul according to reason or involving reason' (1098a7–8), the human good will be 'actualization of the soul according to virtue' (1098a16–17). 'According to virtue' has to replace 'according to reason', because particular human beings might exercise their rational capacities incompletely or perversely, even though, being essentially rational agents, they exercise them to some degree. A good musician exercises his function as a musician completely and correctly, and so achieves his good qua musician; a similar restriction is needed to infer the human good from the human function.[41]

Evidently this account of the human good leaves us with many unanswered questions. We have still not learnt much about what a virtue will require; that is a question for the rest of the *Ethics*. However, Aristotle still thinks we have learnt something; for he defines a virtue in general as a state that will make the possessor perform his function well (1106a15–17). We avoid an uninformative circle of definitions if we can form some reasonable views on what is required for performing the human function well.

Why should facts about the human essence determine what is good for a human being? Why prefer such a normative account of the good to a purely conative account that makes a person's desires determine what is good for him? Aristotle might fairly argue that if we consider the good for a non-human organism, we will find it in fulfilling the function of the organism; a plant or animal flourishes if it fully displays its characteristics as a member of the species it belongs to, not if it displays the characteristics of something else.

Indeed, we will even find it hard to identify the essential functions of the species without some reference to the good of members of the species; for the essential functions will be those that are essential to a normal member of the species, those that teleologically explain the other properties and behaviour of the organism; but a teleological explanation must show how the characteristics and behaviour tend to the good of the organism, and so we need some conception of this to fix the teleological explanations.[42] In the same way, we might argue, we need to fix a human being's good by reference to what a human being is— otherwise we will be describing the good for some other sort of creature; and some of our views about the human good will influence our views about the essential characteristics of a human being.

But if we concede these points to Aristotle, we may doubt their relevance to ethics. Let us suppose we can form a quasi-biological conception of human flourishing and welfare corresponding to our conception of the welfare of another species. Why should we agree that this conception is relevant to the choices of a rational agent? Why should he not be indifferent to the effect of his actions on his welfare as a flourishing specimen of humanity, if he prefers to realize his own particular desires and preferences? Even if we accept a normative account of the human good, we might apparently reply that this has no bearing on human happiness, and no necessary claim on a rational agent.

Aristotle has appealed to the necessary structure of a rational agent's choices and to the essential properties of a human being. In both cases he makes a metaphysical claim that rests on more than pure dialectic. But to reach the result he wants, he needs to combine these claims, and to show that a rational agent has reason to attend to the properties that Aristotle takes to constitute the human function. If Aristotle can show this, he can show that a rational agent has reason to accept a normative account of his good in his own conception of his happiness.

195. RATIONAL AGENCY AND HUMAN CAPACITIES

To see if Aristotle can defend the claims he needs, we may return to his initial conception of a rational agent. Such an agent forms a conception of what is best to do by considering the present and the future, as parts of the same life.[43] I think of myself as the owner of some future desires; but my self is not exhausted by my present and future desires.

Sometimes I can act so that I will or will not have particular future desires, and I must consider which it will be better for me to have. In deciding this I cannot consider simply my future actual desires, since these are precisely the ones I need to decide about. Nor should I consider simply my present actual desires. Perhaps I now have an aversion to buying an expensive violin since I have neither the interest nor the competence to play it. But perhaps it is open to me to form and to satisfy the desire to play a violin well; and after I do that perhaps I will want an expensive violin. It would be unreasonable of me to refuse to set out on the course of action that will result in the desire for a violin, simply because I don't want the violin now. On the other hand, I might decide not to seek a particular sort of job because if I get it and succeed in it I will form the sort of outlook that I now reject, even though I will be quite content with it then.

In neither case can I find an answer to the deliberative problem by simply thinking about desires I have or will have.[44] I have to think of myself as consisting not only of desires, but also of capacities that may or may not be actualized; my deliberative questions are about which capacities I should actualize by forming and fulfilling one or another desire, and about the effect of actualizing one capacity on the actualization of others. Evidently I must deliberate in the light of the values I have, since nothing else is available to me; but I will try to form my desires by considering the interests of my self as a whole, not simply my present or future desires.

Deliberation about the actualization or non-actualization of capacities is an expression of concern for oneself, and it should show itself in the same way as it shows itself in choosing between actual desires. When I think about which of my actual desires I should satisfy, I will intend to satisfy more rather than fewer; and the more I can satisfy, the better, other things being equal. (The reservation here is needed to accommodate the degree of importance that I attach to some desires over others.) If we deliberate similarly about capacities, we have reason to prefer the actualization of more rather than fewer. For we are concerned with the interests of the self as a whole, and if capacities are left unactualized we will be denying them any attention and satisfaction in our plans, and so failing to take account of the whole self in our deliberations.

Here, then, we have argued from the pattern of self-concern shown in deliberation about desires, to show that rational agents will be concerned about actualizing more of their capacities rather than fewer. If a self consists of capacities, and not only of desires, its satisfaction consists in the actualization of capacities, not only in the satisfaction of desires.

This argument does not show that rational agents necessarily act on some concern for the realization of their capacities. But if it is sound, it shows that those who fail to act on such a concern fail to act on the consequences of principles they already accept. Some concern for a conative final good is a necessary feature of a rational agent; and while concern for actualization of capacities is not necessary, it is reasonable for any rational agent.

Aristotle identifies the good with the realization of human capacities; and he takes this identification to explain why we prefer the active to the passive aspects of friendship.

The reason for this is that being is choiceworthy and lovable for all, and we have our being in so far as we are actualized, since we have our being by living and acting; and the product is, in a way, the producer in actuality; hence the producer is fond of his product, since he is also fond of his own being. (1168a5–8)[45]

This feature of our good explains why we should prefer activity to passivity. If we are simply affected by external objects and events, we exercise our passive capacities; but these are relatively simple, and do not involve the exercise of many other capacities.[46]

The distinction between passivity and activity reflects the important difference between those processes that realize more and fewer of our goal-directed capacities. If we choose simply to be pushed around by external objects, we use only the capacities that belong to us as physical objects. If we choose to be mere perceivers, we are leaving unused the capacities that are involved in using perceptions to guide action. Aristotle uses the single term '*energeia*' both for actuality, as opposed to mere potentiality, and for activity, as opposed to inactivity or passivity. The first use explains the second. For the reasons Aristotle suggests in his discussion of artistic production (1168a7–9), we value activity because it is fuller actualization. In goal-directed action we fully display and realize our capacities as rational agents; in passivity we display only the limited range of capacities that are needed for us to be affected.

In these claims about actualization and activity, Aristotle suggests an answer to a reasonable question about his account of the good. His general claims about a rational agent may still leave us unmoved if we do not think they correspond to any of our considered views about a person's happiness or welfare. If we find no correspondence, we must conclude that our common beliefs, and the purely dialectical argument that might rest on them, are quite unconnected with the conception of a person's good that Aristotle tries to derive from metaphysics and strong dialectic. We might concede the truth of a metaphysical account of the human good as the realization of rational capacities, and still deny that we are concerned with any such good in our common judgments about welfare and happiness.

196. RATIONAL AGENCY AND HAPPINESS

For this reason, Aristotle thinks it worth his while to show that the final good and happiness meet the same formal conditions (1097a34, b15–16); even though the identity of happiness with the final good is widely agreed (1095a14–22, 1097b22–4), it is not trivial. For it is important to see that our common judgments about happiness match the metaphysical conditions imposed on the Aristotelian account of the good; if Aristotle cannot show this he will not have given an explanation and justification of our common judgments about happiness.

He suggests that we agree with him in so far as we reject a purely conative or passive conception of happiness.

No one would choose to live with a child's level of thought throughout his life, even if he took as much pleasure as possible in the sorts of things that please children, or to enjoy himself in doing one of the most shameful actions, even if he were never going to suffer pain. (1174a1–4; cf. *EE* 1215b23–6.)

Similarly, we are right to deny happiness to a satisfied person who is satisfied by the wrong things, or lacks the appropriate sort of rational activity.

On these grounds we can rule out the three most popular candidates for happiness—the lives of gratification, honour, and virtue. The life of gratification is fit only for grazing animals (1095b19–20), not for rational and active subjects. The life of honour depends on our being honoured by other people, and therefore makes us passive, not active, in relation to the most important aspect of our happiness; against this we intuitively believe that the good is 'something of our own', expressing our rational agency, not something that leaves us essentially passive (1095b23–6; cf. 1159a12–33). If we identify happiness with virtue, we must claim that someone can be happy when he is asleep or when he is suffering terrible misfortunes (1095b31–1096a2). Aristotle thinks we will agree that this is an absurd claim because both conditions prevent rational activity; when we are asleep we are inactive, and in terrible misfortunes we are victims of circumstances that 'impede many activities' (1100b29–30).

In all these cases Aristotle expects us to agree with him in rejecting a proposed candidate for happiness, because the type of life it defines includes too little rational activity. Either it is largely passive or the activity it involves is non–rational. Indeed these two objections are scarcely separable; for a life that includes very little rational activity will engage so few of the agent's capacities that it will appear to be largely passive rather than active. In rejecting such candidates for happiness, we rely on the intuitive judgments that are explained by Aristotle's appeal to self-realization in ix 7. He argues that if we think a human being's welfare does not require the completion of human nature, we are failing to remember that we are concerned with the welfare of a human being, not of some other kind of thing.[47]

197. SELF-REALIZATION

We can support Aristotle, if we appeal to common judgments about a person's welfare, or about when one person is better off than another. It is useful to begin with a purely hedonist conception, even more subjective than a conative conception, to see the sorts of reasons that incline us in Aristotle's direction. We do not think A is necessarily better off than B if A is immensely pleased because of some false belief about his situation; even though A may think he has got all he wants, he will be wrong, and we normally think this is a cruel deception.

Nor is A necessarily better off than B if A has more desires fulfilled than B has. If A's desires are very few or very foolish, we may think A is worse off than B; we would not necessarily advise B in her own interest to reduce her desires to A's level just because the lower level is more easily satisfied. Nor would we immediately suppose that A becomes worse off if he acquires more desires that are harder to satisfy. If, for instance, A has been content to be ill-treated and abused, but comes to realize he deserves better and to resent the ill-treatment, he may be to that extent better off, even though he has acquired a new unsatisfied desire.

The nature and essence of persons may also affect our judgment about their welfare. We could change someone's desires so that he is able to satisfy them all, and yet might still say that he is worse off now than he was before his desires were changed. A brain operation reducing someone's mental functions to those of a dog might remove all previous dissatisfactions, but we would often be convinced even so that it would involve serious harm to the person, even if he wanted it done—no less harm than he would suffer if he felt like having both his legs painlessly amputated and never felt any regret for them after losing them. In both cases the explanation of our judgment supports Aristotle; when a person is deprived of some essential human function, or the basis of other human functions, he suffers a severe harm. Indeed, if he is deprived of enough of these functions he will have been destroyed.

Similar assumptions about a person's nature seem to support our views about the reasonable expansion of desires. If A expands his desire for steak on Wednesday to a desire for steak on Wednesday, caviar on Thursday, and truffles on Friday, he has acquired more demanding desires, but so far we have no particular reason to think he has increased his welfare. On the other hand, if he comes to resent his patronizing treatment by B, or if he comes to want some more challenging occupation than a boring job followed by mindless amusement, we might well think he is better off. The expanded desires that seem relevant to his welfare are those that are more suitable for a rational agent, and tend to realize a rational agent's special capacities. In so far as we agree with Aristotle in rejecting the life of a child, we reject it as inappropriate for the sorts of rational beings that we are.

Aristotle can claim support in common beliefs for his claim that our judgments about a being's good and welfare are guided by our judgments about the being's nature and essence. On this score the welfare of persons is no different from the welfare of other biological kinds, and Aristotle is justified in claiming that his argument from function to welfare works as well for persons.

We have no reason, then, to dismiss the connexion he wants to find between his metaphysical claims about the essence of persons and our judgments about welfare and happiness. He cannot do without some appeal to common beliefs; but he can fairly claim that his appeal involves more than pure dialectic, in so far as it relies on a theory which has the support of first philosophy.

198. SELF-REALIZATION AND HUMAN GOOD

We have seen some reasons for accepting Aristotle's account of the human good as the actualization of a human being's capacities as a rational agent. Still, the account will be useless if we do not know what counts as a single capacity, and hence do not know whether we have realized more or fewer. If a single capacity corresponds to every true sentence of the form 'I am capable of F', then I seem to realize an indefinitely large number of minimally different capacities, by raising my arm at 10.00 a.m., 10.01, 10.02, etc. If we reply that these all realize just one capacity, the capacity to raise my arm, then surely we can collapse many other capacities into one by providing less specific descriptions.

In reply we may argue that we are interested in counting capacities of widely differing types. Someone may claim to have realized five capacities by raising his arm at five different times; but these may be very similar capacities, in so far as they require very similar thoughts, desires, and bodily movements for their exercise. We can reasonably say that someone who both moves his arm and moves his foot has realized more significantly different capacities than someone who moves his arm at five different times.

If we say this, we need to rely on some understanding of significant difference in capacities, to show why the different times of raising an arm do not constitute a significant difference. Here we can rely on the different processes in the agent himself; though the external conditions differ, the capacity is the same if the same process realizes it. Moreover, in determining difference of process we will fairly pay more attention to the mental cause than to the bodily behaviour it causes. If very similar processes of thought and desire result in two movements M1 and M2, and a very different process results in M3, which looks rather similar to M1 and M2, we will say that we realize more significantly different capacities in M1 and M3 than we realize in M1 and M2, since the causes are so different. With these sorts of restrictions—which no doubt need to be further refined—we can avoid objections that would reduce claims about capacities to triviality. The same considerations will show us how to avoid a foolishly quantitative conception of what is required to realize capacities.

Aristotle's teleological account of capacities implies that a subject has different capacities only if it has states that are explained by different final causes—states that differ in the ways they do because they are for different actualizations.[48] Capacities for slightly different movements count as the same capacity if the different movements have the same explanation. A carpenter can make a chair in two slightly different ways with slightly different movements; but if the slight differences are irrelevant to his craft, he will not exercise different capacities, since the (alleged) two capacities will not be for two different ends. If Aristotle is allowed this fairly systematic way to distinguish capacities, he need not be forced to admit that different human capacities are realized in trivially different activities.

We may still suspect, however, that appeal to realization of capacities will lead to absurdly mistaken conceptions of the human good. If we try to realize as many capacities as we can, then apparently we will always strain for diversity; we will want to hold our breath under water as long as we can; to see how long we can survive at the North Pole; never to do anything very well, since we will always want to do something new; to realize all our cruel and sadistic capacities as well as our sympathetic capacities.

A clearer view of capacities may answer these objections. The objections assume that the range of activities reflects the range of capacities realized; but the assumption is probably false. We may realize more capacities in learning to perform one activity well than in learning to perform several badly; the advice to realize different capacities need not require us to repeat the very similar elementary processes of learning to play several instruments badly, but may require us to develop the wider range of skills involved in learning to play one instrument well. Nor need we agree that immoral or absurd activities realize distinctive capacities. We might realize more capacities if we learn to enjoy playing tennis than if we learn to enjoy playing catch; but we have no similar reason to believe that we realize more capacities in sadistic than in sympathetic pleasure.

To estimate the force of apparent objections we must also remember a rational agent's legitimate concern with the structure of his life as a rational agent. He will have to select from possible realizations of capacities those that are less likely to impede others, those that are more likely to encourage others, and those that allow the fuller exercise of rational agency. If we keep these conditions in mind, we are less likely to suppose that self-realization requires the encouragement of bizarre or immoral activities.

This defence of self-realization does not show that Aristotle's conception of human good is beyond reasonable objection. So far we have found only that it does not collapse immediately in the face of obvious objections, and therefore that we have to examine its implications more carefully to see if they lead to reasonable results or not. His conception of the good rests on strong dialectic, on principles derived from metaphysics and psychology; and so far we have found no reason to dismiss the ethical theory that he seeks to construct on this basis.

17

THE VIRTUES OF RATIONAL AGENTS

199. VIRTUE, HAPPINESS, AND NATURE

Aristotle's ethics rests on his conception of happiness. Still, its primary topic is virtue, not happiness; and it is not immediately evident why an account of happiness should help us to find an account of the virtues. The recognized virtues seem to be those that benefit other people; they are defined by reference to the fine, not to the agent's own good. Aristotle needs to argue that a fuller account of the agent's good will actually explain and justify the recognized virtues that are concerned with the good of others.

It is easy to overlook this question, because Aristotle, quite legitimately, presents another conception of virtue that is derived directly from his claims about happiness. He has argued that happiness is the good performance of the human function, and that therefore it is the realization of the soul in accordance with complete virtue in a complete life. Complete virtue consists of those states and conditions that promote the best sort of realization of human functions. This sort of virtue makes its owner perform her function well (*EN* 1106a14–24, 1139a15–17, *EE* 1218b37), and 'completes' nature (1103a23–6; *Phys.* 246a13, 247a3); it is *eudaimonic* virtue. But since the moral virtues are the primary topic of political science, some further argument is needed to show that the reference to human function explains the nature of the moral virtues as well.

Aristotle does not believe he equivocates when he uses 'virtue' for both the eudaimonic and the moral virtues; for he thinks the two types of virtue are really the same, and this is why he thinks the study of the human good answers some critics of the moral virtues. A full understanding of the eudaimonic virtues should also display the moral virtues, and explain how the moral virtues contribute to the good of the virtuous person.

Virtue is important because it expresses our nature as responsible agents. A person differs from other substances in being responsible for her actions; and we have seen that Aristotle explains this distinctive feature of persons by deriving it from their essential property of rational agency.[1] A person is responsible for her actions and states in so far as they proceed from states that are in her control as a rational agent. By forming her desires, aims, patterns of deliberation, and decisions in a particular way she exercises her capacities as a rational agent, and becomes a candidate for praise and blame. The result of her formation of these states is her virtuous or vicious character. To develop a virtue is to express our essence as rational and responsible agents, and to that extent the cultivation of virtues must be a part of a rational agent's good. To fail to apply rational choice and deliberation to the formation of states of character would be to fail to recognize ourselves as rational agents in this most important respect.

If I rationally choose to form a state of character that reduces the role of my rational agency in my action, I am choosing not to realize my nature as a rational agent any further. But if I choose this in my own interest, I am being inconsistent; for if I understand my own interest, I must understand my own essence; and if this consists in rational agency, I am inconsistent if I choose in my own interest not to realize my own essence. The rational person, therefore, will choose the states of character that involve rational control over his other states and actions.[2] The eudaimonic virtues will be the states that embody this sort of rational control.

200. VIRTUE, REASON, AND DESIRE

Aristotle sees these connexions between his conception of the human function and the foundations of an account of eudaimonic virtue. He first describes the human function as a life of action of the part of the soul that has reason. He divides this part into two, one part that obeys reason and the other that has reason and thinks in its own right (1098a3–5). These two parts reappear in the introduction to the account of virtue (1102b13–1103a3); virtue is identified with the harmony in which the non-rational part obeys and agrees with the correct reason in the rational part (1102b25–8). The virtuous state of character is the one that fully embodies rational agency, by fully expressing the control of rational desire and deliberation over our choices. In so far as we control our choices in this way, we realize our essential capacities as responsible rational agents.

Aristotle outlines his general view of virtue of character by describing it as a mean state between excess and deficiency of action and feeling. His interpretation of 'excess' and 'deficiency' makes it clear that he intends to describe eudaimonic virtue; for the mean states are those that realize the human function by fulfilling the capacities of human nature. Virtues of character resulting from habituation are needed to fulfil the human function, because nature does not infallibly complete itself

(1103a23–6). To complete nature we have to realize our essential capacity of rational determination of human choice and action.

In contrast to the virtues, ordinary capacities are capacities for contraries (1106a6–11). These are capacities we have in the weak sense in which we are capable of being either healthy or sick. In this same sense we are capable of being either virtuous or vicious, and virtue actualizes our capacities no more than vice does. If 'actualize' is to be taken in this weak sense, and if 'complete' just means 'actualize', then virtue actualizes and completes nature no more than vice does.

In Aristotle's view, however, a doctor has a strong or proximate capacity (potentiality) for, or a capacity primarily for, healing, and a weak capacity for, or a capacity secondarily for, killing his patients.[3] Similarly, a hammer's primary capacity is for hammering. For organisms, some actualizations complete their natures and others do not, and the ones that complete their nature correspond to their strong capacities. These are the actualizations that promote and actualize the capacities essential to organisms of those kinds.

Similarly, Aristotle can fairly argue that some capacities are essential to human beings, and some realizations of these capacities are essential activities of human beings. These realizations can fairly be taken to complete a human being's nature. Hence the realization of the capacity for rational direction of actions will complete a human being's nature; and in so far as virtue realizes this capacity it can claim to complete human nature.

This goal of completing human nature determines the distinctive features of the doctrine of the mean. To achieve the goal we must determine our human choices and actions by reason. But we should not simply impose some sort of rational order on them, irrespective of what they are like in themselves, as if they were raw material to be shaped or discarded as we please. Our material is human choice and action, present in an agent with non-rational as well as rational desires; and so these non-rational desires and impulses must be properly trained, neither suppressed nor left alone. If we leave them untrained and unregulated they will tend to dominate us (cf. 1109b1–7), and to distract us from our essential functions of practical reasoning; but practical reasoning does not try to suppress them.[4]

The virtuous person, therefore, allows reasonable satisfaction to his appetites; he does not suppress all his fears; he does not disregard all his feelings of pride or shame or resentment (1126a3–8), or his desire for other people's good opinion. In the good person the non-rational appetites cooperate with reason, not because they have been forced to be accomplices in their own suppression but because they recognize that they are being allowed reasonable satisfaction. Hence the brave person is appropriately afraid of serious danger (1115b10–20), and if the cause is not worth the danger he withdraws; but when the cause justifies his standing firm, his fear is not so strong that he has to struggle against it.[5]

The Aristotelian virtue of character lies in a mean determined by reason, and by the reason by which the wise person would determine it (1106b36–1107a2). The virtuous person must decide on the virtuous action for its own sake (1105a32, 1144a19); but decision rests on wish and deliberation, and correct deliberation is the task of the wise person (1140a25–31); hence genuine virtue requires wisdom, to order non-rational desires by correct reason (1144b21–5).[6] In requiring wisdom Aristotle requires the virtuous person to realize fully his capacity for rational determination of his actions and choices. He has described eudaimonic virtue of character, and derived his account from his conception of the human function.

This general schema of eudaimonic virtue does not yet describe any definite patterns of choice and action. The particular Aristotelian virtues of character are the moral virtues recognized by common sense; and if Aristotle fulfils his aim in the *Ethics*, he will show that they are eudaimonic virtues too.

201. CONCERN FOR A SELF

Aristotle argues that the virtuous person loves himself, because 'he acts for the sake of his reasoning part, which is what each person seems to be' (1166a16–17). His self-love differs from other people's 'as much as life in accordance with reason differs from life in accordance with feeling (*pathos*)' (1169a4–5). These claims imply that the person who is rationally concerned with himself, and whose concern rests on a true conception of himself and his nature as a rational agent, will practise the virtues.[7]

The virtuous person is supposed to have the same sort of concern for himself that he has for his virtuous friend. He is concerned for the friend for the friend's own sake; and this altruistic concern, in Aristotle's view, requires concern for the friend 'in himself'.[8] The right sort of concern is concern for the friend as what he essentially is, not simply in so far as he has some coincidental property that appeals to us (1156a16–19).

Concern for a person's essence seems to Aristotle to require concern for him as having the character he has. In the best type of friendship,

each wishes good to the other in so far as the other is good; and he is good in himself; and those who wish goods to a friend for his own sake are friends most of all; for they take this attitude because of himself and not coincidentally. (1156b8–11)

Aristotle implies that if Al loves Ann for what she is in herself, he loves her for her virtue, and that therefore her virtuous state of character is intrinsic to what Ann is. If this were not so, then the connexion between Al's loving Ann for herself, for what she is, and for her virtue, would be unintelligible. Al loves not simply the instance of rational agency found in Ann, but the particular virtuous states in which it is found.

Aristotle must claim, therefore, that Ann's essence includes her virtuous state of character. It cannot simply include those properties that make her a human being or a rational agent, but must also include those that distinguish rational agents with different characters.[9] Al's concern for Ann herself includes concern to do what Ann wants; but this counts as concern for Ann herself only in so far as her desires express her character, and therefore express her essence.

Self-love, therefore, ought also to include concern for one's own essence, and hence for one's own character. The virtuous person's virtues constitute the character that is himself, and is therefore the proper object of his rational concern.

202. SELF, ESSENCE, AND CHARACTER

Aristotle, however, seems to assume a closer connexion between a person's essence and his character than we can readily defend. A particular person is a particular form present in a sequence of bits of matter. The form is the essence that persists through changes in material composition and in other states; nutrition is a state of a continuing substance rather than the mere replacement of matter because 'the form remains' (cf. *GC* 322a33).[10] Persistence of the particular form does not require any unchanging shape or size, but a persisting and coherently changing system that absorbs the matter in goal-directed processes.

The particular form of a rational agent is the first actuality that is his soul. If it is like other particular forms, it does not require the persistence of any determinate state of character, but just the persistence of a coherently changing system of desires and aims. A particular person's persistence does not consist in the persistence of any particular first-order desires or aims, but in the persistence of the same particular soul that organizes them. The organizing desires are the agent's conception of his good; but this may change without his ceasing to exist. Even very general desires can be modified, sometimes by reflexion on their consequences for satisfying lower-order desires that he is strongly attached to; the persistence of the person does not consist in the fixity even of some very general desires peculiar to him, but in the continuity and suitable causal connexions between earlier aims and the later products of their modification. The persisting self, therefore, cannot be identical to the character.

Aristotle, however, thinks that the connexions between essence and persistence actually support his claims about character, friendship, and self. For he insists that virtuous character is persistent and stable (cf. 1100b11–17, 1105a32–3, 1152a30–3), and that therefore this type of friendship is stable also. Such stability is what we expect in a friendship that involves concern for the person himself (1156b9–12); for since the person himself is stable, genuine concern for him should be as stable as he is. The lower types of friendship dissolve when the situation changes to remove the previous pleasure or advantage; but the best type of friendship should dissolve only when one of the people in it has changed enough to be no longer the same person (1164a8–13, 1165b1–4, 1165b20–31).[11]

Aristotle therefore suggests that Al appropriately shows concern for the permanent, stable thing that is Ann herself by loving Ann for her permanent and stable character. Though her character cannot be as persistent as Ann herself, and therefore cannot be identical to Ann, it is persistent enough to be the appropriate focus of concern for someone concerned about Ann herself.

This concern for another clarifies the virtuous person's concern for herself. My character results from the relatively stable way in which my rational agency, working through wish and decision, shapes and controls my desires and action. If I have developed no character at all, I am still a rational agent; but since my conception is unstable, I cannot predict much about my future desires, and so cannot plan very effectively for the satisfaction of my future self. The less I can plan for it, the less I can take account of it in my present actions, and the weaker my concern for it will be; I will have no stable view about whether the aims of my future self are reasonable or unreasonable. If concern for myself is to be a prominent and effective part of my life, I have reason to form a more stable character; then I will know what to do if I want to express my concern for my future self.

Aristotle's views about the virtues are therefore closely related to his views on self-concern. A virtue is worth acquiring partly because it is a firm and unchanging state (1105a33) that gives us a stable and persisting future self to be concerned about.

The virtuous person values most of all the expression of rational agency in virtuous action. He is not so concerned about other goods that in order to get them he is willing to change his state of character for the worse. More of his traits of character will persist than would persist in an unstable person, and hence he secures *his own* future good more than the unstable person does. Particular goods are no part of my good unless

I exist; but the less stable person does not understand this, and so secures the goods, without the right self to possess them.

It is not simply ignorance that weakens my concern for myself if I lack a stable character; there will also be less to justify my concern. I am reasonably concerned about my future self to the extent that its plans and decisions will be continuous with my present ones and will fulfil or improve them; and if less of me persists, I have less reason for concern. Aristotle assumes that an unstable person preserves less of himself than he would if he were virtuous.

203. SELF-LOVE AND SELF-REALIZATION

Aristotle expects the person with a eudaimonic virtue to be correctly concerned for himself for his own sake, and so to be concerned for himself as a rational agent.

Hence he wishes goods and apparent goods to himself, and does them in his actions, since it is proper to the good person to achieve the good. He wishes and does them for his own sake, since he does them for the sake of his thinking part, and that is what each person seems to be. He wishes himself to live and to be preserved. And he wishes this for the part by which he has intelligence more than for any other part. For being is a good for the good person, and each person wishes for goods for himself. (1166a14–20)

He is not in conflict with himself (1166a13–14), and he has practically no regret for what he has done (1166a27–9).[12] For what he always wants to do most is to exercise his practical reason in rational decision, and he always succeeds in doing this.

The vicious person 'is at variance with himself, and has an appetite for one thing and a wish for another, as incontinent people do' (1166b7–8). Some vicious people refrain from doing what they think best because of cowardice or laziness (1166b10–11); and those who have done many terrible actions come to hate being alive, and even kill themselves (1166b11–13).[13] Their conflicts appear both at a particular time, when they make a decision, and at a later time, when they reflect on the decision they have made. They are not incontinents who act on appetite against their rational decision.[14] Their rational decisions expose them to the conflicts that the virtuous person avoids.

Someone with the proper concern wants to arrange his life so that it allows him scope for exercise of rational agency in a stable character. He therefore does not want his ultimate end to be a state that is to be achieved by being passively affected by external conditions and his own non-rational desires. Nor does he want it to be the sort of end that requires constant change in his character to adapt him to the conditions needed for success. If his goal in life requires honesty at one time, cheating at another, kindliness now, and cruelty later, it does not secure happiness for him. For in order to achieve such a goal he has to sacrifice some of himself, and relatively little of him will persist into his future states of character; such a degree of self-sacrifice is inconsistent with proper concern for himself.

The vicious person values practical reason only for its efficiency in achieving goals that do not essentially involve its exercise. He must therefore suffer regrets and conflicts from which the virtuous person is free. If the virtuous person chooses to deny himself some pleasure that he rationally prefers to avoid, he does not regret his action, though he may be sorry that he cannot have the pleasure; for he values for its own sake the exercise of practical reason and the expression of stable character in that choice. But when the vicious person chooses between his rational plan to rob the bank and his fear at being caught, he has no reason to prefer the first desire as an expression of stable rational agency; his decision must be based entirely on the comparative strength of his desires, and he regrets the frustration of some of his desires. Equally he lacks the virtuous person's reason to be pleased and free of regret about his past rational choices; for since all he cares about is their instrumental efficiency, he regrets his actions if things turn out badly.

Similarly, there is no reason why different elements of a vicious person's good should not conflict and cause him regret; he cannot remove the regret by reflecting on the rational order that requires the satisfaction of one desire over the other. He must be equally prepared to pursue his ends even when they require him to perform actions and to develop traits that previously repelled him and that will come to repel him again in the future. Though he is permanently vicious, he does not have a stable character. For his permanent aim of pursuing the pleasure at hand will require him sometimes to be sympathetic to another person, sometimes cruel, sometimes cooperative, sometimes a double-crosser, sometimes ready to inflict severe future pain, sometimes angry at his past indulgence. Aristotle does not exaggerate in alleging that the vicious person who fails to consider himself as a stable rational agent is liable to hate himself.

If we simply prefer psychic equilibrium over psychic conflict, the vicious person may fairly reply that he prefers the higher level of pleasure and excitement even at the cost of psychic conflict.[15] But Aristotle does not merely appeal to this purely conative conception of happiness. Synchronic and diachronic conflicts result from the vicious person's failure to love himself as a rational agent; and this is the condition that Aristotle describes as wretched (1166b26–9). The vicious person's distress and inner conflict is a symptom of this condition, not itself the proof that he is less happy than the virtuous person.

The virtuous person's attitude to herself is the norm for correct self-concern, because it rests on a true conception of herself (1166a10–13). Since Aristotle accepts a normative conception of a person's good, he believes that self-concern aims at a person's actual good only if it expresses her real nature. While some self-concern seems necessary to distinguish rational decision from animal desire, the degree of self-concern may be slight and uninformed, corresponding to the minimal rationality of the intemperate person. The good person has correct concern for herself, since she is concerned for herself as a rational agent. She cares about herself as a rational agent who has desires for particular objects, but is not identical to these desires.

204. RATIONAL CONTROL AND SELF-REGARDING VIRTUES

Aristotle's general remarks about virtue have now allowed us to form a more definite view of a eudaimonic virtue and of the way it promotes happiness. (1) A virtue of character is a state promoting and expressing the agent's self-realization as a rational agent with both rational and non-rational capacities. (2) Rational agency is primary in the virtuous person's conception of her end; she does not treat rational agency as simply a means to the satisfaction of her other desires. (3) Concern for herself as a rational agent requires her to cultivate and maintain a stable character, not to adapt her outlook to be more efficient in the pursuit of other ends.

The later conditions by themselves allow states of character rejected by the first condition. I might accord primacy to rational agency and pay too little attention to any other aspect of my nature; then I would not be aiming at the realization of myself as a whole. Again, I might develop a highly stable character simply by cultivating irrational and immovable attachments unaffected by rational judgment, let alone by rational judgment concerned with self-realization.[16] To get the right results we must regard the second and third conditions as partial explanations of the first.

The Aristotelian virtues of character are concerned with my relation to my own non-rational desires and impulses, with my use of external goods, and with my attitude to other people and their interests. Temperance and bravery are concerned with non-rational desires, generosity and proper pride (the nameless virtue of iv 4) with external goods, and justice with the interests of other people. However, my attitudes to my non-rational desires and to external goods will influence each other (1121b7–10); and we will see later that all the virtues of character are concerned crucially with the interests of others.[17] The three concerns, then, do not mark a division of labour between different virtues; but they usefully identify different aspects of a virtue, and the three conditions for a eudaimonic virtue apply to each concern.

Since the other-regarding aspects of moral virtue seem to raise special difficulties, it is best to begin with the apparently self-regarding virtues. For present purposes, we may concentrate on the self-regarding aspects of courage and temperance. Once we fix the conception of self-realization that makes these eudaimonic virtues, we may also change our view about the other-regarding virtues.

Even a purely conative conception of happiness seems to support courage and temperance. A rational agent has some concern for his own good as a whole, distinguished from the satisfaction of this or that immediate desire, because he has some conception of himself as an agent beyond particular desires. Temperance requires some concern for my good as a whole in contrast to present pleasures that might distract me from the pursuit of it, and courage requires such a concern in contrast to present fears that might paralyse my pursuit of it. Even a conative conception of the good shows why a rational agent values these minimal virtues.

This minimal degree of virtue requires only a slight degree of courage and temperance. For even if I agree that I should pursue my rational plan for my good as a whole, my rational plan may simply tell me to do whatever I have the strongest non-rational impulse for. In that case I will not try to modify my desires or to restrain my impulses; for practical reason has only a tactical role, in planning the satisfaction of a particular desire, with no larger strategic role in deciding which desires to pursue. This is the condition of the 'intemperate' or 'unrestrained' (*akolastos*) person. He acts on a rational plan, since he acts on a decision, and hence on wish and deliberation; but he sees no point in restraining his appetites or resisting his fears.[18] He will perhaps argue that resistance to appetites or fears causes pain, and that such pain never results in corresponding benefits. Aristotle needs to show how such a rational plan fails to express the agent's rational agency, even though it shows that he is a rational agent.

This minimal planner has already conceded a vital point. He has agreed to consider what benefits him in his life as a whole. He therefore recognizes himself as a rational agent extending over time; but if he recognizes this fact about his essence, he should not ignore it in considering his good, since his good depends on what he essentially is. Since he is essentially a rational agent, his good requires the exercise of rational agency; and when he claims that no good could compensate for the pain of restraining appetite, he overlooks the benefits that consist in the exercise of rational agency in planning for his life.

For similar reasons he overestimates the pain involved in the exercise of temperance. The doctrine of the mean shows that the virtuous person does not have to suffer the sorts of pains that intemperate people will suffer if their appetites are frustrated; for since her appetites conform to reason, they will not have to be frustrated all the time, and when she does frustrate them the pain will not be unbearably severe. The same argument applies to bravery. The brave and temperate person's exercise of rational agency does not cause the pain that intemperate and cowardly people suffer in restraining their desires. Aristotle rightly remarks that pain at doing the virtuous action is a sign of vice (1104b3–8).

205. DEGREES OF RATIONAL CONTROL

These objections may refute the utterly intemperate and cowardly person, who rejects any restraint of his appetites at all. But they will not work so easily against a 'prudently intemperate' person who plans rationally to satisfy his bodily satisfactions over time, and sacrifices some gratification of his appetites now to gratify more or stronger appetites later. Similarly, a 'prudent coward' will plan to minimize his exposure to danger over time, and will incur minor danger to avoid greater danger. The prudently vicious person agrees that it is right to use practical reason to order and arrange the satisfaction of his appetites. He allows this role to practical reason because he regards himself as a persisting rational agent, and hence thinks his plan is better than the plan of the totally intemperate person. But he allows no role to practical reason in the choice of the types of ends that are to be pursued; these are to be determined by his non-rational appetites.[19]

In Aristotle's view, this prudently vicious person cannot justify his restriction of the role of practical reason. Such a person recognizes that practical reason is competent to judge between different conceptions of the good that require different proportions of different satisfactions. He needs practical reason to decide whether to pursue these pleasures at one time or a different set of pleasures at another time. To decide this question, practical reason must form a conception of his life as a whole and of the relative importance of different pleasures and different degrees of satisfaction at different times. If practical reason is capable of this, why should it not also be capable of deciding between bodily appetites and other desires? If practical reason can make these further decisions, the person who is guided by it will express himself more fully as a rational agent than the prudently vicious person will.

Both the prudently vicious and the utterly vicious person unjustifiably limit the scope of practical reason.[20] Since the prudently vicious person allows his non-rational appetites to determine his choice of ends, he must make his character adaptable enough to pursue those ends efficiently; and he must expect that this efficient pursuit will require him to act in ways that he later finds repellent. He will be liable to the self-hatred that Aristotle takes to be a sign of disunity and instability in a self (1166b11–18). Someone who is really concerned with his persistence has reason to reject the self-sacrifice imposed on him by prudent vice.

The same objection works against the vices concerned with external goods. These vices require us to take the external goods as ends to which our rational agency and character are merely instrumental. Sometimes the external goods are themselves instrumental, and we are attached to them because of our non-rational attachment to the satisfaction of non-rational desires. That is why a grasping but also wasteful attitude to wealth often results from intemperance (1121a30–b10); and for similar reasons an intemperate and grasping person will often want to cultivate other people's favour by flattery (1121b6–7, 1127a8–10). Other vices may result from attachment to an external good for its own sake; if we want to be honoured or liked by other people, we may take these as ends to which we subordinate our rational agency.

Aristotle agrees that some level of external goods, and some level of satisfaction of non-rational desires, is genuinely good; they have a proper place in a life designed by practical reason for self-realization controlled by practical reason. But excessive attachment to external goods both displays and encourages disregard for one's own stable character. The person who takes honour as his end will be ready to do anything, no matter how much he disapproves of it, to win honour from other people; and if others are inconstant in their judgment, he will have to change his character and his attitudes to suit them. He will have to be equally adaptable if he wants to be liked by others. Such dependence on others in the pursuit of his general aims easily makes him unstable; if he must always change himself to adapt to external conditions and other people, he does not leave very much of himself to be the object of his rational concern.

Aristotle can therefore explain why self-realization requires courage, temperance, and the virtues concerned with external goods, rather than their utterly vicious or prudently vicious rivals. The virtuous person expresses his rational agency in choosing the ends he pursues and in guiding his actions in accordance with that choice. In subordinating other ends to his rational agency, he forms a stable self for which he has the proper sort of concern. A true conception of the good for a human being justifies Aristotle's selection of these states of character as eudaimonic virtues.

206. THE SCOPE OF RATIONAL CONTROL

The Aristotelian virtues essentially include the regulation of non-rational desires and external goods by practical reason. But Aristotle assumes that the virtuous person will exercise rational control 'in a complete life'.[21] We might have assumed that we fully exercise reason in a 'minimalist' plan, reducing our desires and planning for their satisfaction at the lower level. A minimalist plan might even seem the best for a stable character; the fewer things I aim at, the fewer conflicts I face, and the less adaptation to circumstances is forced on me. Moreover, a higher level of concern for external goods also makes bravery and temperance more difficult; for more external goods require more hazards and dangers, hence more situations inspiring fear, and more actions that require some restraint of appetite and inclination.

Aristotle believes a minimalist plan cannot produce a 'complete life'; for he expects the virtuous person to make more than minimalist demands on external resources. The temperate person should not reduce his bodily appetites to the psychologically possible minimum, even if he feels no pains of deprivation; Aristotle condemns 'insensible' people, without suggesting that they suffer pains of frustration (1119a5–11). The temperate person requires more external goods than the minimum necessary for survival; he wants opportunities for bodily pleasure that require more generous external resources.

The virtues concerned with external goods also avoid a vice of deficiency, by avoiding a stable minimalist plan. If I refuse to compromise my own views by adapting them to other people's, I might cultivate indifference to honour, and to other people's opinion. Aristotle's virtuous person, however, rejects these attitudes as vices. The virtuous person is not so indifferent to honour that he withdraws from competitions for honour altogether. Nor is he indifferent to wealth; he wants it for the practice of generosity, but also to secure other pleasures and honours. He does not cultivate such independence of other people's opinions that he never gets angry with them, and never wants to be pleasant to them; such reduced concern for external goods is a vice of deficiency.

To justify the virtuous person's attitude, Aristotle must argue that the external goods are, or are means to, genuine goods, and that the extent of genuine goods is not determined by the range of a particular person's rational desires. A rational agent has reason to be concerned with himself as a source of capacities capable of realization; and his good consists in the realization of his capacities. This normative conception of the good requires external goods, if some worthwhile capacities cannot be realized without them.

Wealth and honour are resources for the development of someone's capacities. If I attend only to basic necessities, I am 'vulgar' or 'menial' (*banausos*) and slavish; and virtuous people should have more wealth than this, since surplus wealth is useful for virtuous actions.[22] Similarly, a position of trust or responsibility allows me to extend my interests and realize my capacities in ways I otherwise could not; and to win such a position I need honour and reputation. If I care about this, I cannot be indifferent to other people's good opinion of me.

To see that these are worthwhile capacities, I must regard myself as a natural organism with a body and non-rational mental states. The human form is rational agency in a human rational soul that also includes perceptual and nutritive capacities. The conditions that make a person flourish as a biological organism and as a creature with sensory and appetitive states will be among those that a wise person values for his self-realization and the fulfilment of his function.

Moreover, the conception of my good that demands more external goods also develops rational agency further. If I form only the plans that assume a very low level of external goods, I renounce any effort at rational control over my possession of external goods above that level, and over the activities that depend on possession of more external goods. My relation to external goods affects my life anyhow; and if I give up efforts to control it above a minimum level, I contract the scope of my rational agency. Even though my rational control over external goods is incomplete, I need not leave them to chance. If I plan for more activities and contingencies, and do not meet them with indifference or resignation, I realize my rational agency further and make more of my life the expression of my rational agency.

It is wrong, therefore, to appeal to the importance of stability as a reason for minimalist plans. If my character expresses very little of me, then even if it is stable, its stability does not guarantee a stable object of appropriate self-concern; concern for a stable character that expresses a mere fragment of myself is not proper concern for myself. If minimalist planners argue against a more expansive plan by appeal to the dangers resulting from it, then they are moved by fear, not by a correct conception of themselves.

Courage, temperance, and the virtues concerned with external goods all seek the full realization of rational agency in a human life that is fully controlled by it. The 'complete life' that Aristotle demands for a happy person must include a complete range of human activities under the complete control of practical reason. Such completeness does not mean that my life must include every possible human activity, or that practical reason must control it entirely. It means that the activities must include enough to realize the appropriate range of human capacities, and that practical reason must control them to the full extent that is compatible with their appropriate range. Though these demands for completeness do not supply an exact criterion, they rule out minimalist plans.

207. THE DEFENCE OF COMMON BELIEFS

So far, Aristotle's ethical theory relies on arguments ultimately resting on first philosophy, and in particular on his account of the human essence. To this extent the account of the virtues relies on more than pure dialectic. Still, the account does not cease to be dialectical; for he tries to explain and justify the most important common beliefs about the virtues by showing how they should be understood in the light of a true account of a human being's essence and good.

To confirm this claim it will be useful to list the common beliefs and to remind ourselves of Aristotle's explanation of them.

1. We believe that virtue is a stable condition of a person, not the sort of thing that we forget or easily change (1100b11–17). Our belief is justified because a rational agent has proper self-concern for himself as a stable agent with relatively fixed states of character, and therefore has reason to cultivate states that are as stable as the virtues are normally thought to be.

2. We believe in some general way that virtue is distinctively guided by correct reason (1103b31–4). At first sight, correct reason seems no more characteristic of virtue than of prudent, calculating vice that relies on correct instrumental reasoning. But Aristotle argues that the virtuous person correctly values himself as a rational agent, and forms his conception of the end by thinking of himself as a rational agent, not a mere instrument for satisfying his non-rational desires. The virtuous person is therefore distinctively guided by correct reason.

3. We believe that some of the virtues are essentially virtues of character acquired by habituation (1103a14–18). We might reach this belief by observing the training normally required for a virtue; but Aristotle's theory supports the belief by appeal to the role of virtue in a rational agent. Habituation is needed because virtue must harmonize a person's non-rational desires with her rational conception of her ends; and habituation should produce a persistent habit, because virtue has to be stable and persistent.

4. Aristotle's doctrine of the mean rests on the common and apparently truistic belief that some virtues require us to strike the right area on a continuum where both excess and deficiency are possible (1104a11–27, 1106b5–16). This seems plausible for the training of such feelings as anger and fear, where some quantitative model seems

suitable, but less plausible as an account of every virtue of character; hence common sense has no name for some of the mean and extreme states that Aristotle claims to discover (1125b17–18).[23] His theory, however, gives a general reason for thinking that the mean will apply to each virtuous state of character. The virtuous person will not regard his practical reason as a mere instrument for the satisfaction of other desires, and hence he will avoid the vice of excess. On the other hand he will not make stability his only aim, and hence he will avoid the vice of deficiency.[24] That is why Aristotle can supply more precise instructions for finding the mean state in cases where common sense cannot identify one; the precision results from the account of the virtuous person's aim.

5. Common sense sees some connexion between the virtue of F, being a good F, and performing the function of F (1106a15–24). The connexion is easy to see for artifacts and for things designed or used for a purpose; but if human virtues simply reflect the functions that a human being may be used for (as citizen, soldier, parent, etc.), they will not thereby realize his nature as human being. Aristotle seeks to show that the virtues of character fulfil a person's function in a stronger sense than the commonsense analogies make clear; for he argues that a human being's essential function is realized by the virtues of character, because they 'complete' us in the right way (1103a23–6). Common sense sees the connexion between the recognized virtues and functions, and between essential function and eudaimonic virtue; Aristotle completes common sense by arguing for a connexion between essential function and the recognized virtues. He argues that the essential human function requires the rational, stable states of character that common sense already recognizes as virtues of character.

Hence the account of the virtues follows the same line of argument that we found in the account of the good. Aristotle relies on his metaphysical theory of essence as form and function, and on his psychological theory of the human function as rational agency; and he uses these theories to organize, explain, defend, and modify common beliefs. In doing this he shows that his ethical theory is not purely dialectical, but counts as strong dialectic.

18

THE GOOD OF OTHERS

208. ALTRUISM AND THE MORAL VIRTUES

The Aristotelian virtues of character are moral virtues, in so far as they are all concerned with the fine, and therefore with the good of others. Some virtues, especially friendship and justice, make this concern clear and explicit.[1] If these moral virtues are eudaimonic virtues, Aristotle must show why the rational person will develop the moral virtues.

This task is formidable if we begin with a purely conative account of happiness; for we seem to be able to conceive a rational agent with a rational plan for his own life that includes no intrinsic concern for the good of others. If his good just consists in the fulfilment of his rational desires, and these need not include any intrinsic concern for the good of others, the moral virtues are not essential for his good.

Aristotle, however, identifies our good with the realization of our capacities as rational agents, and is therefore free to claim that a rational agent may fulfil a mistaken rational plan that fails to realize his good as a rational agent. He agrees with the critics of conventional morality who demand to be shown that a moral virtue is also a eudaimonic virtue, and thinks their demand can be met if we have the right conception of happiness.

If the final good is self-sufficient, it must, in Aristotle's view, include the good not only of the agent himself, but also of family, friends, and fellow-citizens, since a human being is political by nature (*EN* 1097b8–11). At this stage Aristotle does not defend his claim that a complete and self-sufficient good must extend beyond the agent. But he does not forget that it needs defence; for he argues that friends are needed for a self-sufficient life. He recognizes that someone might argue that since the happy person is self-sufficient, he has no need of friends (1169b3–8). But he replies that the happy person is self-sufficient, not by being sufficient all by himself, but because he has a complete and self-sufficient life, which must include friends.

If, then, for the blessedly happy person, being is choiceworthy, since it is naturally good and pleasant, and if the being of his friend is closely similar to his own, then the friend will also be choiceworthy. Whatever is choiceworthy for him he must possess, since otherwise he will to that extent lack something. Anyone who is to be happy, then, must have excellent friends. (1170b14–19)

Aristotle assumes that his normative account of the good justifies his claims about friendship.

This normative account implies that the virtuous person loves herself as she really is, as a rational agent with a stable character that accords primacy to practical reason in the choice of ends. We tend to think that highly developed self-love will be selfish, and hence that concern for others requires some self-sacrifice; but Aristotle argues that we are wrong, because correct self-love does not allow selfishness, and proper concern for others does not require self-sacrifice.

209. FRIENDSHIP AND ALTRUISM

The virtuous person's attitude to his virtuous friend is the same as his attitude to himself, since he is his own friend (1166a1–2, a29–b2). The virtuous person does what he does for his own sake (1166a16), and wishes good to a virtuous friend for the friend's own sake (1156b7–12), for the sake of the friend himself. We have already discussed the virtuous person's attitude, in trying to understand his concern for himself. We should now re-examine it, to see why Aristotle demands it in the best sort of friendship.

The starting-point is dialectical. Aristotle accepts the common belief (*phasi*) that friendship involves altruism, and active goodwill, which requires concern for the friend for the friend's own sake (1155b31–4). But in his treatment of the common belief, he appeals openly and with surprising results to his own metaphysical outlook. In his view, and contrary to common sense, only the virtuous person takes the attitude proper to genuine and complete (*teleia*, 1156b7) friendship. Only the virtuous person is concerned for the friend for the friend's own sake, because only he is concerned for the friend 'in himself' (*kath'hauton*; cf. 1156a10–11), 'because of himself' (*di'hauton*, 1156b10), and 'in so far as he is who he is' (1156a17–18).[2]

We might be surprised at this intrusion of Aristotelian metaphysics into the apparently straightforward commonsense demand for altruism. Aristotle understands 'for his own sake' with the emphasis on 'his own' so that it means 'for the sake of his essence'. But we might think we have properly altruistic concern if we simply count the other person's own desire for some good as providing a reason in itself, apart from any self-confined concern of ours, for trying to get that good for him. This commonsense understanding of 'for his own sake' is a form of 'simple altruism' that implies none of the Aristotelian metaphysics of essence and coincident; and we might conclude that the 'metaphysical altruism' described by Aristotle is a gratuitous addition.[3]

If, on the other hand, simple altruism is focused on the other person's desires, it may not be the right sort of concern. Even a purely conative account of a person's good challenges simple altruism. If Al thinks of himself as a temporally extended rational agent for whom he has rational concern, Ann's simple altruism towards him may be bad for him; for if she simply tries to get him what he wants, she may get him something that he ought to refuse if he considered his other desires more carefully. If Ann is really concerned for Al's interest, she will need more than simple altruism; she must distinguish the desires that express the interest of Al himself from those that do not.

Aristotle has a still stronger argument against simple altruism, since he rejects a purely conative account of the good, and argues that a person's good is determined by his function and essence, by the sort of being he essentially is. Our altruistic actions will be morally reliable only if they are informed by metaphysical altruism. If friendship should be concerned with the friend himself and with his own good, we have no escape from metaphysical altruism.

Aristotle regards a stable character as the appropriate object of a rational person's concern for her continuing self; and similarly, the best kind of friendship, expressing concern for the other person herself, must include concern for her character. If she had no stable character, our concern for her would have to be rather generalized and indeterminate. We could assume very little about her future desires, and therefore we could do very little to promote their satisfaction; we would be restricted to some very general concern for the sorts of resources that might be necessary for every rational agent. Such generalized concern hardly supports the specific concern for a particular person's aims that we expect in friendship. Concern that ignores a person's character is not clearly concern for the person himself, and, as Aristotle says, it is friendship with that particular person only coincidentally. Metaphysics is needed to tell us what the person himself is, and hence to tell us what attitude is appropriate for genuine friendship.

210. SELF-LOVE AND ALTRUISM

Aristotle must justify the extension of the virtuous person's self-love to someone else.[4] He argues that the right sort of self-love requires love for a friend because the friend is another self.

> The excellent person is related to his friend in the same way as he is related to himself, since a friend is another self; and therefore, just as his own being is choiceworthy for him, the friend's being is choiceworthy for him in the same or a similar way. We agreed that someone's own being is choiceworthy because he

perceives that he is good, and this sort of perception is pleasant in itself. He must, then, perceive his friend's being ⟨together with his own⟩, and he will do this if they live together and share rational discourse (*logos*) and thought. For in the case of human beings, living together seems to consist in this sharing of rational discourse and thought, and not, as in the case of grazing animals, in sharing the same pasture. (1170b5–14)

Being 'another self' is distinctive of friendship, as opposed to mutual admiration or goodwill; but what does it involve?[5]

Rational discourse and thought are characteristic of the shared life of the best type of friends, because each loves the other for what he essentially is, and each of them is essentially his reasoning and thinking part. My thought and deliberation belong to myself in so far as they are connected with each other in the structure of wish, deliberation, and decision that expresses my conception of happiness. My actions belong to myself in so far as they are the products (and also to some extent the causes) of the same structure of wish, deliberation, and decision.

In so far as I treat my friend as I treat myself, my reasoning and thinking are related to his reasoning, thinking, and action in the same way as they are related to mine. We share the same goals and the same conception of happiness, since each of us wants the good of the other as part of his own good; we cooperate in deliberation, decision, and action; and the thoughts and actions of each provide reasons for the future thoughts and actions of the other.

Aristotle claims that this mutual attitude of friends involves concord and goodwill. Concord requires friends to share the same views on important questions about benefit and harm (1167b4–9). Since the good person is in concord with himself, and he regards his friend as another self, he will also be in concord with his friend. Concord does not imply that two virtuous friends will immediately give the same answer when asked, or that each will automatically defer to the other; for this is not the good person's attitude to himself either. Concord implies an extra participant in rational deliberation, and hence further considerations to take into account; it does not involve conflict or compromise between competing interests.

Goodwill explains why there is no competition in a friendship between virtuous people. The virtuous person is concerned with the friend's good for the friend's own sake; if Al is Ann's friend, he wishes good to Ann for Ann's own sake, not just as a means to his own good (1167a10–14; cf. 1155b31–4). Al cares about himself for his own sake, not merely as a means to anyone else's interest; and so he sees that the same treatment of Ann will involve caring about her for her own sake, since she is another rational agent who counts for Al in the way Al counts for himself.

Once we agree with Aristotle that friendship requires goodwill and concord, and that the virtuous person has friends, we can agree that self-love and altruism do not necessarily conflict as they are popularly supposed to (ix 8). The virtuous person values himself as a rational agent; hence he values his own rational plans and choices; these include other-regarding plans and choices; hence the fulfilment of his self-love requires concern for others.

211. THE DEFENCE OF FRIENDSHIP

We may grant, then, that if the virtuous person is rationally justified in having friends, his concern for them is part of the virtuous action that is a part of his happiness. But why should we grant the antecedent of the conditional? Aristotle suggests that it is choiceworthy (*haireton*) for me to be aware of my friend's actions, in the same way as it is for me to be aware of my own. But why is it *more* choiceworthy to be aware of his actions than simply to be aware of my own?[6]

Aristotle argues that a human life of conscious perception and thought is good and pleasant in itself for a human being, and will seem so to a virtuous person. If Al treats Ann as another Al, then Ann's perception and thought will be as good and pleasant as Al's own perception and thought are to Al (1170b5–10). A rational agent with the correct self-concern chooses to realize himself as a rational agent; he prefers more self-realization to less. If Al has Ann as a friend, and cares about Ann for her own sake, just as he cares about himself, then Al will realize himself more fully than if he had no friend; hence friendship will be part of his good.

If Al is virtuous, he is concerned with himself as a rational agent, and values his states of character as expressions of his rational agency. He has reason to take the same attitude to Ann's states of character, if he can regard them as expressions of his rational agency. Friends share rational activity; and the resulting concord in rational deliberation and decision ensures that each friend's deliberation will affect the actions of the other and the joint actions of both. In so far as Al realizes more capacities as a rational agent in this friendship with Ann, he has reason to recognize this friendship as part of his good.

Friendship promotes self-realization through the different causal roles of friends. Ann's (Al's) help may allow Al (Ann) to do something he (she) could not otherwise have done (if, e.g., Ann (Al) thinks of a way for him (her) to realize his (her) ambition to sail across the Atlantic). On other occasions their mutual aid may help both of them to do together something that neither of them could have done separately. Aristotle notices these different functions of friends when he remarks that our friends allow us to be more continuously active; to develop virtue (1170a4–13); and to act in cooperation (1171b29–1172a8). In each of these ways friendship allows the realization of capacities that would otherwise be unrealized. Al can value what Ann does because he regards Ann as another Al, and Ann's actions realize his own rational agency.

Friendship most fully promotes self-realization if and only if Al wishes Ann's good for Ann's own sake; for then he has many opportunities for rational action, in the goals and interests he would otherwise lack. If he cares only about his own condition, he will not care if Ann breaks her leg, unless that results in some further harm for him; and so he will not care about helping her when she is hurt or about helping her to avoid doing it. These areas of rational activity will be of no interest to him. If he cares about her for her own sake, he will want to cooperate with her on occasions that would otherwise be indifferent to him. If he wants her part of a joint enterprise to succeed, he will do more than he would have been willing to do if his concern had been self-confined. Someone who can form the best type of friendship opens for himself occasions for self-realization that would otherwise be closed to him.

This friendship must involve virtuous people. For they will be reliably and correctly concerned for themselves as rational agents, and therefore will see the possibilities of self-realization opened in the best friendship. They will not be tempted by false notions about their good to betray a friend, or to exploit her without regard for her interest, for some benefit to themselves. When each friend knows this about the character of the other, suspicion or caution will not prevent joint activities that realize the capacities of each. Moreover, if each is virtuous, they will decide and act in concord, on the same projects; they will not waste their time in antagonism, conflict, and compromise.

The cooperative aspects of the best kind of friendship promote self-realization by forming a complete life. Aristotle claims that without this friendship our lives are not complete and self-sufficient (1169b3–10, 1170b14–19); and the reasons for demanding external goods are equally good reasons for requiring friendship. We explained why each of the apparently self-regarding virtues is a eudaimonic virtue, by showing why it is part of a complete life for a rational agent. When we saw what such a life requires, we could see why the virtuous person is justified in pursuing a way of life that makes more than the minimal demands for external goods.[7] By planning for the use of external goods he extends his rational control into areas that otherwise he would leave uncontrolled by his rational agency. Though rational agency cannot guarantee the supply of these external goods, it is still reasonable to plan for their use. The best kind of friendship is reasonable in the same way, since it extends the aspects of our lives that are subject to control by practical reason.

In Aristotle's view many aspects of my welfare are subject to fortune and external conditions, because there are genuine goods that I cannot control by practical reason. Cooperation makes some of these subject to our joint efforts. I need not rely on chance or mutual advantage to find financial aid if I have bad luck. The service provided by a friend is good for me not simply because it provides me with something I want, but also because it allows me to count on having the material resources I need, and therefore allows me to make rational plans for aspects of my life that I would otherwise have to leave to chance. For these purposes it does not matter if in fact chance is favourable (1169b7–8); I still have a reason to want to control those aspects of my life, as far as I can, by rational agency, and hence I have reason to want virtuous friends.

212. THE FRIEND AS ANOTHER SELF

These benefits of friendship are relevant, however, only if we can reasonably regard friends as other selves. Aristotle argues that Al will enjoy and value Ann's rational activity of perception and thought as he values and enjoys his own; but how is this possible? Aristotle answers that if Al can regard Ann as another Al, he has no reason not to take the same pleasure in Ann's activities as he takes in his own. His valuing of Al's activities is valuing of those activities as done by Al; and so when they are done by Ann, another Al, Al also values them as Al's activities.

Can Al justifiably regard Ann as another Al in the strong sense that is needed for the conclusion? We might argue that 'Al' is a proper name with a singular reference to one particular—Al himself—and not shorthand for a definite description designating a shareable set of properties—'person with Al-type characteristics'. If we understand that Al is the particular referent of the proper name 'Al', then Ann cannot be in any strict sense another Al. In calling Ann another Al, Al perhaps means nothing more than that he shows to her the goodwill he shows to himself; and surely this falls some way short of the conclusion Aristotle needs.

We might say, for instance, that Al is the human essence as instantiated in this piece of matter, from this egg and sperm, born at this time, and so on; but this conception of particular substances and their essences is inadequate. Continuous human functioning in the same bit of remote matter is not sufficient for the persistence of the same human being, if his traits of character become too radically and suddenly different. A person's essence has to consist in the traits of character that are his determinate ways of embodying rational agency. But these determinate traits are logically repeatable; we might find a Socrates in two different bits of matter.[8]

Once we recognize distinct essences corresponding to different people with different character-traits, we still need not say that 'Socrates' is simply the name of a universal, of determinate traits that are embodied in the son of Sophroniscus but can logically belong to several Socrateses. We can say that only one Socrates is logically possible, because Socrates must have not only the traits that are Socratic, but also a definite spatio-temporal position, associating him with one piece of matter as opposed to others.

If Al loves himself, he does not value simply his spatio-temporal uniqueness; and he does not attend simply to the rational agency that he shares with other human beings. He loves himself as the agent who has developed human capacities in this determinate way to form these determinate states of character. If he is a virtuous person Al does not love his character.for its idiosyncrasies; the fact that it is different from anyone else's because of his particular tastes and circumstances is not in itself a reason for loving or valuing it. Al loves himself since he loves his character as a particular correct way of realizing human capacities in rational agency.

Al's friend Ann is not another Al in the way that a clone of Al might be. She has her own idiosyncrasies that are different from Al's. But Al can still regard her as another Al in so far as she has the same correct realization of the human capacities that results in virtuous traits of character. Ann is another Al in so far as she has what Al loves about himself; these virtues are necessary, though not sufficient, for Al's being the person he is. Al sees in Ann the traits of character of the very same type as those that justify him in loving himself. To be another Al Ann need not be a replica of Al; she simply needs to replicate him far enough to have traits with the properties that make Al's traits lovable to himself. Al's traits are formed by his own deliberation and decision; and when Al and Ann are friends, each contributes in the same way to forming the traits of the other. They have the same reasons for loving each other that they have for loving themselves.[9]

We have appealed, then, to the connexion Aristotle sees between a person's good and the exercise of practical reason. From this we can see how he justifies the best type of friendship as a component of a rational agent's happiness, and why he insists so strongly on a common life, and on shared rational agency, as a crucial part of such a friendship. Aristotle can defend himself, not merely from common sense, but from his general views about the human essence and rational agency. Hence this crucial element of Aristotelian ethics can be defended as part of a systematic moral theory resting on metaphysical and psychological support. Here we are not inventing a defence for Aristotle. In his account of friendship he sees that we must consider it 'from the point of view of nature' (1167b29, 1170a13). He relies on claims about human nature and about realization of capacities; and we have seen that these claims are crucial in his normative conception of the good and of happiness.

213. EXTENDED ALTRUISM AND THE MORAL VIRTUES

The friendship of virtuous people requires highly developed altruistic concerns; but the concerns extend to very few people. We may think that the sort of altruism required by justice and the other virtues of character is so different from the sort required by friendship that we need a different account for these other virtues. Aristotle, however, seems to offer no defence of the other-regarding aspects of the virtues beyond the defence of friendship; and so he seems to face a serious difficulty in justifying them.

The case of justice shows how serious the difficulty is. For Aristotle accepts the general view, stated by Thrasymachus in the *Republic*, that justice is another's good (*Rep.* 343c3–5). He must reject Thrasymachus' further point, that justice is harmful to the just agent. For if justice is a genuine virtue, the just person must choose just action for its own sake; and since the fully just person is also wise, the wise person must choose just action for its own sake. The wise person deliberates well, so that he reaches a true conception of his happiness, and of the actions that achieve it; if justice is a virtue he must include just action as the sort of action in which his happiness consists. If justice essentially benefits others, the wise person must believe that benefiting others is a good in itself that partly constitutes his happiness.

Aristotle's theory does not explain why the wise person will believe this about justice, unless his defence of friendship suggests an explanation of the extended altruism needed for justice. Extended altruism will be intelligible if the reasons that justify the concerns of friendship also justify the wider concerns of justice and the other virtues.

214. THE EXTENSION OF FRIENDSHIP

The best type of friendship holds only between a few, highly selected, and untypical people. Aristotle insists very strongly that it must be a relation between only a few people who are all virtuous, who know each other well, and who can spend a good part of their lives in shared activities (ix 10). This sort of friendship is contrasted with 'political friendship', the friendship for fellow-citizens, which we can have for many people; 'because of virtue and because of themselves it is not possible towards many, and we must be satisfied to find even a few with such characters' (1171a19–20).

If political friendship is to support justice, it must extend beyond the limited circle of complete friends.[10] On the other hand, it must be distinguished from the general attitude of mere goodwill, which we can feel to others with no desire to help them or to put ourselves out for them (1167a7–10). Such goodwill cannot support political friendship and justice; for these require the positive desire to help that need not result from mere goodwill.

If political friendship supports the just person's concern for just action for its own sake, it must involve concern for the friend for the friend's own sake. Only complete friendship seems to justify such intrinsic concern for the other; and political friendship cannot be complete friendship. Still, complete friendship may help us to understand the basis of the intrinsic concern found in other relations. For some of the features of complete friendship are present in other relations to a degree that justifies the sort of intrinsic concern that Aristotle assumes.

The first reason for believing that complete friendship may help to explain other friendships appears in Aristotle's account of friendship within families. The child counts as his parent's 'other self' because of their family connexion (1161b27–9). Since the child is the parent's other self, the parent is intrinsically concerned with the child's welfare, not simply with the parent's own pleasure or advantage (1159a28–33, 1166a2–6). These are the attitudes characteristic of the best friendship between virtuous people.

The parent and child bound by such ties, however, need not be virtuous people. The virtuous friend is 'another self' because he is a virtuous person, sharing the aims and pleasures of his friend because they are both virtuous. The child, by contrast, is another self, and therefore a proper object of intrinsic concern, because he is dependent on the parent and his character is formed by the parent, expressing the parent's own aims. It follows that intrinsic concern for another person does not presuppose that she is virtuous.[11] A parent extends himself and the scope of his practical reason through his relation to his child; and for this reason his natural attachment to the child produces an element of his own good.

Friendship is extended in another direction, through a 'nameless' virtue of character that is similar to friendship, but lacks the right affective features (1126b20–5). (Let us call it 'friendliness'.) This virtue resembles the best kind of friendship, in so far as the friendly person does what is expected of a virtuous friend, and his attitude to others does not rest on consideration of his own pleasure or advantage. Aristotle does not explain this attitude; but the account of complete friendship may explain it.

Friendliness is displayed in social intercourse and common life (1126b11–12), to all fellow-citizens, whether or not they happen to be friends or relatives or acquaintances (1126b25–8). A fellow-citizen may not be a virtuous person, and therefore may not be another self in the way one virtuous person is for another. Nor does the virtuous person share his life with a mere fellow-citizen to the extent he shares it with a virtuous friend. But if the fellow-citizen is virtuous enough to share some similar aims, the virtuous person can extend his practical reason in the same way as with a virtuous friend.

The basis of the best friendship is the virtuous person's ability to take the sort of interest in someone else that allows him to extend his own concerns, and so to realize capacities that would otherwise be left unrealized. In the best kind of friendship Al knows Ann well, knows what she wants, knows she is virtuous, knows that she knows about him what he knows about her, and knows that she has the same desire for his welfare that he has for hers. All these facts make it easy for each to have intrinsic concern for the other, and make the extent of the concern necessarily wider than in other cases; the more Al knows about what Ann wants and the more he agrees with it, the more he will want to do for her; and his concern for Bert, whom he sees on the bus each day, or for Curt, who occasionally passes him in the street, will be narrower.

Still, the reasons that allow Al to be concerned about Ann may also apply to Bert and Curt to some extent. If Al knows that they are virtuous people and shares their virtuous aims, knows of ways to cooperate with them, and can share in their deliberation, then he has reason to be interested in their aims as in his own. Since their aims are virtuous, he approves of them, and can affect them by his own rational planning and deliberation. If they all know this about each other, they will be able to make plans and enter cooperative schemes that would be too risky if each believed that neither of the others had any intrinsic concern for the welfare of each of the others.

215. THE POLITICAL COMMUNITY AND THE HUMAN GOOD

To understand the extension of altruistic concern that results in justice, we must now consider the distinctive role that Aristotle attributes to the *polis*, the political community. For the primary concern of justice is the good of the political community (1129b17–19); and if rational agents have good reason to be concerned about the good of the political community, they have good reason to extend their altruistic concern in the particular direction that leads to justice and to the choice of just action for its own sake.

The *Ethics* identifies the final good as the object of the supreme science, the end that includes the ends of the other sciences; and political science has the all-inclusive end because it prescribes the proper pursuit of all the other sciences (1094a26–b7). The *Politics* claims that the most controlling and all-inclusive community aims at the most controlling good (1252a1–6), which is the final good, happiness. The city is the all-inclusive community, of which the other communities are parts, since it aims at advantage not merely for some present concern but for the whole of life (*EN* 1160a9–30). Since happiness is complete and self-sufficient, the city is a 'complete community' (*Pol.* 1252b28) aiming at a complete and self-sufficient life (1252b27–30, 1280b29–35). It is self-sufficient in so far as it includes all the goods that are needed for a happy life (1256b2–10, 26–39, 1257a28–30, 1326b2–11).[12] It is 'a particular kind of community of similar people, for the sake of the best possible life' (1328a35–7).[13]

Aristotle argues for the completeness of the city by presenting it as the natural goal and completion of the smaller human communities. He compares the city to the full-grown plant or animal that is the goal of its earlier stages (1252b30–4); and so he supports his view that a human being is naturally political (1253a1–7). Though people need not have had any conscious conception of their happiness, their inarticulate search for happiness has rightly led them to form cities (1252a26–34, b15–16, 27–30). The initial motive for more than a temporary union is safety (1252a30–1); concern for more than short-term interest leads to the village (1252b16); and the desire for happiness leads eventually to the city that is formed for the sake of living, but remains in being for the sake of living well (1252b29–30, 1278b20–5).

The analogy with natural growth is useful only within limits. We might agree that the mature oak is the natural completion of the acorn and the sapling, because it gets no bigger than its mature, natural size. Aristotle cannot use this argument, since he admits that the city is not the largest community.[14] He might argue that an animal may grow beyond its natural size; if we say it is too big, we have some conception of the proper functions and activities that are the final cause of normal growth and are impeded by excessive growth (1256b31–9, 1326b2–11).[15]

If Aristotle appeals to this conception of natural growth, he must identify the appropriate functions and activities of the city, and show that these complete human happiness, so that no further community supplies a further part of happiness.[16] He relies on his conclusion in the *Ethics*, that human happiness requires the sorts of activities that fully realize human capacities; he should show why the city, not some narrower or wider community, realizes them.

He repeats his claim in the *Ethics* that a human being is naturally political (*EN* 1097b8–11, 1169b16–19), but now gives a new reason, that a human being is the only animal capable of rational discourse.[17] Other animals have voice, which is a sign of what is pleasant or painful (*Pol.* 1253a8–12):

for their nature has gone as far as having perception of what is pleasant or painful and of signifying this to each other. But rational discourse is for making clear what is expedient or harmful, and hence what is just or unjust. For this is special to human beings in comparison with the other animals, that they are the only ones with a perception of good and evil, and of just and unjust, and so on; and it is community in these that produces a household and a city. (1253a12–18)[18]

Aristotle claims that awareness of good and evil is an essential capacity of a human being, and hence that the realization of this capacity is part of a human being's good; but why would rational communication between enemies and rivals not be a sufficient realization of the capacity? Aristotle needs to show that a human being's essential capacities are fully realized only in cooperative communication about what is beneficial and just.

The good of complete friendship with another virtuous person consists in awareness of his virtuous life and character, which requires living together and sharing rational discourse and thought (*EN* 1170b10–14).[19] The *Politics* suggests that the rational discourse and thought should be about what is beneficial and just; such communication essentially contributes to the virtuous person's self-realization, because it extends the scope of his practical reason and deliberation beyond his own life and activities.

Each of the communities Aristotle considers is more comprehensive than the previous one. A marriage is 'for every day' (*Pol.* 1252b13), and a village is formed for 'intercourse for more than a day' (1252b16).[20] Marriage is characteristic of human beings, because it includes communication about the beneficial and just; unlike animals that simply mate with the unconscious end of reproduction (1252a26–30), human beings have foresight (1252a31–2), and consider the rest of their lives (*EN* 1162a19–24). The village is more comprehensive than the household, both in time and in scope; it is not limited by the lifetime of individuals, and it can make plans that would be pointless for individuals or temporary associations. Since the city is comprehensive, seeking to plan for everything that is needed for the complete good, a rational agent has good reason to want to share in its deliberations.

This argument implies that a virtuous person does not value the city simply because of its general concern with the expedient (cf. *EN* 1160a9–14). Aristotle suggests that essentially political activities are themselves part of the complete and happy life. If the city provides only the instrumental resources needed for a complete and happy life, it is not clear why the virtuous person values just action for its own sake.[21] Aristotle's explanation of the good of friendship allows him the sort of argument he needs for the intrinsic goodness of essentially political activity.

216. POLITICAL ACTIVITY

It is important to decide whether or not this is Aristotle's consistent view in the *Politics*. If he ascribes intrinsic value to political activities, then some institutional and constitutional arrangements that might seem to raise only questions of efficiency will in fact be open to another kind of evaluation. We might think that in deciding how many citizens should take what sort of part in government, we need only consider the instrumental function of one or another arrangement, and need only ask how efficiently it secures some benefit that is its causal result. But if a particular sort of political activity is itself part of the human good, then the argument for its presence in a city cannot be purely instrumental, and we need not, and should not, defend it on purely instrumental grounds.

Aristotle argues against a restricted instrumental function for the state—safety, or mutual protection, or the safeguarding of what justly belongs to each person (cf. 1280b8–23). These aims might explain an association 'for the sake of staying alive'; but they do not explain why there should be a permanent association for the sake of living well. For 'even when they have no need of help from each other they nonetheless want to live together' (1278b20–1). Living together (*suzên*) is to be valued for itself, apart from any instrumental benefit; and if this claim is to be relevant to the city, the city's specific form of living together and sharing in reason and thought must be intrinsically valuable.

The end of the city cannot be simply living together. Friendship is 'the decision to live together' (1280b38–9), and we can live together by forming groups smaller than a city (1280b36–9).

The end of the city, then, is living well, and these ⟨smaller associations⟩ are for the sake of the end. A city is the association of families and villages in a complete and self-sufficient life. And this, we say, is living happily and finely. Hence we must take the political association to be for the sake of fine actions, and not for the sake of living together. (1280b39–1281a4)

'Living together' has different roles in different stages of this argument. First (1278b20–1) Aristotle points to living together to show that the state has more than a protective role. Later (1280b39–1281a4) he argues for an extended function for the city, by arguing that it cannot be confined to living together. His claims are consistent if we distinguish living together in general, which is secured by the smaller associations, from the particular form of living together that requires the political association.

This second form of living together involves sharing in deliberation and choice about the beneficial and the just; and in so far as this shared activity is essential to the city, a more restricted conception of its function cannot be correct. When Aristotle, therefore, contrasts fine actions with living together, he ought to say that he contrasts one form of living together with another. He claims that living together in the smaller communities aims at happiness, and so aims at the complete community that is the city (1280b39–40).[22]

The view that political activity is merely instrumental to fine actions conflicts with Aristotle's argument for treating some people as parts of the city and excluding others.

But in fact the city is not for the sake of simply living, but for living well. For otherwise slaves and the other animals could belong to a city, whereas in fact they do not, because they have no share in happiness or in living in accordance with decision. (1280a31–4)

Instrumental means to happiness are not parts of the life of the city, and those wholly concerned with them are, to that extent, not parts of the city.[23]

This argument would be unconvincing if the city simply provided resources for living well; in that case anyone who could contribute efficiently to the provision of these resources would have a claim to membership in the city. Aristotle's argument for the exclusion of slaves and animals does not claim that they are useless to the city. Their inability to live according to decision incapacitates them for happiness; and if this is a ground for excluding them from political activity, Aristotle must assume that political activity itself is part of happiness.

Aristotle confirms this in Book vii, in his description of the ideal state.

The citizens must live neither a menial nor a commercial life; for such a life is base, and contrary to virtue. Nor must those who are to be citizens be farmers; for they need leisure both to develop virtue and to perform political actions. (1328b39–1329a2)

If political actions themselves were purely instrumental to some further goal, a life including them would be unleisured, and so inappropriate for the citizen of the ideal state. In requiring a life suitable for the practice of virtue and political action, Aristotle must assume that such a life includes constituents of happiness within itself. The sort of work that is dismissed as ignoble is the sort that does not require the exercise of virtue (1258b38–9), whereas the life that exercises the virtues in political activity is taken to realize the agent's good.

In describing the political life Aristotle assumes that the good depends on free cooperation of equal citizens in ruling each other (1325b3–14); this achieves the common happiness that is the aim of the community (1325a7–10, 1328a35–7). The attitude displayed here is characteristic of friends who care about the welfare of each other for their own sake; and the value of friendship explains the value of the citizen's life. Friends exercise their virtue in activity: 'for happiness is action, and moreover the actions of just and temperate people possess the end of many and fine things' (1325a32–4). In speaking of these actions as fine, and therefore good in themselves, Aristotle assumes that they achieve happiness non-instrumentally.[24]

217. THE COMPLETE COMMUNITY

If we have correctly understood this line of argument about the value of political activity, we will better understand Aristotle's further, and initially surprising, claim that the city is naturally prior to the individual just as the whole is prior to the parts; the parts are no longer what they were (e.g. hand, foot), except homonymously, once they are severed from the whole (1253a18–29). This claim about homonymy cannot be taken seriously for human beings, if it is supposed to imply that a person who is severed from a city or from his city is no longer the same person, no longer even a human being, except homonymously.

In support of his claim, however, Aristotle urges two weaker claims. First he says I am not self-sufficient in a separated condition (1253a26–7), but this claim cannot be true if 'self-sufficient' means just 'capable of survival'; for Aristotle knows that human beings can survive in smaller communities than cities. His claim is reasonable, however, if 'self-sufficient' means 'achieving my complete and self-sufficient good'; the city is necessary not for our survival, but for our happiness.[25] The second claim modifies the initial suggestion in the same way: 'Someone who is not capable of association, or because he is self-sufficient has no need of it, is no part of a city, so that he is either a beast or a god' (1253a27–9). A human being's nature, on this view, involves a capacity to belong to a city, not actually belonging to one.[26]

To defend this claim Aristotle will appeal again to his conception of human nature, and to the unique role of the city in fulfilling a human being's capacities. The weaker claims in this passage rest firmly on Aristotle's ethical theory, which rests on strong dialectic; but any strict analogy with other wholes and parts rests on an exaggeration that becomes clear once we examine Aristotle's own arguments. He is capable of misusing the conclusions of his own theory; but once the misuse is discounted, the theory still proves something important.

Aristotle, therefore, draws heavily on strong dialectic in his argument to show that the city is the complete community achieving the complete human good. His claims about its specific role in the realization of human capacities support his conception of the citizen and the qualifications for membership in the city. He argues that political activity is part of a human being's good, not merely instrumental to it, because it realizes the same capacities of rational agency that are realized in friendship. If we are persuaded that friendship is a desirable extension of rational agency, we should be persuaded that the city offers a further desirable extension.

The comprehensive character of the city gives a virtuous person reason to value it for its own sake, not simply because it is useful to him for other aims he already has. It extends the scope of practical reason and deliberation, as friendships do. Without the city I have to leave many aspects of my life to chance and external circumstances, since they will be out of my rational control. Protagoras indicated the dominance of chance over rational agency by remarking that we would be the prey of wild beasts (Plato, *Pr.* 322a8-b8). In Aristotle's view of the human good, this exposure to chance is not merely inconvenient, but a positive frustration of the rational agency characteristic of a human being. The virtuous person has reason to value the extension of rational agency in the city for its own sake, not simply because it allows him to plan more efficiently. He has the same reason to share in the deliberations of the city, not simply to take its benefits passively for granted; for what he values is not simply the services provided by the city, but the practical reason that is exercised in providing them.

This same comprehensive character of the city gives its virtuous citizens reason for intrinsic concern for each other. A virtuous person has reason to regard another virtuous person as another self in so far as he extends his own concerns and self-realization by sharing the virtuous aims of the other. If I know another person is a virtuous fellow-citizen, I know, without knowing anything else about him, that I have reason to regard him as another self; for I know that I share with him the virtuous aim of maintaining the comprehensive community of the city. In a friendship each of us cares about the other for his own sake, not just for his contribution to the good of the city; but our shared concern for the city gives each of us a reason for intrinsic concern for the other. The relation between fellow-citizens expresses, instead of simply facilitating, the extended concern and interest that realizes each person's capacities. That is why relations within a city are a part of each person's happiness, and not simply a means to it.[27]

Aristotle, therefore, can explain why a virtuous person with a true conception of his own happiness will also be just. To be just he must decide to do just actions for their own sake, because they are just, and not for some coincidental feature of them. The actions are just in so far as they benefit the community; the virtuous person is intrinsically concerned with action for the benefit of the community; and therefore he will be intrinsically concerned to do just actions. He will also be intrinsically concerned for the good of the other people who are benefited by the just actions; and for this reason too he will choose the just actions for their own sake. A city is not the only community whose members will see reason to do the actions that a just person does; but the city and the other communities resting on similar altruistic concerns will be the only ones in which people see reason to be just.[28]

The extension of altruistic concern to justice relies on the assumptions about rational agency that supported claims about friendship. Aristotle argues that friendship is necessary for the self-sufficiency of a complete life that secures a rational agent's good (*EN* 1170b17–19). Similarly, the city is the complete community, securing a complete and self-sufficient life. The same conception of the human essence and the human good that forms Aristotle's conception of the self-regarding virtues also supports his defence of friendship and justice. He does not concede the truth of Thrasymachus' charge that justice is another person's good and a harm to oneself; he argues that it is a good to oneself *because* it is another person's good, when the other person is a fellow-citizen. Nor does he simply rely on common beliefs to answer Thrasymachus; he relies on strong dialectic.

19

THE STATE

218. CONCEPTIONS OF THE STATE

Aristotle's account of how the political community promotes the human good supports an account of the ideal state, and of the way actual states fall short of it. For a correct conception of happiness shows how a particular type of state promotes the human good, and gives a virtuous person reason to care about it for its own sake; but it also shows what the right sort of state must be like, and why many states cannot make this claim on the virtuous person's concern.

To find the ideal state, and to decide the institutions and external conditions to be included in our description, we need some clearer conception of the composition of happiness.

For if this ⟨sc. the most choiceworthy⟩ life is unclear, the best political system is bound to be unclear also. For it is appropriate for those who have the best political system to do the best actions from what is available to them, if nothing unexpected happens. (*Pol.* 1323a16–19)[1]

The constitution is the way of life of the city (1295a39–b1); and the correct aim for the city will identify the correct constitution (1280b39–1281a4, 1323a14–19, 1328a37–b2).

A view about happiness forms the 'basic assumption' (*hupothesis*) of a political system (1317a39–b2; cf. 1271a39–b3).[2] Errors about happiness explain some of the characteristic errors of non–ideal states, and a correct conception is necessary for avoiding these errors.

Since happiness is the best thing, and it is a complete activity and exercise of virtue, and since it turns out that some people are capable of a share in this, and others are capable to a small extent or not at all, clearly this is the cause of the emergence of different types of cities and of a number of political systems. For since different people pursue happiness in different ways and by different means, they make their ways of life and political systems different also. (1328a37–b2)[3]

Even if people do not explicitly conceive the state as a community aiming at happiness, their conception of happiness influences their expectations of the state, and hence the errors that they make in forming political systems.

Aristotle suggests that most people take happiness to consist in a life of gratification of appetites or in a life of honour (*EN* 1095a19–23). These views share the assumption that happiness consists in, or requires, the unlimited accumulation of 'contested' external goods (1168b15–19). It follows that happiness appears to involve conflict and antagonism; we want a share of external goods that has no definite limit, and so threatens the share available to others. Hence the rich and the poor are in conflict. Since the rich want to get richer, the poor want to protect themselves from further impoverishment at the hands of the rich, and to enrich themselves at their expense.

While this conception of happiness already helps to explain the characteristics of non-ideal political systems, Aristotle also tries to attach a different conception to each of them. Oligarchs think happiness requires wealth, and that the state is a large business partnership for the accumulation and distribution of wealth. The rich are regarded as the large shareholders who put up the largest amount of capital for the enterprise; and hence it seems only reasonable that they should get the largest share of the profits (*Pol.* 1280a25–31).

In contrast with the oligarchic appeal to wealth, the basic assumption of democracy is freedom (1317a40–b17). Democrats argue that if people are equal in the one respect of being free rather than slaves, they are equal altogether, and should have an equal share in ruling (1280a24–5).[4] Freedom matters because happiness consists in gratification of our desires, and hence requires us to live as we wish; we achieve this best if no one rules us, and the next best is to take our turn in ruling and being ruled (1317b12–17).

Though the pursuit of gratification is the primary source of the oligarchic and democratic outlooks, the pursuit of honour is the source of competition even beyond what is needed to secure the resources needed for a life of gratification. Love of honour is traditionally characteristic of the Greek upper classes, and so Aristotle normally thinks of it as a motive for the few (1266b38–1267a2; cf. 1302a31, 1311a5–7), explaining the rivalries and competitions that may threaten an oligarchy, or encourage the pursuit of tyrannical power. The many, however, are also moved by honour. Though they are not eager to maximize their wealth, they want to protect it for their enjoyment; and similarly, though they are not eager to compete for honour, they will not easily put up with a dishonoured and slavish condition (cf. 1274a15–18, 1281b28–30). Competitive pursuit of honour in one class conflicts with aversion to dishonour in the other.

Aristotle argues that these mistaken conceptions of happiness explain much of what is wrong with the prevalent political systems. But he also intends them to support his conception of happiness, since it shows how they grasp part of the truth or result from an intelligible mistake. In Aristotle's view, honour and sensual gratification are genuine intrinsic goods; but the right sort of honour does not require competition for external goods, and the right extent of gratification does not require an unlimited supply of them. Virtuous action, which most people take to be at best an instrumental good (1271b6–10), is the primary constituent of happiness; and ignorance of this explains the mistaken classification of goods in different political systems.

Democrats turn out to be right to prefer a system in which all the citizens take turns in ruling and being ruled. But they are wrong to prefer it simply as a means to being left alone to gratify their desires as they please; for in fact political activity is an intrinsic good, part of the virtuous life. Once we find the right reason for valuing political activity, we find further reasons for disagreeing with the democratic belief in lax qualifications for citizenship and in minimal government.[5] Oligarchs are right to reject these lax qualifications, but they are wrong to make wealth the condition for citizenship, since they have the wrong view of the place of wealth in happiness. A correct view of happiness and its political consequences will allow us both to learn from these mistaken views and to correct their mistakes.

219. THE HUMAN GOOD AND THE CITIZEN

The requirements of Aristotelian happiness determine some of the conditions for citizenship. A rational agent wants to have the right character and to do the right actions himself, but also wants the characters and actions of other people to be appropriately related to his own. Happiness requires extended concern for people of equal virtue, and the virtuous person has this concern for friends, including fellow-citizens. Hence Aristotle often insists that citizens of the best city should be equal and similar, and that in general citizens should approximate to this relation (1277b7–16, 1325b7–10, 1332b12–41).[6]

On the other hand, friendship benefits me partly because it extends my concerns into the concerns of others. For this purpose it is important that friends should have different interests and concerns. Though I may not have time to be both a musician and an athlete myself, I will benefit from my concern with a friend's musical projects, and he will benefit from concern with my athletic projects. Since I cannot achieve a complete and self-sufficient life by myself, I need a city; and the city adds what I lack only if its different members contribute something different; I would not gain a self-sufficient and complete life if all of us were merely musicians or merely athletes (1261b10–15, 1263b29–35). If the city secures a happy life, it must secure it for individual citizens.[7] Citizens should therefore have some different aims and concerns.

The appropriate degrees of similarity and difference between citizens are captured in Aristotle's general account of a citizen. He argues that citizenship is having a share in judging and ruling (1275a22–33). He recognizes that this definition will not fit all political systems exactly, but replies that we must not expect to find a single definition that exactly fits all cases (1275a33–b5).[8] If he had chosen some lower qualification, his account would have applied to more political systems.[9] But he picks the higher qualification, because he wants to understand the other cases as approximations to it.[10]

The definition shows the place of citizenship in a happy life in the ideal state. Happiness includes essentially political activities, and the account of citizenship describes some of these activities; ruling and judging are parts of the virtuous person's concern for the common good.

Aristotle's conditions for citizenship are demanding because the citizen has to be the virtuous person, whose activities are possible only in the ideal state. In general, the virtues of the good man and the good citizen are distinct. The completely good man will have the virtues of the ruler, but the good citizen only needs the virtues of the subject; hence he needs only true belief, not wisdom (1277b25–32), and will be a good citizen without being a good man. This distinction will not apply, however, to the ideal city, where each citizen both rules and is ruled (1278a40–b5). Here the good citizen will also be the good man, since his role as citizen requires him to have all the virtues (1288a32–b2).[11]

These claims about the good man and the good citizen do not imply that the non-ideal states include good men who do not fit into that system as good citizens. Someone cannot be a good man without being a good citizen and without having the relations to others that make the full range of virtuous actions possible and reasonable. Without the ideal city there will be no good men. Aristotle's views about human nature and happiness imply the necessity of an ideal city for individual happiness.

In arguing that the good man and the good citizen must be identical, Aristotle recognizes essentially political constituents of happiness. Happiness includes virtuous activity, since this fully realizes rational agency; virtuous activity must include the extended deliberation and rational action that results from friendship; and the same argument justifies the further extension to political activity. The good citizen in the ideal state is not merely doing what is instrumentally necessary for his good; he realizes it in his political activities themselves.

220. THE HUMAN GOOD AND LEISURE

Aristotle's conception of happiness requires an active conception of citizenship that is best satisfied in a democracy (1275b5–6). On the other hand, his narrow conception of the qualifications for citizenship implies a criticism of democracy. For citizens must be equal and virtuous, and able to engage in the right sorts of activities. Natural slaves cannot be citizens, since they have no conception of happiness (1280a31–4), and lack the capacity for deliberation and decision that is required for virtue and happiness (1260a12; cf. 1254b22–4). Moreover, manual workers should be excluded from citizenship, and not regarded as parts of the city at all, because their way of life deprives them of the freedom and leisure (*scholē*) that are necessary conditions for the right sort of virtuous life. This stage of Aristotle's argument needs discussion, to see if his account of the human good really supports his restriction of political rights to a leisured elite.

A free person differs from a slave in so far as a slave is for the sake of another and a free person is for his own sake (*Met.* 982b25–6). A master is a slave's master, but does not belong to the slave, while the slave belongs to the master in the way the master's parts or tools belong to him (*Pol.* 1254a8–17). 'Belonging to oneself' does not refer simply to a legal status, but to the agent's control over his actions, and to the ends for which he acts. The slave acts wholly in the interest of another; and the other's interest is independent of and insensitive to his own interest, even if it coincidentally promotes his own interest (1278b32–7).[12]

Hence it seems slavish to live entirely in dependence on someone else and his interests (*Rhet.* 1367a32–3), and the free person is one who is neither forced to do this nor has the slavish inclination to do it. The virtuous person chooses freedom for himself; for he wants to guide his life by his own rational agency, not by mere conformity to the will of another. The magnanimous person refuses to form his life in relation to someone else, except for a friend (*EN* 1124b31–1125a2); and in that case the friend does not impose his will. For a friend is another self, and the aims of a friend will themselves be the result of the deliberation and choice that both have shared.

Aristotle holds that freedom and independence require leisure.[13] Leisure is not 'being at leisure', if that suggests being unoccupied; nor is it recreation as opposed to serious business (cf. *EN* 1176b27–1177a6). It is contrasted, however, with being occupied in the production of necessities (*Pol.* 1333a30–6); the self-sufficient city has to provide enough resources for a life of leisure, which is not occupied in securing the necessary resources (1326b26–32).

Leisure is not necessary for virtuous action (1334a22–8); but Aristotle thinks it is necessary for the sort of freedom that the virtuous person values. Necessary occupations allow some choice, in so far as I can be an unjust or just farmer or electrician, and I can perhaps choose which occupation to enter. But my choice is limited; I have to do something to make a living, and I have to conform to the demands of my occupation if it is the source of my living. Though my choices and decisions are important, they make less difference, and are less free, than they are when I am not constrained by the demands of necessity. Occupations involve some 'mixed' actions that are a mixture of voluntary and involuntary elements; and though these allow choice and decision, the difference between the virtuous and the vicious decision is not as clear here as elsewhere (cf. *EN* 1110a11–19, 1115b7–10, 1116a29–b3). The virtuous person will act virtuously as far as he can; but his virtuous decision cannot design his life as it can if he has leisure.

Leisure implies the freedom from constraint that is important for the exercise of the virtues, as Aristotle conceives them. Generosity and magnificence require a comfortable surplus that allows the appropriate uncalculating attitude; the generous person's virtue forces him into disagreeable choices if it threatens the necessities of his life (cf. 1121b24– 6). Magnanimity harms the magnanimous person if his external resources are so limited that any envy or resentment threatens his supply of necessities. Friendship requires friends to choose to share their lives and common pursuits. If necessities make it difficult to share their lives, or require them to follow different pursuits from those they would prefer, then the life of friendship is not fully achieved.

If necessity does not constrain the virtuous person, then the shape of his life more completely expresses his decision. A rational agent who chooses effective rational agency in the whole of his life wants to make as many choices as possible in conditions of leisure, to the extent that this is consistent with the requirements of virtue. Hence we are best off in a community in which the requirements of virtue and necessity do not constrain our choices, and so our characters and decisions have maximum effect.

Leisure distinguishes a free person's life from a slave's. If a virtuous person becomes a slave, he will still have opportunities to be virtuous, as Epictetus would be pleased to point out. But he will have to live a slavish life, to the extent that he must devote his energies to securing necessities for himself; his life is prescribed in a series of tasks that he must fulfil on pain of some grave penalty. For someone naturally suited to be a slave, lacking the capacity to shape his life by decision (*Pol.* 1260a12), the pressure of necessity is no harm; but for someone with the capacity that the natural slave lacks it is a serious harm.

221. LEISURE AS A CONDITION OF FREEDOM

Part of Aristotle's interest in leisure reflects the narrow range of activities open to a person constrained by necessity. The necessities of life characteristically require dull, repetitive work making minimal demands on rational agency and virtue. If a person's life is occupied with these, then, even if he chooses and pursues them virtuously, much of his capacity for rational agency goes unused. Without denying value to the virtuous action in constrained conditions, Aristotle rejects the Stoic view that the realization of rational agency in virtuous action is the only realization needed for happiness.

While we want rational agency to be exercised in our lives, some types of exercise are preferable to others. We may exercise it even when we decide to make the best of a bad job, and when a less virtuous person would make the same choice. But we prefer the exercise of reason when we are free to do more than adapt ourselves to disagreeable conditions that we would rather avoid. We prefer the exercise of rational agency in conditions that allow its maximum extension and development in forming the character of our lives.

Aristotle values an aspect of freedom to which a Stoic such as Epictetus is indifferent. The Stoic cares about the actual causal relation of rational agency to the agent's actions; if my action is the result of my virtuous decision, then, in the Stoic view, the demands of self-realization and rational agency are satisfied, even if I would have had to do the same action for some other reason if I had not done it for this reason, and even if the same result would have happened from some other cause. Aristotle agrees that this Stoic agency is a genuine and important expression of rational agency, since even in highly constrained circumstances 'the fine shines through' (*EN* 1100b30–3); but he denies that it is the only valuable aspect of rational agency. He implies that it is reasonable to want our rational agency to make a difference to what happens, so that the result is different from what it otherwise would have been. This is another reason why happiness requires circumstances much more favourable than those that permit virtuous action (*Pol.* 1332a7–27).[14]

Aristotle's conception of a person as a designer or craftsman suggests why he values making a difference. A friend sees his own rational agency especially realized in what he does for his friend, as a craftsman finds himself realized in his product (*EN* 1168a5–8).[15] The craftsman reasonably values the *distinctive* realization of himself in the world—something that exists because of him and would not have existed otherwise. The same sort of concern seems reasonable for the rational agent concerned with his own individuality and distinctiveness; and to the extent that this concern is reasonable, so is Aristotle's concern with leisure.

Aristotle has good reasons, then, for his preference for leisure. It reflects what he takes to be a central requirement for rational agency. Since Aristotle is describing the ideal state that fully achieves happiness, he is justified when he insists that the citizens must have leisured lives, free from the demands of necessity.

222. ARISTOTLE'S MISUSE OF HIS ARGUMENT

Do these points about leisure show that manual workers, and especially menial (*banausoi*) workers, should not be citizens of the ideal city?

Aristotle rejects the menial character that is 'unleisured and abased' (*Pol.* 1337b14–15). A menial and abased person is so concerned about necessities and his provision for them that he is timorous and lacking in initiative, and so resorts to slavish flattery (*EN* 1125a1–2), since he lacks the confidence that is needed for the growth of magnanimity. He displays the insecure and suspicious attitude that encourages meanness (cf. 1121b21–31). In circumstances of leisure and affluence he cannot use his good fortune properly, but simply becomes insolent and aggressive (*Pol.* 1334a22–40).[16] The only goods he values are the contested goods that supply necessities; and when he has enough of these, he can think of nothing better to do than to go on accumulating them (1271b2–10).[17]

Aristotle rejects not only the menial character, but also the menial life (1328b39–1329a2).[18] We cannot practise the actions that belong to virtue if we live the life of a menial worker or a hired labourer (1278a20–1), since none of their actions involves virtue (1319a26–8).[19]

Menial activities by themselves do not make a person menial. A citizen may do some menial services for himself without becoming menial (1277b3–7); and the subordination of the young to their elders may involve menial services, but it is not menial, since it is for a fine end (1333a6–16, 1337b17–21). It is only an unworthy end that makes the action base (1341b10–17; cf. *Rhet.* 1419b7–9). Aristotle reasonably comments: 'In relation to what is fine or not fine the actions do not differ so much in themselves as in the end and what they are done for' (1333a9–11). If the right end changes the nature of the action, then apparently someone with the right moral education could do menial actions for the right end, without living a menial life and without forming a menial character.

It might be true that we are likely to form a menial character if we are compelled to spend all our time, without countervailing influences, in occupations where success requires the subordination of virtue to other aims. But if menial work is not our full-time occupation, it is consistent with the leisure and wealth needed for the development of virtue; and if we have some material security, we might apparently have a chance of cultivating the virtues.[20]

The circumstances of the ideal state make it reasonable to consider this possibility that Aristotle neglects. For if the citizens are freed from menial labour altogether, they must use the labour of non-citizen menial workers—natural slaves and foreigners.[21] If they do this, they will be admitting potentially discontented and dangerous non-citizens into the state. Since they cannot pretend to consider the interests of the menials, they must rule them by force, threats, and incentives that make them even more menial and potentially dangerous than they were already.[22] Aristotle seems to have a choice between this sort of relation to non-citizen labourers and a relation of friendship among citizens who share menial work among themselves. It is not clear why the ideal character of the city allows him to reject the second option.[23]

Indeed, perhaps the argument for the second option can be strengthened. The argument for extending friendship from a small group of virtuous individuals to the more heterogeneous association of the state assumed that a virtuous person will want to be on terms approximating to the best type of friendship with more people rather than fewer. He wants to extend his concern because he realizes his own capacities more fully to the extent that he shares in the cooperative deliberation and action of a community.

If Aristotle relies on this argument, he ought to conclude that it is desirable for citizens to cooperate with each other as widely as possible in the activities that they have to manage; such a cooperative arrangement seems far preferable, on ethical grounds, to the relation of citizens to their non-citizen menial workers.[24] It is not clear why this arrangement is empirically impracticable.[25]

Aristotle's own total rejection of menial labour for the citizens has, therefore, no sufficient basis in his ethical theory; it reflects an implausible empirical assumption, or a social prejudice, or the first supported by the second. He is right to suppose that immersion in the outlook of someone who must struggle for a precarious living, with no opposing influence on his character, is likely to conflict with the attitude required by virtue. He is equally right to insist on a life of leisure for his ideal citizen. But he is not justified in proscribing all menial work for the citizens, since menial work does not by itself always constitute a menial life, and the ideal state may actually be harmed by the arrangement Aristotle prefers.

Since Aristotle's ethical principles do not support his conclusion about manual workers, disagreement with his conclusion does not justify rejection of his ethical principles. Indeed we can use the principles to correct some of Aristotle's political recommendations.

223. MORAL EDUCATION AS A TASK FOR THE STATE

Aristotle has found that a city is necessary for happiness not simply because it provides security and conveniences, but because happiness includes activities that are essentially activities of virtuous citizens concerned about the common good. If this is the city's role in happiness, then the functions and tasks of the city will be different from what we would take them to be if we held a narrower conception of its role.[26]

Aristotle argues that happiness essentially includes virtuous character and actions, and that these include essentially political activities. The virtues of character that are components of happiness cannot be reliably secured without a systematic programme of moral education, and the state is by far the most suitable community to undertake moral education (*EN* 1180a14–32).[27] Not every state fulfils this function equally well; some do not bother about moral education at all (1180a23–9), and each political system encourages different sorts of relations between citizens (viii 10). Aristotle ascribes an explicit concern for moral education only to the cities that care about good laws and good order, and criticizes the cities that ignore public education.[28] For this reason also, we should study the differences between political systems, and find the one that is best for the proper task of the state (1181b15–23).

Despite these variations between states, Aristotle suggests that they typically care about the character of citizens, not merely about the avoidance of injustice (*Pol.* 1280a40–b8). He even claims that this moral concern distinguishes the state from some narrower communities.

Hence it is evident that a city that is correctly, not just verbally, so called must be concerned about virtue. For otherwise the community turns out to be an alliance, differing from the other alliances, those between people at a distance, only in the proximity of the allies, and law turns out to be a contract, and, as Lycophron the sophist said, a mutual guarantor of what is just, but not such as to make the citizens good and just. (1280b8–12)

If we deny that the city has any moral concern, Aristotle challenges us to explain why a city is more than a mere alliance.

If Aristotle's claim is to be plausible, even states that neglect moral education must show enough moral concern to distinguish them from Lycophron's minimal state. And indeed some of them regulate the permissible occupations for citizens, and all of them hold some occupations more than others in public honour and esteem (1293b12–14). In so far as a state takes any of these attitudes, it does not fit Lycophron's conception.

Aristotle must also refute Lycophron's view even for a state that consciously, even conscientiously, refrains from public moral education. Such a state actually confirms Aristotle's claim, if it argues that people will live best if they are free from coercive or persuasive interference. This argument appeals to a conception of the good life to defend a policy of inactivity; but if we simply form a trading partnership, we need no such defence of its limited aims, since we take the limits for granted. The city is different, in so far as limitation of its concerns needs some defence that will itself appeal to the happiness of the citizens. The democratic states that regard freedom as the major good, and identify freedom with living as one pleases (1259a39, 1307a34, 1310a32, 1317b1, 1318b39, 1319b30), avoid interference on principle. Modern states that limit the functions of government often assume that individuals get on better if left to themselves.

Defenders of Lycophron need not say this; they could consistently argue that the limited state is the only just arrangement, even though it leaves all its members worse off than they would be under a less minimal state. In fact, however, advocates of a minimal state have been noticeably and understandably reluctant to make such a concession.[29] If non-interventionist policies argue from the good of the citizens, they are not counterexamples to Aristotle's claim.

Aristotle suggests that Lycophron's account cannot describe the essential functions of the state. If in fact the state should behave as the minimalist principles say it should, these principles must be secondary principles, derived from a broader conception of a state as a community pursuing happiness. Aristotle believes that once we recognize the essential aim of the state, the minimalist principles will not even seem to be plausible secondary principles.

When Aristotle, therefore, contrasts Lycophron's minimal state with the law that is 'such as to make citizens good and just' (1280b12), he really collapses two contrasts into one. The state's concern for the happiness of some or all of the citizens refutes Lycophron; and a state shows this concern even if it refrains from public moral education, as long as it argues for such a policy by appeal to the good of the citizens. Aristotle's more specific concern is concern for public moral education; and he argues that this specific concern is the right expression of the general concern for happiness.

Aristotle explains the defective attitude of some states to moral education by referring to their defective conception of happiness; for a state's conception of happiness is the basic assumption of its political system (1317a40–b17), and its attitude to moral education reflects its views about happiness. Aristotle sharply distinguishes happiness, as the proper concern of the city, from wealth and security, which are necessary means to happiness, and hence define a purely ancillary function of the state (vii 8).[30] Non-ideal states do not recognize that happiness consists in virtuous action, and so they cannot have the right reasons for undertaking moral education; they undertake it for, at most, instrumental reasons, to make their citizens fit the constitution better, not because the result will in itself be good for the citizens.

224. THE DEFENCE OF MORAL EDUCATION

Even if we agree with Aristotle's claim that a state is characteristically and properly concerned about the character of its citizens, we need not yet agree that it ought to educate them itself. For perhaps systematic moral education will do more harm than good. Perhaps the sort of character we want to form is not best formed by the sort of training offered by public education; or perhaps, as the democratic assumption holds, freedom is itself such an important good that we should not interfere with it as we would by public moral education.

Aristotle answers the first objection by appealing to the nature of the virtues to be acquired. If we did not think the virtues of character were very important for happiness, we might excusably underestimate the importance of systematic moral education. Or again, we might think the virtues are valuable only because they produce these habits of conformity that are the legislator's concern. Aristotle, however, insists that the virtues and the actions they cause, not merely the conforming actions, are constituents of happiness; and so the legislator ought to care about the character of the citizens (1280b2), not simply about what they do. Since the Aristotelian virtues depend on the proper formation of habit, emotion, and immediate response, we cannot sensibly wait to learn them until we are old enough to decide for ourselves.

Moreover, habits and responses will be weak and confused if they are encouraged only by, say, parents, but discouraged by the attitudes prevailing in social life. If parents encourage a child to regard wealth and honour as comparatively unimportant, but she grows up in a state that values these goods to excess, she will find it hard to form any stable character, let alone the right one.[31] If Aristotle is right about the nature of the virtues and the training they require, and right also about the influence of the state on the habits and characters of its citizens, he has made a strong prima facie case for public moral education.[32]

These arguments show why it is in my interest to undergo public moral education in the ideal state. But it is also in my interest for other citizens to undergo it. For since happiness requires friendship with virtuous friends, I have reason to want other people to be virtuous. In the best city citizens are associated by the mutual admiration and concern that is characteristic of the best type of friendship; hence each of us has an interest in having fellow-citizens who are virtuous enough to be associated with us in the proper relations.

225. THE APPARENT CONFLICT BETWEEN FREEDOM AND MORAL EDUCATION

Aristotle's argument for public moral education is not conclusive. For if the bad effects of public moral education are serious enough to outweigh the advantages described by Aristotle, he will have failed to make his case.

He requires the virtuous person to act on an intelligent and informed decision that causes her to choose the virtuous action for its own sake, not from blind habit or fear of social pressure (*EN* 1144a13–20). If there is strong social pressure for conformity, then other motives will make me conform if the virtuous motive does not; but I may also be moved by the virtuous motive, and it may still be sufficient for my action in conditions (actual or counterfactual) where other motives are insufficient. We must realistically allow the virtuous person more than one motive for her action.

Elsewhere, however, Aristotle rejects an apparently parallel argument. In his defence of leisure he is unimpressed by the fact that we can perform a necessary task both because it is necessary and because we decide that it is fine. The best activities must be chosen when they are not necessary; for we want our rational agency to make an actual difference to our lives, to shape them without the pressure of necessity. If this is Aristotle's view of leisure, should it not also be his view about moral education? Should he not, therefore, require a degree of freedom that precludes public enforcement of moral education?[33]

Leisure secures freedom, in so far as it leaves a person independent of the pressures of necessity, to live in ways that most fully express and realize her own will. Public moral education seems to violate Aristotle's conditions for freedom, even if my own will also endorses it.

The important good that Aristotle seems to forget in his defence of public moral education is fully recognized in a conception of freedom that he seems to dismiss rather hastily. Democracy is the political system that, on his own account of it, seems to come closest to assigning the right status to a free person. A fundamental assumption of democracy is freedom, interpreted as 'living as one wishes' (*Pol.* 1317a40–b17; cf. 1259a39, 1307a34, 1310a28–36, 1318b39, 1319b30, *Rhet.* 1366a4).

Aristotle is surprisingly hostile to this democratic conception of freedom: 'But this is unworthy; for living in relation to the political system (*pros tên politeian*) must be regarded, not as slavery, but as safety' (1310a34–5). In mentioning slavery Aristotle shows how we might argue from his own conception of freedom to the democratic conception. He does not satisfactorily answer the argument. Even if less freedom to live as one wishes were safer, it still might be slavish; it might involve a sacrifice of freedom under the pressure of necessity, and the democrat might argue that such sacrifices should be as small as possible.

Aristotle's defence of public moral education may increase our suspicions. Since the whole city, he says, has one common end, it should also have one common system of education aimed at it.

And at the same time none of the citizens should think he belongs to himself, but all should think they belong to the city, since each is a part of the city; and the treatment of each part naturally aims at the ⟨proper⟩ treatment of the whole. (1337a27–30)

Aristotle alludes to opponents who allege that his policy on moral education conflicts with his conception of a free person as belonging to oneself. He explains that since I am a part of the city, I should suppose that I belong to the city, not to myself.[34]

This argument requires a strong organic conception of the state and the individual; if the end of each individual consists wholly in her contribution to the end of the city, and the converse does not hold, nothing need be considered in her moral education except the interests of the city (1260b13–18). But Aristotle's conception of happiness supports only a weaker organic claim, that an individual cannot achieve her complete happiness without the city. This weak organic conception does not imply that my whole essence is my belonging to the city; and therefore it does not support Aristotle's strong claim about moral education.

Aristotle's opponent suggests that public moral education reduces free persons to the condition of slaves, in so far as they will no longer belong to themselves. Aristotle's attempt to meet this objection by appeal to the organic analogy only makes things worse for him; for the strong organic conception of the individual and the state is open to criticism precisely because it seems to overlook the vital difference between a free person and a slave or an organ (cf. 1254a8–13). In answering the objection Aristotle seems merely to confirm it.

226. ASPECTS OF FREEDOM

These objections to Aristotle's defence of moral education appeal to his own view of freedom, leisure, and independence. His reply will show if we have found serious difficulties in his position.

Aristotle argues that it is slavish to live for another, with the crucial exception of a friend. The magnanimous person follows this principle (*EN* 1124b31–1125a2); only the stubbornly wilful person is so disdainful of others that he refuses to be guided by their desires at all (*EE* 1233b34–8). Aristotle notices that actions that would otherwise be menial are not menial if I do them for myself or for a friend (*Pol.* 1277b5–7, 1337b17–21). Myself and my friend are the two exceptions, since a friend is another self; in living for him I cease to live for myself alone, but I still live for myself since I live for someone who is another self.

Living for a friend imposes some constraints on my life that I would be free of if I were not attached to him; but it does not reflect an extension of necessity or a contraction of freedom and leisure. The constraints are those I have rationally chosen for my own happiness, without the pressure of needs and necessities; and whereas I would prefer a life that was free of the necessity of earning a precarious living, I would not prefer a life without the constraints imposed by friendship.

If the ideal city rests on an extension of the best type of friendship, the virtuous person's relation to the city is not slavish. A virtuous citizen who regards his fellow-citizens as his friends is concerned about the common good of all of them as a part of his own good. In so far as his actions are regulated by the common good, he is not being made to live for another as the slave is; for the slave's interests have no independent weight (cf. 1278b32–7). None of this is true of citizens.

Each citizen, therefore, wants his fellow-citizens to be virtuous, and each wants all of them to share the common moral education that makes them all virtuous. A common moral education is not a disagreeable constraint or an arduous burden. Virtuous citizens welcome it as part of the good that they choose for the ideal state. Hence it does not violate the conditions that make leisure more choiceworthy than necessity.[35]

To some extent Aristotle agrees that freedom is living as one wishes; but he denies that living as one wishes requires freedom from the constraints of law or moral education.

In a household the free people are least at liberty (*exeinai*) to act at random, but have everything or most things ordered, whereas slaves and beasts have only a little ordered to the common end ⟨of the household⟩, and mostly ⟨are at liberty to act⟩ at random; for that is the sort of originating principle (*archê*) that the nature of each of them is. (*Met.* 1075a19–23)

This claim is intentionally paradoxical. It is natural to connect being free (*eleutheros*) with the maximum extent of freedom or liberty (*exousia*) to do as one pleases, and hence to agree with the democratic conception of what suits a free person. In fact, however, we should identify greater freedom with the greater extension of my rational control over the conditions of my life.

Democratic freedom leaves me with an area of private life under my control, and democratic education encourages me to think that the state's constraints on me are impositions of necessity, to be kept to the minimum. In the ideal state, however, the system of education, and the whole political system itself, are the expression of my own rational will, since friendship associates me with the rest of the community.

I should therefore not regard the system of education as interference, but as part of the system that I rationally choose by identifying my own interest with the common interest. The law is not imposed on citizens in someone else's interest; it prescribes what is required for the common good, which is part of each citizen's good. Hence no virtuous citizen has any reason to believe that the law reflects anyone else's interest or will in opposition to his own.[36]

227. THE RECONCILIATION OF FREEDOM AND MORAL EDUCATION

Aristotle's high estimate of freedom is therefore consistent with his apparently anti-libertarian claims about moral education. To show that he is wrong about the ideal city, we must either reject his attempts to show how friendship is its basis, or argue that, despite everything he says, each citizen has a right to freedom that prohibits interference in his education.

Aristotle might reply that complete non-interference is impossible towards a child, and that considerable interference is inevitable for anyone who grows up and lives in a society. If we are not to replace the authority of the state with the authority of parents, we must defend the minimum feasible degree of interference. But this may not affect people any less than systematic training would affect them. Aristotle suggests that in the absence of systematic training, people tend to exaggerate and to adopt the prevalent habits and characters of their political system, to their own harm and the harm of the system (*Pol.* 1310a19–28, 1318b39–1319a1, 1319b27–32).

He can argue further that the alleged right to non-interference harms individuals, since they lose the opportunity to become virtuous, which usually or often requires the appropriate upbringing and habituation (1334b6–17), and is always aided by it. It is useless to say that the choice is left to individuals; for if they have been very badly brought up, the choice that is most in their interest may not attract them. Minimizing interference seems hard to justify if it prevents or hinders the choice that really benefits the individuals.

Still, Aristotle's discussion of the issue is unfair and misleading. He does not admit that democratic freedom includes anything important; but Aristotelian freedom is an empty fraud without some democratic non-interference. For reasons that Aristotle himself insists on, the citizen will not escape a slavish condition if he simply gives his rational assent to a way of life that is independent of his will, or if he is not allowed to develop his own will by comparing alternative ways of life. It is hard to see how he can be properly free of the constraints of necessity without some principles of non-interference.[37] The ideal city, at least as much as any other, must avoid thoughtless conformity, hypocrisy, and intolerance of reasoned dissent; it must leave a citizen some room to 'live as he wishes'.

Aristotle has not arbitrated fairly between the conflicting common beliefs, and his presentation of democratic freedom is one-sided.[38] But his own theory shows us how to correct his exaggerations. His arguments about friendship and self-sufficiency explain what is defensible in the organic conception of the state and the citizen, and therefore show us what is right in his criticism of democratic non-interference. On the other side, his advocacy of self-determination and leisure, as the proper expressions of rational agency, show us why he is committed to more democratic freedom than he recognizes. Reference to the foundations of Aristotle's political theory helps us to correct his own exposition of it.

20

JUSTICE

228. GENERAL JUSTICE

Aristotle's views about happiness, virtue, and friendship determine the shape of the ideal state. No virtue is more important in his argument than justice, since it aims at the common interest of a community. Rational agency requires concern for members of a community aiming at the common good; it therefore requires a just community. Aristotle's conception of justice describes the different principles that display this concern for the common interest. He should explain both how they promote the interest of the community and how a rational person has reason to follow them.

Aristotle argues for two distinct virtues, general and special justice, where common sense sees only one. To correct and explain the common beliefs, he appeals to homonymy. One virtue, general justice, is concerned with the good of others and, more exactly, with the common good of the political community (EN 1129b17–19).[1] The other virtue, special justice, is concerned with equality and fairness, and the avoidance of *pleonexia*, greedy encroachment on the goods justly assigned to others (1129a31–b1, 1130a14–24, b6–16).

Aristotle denies the assumption of common sense that some one particular virtue of character differs from the others in all the features that belong to the two forms of justice. The features of general justice, in his view, are not features of one virtue as opposed to the others, but features of virtue of character as a whole. General justice turns out to be the same state of character as virtue as a whole, and in calling it general justice, we refer especially to the concern of the virtuous person for the common good of the political community (1129b25–7, 1130a7–13).[2]

Common sense is wrong because it suggests that concern for the common good is separable from the other virtues of character. We might have thought that we could be brave, temperate, or good-tempered, even if we were indifferent to the common good. But Aristotle believes that we cannot have any virtue of character without having them all (1144b32–1145a2); and therefore we cannot have any without having justice. Aristotle thinks every virtue, not only justice, is another's good; for each of them has its appropriate concern with the common good.

This result is not surprising. Wisdom is required for any genuine virtue (1144b14–17); each virtue is defined by the rational account by which the wise person would define it (1107a1–2); the wise person deliberates by reference to a true conception of his happiness (1140a25–8); a true conception of his happiness requires concern for the common good of himself and his friends and fellow-citizens; hence a virtue that refers to his happiness will also refer to the common good. To justify the connexion between justice and the other virtues of character, Aristotle needs his argument about happiness and concern for the common good. His account of general justice revises the common beliefs in the direction required by his systematic account of happiness and virtue. Strong dialectic has shown the connexion between the human good and extended altruism; the virtues of character assume the same connexion; hence Aristotle reasonably refuses to count general justice as a virtue distinct from the other virtues of character.

229. THE PROBLEM OF SPECIAL JUSTICE

Aristotle also recognizes a distinct virtue of special justice. We will understand him better if we attend to an ambiguity in his view of extended altruism.

The virtuous person's concern is extended beyond himself. But is it extended to concern for the good of each other person in the community, or to concern for the community? Certainly the good of the community must be closely related to the good of the people in it, as Aristotle insists in his criticism of Plato (*Pol.* 1264b15–22). But it does not follow that the two sorts of concern are the same, or require the same actions. The community persists even if it loses one of its members; and concern for the community might sometimes seem to justify the sacrifice of the interest of some of its members. But if we are concerned for each member, we may be less inclined to agree to such a sacrifice.

These questions are familiar in modern disputes about justice, arising from apparent conflicts between the collective interest and the rights and interests of individual persons. Deontological theories characteristically appeal to rights and duties, and teleological theories characteristically appeal to a collective interest. Kantian theories are characteristically of the first type, and utilitarian theories characteristically of the second type.

We might expect Aristotle to hold some sort of utilitarian theory. For his general ethical position is teleological, in so far as it is guided by concern for an ultimate end, happiness; and his description of justice as the common advantage readily suggests a utilitarian conception of the public interest. Friendship, on the other hand, requires concern for the other person for the other person's own sake; if justice rests on the same sort of concern, it seems to prohibit the sacrifice of the individual person's interest for a collective interest. If Aristotle cannot explain his position further, he has left a serious question about the implications of his argument for extended altruism.[3]

The account of general justice might suggest concern with the collective interest, since general justice is focused on the common good of the political community, not on the good of individual members. But Aristotle attaches a distinct sort of altruistic concern to special justice.

He distinguishes the two forms of justice, because he thinks that sometimes when we speak of justice or injustice we are not referring to a generalized concern for the common good, manifested in some one of the virtues of character, but to a more specific state of character manifested in justice, rather than some other virtue. In one way justice is not parallel to bravery, but superordinate to it; in another way it is parallel and not superordinate.

Aristotle connects special justice with fairness and equality, and with the avoidance of greed (*pleonexia*). This greed implies a comparative, indeed a competitive, assessment.[4] Special injustice is restricted to external goods; these are objects of competition (*EN* 1168b15–23), precisely because the supply of them is limited and if I get some of them there is less left for you.

If the comparative aspects of greed are essential to special injustice, they distinguish it from the other vices. Fred is a coward who wants to avoid military service because he wants to avoid the danger to himself. Bert, however, is unjust because he wants to avoid military service so that others face the dangers he avoids. He wants to gain a comparative advantage over them by escaping the burdens that he and they would justly share. Fred need not have any such desire; he might even regret the fact that others bear the burden that he shirks. The desire to win at other people's expense is characteristic of special injustice.[5]

This type of greed is not a necessary part of the other vices; and it reflects a distinct desire that needs to be curbed. Social life with limited resources distributed according to some conception of fairness encourages the legitimate desire not to be cheated out of what is due to me; but if this desire is unregulated, it may encourage me to benefit myself at the expense of others (cf. 1133b30–1134a13). This is a legitimate area for a distinct virtue.[6]

If I am too cowardly to face danger in the appropriate cause, then the common interest suffers, and so everyone's interest suffers. But it does not follow that I have inflicted a harm or committed an injustice on any particular person in violation of what was justly due to him; there may have been no one in particular to whom my standing and fighting was justly due. Special justice seems to be concerned with particular people in a way that general justice is not; it insists on proper respect for particular people in the fair allocation of external goods.

Some argument is needed to show that concern for the common benefit is either necessary or sufficient for proper respect for others, or that concern for the interests of particular others is automatically concern for the common interest. Aristotle's theory ought to show not merely that the two sorts of concern are consistent, but also that general justice supports the particular concern of special justice.

230. CONDITIONS FOR JUST DISTRIBUTION

Distributive justice concerns the distribution of goods, especially political power and office, by the state to individuals.[7] Aristotle argues that the right distributive criterion should be fixed by worth, *axia*. But what is the just way to assess someone's worth? He recognizes that this question is disputed between supporters of different political outlooks; indeed he sees here the origins of the different types of constitutions and of the struggles between their partisans in a single state (1131a24–9). In the *Politics* he suggests that this dispute should be settled by reference to the proper function of a state (*Pol.* 1280a7–25).[8] We need a state for living well, for achieving the self-sufficient happy life (1280b29–35). If we are concerned for the happy life, we will be concerned for a common good, and especially for the common good of a political community. Distribution, therefore, seems to be regulated by forward-looking teleological considerations; it seems reasonable to distribute power and office to the virtuous people, those who are competent to rule well with an eye on the end of the city.

Prospective arguments, however, seem to lead to further grounds for distribution. Some people will feel aggrieved and excluded if they are denied a share, and will be rebellious and disaffected if their demands are ignored. Aristotle thinks it is sensible to recognize the claims of those who will feel aggrieved if they have no share of power and office. Those excluded from them will rightly resent the exclusion because it is a denial of honour (1281b28–30). A citizen of a state has an interest in having a share of this as of other shareable goods, and in having his worth recognized by the award of it. Aristotle suggests that the true principles of distributive justice will recognize this interest, and protect the citizen's claim to recognition of his worth. He therefore seems to introduce a further prospective criterion for distribution.

But he does not seem to accept a purely prospective approach to distribution. He argues:

Hence those who contribute most to this sort of community, these have a greater share in the city than those equal or greater in free status and birth but unequal in political virtue, or those superior in wealth but inferior in virtue. (1281a4–8)

If we consider the past contributions of different people, our attitude seems to be retrospective.[9]

Aristotle recognizes competence, social stability, and reward for merit, as three different grounds of distributive justice. We might think that these grounds will conflict. The principle of recognizing merit is retrospective, and does not seem certain to reward the people who will be most competent in the future. And if power and office go to people who will otherwise be aggrieved, that may be a sensible concession to expediency, but we might wonder if it is really just. The common good of the community seems to suggest two conflicting prospective criteria, and each of these seems to conflict with Aristotle's own retrospective criterion.

He argues, however, that wealth, free status. and numbers do contribute to political competence, and that distributive justice requires their recognition in the assignment of wealth and power (1283a17–20); in the right circumstances the collective opinions of the individually mediocre many may be better than the opinions of the wise few (1282a14–41). A concession to wealth, birth, and numbers is not necessarily a sacrifice of justice to expediency.

Aristotle argues that there is no conflict between the just demands of individuals and the requirements of the common interest. His basis for distribution is virtue and competence; but he avoids a conflict between fairness and the common interest by associating fairness with virtue and by interpreting virtue widely enough to allow a share in ruling when general justice requires it. Distributive justice, therefore, ensures distribution of external goods according to worth, and specifically according to virtue. Since virtue is in our control, and we have reason to be virtuous, we have reason to be satisfied with this pattern of distribution.

231. RETROSPECTIVE JUSTICE

The main difference Aristotle sees between corrective and distributive justice is the different role of equality. In corrective justice we are not concerned with the worth and virtue of the parties involved in an injustice; when we consider Y's crime against X, we do not ask whether it is just for X to have had more than Y in the first place. We treat X and Y as equals (1131b32–1132a6), in so far as we restore the *status quo ante* by imposing a loss on Y and transferring what is taken from Y back to X (1132a24–b9).[10]

Corrective justice protects each citizen from *pleonexia* by another. It must ensure that as far as possible X does not lose by Y's crime against him and that Y does not profit by his crime against X. Since it is a form of special justice, it is concerned with what is fair and equitable to a particular person, and with the particular aspects of fairness that require the correction of any disturbance resulting from *pleonexia*. Its focus is restricted and retrospective; it does not consider either the common good, or even the principles of distributive justice, but considers only the harm that has been done and the means of restoring the *status quo ante*.

Corrective justice guarantees each person some compensation and protection against the *pleonexia* of others, since it is intended to prevent your losing, and my gaining, by my *pleonexia*. The virtuous person will not lose by refraining from *pleonexia* himself, and the others he cares about will not lose by being its victims.

A commercial transaction has its own proper type of special justice; it should involve exchange at a just price, which is measured by the need of the parties involved (1133a25–7).[11] Though Aristotle does not explain how to measure degrees of need, he might be able to appeal to the relative importance of different components of our good. If, for instance, someone correctly finds more of his happiness in painting than in eating, a just arrangement will make the price of painting higher than the price of eating. When exchange conforms to commercial justice, then I will not find that I have greatly increased your supply of external goods, and hence your prospects for happiness, with only a slight increase, or even an actual decrease in my own. If these unbalanced transactions are allowed, then they will allow successful *pleonexia*, and a citizen cannot enter into the transaction with confidence about his own prospects.[12]

We need to exchange these goods, because the same goods are not always useful to different people or to the same person all the time (1129b1–4), and because they are contested goods, since one person cannot have more without another having less (1168b15–23). Since there must be exchange, commercial justice guarantees that the exchange will serve its intended purpose, of increasing the absolute level of external goods for each person and protecting his relative position in relation to others.

Commercial justice is a part of special justice, because it offers these definite guarantees and protections against *pleonexia*. Without a just system of prices, exchange would be an opportunity for *pleonexia*, since an astute person could manipulate it to improve his own competitive position at the expense of another. Though Aristotle does not describe the workings of the intended system of prices and exchange in any detail, he says enough to show how it is meant to display the characteristic features of special justice.

232. THE RELATION BETWEEN GENERAL AND SPECIAL JUSTICE

Special justice offers guarantees based on a retrospective attitude that seems liable to conflict with the prospective attitude we would expect from general justice. If we are to show on Aristotle's behalf that the two attitudes do not conflict, we should be able to show that his account of altruism both explains and reconciles the two types of concern for others.

I am justified in finding part of my good in the good of another, in so far as I value cooperative activities for ends that we both value. My conception of my own good does not become entirely other-regarding, since I remain concerned about the distribution of goods between us in a way that I need not be concerned about distribution between stages of myself. Indeed this persistently self-confined concern ensures that friendship involves concern for the other person, not just a generalized concern for the sum of interests of two people.

Since I do not make my friend a part of myself, and do not make the two of us into one self, I am not indifferent about which of us gains the benefit.[13] If Al sacrifices his life for Ann, there is clearly a benefit that Ann gains and Al does not, and this is a benefit he wants to secure for her. The happiness of each consists partly in the happiness of the other, but includes other elements also; that is how Al knows what to do to promote Ann's happiness. We expect Al to be aware of the self-confined aspects of his own happiness as well as of Ann's, and to maintain his rational concern for these self-confined aspects.

If the same sorts of reasons justify concern for the common interest of a larger community, the rational citizen does not care only about maximizing the total. He distinguishes the self-confined interests of different people, and wants some protection against being required to sacrifice his own self-confined interest to other people's. If the common interest supports a virtue of general justice that he can value for itself, the common interest must include some protection for the self-confined interest of each citizen. Special justice protects this self-confined interest. It is concerned with external goods, which clearly belong to a person's self-confined interest; it is not concerned with the goods that I secure for myself in so far as I secure the self-confined good of others.

Special justice does not protect us from all forms of interference with our self-confined interest. Aristotle does not assure us that if we refrain from *pleonexia*, our self-confined interest will be left undisturbed. He rejects this contractual conception of the state because it misses the state's essential function (*Pol.* 1280a40–b23). Since the rational agent is interested in the common good as part of his own good, he will be willing to sacrifice some of his self-confined interest to the common good; and he may be willing to sacrifice some of the self-confined interest of others for the same reason.

Aristotle does not insist, then, that a law or policy satisfies general justice only if it advances everyone's self-confined interest more than any alternative would advance it. Sometimes a sacrifice by me may be justified because of some common goal that is in everyone's interest, though not in my self-confined interest. A state that tolerates some inefficiency so that its members can take a wider role in government, or that imposes sacrifices to build temples, may be pursuing the common interest without achieving everyone's self-confined interest as fully as a different state might. Aristotle's theory is firmly teleological; it is concerned with the common good of a community, which is the goal that justifies the requirements of special justice.

In the extension of Aristotelian friendship, concern for particular individuals is extended into a concern for the common good of many individuals. But this concern is not indifferent to the distribution of goods between them. If I am concerned about the self-confined good of other individuals as I am concerned about my own, then I will want the same sort of protection for it that I want for myself. Hence the type of regard for others that Aristotle can justify will also justify the requirements of special justice.

We find the system in Aristotle's account if we relate it to first principles. We have to see the connexion between justice, friendship, and altruism; and we have to see the account of altruism that emerges from Aristotle's account of rational agency and his normative theory of the good. We can then explain his claims about justice, and we can see why they are an important part of a defensible theory. Aristotle identifies justice with the common interest of a city, and defends the city by appeal to its role in a complete and happy life; he therefore defends justice by its relation to the good of a rational agent. The account of justice confirms our claims about the aim and structure of Aristotle's ethics.

233. ERRORS ABOUT JUSTICE

Aristotle's views on justice explain why the rational person will justifiably have the appropriate concern for the good of others, and what principles should underlie the laws and institutions of a state that displays the right sort of concern for the common interest. A correct conception of justice has a further critical function; for, in Aristotle's view, mistakes about justice partly explain the errors of actual states.

At the most general level people seem to agree about justice. For everyone recognizes that the system should be just, and that the just distribution will be equal and fair; but not everyone understands fairness correctly.

First we must understand the received definitions of oligarchy and democracy and the oligarchic and democratic ⟨views of⟩ justice; for they all fasten on some sort of justice, but make only limited progress, and do not describe the whole of what is fully just. For instance, justice seems to be equality; and so it is—but for equals, not for everyone. Again, inequality seems to be just; and so it is—but for unequals, not for everyone. But these ⟨partisans of each view omit⟩ this part—equality or inequality for whom—and so make the wrong judgment; this is because they are giving judgment in their own case, and most people are practically always corrupt judges in their own cases. Now justice is justice *for* certain people, and the division in the things ⟨to be distributed⟩ corresponds to the division in those to whom ⟨they are disturbed⟩, as we have said before in the *Ethics*. Hence all sides agree about the equal amount of the thing ⟨to be distributed⟩, but dispute about who should receive it. They do this mainly because, as we have just said, people are bad judges in their own cases, but also because each side makes some progress in describing a sort of justice, and so thinks it describes unconditional justice; for ⟨oligarchs⟩ think that if they are unequal in some aspects, e.g. wealth, they are unequal unconditionally, and ⟨democrats⟩ think that if they are equal in some aspect, e.g. free status, they are equal unconditionally. (*Pol.* 1280a7–25; cf. 1282b14–23, 1301a25–36.)

Both democrats and oligarchs neglect the relevant qualifications that are needed to correct their views of justice.

To say no more than this would be quite unhelpful, since we still need to fix the respects relevant to distribution of power and office, the basis of the 'worth' (*axia*) that is the proper measure of equality and fairness. Aristotle, however, can also explain how to find the right measure; we will find it if we see that special justice depends on general, and we have the correct conception of general justice. The proper basis for assigning worth in distribution will be whatever is relevant for the common good, since that is the aim of general justice. Since a correct conception of the common good requires a correct conception of happiness, a correct answer to the question about distribution must appeal to a true conception of happiness.

This is why Aristotle rests his criticism of erroneous constitutions and false conceptions of justice on his own views about happiness and the functions of the state (1278b15–30, 1280a25–1281a4). The happy life requires leisured and virtuous action with a sufficient supply of external goods; hence the common interest will be what promotes that sort of life. Since the best life does not consist in the accumulation of external goods, or in freedom from direction by the state, we need not accept either the oligarchic or the democratic conception of happiness, and we can see what is wrong with the conception of special justice and equality that results.

The intrinsic goodness of political activity makes an important difference to the distribution of political power and office. Political activity is part of happiness, because extended rational deliberation and collective action on it extends the realization of a particular person's capacities as a rational agent. This political activity should be open to everyone capable of it who values it correctly. If Aristotle were right to claim that menial and commercial workers cannot acquire virtuous characters, he would be justified, as far as this argument goes, in excluding them from political activity; since they would care about it only as a means to their other ends, it would not be a constituent of their good.

A true conception of the value of political activity makes it clear how a false conception shapes the oligarchic and democratic views about distribution. For both sides take a purely instrumental attitude to political activity; while the oligarch thinks it should be designed to promote the state's function of promoting private accumulation, the democrat thinks it should be designed to promote the state's function of providing conditions for living as we please. In both cases political activity is doubly instrumental, since it is instrumental to the working of the state, and this is instrumental to sóme further end; neither political activity nor the state is accorded any intrinsic goodness.

234. POLITICAL SYSTEMS AND THEIR ERRORS ABOUT JUSTICE

Aristotle is right to claim that if his conception of political activity and the functions of the state is correct, it must make a difference in principle to the distribution of political power and to the institutions controlling its exercise. For the deviant political systems, questions of distribution are questions of instrumental efficiency. For Aristotle, some of the questions must also be questions about intrinsic goodness; if shared political activity is an intrinsic good, we have an argument for organizing the state to secure it, even if it is not maximally efficient for some other purpose. We should even be willing to accept some cost in efficiency if that is needed to promote further political activity at a desirable level.

A true conception of the place of political activity in happiness shows, in Aristotle's view, that we should actually be more strongly committed to the political principles underlying oligarchy and democracy than either oligarchs or democrats are. Oligarchs favour selective qualifications for ruling, but only on instrumental grounds; if the state were a more efficient instrument of accumulation with a larger ruling class, oligarchs would favour a larger ruling class. Aristotle, on the contrary, favours selective qualifications because these are needed to secure the intrinsic good of political activity, confining it to those who benefit from it.

Democrats, on the other hand, think all citizens should share in ruling, but only for instrumental reasons; if a different regime would be better at allowing us to live as we please, they would favour that. Aristotle wants all citizens to rule because ruling is an intrinsic good for each of them. The deviant systems, in his view, have developed in their different ways because they have overlooked important questions about the point of a state and a political system, and have wrongly assumed that a system is to be evaluated only on instrumental criteria.

Aristotle is quite justified in deriving his criterion from his conception of the human good, and hence from the metaphysical and psychological premises on which that conception relies. To agree with him this far is to agree that there is something wrong in principle with the defences that he considers for the deviant political systems. It is not necessarily to agree that none of these systems can be justified; for we may find that democracy is defensible on Aristotle's principles, and that democrats have erred simply in the defence they have offered. We will be all the more inclined to believe this if we are doubtful about his argument to disqualify menial workers from citizenship. The reasonable conclusion of Aristotle's arguments may not be the one he actually draws.

It is equally doubtful that Aristotle's favoured distributive criterion actually follows from the moral and political principles used to attack other criteria. In so far as he seems to believe, for instance, that superior virtue and service to the community justly claims greater goods as its reward (1281a4–7, 1282b30–1283a3), he argues too quickly.[14] The principle that virtuous political activity is the goal of the state does not imply that past achievement in this activity should be the standard for distribution of goods. More needs to be said to show that such a criterion of distribution will best promote the goal of the state, and Aristotle does not say all that is needed. Our views on his distributive criterion should not prejudice us either for or against his views on the significance of political activity and the function of the state.

235. THE EFFECTS OF ERRORS ABOUT JUSTICE

Every regime claims that its distribution is just because it is fair and equal in the appropriate way. But not every such claim is true; for all the non-ideal systems have a false conception of happiness, which deforms their conception of justice, and explains their characteristic types of injustice.[15] The institutions of a political system shaped by the wrong conception of justice will themselves be unjust; they fail to prescribe what is 'strictly' or 'fully' (*kuriôs*) just (1280a9–11).[16] Moreover, the injustice of the system encourages particular forms of injustice in individuals, either because they are useful to someone with the characteristic outlook of the system, or because the system does too little to discourage them. These are the characteristic vices of oligarchy and democracy.[17]

The source of injustice and of vice in general is a false conception of happiness and of what is needed to achieve it. In the *Ethics* Aristotle distinguishes the lives of gratification and of honour. A life devoted to either of these ends mistakes a part of happiness for the whole, and so overlooks the proper restraints on the pursuit of each. Since the two mistaken lives share some common features that distinguish them from the correct life, they share some vices (cf. *Pol.* 1271a16–18). They also differ in certain ways producing distinct vices. Aristotle relies on this difference when he attributes the vices of the honour-loving life to the few and the vices of the life of gratification to the many (1308a9–10, 1315a16–20, 1318b6).

If our conception of happiness concentrates on the expansion of desire and the increased accumulation of external goods, we reach the oligarchic conception of the state as a partnership for the production of wealth. In an ordinary partnership the smaller partners agree that it is in their interest to allow the large partners to have a larger share of the profits. This oligarchic conception of justice explains the characteristic oligarchic injustice—the pursuit of ever larger accumulation, either by illegal injustice against the many, or by constitutional tricks and changes that will weaken the position of the many, and hence make it easier for the few to profit at their expense.

Aristotle claims that the deviant conceptions of justice have hit on something that is just (*dikaiou tinos*, 1280a9), even though they fall short of complete justice.[18] The oligarchic conception would be quite reasonable if a state were a business partnership for the accumulation of wealth. Wealth is a legitimate external good, to be pursued to the right degree; but it promotes the good of the individual or the community only in so far as it is limited by the pursuit of the final good. Hence the association seeking wealth needs to be limited by the proper aims of the association seeking the final good; as Aristotle says, political science has to supervise all the other sciences and pursuits, and determine their proper limits (*EN* 1094a27–b7). These are the limits that oligarchic justice fails to acknowledge.

If, on the other hand, we concentrate more on gratification than on accumulation, we reach the democratic conception of the state as a way of sharing the resources and arranging the laws so that individuals can gratify their own desires. This is part of Aristotle's reason for treating freedom and equality as basic assumptions of democracy.

The democratic mistake is not the same as the oligarchic mistake of confusing a limited association with the political association. The democratic conception of justice, prescribing numerical equality, is extensionally correct, if the individuals being treated equally are equal in the relevant respects (*Pol.* 1280a11–12). The democratic conception of happiness is also extensionally correct for the right people; for if virtuous people are left alone to live as they please, they will want the institutions and pursuits of the ideal state.

Democrats ignore these background conditions, and so do not see why and in what circumstances their conception of justice is extensionally correct. Since they do not see that virtuous activity, and especially political activity, is the end, they do not see that this is the right basis for the claims of numerical equality. They assume that numerical equality fits those who are equally capable of gratification, and so they misunderstand the proper scope of their principle of equality.[19]

Comparison of oligarchic and democratic conceptions of happiness and justice shows that they make some of the same mistakes. They do not disagree on the nature of the end or on its necessary conditions. The oligarch does not deny the importance of freedom to gratify one's desires; and the democrat does not deny the importance of accumulating enough external goods. They disagree about relative importance and relevance, the oligarch appealing to conditions for accumulating the means and the democrat to the conditions for enjoying the end. Neither side sees that this is the nature of the dispute; and neither sees that the error in the other side lies in a mistaken conception of the good.

From this perspective, however, the democratic conception turns out to be more nearly correct than the oligarchic. Oligarchs are far from finding the right principles to govern the enjoyment of the end; but democrats have found some of the correct principles, and simply fail to see when and why they will be correct. Their conception of political justice is closer to Aristotle's; for his ideal state expresses the conditions in which it would be reasonable to follow the democratic principles, though not for the democratic reasons.

236. ANSWERS TO PUZZLES ABOUT JUSTICE

Aristotle assumes that a conception of special justice is properly examined by appeal to general justice, and that the right basis for principles of general justice is a conception of happiness. He infers that the partisans of oligarchic and democratic justice rely on a mistaken view of happiness. The partisans might therefore reply that their view of justice does not rest on the teleological ground that Aristotle assumes in his criticism, but on some independent principle that is not to be tested by Aristotelian general justice.

The oligarch might argue that it is just for people to be rewarded in proportion to their contribution, and the democrat might argue that it is just for each person to have equal political rights simply because he is a (free, male, native-born) person. Aristotle looks for a further end, a conception of happiness to support these claims about justice; but the partisan may reply that Aristotle is looking for the wrong thing. In attributing a goal and a conception of a way of life to the deviant conceptions of justice, Aristotle ascribes more to them than their partisans have stated.[20] Partisans may reply that he distorts their meaning.

In that case Aristotle challenges the partisans. He offers them a conception of happiness that would support their views on justice if it were correct, and argues that it is not correct. In doing this he explains the false beliefs in the light of the true theory (*EN* 1154a22–5).[21] For he shows how we might form a deviant conception of justice through grasping part of the truth about happiness and the means to it.

Our grasp of the truth is partial partly because of the sort of people we are and our material circumstances. We tend to be prejudiced in our judgment when our material condition disposes us to favour one side or the other (*Pol.* 1280a14–16, 1287a41–b3), even though a truer conception of justice would also give us a truer conception of our real interests. Partisans who reject the Aristotelian diagnosis must show that some plausible principle overlooked by Aristotle justifies their position. Aristotle's challenge is a legitimate dialectical argument.

Aristotle has appealed to strong dialectic; for his diagnosis of the partisan views rests on his own moral theory, and therefore on the principles supporting it. The diagnosis is also an argument for the theory, since the theory is expected to explain common beliefs and to solve puzzles they raise. The oligarchic and democratic conceptions of justice clearly conflict, and the apparently irresoluble character of the conflict may suggest that considerations of justice are either too indefinite or too partisan to solve the conflict. Aristotle concedes that the general commonsense maxims about justice, equality, and fairness are too indefinite, but he argues that they become definite enough for the purpose when they are supported by his theory of general justice and of happiness.

The partisans of different views of justice make the mistake that Aristotle often warns against; they have overlooked important preliminary questions about justice that arise from their conflicts and disagreements.[22] Study of the preliminary questions in the light of Aristotle's moral theory and its foundations helps to resolve the puzzles that underlie the conflicts about justice.

THE CONSEQUENCES OF VIRTUE
AND VICE

---

237. THE VIRTUES OF CHARACTER

We began our discussion of the virtues of character by distinguishing eudaimonic virtues—those that promote the agent's self-realization—from moral virtues—those that promote the good of others.[1] Aristotle believes that these are not two seperate lists of virtues, and that the moral virtues are eudaimonic virtues also. We have followed two stages of his argument for this claim, in his defence of altruistic friendship, and his extension of altruism from friendship, to justice. We now come to a third stage, in the defence of the virtues of character as different forms of extended altruism, and hence of rational self-realization.

If Aristotle simply takes over the list of virtues from common sense, and does not try to show how they promote the agent's good and the common good, he has not shown that they are genuine virtues, and he has left the sceptic and the critic unanswered. If, however, he connects the recognized virtues with the good of a rational agent, and with the common good of her community, then he answers the sceptic and the critic; he relies on strong dialectic, appealing ultimately to his metaphysical account of the human essence to justify the common beliefs about the virtues.

Aristotle's descriptive sketches of the virtues of character may not initially suggest any appeal to strong dialectic.[2] But his argument rests on some common features of the virtues:

1. They all satisfy the doctrine of the mean and hence must be defensible by the reasoning of the wise person (*EN* 1107a1–2).
2. They are inseparable, since virtue in the full sense is impossible without wisdom (1144b32–1145a2). Since they all require wisdom, they will not give conflicting advice (*MM* 1200a5–11).
3. Virtue of character as a whole is the same state of character as general justice (*EN* 1130a8–13). Each virtue of character will therefore be a part of general justice, and will aim at the common good.
4. They all aim at the fine (1122b6–7), and hence at the common good.

Each of the later claims explains the earlier ones. The wise person's deliberation focuses each of the virtues on his conception of his good;

and since he values the good of his community, he focuses the virtues on the common good. This is why the virtues are aspects of general justice. The common good is central in the wise person's conception of his happiness; since he forms his character by deliberation from this conception, the common good will be central in the virtues of character.

If concern for the common good is part of the agent's good, we cannot expect to describe the particular virtues without constant attention to the common good. In a community many of my actions and omissions affect the common good, and the nature of the community affects the actions open to me, and the ways they will influence my happiness. Even those actions that do not directly promote the common good are regulated by it, if I systematically exclude actions that harm the common good.

Aristotle ascribes concern for the fine to all the virtues, since they all produce actions that are done because they are fine (1116a11), and for the sake of the fine (1115b12–13). If this concern for the fine includes concern for the common good, concern for the common good is essential to each virtue.[3]

Aristotle assumes that if an action or state of character is fine, it thereby benefits others. Conferring a benefit is fine, and receiving it merely expedient (1168a9–12); that is why it is finer to have friends in our good fortune (1171a25–6), because it is fine to confer benefits (1171b16). Such active concern for the fine rather than the merely expedient is characteristic of the virtuous person (1162b34–1163a1, 1169a4–7), and it explains his concern for the common good. The magnificent person spends his money on objects that provoke competition promoting the common good (1122b21–2), and 'does not spend freely on himself, but on common goods' (1123a4–5).

Such concern for the fine and for the common good is a general feature of the virtuous person.

Hence it is proper for the generous person to give to those he ought to give to, more than to take or avoid taking from where he ought or ought not. For it is proper to virtue to confer benefit more than to receive it, and to do fine actions more than to avoid base actions. (1120a9–13)[4]

Concern for the fine is characteristic of reason (1117a18, 1162b35, 1169a4–6, 1180a4–5, 10–12, *EE* 1229a1–9), and especially characteristic of the correct reason that fixes the mean appropriate for each virtue (e.g. 1115b17–20).

Hence the community benefits from the concerted actions of virtuous people.

When everyone is contending towards the fine and straining to do the finest actions, the community will gain everything it ought to (*deonta*), and each individual will gain the greatest of goods, if that is the character of virtue. (1169a8–11)

In seeking the common good the virtuous person certainly seeks the good of others besides himself, and on some occasions has to sacrifice his own self-confined good to the fine and to the good of others (1117b7–15). But Aristotle denies that he really sacrifices his own good. Though some people may reject the fine because they act on calculations of expediency, their calculations are wrong, and they simply act on what seems expedient (1169a5–6).

The right kind of self-love requires a true conception of oneself; and if we have this true conception, we will also be concerned to do fine actions. The virtuous person who gives up his life for his friend or his fellow-citizens does not sacrifice his own interests. On the contrary, the praiseworthy (1169a8) type of self-love requires a character that pursues the fine.

Such efforts to connect the fine and the common good with the agent's good would be groundless if Aristotle had no systematic argument to connect eudaimonic with moral virtues. But his claims about self-love, the fine, and the good of others show that he relies on his systematic argument from the human good to the moral virtues. He intends each virtue of character to aim at the fine, and therefore at the common good that the wise agent recognizes as part of her own good.

238. THE PARTICULAR VIRTUES AND NON-RATIONAL DESIRES

If Aristotle intends these general claims about the virtues of character, we may still fairly ask if his descriptions of the virtues reflect the general claims.

Aristotle resists the natural suggestion that anyone who is fearless in facing danger is thereby brave.[5] Even citizen soldiers who promote the common good in facing danger, but face it because they want honour and fear disgrace, are not brave (1116a16–29). Even if someone is ready to sacrifice himself for the common good without hesitation, he may not be brave; for he may not have the right conception of the fine if he values his own life too cheaply (1117b17–20).

The brave person sacrifices his life in the right cause for the sake of the fine. He must care about the common good, but he must also care about the self-confined elements of his own good. This self-confined concern itself promotes the common good. For we would all be worse off if we cheerfully faced any life-threatening danger or marched off to war when we were told to, without a second thought; such carelessness might involve us in hasty adventures from which we would all lose. Both the self-confined and the other-regarding aspects of happiness make Aristotle's view of bravery intelligible.

For similar reasons, Aristotle rejects the natural view that people are temperate if they simply restrain their bodily appetites, and accustom themselves to not minding the loss of some satisfactions. He requires temperate people to have moderated their appetites, but for the sake of the fine, and as correct reason prescribes (1119a11–20). Such people are pleased to have moderated their appetites, and displeased at the thought of immoderate pleasures, because of their view of the fine.

The appetites that concern temperance share an animal character (1118b1–4). Someone who occupies himself with them is concerned with the sorts of goals that might interest an animal, not with the intrinsic value of distinctively human characteristics. Hence he will use practical reason only to find ways of securing the pleasure at hand, following his strongest appetite. If he is indifferent to practical reason, he will be indifferent to the arguments from his own good to the common good, and hence indifferent to the fine (1169a3–6). He will also be positively hostile to the fine and the common good. Intemperance requires contested goods; and when these are in limited supply, it encourages me to take them from others. Hence intemperance will be one form of general injustice, and one source of special injustice; Aristotle remarks that most people are greedy because these are the kinds of goods they pursue (1168b19–21).[6]

Bravery and temperance, as Aristotle conceives them, involve a normative, not merely a conative conception of happiness.[7] Since a correct normative conception of my own good involves the good of others, the common good, and the fine, these must also concern the virtues. Bravery and temperance might seem to be purely self-regarding; but in fact they refer to the fine, and hence to the good of others.

239. THE PARTICULAR VIRTUES AND EXTERNAL GOODS

Generosity and magnificence, the two virtues concerned with money, are not exclusively other-regarding, since they cover expenditure on the agent himself as well as on other people. But they still pursue the fine (1120a9–15, 1120a23–b4, 1122b6–7), and hence the common good. Concern for the fine does not require me to think about the common good in all my actions. Virtue requires only that my actions should be regulated by the common good, so that I will be keen to advance it, and pleased to avoid any self-confined action that conflicts with it.

The generous and the magnificent person avoid spending money on intemperate actions, on flatterers, and on ostentatious displays that appeal only to those who compete with others for honour and status. Since their use of external goods is regulated by the fine and the common good, they display moral virtues that also prove to be eudaimonic virtues.[8]

Magnanimity takes the correct attitude to great honours, and hence to other external goods. The magnanimous person appropriately demands great honours, but only when he knows he deserves them. He seeks honour when it advances the common good (1122b21–3); for he wants to be honoured only by the right people, for his virtues (1124a4–12). He does not regard honour as the supreme good, and so he will not sacrifice virtue for honour; for he cares about the common good, not primarily about being honoured for seeming to advance it.

On the other hand, he does not accept just any danger as a reason for risking his life (1124b6–9); he is ready to sacrifice his life, but only for a properly important cause (1124b24–6). The wise person does not abandon his own self-confined good in favour of the common good, and does not expect the community to ignore the self-confined good of individuals. Aristotle ascribes to the magnanimous person the virtue that expresses a correct normative conception of his own good.

A virtue concerned with external goods embodies the right attitude to their role in a virtuous life. The virtuous person wants wealth for generous and magnificent actions. He wants honour as a sign of mutual respect; for he values his fellow-citizens' judgment on him, in so far as he thinks they are virtuous, and that by honouring him they show their respect for him. Mutual respect and honour result from the friendship and goodwill that should be present in virtuous fellow-citizens. The virtuous person pursues and values the external goods as both instrumental and intrinsic goods, within the limits set by his conception of his own good and the common good.

The other social virtues—good temper, friendliness, and wit—concern the appropriate attitude of one person to another in the relatively informal social encounters that are not covered by the specific obligations of justice, friendship and the other major virtues (cf. 1127a33–b3). In such encounters virtue requires some self-assertion against others and some accommodation to others. The virtuous person develops these tendencies to the right extent; and Aristotle insists that the right extent is to be fixed by 'the expedient and the fine' (1126b28–30).

Excessive self-assertion makes us prone to anger and disputes; but fear of failure in competitions of self-assertion makes us ready to belittle ourselves and to demand less than the appropriate honour. Unwillingness to accommodate makes us unsociable and ill-humoured; but excessive accommodation makes us too eager to please. Sometimes apparent eagerness to please conceals willingness to benefit at another's expense, and someone who makes himself agreeable to me may be aiming at his own advantage; by pleasing me with jokes that wound you, he may be getting an advantage for himself over both of us. If I am susceptible to the flatterer or obnoxious joker, I show a weakness in my own character; I am too fond of the sorts of pleasures that a flatterer offers me, and I am too little concerned with the feelings of the victim of an insulting joke (cf. 1128a33–b1). Vices encourage each other, both in the same person and in other people.

The right attitude in these cases results from proper consideration for myself and for the good of others. Proper consideration for myself makes me ready to demand honour from others and to be angry with them when they harm me unjustly; I will not be slavishly pliant (1126a3–8), and I will not understate my own merits (1127b3–7).[9] This is the same sort of self-assertiveness that makes me value special justice in the community. Still, I will be considerate to others; I will want to be agreeable to them if I am not treated unjustly, and I will want to spare them pain that is inflicted simply for my own or other people's amusement.

If I am concerned for the fine, I will be concerned about the good of the other person; I will not want to cause him pain and I will want to give him pleasure, except when the pleasure would be contrary to his longer-term interest (1126b28–1127a6). This same outlook will help the virtuous person to decide when a joke becomes an unwarranted insult (1126a16–22). Consideration for another person, displayed in gentleness, friendliness, and wit, reflects the general consideration for the common good that we expect in the virtues of character.

These ostensibly minor virtues of character, no less than the others, express Aristotle's theory of the virtues. The eudaimonic virtues are the states of character that secure a rational agent's happiness by achieving his self-realization. But his self-realization requires concern for the good of others, and in particular for the common good of the members of a community. Hence the virtues of character must be moral as well as eudaimonic virtues. They pursue the common good, because they aim at the fine, and constitute general justice.

If this is so, then one large part of the *Ethics* that might appear to be merely dialectical turns out to be the strong dialectic that appeals ultimately to first philosophy. The common beliefs are prominent, because Aristotle begins with them and wants to defend them as far as is reasonable. But he is not confined by them; he examines, arranges, and criticizes them in the light of his general theory. The account of the virtues is clearly ethics, not metaphysics of ethics, but it is ethics that relies on metaphysics.

240. VIRTUE AND THE LOSS OF EXTERNAL GOODS

Aristotle has undertaken to explain and to justify common beliefs about the moral virtues. The promotion of the common good or a friend's good is in itself a part of happiness, and the virtuous actions that express this sort of concern will themselves be actions that constitute a happy life. Other virtuous actions will, if Aristotle is right, promote happiness instrumentally by providing the right external goods and encouraging the right relations among fellow-members of a community.

This argument has not yet answered one apparent difficulty in common sense. We normally expect a virtuous person to stick to her moral principles even when they are costly to her. Like Plato's just person, she chooses the virtuous life despite its penalties. Sometimes this means simply that I am not as well off as I otherwise might have been; sometimes, however, it may mean that disaster strikes us through no fault of our own. Sometimes, indeed, virtue itself seems to cause disaster, if it requires us to sacrifice our life or our prospects of happiness, for the sake of some moral requirement. Common sense seems right to assume that the virtuous person is willing to sacrifice her own interest to the requirements of virtue and morality (cf. *Rhet.* 1359a2–5).

Aristotle cannot agree completely with common sense. For he has argued that the moral virtues are justified in so far as they are also eudaimonic virtues. He cannot therefore agree that the choice of virtue is reasonable and yet contrary to the agent's happiness. On the other hand, he cannot argue that virtue is itself sufficient for happiness; indeed, he remarks that no one would maintain this view except from the desire to maintain a philosophical thesis without regard for its plausibility (*EN* 1096a1–2; cf. 1153b19–21). Happiness requires both the activity of complete virtue and a complete life (1098a16–20); and both of these components require external goods.[10]

Unfavourable external conditions impede virtuous activities (1100b29–30), most obviously those characteristic of magnificence and magnanimity. Moreover, by depriving us of other intrinsic goods besides virtuous action, external conditions can take away our happiness, as they took away Priam's (1100a5–9). We may suffer Priam's fate despite being virtuous; but we may also suffer loss of external goods because we are virtuous; bravery may require the brave person to end his happy life for the sake of acting finely (1117b9–15).

The moral virtues share their focus on the fine and the common good; and this focus requires the virtuous person to be inflexible about his commitment to virtue. The brave and magnanimous person is ready to sacrifice his life on the right occasion; generous and magnificent people are ready to spend freely, even to risk their own security, in the appropriate cause. The prospect of losing external goods will not make them shrink from the actions required by the common good; for they do not think the loss of these goods justifies the sacrifice of virtue.

Such inflexibility seems to conflict with the agent's own good, if his good is not exhausted by promotion of the common good. Sometimes we may have to choose between virtue and the other goods; and sometimes if we are virtuous we will actually be more exposed to external hazards. In these cases why should we always choose virtue over the other goods?

Aristotle agrees that a virtuous person may be happy and then lose his happiness (1101a9–11); but he denies that the virtuous person will ever be miserable (*athlios*; see 1100b33–5, 1101a6–8), and denies that he will ever have reason to choose anything else rather than virtue.

If they are great misfortunes, they oppress and spoil his blessedness, since they involve pain and impede many activities. And yet, even here what is fine shines through, when he bears many severe misfortunes with good temper, not because he feels no distress, but because he is noble and magnanimous. And since it is activities that control life, as we said, no blessed person could ever become miserable, since he will never do hateful and base actions. For a truly good and intelligent person, we suppose, will bear strokes of fortune suitably, and from his resources at any time will do the finest actions he can, just as a good general will make the best use of his forces in war, and a good shoemaker will produce the finest shoe he can from the hides given him, and similarly for all other craftsmen. If this is so, then the happy person could never become miserable. (1100b28–1101a7)

If these claims are correct, virtue must be the dominant component of happiness, so that someone who chooses it always comes closer to happiness than he could have come by choosing any other good without virtue. But since lack of external goods prevents us from acquiring and from exercising some virtues, the virtue that is reliably dominant cannot be complete virtue, but must be the degree of virtue that is in our power; why should this be dominant?

Aristotle cannot expect the virtuous person to *consider* whether she should sacrifice her virtue for other goods; she refuses to consider this choice. Aristotle insists that a virtue cannot be lost; someone who was willing to abandon a virtue would simply show that she lacked the sort of inflexible and stable state of character that is necessary for virtue (1105a33). Rather, the virtuous person will have formed a state of character that makes her refuse to give up her virtue in a crisis; we will not expect her to hesitate and consider carefully on each occasion, any more than we will expect the brave person to reflect about how to face a sudden emergency (cf. 1117a17–22). Why, then, should someone form this inflexible state of character?

241. THE SUPREMACY OF VIRTUE

Aristotle has explained why the virtuous state of character is choice-worthy in itself. A human being has reason to seek the fullest realization of his capacities as a whole, in so far as they are his capacities as a rational agent, and in so far as they allow the maximum role for rational agency. I want not merely the results of intelligent rational agency, but also the rational agency itself, and I will prefer one life over another in so far as it allows a larger role to rational agency.

If I agree with Aristotle, I will not accept a conception of my good that identifies my happiness with being well-born or blue-eyed or seven feet tall, since none of these goods can be an end for rational agency at all. Nor will I accept a conception that makes happiness consist in winning bets on games of chance, since the contribution of rational agency to this end is quite small, and the contribution of chances beyond my control is dominant.

Nor will I accept a conception that allows rational agency a large but purely instrumental role, the sort of role it has in some intemperate lives. That conception fails to accord to rational agency the place that the human essence requires. In so far as the virtues form the sort of life that develops and realizes rational agency most fully, they are choiceworthy in themselves, and the actions that express them are also choiceworthy in themselves.

This argument by itself does not show why the wise person should choose the inflexible commitments characteristic of the virtues rather than the flexible and adaptable attitude that would be readier to compromise for the sake of external goods. To defend inflexibility Aristotle needs to appeal to the rational person's concern with himself as a stable and persistent rational agent.[11] The wise person wants more of his definite and specific commitments to persist through his life, since their persistence will be his persistence. Concern for himself justifies him in forming a relatively fixed character with determinate and inflexible aims.

It still remains to be shown that his fixed and inflexible aims should be those that are characteristic of the Aristotelian virtues. Aristotle argues for these by arguing that promotion of the good of others and of the common good is a prominent component of the wise person's conception of his own good. The Aristotelian virtues rationally pursue the common good, and, in moderately favourable external conditions, secure it. They secure it all the better if virtuous people are inflexibly committed to it even in unfavourable conditions. And since inflexible commitment, rather than adaptability to conditions, is in our interest, the virtues do not demand of us a commitment that is contrary to our interest. Since they attach greater value to the exercise of practical reason in states rationally aiming at the common good than to the results themselves, they express the wise person's correct conception of what is most important for him.

It follows that the virtuous person will not count the prospect of further external goods as a reason for deviating from virtue and the common good. The prospect of honour or influence or wealth that causes the vices of flattery, vanity, and honour-loving will not entice the virtuous person, since these vices promise no sufficiently large component of his good. He does not have to resist the temptation to prefer his own happiness to the common good; he sees that the temptation should not tempt a rational person.

The virtuous person can defend his inflexible attitude to virtue and to external goods, by arguing that this attitude secures *his* good, in so far as it is up to him; the goods he would obtain by becoming vicious would not make the change worth his while. I have no reason to become vicious in order to let someone else enjoy external goods; and I have no reason to compromise my own rational agency so that my later self, having lost some major component of me, will gain external goods. If Aristotle is right in connecting the persistence of a person with the persistence of his character, then a good person with a stable character has no reason to sacrifice his character to other goods. Such self-sacrifice would deny any prospect of happiness to himself.

The virtuous person is not the most stable person possible. The minimalist planner ensures a stable character by seeking only what he can achieve without danger of loss; but he does not achieve happiness, since happiness is complete. The virtuous person wants the traits of character that allow him to realize his rational agency in acquiring the complete good; and these require more than mere stability. But he will have good reason to value rational agency most highly, and hence good reason to refuse to sacrifice it for any other good.[12]

Study of Aristotle's account of happiness, and of the underlying conception of self and common good, shows how he can justify one central common belief about virtue. We share with Greek common sense the belief that the virtuous person is ready to sacrifice other goods to observe moral requirements, and the suspicion that such inflexibility requires the sacrifice of his own good to morality. Aristotle argues that the common belief is true and the associated suspicion is false. His account of happiness rests on his conception of a human being's essence as a rational agent. This conception supports the major recognized virtues, and removes the appearance of conflict between morality and happiness. The examination of common beliefs by appeal to metaphysics and psychology does not merely systematize them; it does not justify them quite as they stand; it does better for them than they can do for themselves.

242. VICE IN A POLITICAL CONTEXT

If Aristotle argues that the moral virtues, as he understands them, are a dominant component of a person's happiness, he should be able to confirm his conclusion by showing that the corresponding vices harm the vicious agent himself and the community he belongs to. In the *Ethics* he indicates only briefly (*EN* ix 4) the sort of harm that results from vice. In the *Politics* he argues more fully that the vices of individuals are responsible for some of the basic flaws in non-ideal states. Though I have already discussed some of this line of argument in the *Politics*, especially in connexion with justice, it is useful to examine it more fully.[13]

Aristotle intends his moral principles to contribute to empirical political analysis. For his principles rest on claims about human nature and the function of the city, no less than on common ethical beliefs. Claims about human nature and the city are not straightforward empirical claims; but something would be seriously wrong if they were totally useless or misleading in the explanation of actual behaviour by states and individuals. The three empirical books of the *Politics*, Books iv-vi, offer to analyse and explain the variety of political systems, and the sources of instability and stability in them. If Aristotle succeeds, we should come to believe that his ethical principles contribute to understanding and explanation; and to this extent we should be readier to believe the principles.

Aristotle argues that the variety of constitutions results from different conceptions of justice. The false conceptions are related to the social and economic conditions of different groups, because people tend to make unjust judgments when their own interest, as they see it, is at stake (1280a14–22). The structure of a state may embody injustice to such an extent that it provokes resentment and conflict that is not removed by goodwill or generosity on either side.

Aristotle mentions both different conceptions of justice and the different socio-economic composition of different communities, to explain the difference in political systems.[14] He does not mean that a person's or state's moral outlook is formed quite independently of the social and economic environment. On the contrary, he recognizes— perhaps, as we have seen, he exaggerates—the effects of occupation and social status on moral outlook and character. And he recognizes that one or another type of upper and lower class makes a specific conception of justice, and a specific type of political system, easier to form and to maintain.

Aristotle does not infer that moral outlooks are simply epiphenomena with no causal role of their own. Even though external conditions make people more likely to share one moral attitude rather than another, the moral attitude is still needed to explain the different political institutions. Moreover, a dominant group in a city can change their views on justice, and change the political system to suit, even though external conditions remain unchanged. Indeed, one of Aristotle's purposes in Books v–vi is to show why it is sometimes sensible to change our views on justice. Attitudes to justice have independent weight as explanations of the difference between political systems.

243. THE VARIETY OF POLITICAL SYSTEMS

Though he takes these features of a state—social, economic, moral, and political—to be the primary grounds for distinguishing political systems, Aristotle also considers commonly accepted grounds for distinguishing constitutions. These differentiae mention number of rulers; wealth and poverty; rule of law; consent or force (1295a22–4). Each differentia has some role in his own analysis, but they are not all of equal value, and none is as important as the Aristotelian differentiae are supposed to be. Since rich and poor, few and many, tend to hold different conceptions of justice, the subordinate criteria may be useful indications.

The treatment of democracy and oligarchy illustrates Aristotle's attitude to the subordinate differentiae. Though he disagrees with those who think democracy and oligarchy are the only two systems worth discussing, he seems to agree that in some way they are fundamental. Their fundamental feature is the wealth or poverty, not (as commonly believed) the number, of the ruling group (1279b26–1280a6, 1290a30–b20, 1302a1–2). Wealth or poverty is important because it disposes us towards the oligarchic or democratic conception of justice. As we have seen, Aristotle thinks democrats are right to suppose that justice should imply equality for all citizens, and that unequal possession of some kinds of good is not a relevant basis for inequality; hence they are right to reject wealth as a criterion. Oligarchs, on the other hand, are right to reject the claims of just any citizen to a share in ruling; but they are wrong to suppose that the good they have, wealth, is a proper basis for inequality. Wealth and poverty make these mistaken conceptions of justice seem attractive; and the errors about justice explain the systematically distorted character of the political system.[15]

Aristotle argues, then, that his criteria are better than others, because none of the others properly identifies the features of a state that adequately explain its institutions and practices, and none of them distinguishes the different degrees of justice in different systems. We cannot say that a constitution is just if it follows its laws or if it is ruled by the few or by the many. Each of these constitutions may very well be unjust; and to decide whether it is or not we must turn to Aristotle's basic criterion. Aristotle criticizes those partisans of existing constitutions who support their own favoured constitution as the only just and correct one. His analysis shows why there is something plausible in their view, while at the same time the view is basically mistaken. This is just what he promises to do with common beliefs.[16]

244. VICE AND CONFLICT

The virtues rest on a true conception of happiness, and so promote the common good. The vices rest on a false conception of happiness; and since this fails to connect happiness with the common good, the different vices harm the common good by promoting injustice. In applying his moral theory to the explanation of political variation and change, Aristotle explores the bad social effects of the vices. Each of the virtues is the virtue it is partly because it is fine, because it promotes the common good of the community; and each of the vices is vicious and shameful partly because of the way it harms the common good.

The *Politics* defends these claims in more detail. Its empirical books (iv–vi) rely on the canon of virtues and vices, and confirm Aristotle's claim to have found the right canon. If injustice and the other vices have the bad effects that are displayed in the account of political instability, common sense gives us reasons for agreeing with Aristotle's judgment that these are indeed vices. The appeal to common sense is not the whole of Aristotle's defence of his theory; but it is a reasonable confirmation.

Mistaken conceptions of happiness harm the common interest through the types of moral education, formal or informal, that are practised in some states (1266b35–8, 1318b4, 1324b10, 1333b10). If I have one of the deviant conceptions of happiness, I have no reason to pursue just action for its own sake as part of their own good; hence I lack any overriding reason to follow even a correct principle of justice if it benefits another person and seems, judged by my false conception of happiness, to harm me. Moreover, my belief that justice harms me for someone else's benefit is quite justified, if I reach it from a deviant conception of justice and a true conception of happiness.

The combination of these errors weakens commitment to justice.[17]

The political system loses the necessary conditions for friendship between the citizens. For one important aspect of friendship in a state is concord about what it is expedient to do (*EN* 1167b2–4), but in deviant states this concord is replaced by struggle and competition. The observance of the (supposedly) just policy benefits some at the expense of others; and Thrasymachus' description of justice as simply another's good is true of the prevalent conception of justice.[18]

If so much injustice is built into the system, and if the prevalent conception of justice encourages a prudent person to be unjust, these deviant systems encourage injustice. When one side in an oligarchy or democracy try to exclude the other from political life altogether, or use the judicial system against their opponents, they violate both genuine justice and oligarchic or democratic justice. But the character of the citizens and the institutions of the state tend to encourage violations of the prevalent standard of justice.[19] Those who have developed the vices that are encouraged in deviant states will be greedy to win advantage at each other's expense (1167b9–16), and their injustice is a source of discord.[20]

The discord that results from belief in a conflict of interest between citizens is to be avoided in the ideal state (*Pol.* 1330a16–23). But not all deviant systems even try to avoid it, since their existence depends on the discord that threatens to destroy them; the partisans of one side try to secure loyalty through shared hostility to the other side.[21] They cannot plausibly claim to promote the common interest.

This is the attitude Aristotle sees in those who regard domination of the constitution as a prize of victory, and have no interest in forming a regime that allows common participation and benefit and is fair to everyone (1296a27–b2). Lack of justice and friendship is both cause and effect of this attitude to the constitution. When rich and poor find that their aims have nothing in common, they see no common interest; and when they see no common interest, they do not care about treating each other justly (1295b21–5), but struggle for the contested goods in which they see their whole happiness. Struggles and conflicts in the deviant systems reflect these general errors about happiness and justice; and Aristotle claims that the characteristic vices of oligarchy and of democracy explain the particular forms of conflict and instability to be found in each of these systems.

245. VICE AND AGGRESSION

An oligarch aims at the accumulation of wealth; but he wants it not simply for its own sake, but also as a source of honour. Since he has no true conception of the nature of happiness to impose a limit on his pursuit of wealth, he thinks greater wealth deserves greater honour; hence his love of honour (*philotimia*) produces a competitive attitude (*philoneikia*). This competitive side of the oligarchic outlook explains the characteristic injustice of the rich against the poor—wanton aggression (*hubris*).[22] Aggressiveness is a result of vanity, the vice of excess corresponding to magnanimity. The vain person tries to show that he is magnanimous and deserves honour; but instead of virtue, all he has to display is his good fortune, and this makes him overbearing and aggressive (*EN* 1124a29–b2).[23]

Aggression is different from greed, but the two are often connected (*Pol.* 1302b5, 1307a5–33).[24] When aggressiveness makes me want to profit at your expense, it causes me to do special injustice; but I can commit either one of aggression and special injustice without the other. Aggressiveness reflects the desire to display my superior status in one of the most striking ways—by disregarding what is justly due to you and humiliating you with impunity. Part of my reason may be a desire to show my superiority over the person I humiliate. But I may also humiliate a third party to convince you of my superiority. The particular intention of humiliating another results from the competitive attitude that is part of the oligarchic pursuit of honour.[25]

Aggressive tendencies promote oligarchy and (in extreme cases) tyranny, but also threaten the stability of these systems, since they cause oppression by the few and resentment in the many. The destructive effect of the character formed by the system on the system itself is part of the reason for believing that the system is deviant, resting on a false conception of justice and the other virtues. A genuine virtue should not undermine the system that is founded on the conception of the good underlying the virtue itself.[26]

The vices resulting from love of honour and competition are characteristic of the rich, few, and well born. Aristotle's account of these vices shows both why they should be characteristic of the oligarchic outlook, and how they encourage the actual behaviour of oligarchies and oligarchs.

246. VICE AND SLAVISHNESS

The lower classes, in Aristotle's view, are characteristically menial, and so display the slavish attitude of the menial character.[27] A slavish person's outlook would be suitable for him if he were a natural slave. He has never learnt that anything is worth doing or pursuing apart from what fulfils his bodily needs and appetites. The lower classes are often like slaves, if they have little leisure apart from the pursuit of necessities (1292b25–9, 1318b9–16); and in all circumstances their slavish outlook pursues the life of mere gratification (cf. *EN* 1095b19–22).

Slavishness results in ungenerosity or illiberality (*aneleutheria*), the attitude that is unsuited for free citizen (1336b12, 1337b6), and in an 'abased' (*tapeinon*) outlook (1295b18–21, 1315b6, 1337b14–15), turning away from honour to the exclusive pursuit of one's own gain (1266b40, 1297b6–8, 1318b16–17). These are the people the tyrant likes to encourage (1313b18–29, b41, 1314a15–17; cf. 1295b5–21). Since they care only about their bodily needs, they can be persuaded that it is in their interest to submit to superior force, and their sense of honour will not move them to resist.

Increased slavishness should encourage both slavish intemperance, extreme lack of restraint in the pursuit of bodily satisfaction, and slavish abasement, a diminished sense of honour and dignity. But extreme democracy displays extreme intemperance without any slavish abasement; and Aristotle does not explain why this happens.

The slavish intemperance of the people in extreme democracies explains their tendency to commit injustice against the rich, because of the flattery of the demagogues. The tyrant lives a life of gratification, and so he is willing to listen to anyone who will serve him in it, no matter how dishonourable the service may be (1313b32–1314a4). In democracies the people correspond to the tyrant and the demagogues to the flatterers (1304b20–1305a7; cf. 1274a3–11, 1292a13–38). Though demagogues can arise in different sorts of constitutions, including oligarchy (1305b22–39), they are most readily accepted in extreme democracies because they flatter the demos.

Intemperate people pursuing their own gratification are an easy prey for flatterers (*EN* 1121a30–b10).[28] Since the demos are slavishly intemperate, they care only about gratifying their appetites, and so they are attracted by unjust demagogic measures. The demagogues enrich the demos unjustly, by confiscating property from the rich, imposing heavy levies on them, and attacking them in the courts. Aristotle thinks such disregard for justice is characteristic of slavish people who have the leisure and resources to satisfy their slavish appetites. Such a democracy relaxes the normal and proper restraints over women and slaves (1313b32–8, 1319b27–32), so that everyone can live intemperately, and all restrictions on living as one pleases are removed.[29]

If this is the character of the people in extreme democracies, why do they not also display slavish abasement? Normally the person with a slavish and menial character is little concerned with his honour or status; if he can gratify his appetites he will not complain. A tyrant should apparently be pleased to maintain an idle proletariat, gratified by bread and circuses. But this is not how Aristotle describes the tyrant. To neutralize the demos the tyrant tries to reduce their intemperance, by making them poor and hard-working (1313b18–29). He does not assume that the most slavish demos will be the most intemperate. Nor does Aristotle think so; indeed he thinks a poor and hard-working demos is the best kind (1292b25–1293a10, 1318b6–27), though he acknowledges that extreme poverty makes someone abased and ready to be ruled as a slave (1295b18–21).

Aristotle could not plausibly claim that extreme democracy causes slavish abasement. Far from being ready to be manipulated in return for bread and circuses, the demos in this system show the keenest awareness of their own status and honour. They insist on greater equality for all citizens, and punish anyone who compromises the dignity of the people. Though individual members of the demos may not be competitive in their private aims, they are collectively concerned with their honour—indeed too concerned for Aristotle's liking.

Aristotle assumes that menial work makes a character menial; and this is why he thinks menial workers have no place in the ideal state. Moreover, he thinks the bad condition of some democracies is to be explained by the menial character of the citizens. But unfortunately (for Aristotle's theory) citizens of extreme democracies do not display the menial character that Aristotle expects. If this is so, then menial work by itself cannot degrade someone's character in the way Aristotle claims. He recognizes that citizens of democracies are concerned for honour and justice, and insist on running their own lives.

If Aristotle has been influenced more than he should have been by his views about the effects of menial occupations, he has been influenced less than he should have been by his account of the democratic outlook. He acknowledges that freedom is a mark of democracy, and that the democrat conceives freedom as living as one pleases. He describes the character formed by this belief in freedom as slavish, because he thinks the belief explains why democracies reject restraints on gratification. He unfairly overlooks the other likely effect of the democratic belief in freedom—refusal to be ruled by someone else more than is necessary (1317b10–17). Since a person influenced by this outlook is not likely to be slavishly abased, the demos in extreme democracies are self-assertive.

Aristotle must in consistency recognize the possibility of countervailing influences that may prevent the normal effects of menial work.[30] In democracy the countervailing influence is the outlook resulting from the democratic conception of justice. Someone who grows up with this outlook thinks he is justly entitled to consideration in distribution of goods, and regards it as a slight and dishonour if he is deprived of his equal share in government.

Aristotle's belief in the destructive effects of menial labour leads him to predict that the demos will be slavish and abased; but his account of the democratic belief in freedom and independence should lead him to predict that the demos will be self-assertive. He speaks as though the first prediction is fulfilled, but the evidence he cites supports the second prediction.

These results confirm two previous judgments about Aristotle's theory. We argued that his views about menial labour should be rejected, and that he undervalues the conception of freedom as independence and living as one pleases.[31] Both these objections focus on errors that are evident in the criticism of democracy. Since these errors cause such damage to Aristotle's other claims, we have further reason for concluding that his theory is better off without them, and that they are not warranted by his central political principles.

247. INSTABILITY IN POLITICAL SYSTEMS

After explaining, in Book iv, why there are different constitutions and what they are, Aristotle turns, in Book v, to a discussion of a feature of them that would immediately strike any Greek student—their tendency to change into one another as a result of peaceful developments or as a result of violent revolution arising from conflict within the state.

Many constitutional changes result from features of a state quite apart from its constitution.[32] Aristotle insists in the *Ethics* that rational planning cannot expect to secure every necessary condition of the happy life, and that some of its conditions are exposed to chance and to external conditions. Similarly, political scientists must recognize the role of external circumstances in political change, so that they can more realistically plan for the preservation or change of a particular system.[33]

Still, these external conditions do not fully explain political change. Change depends on the nature of the constitution itself and of the people who live under it, and especially on their relation to justice and the common interest. The character of the people affects the form of the constitution, and the constitution in turn affects them; the laws explicitly reward some people over others, and one constitution suits one type of character more than it suits another. The effects of the constitution may be deep enough to survive an actual change of constitutions, so that the habits and characters encouraged by an oligarchy survive under a democracy (1292b11–21). The interaction of characters and constitutions supports Aristotle's advice to states to attend to the characters and outlooks of their citizens.

Aristotle argues that constitutional changes are the results of the vices encouraged by the unjust aspects of each constitution.[34] He argues that deviant conceptions of justice fail to secure the common good, both because they rest on false conceptions of the good, and because they are systematically biased towards the good of some people against the good of others.

Admittedly, the dominance of such a conception of justice does not imply instability and conflict; people may either be deceived into thinking their interests are being promoted, or apathetic about asserting their interest, or persuaded that their efforts will be fruitless. Still, Aristotle claims that in so far as people recognize their interest and think they can do something about it, they will find legitimate grievances in the political systems controlled by deviant conceptions of justice. Moreover, the deviant conceptions will encourage the pursuit of unjust gain, and so will provoke both justified and unjustified revolts and challenges.

248. VIRTUE AND POLITICAL STABILITY

The *Ethics* describes the virtues of character that achieve happiness in the right external conditions; and the *Politics* describes the external conditions and the community in which the virtues have their proper result. Aristotle, however, does not recommend the virtues only for these conditions and this community; he believes that the virtuous person makes the best of the circumstances (1332a19–27), and that virtue is worth our while even in bad conditions.

In bad conditions we cannot exercise the virtues properly, and so we may be unable to acquire them; but still, Aristotle thinks, we should be as virtuous as we can be in the circumstances. The virtues express a person's decision to guide his life by his rational agency, and to follow the same principles even if he lacks the external goods necessary for happiness; and this is the dominant constituent of his happiness even in unfavourable conditions.[35]

The *Politics* shows that this claim needs some explanation. What virtues should we try to cultivate as far as we can? Should we aim at the virtues of a man or at the virtues of a citizen in a particular political system? The second type of virtue is (for all Aristotle says) fully achievable in actual conditions, while the virtue of a man is not; but that hardly seems a reason for renouncing the virtue of a man in favour of the virtue of a citizen. Aristotle claims that in bad conditions the good person will not give up the virtue that is left to him. The virtue that justifies such inflexibility is the virtue that affirms the primacy of rational agency; and this is the virtue of a man.

Aristotle implies, then, that if the virtue of a citizen conflicts with the virtue of a man, we should give up the virtue of a citizen. He believes, however, that this is only a logical, not a practical, possibility. He is right to believe this if the best way to cultivate the virtue of a man, as far as we can, is to cultivate the virtue of a citizen in the political system we live in. Part of human virtue consists in the right relations to fellow-citizens; and some of these relations are promoted by the virtues corresponding to each system.

On the other hand, Aristotle admits that both tyranny and extreme democracy tend to encourage degraded and vicious attitudes and practices in citizens (e.g. 1311a8–28, 1313b32–1314a29). As Plato argues, wise people are better off without the type of character that is needed for success in a democracy (*Rep.* 496c5–e2), because (Plato supposes) it excludes the practice of genuine virtue. Even in less thoroughly bad systems the city rewards and encourages love of honour, competitiveness, extravagance, meanness, insolence, abasement, and so on. Aristotle seems to violate his own principles, if he advises us to be good citizens in these conditions. At best, his advice seems to encourage uncritical acceptance of 'my station and its duties'. Bradley argues:

To the question, How am I to know what is right? the answer must be, By the *aisthêsis* of the *phronimos*; and the *phronimos* is the man who has identified his will with the moral spirit of the community, and judges accordingly.[36]

In a bad constitution, encouragement of the virtue of a citizen seems to support active complicity in vice.

This objection misunderstands Aristotle's conception of the virtue of a citizen that is relative to a political system. Justice and temperance relative to an oligarchy are not justice and temperance as oligarchs conceive them, but the degree of justice and temperance that are consistent with the preservation of an oligarchy. Aristotle believes that these will actually tend to preserve a fairly reasonable oligarchy (1310a19–22); he implies that an oligarchy that is undermined by the observance of oligarchic justice does not deserve to survive. The virtues of a citizen are not tactics for adaptation to the regime, but the proper way to exercise the genuine virtues in these political systems.

Aristotle believes that since injustice is a source of instability, justice will restore some degree of stability to a state. The more just the state becomes, the more the citizens will develop the virtues relative to that political system; hence the virtues relative to the system will be the best that we can do in those conditions to approach genuine virtue.[37]

This argument implies that *some* devices tending to restore stability to a state also tend to make it more just, since *some* types of instability result from injustice. But injustice by itself is neither necessary nor sufficient for instability; and, similarly, greater stability will be neither necessary nor sufficient for greater justice. We are right to pursue greater stability for a political system only if we attack the specific type of instability that results from injustice.

Aristotle compares the politician to a doctor who advises patients who refuse to do what is needed for complete health (1288b10–21).[38] The politician must assume that this particular non-ideal system is to remain in being.[39] But Aristotle does not imply that a deviant system always can or should be preserved, any more than all a doctor's patients can or should be kept alive.[40]

Nor does the politician simply give advice on ways to protect the constitution from change.[41] If he did that, he might advise oligarchs to demoralize the poor, or democrats to eliminate the rich by judicial murder, or tyrants to divide and discourage the people more thoroughly. Aristotle rejects these popular, and (for all he says) sometimes effective, devices for maintaining a regime (1309b18–1310a2).[42] Instead he recommends the cultivation of the virtues that are contrary to its distinctive vices (1319b37–1320a4). He advises deviant states not merely on ways to achieve stability, but on ways to achieve justice.

This practical advice is meant to show how Aristotle's own conception of justice and the other virtues explains, justifies, and corrects the common beliefs. We tend to believe a political system is better if it is more just, but this belief seems to conflict with our experience of justice. For democratic and oligarchic constitutions may well seem to be worse the more thoroughly they incorporate their favoured conceptions of justice; and these conceptions of justice also seem to conflict. Hence a survey of common beliefs and normal political practice may shake our confidence about what justice is and about whether it is good for a state.

Aristotle replies that the oligarchic and democratic conceptions of justice are false. We find the true conception of justice from the true account of the state, hence from ethical theory, hence from the correct conception of human nature. The true conception of justice shows that the best democratic and oligarchic conceptions are not the most democratic and oligarchic, but the most just (cf. 1320a2–4). The ideal state and its true conception of justice provide the norm for other states, even though they cannot fully realize it (1296b2–12). Common sense, therefore, contrary to initial appearances, supports Aristotle's claim that justice promotes the common interest. His technical and therapeutic advice is part of the argument for his conception of justice and the other virtues.

Aristotle seeks to mitigate the distinctive character of a particular type of regime, and so disagrees with the advice of single-minded partisans (1320a2–4). His advice seeks to reduce the error implied in the conception of justice underlying a particular constitution, without removing the error altogether by removing the constitution. Hence the advice presupposes the truth of Aristotle's account of justice; it does not involve simply splitting the difference between common beliefs.

Aristotle's suggested modifications of democracy are not intended to add oligarchic elements, which would simply add further injustices.[43] Each deviant system rests on a partial conception of justice that results in consideration of only some of the interests that ought to be considered. The remedy for this bias is to pay particular attention to the interests that are not primarily served by the system.[44] That is the way to bring the state closer to justice, which is in the common interest, and hence is in the interest of the dominant and of the defeated class (1320a35–b4).[45]

To achieve the appropriate concord and harmony in the state, Aristotle insists on the importance of the right kind of education to suit the laws and the constitution.[46] Though this education, and hence the corresponding virtue, must be relative to the constitution, it is not simply a support for the *status quo*. It ought to include the virtues, in so far as these are consistent with the maintenance of the existing constitution; and since the virtues will add up to general justice they will be in the common interest. The Aristotelian virtues are found to be appropriate not just for the ideal state in its favourable conditions, but also for non–ideal states in more realistic conditions.[47]

Aristotle recommends the virtues as sources of stability and of other benefits for a state. When he stresses the importance of justice and the common advantage (1320a11–17), resulting in concord (1306a9–12, 1310a2–12), he recommends the virtues to common beliefs. This is not the only recommendation that can or should be offered for the virtues; but Aristotle sees that it is an important part of a dialectical argument for them.

249. STABILITY AND THE MIDDLE CLASS

Aristotle argues that the best non-ideal state will have a large middle class, between the extremes of wealth and poverty, and that the constitution should give this class a large political role. He even appeals to the ethical doctrine of the mean to support his advocacy of the intermediate class. The ethical doctrine is misapplied, and Aristotle's argument may well appear to be mere propaganda dressed up with an appearance of theory.[48] But since he intends to argue from reasonable theoretical assumptions, we should examine his argument, if we are to evaluate the theory on which the argument is supposed to rest. We should hesitate to take Aristotle's word for it if he asserts that his theory justifies his particular recommendation; and often this is all the better for the theory.

Aristotle argues that a large middle class reduces tension between the classes in the state. He suggests that the middle class will avoid the competitive and aggressive tendencies associated with extreme wealth, and also the slavish abasement resulting (allegedly) from extreme poverty (1295b13–25). If he is right about the effects of extreme wealth and poverty, we might agree that it is desirable to reduce the number of the honour-loving rich and the slavish poor, to reduce their influence on the constitution. Aristotle will then be right to claim that many citizens should be rich enough to belong to the middle class; both democracy and oligarchy will be better off without extremes of wealth and poverty.[49]

But this reasonable argument is not exactly an argument for Aristotle's political recommendation. For why is it better to have three grades rather than two or one? If it is good for the state to have many citizens at the level of the middle class, it does not follow that they should constitute a middle class—that there should be extremely rich and extremely poor citizens above and below them. In fact, Aristotle's remarks suggest that if extreme wealth and poverty are bad, they will still be bad (though their bad effects will be reduced) in a state with a large middle class; it is not clear how the argument supports three classes. The class structure Aristotle prefers seems inferior, in the light of his own arguments against extreme wealth and poverty, to restrained democracy at a high material level; this would be a democratic variation on the polity.

The arguments that allegedly support the middle class turn out to be arguments for something different. Aristotle argues that a state should reduce the extent of social and economic inequality, but seems to be committed to one class, whereas he takes himself to be arguing for three classes. To justify his own recommendation he needs to rule out the one-class alternative. Presumably he might argue it is not worth considering as a practical solution. If some considerable degree of inequality must often be accepted, then (he might argue) the best way to avoid the ill effects of inevitable inequality is to ensure a strong middle class. But these claims need further defence; it is not fair to assume without argument that the one-class alternative is impractical, or that the good effects of the middle class compensate for the bad effects of inequality. The further premises needed to justify Aristotle's recommendation are themselves open to doubt.

Examination of Aristotle's argument allows us to identify more clearly the empirical premises that connect his ethical principles with his practical recommendations. In this case, no less than in his exclusion of menial workers and his defence of private property, Aristotle's empirical premises are highly dubious, and the empirical parts of the *Politics* do not support them. We are free to draw different conclusions from his ethical principles.

The tendency of Aristotle's empirical over-confidence in these cases is strikingly uniform. All the recommendations that rest on the dubious premises tend to support wealth and inequality against the claims of the radical democracy familiar to Aristotle. It is unlikely that Aristotle's own political preferences and prejudices play no role in his interpretation of the empirical evidence, and in his failure to look for the empirical evidence he needs. Since his political preferences encourage his empirical over-confidence, they affect his interpretation of his moral and political principles.

We should not infer that the principles themselves reflect the same preferences and prejudices. On the contrary; we have found that the principles rest on reasonable grounds that are independent of Aristotle's own prejudices; and attention to these grounds allows us to expose the prejudices.

250. THE DEFENCE OF PRIVATE PROPERTY

A further specific recommendation allows us to test several of Aristotle's theoretical principles, and illustrates the difficulties in reaching conclusions about political practice from them. Though Aristotle denies that the state or the citizen should aim at the accumulation of wealth, and though he forbids the citizens to engage in commercial activity, he insists that they should hold private property, and that its abolition would be a serious harm and injustice to them. We can fairly ask if Aristotle really justifies his defence of private property by appeal to his principles. We should also ask if a state allowing private property is free of the sources of instability that Aristotle criticizes in the deviant systems; for in measuring deviant systems by this criterion, he licenses us to apply it to his own ideal state.

In his defence Aristotle can appeal first to his conception of happiness. Though he rejects the democratic conception of happiness as the sort of gratification that is secured by living as we please, he must himself attach considerable value to freedom and independence, as the sources of individual initiative. The free person, unlike the slave, is not constrained by necessity, and in his life he is independent enough for his rational judgment and choice to make some difference to what he does.[50]

Aristotle appeals to these goods in his arguments to show that public ownership (of the sort advocated in Plato's *Republic*) is inferior to the friendly sharing of private property (1263a27–40).

He thinks private property is better than public ownership because it allows me to retain the enormous pleasure of thinking something is exclusively my own. This pleasure results from the self-love that is natural and human, and not to be condemned.

Further, it is unbelievably more pleasant to count something as our special possession. For each person's love of himself is not pointless, but a natural tendency. While selfishness is quite rightly blamed, it is not love of oneself, but excessive self-love; and the same distinction applies to love of money, since practically everyone loves himself and loves money. (1263a40–b5)

The sense of exclusive possession is an important support for the sense of freedom and independence sought by a rational agent.

Aristotle claims that the pleasure we get from helping our friends depends on our having something of our own at our disposal that we can usefully give them (1263b5–7). He suggests that we also need private property to leave room for the actions characteristic of other virtues; for temperance presupposes wives belonging to other men, and generosity presupposes some property to be generous with (1263b7–14). This belief in the value of exclusive possession makes the friendship in Plato's city seem watery by comparison with private and particular friendships (1262b7–24).

Aristotle quite fairly assumes that if I have my own supply of external goods under my own control, my choice and decision determine what happens to it. If I do not control it, I must depend on someone else for the necessities that I need and for goods that I can give to the recipients of my generosity. But such dependence conflicts with the initiative that a rational agent needs if she is to make a difference with her decision and action. Even if the result of private generosity is the very same pattern of distribution that the wise legislator would prescribe, the fact that it results from the private generosity of many people is a further good feature of it.[51]

Private property should also, in Aristotle's view, answer one of the demands of special justice. For special justice is intended to protect self-confined interests, so that the state does not impose on any citizen an unreasonable degree of sacrifice for the benefit of other citizens. Since the virtuous person's good consists in more than his purely self-confined goods, justice need not assure him a higher level of self-confined goods than he could achieve under any other arrangement; he will legitimately accept some sacrifice for the sake of the common good that is also part of his own good. However, he will not accept the neglect of his self-confined interest beyond the point where his own interest justifies it.

The self-confined aspects of a person's good imply that he is not simply a natural resource for promoting other people's interest; that is the status of a slave.[52] Since part of his good consists in taking initiatives in the distribution of external goods, special justice should assure to everyone not only the external goods he needs to keep himself alive in moderate affluence, but also the goods he needs to support the initiatives he takes in his leisure. Hence Aristotle will not think the demands of justice are satisfied if everyone simply gets what he needs, as far as this can be achieved without reference to the legitimate demand for protection of initiatives. This protection is secured by private property.

251. OBJECTIONS TO THE DEFENCE OF PRIVATE PROPERTY

Aristotle's defence of private property appeals to quite basic principles of his ethical and political theory. But we should not assume too readily that these principles support conclusions quite as specific as those he draws. It is not clear that private property is even desirable in the ideal city. The citizens are ready to resign the task of moral education to the state, and to accept their own moral education as an expression of the common interest that they identify with their own. Why should they not take the same attitude to the distribution of external goods?

On this view, if external goods are distributed in accordance with need, a virtuous person participates in the action of the state, and so does not think some significant initiative has been removed from him. Aristotle can apparently rely on the argument he uses about moral education; the citizen willingly accepts the state's action, which is also an expression of his own rational design. Why should someone demand individual initiative in private generosity more than in moral education?

Aristotle might claim that the two cases are different. A virtuous person's own rational preferences will require public education, since he will want himself and others to have been trained for the virtues without which the rest of the ideal city will not secure happiness. This is too important to be left to unregulated private initiative. Private property, however, in an ideal city is a rather different matter. Here there is nothing to be lost and something to be gained by allowing individual initiative. An individual's own self-love and pleasure in what is exclusively his own can be used to good effect, to strengthen friendly relations and not as a threat to them.

Happiness, on this view, requires an individual to attach the right weight to the common interest, but also to protect his self-confined interest. Public moral education and private property reflect these two aspects of a person's interest. In the ideal state they support each other.

Public moral education encourages the desire to use private property in the right way; and the right use of it strengthens the friendship that is needed to maintain concern for the common interest.

Aristotle's own account of human nature, however, may not support his claims about property. He argues that Plato's abolition of private property conflicts with basic tendencies in human nature, and will create quarrels and dissensions, destroying concord in the ideal city, no less effectively than greed and competition destroy it in deviant cities. But Aristotle's arrangements seem to encourage the natural tendency to greed, cupidity, and competition. Aristotle's criticism of deviant systems exposes the destructive effects of these tendencies, and the abolition of private property might seem a small price to pay for their removal.

Aristotle might answer that moral education will prevent any dangerous growth of these tendencies if private property is allowed; but then why should moral education not remove the tendencies to quarrels and dissensions that are supposed to result from abolition of private property? Arguments about moral education counter arguments about human nature; and neither claim seems more legitimate than the other.

Aristotle himself gives us some reason to argue that he puts too much weight on moral education, and too little weight on the effects of actual concern with private property. He implies that it is folly to pretend we can talk ourselves out of deeply ingrained habits; for he admits that generous people may be worse than others at managing their assets (*EN* 1120b4–6, 14–20), and that the process of acquisition tends to make people more acquisitive and less generous (1120b11–14). More important, his own refusal to allow citizens to be menial workers seems to assume that the work itself is corrupting, beyond the influence of any moral education.[53] In his defence of private property, by contrast, Aristotle seems to take very little account of the motives that are encouraged by the objective nature of accumulation and possession.

It would be unwise, however, to rest our case against Aristotle's defence of private property on the claim that he expects too much of moral education in this case. For we might argue that he is nearer the truth here than he is when he assumes that menial workers are beyond the help of moral education. If we are more optimistic than he is in that case, we should not be too ready to accuse him of over-optimism about private property.

Citizenship for menial workers would benefit the city enough to justify the risks. Is the same true of private property? Are its benefits so great and so special to it that the ideal state ought to accept the risks? Aristotle appeals to the value of freedom and individual initiative. But in the ideal state it is not clear that private property is needed to secure these goods. The citizen contributes his own deliberation to the deliberation of the community about the common good; and these deliberations should take account of the self-confined good of each citizen.

Since the political institutions of this city require this exercise of individual initiative, it is not clear why private property should be needed as well; though it may be a useful expedient for encouraging individual initiative in inferior political systems, it seems to be superseded in the best system.[54] Aristotle urges that a person should develop a conception of himself as an individual, a source of desires, interests, and claims, distinct from those of other individuals. But it is hard to see why, in the ideal state, the desirable sort of independence should require exclusive ownership.

If this is true, then Aristotle's principles about friendship, justice, and freedom do not support private property in the ideal state. He fails to take proper account of the ideal character of the ideal state. He properly urges the benefits that might, in some conditions, be secured by private property, and properly insists that the ideal state ought to secure these benefits; but he does not see that it could secure them without private property. He thinks his ethical principles justify a more definite recommendation than in fact they seem to justify. If Aristotle's principles do not support his specific recommendations about property, then our doubts about his recommendations need not undermine our confidence in his principles.

252. MORAL AND POLITICAL THEORY IN ARISTOTLE'S SYSTEM

We have now seen where the *Ethics* and *Politics* rely on 'strong' dialectic, introduced in *Metaphysics* iv to fulfil the tasks for which 'pure' dialectic proves inadequate. Pure dialectic follows the prescription of the *Topics* in picking its premises from among the common beliefs, leaving the interlocutor free to accept or reject them; its conclusions express a systematic and consistent account of the common beliefs, but do not pretend to correct them, or to replace them with objective principles.

Strong dialectic also relies on common beliefs. Since a dialectical argument, strong no less than weak, seeks to lead us from what is known to us to what is known by nature, the argument must begin from premises that we can accept, and must continue to rely on them as the argument proceeds. Here as elsewhere, dialectic follows the pattern of the Platonic dialogue, where the reflective assent of the interlocutor is always required. Strong dialectic, however, confines itself to those premises we have strong reason, apart from the range of common beliefs currently being considered, to take to correspond to independent reality. The argument to show that a premiss is privileged in this way is different in different cases.

The basic privileged premisses belong to first philosophy, described in *Metaphysics* iv; some premisses cannot be denied unless we are to make ourselves incapable of thought and speech about any persisting subject. The privileged premisses derived from *Metaphysics* vii–ix rest on general assumptions about the nature of the world and the task of explanation; while we could deny them without the crippling effects described in *Metaphysics* iv, we could not deny them without losing the explanations and the types of understanding that result from Aristotle's metaphysical outlook. Once these privileged premisses are secured by metaphysical argument, Aristotle uses them to support his conception of the soul and the human essence; and he uses this conception as the basis of his ethical theory.

The justification, however, does not go only one way. The metaphysical and psychological claims are defensible independently of the ethical common beliefs, and hence provide some external justification for Aristotle's ethical theory. Without form, matter, essence, soul, and rational agency we could not appropriately explain or understand the phenomena that we need to explain. But if these metaphysical and psychological claims were diametrically opposed to our basic ethical beliefs, we would have to reject something; and why should we give up our basic ethical beliefs? We would need some reason for thinking them less warranted than the competing beliefs; and Aristotle's arguments give us no reason for thinking so. A diametrical opposition would raise justified doubts about all the opposed beliefs. When we find that these doubts are unwarranted, we help to justify the non–ethical as well as the ethical beliefs.

The cumulative force of Aristotle's arguments is not confined to ethics, narrowly conceived. We have tried to take seriously his claim that ethical inquiry is part of political science; and we have looked for a continuous line of argument in the *Ethics* and *Politics*. We have found that Aristotle is largely justified in his claims, and that his ethical theory is properly completed in his political theory.

Moreover, his political theory is not merely ideology, depending for its premisses on the special assumptions of one or another political system. On the contrary, Aristotle has a systematic philosophical argument; for the *Politics* transcends mere ideology to the extent that it relies on ethical theory, and ethical theory transcends mere common beliefs to the extent that it relies on psychology and metaphysics. Aristotle's dialectical method is capable, therefore, of finding results that we have reason to believe are true, not merely coherent with common beliefs. The capacity of his ethical theory to explain political phenomena and to justify the most important common beliefs is a legitimate dialectical argument in its favour.

253. THE EVALUATION OF ARISTOTLE'S CLAIMS

In these ways the *Politics* confirms the expectations we have formed in our examination of the *Metaphysics, De Anima,* and *Ethics.* A proper understanding of Aristotle's method allows us to understand the structure of his theory better than we might otherwise have understood it. Equally, we are confirmed in believing that the method is sound if we find that it yields well warranted conclusions.

We should not be surprised, then, to find that the argument of the *Ethics* and *Politics* is dialectical, and that sometimes Aristotle claims more than pure dialectic would allow him. The difference between pure dialectic and strong dialectic is reflected in the appeals to human nature and the human essence; and these appeals determine the direction of the argument. The order of topics is the order that Aristotle thinks most suitable for a dialectical argument from what is known to us; but he selects the common beliefs that fit his systematic argument.

Aristotle thinks strong dialectical argument is no less possible in ethics than elsewhere. Knowledge of a human being as essentially a rational agent is the basis of an account of the human good and of responsible rational agency from which the rest of the account of virtue is derived. When we understand the place of rational agency in the human essence, we can describe the complete good and identify its dominant component. When we have justified 'the most and the most important' ethical common beliefs, we have shown that ethics is a part of philosophy secured by strong dialectic. At the same time we have defended in one important area the claim of strong dialectic to be a method of philosophical argument that can justify claims to knowledge of an independent reality.

The result of approaching Aristotle from this point of view should not be uncritical acceptance of his conclusions. For sometimes we can see that they rest on prejudice, or on a disputable assessment of empirical evidence, or on an appeal to common beliefs with no broader support. We have seen that this is true in Aristotle's defence of a restrictive qualification for citizenship, of private property, and of a mixed constitution allowing predominance to the middle class. In all these cases we can see that Aristotle's theory proves less than he wants, and that dubious assumptions are needed to fill the gaps.

Discovery of these weaknesses may properly strengthen our confidence in the general soundness of Aristotle's method and doctrine. For since his general principles commit us to something less specific and more plausible than he wants, we need not reject the general principles because of doubts about the conclusions he draws.[55] If we examine Aristotle's arguments to find those that rely on strong rather than weak dialectic, we find some grounds for criticism of his conclusions.

We should not conclude that Aristotle's principles are too unspecific to yield any interesting conclusions or to justify any distinctive moral and political recommendations. His conception of happiness as self-realization relies on his conception of the human essence; and it supports the claims for friendship, and thereby the account of citizenship, moral education, and the proper extent of individual freedom and state action. The argument relies partly on assumptions that are capable of being false; but with weak and reasonable empirical assumptions it is hard to deny all force to his argument. While the warranted conclusions of Aristotle's philosophical system are less specific than he sometimes takes them to be, they are not so general as to be uncontroversial. Aristotle's own method of argument shows us a fruitful way to conduct the appropriate controversy.

22

RECONSIDERATIONS

254. ARISTOTLE'S SILENCES

It may be helpful to readers who have tried to follow the argument of this book if I review some of its main claims, and comment briefly on some of the questions that they raise. In particular, I will try to distinguish some of the different claims I have argued for, and suggest how they do or do not depend on each other. While I think the main arguments of the book support each other, and that the detailed discussion supports the main arguments, I do not think it all forms a single package that has to be taken or left as a whole; and in recognizing some objections to some of my claims, I would like to see how far the force of these objections really spreads.

I have explored Aristotle's conception of the status of first principles, and of the sort of argument he thinks can be given for them. I have suggested that the conception developed in *Metaphysics* iv expresses a quite significant change of mind from the view in Aristotle's earlier works, and that this conception underlies his argument in psychology, ethics, and politics.

One might wonder why Aristotle says so little about all this. Though he certainly introduces first philosophy, he does not say in general terms what an argument has to be like if it belongs to first philosophy; and he never asks if any of his psychological or ethical principles can be defended by this sort of argument. He never explicitly raises the main questions that have occupied us in Part III. This might suggest that I have raised the wrong questions, and that Aristotle does not hold the views I have attributed to him.

Aristotle's silence partly reflects his rather narrow conception of what is relevant to a particular discussion. In his inquiries into, say, physics or ethics, he quite often alludes to an issue only to dismiss it as inappropriate to the present discussion.[1] In refusing to discuss these issues at length, he does not always mean that they are irrelevant, or that our view on them makes no difference to our view of the subject under discussion. It certainly makes quite some difference to our views on physics if we do not believe in change, and it may make some difference to our views on ethics if we hold a Platonic rather than an Aristotelian view of the soul. Aristotle does not deny this. But he thinks it better to assume that we grasp these issues before we discuss physics or ethics, and he prefers to keep them out of his physical or ethical argument.

Similarly, then, we should not be surprised if he approaches ethics with some quite specific assumptions about the nature of first principles and the sorts of arguments they allow, but thinks it inappropriate to explain or justify his assumptions in a ethical work.[2] We have Aristotle's own authority for supposing that he will assume quite a lot, and that we have to turn to his other works to evaluate his assumptions.

And yet, Aristotle's silences do not simply reflect his views about appropriateness in a particular work. It is a more general feature of his works that the importance of a claim is often inversely proportional to the amount of space he gives it. He is in no doubt about the importance of understanding the first principles and getting them right. We should investigate first principles;

for they have great influence on what comes next. For it seems that the origin is more than half the whole, and that many answers to the questions we investigate become clear through the origin. (*EN* 1098b6–8)

For similar reasons, the study of the soul ought to contribute to knowledge of nature, since the soul is a first principle (*DA* 402a4–7). But Aristotle does not characteristically examine them in the detail that their importance might seem to warrant. His admission in the *Ethics* that his account is rough and sketchy (*EN* 1098a20–2) applies equally to some of his other discussions of first principles.[3]

The difficulty is not that Aristotle is never willing to go into detail. Characteristics of animals, senses of words, varieties of political systems, all move him to full and precise description; but on the most important issues of all his remarks are often brief, inexplicit, and inconclusive. Some of the best-informed modern students of Aristotle recognize the frustration that many readers must feel in trying to fix his view on some fundamental issues.[4] Perhaps his sketchiness about first principles reflects his awareness of the obscurity and difficulty of the questions they raise, and some tentativeness in his answers.

But whatever the reason for Aristotle's silences, we should not take them to count against an attempt to attribute to him the sorts of views I have described in the previous chapters. A philosophical reader may in any case want to know how Aristotle might deal with the questions I have raised. I have tried to answer that question. But I also claim to describe views that Aristotle explicitly or implicitly holds, not simply views that he might have formed if he had faced certain questions. His silences, at any rate, do not show that he does not hold these views; they should not surprise us, if we are familiar with the general character of Aristotle's works.

255. THE TREATMENT OF ARISTOTLE'S EARLY WORKS

I have described some contrasts between the *Metaphysics* and the *Organon* and *Physics*; and I suggest that the contrast reflects a development in Aristotle's views, both on methodological questions about dialectic and science, and on more specific questions about substance, form, and matter. I take the contrast to be a good reason for supposing that the *Metaphysics* is a later work than the other works (which I will continue to call 'early', simply for convenience).

Arguments about Aristotelian chronology are, admittedly, hazardous. We have no firm non-philosophical grounds for ordering the treatises in the Corpus; and philosophical arguments are liable to be inconclusive on this issue. In this particular case my argument may appear especially inconclusive, in so far as it rests partly on silences in the early works. They do not describe first philosophy, as the *Metaphysics* conceives it. But they do not deny its existence; the *Organon* explicitly rejects only a demonstrative science, without considering a non-demonstrative alternative. Nor do the early works offer the elaborate account of substance that is worked out in *Metaphysics* vii–ix. But their failure to say certain things may simply reflect the fact that they are more elementary treatises; or Aristotle may be following his rule of not mentioning more than he takes to be necessary for the questions currently at issue.

I do not think this is a good enough explanation of the difference between the early works and the *Metaphysics*. The difference is especially clear in Aristotle's early views on the relation between subject, this, essence, and form (in his discussion of substance), and in his claims about knowledge and demonstration (in his remarks on science and dialectic). In both cases, the argument of the early works is far less intelligible if we take them to rely on views similar to those in the *Metaphysics*. On the contrary; they raise just the puzzles that are set out in *Metaphysics* iii. It is reasonable to infer that Aristotle sees the puzzles arising from his early views, and that he changes his mind.

Still, I do not want to make my account of Aristotle depend entirely on the claim that his views actually develop in the direction I have described. Let us, then, assume for the sake of argument that he had already formed the outlook of the *Metaphysics* when he wrote the early works. How ought we, on this assumption, to understand the relation between the different works?

I believe that in this case we must say that Aristotle fails to understand some of his views. If he takes his early works to offer an elementary, intuitive, or selective statement of the very same doctrine that he expounds in the *Metaphysics*, he is wrong. Commonsense distinctions by themselves do not support, or do not uniquely support, Aristotle's views about substance. Moreover, a natural development of the views in the early works leads to conclusions (e.g. about the claims of matter and form to be substance) that conflict with the views in the *Metaphysics*. Similarly, we must say that Aristotle's foundationalism in the *Analytics* results from a one-sided view of science and objectivity, and that this view needs considerable modification in the light of Aristotle's views on first philosophy. Any attempt to treat these different parts of the Corpus as different expositions of the same body of doctrine conceals major differences—whether or not Aristotle himself sees the differences. Even if we refuse to explain the differences chronologically, we ought to recognize them.

Still, I do not want my argument to depend wholly on claims about doctrinal differences between different works. Even if we believe that the *Metaphysics* is simply a fuller exposition of the doctrine of the earlier works, it is useful to see what it adds to them. For I have claimed that the early works do not by themselves explain how dialectical argument leads to objective principles, though they assume that they have found objective principles and suggest no method of discovery besides dialectic (in cases where empirical inquiry is not appropriate). On this issue the early works raise a legitimate question that they do not answer; but the *Metaphysics* answers the question.

If I am right, then we must appeal to the arguments of the *Metaphysics* if we are to explain why the early works find objective principles. To show that the principles found in the early works are objective principles, we must defend them by a form of argument that the early works themselves do not provide.

Whether I am right or wrong about these questions does not depend on claims about the order or consistency of the Corpus. The issue can be settled only by an examination of the argument in the *Metaphysics* in comparison with the early works. This is why I have not confined myself to the methodological parts of the *Metaphysics* (in Book iv), but have also examined some of the discussion of substance. Only the details of the argument show the difference, if any, that results from Aristotle's effort to offer arguments that are proper to first philosophy. I have argued that Aristotle's treatment of subject, essence, potentiality, actuality, matter, and form, relies on premises drawn from first philosophy; even if the doctrine of the early works were just the same, only the arguments of the *Metaphysics* justify it.

256. THE TREATMENT OF ARISTOTLE'S LATE WORKS

Part III may reasonably raise doubts, partly similar and partly opposite to those raised by Part I. In Part I I have been quite strict about taking the early works on their own terms, resisting any attempt to interpret them in the light of the *Metaphysics*. I have refused, for instance, to appeal to *Metaphysics* iv to explain what Aristotle has in mind (in *Topics* i 2) in ascribing a constructive role to dialectic. Similarly, I have been cautious about the references in the *Physics* to first philosophy, and to a discipline common to the sciences; I have refused to interpret these remarks in the light of *Metaphysics* iv. But in discussing the *De Anima*, *Ethics*, and *Politics* (which I will call, for convenience, the 'late' works), I have freely appealed to the methods and doctrines of first philosophy, despite Aristotle's silences.

This policy might be defensible if we knew for sure that the late works are indeed later than the *Metaphysics* and that the early works are earlier than it. But since we do not know this for sure, my interpretative assumptions may reasonably seem contrived, and liable to convey a misleading impression of actual difference between the early and late works; the apparent difference may simply be the result of different policies about interpreting one work in the light of another.

Such doubts might arise especially about my treatment of the *De Anima*, in comparison to the *Physics*. Both belong to natural philosophy, and both refer briefly, in quite similar terms, to first philosophy.[5] If I had discussed them together, instead of interpolating a discussion of the *Metaphysics*, the two works would appear quite similar on some of the relevant issues. If it is reasonable to pass directly from the *Physics* to the *De Anima*, it seems no less reasonable to go on to the other late works. It is not obvious that first philosophy, as opposed to natural philosophy, provides the necessary foundation for understanding Aristotle's moral and political theory.

In reply to these doubts, I would in fact be ready to defend the actual lateness of the late works; I think it is historically, as well as philosophically, reasonable to interpret them in the light of the *Metaphysics*.[6] But I would defend this chronological claim with much less assurance than I would defend the early date of the early works. A proper defence involves discussion of the relation between the *De Anima* and the other psychological and biological works; of the order of the three ethical treatises in the Corpus; and of the composition of the *Politics* and its relation to the ethical treatises. I believe a full discussion of these issues would confirm my suggestion about the lateness of the late works; but I have not tried to confirm the suggestion with a full discussion.

In this case, as with the early works, I hope the philosophical point of my argument is worth discussing even if one sets aside the chronological issue. In particular, I have tried to bring out the ways in which the *De Anima* displays the method advocated in the *Metaphysics*. It deals with the initial puzzles by sorting out preliminary questions, and 'makes a new start' from a principle that has more than purely dialectical support. I do not see any parallel in *Physics* i–ii. The *De Anima* also begins from the views about form, matter, this, potentiality, and actuality that are developed in the *Metaphysics*; no such pattern is to be found in the *Physics*.[7]

If we assume that the *Physics* and the *De Anima* were written at the same time, we ought to conclude none the less that only the *De Anima* practises the methods of first philosophy. Whether or not Aristotle realizes it, one line of argument—the one in the *De Anima*—belongs to strong dialectic, and the other—the one in the *Physics*—belongs to pure dialectic. Since strong dialectic uses dialectical arguments, but uses them selectively, it is not surprising that a purely dialectical argument provides, among other things, some of the material of strong dialectic. Hence we should not be surprised to find such material in the *Physics*.

Let us now assume (contrary to fact) that the *De Anima* gives no evidence of any intention to practise strong dialectic. In that case, my account of it suggests how the argument must be understood, and what we must believe about the premises, if it is to conform to the standards for strong dialectic. I believe it is worth discussing whether in fact we can reasonably, in the light of the *Metaphysics*, claim that the argument of the *De Anima* conforms to strong dialectic, and whether in particular the premises can be supported by something more than common beliefs. Readers might agree or disagree with me on this issue, irrespective of what they may believe about the order of the works, or about Aristotle's actual intention in writing them.

Something similar is true for the *Ethics* and *Politics*. Aristotle does not say that his crucial premises derive support from strong dialectic and from first philosophy. But I argue that in fact this support is available for the premises, and that the prospect of this support makes it more reasonable to claim that he has found objective moral principles. I might still be right about this even if I am quite wrong about Aristotle's actual intentions.

For the late works as well as the early, there is room for doubt about my historical claims and assumptions, and I have argued that the correctness of such doubts would still not undermine some claims that might deserve discussion in their own right. In saying all this I do not intend to take back the historical claims; and I do not imply that they are not an important part of a plausible account of a philosopher's views. Moreover, I doubt if a reader could reasonably agree with my philosophical claims without thinking they made some prima facie case for the historical claims too. But such a prima facie case might be overridden by conflicting historical evidence; and I have tried to identify the philosophical claims that do not depend on the historical case that might be overridden. The philosophical claims suggest than an appeal to first philosophy makes quite some difference to the status and the cogency of the arguments in the late works.

257. STRONG DIALECTIC

The structure of this book and of its cumulative argument relies considerably on the claims about strong dialectic, in Part II; and some questions may be raised about whether strong dialectic will bear all the weight. The main questions are these: (1) Does Aristotle's account of the science of being or first philosophy show that he has anything like strong dialectic in mind? (2) Can we give a clear account of the difference between strong dialectic and 'pure' or 'ordinary' dialectic? (3) Does strong dialectic support Aristotle's claim to find objective, and not merely endoxic, principles? (4) Does Aristotle practise strong dialectic in *Metaphysics* iv? (5) Does he practise it in *Metaphysics* vii–ix? (6) Do its methods apply to psychology and ethics, and not just to the area of universal science?

The basic question is the second; if we answer it, we go some distance towards answering all the others. I describe strong dialectic in general terms, simply as a method that differs from pure dialectic in so far as it selects only some of the premisses that pure dialectic allows.[8] Strong dialectic requires us to stick to premisses that we have some good reason for accepting, beyond the fact that they are matters of common belief.

This very general account of strong dialectic does not require very much. Since the strong dialectical premisses are a subset of dialectical premisses, they must be matters of common belief (or suitably related to them). This condition excludes simply treating all results of empirical inquiry, as such, as appropriate premisses of strong dialectic, since there is no reason to suppose that these results will automatically be matters of common belief. But if we simply require *some* good reason beyond common belief, many sorts of propositions count as possible premisses for strong dialectic; and evidently they will result in arguments of quite different degrees of strength.

I introduce strong dialectic to explain the type of argument that Aristotle attributes to first philosophy. I might be right about this even if he thinks there is no scope for strong dialectic in any other area, or he thinks that the premisses of different arguments in different areas of inquiry have no significant connexion with each other. I suggest, however, that Aristotle thinks strong dialectic has a wider scope, and that the arguments of first philosophy provide a foundation for strong dialectic in other areas. The defence of strong dialectic as a possible method for universal science is equally a defence of it in narrower areas; and in fact the conclusions of first philosophy serve as appropriate premises for strong dialectic about the soul and about ethical and political questions.

My account of strong dialectic makes it reasonable to expect that different arguments will have premises of different types. This difference becomes clear in the progress of first philosophy through the *Metaphysics*. In Book iv the premises express basic conditions presupposed by the very possibility of scientific study of an objective reality; and Aristotle argues that those who reject study of an objective reality give up the possibility of rational inquiry altogether. He argues, moreover, that they are wrong to think they must reject claims to know an objective reality; they reject such claims only because they accept epistemological assumptions that we have no reason to accept. To this extent, the argument is transcendental, appealing to the necessary conditions for being justified in believing in something that we cannot rationally abandon. Though Aristotle himself does not explicitly distinguish a priori from empirical knowledge, these arguments in *Metaphysics* iv have a strong claim to embody a priori knowledge.

In so far as strong dialectic also supports the theory of substance in *Metaphysics* vii–ix, its arguments must be less purely a priori than those in Book iv. Once we accept the connexions Aristotle sees between substance, subject, form, essence, cause, and potentiality, we introduce (on a priori grounds) some explanatory assumptions that are empirically falsifiable. I have argued that Aristotle must rely on such assumptions—especially about final causation—to defend his version of the claim that form is substance. Since I have emphasized the wide scope of the initial description of strong dialectic, there is no cause for suspicion in the fact that *Metaphysics* iv and vii–ix rely on different types of premises, even though both arguments count as strong dialectic and as first philosophy.

258. THE USES OF STRONG DIALECTIC

If we go this far with Aristotle, then it is reasonable to regard his account of the soul and of psychological states as part of a continuous argument in strong dialectic. For if his account of the puzzles about the soul is correct, then the explanatory arguments that support the identification of form with substance also support the identification of soul with substance as form.

Further questions arise, however, in the discussion of ethics. If the premises of ethical theory belong to strong dialectic, it does not follow that they also depend on first philosophy, since, as I have emphasized, nothing like this follows from the initial description of strong dialectic. But Aristotle himself shows why the premisses depend on first philosophy. For he makes it clear that he derives ethical principles from premisses about the human essence and the human soul; and we already know that these premisses depend on his theory of substance, and ultimately on first philosophy.

If we (wrongly, in my view) reject this conclusion, we might object that the psychological claims in the *Ethics* are mere matters of common belief, so that the argument is after all purely dialectical. It is hard to refute this objection conclusively, since Aristotle says so little about the status of his premisses. Moreover, the psychological claims ought not to be obscure or technical, if they are to belong to a dialectical argument. But they are not *mere* matters of common belief. Aristotle's specific claims about the essence and function of a human being are highly disputable, if they are interpreted against the background of common sense. They are reasonable, and some apparent objections to them are removed, if they are interpreted by reference to the *De Anima* rather than to common sense.[9] For this reason, it is most reasonable to assign the argument to strong dialectic; and if we agree with this, we connect the *Ethics* and *Politics* with the argument that extends through the *Metaphysics* and *De Anima*.

But even if we admit this connexion, we might suspect that it is not very important. Even if the *Ethics* includes some strong dialectic, this might not play a large role in supporting Aristotle's more specific moral and political conclusions. This suspicion can be removed only by going into some detail; and this is why I have tried to show that the main argument relies indispensably on the premisses about the human essence and the human good. If this is true, then the argument of these treatises as a whole belongs to strong dialectic rather than pure dialectic.

Even if I am wrong to claim that Aristotle introduces anything like strong dialectic, I am not necessarily wrong about the role of first philosophy in ethics; and this role implies an important connexion between ethics and metaphysics, even if it does not rest on strong dialectic. The connexion is clear if we reject strong dialectic, but believe that first philosophy is a demonstrative science with principles grasped by intuition. In that case, the connexions between ethics and metaphysics take ethics beyond pure dialectic by connecting to a demonstrative system.

If, on the other hand, we think the argument of the *Metaphysics* is pure dialectic, then the connexion between the *Ethics* and the *Metaphysics* does not lead us beyond pure dialectic. Whereas the demonstrative view of first philosophy and ethics gives a foundationalist argument to show that ethics reaches objective principles, the purely dialectical view leaves ethics with the general puzzle about pure dialectic and objective principles. But even if all the argument is purely dialectical, it is worth seeing whether the *Metaphysics* and the late works are connected in the way I suggest.

Coherence plays a useful role even in a purely dialectical argument. If some of our metaphysical views undermine our ethical premises, we face a possible source of doubts and puzzles, unless we try to divorce ethics from metaphysics more sharply than Aristotle is willing to do. His appeal to the human essence and function shows that he thinks metaphysics and psychology play a legitimate role in ethical dialectic; and so it is useful to see whether his views in these different areas support each other. I have argued that they do support each other; and this part of my argument is independent of the claims about strong dialectic.

If, however, I am quite wrong about strong dialectic, then I have to say that Aristotle has no answer to the puzzles about dialectic and objective first principles, and in general no argument to remove the apparent gap between his arguments and the alleged status of his conclusions. I assume that the appeal to intuition, restricting dialectic to a purely heuristic role, is not a good answer to the puzzles.[10] If Aristotle offers nothing more than pure dialectic, he has no answer at all. Since the puzzles seem to be reasonable and serious, it is a serious objection to Aristotle's philosophical method if he has no answer to them.

A simple appeal to strong dialectic does not do much by itself to answer the puzzles about how dialectic can lead to objective principles. The credibility of an answer depends on how good a reason beyond common beliefs we can give for accepting the premises of a particular argument of strong dialectic. In this case also, we have no option but to examine the arguments that Aristotle does and can offer on each issue.

A different line of objection to my argument might suggest that I have described strong dialectic correctly, but wrongly supposed that Aristotle in his philosophical works practises what I have called pure dialectic. It might be argued that the restrictions I suggest for suitable premises of strong dialectic are simply those that Aristotle intends for all dialectical argument, and that pure dialectic has no place in his actual dialectical arguments.

It is hard to refute this objection conclusively, since Aristotle is quite non-committal at some of the crucial points in his account of dialectic. He insists that common beliefs should be discussed only selectively, and that we should approach the puzzles by making a new start from an unchallenged premiss. One might suggest that the restrictions implied in strong dialectic are actually implicit in dialectic all along.

I find this suggestion less likely than my own, because it fails to explain the contrast Aristotle sees between dialectic and the method of first philosophy. In his view, dialectic argues 'from the common beliefs alone' (*Met.* 995b24). If first philosophy is dialectical to the extent I have described, and yet does not argue from the common beliefs alone, then Aristotle should not suppose that the premisses of ordinary dialectic are chosen by the criteria of strong dialectic. In that case, we should not take the restrictions of strong dialectic to be implicit in the account of dialectic.

Even if I am wrong about this, however, I still think it is worth considering the place of strong dialectic in Aristotle. Even if it states implicit conditions for all dialectical argument, rather than identifying a special type of dialectical argument, it is worth seeing what the implicit conditions are. If they are the conditions that I ascribe to strong dialectic, then Aristotle's dialectical arguments are not open to some of the objections that would damage them if they belonged to pure dialectic (as I describe it). If my account of strong dialectic gives an accurate picture of the argument in Aristotle's later works, then that argument acquires some interest that a purely dialectical argument would lack.

259. SYSTEMATIC PHILOSOPHY IN ARISTOTLE

The effect of my argument is to support one form of a 'systematic' view of Aristotle.[11] I do not suppose that the whole Corpus expresses a unified philosophical system; and in particular I have argued that Aristotle changes his mind on some fundamental issues about the nature of his argument. None the less, I eventually suggest that his later works develop views that are connected enough to count as systematic.

The mere recognition of a system in Aristotle should not necessarily lead us to think better of him. Philosophers' views on particular issues are sometimes more plausible than the systems in which they try to embed them; sometimes the views evidently do not fit into the system, and sometimes the system distorts the views until they fit. Readers must decide whether this is true of Aristotle, as I understand him, by considering the particular systematic argument I claim to find in him.

I believe, however, that in this case the recognition of a system makes Aristotle look better. By developing it, he exposes the more fundamental issues underlying some of his dialectical puzzles. The argument of the *Metaphysics* exposes more clearly the questions that are really at stake in the dialectical arguments about substance. The early works do not clearly identify the questions that need to be answered if we are to find the genuine basic subjects; but *Metaphysics* vii both raises and answers these questions, because it begins from the discussion of substance and essence conducted in Book iv.

If Aristotle's psychology did not rest on first philosophy, his account of soul and body would not reveal the parallel between problems about the soul and the general problems about form and matter, and it would not show how souls and minds meet reasonable general conditions for being substances. The systematic character of his argument suggests the proper solution to puzzles raised by dualism and materialism, and explains why each of these views seems both attractive and unsatisfactory. It is not obvious that the solution Aristotle offers is as satisfactory as he thinks; but it puts forward some options worth investigating. The options would be far less plausible if they were not embedded in the more general theory derived from first philosophy.[12]

In moral and political theory the issues are more complicated. On the one hand, we may doubt whether Aristotle's system has any important influence on his moral and political views at all. On the other hand, we may think its influence is important and pernicious. I have tried to answer the first objection by describing the pervasive influence of Aristotle's conception of a rational agent in his moral theory. I have tried to answer the second objection by arguing that the influence of Aristotle's metaphysical premisses is not pernicious, because they cannot fairly be held responsible for the errors in his particular political conclusions.

We may have more general philosophical reasons for rejecting attempts to found moral arguments on metaphysical premisses. We may think not that Aristotle carries out his argument badly, but that such a line of argument is misguided in itself. I have not tried to argue directly against this sort of philosophical position; but my argument bears indirectly on it. We are likely to think there is something wrong with Aristotle's type of argument if we find something obviously and badly wrong in every example of this type of argument that we examine. It is therefore useful to show that nothing is obviously or badly wrong with particular examples of such argument. I do not claim to have shown this for Aristotle; I have not examined all reasonable objections to his premisses, or to the further moral and political consequences of his conclusions, in comparison with the conclusions of other theories. But I hope to have shown that his theory is plausible enough to make it worth our while to raise these further questions.

260. METAPHYSICS, EPISTEMOLOGY, AND METHOD

In the first chapter I suggested that Aristotle's views reveal an apparent conflict between his metaphysical realist view of first principles and his dialectical method of inquiry; such inquiry did not seem to give us good reason for claiming to have reached the objective principles that are needed to meet metaphysical realist conditions. A natural response to this puzzle is acceptance of epistemological foundationalism; and I argue that in the *Analytics* Aristotle accepts foundationalism about science. The belief that realism requires foundationalism helps to explain his contrast between science and dialectic.

Aristotle never explicitly gives up the foundationalism of the *Analytics*; and he never explicitly sets out the epistemological position that would make it reasonable to accept the claims of first philosophy. On these issues he shows his inferiority to Plato as an epistemologist; indeed we have to appeal to Plato's account of dialectic to make sense of Aristotle's own metaphysical arguments and of his conception of philosophical method. His inexplicitness about his first principles conceals some of his commitments from him; and, correspondingly, a clearer view of his first principles makes his commitments clearer.

Strong dialectic removes the gap between Aristotle's dialectical methods and his claim to reach objective principles—if we are willing to make the appropriate epistemological assumptions. I add this condition to stress the point that a defence of strong dialectic does not answer the doubts of metaphysical realists who are also foundationalists. Since Aristotle is this sort of metaphysical realist himself in the *Analytics*, it would do him no good, in the light of such assumptions, to think of strong dialectic. For strong dialectic assumes that in some conditions the appropriate kind of coherence between our beliefs constitutes justification for believing them to be true; and in the *Analytics* Aristotle rejects that assumption. In order to take strong dialectic seriously, he has to reject foundationalism. I do not claim that Aristotle ever thoroughly rejects foundationalism. But I claim that the anti-sceptical arguments in *Metaphysics* iv show that at any rate he does not consistently adhere to the foundationalism of the *Analytics*.

Equally, readers who are quite convinced of foundationalism will not be convinced by the defence of strong dialectic as a method for discovery and defence of objective principles. I have not tried to discuss all the more resourceful varieties of foundationalism, or to remove all the doubts about coherence; but discussion of the *Analytics* should have made clear some of the difficulties that foundationalism faces.

Similar epistemological questions arise about the structure of Aristotle's arguments in psychology and ethics. I have argued that these belong to a fairly systematic argument appealing to first philosophy; and I have suggested that the systematic character of the argument supports both the psychology and ethics and the metaphysical premises. If that is so, and justification does not go only one way, then some appeals to coherence must confer justification. But Aristotle does not explain why that should be so; and his explicit epistemological doctrine in the *Analytics* would lead us to expect something quite different. Aristotle's views on metaphysics, psychology, and ethics constitute a rather impressive whole; but we need to add something to Aristotle if we are to explain why we should be so impressed by their systematic character. Aristotle is less than fully self-conscious about his own achievements.

261. DEFENCES OF ARISTOTLE

I have suggested both that Aristotle can defend his method in principle, and that he can defend some of the particular conclusions he actually reaches by it. These two sorts of defences are distinct. We might be satisfied that Aristotle has a good account of how strong dialectic *can* give us reason to believe we have found objective principles, and still decide that Aristotle himself has executed this project badly. We might decide that he is wrong in his selection of principles that he thinks defensible by strong dialectic, or in his inferences from them, or in both ways. Still, a defence of Aristotle on the first point will be more convincing if we can also defend him to some extent on the second; it is easier to make a method seem capable of reaching reasonable conclusions if we can point to some reasonable conclusions that it reaches.

If we set out to defend Aristotle's particular version of strong dialectic, and the conclusions he reaches, it is especially important to face the objection that sometimes his theory leads him to clearly false conclusions. This is why the discussion of the *Politics* is relevant to the main issues examined in this book. We might readily suppose that any sort of dialectical argument relying, even selectively, on common beliefs, is bound to be parochial, mistaking the common beliefs of a particular time and society for objective principles. There is no doubt that Aristotle sometimes speaks as though his philosophical principles justify conclusions that strike us as clearly false, and especially some conclusions that seem to reflect his historical limitations and political biases.

To show that his first principles and his methods are not open to this objection, I have argued that they actually provide a basis for criticism of his more questionable conclusions. If this is so, then, to that extent, Aristotle's principles cannot be charged with being parochial or inevitably biased, and to that extent his practice of strong dialectic turns out to be defensible.

I believe Aristotle's position on these issues has the philosophical interest that belongs to an unsolved problem. Our starting-point is not basically very different from his. For though we benefit from a far longer tradition of reflexion about philosophical argument, we have not found a clearly acceptable alternative to dialectic. The Aristotelian view of philosophical argument is not unfamiliar to us; and we can hardly avoid his difficulties about the status of first principles. We should be interested, therefore, to see how far he can answer these difficulties, and what sorts of conclusions he can justify by the right sorts of dialectical arguments.

It would clearly be foolish to try to reach a definite conclusion about the plausibility of Aristotle's actual views simply by considering what he says. In many cases the sort of view he presents has been frequently discussed; and discussion has led to clearer articulation of the view, and to sharper appreciation of its difficulties. Moreover, further discussion has not always resulted in agreement about how Aristotle's views ought to be elaborated, or about which tend in the right or wrong direction.

It would, indeed, be boring if Aristotle merely said things that strike us as evidently true or false (though some things he says fall into one of those categories). One of his most distinguished modern students writes:

What is true in Aristotle has become part, and no small part, of the heritage of all educated men; what is false has been gradually rejected, so that explicit criticism is now hardly necessary.[13]

Though this remark is probably meant as a compliment to Aristotle, it does not really do him justice. It was not true in 1923 when it was written, and it is not true now; probably we should not want it to be true. A sympathetic and critical student might reasonably find Aristotle's views a stimulus to fruitful controversy, needing further explanation and evaluation, but deserving the effort.

We gain at least one benefit from examining Aristotle's own statement of his views on topics that other philosophers have discussed at greater length and often with greater sophistication. His different works show how his doctrines form a systematic view; and if we examine the system, we can see how the particular doctrines gain plausibility from their place in the system. To this extent it is wise to accept Plato's advice that the dialectician should take a synoptic view. Aristotle did not accept this advice immediately; but he eventually accepted it, to the great benefit of his own philosophical thinking and of those who study it.

262. DIALECTIC AND HISTORICAL STUDY

In examining Aristotle's views on dialectic, I have relied on certain assumptions about the interpretation and understanding of Aristotle, and about reasonable ways to study the history of philosophy in general. Study of his views on dialectic is interesting and useful partly because it helps us to understand Aristotle's views on these questions, and helps us to decide whether his views constitute a plausible approach to the study of past philosophers. His views on dialectic, and on the use of past philosophers in dialectical discussion, suggest how we ought to assess an examination of his own views.

Aristotle thinks he understands his predecessors better than they understood themselves, because he sees what they were trying to say, and articulates it better than they articulate it themselves.[14] This approach to them is meant to make them fruitful contributors to dialectical argument. It is not an uncontroversial approach; it involves dangers of anachronism and of subtler forms of distortion. But it is the best approach we have available.

For Aristotle the history of philosophy is a part of philosophical discussion; it is not a museum of freaks or of primitive mentalities; above all it is an encouragement to further inquiry, not a source of sceptical doubt. If we can treat Aristotle as he treats his predecessors, and find that he does as well for us as a contributor to philosophical discussion as they do for him, we have treated him fairly; and in doing so we have given a further argument in support of his own view of the value of dialectic.

One of the pioneers of philosophical study of the history of philosophy by English-speaking philosophers expresses a broadly Aristotelian view in these terms:

We have been learning of late to know much more about philosophers, but it is possible for knowledge about philosophers to flourish inversely as the knowledge of philosophy. The revived interest which is noticeable in the history of philosophy may be an indication either of philosophical vigour or of philosophical decay. In those whom intellectual indolence, or a misunderstood and disavowed metaphysic, has landed in scepticism there often survives a curiosity about the literary history of philosophy, and the writings which this curiosity produces tend further to spread the notion that philosophy is a matter about which there has been much guessing by great intellects, but no definite truth is to be attained. It is otherwise with those who see in philosophy a progressive effort towards a fully-articulated conception of the world as rational. To them its past history is of interest as representing steps in this progress which have already been taken for us, and which, if we will make them our own, carry us so far on our way towards the freedom of perfect understanding; while to ignore them is not to return to the simplicity of a pre-philosophic age, but to condemn ourselves to grope in the maze of 'cultivated opinion', itself the confused result of those past systems of thought which we will not trouble ourselves to think out.[15]

Green applies these general views to the study of Hume; but they apply as well to the study of Aristotle, and they are Aristotle's views on historical study.

We should not accept either Green's or Aristotle's view uncritically, any more than they accept their predecessors' views uncritically. In particular we may not find Green's Hegelian additions an unqualified improvement over Aristotle. Nor should we be too ready to share Green's complacent assurance that we have reached the position from which we can definitely assess what aspects of past philosophy count as progress. Still, Green rightly regards one form of historical study as a reasonable part of philosophical inquiry; far from being a source of scepticism, it should be part of the philosopher's answer to sceptical doubts about the progress of philosophy. Descartes, as we saw, explicitly draws the sceptical conclusion from historical study.[16] Aristotle challenges us to study and understand the history of philosophy so that it becomes part of constructive philosophical dialectic.

NOTES

CHAPTER 1

1. See also *EN* 1098b3–8, *Top.* 105a16, 141b4, *APr* 68b35, *Phys.* 188b32, 189a5, 193a5, *EE* 1220a15. *Gnôrima haplôs*: see *EN* 1095b2–3, *Phys.* 184a18, *APo* 72a3, *Top.* 141b25; cf. *holôs gnôsta*, *Met.* 1029b11. *Gnôrima phusei*: *Phys.* 184a17, *APo* 72a1, *Met.* 1029b8; cf. 993b11, *ta tê(i) phusei phanerôtata*, *DA* 413a11–12. See Zeller [1897] i 284–9, Grote [1872], i 196, 239, 332.
2. See *DA* 402a3–10, *Met.* 982a1–3, 1029b3–13, *EN* 1095a30–b4, *EE* 1216b26–39.
3. See Burnyeat [1981].
4. Different examples that Aristotle takes to be parallel to 'known by nature' are discussed by Evans [1977], 53–61, 68–73. Some examples and issues are discussed by Evans [1974] and Moore [1975].
5. Grote [1872], 269–71, discusses the contrast between 'known to us' and 'known by nature', against Hamilton's account of Aristotle's appeal to 'common sense'. Grote is clearly right in emphasizing the caution implied in calling something 'known to us' (i.e. the suggestion that it is not necessarily an unchallengeable first principle). But his reply to Hamilton is exaggerated when Grote takes an unduly narrow view of the scope of dialectic and its procedure of arguing from common beliefs; see 274f on *Top.* 100a30, discussed at 2n40.
6. Aristotle's term *archê* often refers to primary and fundamental things, and often to propositions; the second use is secondary to the first, since a propositional principle counts as a principle in so far as it describes a real principle. Wieland gives insufficient grounds for reversing this order, and for his claim that Aristotle replaces a search for things with a search for the right explanatory concepts and (propositional) principles: 'Aristotle puts the problem of first principles on a new level, when he no longer treats principles as independent entities or forces, but as concepts of reflection which do not release one from the duty of detailed inquiry in the individual case.' [1960], 136. Wieland offers false alternatives here, to the extent that 'which do not . . .' does not justify his first claim.
7. On the character of *gnôrima phusei* see Aubenque [1966], 62–5, Wieland [1970], 69–85. Wieland denies that talk of *gnôrima phusei* indicates belief in an 'objektive Seinsordnung'. He claims that the distinction between 'to us' and 'by nature' only makes clear 'was wir immer schon vorausgesetzt haben, wenn wir etwas *aus* etwas anderes begründen' (73). The point seems to be that something becomes known by nature by *serving as* a principle. But this explanation overlooks the role of natural priority in explaining why it is correct for some things rather than others to serve as principles. Wieland claims: 'Aristoteles kennt keine besondere Bewusstseinssphäre, der dann auf rätselhafte Weise eine von ihr unabhängige subjektfreie

Dingswelt gegenüberstehen würde', 73. But I think such a contrast (not necessarily enigmatic, and presumably not involving a completely 'subject-free' world of things, if subjects are themselves part of the objective world) is just the contrast that is needed to explain Aristotle's views on the priority of the *pragma* to the *logos*.

8. Some aspects of Aristotle's views on truth are discussed by Wilpert [1940], though without much reference to the claims about asymmetry in the *Catg.* passage.

9. See § 103 on perception.

10. Putnam [1983] provides a lively summary of some of the issues in recent debates about realism. He states an especially clear challenge to Aristotelian metaphysical realism, in so far as this rests on claims about explanation, 215f. His claims about the nature of explanation, however, are open to some doubt; for a few further remarks see § 52.

11. See Hume, *Treatise* i.3.14, p.167; ' 'Tis a common observation, that the mind has a great propensity to spread itself on external objects, and to conjoin any internal impressions, which they occasion.' Hume recognizes a natural protest: 'As if causes did not operate entirely independent of the mind, and would not continue their operation even though there was no mind existent to contemplate them or reason concerning them. This is to reverse the order of nature, and make that secondary, which is really primary.'

12. Here I use 'intuitive' for beliefs that we hold without *giving* any inferential justification. In discussing first principles that are known by nature I use 'intuition' to refer to beliefs that do not *need*, and in some cases do not *allow*, an inferential justification. This double use is familiar, e.g., at different places in Sidgwick [1907], and I hope it will cause no confusion.

13. On Platonic and Aristotelian dialectic see Ryle [1965] (though he unjustifiably assimilates the Socratic elenchos to eristic contests). Vlastos [1983] gives a far more satisfactory account of the elenchos; but I do not agree with the contrast that he draws, 41–3, between the role of common beliefs in Socratic and Aristotelian dialectic (the contrast results from underestimating their role in Socrates and overestimating it in Aristotle).

14. For quotation and discussion see § 18.

15. On the transition from dialectical debate to dialectical argument carried on by a single author see Greenwood [1909], 128–32, Owen [1968], 222f. Though *Top.* 155b10–11 suggests that question-and-answer is the normal method for dialectic, it is possible for the same person to take both parts; and Aristotle's works characteristically follow this procedure. *Top.* 163a36–b16 shows how preparation for dialectical conversation develops into philosophical exploration.

16. On foundationalism see § 71.

17. See § 78.

18. See e.g. the comments on *Phys.* i 1 discussed at 3n52.

19. This approach to Aristotle is best known from Jaeger [1948], and its application by Solmsen [1929], Nuyens [1948], and Gauthier [1970]. It is sympathetically but soberly discussed by Ross [1957]. See 8nn4, 33, 13n33, 15n2.

20. The best compact discussion of what is wrong with Jaeger's account of the early Aristotle is Owen [1965]. On issues about Aristotle's development and about interpretative approaches see Wieland [1970], 19–41.
21. The best statement of this view is in Owen [1960], [1965].
22. See e.g. 3n12.
23. Arguments against premature appeals to development are offered, e.g., by Ross [1957] on the *Pol.* (see 16n13), by Kahn [1966] on psychology, and by Owens [1963] and Reale [1980] on the *Met.*
24. See § 77.
25. See §§ 94–5.
26. See 8n41 on first philosophy and theology; 16n40 on theology and ethics.
27. See 16n6.

CHAPTER 2

1. See § 2.
2. This description of 'naïve realism' shows that I am not using the expression in the sense that is standard in discussion of philosophical theories of perception.
3. Following Peck [1937] (apparently), and contrary to the OT, Le Blond [1945] , and Balme [1972], 70, I take *ton de*, 639a10=the demonstrative scientist, and *eiê gar* . . . as a parenthesis remarking that it is also possible to be *pepaideumenos* in only one particular science (cf. *EN* 1094b22–1095a2).
4. 'Peirastic' dialectic will be appropriate for the educated person; see n36.
5. On proper principles see 7n15.
6. This similarity between the educated person and the dialectician is noticed (with appropriate reservations about simply identifying the two) by Le Blond [1945]. For fuller discussion see Aubenque [1966], 282–9, and for some doubts see Kullmann [1974], 95–7.
7. The biological, ethical, and political works are different, in so far as they are clearly meant to advance the branch of inquiry that they discuss. But here too Aristotle is concerned with the issues that concern the educated person.
8. *Historia* is applied to empirical inquiry at, e.g., *HA* 491a13, *APr* 46a29, *PA* 646a9, *PN* 438a34–b1, *GA* 719a9–11, 740a23–4, 741a14–16, 750b31–3, 751a8–11, 763b15–16. *DA* 402a4 mentions *historia* about the soul; but Aristotle does not imply (contrast Hicks [1907]) that the *DA* itself is a work of *historia*. The term is not applied to a survey of dialectical *endoxa* or to a dialectical discussion. This is explained by the close connexion between *historia* and *empeiria*, e.g. in *GA* 757b35–758a3 (remarked by Waitz [1844], ii.459).
9. On appearances v. arguments see 3n61, *DC* 293a25–8, *GC* 325a23–8, *PN* 469a23–9, *Met.* 1056a12–14, *EE* 1216b26–8. Perception v. arguments: *Phys.* 262a19, *DC* 287b15–18, *GC* 323b30, 325a23–8; *PN* 468a20–3, *Pol.* 1257b13, 1323a40, 1328a20.
10. 'Appear' (*a*) sometimes implies truth (in constructions that should be translated 'evidently is'; e.g. *DC* 297a2–6, *GC* 325b15, *GA* 729a31–2, 756b23–4, 759b28); (*b*) sometimes just means 'appear to be so', with no

implication that the appearance is true, e.g. *GA* 760b6. (But see Owen [1961], 240n4.)

Sometimes Aristotle speaks of appearances, what we see, what happens (*ta gignomena, ta sumbainonta*), or what is the case (*ta huparchonta*) with no apparent distinction. This failure to mark the distinction is legitimate only if 'appear' has the veridical use. See *APo* 81b23, 88a2–5, *Phys.* 208a34, 210b33, *DC* 297b22, *GC* 316a10, 325a17–29, *Metr.* 346a6–8, *PN* 438b12, 439a27–9, 470b8–9, *PA* 642a18–21, *GA* 742a17–19, 750a21–3, 760b28–32, 765a26–9, *Met.* 986b27–33, 1075b37–1076a4, 1090b19–20, *Pol.* 1257b13, 1323a40, 1328a20, 1334a5, *Rhet.* 1396a28. In all these places Aristotle shows no concern about any possible conflict between the appearances and the truth. An appeal to the *phainomena* indicates modesty and tentativeness at *DC* 287b28–288a1 (*to phainomenon* contrasted with *akribesterai anankai*), 291b24–5. Stocks's OT actually renders by 'probable'. (ROT: 'what seems to be the case'.) He appeals to *IA* 809a24, which, however, gives examples of the apparent as *opposed* to the true, e.g. *Top.* 171b28, *Rhet.* 1402b23.

11. For non-sensory appearances see *DC* 270b5–15, 287b18, 303a20–4, 306a3–5. Indirect testimony: *PN* 462b12–22.

12. For fuller quotation and discussion see § 16.

13. False perceptual appearances: *DC* 290a8–24, *GC* 328a10–11, *DA* 428b24–5, *PN* 442b4–10, 446a7–20, 448b12–15, 460b20–7. While some theorists have gone wrong by neglecting appearances, *DC* 306a3–18, *GC* 314b2–16, 327a15–20, others have erred by naïve and uncritical confidence in them: *GC* 315b9–15, 318b21–33, 320b2–4, 325a23–9, *DA* 404a27–31, 427b2–3, *Met.* 1009a6–1010a9.

14. He argues that Empedocles' claims conflict with appearances, *GC* 315a3–4; but the relevant appearances seem to be simply the belief (*dokei*) that alteration is different from genesis, 315b15–16. Aristotle even regards his own doctrine of the four causes as one of the appearances, *PA* 639a6–11, 640a10–18, and suggests that his predecessors simply failed to 'see' the actual variety of causes, *GA* 778b2–11. Similarly, the teleological belief that nature does nothing inadequate or pointless is taken to be an assumption derived from what we see, *GA* 788b20–3. Aristotle implies that it rests fairly directly on the perceptual appearances. These aspects of Aristotle's view of appearances lead Düring [1961], [1943], 36f, to underestimate the empirical character of his method.

15. The sequence of *gar*-clauses in *APr* 46a17–25 indicates that *empeiria* is needed to grasp the *phainomena*, a20, identified with the *huparchonta*, a23 (cf. *Metr.* 353b17–18), and that these are grasped by *historia*, a24.

Without experience theorists offer wildly inappropriate theories that would soon be rejected on closer acquaintance with the subject: *GC* 315a33–b6, 316a5–14, *Metr.* 349a14–16, 352a17–20, *PN* 470b6–12, *GA* 742a16–18, 747a26–8, 748a13–17, 757b35–758a7. Aristotle thinks that once we have a full description of the appearances it will be quite easy to find the right theory to explain them: *APr* 46a17–27, *HA* 491a9–14. On the importance and nature of experience see Le Blond [1939], 239f, 248–51, Mansion [1946], 217–24, Bourgey [1955], 37–55, 78–83.

16. Non-perceptual appearances are often admitted; but this is because they are the next best thing to direct observation when it is impossible, *DC* 270b4–20. See also 286a3–7, 290a13–18, 292a14–17, *Metr.* 350a15–18, Moraux [1961], 182, 184.

17. On proper appearances and principles see *APr* 46a17, 53a2–3, *APo* 90a38–b1, *GC* 316a5–8, a13 (cf. 325a23), *Metr.* 346a27–31. Cf. 7n15.

18. On the sense of *aporia* see Aubenque [1961], 3–19, Owens [1963], 214–19.

19. Sources of puzzles: (1) The cause of some appearance. See *PN* 464b19–465a2, answered 466a17; *GA* 757a14–17, answered a18; 776a9–10, answered a10; *Metr.* 338a26–339a4; the cause solves the puzzle, *DC* 292a10–22, b25–8; (2) How a process happens. See *GA* 759a8–12; 733b24–6, answered 735a27–9; 736a24–7, 736b5–8, 740b3–5, 752a24–5, 770b27–35; (3) Something unexpected. See *GA* 757a14–17. Cf. 735a30–1; b4–5, answered 736a22–4; 754b20–1, 776a9–10, 745a19–27, *Metr.* 354b19–24, 355b21–33, 358a30–b11; 340a19–33, answered 340b4–6; 362a12–31, 355a33–b4, *DC* 291b24–292a18; (4) The nature of something. See *GA* 735a30–1, b4–5, 741a19–20, *Metr.* 357b26–32; (5) Something undiscovered. See *GA* 740b3–5, 778b23–5.

20. Hamlyn [1976], 169–71, emphasizes the connexion between *epagôgê* and the exposition or explanation of general principles by appeal to particular cases. I do not think this view of *epagôgê* adequately explains the role Aristotle ascribes to it in advancing from *gnôrima hêmin* to *gnôrima phusei*. If Aristotle did not ascribe *epagôgê* a role in the process of discovery, he would have given no account of the process at all.

    Engberg-Pederson [1979], 301–7, rightly resists the suggestion that '*epagôgê*' has different senses in its different uses. He denies that *epagôgê* involves inference, and takes that to explain why 'the question of the validity of a given piece of *epagôgê* never arises for Aristotle'. It could hardly follow that the question of the legitimacy or justifiability of a given piece of *epagôgê* could not arise; on the contrary, the more widely *epagôgê* ranges, the more important it becomes to decide if a given piece of *epagôgê* has been reasonable or justifiable.

21. When Aristotle suggests that the only ways of teaching and learning are induction and demonstration, *APo* 81a38–b6, 92a34–b3, *Phys.* 252a24–5, *Met.* 992b31–3 (adding *horismos* as a way of learning), he perhaps uses 'learning' and 'teaching' in a narrow sense, for the exposition of an existing body of knowledge rather than for the result of an inquiry that produces new knowledge. When he says that learning requires syllogism or induction, he should be using 'learning' in a broader sense to include discovery (perhaps suggested by *APo* 71a9–11). Otherwise his different remarks seem inconsistent.

22. The result of induction will be a universal conclusion; and sometimes Aristotle is willing to call the inference with this result an inductive syllogism, *APr* 68b15–29; he implies, (cf. 68b13–14) a relaxation of the normal conditions for a syllogism, which must have universal premisses. Aristotle recognizes that the conclusion of an induction is universal, *APo* 92a39, and that enumeration of particular cases does not normally allow a deductive inference about the universal, *APo* 86a3–8. Still, he thinks

induction involves an incomplete enumeration of cases, e.g. *Top.* 105a13–16, and reaches the universal, *APo* 81a38–b9, 88a1–3, 90a28–30.

23. On explanatory properties see § 63–4.

24. Conflict with appearances: see also *DC* 293a25–8, 297a4–6, 306a6–17, *GC* 325a17–29, 331a7–10, b24–5, 336b15–19, *Metr.* 344a5–9, *GA* 729b22–3, 756a3–6, 757b34–758a4, 759a25–7, 760b28–30, 765a25–9.

25. The contrast between 'what appears authoritatively to perception' and perceptual appearances as a whole (cf. *DC* 306a3–5) implies that not all perceptual appearances are authoritative, and that a theory need not be rejected simply because it conflicts with non-authoritative ones.

26. Simp. 643.11–12, says reasonably that the *telos* is 'truth in appearances in accordance with perception that is authoritative and correct'.

27. 'Yielding' the appearances: see *Met.* 1073b36–7, 1074a1; cf. *Phys.* 189a16–17, *Metr.* 365a34–7. Appearances as 'witnesses' or evidence for the theory: *Phys.* 213b21, *Metr.* 350b19–20, 360a34, *PN* 460a26–8, *PA* 666a22–4, *GA* 721b28–9, 725b4–7, 727a31–3, 771b8–10. Non-perceptual appearances as witnesses: *DC* 279a33, *Metr.* 359a17–21.

28. On *eulogon* see Le Blond [1939], 241–3, Aubenque [1966], 86f. What is plausible is different from what is necessary, *GA* 763a3–7, *Met.* 1074a14–17; hence the theory is not required to show that only these appearances could be consistent with it. But a good theory should show that it is reasonable to expect the appearances we actually find, *Metr.* 341a29–32, *PN* 446a7–10, a28–b2, *PA* 667b6–10, *GA* 715b7–16, 725b6, 728a25–31, 729a9–14, 731a24–39, 753a27–30, 761a14–19. The theory and the appearances agree with each other in so far as the theory gives an account of the appearances that happen, *DC* 270b5–6, 284a12–13, 292a15–23, b25–8, *PN* 468a20–5, 469a23–b1, *GA* 760b17–22, *Met.* 1087b1–3.

29. It is clear that attention to a wide range of appearances will expose conflicts, *DC* 293a23–30, 303a20–4, 306a6–17, 26–30, *GC* 325a13–16, *GA* 747a26–30. Aristotle acknowledges that in some cases—the heavens being an obvious example—we do not have all the appearances we would like, *DC* 270b13–17, 287b29–288a12, 291b24–8, 292a15–19, *Metr.* 344a5–9, *PA* 644b22–645a4.

30. A theory should 'cohere', *suneirein*, over a wide range of appearances: *GC* 316a5–10; cf. *Met.* 986a6–8, 1093b25–9, *Top.* 158a36–7, *GA* 716a2–4.

31. In Aristotle's view, we should be looking for them, and making a positive effort to test our theory by them, *PA* 644b30–2, *GA* 760b30–3.

32. On Aristotle's realism about perception see § 163.

33. On foundationalism see § 71.

34. On self-evidence see §§ 35, 72.

35. Alex. 29.18–30.12 recognizes that the reference to first principles looks like a fourth purpose of dialectic, but argues reasonably that it may be counted in the third. At 32.9–10 he rightly connects *exetastikê* with *zêtein* and *epicheirein*. Contrast Brunschwig [1967], 116f, who disagrees with Alexander partly because of the use of *kata philosophian* in a27, 34, as opposed to *peri hekastên epistêmên*, a37; but the reference to *philosophia* (cf. 7n14) just distinguishes science from dialectic.

36. Aristotle also distinguishes arguments (1) for gymnastic purposes, (2) for testing, *peira*, and examination, *skepsis*, and (3) for teaching, 159a25–8 (for peirastic cf. 161a24, 165b4, 169b24, 170b11, 172a35–6, 183b1). Only the third function (cf. 143a30, 171b1) seems to correspond to the constructive function of dialectic in finding first principles. Aristotle sometimes associates teaching and learning with the exposition of a completed science, and so with demonstration rather than dialectic, 165a38–b11 (cf. 155b10–16, *APo* 91b15–17; see above n21). But he seems to recognize dialectical argument as constructive and hence as a source of a different sort of learning. At any rate, he recognizes rules for some dialectical argument that seem unsuitable for peirastic and gymnastic. Since peirastic seeks to test someone else's claim to knowledge, it depends on what seems true to the respondent, and the tester is allowed to use premises he believes to be false, 161a24–9, and to reach false conclusions, 169b25–7; but dialectic is sometimes held to the requirement of sincerity that applies to teaching, 156b6–9.

37. For 'undertake' or 'deal with' (*epicheirein*) cf. 162a16, *epicheirêma*, where it is a dialectical as opposed to a demonstrative syllogism, 158b1.

The systematic practice of gymnastic and peirastic (as opposed to constructive) functions of dialectic are probably intended at *Met.* 1078b25–7, on which see Wilpert [1956], who suggests reasonably that 987b32–3 attributes the constructive use of dialectic to Plato.

38. On *exetazein* cf. *Top.* 164a8–15 (and De Pater [1965], 82), *EE* 1215a4–8, *EN* 1095a28–30 (see 16n1), *Met.* 1091a19. In 1095a29–30, *tas malista epipolazousas*, shows that *exetastikê* in 101b3 refers to and explains *dia de tôn peri hekasta endoxôn* in b1. The connexion of *exetasis* with the exposure (*emphanisis*) of conflicts in someone's beliefs is made clear in *Rhet. Alex.* 1427b12–30.

39. On 'redirect', *metabibazein*, cf. *EE* 1216b30, *Top.* 157a29ff, Thurot [1860], 198f.

40. The constructive function of dialectic is emphasized by Wilpert [1956], 250f, citing 171b3–7 (esp. *kata to pragma*, b6), *Rhet.* 1355b15–21. See also De Pater [1965], 78–80, Le Blond [1939], 44–7, Wieland [1970], 216ff, Aubenque [1966], 258f, Weil [1951], 99, Happ [1971], 58–81.

Grote [1872], i.286f, takes a limited view of the function of dialectic. He renders the claim about having a *hodos* by 'is connected by some threads with the *principia* of all the various scientific researches'. This rendering supports Grote's generally unfavourable estimate of dialectic in general, i.95–108. His estimate partly reflects his opposition to Plato's attack on sophistic, and partly reflects his failure to notice that dialectical evaluation of premises requires some judgment about their reasonableness (see Greenwood, cited at 1n15). Grote's generally negative view of Platonic and Aristotelian dialectic is shared by Hamelin [1920], 231–5. A similarly limited view is defended by De Blic [1930]. He speaks as though evidence for the claim that (1) dialectical techniques may be used for other purposes than finding the truth, were evidence for the claim that (2) dialectic cannot be a method for systematic pursuit of the truth. The difference between the two claims is helpfully brought out by Raphael [1974], 164f. See also Descartes, quoted in § 84.

41. Owen [1961] defends the second answer; see 7n10.

42. On *endoxa* see *Top.* 100b21, 104a8–12, 165b3–4, 170a33, 40, b7–11, *APo* 81b18–20, *Met.* 995b23–4. Aristotle uses 'endoxon' to suggest both that something is widely held and that it is also respectable, with something to be said for it, *APr* 62a11–19, 70a3–4, *Rhet.* 1355a14–18, 1356b28–35, *Top.* 161b34–8 (cf. *Rhet.* 1355b8–17). Brunschwig [1967], 113f, gives a good account of *endoxa*, which he renders by 'idées admises'. See also Weil [1951], 97. Raphael [1974], Barnes [1981a], 498–500, render *endoxa* as reputable things', so that to call a belief *endoxon* is to say (not merely, as I have said, to convey or suggest) that it deserves a good reputation. I doubt if this is justified as a translation. (The connexion of *doxa* with reputation does not imply that 'reputable' as opposed to 'reputed' is the right translation; a reputed thief is not necessarily a reputable thief.) If Aristotle meant to say, in using the term itself, that to be *endoxon* is to deserve a good reputation, it would be surprising that he so often treats the terms *endoxon* and *phainomenon* or *legomenon* as equivalent, since these other terms lack the implication of desert that is present in the very meaning of *endoxon*, as Barnes understands it.

   Le Blond [1939], 9–17, considers 'probable' and 'plausible' as renderings of *endoxon*, and thinks both capture aspects of its sense. His argument, like Barnes's, insufficiently distinguishes the sense of the word from what might readily be conveyed or suggested by the use of it. See also Régis [1935], 81–8, De Pater [1965], 74–6.

43. Cf. *Top.* 104a3–11, b22–4, *EN* 1095a28–30, *Rhet.* 1356b35–7. Common beliefs reflect the consensus of many people about the same questions on many occasions, *DC* 270b17–21.

44. Aristotle acknowledges readily that we may not be able to show that all the common beliefs are true, though we should prove the truth of most of them and the most authoritative, *EN* 1145b1ff; see § 12. For false *endoxa* cf. perhaps *Phys.* 253b29, 254a6, 17. He is less ready to assume the truth of the common beliefs, saying instead that they seem to be correct, e.g. *Phys.* 208a34, 210b33, 211a9, though sometimes he seems not to distinguish the appearances from the actual facts, *EN* 1098a8–12, *DA* 403b24–5.

45. Appeals to common beliefs in works that also use empirical methods: see e.g. *DC* 279a30–3, 297a3–6, 303a20–4 (referring to *Phys.* 231a18ff), Le Blond [1939], 251f.

46. Aristotle divides dialectical questions and propositions into three types—logical, physical, and ethical, *Top.* 105b19–29. Here the logical questions are of the type discussed in the *Topics*, belonging to no special subject-matter any more than to another, while the other questions are especially relevant to physics and to ethics. For this use of 'logical' see the reference to the categories, *APo* 82b35–6; to general views about the syllogism, 88a18–19; the distinction between potential and actual, *EN* 1147a24; the concept of essence, *Met.* 1029b13, 1041a28. See also *Top.* 180a26–9, *APo* 86a22, *Met.* 1005b20–2, 1087b18–21, 1090a9–11, *EE* 1221b4–8. They are contrasted

with the arguments from the appropriate subject matter, analytics, *APo* 84a38, 88a30, or the aspects of human nature relevant to ethics, *EN* 1147a24; cf. 1167b17–30, 1168a8, 1170a13–14. In these cases it is unwise to assume that the logical argument is being contrasted with a non–dialectical argument.

47. Dialectic relies on common 'places' or 'topics', those that are not confined to a particular science or discipline. See *Top.* 171b6–7, 172a11–21, *APo* 77a29–35, *Rhet.* 1355b25–34, 1356a27–33, 1358a1–35, 1359b12–16.

48. Sometimes the logical argument is not completely general, as it is in the *Topics*, but belongs to the area being studied. It differs from the 'special' arguments in relying less heavily on the appearances and principles appropriate to that area of study, and relying more on some general assumptions being applied to a particular case, *Phys.* 202a21–b5, 204b4–10, 264a7, b2, *DC* 275b12, 280a33–4, *GC* 316a5–14, 335b24–7, *GA* 747b27–748a17. Such logical assumptions and arguments might be counted in the *Topics* as physical or ethical. (This point is not adequately considered by Le Blond [1939], 193–212, Rodier [1900], ii. 26.)

49. Uses of logical argument: *DC* 275b12, 280a33–4. Criticisms: *Top.* 178b36–9, *DC* 306a7–9, *GC* 315a33–4, 316a5–14, 325a14 (contrast *Phys.* 262a18; cf. 188a3), 335b24–6, *DA* 402b16–403a3, *GA* 747b27–748a17, *Met.* 987b29–32, 1050b34–6, 1069a27–8, 1084b23–5, *EE* 1217b21–2. See also 7n15.

50. On *euporia* and its association with movement forward on a road cf. *APr* 46b22–5, *DC* 291b24–8 (OT translates, 'where it is very difficult to see one's way'), *DA* 403b21–2, Owens [1963], 214n. It is also connected with another aspect of not being at a loss—being well supplied, *Top.* 163b4–9, *Met.* 993a26–7.

51. On the importance of a preliminary survey of the puzzles see *DA* 403b20–4, *Met.* 995a24–b4, *EN* 1145b3–5, 1146b6–8, *EE* 1214a12, 1215a5–7.

52. This account of a puzzle is explained by 145a37–b7, 162a17–18.

53. This issue about raising puzzles is discussed by Evans [1977], 80f, citing 159a37–b35, who does not exactly answer the issue about puzzles, but perhaps suggests the answer.

54. Objective puzzles: *Phys.* 202b30–203a4, 208a32–b1, 217b29–32, *DC* 294b6–13, *Met.* 995a25–7, Aubenque [1961], 7, 9. See § 14.

55. Beliefs taken to be evidently true, but raising puzzles: *Phys.* 209a29–30, 217b32–3.

56. Empirical puzzles in a dialectical work: *DA* 413b16, 417a21. On the *Politics* see 16n16.

57. On conflicting appearances and scepticism see §§ 84, 104.

58. See § 105.

59. Aristotle's readiness to consider rejection of the *endoxa* is underestimated by Aubenque [1961], 13, and Barker (quoted 16n20).

60. Comparisons and contrasts between empirical and dialectical method: Le Blond [1939], 196f.

61. Cf. *DA* 413a11–16, *Met.* 993b7–11, 1029b3–12, *EN* 1138b25–34, *EE* 1216b33–9. We want an explanation of the initial appearances, *EN* 1095b2–8, *EE* 1216b35–9.

62. We are initially familiar with some examples of things to which the name applies, but do not know the difference between men and fathers; and the definition reaches the 'particulars' in so far as it articulates the features that something must have for the name to apply to it, 184a26–b14. The argument of *Phys.* i, similarly, begins with a fairly undifferentiated notion of an 'origin' or 'first principle', and of the different things that seem to be first principles; it gradually explains what is required for something to be an origin, and what different sorts of origins there are.

   Aristotle says his task is to find the principles of scientific knowledge (taking *tês* . . . *epistêmês*, 184a14–15, with *archas*, a16, with Ross [1936] and Simp. 10.1–2, Phil. 9.1–3). He does not claim to be expounding scientific knowledge in the *Phys.* (though Porphyry and Simplicius suppose that he is engaged in first philosophy; see Simp. 9.10–27, citing 193a34–b1, on which see 8n1).

   Simp. 14.30–16.13 and Phil. 9.6–10.22 try to connect Aristotle's claims about the *gnôrima hêmin* and *gnôrima phusei* with his account of demonstrative reasoning in the *APo*. They do not consider the possibility that he is practising dialectic here. See also Le Blond [1939], 286–8, Konstan [1975].

63. Induction in dialectical argument: *Catg.* 13b37–14a1, *Phys.* 185a12–14, 244b3, *Met.* 1048a35–b4, 1054b32–1055a2, 1055a5–6, 1055b17, 1058a8–9, *EE* 219a1–2, 1220a23–9, 1220b30–3, 1248b25–7. Induction and *logos*: *Top.* 105a10–19, *Phys.* 210b8, 229b2, *PA* 646a30, *Met.* 1055b17, 1058a9, *EE* 1220b30. Wilpert [1956], 254, connects induction and dialectic too closely.

64. Undisputed *huparchonta*: *Phys.* 200b26–8, 208a34, 210b33, 211a19, 218b9–219b2, *EN* 1155b17–18, 1174a13–14, *EE* 1226a17–b9, 1235b24–7, 31–3.

65. On making a new start see §§ 94, 111, 192.

66. See Alex. *in Top.* 27.24–31.

67. Some argumentative tactics are rejected as non-dialectical altogether: 108a26–37, 112a7–11. For further discussion see Owen [1968], 223–5.

68. Argumentative tactics (see further Moraux [1968]):

    (1) Appeals to etymology (112a32–8; contrast 148b16–22) perhaps force the interlocutor to say he is using the word in its usual sense, 112a34.

    (2) We may propose a non-convertible property of a subject as the genus, even though we may object if someone else does this, 128a38–b6. Since it is not always clear when such a property is not the genus, though clearly sometimes it is not, the attitude of each side is defensible.

    (3) We should ask whether F is the definition of G without mentioning that Fs are homonymous; it is the defender's task to mention this in his defence of a definition, 148a37–b4.

    (4) Padding an argument with irrelevancies makes it harder for the answerer to realize what he commits himself to. (Padding: 155b24–8, 157a1–5. Concealment; 156a7, 156b8–157a6; see § 100.) This may be necessary if the interlocutor is to reveal his real commitments instead of trying to protect himself against refutation.

    (5) If we say that something is customarily said, the interlocutor will be reluctant to dissent unless he has a specific counterexample, 156b20–3.

The onus is thrown on the interlocutor, but nothing false or deceptive is said.

(6) We should propose something as universally true if it is true in many instances and no obvious objection appears, 158b3–6.

69. Objections, *enstaseis*: *Top.* 153a31–b8, *APr* ii 26, *Rhet.* 1402b13–1403a1, *DC* 294b6–13, *Phys.* 253a32–b6. They may aim at the speaker or at his way of asking questions, *Top.* 161a1–15, or at the argument itself, 160b33–9; cf. 161a14–15. Aristotle considers only the last kind. Sometimes he mentions an objection without comment, 123b17, 27, 34, 124b19, 32, 125a1, 32, 128b6. Sometimes he seems to endorse it, 146b13–19 (cf. 121a30–9), 150b7–13, 15–19, 153b4–12 (cf. 157b14–23). Sometimes he rejects it in whole or part, 115b14–24, b24–9; cf. 156a27–b3, 157a34–b2. Even if a reasonable objection can eventually be shown to be false, this may be a waste of time if the claim provoking the objection is not necessary for our main thesis.

70. Conflicts with appearances: *Phys.* 253b29, 254a8, *GC* 315a4, 325a16–23, 26, 28, *DA* 418b20–6, *Met.* 1091a6, *EN* 1096a1–2, 1145b27–31, *EE* 1236a25–33.

71. If *ha pasi* (OCT) rather than *ho pasi* is read, then *agathon* is the probable complement (so Burnet [1900] ad loc.), and the passage does not express acceptance of universal agreement as a mark of truth. (Appeals to universal agreement are discussed by Kirwan [1981].) Contrast Stewart [1892], Heliodorus 211.26–7, Michael 537.32–3 (whose paraphrases both suggest *ho*), Owen [1961], 243, Grote [1872], ii.276–8. Aristotle's attitude to universal agreement in *EN* 1098b27–9, *Phys.* 196a14–17 is quite cautious.

72. On self–evidence see § 72.

73. See § 19.

74. He rejects empty theories: *EE* 1216b40–1217a9, 1217b21–4. The theory should 'yield' the appearances: *Phys.* 211a7–12, *EN* 1145b4–6, *EE* 1236a25–33. The appearances should 'witness' to the truth of the theory, *Phys.* 265b17–19, *Met.* 1069a25–6, *EN* 1103b2–6, 1113b21–6, 1154b7–9, *Pol.* 1338a35–7, 1340b5–7.

75. This fulfils the promise in 1216b28–32. On making the appearances seem reasonable cf. *Phys.* 220b22–8, *Met.* 1026b4–14, *EN* 1153a23–7, *EE* 1245b9–13, *Pol.* 1279a32–b4. Often the way to make them seem reasonable is to draw a distinction, *dihorismos*: see *EN* 1104b24, 1168b12, 1169b23, Eucken [1870], 13.

76. Importance of puzzles: *DA* 408a11–24, *Met.* 991a8–b1, 1063b30–5, 1076b39–1077a20, 1085a3–9, a26–b7, 1085b34–1086a18, *EN* 1096a10–11, a34–b3, 1097a8–13.

77. Solutions proceed on different lines (see also Aubenque [1961], 14):

(1) Sometimes Aristotle attacks the reasoning that leads to one side of the puzzle, and so rejects the conclusion.

(2) Sometimes he accepts the argument for a puzzle, and agrees that it requires some change in the claim that raises the puzzle, *APo* 91a12, 99b20–100a3.

(3) An apparently absurd conclusion from an appearance is not absurd,

and so gives no reason for rejecting the initial appearance, *Met.*
1004a31–b1, 1061b11–17, *MM* 1200b20–5, 1201b1–1202a18, *Pol.*
1277b39–1278a1.

(4) Apparently contradictory conclusions (e.g. that pleasure is good and
that it is not good) are not contradictory after all.

(5) Sometimes Aristotle combines (1) and (4). He suggests that if the
conclusions are taken to be genuinely contradictory the arguments
are unsound, but the arguments are sound if the conclusions are
qualified in a way that removes any contradiction: *Phys.* 194a15–b15,
EN ix 3, *Pol.* 1268b33–1269a28.

78. Here 'as a whole' and 'any experience' are important. Every concept and
belief might reasonably be said to be used to interpret and understand some
experience. But not every concept is used to interpret and understand the
experience in the light of which it might be modified (e.g. our assumptions
about fish did not wholly control the experience in the light of which we
found that whales are not fish).

79. The problem emerges especially sharply from Wilpert's claim, [1956], 253,
that 'Der Methode nach ist der Dialektiker, so könnte man es überspitzt
vielleicht formulieren, Sophist ⟨sc. because he deals in appearances⟩, der
Intention nach Philosoph' ⟨sc. because he seeks objective truth⟩. The
question is how such a method can fulfil such an intention. A defence
appealing to Aristotelian teleology is considered by Barnes [1981a].

80. Hamelin [1920], 234, remarks, quite plausibly, that if first principles were
made to rest on dialectic, 'Aristote puiserait les principes des sciences dans
les opinions, et non dans les choses'. See also 9n37.

CHAPTER 3

1. Malcolm [1981], 663, 666, supposes that different predicables are meant to
belong to different categories, so that, e.g., genus and definition belong to
the first category. This view is not required if two lists of categories are not
required. See n36. For further discussion see Kosman [1966].

2. New starts: § 22.

3. Dialectical terms: see 4a22, *enstasis*; 8a13, b23–4, 15a18–20, *aporia*; 3b13–14,
schêma tês prosêgorias, 3a29–31, 11a20, *tarattein*. Further parallels are noted by
Husik [1952a], 98–106. See n10.

4. 2a4–10, *DI* 16a9–16, *DA* 432a11–12, Plato, *Sph.* 262bc, on truth and falsity
suggest that 1a16, 1b25 refer to words (though, as Kahn [1978], 256f,
remarks, signifiers need not always be words). 1a16, 20 also seem to
contrast words with things. On signification see Irwin [1982], 243–8.

5. Simp. *in Catg.* 9.4–13.18, summarizes the different views about the *Catg.*:
(a) It is about words, 9.8–19. (b) It is about things, 9.19–30. (c) It is about
thoughts, 9.30–10.5. (d) It is about words, but in so far as they signify
things.

   In modern discussion (a) is defended by Trendelenburg [1846], e.g. 23f, criticized at length by Bonitz [1853], 621–40. Simplicius traces (*d*) back to Alexander (cf. Porphyry, *in Catg.* 58.21–9), and favours it himself, 13.11–18; he argues that it explains why Aristotle begins with words, but continues with things. This view differs from (*a*) in considering words only as signifiers (i.e. apart from their internal structure), and differs from (*b*) in so far as Aristotle is not committed to the reality of the 'beings' signified by the simple words, but only points out that they are what words purport to refer to; signification involves only ostensible realities—'for things are not revealed by the categories in so far as they are in actual existence, *hupostasis*, but only in so far as they are thought of, either beings or ⟨thought of⟩ as beings', 11.10–12. This is how Simplicius explains the fact that the *Catg.* belongs only to logic, not to first philosophy studying being qua being; cf. 9.28–30, 104.6–14. I think he misinterprets the distinction between logical inquiry and first philosophy; see § 94.

The same conception of the distinction between logic and first philosophy underlies the account of the *Catg.* in Owens [1960], 79. Owens argues that the *Catg.* belongs to 'logic' in so far as it speaks of saying and predicating, and to 'metaphysics' in so far as it speaks of being. He explains the double aspect by appeal to the claim that first and second substance belong to the logical order, while only substantial form (neither universal nor particular) belongs to the real order. This explanation hardly shows why Aristotle speaks of second substances as beings, and uses the very same term 'subject' for first substance both in the *Catg.* and in the *Met.* Owens is also committed to a non-realist interpretation of universals in the *Met.*, on which see 12n50.

The main objection to Simplicius and Owens is Aristotle's complete failure to indicate any of the appropriate reservations about the truth of his conclusions. Such reservations would make it hard to understand why he uses the apparatus of the *Catg.* not only in the *Met.* but also in the *Analytics* and in his natural philosophy, and in the criticism of other philosophers. (A similar objection arises against Bonitz's attempt, [1853], 607f, to distinguish the empirical character of the doctrine of the categories from the more strictly ontological doctrine involving form and matter; see also 4n9.) It would be curiously feeble to criticize Plato's or Democritus' metaphysical claims on grounds that Aristotle himself admits are not necessarily a guide to the real nature of things. (The question about Plato does not escape the Neoplatonic critics; see e.g. Simp. 7.29–32.)

6. I see no support for Moravcsik's view, [1967*a*], 131f, that Aristotle intends each one of the things said without combination to signify an item in *only one* category. Only an uncompounded item has to be in only one category, and not all things said 'without combination' in the syntactical sense signify something uncompounded.

7. If Aristotle assumes that all non-substances are properties of substances, a complete list of the possible properties of substances will also be a complete list of non-substances. He might reasonably consider the different interrogative expressions corresponding to these different questions as a guide to different possible properties. If, however, Aristotle's main aim

were to classify the questions or the interrogative expressions themselves (raising questions about a man; see Ackrill [1963], 78f, Malcolm [1981], 662f, Gillespie [1925], 8f, Kahn [1978], 262), we would expect masculine adjectives (*dipêchus, leukos*, etc.) in the answers. The neuters we actually get are explicable if Aristotle is asking the same question as in *Top.* 103b29–35, about substantial and non-substantial *items*.

8. At *Top.* 107a3–12 (cf. *EN* 1096a23–9, *EE* 1217b26–38, Ackrill [1972], 21f) Aristotle argues that goods are homonymous because goodness differs according to the different categories of being; it is hard to believe that he does not intend, here as elsewhere, to mark a similar homonymy in beings. (In *Top.* 107a3 Aristotle does not say exactly why it is relevant to consider the 'genera of predicates', *ta genê tôn . . . katêgoriôn*; but it is plainly relevant if the categories indicate the homonymy of being, which then infects good with homonymy.) Elsewhere he recognizes the homonymy of being, 182b13–27. Just as the question 'What is it?' requires a different type of answer according to the category of the item considered, so also the statement 'x is F' must be understood differently according to the category of x, and being will be defined differently according to the categories.

The homonymy of being is connected with the categories in *APr* 49a6– 10, *APo* 88b1–3, *Phys.* 185a20–6, *EE* 1217b27–8, *Met.* 992b18–24, iv 2, v 7, 11, vii 1. But we need not regard the connexion as a later innovation; we are entitled to use it to explain the point of the categories in the *Catg.* and *Top.* as well. The homonymy of being is discussed at length by Owen [1960], [1965a]. See also Leszl [1970], Loux [1973].

Devereux [1985], 236f, rejects this use of the argument about good, and denies that in the *Org.* Aristotle recognizes the categorial homonymy of being. If, however, Aristotle does not think being is homonymous, he overlooks the fact that his argument about goods allows the construction of an exactly parallel argument about beings. Moreover, his own account of the categories in connexion with the 'What is it?' question (in *Top.* i 9) makes the strategy of the parallel argument easy to conceive, and it is quite surprising if he fails to see this. Admittedly, he never explicitly denies that the different answers to the 'What is it?' question ultimately lead back to one answer specifying the synonymous way in which all the different categorial items are beings. But he never offers such an answer, and his other arguments about goods and beings make it unlikely that he thinks there is one.

9. Aristotle assumes, perhaps, that grasping the sense of a word is grasping an appropriate series of inferences about, e.g., the genus or the contrary of the referent. If different uses of the term are associated with different inferences, that is a good reason for seeing a difference of sense. This sort of argument explains Aristotle's claim to find homonymy in such terms as 'sharp' and 'light', *Top.* 106a9–22, b1–20, 106b34–107a2, 107a18–21, b6– 12. Irwin [1981] discusses homonymy more fully.

10. Aristotle recognizes that ordinary names often fail to correspond to important kinds, but he does not want to reject ordinary names, or most common-sense views about their referents. He criticizes those who

'legislate', who reject ordinary views about Fs because these do not apply to Fs as picked out by the favoured single definition, 148b16–22; see Alexander *in Top.* 181.2–6. Aristotle's preferred solution accepts the ordinary name, 104b36, 109a29, 110a16, 140a3, *APo* 98a13, *PA* 644b1, and recognizes the important differences by recognizing homonymy, *EN* 1129a26–31, *EE* 1236a23–32. See also § 219.

11. These limitations of appeals to multivocity become important in the *Met.* See 8n37.

12. In Aristotle's view Plato's fatal mistake is his assumption that 'tall' refers to some tall object, not a dog or a horse or any ordinary tall object, but still something that is tall. Aristotle thinks he can show that Plato cannot describe any object that could possibly meet his conditions for the Form; every tall object, e.g., must have some determinate size, but the Form of Tall cannot have any. Plato's theory illustrates the dangers of having no doctrine of categories; for (as Aristotle interprets him) Plato first distinguishes the tall object from its tallness, but then regards its tallness as a second tall object, simply reduplicating the thing he wanted to understand (cf. *Met.* 990a34–b4). In distinguishing the categories Aristotle wants to show how Plato's mistake is to be avoided.

    In Plato's view the substances are separated non-sensible Forms, on which sensible things depend for their existence and character; and these basic realities correspond both to men and dogs, items in Aristotle's category of substance, and to white and tallness, Aristotelian non-substances. Aristotle, however, distinguishes substances from non-substances by distinguishing (roughly speaking) sensible objects from their properties. He agrees with Plato about the role that substances should play in relation to other beings; but he thinks a subset of ordinary sensible beings can play that role without appeal to non-sensible beings.

    Though Aristotle uses his doctrines to criticize Plato's Theory of Forms, there is no good reason to believe that he devises his doctrine with these controversial aims in mind. Such aims are rather overstated by Gillespie [1925], and Owen [1965], 206f. On Aristotle's attitude to Plato's dialectic see § 76.

13. Gillespie [1925], 7, rightly stresses the connexion between the *Catg.* and the *Top.*; see also n3 above. But he infers that 'if it ⟨sc. the doctrine of the categories⟩ owes its origin to the logical analysis of predication, its primary meaning is to be sought in such passages rather than in those where it is extended to scientific and philosophical questions'. Here he seems to me to assume a distinction corresponding to nothing in Aristotle, and to mislead us about the character of Aristotle's interests. Dialectic often relies on some general ontological views about the presence of natural kinds in the world, and about their significant properties.

14. On central common beliefs about substance see Dancy [1975a], 346. The passages in the *Met.* might reflect views that differ from those in the *Catg.*; but they are the best available evidence.

15. Aristotle allows elsewhere that these are thought to be the most obvious candidates for substance: 1028b8–15; cf. 1001b32–1002a4.

16. On *Met.* v 8 see further 10n15.

17. *Top.* i 9 seems to include four lists of ten: (1) 103b21–3; (2) b26–7; (3) b28–9; (4) b37–9; and we may add (5) the list in *Catg.* 4. I take all five lists to list the same things, though this assumption is challenged by Frede [1981], Malcolm [1981], Kapp [1920]. The last nine items seem to be the same in all five lists; List 2 mentions the last seven items as *tôn allôn tina katêgoriôn*, 103b26–7, and List 3 uses the same phrase, 103b29, suggesting that both lists list the same items.

   This suggestion is sometimes resisted because List 3 is headed by substance and the other three lists in the *Top.* are headed by what-is-it. In List 3 the ten items beginning with substance provide ten ways of answering that 'what is it?' question, suggesting that List 3 provides ten answers that fall in the first category of the other lists. On this view, however, Aristotle would offer two vitally different types of lists, whereas his other remarks invite us to identify them. List 3 corresponds to the other lists if we can explain why 'what-is-it' should be used especially for the category of substance, as opposed to the others, even though the others also answer the what-is-it question.

18. This division ignores the problem of differentiae, which do not seem to fit into any category. See § 38.

19. He speaks of particulars, e.g. 2a36, b3, 8b3, and intends 'the individual man' (literally 'the some man') to pick out a particular. He also calls this subject 'undivided and numerically one', 1b6–7; numerical unity is apparently identified with being a this (*tode ti*), 3b10–13; and being a this is identified with being a particular, 8b3–6. On thisness see 10n34.

20. Water taken from the same spring is one in species, not in number (103a14– 23); presumably it fails to be one in number because it includes many bucketfuls or pools. See 12nn27, 30.

21. If there were no non-substantial particulars, the non-substance categories would not include particulars as the category of substance does, and there would be no particulars whose essential properties belong in the non-substance categories; but his exposition of the categories in the *Topics* assumes that they answer the question 'What is it?' and so reveal essential properties of different things. Aristotle supposes, reasonably, that if the category of substance reveals an essential property of particular substances, he has a good reason for making the parallel claim about non-substances.

   Since individual non-substances are particulars, they must be numerically one, and therefore cannot inhere in more than one particular substance. Particular relatives include particular slaves and fathers, each of whom inheres in only one particular substance, *Catg.* 6b28–30, and when Aristotle refers to particular relatives, 8b13–15, these particulars limited to one particular substance seem to be intended. Similarly, when he says the same numerically one action cannot be both good and bad, he ought to be referring to an action-token; the point would not be correct for an action-type, 4a15–16. We have several good reasons to believe, and no good reason to deny, that Aristotle recognizes one particular non-substance inhering in each particular substance to which one characterizing adjective is truly applied.

This conception of particular non-substances is presented by Ackrill [1963], 74. It is challenged by Owen [1965b], and the issue has often been discussed. See Matthews and Cohen [1967], Allen [1969], [1973], Duerlinger [1970], Jones [1972], Annas [1974], Hartman [1977], 14f, Frede [1978], and especially Heinaman [1981] (the fullest discussion of the evidence and problems). Owen's view requires a 'particular' white to be a fully determinate shade of white. *DI* 17a39 might seem to imply that such a thing is a universal; this conclusion may be resisted only if we suppose, with some strain, that *epi* in that passage implies *kata*, in the *Catg.* sense. Owen offers no evidence to show that Aristotle will count anything like this as numerically one; indeed the tests for numerical unity seem to exclude Owen's account (see Duerlinger, 188). Some criticisms of particular non-substances (see Moore [1923], followed by Owen) are unduly harsh.

This debate about particular non-substances has often invoked 2b1–3. Ackrill, 83, suggests that Aristotle's formulation is 'compressed and careless', since he should say that an individual instance of colour, not colour itself, is inherent in an individual body. Owen, 254, appeals to this passage to argue against Ackrill's conception of particular non-substances; the argument is developed more fully by Frede, 58–61. However, the passage makes good sense if it means that colour is inherent in some individual body or other, not that it is inherent in this or that individual body. (See esp. Frede, whose argument requires colour to be inherent in each particular body (e.g. this cube) rather than simply in some body or other (this cube or that sphere or . . .).) This is how we must take 'the individual man' in 2a36–b1 (cf. Owen, 257); see 4n20. Once we see this, the passage raises no objection to Ackrill's view of 1a24–5 (and does not require the two senses of 'in' suggested by Duerlinger, 186f). Recognition of non-substance particulars is quite important for understanding Aristotle's belief in the priority of first substance; see 10n6–7.

It is amusing to see the warmth that debates about non-substance particulars provoke in some philosophers. See Berlin [1973], 8: '⟨Austin:⟩ "If there are three vermilion patches on this piece of paper, how many vermilions are there?" "One", said I. "I say there are three", said Austin, and we spent the rest of the term on the issue.' Unfortunately Berlin does not say what conclusion, if any, they reached.

22. See e.g. 8b27, 9a14, 28, 10a11, 11a23. Aristotle does not use the term 'universal' in the *Catg.*; but his normal definition of a universal makes it clear that whatever is predicated of a subject (substance or non-substance) that is numerically one is a universal (cf. *DI* 17a39).

23. 'In' appears in the explanation as well as in the expression to be explained, apparently making the explanation circular. But without this clause inherence would just be existential dependence of something that is not a part; and such existential dependence, in Aristotle's view, follows from strong predication, 2b5–6c. The first clause of the definition of inherence should show why second substances cannot be inherent.

Ackrill, 74, offers examples to illustrate 'belonging in' without appeal to paronymy. Duerlinger [1970], 185, denies that 'in' is needed in the explanation; but his alternative implies that, e.g., an individual man inheres in oxygen.

24. On paronymy see *Phys.* 207b8–10, Ross [1936] ad loc. (his explanation, however, is doubtful; see Hussey [1983]), 245b9–12, *EE* 1228a35–6, *Top.* 109b1–9, 111a33–b4 (cf. 114a27–32, 106b33–107a2), Ackrill, 72. Paronymy cannot be merely a grammatical relation between words (as suggested by Owen [1960], 21; Owens [1963], 111). For *Catg.* 10a27–b11 shows that paronymy requires that (a) the adjective 'F' is applied to the subject x from the quality (or other non-substance) y, and (b) the name of y is 'F-ness' or otherwise grammatically related to 'F'. In the case of the excellent, *spoudaios*, person and virtue, (a) is true, but (b) is not. The ontological relation in (a) is therefore not reducible to the grammatical relation in (b). I will sometimes speak of paronymy with (a) rather than (b) in mind. The non-linguistic aspects of paronymy are stressed by Jones [1975], 120 (without reference to 10a27). These facts about paronymy undermine some of the objections (by Owen, Owens, Kahn [1978], 273n50) to the very plausible attempts (e.g. Ross [1924], i.256, Patzig [1960], 38) to find in paronymy the basis of Aristotle's doctrine of focal connexion; see 8n45.

25. Aristotle has nothing that quite corresponds to the use of the English indefinite article; but his examples seem to reflect our use of it quite well. Some qualification, however, is needed. The claim that strong predication requires a noun does not quite reflect Aristotle's view, since he mentions *to ti leukon*, with a neuter adjective, as a subject of strong predication, 1a27. But since this is parallel to *hê tis grammatikê*, Aristotle probably means the adjective to be (as often in Greek) interchangeable with an abstract noun— i.e. his point would equally well have been captured by *hê tis leukotês* (cf. 10a30). He moves freely from neuter adjective to abstract noun in referring to qualities; at 10b12–17 *to purrhon* and *to ôchron* are said to be colours and called *poia*, and coloured subjects are called *poia kata* them; this is the same relation that is said to hold between subjects and *poiotêtes*, 8b25, 10a27–9, where the *poiotêtes* are referred to by abstract nouns. On 2a27–34 see n27.

26. At 3a36 Aristotle says no predication (or predicate: *katêgoria*) comes from first substance. He does not offer examples to illustrate the error of treating the first substance as a predicate; but his illustration in 8a15–21 suggests how he might argue. It shows that he insists on referring to the first substance as *ho tis anthrôpos* etc., not by a proper name.

27. Aristotle claims that 'it is evident from what has been said' in the definition of strong predication and inherence and of first and second substance, that a first substance has the name and definition of its second substance, but not of its inherent item, predicated of it, 2a19–34. The definition of man and animal are predicated of the individual man, but the definition of whiteness is not. This is a consequence of the definition because inherence underlies adjectival predications, those in which we introduce (e.g.) whiteness, but cannot say that Socrates is a whiteness. On nouns and adjectives see Joseph [1906], 46.

On name and definition see Ackrill, 82, 85. Ackrill is probably wrong in saying that Aristotle tells us to substitute for the name (e.g. 'boxer') the definition of 'the item it introduces'. Aristotle has no reason to deny that 'the individual man is a boxer' introduces the item that is a boxer. He claims that this item is introduced only in so far as boxing is inherent in the man. Hence he has to instruct us to substitute the definition of the *inherent* item introduced. On Dancy's treatment of this passage see n29.

In 2a27–34 Aristotle mentions an exception. Here the 'name' is the adjective, and the case arises only when the subject is neuter. This is not an exception to the point about nouns and adjectives in n14 above. Contrast the case of differentiae, n46.

28. Perhaps *Phys.* 190b24–6 alludes to this point; see 4n31.
29. On sortal and characterizing universals see Strawson [1959], 168, Sellars [1957], 130–3. Strawson, like Aristotle, recognizes particular instances of characterizing universals. He allows that 'his anger cooled rapidly' mentions a 'particularized quality', 168n. Cf. Wiggins [1980], 7 (referring to Aristotle on substance and quality). Ayers [1974] rejects the claim that sortal properties determine identity as a 'conceptualist' as opposed to a 'realist' view. This view that appeals to sortals involve conceptualism scarcely fits Aristotle, who believes that correct judgments of identity reflect the real kinds that things belong to, expressed in the correct sortal predicates. See further § 99.

Dancy [1975a], 350–2, suggests that in 'Socrates is pale' pale is said of Socrates. (He speaks as though Aristotle used proper names such as 'Socrates' to refer to first substances; but see n26.) But in 3a21–8 Aristotle remarks that it is not special to second substances to be said of first substances, and points out that differentiae are said of them too. If he thinks 'the individual man is pale' is a strong predication, why does he confine himself to differentiae?

30. The question '*Poion?*' may seek two quite different sorts of answers: (1) The contrast between *ti* and *poion* is the contrast between asking what something is and asking what it is like. See Plato, *Meno* 71b3–8, *Eu.* 11a6–b1 (on *ousia* and *pathos*). (2) The contrast between *tode ti* and *poion* is the contrast between particular and universal. The '*poion*' question asks us what sort of thing the subject is, and the answer tells us the kind or class or sort it belongs to, not the particular thing it is. Hence it answers the 'What is it?' question. For this reason Socrates often associates '*ti esti?*' with '*poion esti?*' (e.g. *Ch.* 159a3, 7, 10, 160d7, *Pr.* 312d5; in *Meno* 74c3 *poion* = the differentia).

Aristotle seems to distinguish the two uses of '*poion*', when he claims that second substances (a) signify a *poion*, a such, not a this (*Catg.* 3b15, quoted, § 41); (b) do not signify a *poion* and nothing else (*haplôs*), as qualities do, but signify a sort (*poia*) of substance (3b18–21); (c) say what first substances are (2b29–34). The consistency of (a) and (c) rests on (b).

31. Aristotle claims that qualities are multivocal, and that their common feature is only their being 'that according to which people are called such (*poioi*)', 8b25–6). Second substances and differentiae seem to satisfy this rather

generous condition. Aristotle might reply that '*poion*' is multivocal not just within the category of quality, but also between quality and substance; but if he says this he needs to say what the qualitative *poia* share with each other and not with the substantial *poia*. Since *poioi* seems to meet the conditions for homonymy in *Top.* 107b6–12, Aristotle probably means (contrast Ackrill, 104) that qualities (within the category of quality) are homonymous.

32. *Met.* 1020a33–b25 perhaps suggests a helpful distinction between the two types of quality. (1) The differentia of substance is a property that the subject must retain, the stable aspect of the substance. (2) The second type of quality is the property that makes the subject capable of change. Since a subject is capable of change only if it is to some degree stable, the second type of quality presupposes the first.

   Ross [1924], i.p. xci n4, assumes on the strength of this passage that the differentia of a substance is a quality, i.e. a non-substance. But Aristotle does not say that the first type of *poion* belongs to the category of quality.

33. It is especially obscure at *Top.* 178b37–9, 179a8–10, whether Aristotle intends *poia* to be qualities or universals ('suches') or both.

34. Though time and change are not mentioned in the statement of the special property, the examples show that they are intended; see esp. 4a5–17 (cf. 5b30–6a11, *Top.* 167a23–7 on contraries), 4b10–13.

35. Why might not some substances be subjects without being subjects of change? (See Stebbing [1929]; Kneale [1939], 110, citing Hume and Russell.) Aristotle might appeal to the counting function of second-substance terms for subjects across time, not only at a single time. If we have to say why this horse is a single subject, and this horse's leg plus that horse's head is not, we might properly appeal to the role of this horse in change—change happens to it, not to the arbitrary collection of parts of two horses. Aristotle has no general argument, then, to show that every subject must persist through change; rather, judgments about what persists through change provide some basis for judgments about what is a subject. See 11n3.

36. In using 'what-it-is' in a specialized way, as a name for the first category, *Top.* 103b22, Aristotle suggests some special connexion between this category and the 'What is it?' question. He sums up the general use of what-it-is: 'For each of these ⟨sc. substance etc.⟩, if it is said about itself ⟨e.g. 'this man is a man'⟩ or its genus is said about it ⟨e.g. 'this man is an animal'⟩, one signifies what-it-is. But when ⟨it is said⟩ about something else, one signifies not what-it-is, but quantum or quale or one of the other categories', 103b35–9.

   Two assumptions made here reveal the special position of the first category: (1) When Aristotle describes the second case he does not include substance among the things we could mention without saying what something is. (2) Aristotle perhaps assumes that 'saying about something else' is saying something about a substance, so that the substance is the genuine bearer of non-substantial properties. If this is right, we will collect the non-substances by collecting the non-substantial properties of substances. In this way the procedure in the *Top.* leads us back to the procedure in the *Catg.*, where Aristotle seems to be asking different questions about a substance.

37. Moravcsik [1967], 90f, rightly appeals to *idia* to show that the distinction between strong predication and inherence cannot be the distinction between essential and accidental properties. The two distinctions are identified by Trendelenburg [1846], 36. Further relevant distinctions are discussed by Copi [1954].

38. The proprium seems to be defined both in non-modal terms (All and only Fs are Gs) and in modal terms (Necessarily Fs are Gs and Gs are Fs), 102a18–24. However, the non-modal account cannot be adequate; for 128b34–6, 132a34–b3 reject propositions that belong to a subject because of its non-essential relations to other things, 139a10–20. On propria see further Joseph [1906], 90f, 6n13.

39. The further conditions for propria are these: (1) The proprium must always be true of the subject, not true at one time and false at another, 133a12–23. Aristotle wants to identify permanent features, not just distinguishing marks, of the subject. (2) The statement of the proprium must mention the genus, but not the differentia, since otherwise it will state the essence, 131b37–132a21. (3) The proprium must be described by reference to what is better known, 130b38–131a26. Hence we cannot mention the species in trying to state the proprium of the genus. By 'better known' Aristotle must mean 'better known by nature'; for otherwise he would not claim that the species is never better known to us than the genus.

40. We must assume that quanta all have numerable properties making them numerable, if we are to agree with Aristotle's claim that equality and inequality are the proprium of quanta, 6a26–35; cf. *Met.* 1004b10–12, Plato, *Parm.* 140b7–8. But he does not say so in the *Catg.*

41. For *sôma* cf. *Met.* 1020a15, *DC* 268a1–11, 298b3. It is not clear if a particular mathematical *sôma* necessarily has the size it has; if so, it will not be capable of growth or diminution, and so cannot be identical to the organic body that is capable of these.

42. It is not even clear that the second definition is right to imply that being necessary is necessary for being non-coincidental. We cannot say that it is a proprium of men to have two legs, since some men are mutilated, and hence it is possible for men not to have two legs, *Top.* 134a5–17, a26–b10. On this view it will (according to the second definition) be coincidental to men to have two legs, whereas Aristotle believes it is intrinsic and natural, and hence not purely coincidental.

43. He claims that the second definition is preferable because it is self-sufficient, not requiring us to understand the three properties being excluded in the first definition. But this claim is true only if we can grasp the concept of possibility more easily than we can grasp the concepts in the first definition. Why should we assume that this is true? (At any rate it is not because Aristotle takes being possible to be the same as being sometimes true; for he allows that an argument is a proof of possibility, but not a proof of being sometimes, 113b6–14.)

44. For this reason two definitions of the same thing are not allowed, 141b22–

142a2, 139b22–140a2. Though two descriptions may be equally useful for informing different interlocutors, only one definition can describe the real essence. Two definitions of the same thing are perhaps allowed at 128a4–12; but cf. 144a11–15, 151a32–b2, b15–17.

45. Aristotle's failure to mention form and matter in such a suitable context is a good reason for thinking he has not yet formulated these concepts, or at least has not reflected enough about them to see how they apply to this problem; see also 4n19.

46. Ackrill, 86, remarks that Aristotle uses differentia-terms that function naturally in Greek as nouns, citing *Catg.* 14b33–15a7. At *DI* 21a3 he uses the masculine *dipous*, in a context where he is raising a difficulty and deliberately treating *dipous* as parallel to *leukos*. The neuter *dipoun* is used at 20b17, 34, 21a15, 17, where it is closely related to *zô(i)on*. Aristotle certainly can say 'The man is a white thing, *leukon*'; but he also freely uses the masculine adjective here, and normally avoids it for the differentia-term. Here is perhaps a further reason for doubt about Dancy's view that *mousikos* is said of a first substance; see n29 above.

47. Biped is not a proprium, since a proprium is a necessary property and it is possible for a man not to be a biped, *Top.* 134a5–17, b5–7. If biped is a differentia, then at least some differentiae are natural but non-necessary properties (but contrast 144a23–7). In predicating a differentia of a first substance or species, we will be saying that this man belongs to the naturally biped species, or that man is the naturally biped species of animal. On this view, the property of being biped is merely inherent in the species; but predicating the differentia is still strong predication, because it is really predicating the species.

48. On *Phys.* i 1 see 2n62.

49. On *Top.* 101b3–4 see § 18. On argument according to belief see 6n1.

50. Allan's clear statement, [1965], 9f, of a purely dialectical method, relying simply on common beliefs and ways of speaking, underestimates the selective aspect of Aristotle's treatment of common beliefs. The difficulty of explaining how the conclusions of dialectic can be objective principles is ignored in Wieland's account of 'principles as *topoi*', [1970], 202. He argues from the claim that we search for principles by means of *doxa* to the conclusion that the principles rest, in Aristotle's view, on nothing but *doxa*: 'Alle Wissenschaft gründet so in etwas, was selbst nicht der Wissenschaft zugänglich ist', 221 (the context shows that he refers to *doxa*). This raises a difficulty for Aristotle unless we deny that his *archai* are meant to be objective principles.

51. 184b25–185a5 argues: (1) Nature is an origin of change, and the Eleatics abolish change. (2) Monism makes an origin impossible altogether. (See Ross [1936].)

52. 185a2–3 might refer to dialectic or to first philosophy, as described in *Met.* iv. Phil. 27.9–18, Them. 3.20–2, Simp. 47.21–3, 49.6–11, do not decide between the alternatives. Alex. ap. Simp. 49.20–3 takes Aristotle to refer to first philosophy; and Ross agrees. A reference to dialectic is more probable, however (see Berti [1965], 43n93, opposed by Leszl [1975], 339, 505), since Aristotle's approach is purely dialectical, following the methods described

in the *Topics*. In saying that his discussion 'has some philosophy', 185a20,
he does not mean that it is more than gymnastic. On philosophy see 7n14.
On the prospects for a 'common science' see 7n19. He does not intend to
prove the truth of the belief in change, but thinks dialectical discussion of
the Eleatic position will be useful gymnastic exercise. He says the
examination 'has some philosophy' in it, 185a20, but he does not mean that
it is more than gymnastic. On first philosophy see 8n2.

53. See 185a5–12, *Met.* 1009a20–2, *EN* 1146a21–7, *Top.* 105a3–9, 159b30, viii
5.

54. Students of nature justifiably reject challenges to their principles and treat
them as 'assumptions' (*hupotheseis*, 185a12; cf. *EE* 1218b37, 1219a28), for
two reasons: (1) Students of nature, as such, actually define their task partly
by the principles they take for granted; cf. *DC* 298b11–20. (2) It is clear
from induction that things change, 185a12–14; and if a truth is clear in itself,
there is no need and no scope for a proof. See § 72. Only (2) explains why
Aristotle thinks it unreasonable to seek a proof at all.

55. Some of the limitations of Aristotelian dialectic are stressed by Solmsen
[1968], 52–4. On the contrast with Plato see 7n13.

56. See § 69 on the rejection of coherence, §§ 83–4 on proof of first principles.

57. If the one being is substance, then, Aristotle assumes, it must also have
non-substantial properties, and these are further beings, even if they are not
separated from substance. If, on the other hand, we say that the one being is
non-substantial, we talk nonsense; for non-substances depend on substance, and in this way also we find that there must be at least two beings,
185a26–32.

If things are one by being continuous or by forming a single whole, there
can still be many of them, 185b5–19. And if the Eleatics want to say that
everything is one 'in account', as cape and cloak are, the result will be
nonsense. For then they will be committed to the Heracleitean view, as
Aristotle describes it, that contrary properties are really one and the same
property; they will be making everything not one, but nothing, 185b19–25;
all the properties there are would make a self-contradictory property.

Aristotle now argues that even if 'being' has one signification, it does not
follow that there is one being; for if 'white' has a single signification, there
may still be many white things, 186a24–31. Parmenides must take 'Being'
to signify only the very subject that is wholly and exclusively being. If
Parmenides is granted this conception of signification, his monist conclusions follow; for 'being' will be inapplicable to anything except this one
subject, 186a32–b14.

58. If Parmenides' being is the only being it cannot be defined, since the
defining properties would have to be further beings, 186b14–33; and in
general it can have no other properties except that of being wholly and
exclusively being. Aristotle could raise a further question: how can it be
without being something or other, and how can it be anything without
being something other than being? The Eleatic being seems to turn out to
be a non-being. But though this further objection is a natural corollary of
Aristotle's previous points, he does not raise it.

59. See § 74.

60. See §§ 94–5.
61. On *logos*, 188a31, contrasted with *aisthêsis* see 2n9. Charlton [1970], 66, claims: 'This is not an empirical doctrine to the effect that the universe is regular; it is the purely logical doctrine that change is within definite ranges.' But Aristotle does not mean (as Charlton's view would imply) that if not-F is followed by F and the succession is not suitably related to a succession of contraries, that is not properly a change; he means that there are no such successions. Bostock [1982], 186, also seems to me to exaggerate (though he adds some appropriate qualifications) the 'conceptual' character of Aristotle's argument.
62. This passage is not mentioned in Sorabji [1980], 51–4, in his survey of evidence for determinist assumptions in Aristotle, or in Hintikka [1977], 38. Waterlow, however, mentions it, [1982], 6, and takes it to imply rejection of random processes.
63. The contraries involved in becoming and perishing are referred to both by neuter adjectives (*to mousikon* etc., 188a36) and by abstract nouns (*anharmostia*, 188b14). Charlton reasonably remarks, [1970], 68, that Aristotle treats the contraries as properties, not things. However, he also seems to refer to the compound of a subject with a contrary; this is the *hêrmosmenon* in 188b12.
64. Aristotle might insist that only those unmusical things that are also capable of becoming musical are suitable termini of a change resulting in something's being musical; the demand for contraries and intermediates will then be simply a symptom of the demand for reference to the appropriate potentialities. But though potentiality and actuality are prominent in later books of the *Phys.* (and cf. 191b27, 193a31–b8), he omits them here. He simply appeals to common sense, citing ordinary ways of speaking about contraries and intermediates. Some of the difficulties Aristotle causes by his appeal to contraries are skilfully exposed by Bostock [1982], 190f.
65. Aristotle argues: (1) It is hard to see how either of the contraries acts on the other, 189a20–7. (2) We never see the contraries being the substance of anything, and the origin must be said of no subject, since otherwise the subject of which it is said will be the origin of the origin; for the subject is the origin, and seems to be prior to the thing predicated, 189a27–32. (3) Since we do not allow substances to be contrary to each other, we cannot allow them to be constituted by contraries, since that would make non-substances prior to substances, 189a32–4.

These arguments will move us only if we agree that substances are not contrary to each other. But in *Catg.* 3b24–32 Aristotle merely points out that a favoured example of substance, e.g. man, has no contrary, and generalizes the claim to substances in general. (In the *GC* he allows that the four simple bodies are contraries, 331a1–3, but only in so far as they have contrary affections; they are not contraries in themselves, 335a3–6.) He continues to rely on this hasty generalization.

CHAPTER 4

1. If we answer 'What is this man?' by 'He's a son', we invite the further question 'Whose son?'; and if we answer 'How big is this man?' with 'He's tall', we invite the question 'Tall in relation to what?' or 'Taller than what?'. Aristotle implies that if our initial answer invites a further question relating the object of our initial inquiry to something else, then we were wrong in thinking we had identified a substance, quantity, etc., and we have really identified a relative.

2. Aristotle's revised test for relatives claims that if we definitely know some relative, we definitely know what it is related to; heads and hands fail this test, but doubles and halves do not, 8b3–21.

This revised criterion deserves two comments: (1) It does not seem obvious that to know that A is a slave I must know that he is B's slave, or that to know that A is a father I must know that he is B's father. Any questions about whether I 'definitely know' in these cases seem equally relevant to a head or a hand. (2) Aristotle assumes that (*a*) parts of bodies are substances, and (*b*) no substance is a relative. If it is better to revise the criterion for a relative than to give up either (*a*) or (*b*), the class of relatives cannot be determined by the initial grammatical tests that embodied the first criterion. But Aristotle offers us no other way to determine the class of relatives; and hence we do not know what the first and second criteria are meant to be criteria for. The revised criterion is justly criticized by Ackrill [1963], 102f.

Perhaps he could argue that what makes something a hand is something about its internal structure and organization, not about its relation to something else, even though the internal structure and organization make it capable of being related in the appropriate way to something else. This argument conflicts with the view that hands essentially depend on belonging to living organisms, so that dead hands are merely homonymous, *Met.* 1035b23, *DA* 412b20. But Aristotle may not hold that view in the *Catg.*, where he thinks that hands etc. are substances, contrary to *Met.* 1040b5–16.

3. On the problem about descriptions see White [1972]. In claiming that being a man is a coincident of being a master, 7a25–b14, Aristotle need not, and should not, mean that it is not necessary for being a master; but if he allows a necessary property to be a coincident, he violates one of the definitions of coincident offered in the *Topics*.

4. This claim applies to non–compounded things; see 3n6.

5. If 6b2ff is taken with 11a20ff, it seems most plausible to take the 'of' belonging to states as specifying the states, rather than saying who their owners are (as in 'state of Callias' etc.). The second view seems to apply, undesirably, to qualities and quantities no less than to relatives.

6. Elsewhere Aristotle claims that relatives are secondary in the appropriate way; a relative is merely an appendage and coincident of being, *EN* 1096a21–2, and inferior even to other non–substances, *Met.* 1088a21–9. A substance must have a relative property by having some non–relative

property; a father must have begotten, a child must have been born, a double must have a quantity, and so on. A subject has its relative properties by having the non–relative inherent properties it has, and it has these by being the subject and the substance it is. The 'by' relations here must be asymmetrical, and must reflect some ontological hierarchy, independent of the choice of one or another description. The discussion of relatives in the *Catg.* never suggests that they have this inferior ontological status; for the *Catg.* lacks the resources to argue for the appropriate claims about priority.

7. In *DI* 21a14 I follow the OCT in reading *ouk estai to leukon mousikon*. In the light of 'if it is true to say that the white is musical', a12, we must take a14 to mean that it is not the white, but the subject that is coincidentally white, that is the proper subject of the coincident of musicality; see 6n11.

8. On paronymy see 3n24.

9. The apparent fact that 'both the word *hulê* and the notion for which it stands are entirely absent from the *Organon*' (Ross [1949], 639) might be explained by (*a*) the absence of the concept from Aristotle's early thought, or (*b*) its irrelevance to the purely logical concerns of the *Org.*, or (*c*) its inappropriateness in the *Org.* for some other reason. Ross, Bonitz [1853], 608, defend (*b*). Moravcsik [1967] 90, Dancy [1978], 373ff, defend (*a*). Furth [1978], 629–32, defends part of (*c*), by reference to the deliberately introductory character of the *Catg.*; but he does not discuss the general question about the *Org.*

   I am convinced by (*a*). The *Catg.* could easily have introduced matter, and it would quite often be relevant, e.g. at 4a10–13 (see also the examples in the text, and 3n45. (I agree with Ross and Dancy, against Waitz [1844], ii.402, Barnes [1975], 216, Balme [1972], 83, that *APo* 94a21 does not show that Aristotle has the concept of the material cause.)

10. On questions about matter and numerical unity see § 138.

11. Armstrong [1978], i.111–13, imposes stricter requirements on a believer in universals. In his view, the universal is one and the same in all its instances, in a sense of 'one and the same' that is not captured by the sense in which a scattered particular is one and the same (see 3n20); he wants 'one and the same' to imply that the whole universal is present in each of its instances. I think the unity of a scattered object is very close to the sort of unity that Aristotle ascribes to universals.

   Nominalist (in the sense I have indicated) views of Aristotle's doctrine in the *Catg.* are defended by Sachs [1948] (answered by Mure [1949]), Jones [1975], 167. (Jones distinguishes 'class' and 'property' interpretations, but argues only against universals conceived as classes.) Hartman [1977], 17, says: 'When one talks of species and genera, in a first order way, what one says can be translated into talk of their members, according to Aristotle. Therefore nothing he says in the *Catg.* commits him to species or genera distinct from their members.' His second sentence does not follow from the first. For the 'class' interpretation see Lloyd [1966], 259f.

12. The use of 'signify' in 3b10 should not mislead us (as it misleads Jones [1975], 165, and Ackrill, 88) into supposing that Aristotle ought to be

talking about names rather than extra-linguistic items. Signifiers include extra-linguistic items too. See Irwin [1982], 254.

13. The same claim that universals are beings but not thises supports Aristotle's account of a Platonic error. He thinks we avoid the error if we recognize that man and every 'common thing' (*koinon*; i.e. universal) signifies a such rather than a this, *Top.* 178b36–9; cf. 168a26, 169a30–6. See 3n30 on thises and suches.

14. When he says that what is imperishable is found among universals, *APo* 85b15–18, he must refer to a subset of universals, including those for species of organisms, whose everlasting existence is secured by the laws of nature. On everlasting species see 5n25.

15. To support actual instantiation a definition of universal need only say 'is actually predicated of at least one thing and possibly predicated of many'; but this is not a possible interpretation of Aristotle's definition. Either the remark about instantiation conflicts with the definition (taken to require only possible instantiation) or the definition requires actual *plural* instantiation.

16. According to Armstrong's conception of universals, [1978], i.64f, 113, every universal must be instantiated at least once at some time. His view is therefore intermediate between the Platonic belief in uninstantiated universals (compared and contrasted with Aristotle's view by Fine [1984]) and the probably Aristotelian belief in necessary plural instantiation; see § 143.

17. Aristotle might be speaking loosely; perhaps he really means that a universal is not a this because, unlike a this, it *can* have plural instances, and if that is all he means he might still think universals are properties. That is not his usual construal of the requirements for not being one in number; all his other examples are spatially dispersed. Moreover, since we have already seen some evidence for taking him to require plural instantiation, there is no reason to make special efforts to avoid attributing the same requirement to him here. See 12n46.

18. Other types of priority listed in *Catg.* 12 (temporal, 14a26; value, 14b3) do not seem promising ways to explain the priority of first substances.

    'Natural priority' is not used in ch. 12 for asymmetrical dependence. It is used this way at *Met.* 1019a2 (on 1028a33 see 10n8; cf. 6n18). The same relation is referred to without this name at 1077b2–3, *Phys.* 208b33–209a2, 260b17–19, *EE* 1217b11, 1218a4; and 'natural priority' is used to refer to different relations, e.g. at *PA* 646a26 (cf. 'priority in being', *GA* 742a22), and perhaps *EN* 1096a21 (see Ross [1924], i.317, ii.160f). (Owen's account of logical priority at [1960], 186, is over-simplified. The *EE* passages that he takes to discuss natural priority do indeed concern asymmetrical dependence; but they do not use the phrase 'prior by nature' at all.)

19. To show that there can be no first substances with nothing said of or in them, Aristotle needs at least to exclude the possibility of bare subjects. See 3nn57–8, 9n12. To show that there must be a first substance as the basis of a series of predications he needs to argue against the possibility of an infinite series of predications, each involving a subject that is predicated of a further subject. He argues against this possibility in *APo* 83b17–31.

20. Aristotle argues that since animal is predicated of man it is predicated of the individual man; for if it were predicated of none of the individual men it would not be predicated of man at all, 2a36–b1. Aristotle cannot take predication to imply dependence (contrast Ackrill [1963], 83, whose suggested principle makes a genus depend on each one of its species). For animal is not dependent on man—it would exist if there were other species of animal, but no human species; for the same reason it cannot depend on an individual man either. Aristotle might also claim that if F is said of any F it depends on the existence of some F or other. See 3n21. This further claim would imply that animal depends on some animal and man on some man, without implying that animal depends on some man. But Aristotle never states, much less defends, this further claim. See further Harter [1975], 19.

21. Ackrill, 83, remarks that 2a5–6 assign no special status to substances if they are not independent of other beings. Duerlinger [1970], 199–201, and Dancy [1975a], 346, deny that Aristotle means to claim independence, but do not answer Ackrill's point. Moravcsik [1967], 95, Hartman [1977], 14, assume rather too quickly that Aristotle is committed to the asymmetrical existential dependence of other beings on first substances. The problem of mutual dependence is sharply raised by Grote [1872], i.119. On the priority of substance see Stough [1972].

22. Aristotle might reply that a first substance is either a 'moderately bare' particular (if it must instantiate some universal or other, but there is no one universal that it must instantiate), or an 'extremely bare' particular (if it can exist without any universals at all). But he probably does not allow extremely bare particulars. If he thinks a first substance is moderately bare, two difficulties arise: (1) Moderate bareness does not establish the independence of first substances from all universals. (2) Aristotle should say what makes a given moderately bare particular the same thing when it has ceased to be (e.g.) a man, and what would make it the same thing if it exchanged each of its properties for another. In fact he never suggests that the first substance that is an individual man can ever be anything else.

Furth [1978], 628–31, points out that the *Catg.* does not explicitly deny the possibility of moderately bare particulars (i.e. those for which no one property, but some property or other, is necessary). But Aristotle plainly has the concepts of proprium and coincident in the *Catg.*, and he can hardly relate them to 'What is it?' without taking the latter question (as in the *Top.*) to be answered by an account of the essence, which is a necessary property (implied by the second definition of coincident in *Top.* 102b6). This essentialism is consistent with the independence of first substances from second (contrast Furth, 631), if the existence of one specimen does not imply the existence of the species.

23. We might try a different sort of explanation. A first substance, we might say, already includes all it needs; it already has a substantial property, and by being what it is it includes non-substance particulars. It does not depend on anything not already included in it. A particular non-substance, on the other hand, requires something external to it, the existence of a first

substance; and a universal requires something external to it, the existence of a plurality of instances. (Ross [1924], i.p.xci, explains the priority of first substance by reference to completeness. See also Grote [1872], i.136.) But if externality is explained by reference to existential independence, it does not yield existential independence for substances. It might be understood by appeal to definitional or explanatory priority; see 10n7, § 145. Aristotle's unclarity about subjecthood and independence is pointed out by Kneale [1939], 105.

24 . In 190a6–7 we might translate *ek mê mousikou mousikos* by 'musical comes to be from not musical', with *mousikos* as subject and (the understood) *gignetai* taken absolutely. (So Charlton [1970]. Ross [1936], 492, implies this view, but does not imply it in his summary, 345. The OT is ambiguous.) The absolute use, however, is explicitly introduced only at 190a31–3, and 190a6, *tode gignesthai* (after the example in a4–5), suggests that qualified becoming is at issue. We therefore have good reason to take *gignetai* predicatively, as 'from being unmusical ⟨the man⟩ becomes musical'. (So ROT. This explains the masculine *mousikos*.) The same translation works in the rest of the discussion up to a31–3.

25. What is the exact referent of *to amouson* and such phrases? (Cf. n7, 6n9, 10n5, 45.) (1) The referent does not persist, 190a10–13. (2) Hence the phrase should not mean 'the man (etc.) who is coincidentally unmusical', since he does persist. The unmusical might therefore be (3) the subject that is essentially unmusical, or (4) the instance of the property. Both (3) and (4) satisfy (1), and they seem equally plausible. Code [1976], 180f, and Matthews [1982], 225, endorse (3) without considering (4). See also Williams [1985].

 In 190a17 Aristotle says *ou gar tauton to anthrôpô(i) kai to amousô(i) einai*, and if *amousô(i)* is neuter, he claims that *to amouson* is numerically one with the man. If, however, *amousô(i)* is masculine, he may mean that the man and *ho amousos* (i.e. the man who is coincidentally unmusical) are one in number, but not the same in form. This does not imply the parallel claim about *to amouson*. On difference in being see 13n21. On property-instances see 3n21.

26. Charlton [1970], 76f, denies that the matter persists in cases of substantial becoming, appealing to the seed, which is the matter of the plant or animal, 190b4–5, but does not persist in the product. Jones's defence of this view, [1974], 476, is answered by Code [1976a]. Aristotle seems to believe (i) that the organism comes to be from the seed, (ii) that the seed is the matter, (iii) that the organism comes to be from the matter, (iv) that the seed does not persist, and (v) that the matter persists, 192a31–2, 193a10 (*enhuparchein*). But these need not conflict. For (ii) may apply to the seed as a stage of the continuous thing that is the matter of the organism, and in that case (iv) is no objection to (iii) and (v). On *Met.* ix 7 see § 126.

27. In the *GC* Aristotle argues that unqualified becomings are not really just qualified becomings: (1) Unqualified becoming is not by combination and dissolution but 'whenever it changes from this to this as a whole', 317a20–2;

some new whole must come into being. (2) When the whole changes, nothing perceptible remaining as the same subject, there is unqualified becoming, 319b14–16.

These answers are open to objections: (*a*) Can we tell if (1) is satisfied without deciding if a new substance has come to be? If not, we seem to rely on the views we are trying to understand. (*b*) Joachim [1922], pp. xxxiii, 107, suggests that the demand for a perceptible subject is really a demand for a substance composed of form and matter—though the evidence he cites is not compelling (see also Jones [1974], 499n, Williams [1982], 216f). If he is right, then (2) seems to be open to the same objection as (1). (*c*) Why should qualified becoming require the persistence of a perceptible subject? Why should a persistent subject of any sort not imply that the process is merely a non-substantial change? (*d*) The bronze seems to persist when the statue comes to be; and the bronze is apparently a perceptible subject. Hence (2) seems to make the process a qualified becoming. (*e*) Might there, however, still be a change from whole to whole? We seem to be forced back to (1).

Both the *GC* and the *Physics* fail in the same way, by assuming that we can identify substances or subjects or wholes without further argument.

28. 190b9, b25, mention matter casually as though it is understood. 191a7–12 explains 'subject nature' (or 'underlying nature', *hupokeimenê phusis*) by analogy; and one of the examples in the analogy may mention matter. (Some editors, perhaps rightly, suggest the deletion of *hê hulê kai* in 191a10; but 190b9, 25 weaken their case.) 192a5 speaks of matter without further explanation. 192a31 identifies it with the first subject. Bostock [1982], 187, argues unnecessarily for an ambiguity in *hupokeimenon*.

Aristotle seems to take his use of 'matter' to be neither perfectly familiar nor a purely technical use requiring explicit definition. Presumably he appeals to its use for 'raw material' (e.g. Plato, *Phil.* 54c2). See Solmsen, [1961], who contrasts (410) *hulê* with *xulon* (but 193a9–12 counts against such a contrast).

29. 'Said of' relies on *kat' allou legesthai hupokeimenou*, 190a35. I take this to cover both strong predication and inherence, as they are conceived in the *Catg.*; and I assume (see § 39) that it also implies that no compound of a subject and an inherent item (e.g. a musician) can be a substance.

30. I agree with those who believe that in the *GC* (esp. 332a3–18, 334a15–25, b2–7; see Williams [1982], 214f, Sheldon Cohen [1984], 174f) Aristotle recognizes prime matter, the basic matter that underlies the four elements and the most elementary qualities. See Charlton [1970], 129–45, and [1983], King [1956] (against prime matter), Solmsen [1958], Robinson [1974], Williams [1982], 211–19, Sheldon Cohen [1984] (in defence of prime matter). I do not, however, believe that Aristotle is committed to prime matter in all the passages where some defenders claims to find it. On *Met.* vii 3 see 10n27.

We may doubt if prime matter is really a plausible, or even coherently describable, subject. It must have the capacity to acquire the different elementary qualities, but has none of these qualities essentially. It is pure capacity, because its capacity is not further explained by any actual qualities it has; here it violates our normal way of understanding how a subject has the capacities it has. (Sheldon Cohen [1984], 178–81, defends prime matter against the charge of incoherence, but I doubt if he adequately answers the charge about capacity.) If, then, prime matter is the result of applying the common-sense conception of substance, and prime matter is so dubiously coherent, something seems to be badly wrong with the common-sense conception. But even if prime matter is coherently conceivable, it still makes difficulties; Aristotle's initial candidates for substance will turn out not to be substances at all.

31. In i 6 he seemed to take it for granted that a substance would be a subject, 189a27–33; and he has not explained why being a basic subject is not sufficient for being a substance. Admittedly, he contrasts matter with 'substance, this and being', 191a11–12, and says that matter is 'not one or a being in the way that a this is', 191a13. But he has not explained what is wrong with matter; see Bostock [1982], 195. He does not deny that the piece of bronze that is the matter of the statue is a single piece, and therefore numerically one, and therefore a this; cf. 190b24–6.

32. See also *Catg.* 1b6, 3a35–b7, where *atomon* is applied to substances and non-substances alike. It is applied to particulars in contrast to their *eidos* at *Top.* 121a35–9, 122b20–2, 144b1–3, and to the species (since it is not further divisible into species) at 109b13–23, *Phys.* 227b7, 30.

33. *Top.* 135a20–b6 discusses sea and air as examples of homoeomerous things, without reference to any questions of numerical unity, and with none of the biological examples Aristotle uses elsewhere. On homoeomerous parts see *Metr.* 389b23–8, GC 314a18–20, 321b16–19, 328a10–12.

34. The suggestion that *atomon* ('undivided' or 'indivisible') refers to the sort of indivisibility that homoeomerous things lack faces a difficulty. For non-substance particulars are also thises, and therefore *atoma*; for this particular white, e.g., seems to be divisible into particular whites (i.e. patches of white), and large or equal things may also be divisible. We might reply that Socrates' white is not divisible into two Socrates' whites; but in the same way this pint of water is not divisible into two pints of water. It is not easy to say what conception of indivisibility Aristotle might reasonably intend. A piece of bronze seems to satisfy the condition for being *atomon* suggested by Simp., *in Catg.* 51.14–15, of having nothing more partial (or 'less general', *merikôteron*) than itself of which it is predicated as of a subject.

CHAPTER 5

1. Aristotle seems to accept this inconsistent sct: (1) Form and matter are origins of change. (2) The origin of change is the same as the efficient cause. (3) Therefore form and matter are efficient causes. (4) The formal and

material causes are not efficient causes. (5) Therefore form and matter are not efficient causes. (6) Therefore they are not origins of change. To defend (1) he must reject (2) or (4) or both.

2. Alexander, *De Fato* 3, presents the four causes as coordinate causes of the same thing, a statue. While such an account is suggested by *Phys.* 195a5–8, it may still be significant that, as Sharples [1983], 127 remarks, Aristotle himself offers no such example. His own examples illustrate the difference between the different why-questions in a way that suggests that the causes are not coordinate in exactly the way that Alexander's exposition implies. This point is suggested without argument by Sprague [1968], 299. See also Todd [1976].

3. Annas [1982], 321n, mentions these as examples of things cited 'elliptically' as *aitiai*. I agree with her against Moravcsik [1975], 629, who regards such examples as constituting an objection to our attributing a concept of an efficient cause to Aristotle. But Annas surprisingly claims that Aristotle 'does not envisage that a statement might truly pick out a causal relation, but in a quite unexplanatory way', 320. The elliptical examples she cites seem to illustrate the sort of thing she thinks Aristotle does not envisage; still clearer examples are provided by coincidental causation, which she does not discuss; see § 56 below.

4. My account of Aristotle's view implies that the traditional label, 'the four causes', is largely justified. (*a*) It is not always clear what is meant by claiming that the four *aitiai* are really explanations, since it is not always clear what a critic takes the relata of an explanation to be. Sometimes it is assumed that the relata are propositions, or at least that the explanans is; we can then distinguish explanation rather sharply from causation, if we think causation relates events. Hocutt [1974], 388, seems to claim both that (1) a demonstrative syllogism states the *aitia*, and that (2) it is the *aitia*; and he gives no argument for passing from (1) to (2). (This objection is raised by Mure [1975], 356.) Aristotle does not treat either of the terms related by an *aitia* as a proposition; see Moravcsik [1974], 6f, Charles [1984], 44–7. (*b*) If explanations relate events or substances (or other items that are not propositions), then *aitiai* are explanations; but this may actually imply (if we take the relevant kind of explanation to be a causal explanation) that they are causes. (*c*) If an explanation is true and adequate only relative to a given questioner's interests and puzzles, then we could find a true explanation without finding the cause (if the questioner is puzzled about the wrong things, or not puzzled about all the right things). See Sorabji [1980], 29. But there is no reason to suppose that Aristotle attributes such relativity to judgments about *aitiai*. (*d*) Aristotle's examples do not all look like what we would call causes; only the efficient cause (which Aristotle calls the origin of motion) looks like a cause. See Annas [1982], 319. Moravcsik [1974], 9, perhaps goes further than Annas in denying that the *archê kinêseôs* is a cause; he denies that it is a 'mechanical' cause, but does not explain exactly what that is. If our account is right, the efficient cause is central in a way that encourages us to think he is speaking about causes. The other causes are no more rivals to the efficient cause than 'The captain caused the

ship to sink' is a rival to 'The incompetence of the captain caused the ship to sink'. (e) It is true that unchanging as well as changing things may have an Aristotelian *aitia*. If we ask for the *aitia* of a triangle's having angles adding up to 180 degrees or of a syllogistic conclusion (cf. 194b27–8, 195a18–19), there is no change, and no efficient cause, but there are still formal and material *aitiai*. (Moravcsik [1974], 3, mentions this as a reason for denying that the four *aitiai* are causes.) But it does not follow that Aristotle is not looking for causation when he investigates the *aitia* of a change. See Fine [1987], 70–6, Sauvé [1987], ch. 2 (two different views, but with similar conclusions on this particular issue).

5. 'Most exact' renders *akrotaton*, 195b22, literally 'most extreme'. Aristotle does not say that the *akrotaton* cause will be the *energoun* mentioned in b16–20. But the descriptions of the two seems to imply this. On *akrotaton* Ross rightly refers to *Met.* 1044b1. Phil. 258.16–22, Simp. 326.15–30, Them. 47.2–7 explain *akrotaton* by *kuriôtaton kai prosechestaton*, saying why the cause (i.e. the substance with the relevant actualized capacity) is the cause (by referring to the actualized capacity). Simp. 326.15–16 identifies the *akrotaton* cause with the Stoic *sunhektikon* cause. They suggest that this is the *prôton aition*, because any further asking of the question 'Why?' is *euêthes*; Simp. 326.19–20 uses this point to explain *akrotaton* (which he therefore must understand as something like 'highest').

6. On non-propositional first principles see § 1.

7. In 193a31–b18 Aristotle offers three arguments to show that form is nature. (a) 193a31–b8; we do not say something has reached the completion of the craft until it has acquired the form of a bed; so also we should not say that something has reached its nature until it has reached its form. Aristotle needs to convince us that these ways of speaking of artifacts reflect causally relevant features, and then that the same features justify similar ways of speaking about organisms. (b) 193b8–12; man comes to be from man. But equally a musical man comes to be from a white man (if the unmusical man was white); Aristotle has himself pointed out that in 'the F comes to be from the G', 'G' may be a purely coincidental description of the origin, 191a33–b10. (c) 193b12–18; becoming is a way towards nature; the nature towards which it is a way is form; hence nature is form. Organisms certainly come to have a form; but such a weak sense of 'is a way towards' is not enough to show that form is nature. Aristotle needs the stronger claim that growth is to be explained by reference to form, that things grow in order to achieve their form. This teleological sequence is implied in 193b13–16; but he needs to show that the same sort of sequence is found in organisms.

8. At 190b19–22, 28–9 form or shape is identified with the quality instantiated as a result of a change; see also 191a8–12, 15–20, 192a20–1, a34–b2. At 193a31 Aristotle probably does not intend every quality acquired in a change to count as a form; but he has not explained how he distinguishes genuine forms from mere qualities.

In GC 322a2 wet and dry are taken as examples of form, and form is connected with affections, *pathê*, 316b2–5. Form is connected with a this and a positive quality as opposed to a privation, 319b14–18. Like 'this' (see 10n12), 'form' is used in the *GC* for the category of substance, but not confined to it.

9. In Aristotle's discussion of growth, form cannot be simply shape or quality, since growth involves change in these, whereas the form remains the same, 321b28–34, 322a29–33. (The distinction is not so clear when, e.g., the form of wine is being discussed, 328a27–8.) Indeed form is what grows and is nourished, 321b16–28; for it is not every part of the matter that increases, but the form, 321b32–5. Aristotle compares form (1) to a measure that remains the same but measures successive quantities of water, 321b24–8; (2) to a pipe or tube or vessel that grows as new matter is added and flows through it, 322a28–33. Though (2) is better than (1) (since a tube, unlike a measure, can grow while remaining the same tube), it is still not quite right; a tube is constituted of additional matter besides the matter that flows through it, whereas the form is not, and the nature of the tube does not explain the changes in the matter in the way the form is supposed to explain the process of growth.

   If growth is a teleologically ordered process, the formal and final cause has the sort of efficient-causal relevance that is needed for a genuine cause; this connexion between form and growth is clear in *DA* 416a9–18 (see n23), but not in the *GC*. Aristotle identifies the form and essence with the final cause, 335b5–7, but this view does not completely control his account of growth. He attributes growth to a fire, 322a10–16, which is not teleological. Joachim [1922], 134, reads in too much from *DA* 416a9–18 (see Williams [1982], 111).

10. Early in *Phys.* ii 1 substance is identified with subject, 192b33–4. But 193a9–10, 20 refer to the substance of something, i.e. substance as essence, apparently identified with the nature of that thing. 193a23–6, contrasting substance with affections, could refer to substance as subject or as essence. The discussion of substance, form and matter in Book i, by contrast, has no example of 'substance' referring to the substance of something.

11. 198b16–23 concedes that the rain falls not for the sake of anything, but simply *ex anankês*. We might take this to be merely a temporary concession, so that Aristotle still might think rain falls for the sake of something (though not to make the crops grow). See Cooper [1982], 217n; but on his argument from 198b36–199a5 see n18 below. On local and global teleology in Aristotle see Eucken [1872], 81–7.

12. In 196b34 I would prefer to read *komizomenos* or *komisomenos* (i.e. referring to X who has come now to sell his olives, but would have come now to collect the subscription Y owes him if he had known Y would be here now), rather than Ross's *komizomenou* (which would have to refer to Y, the debtor). In 196b35–6 I retain *tou komisasthai heneka*, and explain it: 'it was a matter of coincidence that X came to the market just now and did this now (i.e. got the money off Y) to collect what Y owed him'. If we explain 35–6 in this way, then we must apparently take the occurrence of some form of *komizesthai* in 35 to refer to X also.

13. This account of lucky events supports Torstrik's suggestion, [1875], 445, that we should read *prachthê(i)* rather than *prachtheiê* in 196b22. Them. 51.1,

ginetai, perhaps supports Torstrik. In any case, the better attested reading gives too weak a condition for something's being *heneka tou*, and we can easily explain how lucky events (said to be *heneka tou* in 196b30, 197a6) meet the stronger condition of actually being done from thought. The optative phrase occurs in 197a35, *hos' an genoito heneka tou*. But it does not support the optative in 196b22; for in the later passage Aristotle is referring to both lucky and chance, *automaton*, events, and chance events need not in fact happen for the sake of something. As Aristotle says, chance events are included *en tois haplôs heneka tou gignomenois*, 197b18–19 (i.e. they are events, e.g. escaping danger, of the type that are done for the sake of something). They are not caused by anyone's decision, and are not done for the sake of the end that they in fact promote (197b11–22). They have the wrong sort of efficient cause to be really for the sake of the good result that they actually promote. They have a non-final cause that coincidentally produces the beneficial result. The difference between luck and chance casts doubt on Simplicius' explanation of 196b22, at 335.20–6. Unlike Aristotle, he refers the remark to both luck and chance, and imposes too weak a condition on luck. He rejects Eudemus' and Porphyry's correct (as far as I can see) explanation of *heneka tou* applied to luck, on the ground that it is too restrictive to apply to chance, 336.20–30 (but then seems to imply that it is correct, in 30–3). He is right to say that it is too restrictive to apply to chance, but this is not a ground for rejecting it, since Aristotle does not apply it to chance.

14. It is not clear what X's actual purpose was; probably Aristotle means, as when he first introduces the example, that X came to the market to sell his goods, 196a3–5.

15. 196b24–36 suggests that Aristotle thinks the same event has both an intrinsic and a coincidental cause—e.g. that the same event is both (*a*) X's being in the market at the time he intended, to sell his olives, and (*b*) X's being in the market when his debtor Y is there. Because (*a*) is true of the event, X's decision to go to sell his olives is its intrinsic cause; because (*b*) is true of it, X's decision is its coincidental cause. Though the lucky event, as such, has only a coincidental cause, the event itself also has an intrinsic cause. Aristotle shows no sign of denying that every event has an intrinsic cause. He shows how he might defend the determinist assumption of Book i (see 3n62) against objections based on belief in the existence of lucky and coincidental events. His treatment of these casts doubt on the claim (defended in Sorabji [1980], ch.1) that in *Met.* vi 3 he affirms some form of indeterminism.

We will want to state Aristotle's position differently if we attribute to him different views about the individuation of events; see n33 below.

16. The end or goal of an event is not the same as the efficient cause. In intentional action the end is not the decision, *EN* 1139a31–2, but the result aimed at in the decision; but since the result is part of the content of the decision, 1139b3–4, reference to it explains something about the nature of the efficient cause. Though the end is not the efficient cause, it must be relevant to and explanatory of the efficient cause.

17. If 'as they do' (*houtô*, 198b35) means just (*a*) 'the same way', then Aristotle

simply appeals to uniformity. But the way that is relevant here is (*b*) uniform apparent teleology, 'as if they were coming about for the sake of something', 198b29–30. Since this point is not in dispute with Empedocles, Aristotle can fairly take it for granted. See n18.

I use 'uniformly' and 'frequently' for the purely statistical notions that might seem to be conveyed by *aiei* and *hôs epi to polu*. I use 'always' and 'usually' as translations of Aristotle's terms—and so not as having a purely statistical sense (since I do not think this is always the sense of Aristotle's terms).

18. In 198b36–199a5 Aristotle might seem to argue: (1) Whatever happens always or usually (e.g. rain in winter, heat in summer) is not accidental. (2) Whatever is not accidental is teleological. (3) Hence what happens always or usually is teleological. (4) Hence rain in winter etc. is teleological, Phil. 315.14–16. This argument will secure Aristotle's conclusion against Empedocles, but it relies on the highly controversial premiss (2). Admittedly (2) might seem less controversial if Aristotle illegitimately equivocates on two senses of 'accident', (i) not always or usual, (ii) not for some purpose; the Atomists, e.g., might agree that the present order of the world is non-accidental in sense (i), because it is necessary, but accidental in sense (ii) because it is non-teleological (cf. 196a24–196b5).

However, we can take the argument differently, taking (2) to refer only to apparently teleological things (as in 198b35; see n17). Rain making the crops grow does not count as apparently teleological, since it no more makes the crops grow than it spoils the crops on the threshing-floor. For apparent teleology the benefit must not suffer from these obvious counterexamples. (Contrast Furley's argument, [1985], 180.) If this is right, the *tauta* in 199a4 will be the same *tauta* as in 198b34, i.e. apparently teleological things, and (1) will be a parenthesis, giving examples that are not intended to be within the scope of (3).

Charlton [1970], 123, takes *tauta* this way (but still criticizes Aristotle as though (2) were involved). Furley's argument against Charlton assumes that the always and usual cases in 198b36–199a3 cannot be non-teleological without damage to Aristotle's argument. But we need not accept Furley's assumption. The examples illustrate what is always or usual; and when we have a case of this *plus* regular benefit, we have a case of final causation. On always and usual see n20.

Cooper [1982], 216f, argues that Aristotle accepts (2), without any support from an equivocation, 208n, and that he simply assumes teleology is the only plausible explanation of uniform apparent teleology. Such an inference is dubious if (as Cooper agrees) a teleological claim implies the sort of efficient-causal claim described in the account of chance above. If we take *tauta* in 199a4 so that it does not commit Aristotle to (4), we need not assume that he makes the dubious inference supporting (2). We might none the less have to agree with Cooper, if we can find no more plausible account of what Aristotle might be taking for granted.

If we deny that Aristotle's argument assumes that rainfall has a final cause, we need not also deny that he believes rainfall has a final cause; the final causes he considers are not the most plausible candidates (cf. Them. 60.9–14, Simpl. 374.18–28). The issue is only whether this particular argument assumes or implies that rainfall has a final cause.

19. In 196b36–197a1 and 197a3–5 the addition of *toutou heneka*, 197a4, suggests that a causal connexion is assumed, not merely inferred from the fact of uniformity. Perhaps X and Y both want to catch a bus at 9.00, and so are always or usually at the bus stop at 9.00; but it is still a coincidence that each of them is there at the same time as the other is (i.e. this property of the event is coincidental). Though Aristotle does not discuss this possibility, he has no ground for rejecting it.

20. In his discussion of luck Aristotle uses 'usually' to indicate a causal, lawlike connexion, not a mere uniformity; and this is a frequent, though not the only, use of 'usually'. It often refers to what happens 'by nature', where this indicates a teleological connexion, not mere statistical frequency. See *GA* 727b29–30, 777a19–21, Eucken [1872], 88, Régis [1935], 93–105 (who connects it, wrongly, with the denial of determinism), Barnes [1975], 184. Moreover, Aristotle pairs 'usually' with 'always', which, in this context, he takes to be interchangeable with 'necessarily'; see also *Phys.* 196b12–13, *Met.* 1025a15, 1026b30, *APr* 32b5–6. On the usual and the necessary see Mignucci [1981].

Some have claimed that Aristotle takes mere uniformity to be sufficient for necessity. (See Hintikka [1973], 96, taking omnitemporality to be equivalent to necessity.) But *APo* 73a28–b28 sharply distinguishes mere uniformity, *kata pantos*, from the *katholou*, which must be *kath'hauto*; and being *katholou* is necessary for being *anankaion*, 73b25–8 (cf. 96b1–3). (See further § 63.) Since uniformity is not sufficient for necessity, and Aristotle treats 'always' as interchangeable with 'necessary', he is unlikely to believe that mere uniformity implies 'always'. The passages that Barnes [1977] regards as the best evidence of Aristotle's reducing the necessary to the omnitemporal are *Met.* 1026b27–37, 1088b23–5, *GC* 337b35–338a3, *DC* 281b20–5, *Phys.* 203b20. But they are evidence for this only if 'always' has a purely temporal sense.

If this is true about 'always', we should not assume that mere uniformity implies 'usually'.

21. 'Always' and 'usually' must share the asymmetry of the causal relation, rather than the non-symmetry of the relation between things that are uniformly or frequently associated. (1) B uniformly follows A, and (2) whenever B, then A, imply (3) A uniformly follows B. But the implication does not hold if Aristotle's 'always' or 'usually' is substituted for 'uniformly'.

22. In final causation without intentional action we can still say that the putative goal of a process is the real goal if the properties of the goal explain some aspect of the efficient causation of the process. This condition is met if the theory of evolution is true of natural organisms, since the benefit secured by a particular trait (itself the result of a process with no final cause) explains why the trait persists in later generations. Wright [1973], 61, and [1976], esp. 80–6, presents an account of teleological explanation with this

causal element. Wright's account is criticized by Boorse [1976], and
Cummins [1975], esp. 749–57. I am not convinced that these criticisms
undermine Wright's type of analysis (though they may show that it is
incomplete; see Cummins 752n); and in so far as they raise objections to the
efficient-causal aspects of an account of teleological explanation, they seem
to raise objections to Aristotle's account also. See also G. A. Cohen [1978],
ch.9, Meikle [1985], 166–71, Sorabji [1980], ch.10, Gotthelf [1976],
Woodfield [1976].

23. See also § 158.
24. If this view is right, then 198b34, 'it is impossible for it to be this way', does
    not refer to Empedoclean natural history, but to the conclusion of the
    argument (*logos*, b33) that beneficial teeth etc. are purely coincidental. The
    argument fails, because the teeth example implies the presence of an
    always-or-usual causal connexion that is not implied in the rainfall
    example.
25. To see that Aristotle's teleological claims are compatible with more than
    one, but not with all, of the logically possible empirical accounts, it is useful
    to compare his account and Empedocles' account with Darwin's, which
    combines elements of both their accounts in ways contemplated by neither
    of them. (See also Sorabji [1980], ch.11, and esp. G. A. Cohen [1978], 270–
    2, on teleology and evolutionary theory.) (1) He agrees with Empedocles in
    regarding the appearance of the first creatures with beneficial teeth as a
    random change. The benefit of teeth does not explain why these creatures
    have them. (2) But he agrees with Aristotle's view that the benefit of teeth
    explains why later generations have them; heredity and natural selection
    make the benefit of teeth causally relevant. The Darwinian theory,
    therefore, like the Aristotelian, makes teleological explanations turn out to
    be true.

    Darwin's account, then, is one logically possible empirical account of
    how Aristotle's teleological claim might be right. It could not be Aristotle's
    account; for he does not believe that there ever was a creature for which
    beneficial teeth were coincidental. He can appeal to some extent to
    heredity, since that will eliminate the deviant specimens that violate the
    usual teleological rules. But he does not suppose that the observance of
    teleological rules could be the result of processes that were originally
    matters of chance. He assumes fixity of species, and therefore does not
    allow random mutations (which he does allow) to have the far-reaching
    effects contemplated by Darwin. See *GA* 731b31–732a1, 760a35–b1. *GC*
    338b11–19, *DA* 415a25–b7 stop short of asserting the actual permanence of
    species; Balme [1972], 97f, and Clark [1975], 35f, raise doubts about
    Aristotle's general commitment to the thesis. Lennox [1985], 90f, denies
    that Aristotle is committed to the fixity of species and the everlasting
    continuation of their members. He denies that species-forms are ever-
    lasting, 88, by relying on evidence that seems to me to prove the point only
    for particular forms; see 11n22.

    A Darwinian account explains the causal relevance of benefit without
    assuming that organisms have been designed for their benefit. An account

of intelligent creation appeals directly to design as the basis of teleological regularities. Aristotle's position is different from both of these; for him the universe was never created, and hence nothing explains how organisms originally came to be teleologically ordered, since they never came to be this way. He must express in different terms his belief that organisms have always had their teleological structure non-coincidentally. He needs to say that if the structure they have did not benefit them, they would not have had it and the universe would to this extent be different from how it actually is. The crucial claim, then, for the truth of Aristotle's teleological thesis is the claim about causal relevance; and while this has empirical implications, it does not imply the truth of Aristotle's particular empirical account.

The possibility of teleological explanations without belief in evolution or design is raised as an objection to Wright's causal account of teleology (see n22 above) by Boorse [1976], 74f. I do not see that this objection gives sufficient reason for denying a causal element in teleology; I am not sure how a non-causal account deals with beneficial coincidences (see Wright [1973], 165). In some cases, admittedly, a mechanism may have come into being by accident (not even by Darwinian evolution) and yet be explicable teleologically; but in this case the benefit resulting from it explains its remaining in being rather than its coming into being, and the explanation will still be causal (satisfying the sorts of counterfactuals suggested for Aristotle's account). This conception of functional explanation is considered and rejected by Cummins [1975], 749–51.

26. The other arguments for teleology in ii 8 appeal in various ways to analogies between craft and nature, explored in 199a8–32. We might construe these as purely dialectical arguments, pointing out that we tend to think of natural processes in some of the terms we apply to crafts, and therefore tend to apply teleological notions to them. But these arguments are useless for proving that natural processes are really teleological unless we accept the crucial claim about the causal relevance of the goal. When Aristotle claims that technical and natural processes work in the same way, 199a9–15, he does not mean that if ships grew naturally, the keel and the skeleton would grow first. He means that in both cases the growth and the final state of the object is to be explained teleologically—it grows that way and is that way because that is its function. To understand the 'because' here we must say something about the type of efficient causation involved. In production by a craft we can see that the right type of efficient cause is present. In natural processes the question is harder; to answer it Aristotle must appeal to the arguments against Empedocles. The success of the later arguments, if they are to be anything more than purely dialectical, depends on a claim about causal relevance.

27. This view is present in Dennett [1971].

28. The view that teleological claims involve no efficient-causal claims at all, is held by Von Wright [1971], 83–6, Nussbaum [1978], 88. I believe (without certainty) that it is fair to attribute this view to Wieland [1975], since he claims that '*telos* is a concept of reflection . . . not a universal cosmic or

metaphysical principle' (146). He does not clearly distinguish the question of whether Aristotle is committed to the view that the universe as a whole has a teleological structure from the question of whether he is committed to *some* metaphysical or ontological claim—e.g. to the presence of the right sort of efficient cause.

29. The view that a teleological explanation conflicts with a non-teleological explanation of the same process is held (for purposive behaviour) by Taylor [1964] 40–8, clarified by [1966]. In [1970], he seems to withdraw from the claim about conflict, and to claim instead (quite reasonably) that the same property of a process or event cannot have both types of explanation (see, e.g., 73f (related to his [1967]) and 89–92). This would be a version of the third view of teleology. (Taylor's conception of the individuation of processes and events, and his claims about basic explanations, leave me a bit unsure about his position.) Taylor's earlier view is effectively criticized by Block [1971].

    Gotthelf [1976] defends the irreducibility of teleological explanations and the *dunameis* they essentially refer to. But he also accepts Taylor's earlier belief in incompatibility, without distinguishing this from irreducibility (as Taylor does in his later work). He is rightly criticized by Miller [1984], 142. Incompatibility is also accepted by Balme [1972], 76–80, Cooper [1982], 210n (where he distinguishes his view from Balme's). Sorabji [1980], chs. 9–10 criticizes this view.

    Waterlow [1982], 80–9, argues that for Aristotle the prospect envisaged by his materialist opponents would be empirically so implausible as to be not worth taking seriously. Waterlow describes Aristotle's position in such extreme terms that it is hard to see why Aristotle should offer the material explanations of goal-directed processes that he actually offers. Waterlow's argument, however, does not imply that Aristotle regards teleological explanations as incompatible with non-teleological explanations of the same events (she does not state a view on this issue).

30. The third view results from attributing to Aristotle a view similar to the one developed by Wright; see n22 above.

31. To avoid this argument some believers in the second view about teleology (e.g. Taylor, in his first view; see n29) have denied that explanations referring to intention and purpose are efficient-causal explanations. The argument for this denial are not very good; and they would in any case require considerable revision to Aristotle, since he does not entertain any of the necessary doubts about the efficient-causal character of these explanations.

32. In speaking of unconditional, *haplôs*, necessity in contrast to conditional necessity in teleological contexts, we mean that this necessity is not limited by any teleological condition, not that it is from every point of view unconditional. The necessity of the movement of the heavens is, in Aristotle's view, absolutely unconditional, but the necessity of a particular sublunary contingent material process is conditional, since it depends on the occurrence of the process that is its efficient cause, and this is not absolutely unconditionally necessary. The contrast drawn in *GC* ii 11 does not conflict with the one drawn in *Phys.* ii 9.

33. We may deny that a goal-directed process is the same event as the material processes underlying it, even if we agree that they are necessary and sufficient for it. Such a view, requiring two events to have the same essence if they are to be identical, is attributed to Aristotle by Charles [1984], 30–4. I am inclined to think that Aristotle individuates events in such a way that the goal-directed process and its material basis will be the same event (cf. the treatment of lucky events, n15 above). A narrower construal of event identity requires Aristotle to say that teleologically explained events are not identical to non-teleologically explained events, but the latter sort of event is necessary and sufficient for the former. Similar reformulation will be required if we construe 'explanation' differently from the way I have suggested in n4 above.

34. Other examples make the same point about the possibility of double explanation. (1) Man has the hairiest head among the animals, both because of an unconditional necessity and for some goal, *PA* 658b2–10. (2) An animal's horns have a function, because nature uses their necessary nature (cf. *Phys.* 200a8–9) to achieve a good result, *PA* 663b12–664a8. The necessities mentioned here are unconditional, e.g. the tendency of some matter to move upwards, 663b34; nature uses them for the protection of the animal. To support this claim Aristotle argues that the benefit resulting from horns helps to explain why animals have them (or lack them, 664a3–8). (3) The squid's secretion of dark fluid is necessitated as the discharge of urine is in other animals, but nature uses this necessary effect for the creature's benefit, 679a25–30. In each of these cases the explanatory relevance of the benefit still allows a non-teleological explanation of the same event.

35. The most helpful discussion of conditional and unconditional necessity is Cooper [1985], esp. 158–61. He argues that unconditional necessity operates at stages within larger natural material processes that are themselves *only* conditionally necessary. For these larger processes, then, Cooper still apparently takes teleology to be incompatible with unconditional necessity, on the ground that Aristotle thinks, e.g., that the end product is not explained by the matter, 161. But this does not show that the process identical to the emergence of the end-product cannot be explained non-teleologically. If Cooper allows the compatibility of teleological explanations and unconditional necessity for smaller processes, why not for larger processes too?

36. Le Blond [1939], 29, notices the absence of reference to causation in the dialectical account of essence in the *Topics*. See also 6n12.

37. Waterlow [1982], 90f, rejects some of Gotthelf's emphasis on the empirical character of Aristotle's theory. I agree with her conclusion, though not with her argument. She argues that Aristotle's conception of nature leaves 'no conceptual room for a view of basic physical units whose character is shown in and through all their specific combinations', 91. Even if Waterlow were clearly right about this, it would show only that Aristotle must reject one type of non-teleological law; it would not show that he could not regard any types of non-teleological laws as empirically possible.

CHAPTER 6

1. For 'according to belief' and 'according to truth' see *Top*. 100a27–b23, 105b30–1, 155b7–16, 162b31–3 (cf. 165b1–4), *APr* 43a39, b8–9, 46a3–10, 65a35–7, *APo* 81b18–23 (cf. 72a9–11). On dialectic versus demonstration see *Top*. 162a12–18, *APr* 24a22–5.

2. See § 35.

3. The account of science in the *APo* does not describe a method for discovering scientific truths from experience. See Barnes [1969]. The demonstrative structure is intended to display the epistemological and metaphysical conditions for a science. (Contrast Barnes's view, 77–87 (discussed by Burnyeat [1981], 115–20), that the demonstrative structure is simply an expository or didactic device.) Though Aristotle need not believe that the standards of science have been attained yet, he must give us reason to think they are attainable, if he is not to frustrate his own aims for inquiry.

   Some have suggested that passages in Aristotle's other works actually display the demonstrative form that he expects in a completed science. See Allan [1961], Jope [1972], Barnes [1981]. While there is some reason to see deductive structure, there is no sign that Aristotle intends the first principles to have the status he assigns to first principles of demonstration. See 7n10.

4. On nominalism and realism about universals see 4n11, § 144. According to Barnes [1975], 139, Aristotle means that demonstrative science requires true universal propositions rather than subsistent universals, and any apparent commitment to the reality of universals is a result of failure to 'put the matter cleanly'. There is no reason to attribute any such nominalist intention to Aristotle (least of all in 77a5–9); and the nominalist claim itself is disputable. Statements about universals cannot be reduced to statements about classes of particulars, unless we speak of predicating properties of particulars; and in predicating properties (and not simply applying names) we commit ourselves to the existence of universals. Armstrong [1983], 77–85, presents this argument briefly.

5. These arguments do not distinguish Aristotelian universals from non-particular properties. See §§ 43, 143.

6. In 85b23–5, *kath'hauto* in the *gar*-clause explaining *katholou* indicates that here also the *katholou* is *kath'hauto*.

7. On the demand for necessity see Sorabji [1981], 233–44. He seems to me to under-emphasize Aristotle's explanation of necessity by reference to essential and intrinsic properties. Kosman [1973], 377, appropriately stresses the connexion of necessity with explanation. On necessity see also Barnes [1975], 97; Burnyeat [1981], 108–10.

   Hintikka [1972] (discussed by Frede [1974], with a reply by Hintikka [1974]) claims; 'One is almost tempted to say that Aristotle's views on first principles of a science are predictable on the basis of his syllogistic theory' 55. But Hintikka's prediction fails to deal with the demands for necessity and for explanatory connexion. (The relation to syllogism would be even less close if Barnes [1981] were right to say that Aristotle's theory of demonstration is earlier than his theory of the syllogism.)

8. My remarks indicate that I am inclined to believe (*a*) that the necessity Aristotle has in mind is primarily the (*de re*) necessity of necessary properties rather than the (*de dicto*) necessity of necessary truths (on this distinction see Kneale [1962], who describes it with some scepticism, and Sorabji [1980], 186–91; its formulation for Aristotle requires us also to take account of his use of 'qua'); and (*b*) that he explains necessity through essence rather than the other way round (though his concept of the necessary as what cannot be otherwise clearly does not mention essence). Doubts on these points are expressed by Lloyd [1981a], 163. On genuine subjects see § 39.

9. 'White thing' translates *to leukon*, i.e. 'the white', the neuter definite article plus the neuter adjective. Sometimes these adjectival phrases refer to properties, e.g. to inherent items in *Catg.* 1a27, 10b16, 27, 11a7; see 4n25. Here, as in *DI* 21a20, they must refer to the subject; it is not the quality white that is a log. On these phrases see further 10n45.

10. 'Essentially' renders *hoper*, 83a7. 'x is *hoper* y' means 'x is exactly y', i.e. the sort of thing whose essence is y. This assumes that it means the same as 'y is *touto hoper* x is', as in *Catg.* 3b36, 6a39, 11a25, b26, *Top.* 141a35, *Met.* 1021a28 (retaining *auto ho estin*, against OCT and Ross's note). These examples are appositely cited in *IA* 533b59.

   I follow Barnes in reading *outh' ⟨hoper⟩ leukon on* in 83a7; cf. *hoper xulon*, a14, and *hoper ekeino*, a27.

11. Two tests pick out the genuine subject: (1) If 'The G is H' is true, but the F is G coincidentally and is H, then the F is the subject of the G and the H. (2) If the F is G by being F, then the F is the subject of the G. In Aristotle's example, nothing is a log by being white, but logs have the coincident of being white by being logs, and hence the log is the genuine subject of whiteness, while the white thing is not the genuine subject of being a log. The sentences that have combinations as their apparent subjects are equivalent to sentences that reveal the genuine subject more clearly, *Met.* 1017a7–22.

12. The explanatory aspects of essential properties are well discussed by Kung [1977], 370f. See 5n36. On definition see Bolton [1976], Ackrill [1981]. On essence see 3n39, Kirwan [1970].

13. The properties that are explained by the essential properties are the 'intrinsic coincidents', *kath'hauta sumbebêkota* defined in *Met.* 1025a30–4 (cf. 3n38). See *APo* 75a18, b1, 76b13, 83b19–20, Barnes [1975], 115. Inwood [1979], 323, infers from 85b23–7 that *kath'hauta sumbebêkota* are self-explanatory. But Aristotle says only that the subject (*hô(i) huparchei*) of the intrinsic coincident is itself the *aition* for itself, 85b24–5, which I would take to mean that the essence of the subject explains the inherence of the coincident (see Barnes [1975], 177), rather than that the coincident explains itself. Intrinsic coincidents are discussed further by Barnes [1970], 139f, Wedin [1973], Graham [1975], Hadgopoulos [1976], Granger [1981], Tiles [1983].

14. On homonymy see 3nn9–10.
15. On substance and explanatory properties see § 118.
16. On references in the *Top.* to demonstrative science see Barnes [1981], 48–50.
17. On truth and correspondence see § 2.
18. The passage is quoted and discussed at § 2. 'Natural priority' refers not only to asymmetrical existential dependence, but also to precedence in different natural orders in different contexts; cf. 4n18, 10n8, *Catg.* 14b4–5, *Phys.* 261a13–14, 265a22–4, *PA* 646a25–b2, Ross [1924], ii.160.
19. Some issues about the asymmetry of explanation are discussed by Van Fraassen [1980], Brody [1972].
20. On priority in knowledge see *Met.* 1018b30–7, Barnes [1975], 100.
21. Aristotle is entitled to treat necessity as transitive, if he construes it as the normal purely modal operator. But in the *APo* it is not clear that he has explained it this way. What belongs necessarily to something must belong to it in itself, *kath'hauto* (see n6 above), and 'in itself' introduces a reference to essence that may challenge the transitivity of necessity.
22. See § 106.
23. In 72b13–15 Aristotle claims that for his opponent demonstration 'from an assumption' will count as a demonstration, and this criterion makes demonstration absurdly easy, since 'If p1, then p1' is a demonstration from an assumption. The opponent, however, claims at most to argue 'Since p1, then p1', not merely to argue from the assumption that p1 is true. Hence his condition is not as trivially satisfied as Aristotle suggests.
24. Aristotle's claim that *epistasthai* requires an explanation has encouraged some readers to suppose that *epistêmê* is really understanding (which is supposedly connected especially with explanation) rather than knowledge (which is especially connected with justification). Hence Barnes renders *epistêmê* by 'understanding', and Burnyeat [1981], 102–15, defends this rendering. I think it is a mistake, however, to suppose that Aristotle is not also concerned with conditions for justification, and therefore a mistake to suppose that he is not concerned with knowledge; providing an explanation is a reasonable way of showing that a belief is justified. Though Burnyeat appeals to *APo* i 2 to show that explanation fits better than knowledge, 110, he does not discuss i 3 fully. But the types of demonstration rejected in i 3 allegedly violate general conditions for knowledge, not merely for demonstration; and Aristotle sometimes says that the puzzles are general puzzles about knowledge. See 72b11–15, *eidenai* and *agnôstous*, 26–7, *gnôrimôterôn*; 30, *eidenai*. The three possibilities—infinite regress, circle, and self-evident foundations—are three ways of answering a question about justification. See Chisholm [1982], 129–36. Armstrong [1973], 150–161, traces the three possibilities, which he plausibly supposes to be possible accounts of knowledge, to Plato, *Tht.* 200d–201c; see 7n27.

Even if Aristotle is concerned only with a regress of explanation, he must show why explanations should not form an infinite regress or a circle; and he will have to appeal to those very claims about priority and independence in knowledge that support claims about justification. Even if the issues about justification and about explanation are distinct, they do not seem to be independent in this case.

25. Foundationalism: see Chisholm [1982], 9–15. Aristotle cannot claim merely (as some foundationalists do) that some beliefs have some degree of justification independent of inference. Epistemic asymmetry demands basic beliefs that are actually matters of knowledge or have equivalent epistemic status (the disjunction makes room for *nous*) without any appeal to inference.

26. Scientific knowledge, *epistêmê*, requires demonstration; but Aristotle's conditions for demonstration preclude demonstration of the initial propositions, the first principles; either, then, there is no scientific knowledge of the principles, or not all scientific knowledge is demonstrative. Aristotle speaks in both ways; see 72b18–25, 88b35–7, 100b5–17, Barnes, 108f.

27. See also *Phys.* 185a12–14, 252a32–b6, *GC* 325a13–23, § 16.

28. On begging the question see 9n14.

CHAPTER 7

1. The importance of epistemic asymmetry in Aristotle's view of first principles is not accommodated in Wieland's account [1970] 62–7, [1960], 135 (discussed by Hess [1970], 48–51).

2. On *nous* of first principles see also *EN* 1140b31–1141a8, 1143a35–b3. *GA* 742b30–3 and *Met.* 1011a11–13 (see § 106) do not say that the basis of demonstration must be *nous*.

3. *Nous* is the capacity for conceptual thought and reasoning that is involved in the grasp of universals and the use of universal concepts. See § 169. It is also needed to form the different perceptual judgments about this or that F into the universal judgment about Fs as a whole (68b27–9, 88a14–17. *horan . . . noêsai*). It is not clear whether the *nous* is part of induction or the state we have reached when we have finished the induction. Probably Aristotle has both roles in mind, since the same sorts of abilities will be required at both stages. But these functions of *nous* do not explain Aristotle's epistemological claims for it. Lesher [1973] shows that *nous* has a legitimate role in the formation of generalizations and the acquisition of first principles, and that this role does not require intuition of the principles as self-evident. (See also Engberg-Pederson [1979], 307–10.) But we could agree with this, and still argue that the epistemic status Aristotle assigns to first principles of demonstrative science requires him to understand *nous* as non-inferential awareness of something as true and necessary and better-known than its consequences. Lesher's argument, 65, therefore fails to undermine a 'traditional' interpretation (accepted by, e.g., Sidgwick; see n9 below). A similar objection applies to Kahn's account in [1981]. Though Kahn thinks it is wrong to understand *nous* as 'an infallible intuition of self-evident truths', 386, his account does not suggest an alternative way of explaining the epistemic status assigned to *nous*.

Kosman comments, [1973], 388f: 'understanding these principles *as principles* is just seeing them in their capacity to effect this consistency and coherence in regard to phenomena, their capacity to make the phenomena intelligible. It is, in other words, seeing them in their capacity to *explain.*' Such an appeal to explanatory coherence is completely reasonable, but it is not obvious how it will meet Aristotle's demands for epistemic priority. Kosman does not explain how it avoids circularity of the sort Aristotle rejects (briefly mentioned, 381). For further discussion of *nous* and first principles see Lee [1935] (the parallel with geometry that he suggests, even if it is correct, does not fully explain the epistemic status that Aristotle claims for first principles).

4. Aristotle sometimes seems to be discussing the acquisition of propositions that are first principles, and sometimes the formation of universal concepts. (See Barnes, 249, 254–6, 259f.) Probably he intends the account of concepts to answer the question about principles. See Kahn [1981], 394–7.

5. In treating perception as an elementary cognitive state contributing to the formation of concepts, but not itself involving them, Aristotle seems to ignore the conceptual character of some perception and appearance. See § 166. He makes a parallel mistake in assuming that we begin by perceiving Fs, and then perform the induction that is necessary for any universal judgment about Fs. See § 15. He ignores the fact that if we perceive things as Fs, we must have the concept of F, and surely must already make some universal judgments about Fs.

6. Aristotle's genetic account of the growth of universal principles does not justify his claims about *nous*. When we grasp a universal conclusion that Fs are Gs, we may also (if we have not yet accepted Aristotle's doctrine of justification) want to support the universal conclusion by appeal to our perceptual judgment that this F is G, that F is G, and so on. In that case we do not halt the regress of justification; to show that this must be halted Aristotle needs to add further epistemological doctrines to his genetic account.

7. *Nous* is sometimes rendered by 'intuition', which is too specialized to be a good translation. (Barnes, 257, rejects 'intuition', on the mistaken assumption that such a translation would imply that *nous* was a means of acquiring knowledge.) The wide scope of *nous* demands something like 'understanding' (Barnes uses 'comprehension'). But this point of translation leaves us free to argue that when Aristotle mentions *nous* of the first principles of demonstration, he must have in mind some intuitive awareness of them (see Sidgwick and Descartes, quoted below, n9 and n17); and such an argument is cogent.

8. Le Blond's surprise [1939], 137 that *nous* is not mentioned in the account of acquisition of principles assumes that it should be part of the process, rather than necessary for the product to count as a grasp of the principle. For similar reasons Viano [1958] assumes that *nous* cancels the constructive role of dialectic. The distinction is clearly drawn by Grote [1872], ii.293: 'By referring the principia to Intellect (*nous*), he does not intend to indicate their generating source, but their evidentiary value and dignity when generated and matured.'

9. This role for dialectical argument is clearly stated by Sidgwick [1879], 106: 'To find a way out of this difficulty we require, I think, to take Aristotle's distinction between logical or natural priority in cognition and priority in the knowledge of any particular mind. We are thus enabled to see that a proposition may be self-evident, i.e. may be properly cognisable without being viewed in connexion with any other propositions; though in order that its truth may be apparent to some particular mind, there is still required some rational process connecting it with propositions previously accepted by that mind.' In Sidgwick's example I begin with a limited statement, come to see that the limitation is unjustified, and so come to regard the unlimited generalization as self-evident. But even if we initially regarded the limited statement as a matter of intuition (i.e. we sought no further grounds for it), it is hard to see why we should say the same about the unlimited generalization; why do the reasons for rejecting the limitations not also constitute inferential grounds for accepting the unlimited generalization?

Ross [1924], i.251f, suggests a similar role for dialectical argument about first principles: '. . . the statement of the assumptions is preceded or accompanied by some sort of argument which is not meant to be cogent deduction (*that* works only from principles to their conclusions), but to bring home to the learner's mind propositions which in time he will see to be self-evident though at first he may doubt or deny them.' This account works quite well for Aristotle's remarks on his approach to the Eleatics in *Phys.* i; see § 35. De Pater [1965], 83–5, takes a similar view of dialectic in both Plato and Aristotle: '. . . si selon Aristote la dialectique remplit une fonction à l'égard des principes, ce n'est qu'en tant qu'elle mène jusqu'au seuil de la découverte des principes', 85.

10. On the differences between empirical inquiry and dialectic see § 24. The claim in *Top.* 101b3–4 (see § 18) that dialectic has a road towards first principles does not imply that it is more than ancillary to empirical inquiry. *APr* 46a28–30 refers to the work on dialectic for a discussion of the selection of premisses; it does not imply that dialectical inquiry alone is adequate for finding first principles. Owen [1961], 244, and Evans [1977], 32f, go too far in connecting this passage with, as Owen puts it, 'the claim made in the *Topics* that the first principles of scientific argument can be established by methods which start from the *endoxa*'. Owen refers to *Top.* 101a36–b4; but Aristotle's claims there and in the *APr* fall short of the one Owen ascribes to him.

If Aristotle clearly relied on dialectically established first principles for further demonstration, he would clearly be committed to the strong claim about dialectic. On the possible role of demonstration see Jope [1972]. But Jope does not show that Aristotle thinks the premisses of his deductions have the appropriate status to ground demonstration, strictly so called. Jope fairly cites, 279n, the use of *apodeiknunai* at 233a7, b14, 237a35, 238a32, b16, 26, 240b8; but these passages do not show how strictly Aristotle intends the claim.

11. Since special disciplines do not fully answer the demand to 'give an account' that must be answered in a justified claim to knowledge, *Rep.* 534b3–d1, they do not count as complete knowledge, 533c3–e2. The practitioners of

these disciplines (e.g. mathematics) suppose they have found genuine first principles when in fact they treat their basic propositions as mere assumptions, *hupotheseis*; they simply assume their truth and construct a deductive system from them, without seeking any further justification for them, 510c1–d3. The dialectician looks for first principles that will justify them, 510b4–9, 511b3–c2. His activity is 'destroying the assumptions', 533c8; but he does not undermine the propositions themselves, only their status as mere assumptions.

12. Dialectic will present the metaphysical basis of the special disciplines; it will show that mathematicians and moralists must be talking about Forms, not about sensible particulars or properties; and *Tim.* 27d5–30c1 suggests that the teleological structure of nature is explained as the product of intelligent design that is guided by awareness of the Forms.

13. Aristotelian and Platonic dialectic are somewhat misleadingly contrasted by Solmsen [1968], 66 (who wrongly denies that in Plato's theory dialectic begins from *endoxa*), and by Wieland [1970], 221 (who speaks of 'Diese neue Dignität der Doxa', in Aristotle, as opposed to Plato, whose philosophy 'gipfelt in dem, wovon man nicht mehr reden kann', 222). In my view, the essential difference is not in the starting-point or use of dialectical argument, but in the evaluation of its conclusions. See also Viano [1958], Aubenque [1966], 277.

14. Aristotle's disagreement with Plato over dialectic explains a further disagreement about who deserves to be called a philosopher. Both of them regard the philosopher as the seeker of knowledge and truth rather than mere belief, *Rep.* 480a6–13.

   Minimally, Aristotle finds philosophy in the disinterested study of puzzles apart from any immediate practical need to resolve them, *Top.* 163b4–16, 175a5; *Pol.* 1279b11–15, 1282b14–23, 1299a28–30; and this is the sense in which the gymnastic dialectic of the *Physics* 'has' some philosophy; see 3n52. He also identifies it with the serious and disinterested pursuit of the truth, *EE* 1216b35–9, *PA* 645a3, *DC* 291b24–8; hence the philosopher argues according to truth, whereas the dialectician argues according to belief (see 6n1). Hence the 'philosophical sciences' are demonstrative, *Top.* 101a27, 163b9—though the term is not used in the *Analytics*, it refers to the sciences described there. Demonstrative scientists deserve the name of philosopher because, in Aristotle's view, they fulfil the reasonable aspects of Plato's aspirations for the philosopher in *Rep.* vi–vii. For Plato, the philosophers know the permanent realities opposed to transient sensibles; they have knowledge and not mere belief; they can give an explanatory account stating the cause. Aristotle's demonstrative scientist is the one who satisfies these Platonic conditions.

   Plato, however, also claims that philosophers will be universal scientists and that their method will be dialectical. These two further claims are connected because dialectic is the universal science that understands and justifies the first principles of the other sciences. Aristotle entirely rejects these two further Platonic claims, since he denies the possibility of any universal science, and the claim of dialectic to give scientific knowledge.

The only science is the demonstrative, departmental science that Plato assigns to *dianoia*; and hence Aristotle describes the first principles of demonstrative science as 'assumptions', *hupotheseis*. Aristotle preserves the distinction between *dianoia* and *noêsis* by requiring *nous* to grasp the first principles of science. But *nous* is not dialectical, since it is not ratiocinative at all, but intuitive and immediate. Nor is it a universal science, since different departmental sciences require different, and epistemologically independent, acts of intuition.

On the Platonic and the polemical origins of Aristotle's appeal to *hupotheseis* see Solmsen [1929], 105–7 (who points out the connexion with Aristotle's foundationalism); Ross [1939], 266f (who states the important difference between Plato's and Aristotle's conception of *hupotheseis* and *archai*); Barnes [1981], 35.

15. Derivation from proper principles is one of the conditions for demonstration, *APo* 71b22–3; in fact there is no such thing as a demonstration unconditionally, but only demonstration from the proper principles, 76a13–15, which must therefore be indemonstrable, 76a16–17, 31–2. The proper and primary principles, 72a5–6, are contrasted with propositions that are merely true and *endoxa*, 74b24–6; and a genuine demonstration has a conclusion homogeneous with the primary principles, in so far as it is derived from the proper principles, 76a26–30. The nature of the proper principles determines the appropriateness or inappropriateness of a question addressed to a special scientist, 77a36–40. On proper appearances see 2n17.

Aristotle relies on the demand for proper principles to rule out excessively general arguments, *GA* 747b27–30, 748a7–11, including those involving Platonic Forms, *MM* 1183a39–b8; hence he contrasts *oikeioi logoi* with merely 'logical' argument, *Phys.* 264a7, b2, *DC* 294b11, *EE* 1217a9, *Pol.* 1323b38, *Rhet.* 1396b11. (See 2h46.)

16. This role for inquiry as a preliminary and support to intuition is stressed by Sidgwick [1907], 339–42.

17. Descartes develops Aristotle's view most thoroughly in his account of intuition and deduction, in *Regulae* iii (= AT x. 366–70). He defines 'intuition' (which he admits he uses in an unfamiliar sense, 368) as 'such an easy and distinct conception of a purified and concentrated mind that no doubt at all about what we understand (intelligimus) is left; or, what is the same thing, an indubitable conception of a purified and concentrated mind, arising solely from the light of reason', 368. The objects of intuition are simple and basic truths (e.g. I exist, I think, a triangle is bounded by three lines, etc.). Like Aristotelian *nous*, intuition must be the basis of deduction, if deduction is to transmit truth and certainty from premisses to conclusions, 369. Descartes's objects of intuition seem better than Aristotle's candidates for being intuitive first principles, since they seem less dependent for their justification on inferential connexions. On the other hand, it is hard to derive anything from them that is close to a first principle of a special science.

An empiricist may appeal to perception as a source of beliefs that seem unaffected by inferential connexions. See Hume, *Treatise*, i.4.2, 190: 'For since all acts and sensations of the mind are known to us by consciousness, they must necessarily appear in every particular what they are, and be what they appear. Every thing that enters the mind being *in reality* a perception, 'tis impossible any thing should to feeling appear different. That were to suppose, that even where we are most intimately conscious, we might be mistaken.' Aristotle also picks perceptual judgments as examples of those that are evident in themselves. But he does not think perceptual judgments about particulars can supply the proper foundation for a scientific theory, since the theory describes relations between universals.

Both the rationalist and the empiricist simply postpone Aristotle's difficulties. We may be subjectively certain, unwilling to entertain any doubt about an axiom or a perceptual judgment, it does not follow that we are justified in trusting this subjective certainty. To find some justification for our trust, where can we turn but to inferential connexions with other beliefs? Descartes seems to lead us back into this inquiry when he tries to justify confidence in his clear and distinct perceptions (in *Med.* iii–iv). Hume in fact insists that our subjective certainties have no justification at all, even though our lack of justification does not affect our conviction. See *Treatise* i.4.2, 218: ' 'Tis impossible upon any system to defend either our understanding or our senses; and we but expose them further when we endeavour to justify them in that manner.' Once we look for something more than subjective certainty, Aristotle's difficulties return for versions of foundationalism that initially seem more plausible than his.

18. Only a universal science could demonstrate the axioms, since they apply equally to all reality. But Aristotle insists there is no such science, since a science depends on a special range of appearances (see n15). Moreover, if we demonstrate the axioms, we must demonstrate them from some prior and better known principles, and what would these be? All demonstration relies on the truth of PNC, and hence we can hardly find a demonstration of it. See § 97.

19. Ross [1949], 543, Owen [1960], 190, Berti [1965], 38, Barnes [1975], 143, all take 77a29–31 to be counterfactual, not referring to any science that Aristotle recognizes; it refers to the same science that would be *kuria pantôn* and is rejected in 76a16–25. Philop. 142.20–143.3 takes 77a20 to refer to first philosophy, and alludes to *Met.* iv—this is quite reasonable, since the science that is described only counterfactually in the *APo* is taken to be actual in *Met.* iv. In rejecting such a science Aristotle rejects the possibility of proving (*deiknunai*, 77a29) the common axioms, not merely the possibility of demonstrating (*apodeiknunai*) them. Since *Met.* iv offers a proof, though not a demonstration, of them, it conflicts with the *APo*.

Top. 172a11–13 mentions the universal scientist in the same counter-factual way. Probably *ho katholou* = the universal scientist, rather than the *logos* of a special demonstrative science (so Waitz [1844], ii.552, followed by Owen); cf. *Met.* 1005a34–5 (reading *tou katholou* without the OCT's unnecessary supplement). Alex. *in SE* 93.26–33 identifies *ho katholou* with *ho theologos*, whom he describes in terms similar to those of *Met.* iv, as studying *ta koina*, and the intrinsic properties of beings. But he does not attempt to combine this alleged recognition of a universal science with the claim that beings do not fall into one genus (correctly reported in 94.1–14).

20. The *Org.* says nothing about who, if anyone, studies the axioms. Barnes, 142, cites *Met.* 1004b22, 1005a19–22, and says, 'The easy inference from these two passages, that logic ⟨i.e. dialectic⟩ too investigates the axioms, is drawn explicitly at *Top.* 101a36–b3.' The inference, however, is not drawn explicitly, since the *Top.* passage does not even mention the axioms or common principles; Aristotle suggests only that the way to discuss the special principles, *oikeiai archai*, 101a37–8, is through the common beliefs on each subject, 101b1. The difference from the *Met.* is striking; see § 94. Berti [1965], 44, suggests that the axioms are the premisses of dialectic (but I think he misunderstands *koina* in 170a34–b3, 171b5–6).

21. Aristotle's argument from the homonymy of being against a single science of being assumes that the subject-matter of a single science cannot be homonymous, because a science must be demonstrative. (A syllogism is invalid if the same definition cannot be substituted for different occurrences of the same term in the appropriate places; and the terms in a demonstrative science must meet the necessary conditions for syllogistic validity.) This objection to a universal science rests on the prior choice of demonstration as the appropriate form for science. See 8n51.

22. At 75a42, 76b9–11, 88b3, 27–9 Aristotle suggests that special and common principles have different roles; e.g., the science argues from, *ek*, the special principles and through, *dia*, the common principles, 76b10. (Questions related to the contrast are discussed by Husik [1906].) He does not stick to this contrast; see Ross [1949], 531, and the suitably cautious remarks by Barnes, § 135. And in any case, the claim that common principles have a different role would not remove the question about their epistemic status.

23. For examples of dialectical procedure see 90a36–b1, 91a12, 93a1–3, Aubenque [1961], 10f.

24. On the educated person see § 11.

25. See, e.g., the comparison between 'speculative' and 'scientific' philosophy in Reichenbach [1951], 303f. Speculative philosophy has 'sought to acquire a knowledge of generalities, of the most general principles that govern the universe', and its methods have been a priori. Scientific philosophy gives up this search for generality and for any synthetic a priori truths, 47–9. On this conception, philosophy 'is a logical analysis of all forms of human thought'; it 'is scientific in its method; it gathers results accessible to demonstration and assented to by those who are sufficiently trained in logic and science', 308.

26. Carnap [1956], 206–8, distinguishes internal questions, those arising within a linguistic framework recognizing a system of entities, from external questions, those arising about the reality of the system of entities as a whole. Internal questions are to be answered by the recognized methods of science; external questions are matters of decision and convention, not to be answered by recognized scientific methods. Carnap's distinction between scientific methods, on the one hand, and products of decision, is decisively criticized by Quine [1966], chs. 10–11.

27. The assumption that knowledge must be based on knowledge is important in the last part of Plato's *Tht.*, which provides the source of several of Aristotle's problems in the *APo.* See Kosman [1973], 380f, Fine [1979], Armstrong (see 6n24).

CHAPTER 8

1. *Sophia* in *Met.* i is discussed by Berti [1965], 98–100, Aubenque [1966], 220f, 266f.
2. On *philosophia* see 7n14.
    Though Aristotle's early *De Philosophia* (discussed by Jaeger [1948], ch.6, Décarie [1961], 36–8) is parallel to the *Met.* in several ways (a historical survey, frr. 3–7 (OCT); criticism of the Theory of Forms, fr. 11), it does not seem to be organized around the four causes, or to distinguish *sophia* or *philosophia* as a general science from theology (fr. 8). Its views fit the conception of science in the *Org.*
    Similarly, 'first philosophy' in earlier works is concerned with the substance that is separate from matter and change (*Phys.* 185a2–3, 20, 192a34–6, 194b14, *GC* 318a5–6, *PA* 641a36) with no reference to any universal functions. See Mansion [1946], 217–24. Against Décarie's argument that the 'mature' conception of first philosophy is already present in the early works see Allan [1964].
3. Aristotle rejects the Platonist attempt to find the 'elements of all things', 992b18–24; cf. 986a1–2. The Platonists think the elements will be numbers and they think items in every category have elements in the same way. This failure to attend to the categories is their failure to make distinctions. But he claims later that those who sought the elements of beings were looking for the same things that he looks for in studying being qua being, 1003a28–32; and he then explains how the different categories can be recognized without denying the possibility of a universal science, iv 2. Owen [1960], 192, claims that 992b18–24 is 'out of tune' with 1003a28–32; but *mê dihelontas*, 992b19, and *touton ton tropon*, b20, should remove any suspicion of disharmony. Probably Aristotle writes each of these two passages (in i and iv) with the doctrine of the other in mind.
4. I assume that the *Met.* is doctrinally fairly unified, and in particular that vii–ix are meant to be continuous with i, iii, iv, vi, as Ross [1924], p. xx, thinks; contrast Jaeger [1948], 198–204, Leszl [1975], 14. Some evidence of a connected sequence is detectable, though not obvious, in iv–ix.
    (1) iv 1–2 introduces (a) the science of being qua being, (b) the multivocity of being, and (c) the priority of substance, with no explicit reference to (d) the doctrine of the categories (1003a33–b10).
    (2) v 7 repeats (b) without (a) or (c), and introduces (d) as part of (b).
    (3) vi 1–2, esp. 1026a33–b2, repeats (a) and (b) without (c), mentioning (d) without elaboration as part of (b).
    (4) vii 1 refers to v 7. It asserts (a) and (b) with reference to (d), and

explains (*c*) with reference to (*d*). (Here Aristotle refers to v 7 (rather than to iv or vi) because v 7 explains (*d*), and vi only mentions it.)

(5) ix 1, 1045b32–4 refers to the list of types of being in vi, 1026a36–b2 and 1027b28–1028a4 (it skips the items on the list that were dismissed in the second passage). 1046a4–6 refers to v 12. 1045b27–32 refers to the *prôtoi logoi*. The claim that other beings will have the *logos* of substance recalls 1028a34–6, rather than iv 1–2. (See Burnyeat *et al.* [1984], 48.) On the other hand, *pros ho . . . anapherontai*, 1045b27–8, recalls *pros to prôton anapherontai*, 1004a25–6, rather than vii 1. Whether *prôtoi logoi* refers to iv or to vii, Aristotle recalls both books.

The sequence is intelligible. While iv 1–2 asserts (*c*) without detailed explanation, v 7 and vi 2 introduce (*d*), and so prepare for the explanation and defence of (*c*) through (*d*) in vii 1. In ix 1 Aristotle shows that he thinks he has given such a defence and explanation in vii 1.

Connexion between vii and x is marked by 1053b16 (treated by Jaeger [1948], 202, in a rather arbitrary way). Some connexion is likely between v and vii–ix; for v often arranges problems and summarizes discussions up to the point where the argument of vii–ix begins. See Owens [1963], 86. For connexions between vii–ix and the later books see 1037a12, 1042a22, 1076a8–10, Ross, p. xix, xxvii.

Owens [1963], 332, argues from the cross-references to Book v and the lack of cross-references to the rest of i–vi that vii was probably written earlier than iv and vi. This argument loses force if we see the strategic reasons for beginning vii from a new starting-point. See 10n2.

These are some reasons for thinking that the *Met.* is doctrinally unified. On the importance of the puzzles in iii see n33.

5. See further 10n32.

6. Sceptical use of the history of philosophy: Sextus, *PH* i 88, iii 30–6, *AM* xi 173–4; Cicero, *Ac.* ii 117. Perhaps such use goes back to Protagoras, though definite evidence is lacking (DK 80 B 2, 7 (= *Met.* 997b32–998a6) suggest that he argues destructively against previous thinkers); historical examples could certainly be used to support his claim that there are opposed arguments on every question (Diog. L. ix 51).

7. Descartes, *Regulae* iii, (= AT x 361f). On Descartes on intuition see 7n17.

8. For his views on dialectic see *Regulae* = AT x 360–5; *Principles* = ixb 13.

9. Aristotle, therefore, does not claim to be describing his predecessors' intentions, or to state their position in words that they would themselves have used, 989a30–b6, b19–21, 993a17–24.

10. In *Physics* i–ii Aristotle describes the four causes only in ii 3, after already mentioning them, e.g. 194a18–21, a27–b13. They do not explicitly control the discussion. *PA* i criticizes the Presocratics, and in particular criticizes them for their neglect of the formal and final cause, 640b4–29, 641a14–17, 642a13–31, but does not explain why we must 'see' the different causes, 639b11, 640a13–19, or even distinguish the four causes clearly. The *GC* mentions form and matter, but does not clearly connect them with the conception of a this and a substance. Nor is the connexion between formal and final causation made clear.

11. Some materialists try to explain change by recognizing different material elements, but without clearly explaining the interactions that must be assumed to explain change, 984b5–8, 985a4–b4, b19–20. They are especially at a loss to explain changes with good results, 984b8–22, 985a18–29; cf. 1075a38–b8, and see Ross, i.135f. The Eleatics realize that materialism allows no explanation of non-essential change, and so reasonably, in Aristotle's view, reject such change altogether, 984a29–b1.

12. Substance as subject: 983b7 (matter), 10, 16, 985b10, 986b8. Substance as essence: 983a27, 987b21, 988a35 (cf. *GC* 335b35), 991a13, b1, 993a18. 987a19 connects the two uses. See 9n10, § 107, Owens [1963], 190–3.

13. Here, in contrast to *PA* 642a13–28, *GC* 335b33–336a12, Aristotle does not appeal to teleology to justify belief in the formal cause, presumably because he thinks (as Books iv–vii argue, and as *Phys.* 194b27–8 suggests) form is defensible from more general grounds than those offered in the physical works.

14. See §§ 57–8.

15. On 'mumbling', *psellizesthai* see *Probl.* 902b23–7. It suggests indefiniteness (cf. *GC* 328b9) and poor articulation (cf. 989b5).

16. On several points Aristotle takes the *Phaedo* both as a target and as a model. *Phd.* 96aff argues that the Presocratics were silent about the final cause, and the formal cause, 96d–97b. On Anaxagoras see 97b8–98c2, *Met.* 984b8–20, 985a10–23. Socrates' 'second-best route', involving *logoi* (*Phd.* 99c6–100a7; cf. *Met.* 987b31–3) presents the formal cause, but with the eventual aim of giving an account referring to the final cause; in the *Republic* dialectic is supposed to fulfil this aim, and so to provide first principles for the departmental sciences. Plato displays the self-consciousness about questions of method, and especially about the right form of explanation, that Aristotle himself displays in the *Metaphysics*. He suggests the possibility of Aristotle's second-order science.

 Aristotle's criticism of Plato also reflects the influence of *Phd.* 96ff. (See Fine [1987], 76–81.) He agrees with Plato's search for the cause of an action as opposed to its necessary conditions (*Phd.*98c2–99b2; cf. *Phil.* 26e–27a). But he criticizes Plato's view of the explanatory role of Forms, 990a33–b2, 991a8–11, b3–8, 992a24–b1, b7–9, *GC* 335b9–17. And he argues against Plato for more than one type of genuine cause (he partly follows Plato himself. *Tim.* 46c–e). But again he shows he thinks Plato has raised the right questions.

17. On Platonic dialectic see § 76. The discussions of method in *Physics* i–ii and *PA* i are the concern of the educated person, *PA* 639a4–6; they do not belong to a second-order science. A dialectical survey of particular questions, appearances, and puzzles is all that the educated person needs, since (in Aristotle's pre-*Metaphysics* view) the methods of the particular sciences have no epistemological basis outside pure dialectic.

18. See Kant *KrV* A851/B879. On the name *meta ta phusika* see Reiner [1954], Aubenque [1966], 29, Merlan, [1957], [1968], 238f, Owens [1963], 74n, Routila [1969], 18–23. The *meta* is most plausibly taken to refer to the fact that the study of nature is better known to us, and that the topics of this

work come later than the study of nature. This explanation of *meta*, however, does not imply that the *Met.*'s primary concern is with super-sensible reality (an inference that Merlan, e.g., draws from the title); study of the principles presupposed by the study of nature also comes after the study of nature in the order of discovery. This Kantian conception of metaphysics, applying to the principles presupposed by the special sciences, is not necessarily alien to Aristotle. (Kant also uses the term for the study of the super-sensible.)

19. For further discussion of this passage on puzzles see § 20.

20. The character of metaphysics as something 'sought' is emphasized, with considerable exaggeration, by Aubenque [1966], esp. 250.

21. 997a33–998a19 puts the fifth puzzle in the right place (contrast 995b13–18, 1059a38–b21, 1060a3–4). Owens's arguments, 233, do not undermine the distinction between methodological and substantive puzzles. Jaeger's lack of emphasis on the methodological puzzles leads him to distort the focus of the puzzles as a whole; see [1948], 195, and n33 below.

22. The connexion of the puzzles with Aristotle's own conception of demonstrative science is noticed by Mansion [1955], 151f; but she does not suggest that Aristotle challenges this conception in Book iv.

23. The objection in the first puzzle argues that there can be no single demonstrative science of all the types of cause, since (*a*) causes are not contraries (which are studied by a single science, 996a20–1), and (*b*) the study of the causes can be distributed among the departmental sciences, and need not be assigned to a single science, 996a21–b1 (Ross, i.227, and Owens, 221, offer explanations resting on less plausible assumptions). The objection turns on an ambiguity in 'study the causes', taking it to mean (i) study some instance of e.g. the formal cause (as mathematics does), rather than (ii) study the nature of the causes. (See Leszl [1975], 124.) The objection does not damage a science concerned with (ii). The other side of the puzzle, 996b1–26, shows why it is hard to claim that a particular first-order science is prior and universal.

24. The objector in the third puzzle assumes that wisdom is the science of every sort of substance. Every demonstrative science demonstrates the intrinsic coincidents about its subject; hence the demonstrative science of all substances will demonstrate all the intrinsic coincidents, 997a17–21. ('Science of F' is referentially opaque, implying a close explanatory connexion between something's being F and its being the object of scientific study.) The puzzle clearly assumes that wisdom will be a demonstrative science, and, equally important, that it will be first-order. Owens's suggested solution ('the reduction in a non-generic way of all Entities ⟨i.e. substances⟩ to the one primary type', 231; cf. Reale [1980], 85) does not explain how a universal science of substance fails to threaten the autonomy of the special sciences; and once we explain this, by showing that the universal science is second-order, Owens's solution is unnecessary.

25. The initially surprising assumption that a science of substance would have to demonstrate the nature of substance is explained by 1059a32–4 (see Ross, i.231). Once again Owens's suggestion (232; the coincidents must in some

way be reduced to substance, since 'only in this way could there be demonstration within the realm of Entity ⟨i.e. substance⟩ itself') fails to meet the main difficulty raised by the puzzle.

26. The role of substance in Book i makes it reasonable for a putative universal science to study substance; see n12, Reale [1980], 70, 85). The objector in the second puzzle asks: since it is not the task of any other single science, or of all the sciences, to prove the axioms that are used, why should it be the task of the science of substance, 996b33–997a2? Moreover, to demonstrate the axioms, we must demonstrate them from principles assumed as true, and these will be further axioms; if wisdom has to demonstrate these further axioms too, there will be an infinite regress. Apparently, then, the more ultimate axioms from which we demonstrate our initial axioms are undemonstrated, and the universal science cannot after all claim to demonstrate all the axioms, 997a5–9. In any case, the genus of the science of the axioms cannot be narrower than everything, since all the sciences use the axioms, 997a9–11; but there is no universal genus. The objection assumes throughout that the universal science must be demonstrative.

27. In some cases we seem to learn the nature of something by mentioning its constituents and the way they are combined, 998a20–b3; but in other cases we know things through definitions involving species whose first principles are genera, 998b4–8. The references to constituents and definitions readily suggest material and formal principles, so that the thesis and the antithesis of the puzzle need not be mutually exclusive.

28. An infinite series of perishable principles might seem to involve an infinite regress that must be rejected in favour of a first cause, 1000b24–9. But we need to know what sort of cause the first cause would need to be, and what sorts of causes can or cannot form an infinite series; neither side of the puzzle is cogent before we consider the types of principles that are relevant.

29. Several of the puzzles suggest that particulars and universals are rival candidates for being principles. The eighth puzzle asks whether there is anything besides particulars, 999a24–b24, and the fifteenth asks whether the principles are particulars or universals, 1003a5–17. Questions about universals also arise when we consider the existence of non-sensible principles (fifth puzzle, 997b34–998a19), when we ask if the principles must be numerically one (ninth puzzle, 999b24–1000a4), and when we consider the status of being and one, apparently the most generic universals (eleventh puzzle, 1001a4–b25).

The antithesis of the eighth puzzle, 999b17–24, suggests a possible solution, since it suggests that we find it hard to believe in universals because we assume that they must be separated Platonic Forms. Aristotle argues that many of the difficulties about the Forms result from mistakes about universals, 997b3–12, 999a19–22. Aristotle suggests that universal predication does not imply separation; if it does not, the problem of separate existence should not be combined with the problem of universals, and the two problems will become more tractable.

30. The fifth puzzle asks if there are any non-sensible substances; the eleventh and twelfth ask about the claims of mathematical objects to be substances;

and the fifteenth asks how universals can be principles if they are not substances.

31. On the relation of first to second substances see §§ 42–3, 48, 60. If (as *Phys.* i 7–8 seems to suggest) we identify the particular subject with matter, and the universal with form, the only sort of independent particular seems to be formless matter. Aristotle's earlier views do not dissolve the puzzles in *Met.* iii.

32. Aristotle credits Plato with the discovery of the formal cause, and rejects Plato's conception of it as both (i) a separable particular substance, and (ii) a universal. But he does not necessarily reject either (i) or (ii); in Bk iii he raises a doubt about whether they can both be true of the same things. Cf. 1040b26–30, § 140 below.

33. Books vii–ix never refer explicitly to the puzzles, and never answer any of them directly; see Jaeger [1948], 196–201, [1912], 102. We might infer that the puzzles represent an earlier plan that was abandoned; Jaeger attributes it to Aristotle's Platonist phase. Aubenque [1966], 310, also ignoring the emergence of the preliminary questions, sees two conflicting perspectives in Aristotle. Books vii–ix, however, deal with highly relevant preliminary questions; and the puzzles are all eventually answered by the end of the treatise; see Ross, p. xxiii. To this extent they provide further evidence of the unity of the treatise; see n4. Owens, 256f, goes too far in denying that iii presents a plan or programme for the rest of the treatise, though his further remarks about its role are quite just.

34. Kant says it was the Antinomy of pure reason that 'first awoke me from the dogmatic slumbers and drove me to the critique of reason itself in order to end the scandal of reason's ostensible contradiction with itself' (Letter to Garve, 21 Sep. 1798 (= Zweig 99n). For references to comparisons between *Met.* iii and Kant's Antinomies see Reale [1980], 94–6.

35. See the quotation from Descartes in § 84.

36. Kant, *KrV* B22–3. The result of dogmatic assertion is the sort of *anepikritos diaphônia* that Sextus describes, *PH* i 98.

37. In iii Aristotle avoids the standard dialectical device of appealing to multivocity in, e.g., 'principle' or 'substance'. He certainly thinks multivocity is relevant; for *Met.* v is entirely concerned with multivocals. (There are no good reasons for doubting that Aristotle intended it to be part of the *Met.* See Owens, 86f. Ross, p. xxv, is more sceptical.) But the dialectical appeal to multivocity will not answer the questions that are raised in iii. For judgments about when and how a term is multivocal are not neutral and independent of theory; they rest on common beliefs that may themselves be challenged (see § 27). Aristotle sees that arguments against the assumptions underlying common beliefs are not answered by dialectical argument relying on the very assumptions being challenged. Gewirth [1953], 579, argues cogently (with reference to questions about translation) against attempts to solve such problems by appeal to homonymy.

38. On 'new starts' see 2n65.

39. In 1003a27 I understand *phuseôs tinos* ⟨*aitias*⟩, i.e. 'they are the causes of some

nature *kath' hautên'* (and so not its causes because of some coincident of it), not simply properties of it *kath' hautên*. Ross's note is clearer than his and Kirwan's translations.

40. On elements of being see n3.

41. 'Being qua being' is not (a) the name of a proper subset of beings, but (b) a description of a subset of the properties of a being, and hence derivatively (c) a description of the study that is prescribed. On the phrase see Merlan [1968], Routila [1969], 103–21, Happ [1971], 385–404. Kirwan [1971], 77, prefers (c) to (a), but does not consider (b). Owens, 266, defends (a), arguing that non-substances are not beings qua beings. But non-substances can be studied qua beings, in so far as they depend on substance; hence they are included in the study of being qua being. Ascl. 124.5–6 also accepts (a).

42. Aristotle claims that the science of being is both (a) a general science concerned with all beings, and (b) the science of the primary beings, those studied by theology. See 1005a33–b1, 1026a10–32, 1064a28–b14, Le Blond [1939], 51ff, Patzig [1960], 35–7, Décarie [1961], 177–82, Merlan [1960], ch.7, [1968], 248–58, Owens, 298–300, Berti [1965], 102–5, Leszl [1975], 21–47, Frede [1987]. If first philosophy studies being qua being, abstracting from the additional properties of natural and mathematical beings, then it will have some special objects of its own, *if* there are beings that have only the properties of being qua being (they are persisting subjects of properties) and lack any further properties to make them changeable and inseparable from matter; these special objects will be eternal and separable. This is the sort of special object intended in 1026a13–16 (reading *achôrista* with the mss. in a14, against OCT and Ross; see Owens, 296 n44), 1064a28–b1 (where 36–7 indicates the condition on which the science of being will have special objects).

It does not follow that (i) being qua being is eternal and separable; or (ii) that the content of the science of being depends on whether there are special objects for theology; or (iii) that the proper study of beings qua beings requires study of them qua eternal and immaterial beings.

Aristotle suggests that if there were no beings higher than natural beings, then physics would be the primary science, 1026a27–9, 1005a33–b2. There would still be a universal science; but since there would be no special beings with only the properties of being qua being, the universal science of being could not completely describe any actual beings, but would be a part of physics.

43. On abstraction 1061a28–b7, taken with 1077b17–1078a31, *Phys.* 193b31–5 (where 'qua' expressions often occur), offers a helpful comparison. Abstraction is discussed by Mansion [1958], 206f, Leszl [1975], 26, Happ [1971], 395–9; see also 14n49.

44. In 'being qua being' Aristotle might intend any of four conceptions of being: (1) Predicative: we study beings as items about which we can say something. (2) Ontological: we study them as things that are something, that have properties. (3) Existential: we study them as existents. (4) Epistemological: we think of beings as items that really are, and do not just seem, some definite way. Even if Aristotle uses 'to be' in a univocally

copulative sense (so that it always means 'is . . .' with some predicate-place to be filled; see Owen [1965a], 260f), he may intend any one, or more than one, of these four conceptions of being. But the second seems most prominent in his conception of being as the object of a science, in 1003a23–6, 1025b9, 1061b6, 28–30. He assumes that a being is something with essential properties and coincidental properties derived from them.

45. 'Focal connexion' renders *pros hen kai mian tina phusin*, 1003a33–4. Owen [1960], 184, uses 'focal meaning' and Owens, ch.3, speaks of '*pros hen* equivocals'. See further Hamlyn [1977], Irwin [1981], 531, esp. n12.

46. This dependence may be existential or, as in 1003b6–10, logical or definitional; see further § 108.

47. On substance as subject (the Presocratic candidate) and essence (the Platonic candidate) see nn12, 31.

48. On logical questions see 2nn48–9. The connexion between (*a*) studying everything, (*b*) studying logical questions, and (*c*) studying being qua being is marked by *ei gar mê* . . ., 1004b1, and *epei oun*, b5.

49. The student of being qua being is called the philosopher, 1003b19, 1004a34–b26. 1004a4 introduces 'first philosophy', studying the first type of substance—i.e. the type conceived as being qua being, not the type conceived by physics (being qua changeable). 1004b5–17, 1005a23–b2 explain the firstness of first philosophy by the universality of its concern with being qua being; and 1005a35 explicitly connects firstness with universality (*Top.* 172a13 supports Ross's text). If this is what 'first' substance means, the science of being qua being and first philosophy are the same science, and Aristotle does not imply that first philosophy studies only the beings that are eternal and unchanging. Contrast, e.g., the account of first substance in Mansion [1958], 171–3, and see n42 above.

50. This explanation of 'second-order' is meant to avoid the suggestion that a second-order inquiry has no ontological commitments. For such a suggestion see Wieland, quoted in 1n6 above.

51. Aristotle argues that multivocity by itself does not preclude a single science, as long as we can rely on focal connexion, 1004a22–5, 1005a5–11. But his argument does not undermine the claim in the *Organon* that a *demonstrative* science cannot have a multivocal subject-matter; for a demonstrative science requires demonstrative syllogisms, and a syllogism is invalid if it includes multivocal (even focally connected) occurrences of the same term in the wrong place (see 7n21). In suggesting that focal connexion is sufficient for a single genus studied by a single science, Aristotle ought to be thinking of a non-demonstrative science. See Owen [1960], 192, [1965], 216f; his exact view on the relation to the *Org.* on this issue is not clear. Routila [1969], 98–102, agrees with Owen in stressing the importance of focal connexion in claiming scientific status for dialectic; I do not think he answers all the challenges to scientific dialectic. The same question arises about Ferejohn [1980].

52. On *ek tês toiautês epagôgês* I follow 1064a8 (contrast Owens, 288, Ross, i.352). Cf. 1064a8–10, *GA* 742b32–4.

53. To demonstrate the axioms we would have to assume some prior truths

about being qua being and demonstrate the axioms as intrinsic coincidents (997a2–11); but no truths about being seem to be prior to the axioms (997a11–15); hence the axioms are indemonstrable.

54. This may be the point intended in 1005b2–5. If so, the passage is in the right place (as Ross, i.263, following Bonitz [1848], argues; Alexander and OCT think the passage misplaced).

55. At 1004b17–26 dialectic and sophistic indicate the scope of philosophy, because they have the universal concerns that Aristotle has in mind for philosophy.

56. In *Top.* 159a25–37, 169b22–7, 171b3–12, 172a21–36, peirastic is one, but not the only, function of dialectic. (Ross, i.260, and Kirwan, 85, wrongly claim that he always or sometimes fails to distinguish dialectic from peirastic.) 1004b25–6 is consistent with this distinction. Aristotle does not say (contrast Owen [1965], 216) that dialectic is only peirastic, but that its only function *in the area* where first philosophy seeks knowledge is peirastic. The force of 'in the area', *peri hôn*, is brought out by Colle [1924]: 'Sur les mêmes objets, la Dialectique s'applique à éprouver le savoir, la Philosophie à le produire.' His commentary, however, 59f, is dominated by the assumption that philosophy must be demonstrative.

Wilpert [1956], 255 (agreeing with Bonitz [1848], ii. 181f), identifies the contrast between dialectic and philosophy with the contrast between dialectical discovery and demonstrative presentation; but I think this answer fails to face the real difficulty. Alex. 260.2–5 also refers to the non-demonstrative character of dialectic; though at 273.3–19 he recognizes that 1006a11ff argues non-demonstratively, he does not try to reconcile the two comments. See further Thurot [1860], 205, Le Blond [1939], 50–5, Berti [1965], 171–3, Leszl [1975], 293–301.

57. 1061b6–10 explains how the dialectician and the sophist do not study being qua being. Dialectic, in its 'logical' function, is concerned with subjects common to all the sciences. But it is concerned with the coincidents of being, not in so far as it is being, but in so far as they are commonly believed to belong to being.

58. See §§ 35–6.

59. Contrast the apparent suggestion of Owen [1965], 216, that 'the science of being' is just a new name for dialectic: 'The new science is not an axiomatic system; and lest it seem curiously like those non-departmental inquiries which Aristotle had previously dubbed "dialectical" or "logical" and branded as unscientific, dialectic is quietly demoted to one department of its old province so as to leave room for the new giant (cf. 1004b17–26 with *SE* 169b25 etc.).' On 1004b17–26 see n56.

60. The close relations between metaphysics and dialectic are most strongly emphasized by Aubenque [1966], esp. 295; he takes the dialectical character of Aristotle's argument to indicate the essentially inconclusive and permanently aporetic character of his inquiry, and he argues, 299f, that the distinction drawn in 1004b25 would be justified only if philosophy were a complete demonstrative system. Some of Aubenque's arguments are well discussed by Brunschwig [1964], 185–96. Brunschwig, however, 196–200, regards Aubenque's view as substantially correct, as a claim about the

actual character and results of Aristotle's argument, as opposed to Aristotle's view of them.

61. See § 19.
62. He signals the agreement with Plato in *anhupotheton*, 1005b14, and *bebaiotetê*, 1005b17; cf. *Rep.* 511b6, 533d1. Aristotle agrees with Plato on the crucial point that differs from the *Organon*; he thinks there is a universal science that has the task of presenting scientific, though non-demonstrative, proof, by dialectical methods, of non-hypothetical first principles. On the relation to Plato see Berti [1965], 159f; the degree of similarity is considerably exaggerated by Décarie [1961], 79–84.
63. On 'philosophy' see above n2, 7n14.

CHAPTER 9

1. I discuss the 'ontological' formulation of PNC; see Lukasiewicz [1910], 51. The 'logical' version (it is not possible for contradictory statements to be true, 1007b17–19, 1011b13–14) is equivalent to the ontological version if the two statements are about the same subject (*kata tou autou*, 1011b16). On 1005b26–34 (not a 'version' or a proof of PNC, but an argument to show we cannot be mistaken about PNC) see Lukasiewicz, 52, Barnes [1969a], Lear [1980], 99–101.
    Probably (cf. the reference to an extreme view, 1009a3–5) the opponent holds that PNC may always break down (i.e. Poss [(x) (Fx & not Fx)]); hence Aristotle needs to claim that PNC cannot always break down (i.e. Nec [Ex (not (Fx & not Fx)]). (See Dancy [1975], 59–61, Kirwan [1971], 102f.) And probably the opponent holds that PNC may fail for every predicate (i.e. Poss [(x) (F) (Fx & not Fx)]. The denial of that would be to claim that PNC cannot fail for every predicate (i.e. Nec [(Ex) (EF) (not (Fx & not Fx))]); and this denial is the conclusion Aristotle defends in iv 4, arguing that PNC must be true for essential properties of the subject. (See Anscombe [1961], 41, Kirwan, 93.) Even if, with Kirwan, we think Aristotle does not always confine himself to rejecting these extreme theses, an answer to them will be sufficient for the point he wants to make about subjects.
2. It is important to stress the grounds for believing that Aristotle intends iv 4 to *practise* the scientific argument of first philosophy, not merely to prepare for the science by dialectical argument. The 'preparatory' view is suggested by Ross, i.252, by Frede [1987], 94f, and perhaps by Code [1986]. I do not think it fits the implied claim in 1005a29–31, that the first philosopher, as such, will offer non-demonstrative, non-dialectical defence of the axioms. Once we admit that Aristotle claims this, it is hard to maintain that iv 4 is not meant to justify the claim. If iv 4 is not part of first philosophy, something like it must be, if the claim in iv 3 is to be defended; so we still face the same difficulty that we face if we regard iv 4 as a part of the science Aristotle describes.
    To claim that first philosophy is to this extent non-demonstrative is not

to claim that it is wholly non-demonstrative. As Frede remarks, many of its propositions could well be presented in demonstrative form. It differs from the special sciences in not regarding its first principles as unargued assumptions.

3. The argument proceeds: (1) First O speaks of something, 1006a12–13. (2) We ask O to agree that he signifies something, a18–22. (3) O agrees that he does signify something, a26–7. (4) We consider the consequences of signifying something, a29–30. (5) We consider the consequences of signifying one thing, a30–1. (6) Aristotle explains parenthetically why the move from (4) to (5) is justified, because signifying something requires signifying one thing, b5–11.

4. Aristotle undertakes to show the impossibility of O's thesis, 1006a11–12, which is that PNC is false and O believes it is false. In fact he argues against both parts of O's thesis, and the first lengthy argument concludes by asserting PNC, 1006b33–4. This is not surprising, since Aristotle has already implied that first philosophy will undertake to say that the axioms are true, 1005a29–31 (see above n2). He is unlikely, then, to be concerned primarily (as Code [1986] claims) with the indubitability of PNC; see Cohen [1986], Furth [1986] (both expressing reservations about Code's view).

5. I assume that the significate is (a) the subject—man—of which O predicates contradictory properties, rather than (b) the sense of 'man'. Dancy's objections to Aristotle ([1975], ch.6, criticized by Lear [1980], 108f) assume (b). On signification see Anscombe [1961], 39, Noonan [1976], Kirwan [1971], 95f, Irwin [1982]. Aubenque's interpretation of the defence of PNC, [1966], 124–9, captures its transcendental aspects well, but seems to me to overestimate its concern with language and with senses of words.

6. Aristotle rightly sets aside appeals to multivocity, 1006a34–b5. If O claims that 'man' is multivocal, but refuses to distinguish different significates, we cannot say if O is really denying PNC, 1006b5–11.

7. This does not mean that O must have any beliefs about what the essential property is, or that anyone must have such beliefs.

8. If we were only concerned with signifying of one subject, in the way that 'musical', 'white', and 'man' may all signify of one subject that has all these properties, we could not insist that being man cannot signify not being man. For 'man' could easily be predicated of something of which 'not man' could also be predicated. (Suppose, e.g., that something is both a man and white, and white is not the same as man; then 'man' and 'not man' would be predicated of the same subject, and would signify the same thing, if signifying of the same subject is sufficient for signifying the same thing.)

9. O might perhaps say that he is not denying that man is biped animal, and therefore is not denying that it is the same subject; he is only saying that this subject is also not biped animal. But he can hardly maintain this with the standard conception of negation, which we need to use to understand O's thesis as he intends it to be understood in the first place (in asserting that man is not F).

10. 1007a21, 27, 31 refer to substance as essence. But a34, 35, b10 (*hen ex*

hapantôn), refer to substance as subject. As before (see 8n12) Aristotle assumes a connexion that needs to be defended; see § 107.

11. This point needs a more complex statement to take account of the difference between necessary and essential properties; but the complications will not affect the main point.

12. Aristotle does not, e.g., rule out every sort of 'bare particulars'; see 3nn19, 57–8, 4nn19, 22. The minimal character of his claims counts against those (see Lear [1980], 109, Code [1986], 346) who take the reference to essence and substance to show that the argument against PNC assumes distinctively Aristotelian metaphysical claims. (Code uses this alleged feature of the argument to show that it cannot embody what I have called 'strong dialectic'.)

13. On the dialectical character of this argument see Ross, [1923], 57 (who cites it as 'the best specimen of an establishment of first principles by dialectic', of the sort promised in *Top.* i 2), Berti [1965], 42, 146f, 158. See also 7n20 above.

14. Aristotle is concerned with dialectical question-begging, assuming something not conceded by a particular interlocutor. An attempted demonstration will beg the question 'according to truth' only if it tries to prove through itself something that is not known through itself, *APr* 64b34–65a4, *Top.* 155b10–16, 158a7–13, 162b31–163a28, *APo* 91b15–17. We might, therefore, claim that a purported demonstration of PNC through itself is not question-begging. But such a defence against the charge of question-begging has to concede for a different reason that we have not demonstrated PNC; for we cannot demonstrate a proposition through itself, but only from prior and better-known ones. On question-begging see Lear [1980], 100f, who offers a different defence of the non-question-begging character of an attempted demonstration of PNC. Hamblin [1970], 74f, stresses the context-dependent character of allegations of begging the question.

15. Lukasiewicz [1910], 55, argues that Aristotle contradicts himself in claiming both that PNC is indemonstrable and that it can be demonstrated elenctically. His argument fails to distinguish syllogism from demonstration. (See also Maier [1896], iia. 359.) If we show that PNC is implied by something the respondent says, that is no flaw in an argument by refutation for PNC. A refutation is a 'syllogism of the contradiction', *APr* 66b11, *Top.* 170b1, and we have no syllogism unless the respondent concedes some premises, *APr* 66b4–17. The premiss he concedes must conceal its implications from him (cf. *Met.* 1062a5–9, *Top.* 156a7, 156b18–157a6); this is a normal dialectical tactic that would be out of place in a demonstration.

1062a2–11, 30–5, speaks of demonstration ad hominem, which, unlike an unqualified demonstration, relies on a principle conceded by the interlocutor. On argument ad hominem see Aubenque [1966], 129f, Dancy [1975], 14–16. On demonstration by refutation Aubenque, 124, aptly cites *Phys.* 254a27.

16. On concealment see 2n68. On refusing to allow the question to be begged see below § 104.

17. Sextus concedes the truth of a similar charge against the sceptic, *AM* xi 163.

18. Code [1986] offers a different account of Aristotle's aims. I am not sure if he denies that Aristotle aims to give a reason for believing PNC to be true, since he does not consider precisely this possible aim. When he claims an elenctic demonstration does not yield the knowledge of why PNC is true, he appeals to the fact that it does not demonstrate from prior principles. But such a demonstration would not be the only way to give a reason for believing PNC to be true. See also Furth [1986].

19. Nussbaum [1986], 254, denies that Aristotle intends the realist conclusion 'that can be known to hold independently of all experience and all ways of life, all conceptual schemes'. But her argument only shows that Aristotle uses *evidence* drawn from experience, ways of life, and conceptual schemes. The use of such evidence (who could reasonably avoid it?) does not preclude maintaining the realist conclusion I have described.

20. The problem of conflicting appearances arises as follows:
    (1) The senses are the criterion of truth.
    (2) Sometimes the senses report that an object has both a property and its negation (the water is hot and cold, the tower is round and square, etc.), 1009a33–b4.

    As Aristotle reports him, Democritus inferred:

    (3) The senses' reports in (2) imply that things violate the Principle of Non-Contradiction.
    (4) But things do not violate the Principle of Non-Contradiction.
    (5) Therefore we cannot trust the senses.
    (6) Therefore, by (1), we have no access to how things really are, 1009b11–12.

    (See Burnyeat [1979], 76–9.) Democritus rejects the claims of the senses, and, left with no other criterion, seems to be driven to scepticism. Protagoras accepts (1), and wants to reject (6), by denying (5). Since he accepts (2) and (4), he must reject (3). Aristotle's claim that Protagoras or his followers 'must' deny PNC, 1007b20–3, 1009a6–15, probably means not that they explicitly deny it, but that their position commits them to the denial of it even against their will.

21. I assume that Plato's *Tht.* gives a good account of the doctrine that Aristotle ascribes to Protagoras; see 152b–e, 153e–154a, 156c6–157c3. On this view, an apparent contradiction such as 'Socrates is tall and short' turns out not to be a real contradiction because it is covertly relational, *Phd.* 102b3–6, and does not count against the veracity of the senses. Protagoras applies the same strategy to heat and cold, *Tht.* 152b, to quantities, 152d, and to all sensible qualities, 153e.

22. On the interpretation of Protagoras' position see Fine [KPC]. The sceptical thesis appealed to ancient sceptics as well as modern. On the subject see Sextus, *AM* vii 167, 177, 248; *PH* i 48. Doubts about external existence: *AM* vii 191, 194, 297; *PH* i 19, 22, 212. Burnyeat [1982], 36–43, seems to

me to underestimate their scope (i.e. their logical implications, as distinct from the consequences that the doubters explicitly mentioned).

23. Aristotle does not explicitly connect 1010a1–15 (on flux) with Protagoras. But the *Tht.* and Sextus, *PH* i 217–19, make the connexion clear. Cratylus, 1010a10–15, represents the comic extreme of Protagoras as well as of Heracleitus.

24. *Tht.* 156c6–e7 calls these two types of objects 'parents' and 'offspring'. This passage justifies Sextus in claiming that Protagoras believes in some underlying matter, *PH* i 218.

25. On prime matter see 4n30.

26. Cf. 1063a27; Aristotle does not mean to prohibit all qualitative change, but to draw attention to the particular kind of quality that constitutes the form and essence of the subject.

27. In his first argument against total change, 1010a15–22, Aristotle argues that even ceaseless change requires some stability: what is ceasing to be white must still be partly white, and so must be stable to this degree, a18–19. But Protagoras cannot afford to allow this, since the subject could appear to be not partly white; and if this appearance were false, the senses would deceive us. To avoid admitting this Protagoras must believe in change in every respect; but this is inconsistent with the stability in some respect that is presupposed by change. Moreover, to say what change this is we must identify the termini, *EN* 1174b5, *Phys.* 224b1–10. But any description we use to identify them must also be restricted by Protagoras' demands, 1063a21; the termini must also be changes, and therefore identified by further termini, and Aristotle claims that this is a vicious infinite regress, 1010a19–22.

28. At *Tht.* 182d1–e5 Plato relies on points similar to those Aristotle makes about the termini of change (n21 above). The Heracleitean has to say 'not thus' about any terminal property, 183a9–b5. This is 'not thus' said to infinity, about any description of a terminus, 183b4–5, and Aristotle insists that this refusal to characterize the terminus cannot go on to infinity, 1010a21–2. Plato now takes himself to have refuted Protagoras, 183b7–c4. He has failed, however, to explain exactly what is wrong with the view he has rejected. Aristotle offers an explanation, by arguing that change requires a single subject, and someone who cannot allow essential properties cannot allow a single subject.

29. See § 161.

30. On the Megarians see § 123.

31. See § 2.

32. For these tropes see Plato, *Tht.* 157e–158e, Sextus, *PH* ii 51 ff, Long [1981], 90f, Annas [1986], 85f.

33. Instead of saying that whatever appears is, the Revised Protagorean must say that it is to the perceiver to whom it appears when it appears, in the respect and the way it appears, 1011a22–4. If it appears white to me, then it is white to me now, in respect of this appearance. The RP reduces his position to near-tautology, once the force of the qualifications is understood. In 1011a25–b1 Aristotle argues that the retreat from Protagoras to

the RP position is (a) necessary, a25–8, and (b) sufficient, a28–b1, to avoid violation of PNC.

In a28–34 I follow Bonitz [1848] in accepting the ms. text and treating *all' ou ti tê(i) autê(i)* ⟨*sc. tanantia phainetai*⟩, a34, as the RP's defence, showing that the RP need not violate PNC. In 1011b1, *hôste tout' an eiê alêthes*, Aristotle endorses the RP's claim to avoid violation of PNC, but at once goes on to insist that the RP himself cannot regard his claim as true without qualification.

1011b4–12 mentions consequences of RP, first (a4–7) for the account of becoming, and then (a7–12) for the account of the perceiving subject. The RP's statements about perceivers must be qualified by reference to perceivers, causing an infinite regress, b12. Aristotle does not present this as an inconsistency in the RP.

34. Aristotle's appeals to examples (cf. *PH* ii 54) all fall victim to the sceptical tropes, involving circular argument (i 169), and infinite regress (i 166, 173).

35. The rejection of demonstration leads Aubenque to pure dialectic, and Berti to intuition; see 8n60 and n36 below.

36. For the second type of *nous* cf. perhaps *EN* 1143a35–b5 (but there is no reason to think that Aristotle regards this as intuitive knowledge independent of inferential justification). A large role is assigned to *nous* in Book iv by Berti [1965], 185f; in his view, philosophy 'non procede dimonstrativamente e si identifica col nous essa stessa', 156. But he recognizes a role for dialectic, 157f.

37. An appeal to *nous* is read into the argument by Hamelin [1920], 235, on the ground that if Aristotle had founded a first principle of science on dialectical argument, 'il aurait contredit la distinction capitale qu'il a si définitivement aperçue et posée entre la dialectique et la science'. See 2n79.

38. See §§ 68–9.

39. In *Phys.* i, by contrast, Aristotle does not offer dialectical arguments to prove his first principles, but only to prevent common sense from being taken in by Eleatic arguments. In his own arguments he is rather indiscriminate about the sorts of common beliefs he appeals to; among them he includes his own doctrine of the categories, taken to reflect common sense. In appealing to common beliefs he never suggests that any of them has any further feature that makes them suitable for the defence of a first principle. See § 36. On all these points *Met.* iv is different; and each difference helps to explain the others.

CHAPTER 10

1. I take 'always' to refer to the present and past, not to imply that the puzzles will continue in the future (contrary to the suggestion of the present participles); see Brunschwig [1964], 190n, 192. But I do not agree with Brunschwig's view that *ti to on* and *tis hê ousia* ask about the extension of 'being' and 'substance' rather than for a definition. Though certainly the

Presocratics had explicitly discussed the extension without raising the Socratic question about the definition, and though vii 2 is concerned with the extension, Aristotle might reasonably claim that the Presocratics had been implicitly concerned with the definitional question. Brunschwig agrees, 194, that the Socratic question is raised at the beginning of vii 3. But if we admit this, we can hardly say it is absent in vii 1; for the initial outline in vii 3 answers the question in vii 1, and is itself discussed further in the rest of vii.

2. Book vii does not refer explicitly to iv, but only to the division of the categories in v 7. See 8n12. But failure to mention iv is intelligible in the light of Aristotle's aim. For he wants to show that the doctrine of the categories provides a new starting-point, apparently independent of the starting-point of iv, from which we raise some of the questions that were raised in iv.

3. On the two criteria for substance see § 28.

4. On the independence of substance see § 43.

5. In 1028a24 *to badizon* etc. are grammatically suitable for referring to an ordinary subject, e.g. a man; cf. *Top.* 103a30, b30, 4n7, 25, 6n9, 10n45.

6. Leibniz (= Alexander), 70, states clearly this claim about the dependence of particular non-substances on particular substances: '. . . two individual subjects . . . cannot have precisely the same accidents; it being impossible, that the same individual accident should be in two subjects, or pass from one subject to another.' See Clatterbaugh [1973], 3f, 65f, Mates [1986], 196f. On non-substantial particulars see 3n21.

7. If this point is conceded to Aristotle, it still leaves further questions: (1) A substance still seems to be inseparable from its propria or intrinsic coincidents, which are necessary but non-substantial; cf. § 32. It is not clear, however, that this must be, e.g., some particular determinate capacity for learning grammar, as opposed to some instance or other of that type of capacity. (2) It still seems to require the existence of some non-substance or other, even if not of any particular one. (3) If universals are separable from particulars, particular substances may not be prior to universal non-substances. None of these questions necessarily refutes Aristotle. His claims about priority amount to a statement of apparently necessary conditions for being a substance. The rest of his discussion should show how many of them, under what interpretation, are genuinely necessary conditions. See §§ 139, 144. On separation and priority see Fine [1983], 25–9, [1984], 34–9, Morrison [1985], 130–8.

8. In 1028a32–3 I prefer the text of Asclepius, 377.7–8 which reads *kai phusei kai logô(i) kai chronô(i) kai gnôsei* (but I would delete *kai chronô(i)* as an inexact gloss on *phusei*), to OCT's *kai logô(i) kai gnôsei kai chronô(i)*. Reasons: (*a*) Asclepius explains only three of the four types of priority, the first explanation being concerned with *chôriston*, derived from 1028a23–4. (*b*) Separability is more usually connected with natural priority. See 1019a2, 4n18, 6n18. (*c*) If we delete *chronô(i)* from Asclepius' text, then the three types of priority are explained in the order of introduction; and we expect either this order (ABC/ABC) or chiastic order (CBA/ABC) (hence

Alexander gives CBA, 460.35, and ABC, 461.29). The ms. order (CAB/ABC) is open to suspicion.

9. This comment shows nothing about priority unless he means that the converse is not true.

10. The explanation shows that Aristotle appeals to the frequent use of 'ousia' to refer to essence; and his claim about the role of essence in knowledge is correct. But this does not seem to show what is needed about substance; non-substances also have essences, and in finding them we do not seem to refer to substance. Aristotle refers to substance-as-essence to defend a claim that has seemed to concern primarily substance-as-subject.

11. On the relation between the subject-criterion and the essence-criterion in the *Catg.* see § 42.

12. In *Phys.* 200b27, 35, 201b26, *GC* 317b9, 21, 27, 31, 318b1, 319a12, *DA* 402a24, 'this' is used for the category of substance (cf. 5n8). 'What is it' or 'what' is used at *Top.* 103b22 (see 3n17), 178a7, *APo* 83a21, 85b20, *GC* 381a15, *Met.* 1017a25. See Ross [1924], i.p.lxxxviii, Apelt [1891], 140. Only *Met.* vii 1 juxtaposes the two terms.

13. In vii 2, in contrast to earlier works, but in harmony with the aporetic starting-point provided by Book iii, Aristotle does not take the claims of any candidate for granted; he mentions candidates favoured by common sense (animals, plants, and their parts), Presocratics (the four elements), and Platonists (Forms, mathematical objects), without any initial decision between them.

14. Ross translates 1028b33–4, 'if not in more senses, still at least to four main objects'; and one might (cf. Alex. 463.18–19) take *en tetarsin* as = *tetrachôs*. But Aristotle shows no sign of conceding that these are four acceptable definitions of *ousia*, which would be needed for a *pollachôs legomenon*. Probably *pleonachôs* is equivalent to *pollachôs*, and *en tetarsin* implies that *ousia* is not being treated as a *pollachôs legomenon*.

15. In the *Organon* Aristotle assumes with little argument (1) that there are first (particular) and second (universal) substances; (2) the subject-criterion (see § 28); (3) successful candidates (particular men, horses, and their species and genera; occasionally stuffs). In the *Phys.* and *GC* (1) the status of universals is not clear; (3) candidates include form, matter, and compound; but (2) alternatives to the subject-criterion are not discussed, even though it seems to favour matter. See § 47.

   Met. v 8 makes a useful transition from the relatively unself-conscious and inexplicit discussions in earlier works to the fuller statement of the problem in *Met.* vii. It seems to offer (A) four candidates: (A1) simple bodies and their compounds; (A2) their internal cause of being; (A3) limiting and defining parts; (A4) essence, 1017b10–23. (B) Two apparent criteria follow: (B1) 'the last subject, which is no longer said of another'; (B2) 'whatever, being a this, is also separable—such is the shape and the form of each thing', 1017b23–6.

   The relation between the candidates and the summary in 1017b23–6 is not clear. (B1) seems to repeat (A1); (B2) best fits (A2) and (A4), if we can understand how an essence can be a this. But (A3) is harder. Ross ad loc.

and Dancy [1975], 96, suggest it is included in (B2); Kirwan [1971] thinks it is omitted in the summary. Perhaps, however, it is included in (B1). It is also not clear why (A4) is a candidate rather than a criterion; or whether the two criteria are supposed to be equally legitimate; or how (B2) is justified. Book vii clarifies these issues.

16. Aristotle's rejection of the view that 'substance' has different senses or radically different types, legitimately puzzles some critics. See, e.g., Cousin [1935], 168: 'No doubt it is human to find difficulty in believing that things meant by the same word can be in any important sense different. But in Aristotle, despite the masterly analysis of which he is capable, the disease reaches such a height that I can only envy the moderation of the Provost of Oriel ⟨i.e. Ross, ii.161; cf. i.p. xcii⟩ when he remarks that in the notion of substance two notions "are somewhat unsatisfactorily blended".' On the other side, both Owen [1978], 280, and Code [1984], 7, reject the solution invoking different senses of 'substance'.

17. In the predication-formula (cf. 1017b23–4) 'said of' should include both strong predication and inherence, as the *Catg.* construes them. More important, 'it is no longer ⟨said⟩ of another thing' corresponds to the *Catg.* account of a first substance, 1b3–6. In the *Catg.* this second clause is not necessary for being a subject or for being a substance. (Contrast Furth [1985], 104.) *Catg.* 2b15–22, 2b37–3a6 counts second substances as substances, on the assumption that they are subjects; but they are not subjects according to vii 3.

18. On the translation see n24 below. Alexander's fairly loose paraphrase of 1029a1–2 (463.24–6) omits *prôton*; but since he has *to hupokeimenon pasi* where Aristotle has *hupokeimenon* alone, he may have thought *prôton* superfluous after this.

19. *Phys.* 191a19–20 contrasts the subject, i.e. the matter, with the form, and contrasts each with the compound (not so called), which is 'substance, this, and being', 191a8–12. Here the form and the matter seem to be prior in definition to the compound, which seems to exist because the form (universal) is predicated of the particular bit of matter. From most points of view, then, matter seems to be prior, and it is hardest to see how form could be a prior subject.

    Met. v 8 distinguishes the ultimate subject from the form, which is separable and a this, 1017b23–6. Unlike the *Phys.*, it treats the form as a this, but, like the *Phys.*, it still contrasts the form with the subject.

20. Bonitz [1848], ii.301, finds the suggestion that form is subject so surprising that he suggests it is an oversight caused by Aristotle's habit of mentioning matter, form, and compound together. He comments correctly that Aristotle discusses form only when he discusses essence, not in his explicit discussion of the subject-criterion; but that is the whole point of Aristotle's solution. As Ross, ii.164, and Frede [1985], 75, remark, the connexion of form with subject is reasserted at 1042a28. See also Owens [1963], 328n.

    Aristotle's acceptance of the subject-criterion is rightly stressed by Cousin [1933], 327, and by Frede. It is overlooked by Haring [1956], 315.

21. On making a new start see 8n38.

22. Burnyeat [1984], 1f, presents some exaggerated objections to the view (see Ross, ii.226) that viii 1 summarizes vii. Some of them rest on dubious claims about the treatment of the different candidates for substance in vii. The claim that 'nothing is said to recall the challenge to *hupokeimenon* as substance' wrongly assumes that Aristotle has challenged the subject-criterion. The claim that 1042a27–8 'blandly accepts *hulê* with a justification in terms of the actual/potential distinction to which again nothing in vii corresponds' ignores 1035a1–2, 1038b6, 1040b5–10, which prepare for viii 1 quite well.

23. For different views about the strategy and conclusions of vii, and its connexion with viii and ix, see, e.g., Owens, 415f, Rorty [1973], 393–5. Owen [1978] and Code [1984] raise general issues about Aristotle's intentions. I do not agree with Owen's view (287) that in Aristotle's view (*a*) pursuit of the subject leads to prime matter, and (*b*) pursuit of essence leads to the universal. On the contrary, I think Aristotle believes that (*a*) and (*b*) seem to be true only if we misunderstand subject, 1029a9–10, and essence, 1038b4–5. For similar reasons, I believe Code exaggerates the degree to which vii is an exposition rather than a categorical solution (which I would find in, e.g., 1028b31–2, 1029a7–9, 1032a10–11, 1035b3, 1037a21, 1038b1–6, 1041a3–5) of the puzzles in iii.

24. This passage forces attention on some connected ambiguities (marked by (*a*) and (*b*) below) in vii 3, affecting points of translation. Two versions are possible:

  (1) 1029a1: (*a*) It seems most true to call the first subject (i.e. the subject) substance. (*b*) The first subject (as distinct from the subject) seems to be substance to the highest degree.

  (2) 1029a10, 26–7: Matter turns out to be (*a*) an instance of substance; (*b*) . . . identical to substance.

  (3) 1029a27–8: (*a*) It seems most true to ascribe separability and thisness to substance (i.e. every substance is separable and a this). (*b*) Separability and thisness seem especially characteristic of substance (i.e. the mark of a substance par excellence).

  (4) 1029a29–30: (*a*) Form and compound rather than matter would seem to be substance (i.e. matter would not seem to be substance). (*b*) Form and compound would seem to be substance more than matter (i.e. to a higher degree than matter).

Since the (*a*) versions conflict with 1029a32–3 (where *tritês* = *tritês ousias*), and since 1029a19 takes (2*b*) rather than (2*a*) to be the issue, it is reasonable to accept the (*b*) versions, which yield a clear and consistent argument for the whole chapter.

Ross in the OT accepts (4*a*). In [1924], ii.165f, he accepts (3*b*) and (4*b*), but seems to think (n. on 1029a27) that (2*a*) is the thesis under discussion (and see i.p.xciv). Owens, 332f, is close to (*b*). Cousin [1933], 325, and Haring [1956], 316, accept (*a*). Owen [1978], 13, accepts (2*a*) and (4*a*).

The very helpful discussion in Kung [1978] defends (2*b*), (3*b*) and (4*b*). Against her claim that Aristotle intends the subject-criterion, separability, and thisness to be independent sufficient conditions for substance: (i) Aristotle's claim to have given the answer in outline, 1029a7–8, usually means that it needs clarification, not that it gives only a sufficient condition (cf. *EN* 1098a20–2). (ii) 1038b15 suggests (as Kung says) that the subject-criterion is sufficient and not merely necessary; but 1042a26 suggests no other sufficient conditions (see 12n30). (iii) She overlooks the connexion, implied by vii 4, between the subject-criterion and thisness.

25. It is important that he does not say the predication-formula vindicates the claim of matter to be substance. See n39, 12n30.

26. In 1029a23–4 he explains that (1) all the non-substantial properties are predicated of substance (i.e. the ordinary putative substances) and (2) substance is predicated of matter (cf. 995b35, 1049a35). 1029a21–3 explains that this requires a subject distinct from the categorial properties, because (*a*) each non-substantial property is predicated of a putative substance as its subject, and (*b*) this putative subject is in turn predicated of a further subject, its matter. The two subjects of predication correspond to the two stages of the removal described above.

27. In saying this Aristotle is free to insist that it is necessary for any bit of matter at any time to have some categorial property or other; he is not describing some strange entity that is capable of existing without any categorial property. Nor does the denial of categorial properties imply that the subject cannot essentially have, e.g., some definite material composition. If this is so, the passage offers no prima facie evidence for a doctrine of prime matter. Among those who claim to find such prima facie evidence here see Cousin [1933], 326, Haring [1956], 316, Sokolowski [1970], 276, Charlton [1970], 138 (who takes this to be an opponent's line of thought), Schofield [1972], Robinson [1974] (discussed by Stahl [1981]), Owen [1978], 288, Kung [1978], 151, Williams [1982], 212, Charlton [1983], Sorabji [1985], 3–7 (who discusses views connecting prime matter with extension). If Aristotle believes in prime matter (see 4n30), that will indeed turn out to be the ultimate subject; but the argument of vii 3 is quite neutral on what the basic type of matter will be—it is as non-committal as 1044b2, 1049a24–7 are.

28. On the puzzling character of form see § 49.

29. The passage is quoted and discussed at § 138.

30. This claim might seem to conflict with 1049a29–30, where the example of the first type of subject is 'man, both body and soul', which might seem to be the compound rather than the form. But this is not a serious objection, if body = proximate body, since proximate body = soul. See § 132.

31. Bonitz [1848], ii.303 (followed by Ross, ii.166, and Jaeger [1948], 199) gives two reasons for transposing 1029b3–12 to follow 1029a34: (1) The transposition provides a clearer antecedent for *enia peri autou* in b13. (2) The essence is not better known to us. Von Arnim [1928], 39f, followed by Owens, 347n, moves b1–3 to before *homologountai*, a33, following Bonitz on (2), but not on (1). See also Arpe [1938], 31, Leszl [1975], 467.

    Against (1): *autou* = essence is not too strained, if b3–12 is an explanatory parenthesis. Against (2): the concept of essence is quite familiar from dialectic, and Aristotle introduces it with some 'logical' remarks. (For 'logical' cf. 1041a28, without OCT's deletion.) He approaches the puzzling (1029a33) notion of form by referring to familiar views about essence (Ascl. 383.17). Hence b3–12 need not be transposed.

Critics who favour the transposition take b3–12 to be contrasting the cognitive and ontological status of sensible substances with that of non-sensible substances (see Owens, 347f; the view is present in Alex. 465.19–22, Aquinas, *in Met.* 1300). The passage justifies no such contrast, since the ms. order is quite intelligible.

32. Owen [1960], 189n, rightly connects (a1) 1030a27 on 'how one should speak' with the 'logical' (i.e. dialectical) remarks promised at 1029b13, and contrasts it with (b1) saying how things are, which belongs to philosophy. I think he is wrong to identify this contrast with that between (a2) exhibiting the relation between beings by addition and subtraction, 1030a33, and (b2) exhibiting it by focal connexion, a35. Aristotle says the difference between (a2) and (b2) does not matter for his present purposes, 1030b4. But the difference between (a1) and (b1) matters a lot; (b1) shows that essence primarily belongs to substance, whereas (a1) attributes it 'logically' (1030a25) to all sorts of things, even to not-beings, 1030a21–7 (see Ross ad a27–8). This fact about essence and substance can be expressed either by (b1) or, more correctly, by (b2); neither (b1) nor (b2) is intrinsically dialectical or philosophical, but either may be defended on either sort of ground, and in this case Aristotle defends both on philosophical grounds.

　　Woods [1974], 170f, argues that since not everything up to 1030a27 is merely logical discussion, 1030a27 does not refer back to 1029b13. His premiss is true, but his inference is unwarranted. 1030a2 introduces philosophical rather than logical considerations, and a21–7 reasserts the contrast between 1029b13ff and 1030a2ff.

33. On change see § 45–6.

34. In *tode ti* I take *tode* to be the demonstrative and *ti* to be the indefinite article—hence 'some this' (cf. *tode toionde* in e.g. 1033b23–4, where *tode* seems to be some definite particular and *toionde* the character it acquires). For other views see Smith [1921], 19 (*tode* is the demonstrative and the *ti* refers to the kind), Preisewerk [1939], 85f (*ti* is the kind, and *tode* the indefinite individual within it), Owens, 386f.

35. At *Catg.* 3b10–13 numerical unity seems to be sufficient for being a this, and some non-substances are numerically one (1b6–7); hence some non-substances seem to be thises (see 3n19). Though 'this' is used to name the category of substance (see n12 above), it is also applied to the form (which need not be a substance), in contrast to the privation (GC 318b32; cf. *Phys.* 190b24–7). The reason for associating thisness with substance is perhaps similar to the reason for associating what-it-is with substance; just as the first category tells us what things basically are, it tells us what the basic numerical unities are. On whether thises are particulars see 12n2–3 below.

36. Brunschwig [1979] agrees, 146, that this is the sort of predication Aristotle intends in 1041b11, but he denies, 149–52, for insufficient reasons, that it is intended in 1049a18–b2. 'The statue is wooden' does not itself predicate

form of matter; it expresses the fact that underlies the predication 'The wood is a statue' (where the 'is' indicates constitution, not identity; see § 139 below).

37. The distinction between the two formulae helps to answer some of the questions raised by Ross, ii.170, and Burnyeat *et al.* [1979], 22f.

38. If x's being inseparable from y is sufficient for y to be part of the account of x, then natural priority is sufficient for priority in account; if not, then these will be two distinct but related demands. However they are related, they impose the same conditions that are imposed by the narrow predication-formula, but they do not necessarily agree with the broad formula.

39. It is important to remember that Aristotle does not claim that the broad formula vindicates the claim of matter to be substance; see n25 above, 12n30.

40. Though the argument of vii 5 is puzzling in places (see further Hare [1979]), the conclusion is fairly clear, 1031a1–14; it reinforces the conclusion of vii 4 that substances are the primary bearers of essences. Aristotle reinforces this conclusion by appealing to such terms as 'snub', which differ from 'white' in implying a reference to a definite type of subject (e.g. a nose), 1030b16–26. In their case also we have to recognize that the subject is distinct from (e.g.) the snub and the bearer of the essence of the snub, and the snub turns out not to be a subject in its own right (this is the point of the puzzle in 1030b28ff, which is solved only by recognizing this fact about the snub; *Top.* 140b27–141a2, 181b37–182a6). Given the comparison in 1025b30–1026a6 between the snub and natural substances, the claims about the snub raise a difficult problem; how can natural substances escape the sort of analysis that (in ch.5) shows that compounds of form and matter are not substances in their own right? See § 138.

41. Since 1032a4–10 applies a previous solution to a problem about a particular, Aristotle probably does not suppose that the previous solution was confined to particulars (Ross, 177, goes too far in arguing that it must have been confined to universals); the points about primary and intrinsic beings did not assume any definite view about the successful candidates for this status. But since he thinks the solution applies to a particular, he probably assumes that a particular such as Socrates is a primary and intrinsic being. (The resolution of the previous problems in vii 6 resolves this one too.) See further n47.

42. On Woods's challenge to this argument see n47.

43. Aristotle does not actually say that if x is numerically one, the essence of x is numerically one also (i.e. it is linguistically possible to interpret: 'the substance of something numerically one is specifically one'). But if he does not mean to say this, his argument is blatantly faulty, and the introduction of a substance (=essence) that is numerically one is quite unexplained. The passage, therefore, strongly suggests that *if* Aristotle thinks particulars have essences, he believes in essences that are particulars.

44. The first part of vii 6 (to 1031b18) seeks to show that certain putative substances, Platonic Forms, must be identical to their essences. Aristotle stipulates that Forms and the essences corresponding to them must be

'severed', so that (*a*) what it is to be good is not present to the good itself, and (*b*) being good is not present to what it is to be good, 1031b4–6. Here (*a*) follows from the assumption that Forms are not identical to their corresponding essences. He can defend (*b*) from the initial assumption that if x is F, then the essence of F (EF) is not identical to x; for if EF is also F, the essence of EF will not be identical to EF, and if the essence of EF is also F, we face an infinite regress of essences, which we prevent only by accepting (*b*). Aristotle appeals to some of the argument underlying the Third Man regress, in Plato, *Parm.* 132a–c. He argues that the self-predication (i.e. being instances of the property they correspond to) that Plato ascribes to Forms cannot be ascribed to essences, if we accept the initial assumption (corresponding to the Non-identity assumption implicit in Plato's argument).

The first bad result of severance is supposed to be that the Form of F (FF) is unknowable, because we know something when we know its essence, 1031b6–7. Since EF, not FF, is the essence of F, we cannot know about F by knowing FF, but only by knowing EF. Plato assumed that Forms, rather than sensibles, are objects of knowledge; but now Forms turn out to be no better off than sensibles. The second bad result follows from (*b*), which implies that the essence of being will not be a being; since there is no reason for one essence more than any other to be a being, none of them will be a being, 1031b7–10. Since we must reject (*b*), and since (*a*) without (*b*) involves an infinite regress of essences, we must also reject (*a*).

Aristotle infers that things that are beings in themselves and primary, not one thing said of another, must be identical to their essences, 1031b11–14. This point is meant to have been made clear by reference to Forms, since, as the Platonist conceives them, they are primary and intrinsic beings; as Aristotle stresses, they are not what they are by having sensible particulars participate in them, 1031b17–19. If Forms are not identical to their essences, then we face the dilemma explored in the previous argument. The argument will work for any other subject; either we allow the essence that is not identical to the subject to be another instance of the property and so face an infinite regress, or we prohibit this, and face impossible results about the essence.

45. Aristotle clarifies his position by rejecting an attempted *reductio* of the view that coincidental beings are identical to their essences. The attempted *reductio* offers to derive an absurd conclusion from the view in question, as follows:

(1) The pale man is the same as the man.
(2) The man is the same as his essence.
(3) The pale man is the same as his essence.
(4) Hence the two essences are the same, 1031a21–4.

Aristotle points out that (1) involves merely coincidental identity, from which the conclusion in (4) cannot be derived, 1031a24–5. (1) is true because it is true that

(1a) The (particular) man who is coincidentally pale is the same as the man.

From (1a) we can validly derive (3) if it is understood as

(3a) The man who is coincidentally pale is the same as his essence.

But (4) asserts not the identity of the man and his essence, but the identity of the two properties of being a pale man and being a man; hence (4) does not follow from (3a). (4) does follow from

(3b) The pale man is the same as being a pale man.

But (3b) is inconsistent with (1); the subject of (3b) essentially has the property of being a pale man, and hence cannot be identical to the man who is coincidentally pale.

As Aristotle remarks, 'the pale' signifies two sorts of things: 'for both the ⟨subject⟩ which has the coincident and the coincident ⟨are pale⟩, so that in one way the thing is identical to its essence, and in one way not; for ⟨being pale⟩ is not the same as the man or the pale man, but is the same as the affection ⟨pale⟩', 1031b24–8 (OCT and OT). We can use 'the pale' to refer to the man who is coincidentally pale; but he is not identical to what it is to be pale (since he can persist without being pale). However, the pale (i.e. the essentially pale quality) is identical to this affection, and so identical to what it is to be pale. Similarly, if 'the pale' refers to an essentially pale subject, it is identical to what it is to be a pale thing. On 'pale things' see further 4n25. On the application of this doctrine to compounds of form and matter see 11n37.

46. If 1030a11–12 meant 'nothing, then, that is not a species of a genus has an essence', it would immediately imply that substances must be species. (See Ross, ii.170, Lloyd [1981], 37, Code [1984], 15. Bonitz [1848], ii.308 is less definite: 'eas res quae a natura a genere ad species descendente sine ulla vel accidentis vel fortuiti admistione definitae sunt'.) Nothing at all, however, has been said at this point to show that only species, as opposed to particulars, could satisfy Aristotle's requirements for being primary. It is no less reasonable to take the remark to mean that no essence is found outside species of genera, i.e. only members of basic natural kinds have essences. (Non-substance species are excluded, as Alex. 472.9–11 suggests.) Alex. 472.10–14 sees the difficulty in speaking of species as opposed to particulars, and insists that Aristotle is really speaking of particulars; but he relies unnecessarily on nominalism to reach this conclusion (*tauta de ta eidê epeidê ouden allo eisin ê ta kath'hekasta*, 472.11–12).

47. Ross, ii.176, suggests two other views about the conclusion of vii 6: (a) the intrinsic beings identical to their essences are genera and species (cf. i. p. xcv); and (b) the essence of man, 'to be a man', is identical to each and every man. Owen [1965], 209, and Woods [1974], 167ff also accept both (a) and (b) (as S. Marc Cohen remarks, [1978], 82; see also Kung [1981], 228f). Woods argues for (b): 'When we use a proper name like "Socrates" to pick out an individual man, (i) what we pick out is always the form; though (ii) we pick it out as it occurs in a particular piece of matter. (iii) The essence of Socrates is simply the form man, an essence which he shares with Callias', 177 (reference-numbers added). Contrary to (i), however, 'Socrates' seems to pick out something that, unlike the species-form, undergoes Socrates' birth and death. If Woods agrees, and appeals to (ii), he casts doubt on (iii). On 1034a6–8, cited by Woods, 177, see 12n13. On the alleged connexions between Aristotle's views and the Third Man regress see Fine [1982].

Owen claims that (b) helps to persuade Aristotle of (a)—'that the primary subjects of discourse cannot be individuals such as Socrates, who cannot be defined, but species such as man', [1965], 209. If, however, (b) is true, Socrates turns out be definable after all, and (a) will be false. Cousin, [1935], 175n5, notices the conflict between (a) and (b) in Ross, and Owen and Woods do not answer his objection.

Owens, 352–7, assumes (relying, without warrant, on 1017b33–4) that the essence must be something of which there is universal knowledge, and argues that since there is no universal knowledge of the particular sensible thing 'the form is one with the thing, but not entirely so', 356. Owens, therefore, cannot agree that Socrates is identical to his essence, and cannot explain 1032a6–10 (cited without discussion, 357n). His assumption about the connexion between essence and universal knowledge has no basis in vii 6. (He does not comment on the apparent particular essence 'being you' in 1029b14–15.)

48. See § 64.

CHAPTER 11

1. See § 37.
2. See § 103.
3. Traits persisting through change in the subject are not required for a persisting subject in general, since an absolutely unchanging subject needs no potentiality. (Cf. 3n35.) But it is reasonable to require them if the persisting subject is to change.
4. The ordinary dialectic practised in *Phys.* i and *GC* i relies on intuitive beliefs about becoming and perishing; see § 37, 4n27. Different degrees and types of form are explored by Williams [1958], 302–12.
5. See Shakespeare, *Henry IV, Part I*, V. iv.84–6: ((Hotspur) No, Percy, thou art dust, and food for—(Prince) For worms, brave Percy. Fare thee well, great heart.
6. Aristotle does not report the Megarians' argument against unactualized potentialities. Perhaps they believe that (1) possibility is necessary for potentiality, and (2) there are no unactualized possibilities (for the reasons given by Aristotle's opponents in *DI* 18b9–25).
7. The Megarians might say that in denying that x is capable of (F at t), when x does not F at t, they are not denying that x is capable of F. (See Burnyeat *et al.* [1984], 62f.) But, in Aristotle's view, what makes x capable of F is some persistent potentiality of x. To be capable of (F at t) x needs this very same potentiality; hence if we deny that x is capable of (F at t), we must say that x has lost the potentiality to F, and if x is capable of (F at some later time) x must have recovered this potentiality. The apparently more moderate Megarian claim, together with Aristotle's conception of potentiality, turns out to require the stronger claim.
8. Aristotle uses the adjective *dunaton*, cognate with *dunamis* ('potentiality') for both substances (hence meaning 'capable') and states of affairs (hence

meaning 'possible', equivalent to *endechomenon*). Aristotle's distinctions between potentiality and possibility are fully explored in Ide [1987], ch. 1.

9. Cf. *Phys.* 251b1–5. This construal of 1048a15–16 is supported by the ms. text. Ross and OCT delete *poiein*, making the presence of the passive object necessary for the agent to have the potentiality to act on it. Hintikka [1977], 19–20, follows them, taking the passage as evidence for the view that all total possibilities are realized. If it is about potentiality, it does not support Hintikka's thesis. See also Burnyeat *et al.* [1984], 120f, defending *poiein*, but still conflating possibility and potentiality. Moline [1975], 247, translates the emended text, though his view, 253, seems to fit the ms. text better.

Support for the ms. text: (1) 1048a18–20: we need not add the clause 'no external conditions preventing' to the statement of the potentiality, since the clause is already presupposed in the statement. (2) 1049a5–7: the wood is potentially a house if someone's (i.e. the builder's) choice will make it a house, nothing external hindering. 'Nothing . . .' is part of the condition for actualizing the potentiality, not for having it; cf. 1049a13–14. (3) The paraphrase in Alex. 577.26–7 is closer to the ms. text.

Contrary to Burnyeat *et al.* [1984], 121, *poiein ou dunêsetai*, 1048a16, may also refer to potentiality; it will then mean 'if the agent will not act on the patient in the right circumstances, it lacks the potentiality to act on it'.

10. Potentiality therefore requires an 'internal' possibility (i.e. x's potentiality for F must make it possible for x to F if we consider x's other characteristics). This in turn depends on some 'standard' external conditions (since some internal possibilities are possibilities for interacting in particular ways with other things), which need not always be the prevailing ones. (The role of standard conditions is noticed by Mourelatos [1967], 101, replying to Manicas [1965], with some unwarranted inferences about the conflict between Aristotle's account and a counterfactual analysis of powers. A plausible counterfactual analysis will also involve some reference to standard conditions.) Amphibians stuck on dry land far from water still have the potentiality for swimming, and swimming is still internally possible for them, though external conditions make it impossible for them to swim. (For the restrictions imposed by external conditions see n11.) It follows that not every logically possible situation makes it equally reasonable to attend to Aristotelian potentialities. If we have been trained as thatchers, but there are no houses left for us to thatch, our potentiality as thatchers may not explain much.

11. To explain the relation of potentiality to possibility Aristotle adds 1047a20–6: 'And so it is admissible for ⟨something⟩ to be capable of being something, but not to be it . . . Something is capable to which if there belongs the actuality of that of which it is said to have the potentiality, nothing impossible will be the case.' 'Capable' (rather than 'possible') for *dunaton* is supported (i) by *hôste*, 1047a20, drawing a conclusion from his previous remarks about the potentialities of substances, 1047a10–17; and (ii) by the fact that the subject of *dunaton* is also the bearer of a *dunamis*, i.e. a substance with a potentiality. 'Impossible' in the last clause is justified by 1047b12, referring clearly to the impossibility of a state of affairs (*to*

metreisthai), and relying on the definition in ix 3. On 1047b3–6 I agree with the view attributed to Kneale and Owen by Hintikka [1973], 107f (and defended by McClelland [1981]), against Hintikka and Furth [1985], 134.

1047a26–8 expands the formula: 'If something is capable of sitting, and sitting is admissible, then if sitting belongs to this, nothing impossible will be the case.' The antecedent treats the admissibility, i.e. possibility, of x's sitting as a further condition beyond x's potentiality for sitting; this clause accommodates the reference to external conditions in later remarks about potentiality, e.g. 1048a15–16 (see n9). If x has a potentiality for F, then x's actual F-ing in the right external circumstances must result in no impossibility—i.e. it must be compatible with all the other possibilities there are. This necessary condition for potentiality does not imply that the actualization of every potentiality is possible.

Ross, ii. 245, Burnyeat *et al.* [1984], 67, Hintikka [1977], 22, Furth [1985], 133, take the passage to give an account of possibility. In disagreeing with them I agree with part of Waitz's claim, [1844], i.398f that *dunaton* and *endechomenon* are not interchangeable (accepted by Bonitz [1848], ii 387), though I do not think he is right about every use of *dunaton*. The criticisms by Maier [1896], i.193, Ross, and Le Blond [1939], 419, are too sweeping.

12. It is misleading, then, of Aristotle to suggest that I acquire the potentiality to F by previously exercising *it*; he presumably means that I acquire the potentiality to F by doing some of the sorts of actions that I will also do once I have acquired the potentiality to F. In *EN* 1105b5–12, 1144a13–20 he clarifies his view.

13. Kosman [1984], 132, stresses the importance of the distinction in 417a30ff, though without appeal to the distinction between potentiality and possibility. The discussion in Burnyeat *et al.* [1984], 136f, comes closer to making the distinction.

14. 1050a5–16 stresses this explanatory role for actuality, discussed by Sellars [1967], 122f.

15. A doctor-turned-poisoner and a trained poisoner have different potentialities, since different activities explain their acquisition of the traits they have acquired, even if they exercise these traits in the very same actions.

16. Similarly, the brickmaker need not know about houses if he is to make bricks competently (though the nature of his craft is no doubt affected by facts about houses), and the bricks will be made in just the same way even if they do not happen to be used for building a house; his potentiality is for making bricks.

17. 'Through it', 1049a14, is explained by 'through its own origin', a15–16. On the body as potentially alive see § 152.

18. GA 735a4–8 explains that the seed from which a human being develops potentially has a human soul; but 735a9–11 appeals to the distinction between remote and proximate potentialities; the embryo already has some of the relevant organs, and has a proximate potentiality to grow, 735a12–26, into the full-grown body that has the more proximate potentiality for the activities of the adult F.

19. Aristotle adds to ix 6 a further illustration of the ways in which potentiality and actuality can be detached from change. Not all actualities are changes; in fact change is merely an incomplete actuality, and the most complete actualities are not changes, 1048b18–23. A change is incomplete and does not have its end within itself, but an actuality is complete and self-contained, b21–2. In describing complete actualities we can apply both present-tense and perfect-tense verbs whenever we can apply either, b23–7 (since the perfect tense indicates present completeness). With a change, however, the perfect tense is inappropriate at times when the present tense is appropriate, because changes are not complete until they are over, b28–34. The importance of this aspect of changes is especially stressed by Kosman [1984], 124–9 and [1969]. Among the most helpful earlier discussions of the contrast between change and actuality are Ackrill [1965] and Penner [1970], esp. 405–22.

    This contrast is relevant to the relation of potentiality to form and matter. When we say that F is potentially G, we need not be referring to any tendency of the subject to change from F to G. Nor need G itself be any sort of change or process. The sorts of actualities that Aristotle identifies with forms are described in terms that make them complete actualities rather than changes. 'Is a statue', 'is alive', 'is human', 'is a perceiver', and so on all satisfy the present-and-perfect test.

20. Hartman objects, [1977] 98, that 'Aristotle does not need both the conception of person and that of human body'. He thinks Aristotle is wrong to treat the body as matter at all.

21. Aristotle does not want the cause of some event or change, but the cause of being, 1041a31–2. If this question has a non-trivial answer it must be the question 'Why is x x?', understood in the non-trivial way; 'Why is x-qua-F also x-qua-G?', e.g. 'Why is this (i.e. bricks and mortar) this (i.e. a house)?'. The answer to this question states the form and the substance.

22. In vii 7–9 Aristotle describes production by craft; the house with matter comes into existence from the matter and from 'the house without matter', 1032b11–12, also called 'the form in the soul', 1032b1 (the house is conceived in the craftsman's soul, though not embodied in any matter there; see 14n3). It is not a particular *house*, since a particular house must be embodied in matter. But it is not clearly a universal either. For what is needed for *this* house to come to be is the particular instance of a conception of a house; the universal house, and the universal conception of a house, will not explain the coming-to-be of this particular house. It is reasonable to regard the form that is an element of becoming as a particular.

    Admittedly, Aristotle remarks that the form does not come to be, 1033a31–b16. But he argues only that some form must precede each becoming of an informed thing (for if the form has to be produced, it must also be produced from form and matter, hence from another form which must also be produced, and so on to infinity, 1033b3–5). It does not follow that every form must always have existed. Rejection of an infinite regress is therefore consistent with the belief there are particular non-everlasting forms. Heinaman [1979], 252–7 argues this point well. Contrast Haring

[1956], 325, 330, Code [1984], 16, Ross, ii.188 (more cautious, believing in the everlastingness of substantial forms, but not inferring it from this passage by itself), Owens, 360. Owens's appeal to 999b5–16 actually tells against him; the absence of any claim about everlastingness and absolute ingenerability from vii 7–9 marks a striking contrast with iii, and suggests that Aristotle deliberately fails to rule out particular forms.

Just as in production the form is the particular in the soul of the producer, in natural generation the form involved seems to be the one peculiar to the progenitor (cf. 1070a4, 1071a19, GA 767b29). It is Peleus' form, not the universal human form, that is part of the process resulting in the coming-to-be of Achilles.

23. In speaking of matter, I refer to sensible matter, not to the intelligible matter that is relevant to mathematical objects. Some questions about it are raised by Ross.ii 199.

24. Lloyd [1970] 524, relies on 1035a7–9 to argue that 'the form of x' and 'the matter of x' should be understood as 'x qua form' and 'x qua matter', so that 'both expressions are *about* the composite'. The same view underlies the claims of Wiggins [1967], 48 (criticized by Ackrill [1972a], 119–22, and not reappearing in Wiggins [1980]), Charlton [1970], 72f (criticized by Harter [1975], 12; I think Charlton is probably wrong about *Phys*. i—see § 48–9—but right about the *Met.*).

Anscombe [1961], 53, takes *hekaston*, 1035a8, to extend, e.g., to lumps of matter, and to imply that we must apply a form to them in speaking of them. I think *hekaston* might extend only to such things as statues; it need not imply a general claim about the impossibility of speaking of matter in its own right.

25. It follows that 1035b27–8 need not be distinguishing the species horse (a compound) from the species form. (See Loux [1979], 3, 14; Driscoll [1981], 136; Code [1984], 15.) For Aristotle must also identify the species form with (one sort of) compound if he is to distinguish the (materiate) essence of horse from the (immateriate) essence of circle, and must identify the species with (one sort of) form if he is to distinguish it from bronze ball. No difference emerges between species and species form.

26. I rely on Sellars's explanation of how the form includes matter, in [1957], 135; 'the form . . . is . . . these qualities determined in reference to substance (i.e. as criterion qualities for a thing kind name) *in some appropriate material or other*. Thus Aristotle can say that the form of this shoe is, in a certain sense, the shoe itself.' The different types of form, matter, and compound are carefully examined in Whiting [1984], chs.3–4.

Heinaman [1979] (see also Harter [1975]), argues that Aristotle (e.g. 1036b21ff) allows definitions of the compound, but not of the form, to include matter. Heinaman's view (*a*) makes it hard to distinguish circles, men, and bronze balls in the way Aristotle wants to (since Heinaman's view will make the immaterial form the essence of all of them); and (*b*) becomes less attractive once we admit different types of matter. See further § 134.

27. Falstaff, unlike Hotspur (see n5 above) grasps the point about homonymy: '. . . to die, is to be a counterfeit; for he is but the counterfeit of a man, who hath not the life of a man' (*Henry IV Part I*, V.iv.116–18).

28. The passage is quoted at § 122.
29. On proximate and remote matter see Loux [1979], 10 (who identifies proximate matter with any non-prime matter); Sheldon Cohen [1984], 188–94; Owen [1978], 287f (citing *GA* 741a10–11, 734b24–7, 726b22–4); Ackrill [1972a], 69f (whose arguments against Aristotle apply to proximate matter; his arguments at 73f to show that remote matter cannot be the matter of an animal show only that it cannot be the proximate matter); Kosman [1984]. 143 (whose claim that 'there is no thing which is the matter of a human being' applies only to proximate matter; he does not consider remote matter).

     In *GC* 321b19–22 (flesh as matter v. flesh as form), *Metr.* 389b28–390a19 (different material parts satisfying the homonymy principle to different degrees) Aristotle draws distinctions related to, though not quite the same as, the one between proximate and remote matter.
30. The passage is quoted and discussed at § 133.
31. Aristotle appeals less readily to the possibility of different material compositions than do modern philosophers who want to distinguish functional from compositional properties. (The strategy of such arguments from 'plasticity' is summarized by Boyd [1980], 87–91.) In fact he is more often impressed by the fact that only one sort of stuff is actually suitable for the function, *Phys.* 200a30–b8. But 1036a30–b3 refers to the right sort of possibility.
32. I have quoted selectively from Locke, to bring out his implicit conditions for the persistence of the same living body. He does not state explicit conditions; but he clearly thinks it lasts as long as, and no longer than, the creature whose body it is. He contrasts it with a mass of matter, which has to retain all the same material parts to be the same mass, 27.4.
33. On 1043b1–4 see Ackrill [1972a], 68, Loux [1979], 4, who both rely heavily on the distinction Aristotle alludes to, but do not say why Aristotle should think it so unimportant for his present purposes. The distinction between form and compound is unimportant, as Aristotle says, only for sensible substances. If non-sensible substances do not essentially include matter, their forms are not the essences of formal compounds, but they are immateriate forms; if they were embodied in matter, it would be very important to distinguish the compound from the form.
34. On life histories see Wiggins [1980], 30–5. If proximate matter is distinguished from remote, then Hartman's suggestion, [1977], 99, that Aristotle thinks form and matter are 'accidentally identical' (a 'weaker sense' of 'identity' (103) than 'full' (75) or 'perfect' (76) identity, and holding between Socrates and the musical man) becomes less attractive, since a 'weak sense' of identity seems to fit neither type of matter (the proximate matter is fully identical to the form, and the remote matter is not identical to it at all). See also n37 below. On the identity of form, matter, and compound see 13n21.
35. In 1035a23 I follow Ross, and retain *an mê ê(i) tou suneilêmmenou* (bracketed as a gloss in OCT), taking *to sumeilêmmenon* to be, e.g., the statue as material compound, as opposed to the statue as form (intended in *tôn d'ou dei eneinai*).

36. See 10n45.
37. In saying that Socrates and the musical are coincidentally one, 1037b6–7, Aristotle means that Socrates is identical to the thing that is coincidentally musical (i.e. Socrates) because it is a coincident of Socrates to be musical. 'Coincidentally' does not modify or weaken the claim about identity, but gives the grounds for claiming (strict, full) identity. (Contrast Hartman [1977], 99, also discussed in n34 above.) If, however, 'the musical' signifies the compound that is essentially musical, then Socrates is not identical to it at all, since he can exist without it.

    Our previous explanation of Aristotle's claim that coincidental compounds (man and musical) are not identical to 'their' essences also explains the corresponding claim about material compounds. For if we take man to be a material compound, his persistence depends on the persistence of the form (= the formal compound), but the converse does not hold; hence the essence of the material compound depends on the essence of something other than it (the form). 1037b5 (retaining the ms. text, *oude*, supported by Ascl. 422.28–32, which contrasts compounds with coincidental unities) implies that the material compound is not a coincidental unity, as Socrates and the musical are. Perhaps (cf. 1030b16–23) Aristotle means that the form and the remote matter are more closely connected, as snubness is to nose; a form needs some remote matter or other (just as a nose must be either snub or aquiline or . . .), though it need not have matter of just this type.

38. It is useful to see how vii 12 completes the argument of 10–11, and shows why formal compounds are identical to their essences, not coincidental unities. In ch. 12 Aristotle wants to show that genus, differentia, and species together constitute one natural kind, and not a coincidental combination in which the genus is the basic subject, and the differentia and species are coincidents of it, as musicality is a coincident of man. The difference is that whereas a particular man who at one time is musical can persist even if he ceases to be musical, a particular animal who at one time is a man cannot persist if he ceases to be a man. Hence the genus is not a more basic subject than the species, and the species is a unity, 1037b21–3. The universal defined in the account of the species is a single universal, not a coincidental combination, because the this, i.e. the particular instance of the universal (see 10n34–5) is a unity, 1037b24–7, not spoken of by one thing being said of another, 1030a10–11, and therefore belonging to a species of a genus, 1030a11–14.

    This conclusion is relevant to the argument of 10–11. For an exactly parallel argument will show why the formal compound universal is a genuine unity and not a mere coincidental combination, and why the particular instantiating the compound universal is a genuine unity and not a mere coincidental combination (of matter as the more basic subject and form as the coincident). Aristotle sees the connexion between the problem about genus and species and the problem about matter and form, since he compares genus and species to matter and form, 1024b8–9, 1038a5–8, 1043b28–32, 1045a33–5, 1058a23–4. In this comparison he shows that the problems about genuine unities apply directly to the substances that are his main concern in Book vii.

39. In 1036b28 I read *aisthêtikon* for the ms. *aisthêton*. The other claims follow naturally from an animal's being capable of perception (given Aristotle's teleological views about psychic faculties; see § 159), but not from its being perceptible. Most commentators assume that *aisthêton* simply reflects the fact that the object is material (cf. 1026a2–3; Alex. 514.22). But then (as Ross remarks) *echontôn pôs* becomes irrelevant. But *aisthêtikon*, referring to the definition of an animal, makes the following remarks relevant (as Ascl. 420.25 and Aquinas *in Met.* 1519 ('animal enim discernitur a non animali sensu et motu'), show in their paraphrases, though both read *aisthêton*). For 'just any condition', *pantôs*, 1036b30, cf. *ho pantôs echôn daktulos*, 1035b24.

40. See 14n3.

41. Since no similar explanatory relation holds between geometrical properties objects and their sensible matter, having sensible matter is not essential to them; circularity is not an actuality of sensible material bodies as such, even if particular circles can exist only in material bodies. Young Socrates overlooks this distinction. Nussbaum [1984], 201, rightly argues from 1036b26ff to show that the functional organization of a natural substance is necessarily enmattered. She does not explain why Aristotle should think the connexion with matter is stronger in this case than with mathematical objects.

CHAPTER 12

1. Sellars [1957] has introduced particular forms into recent discussion. For earlier discussion see Cousin [1935], 172, who cites 1022a25–9, 1029b14, 1037a7–10, 1071a28; Ross [1923], 170n3; Cherniss [1944], 506, who adds 1032a8.

   The main putative evidence that has been adduced is as follows: (i) A form is a this, and hence a particular (Sellars). (ii) A particular form is needed as the essence of a particular substance (Hartman [1977], 62). (iii) 1070a21–6, 1071a1–3, 20–9, 1075b35 on particular causes (Albritton [1957]). (iv) 1035a7–9, b14–24, 27–31, 1036a16–17, 24–5, 1037a5–10, 27–33, 1043b2–4 on souls (Albritton). (v) *Catg.* 1a27–9, *Met.* 1087a19–20, *Phys.* 228a6–9 on particular non-substances (Lloyd [1981], 24). (vi) 1029b23–6, 1043b15, 1044b21–6 (cf. 1002a30, 1026b22–4, 1027a29–32, 1033b17, 1070a1–4); forms that are destructible without being destroyed. (vii) *Phys.* i and v, *Met.* xii 4–5 imply that the form is a principle of change, and principles of change must be particulars, so that the form must be particular (Harter [1975], 11–15). (viii) Forms are perishable, 1060a21–3, *Phys.* 192b1–2, 246b12–16, *GA* 731b31–5 (cf. *GC* 328a27–8, 338b14–17, *Met.* 1059a6–7, 1071a21–6, *DC* 306a9–11) (Heinaman [1979], 268f). (ix) The perishability of souls, 1070a24–6, *DA* 408a24–6, 413a3–7, b24–9, 430a24–5, *PN* 465a27–30, 479a7–9, 22, *GA* 736b21–4 (Heinaman).

   Among these arguments I am persuaded by (i)–(iv), (vii), and (ix), and regard (v), (vi), and (viii) as indecisive. (On (i) see n2–3 below. On (v); the evidence refers to non-substances. On (vi); as Lloyd himself notices, 54, if the existence of the universal depends on a plurality of instances, some universals will be capable of ceasing to exist (see n46 below)).

Albritton presents some of the major objections to particular forms: (1) The evidence secures at most particular forms for living substances. (2) In calling the form a this Aristotle need not imply that it is a particular. (3) In 1039b25 the essence of this house cannot be a particular form, since it is generated and destroyed. (4) The arguments in vii 13 do not require Aristotle to deny that universals are substances. Other objections: (5) Loux [1979], 13; since the form is predicated (e.g. 1049a35), it must be a universal. (6) He suggests that the form is a this only in so far as it makes something a this. (See DA 412a8–9, n10 below, Ross, i.310, Lacey [1965], 66.) (7) Code [1984], 13–16; particular forms cannot be essences, since essences are definable (and hence universal) in a way particular forms cannot be. For further discussion see Lewis [1984].

In reply to these objections: (a) (1) does not count against the view that every substance has a particular form, if Aristotle himself doubts (see Albritton [1957], 704n1) if there are any inanimate substances, 1032a18–19, 1034a4, 1041b28–30, 1043b19–23, 1040b5–16, 1043a2–7. (b) On (2), (4)–(5), see n3, 35–7 below. (c) (3) is answerable if the essence of this house is a particular formal compound. (d) Against (6) see Cherniss [1944], 352n, Lloyd [1981], 39. If there is other good evidence that the form is itself a this and a particular, (6) is too weak an interpretation. (e) (7) is not so powerful if essences may be instances of essential properties, not necessarily the properties themselves; see § 117.

2. Further reasons (cf. 10n34–5) for thinking Aristotle takes a this to be a particular: (a) It is clear in the Catg. that thisness implies particularity (see 3n19). (b) Top. 178b38–9 says that nothing common (sc. to more than one thing) is a this, and the this is clearly the particular (178b37, kath'hekaston) just referred to (cf. 1014a22). This argument, to expose the Platonist mistake in treating a such as a this, recurs in Met. 1039a1–2. (On Driscoll's discussion of these passages see n40.) (c) Met. vii 1 connects thisness with substance, identified with the definite particular subject, 1028a27. At this stage Aristotle has no doubt that a this and a definite subject is a particular. (d) Since his appeal to thisness in 1029a28 is part of his discussion of substance as subject, he should still be talking about particulars.

3. Reasons for denying that thises must be particulars (see Owens, 389f): (a) Aristotle says the form is a this that is predicated of matter, 1049a35–6; see Loux [1979], 13, Driscoll [1981], 136n. (b) Albritton [1957], 701f, argues that universals may be thises from 1042a29, 1049a35–6, 1070a14–17. (c) Aristotle is alleged to contrast the this with the particular, in contexts where he says the form is a this; see 1017b24–6, 1042a26–31, 1070a9–15, Cherniss [1944], 352.

Replies: (a) While nothing predicated of a plurality is a this, a particular form is predicated of just one subject, and so is not a universal. (b) 1070a14–17 may well refer to a particular form in the soul of the craftsman (as in vii 7–9; see 11n22). 1042a29 readily applies to the particular form, since this is separable in account. (c) These passages mention thisness and particularity separately, but do not imply that a this cannot or need not be a particular.

4. I follow Sellars (see 11n26) in identifying a particular form with a formal compound. Albritton, however, assumes that it must be 'an abstract particular . . . which . . . would not be a material thing', [1957], 703; and Harter [1975] and Heinaman [1979] agree in taking the form to be immaterial. I think the immaterialist views have difficulty with 1037a1–2. Whiting [1984], chs.1–2, argues convincingly that particular forms are formal compounds.

5. Anscombe [1961], 53f, takes 1035b27–31 to refer to Platonic Forms; contrast Furth [1985], 120. We remove the difficulty in supposing that Aristotle means to refer (as Ross, 199, rightly assumes) to his own universal forms, if we take him to intend the formal compound. Chen's argument, [1964], 56f, that the universal compound is an undesirable intruder into Aristotle's ontology, loses its force if we distinguish formal from material compounds.

6. On 1035b31–1036a8 see Owens, 360. His conclusion (that the per se being identified with its essence is the form without matter, which is 'the same in all its singulars') would be justified if we could fairly assume that Aristotle refers to only one type of form and one type of compound.

7. On 1043a37–b1 see § 132. In 1037a9 I follow the ms. text, *kai sôma tode*; Ross and OCT insert *to* after *kai*, yielding 'if Socrates is unconditionally this soul and this body' (which will also, on my view, introduce the formal compound). The ms. reading implies the identification of the soul (the materiate form) with the body (the proximate matter), and therefore justifies Aristotle's conclusion that Socrates is the (formal) compound. Here, as in 1036a16–25, 1043a29–b4, Aristotle does not seem to decide if the soul (universal or particular) is identical to the animal or not; but his indecision is reasonable, since we will be talking about the same thing both times.

   Lloyd's appeal to 1036b24–30 to show that Aristotle could not identify Socrates with his soul ([1981], 38) fails, once we distinguish the formal from the material compound. The same distinction shows why we need not follow Hartman [1977], 69f, in denying (against *dêlon*, 1037a5) that the universal man is meant to be a compound of soul and body.

8. I am assuming that persistence is consistent with the eventual replacement of all the original remote matter. Whether such persistence is also sufficient for identity depends on questions about such puzzles as the Ship of Theseus, on which see Wiggins [1980], 90–9. Wiggins's discussion suggests reasons why Aristotle might doubt whether anything besides a natural substance is a substance; see 1041b28–31, 1043b21–3. Perhaps he believes that because artifacts do not replace their own matter, and need to have distinguishable bits replaced, they are more like heaps of constituents. These points suggest that organisms are better wholes, and hence are basic subjects to a fuller extent, than artifacts are; it does not follow that there is no important difference between artifacts and mere heaps or that artifacts are not substances to a high degree. Most of what is true about the irreducibility of genuine substances to aggregates of their parts is true about artifacts as well. Moreover, on this view, a normal artifact fails to be a substance because of its relation to its parts, not because it is an artifact. If an

artifact nourished and maintained itself as an organism does, it is not clear why Aristotle should deny that it is an organism, and hence a substance.

9. Albritton (see n1 above) and Code [1984], 17n, argue that since (1) the essence of this house, 1039b24–5, is generable and destructible, and (2) all such things have matter, (3) the essence of this house must have matter; but since (4) whatever has matter cannot be a form, it follows that (5) the essence of this house cannot be a particular form. Heinaman [1979], 253n, agrees, but argues that 'being house' refers to a particular form (not, as Albritton, Code, and I suppose, the universal) and 'being this house' to a particular composite (cf. *DC* 278a8–10). A believer in formal compounds should reject (4).

10. At 412a7 I read *kath'hauto men*; some mss. omit the *men*. The *men* is justified, since it receives the equivalent of its answering *de* in *kath' hên êdê*, a8. (Hicks [1907], 305, does not quite do it justice in calling it a *men solitarium*.) The matter as such is not a this, but it is a this in so far as it is a form. I take *hulê* to be the subject of *legetai*, following Alex. *Quaest.* ii 24 (p. 75.3–16, cited by Rodier [1900], ii.165f), who makes it clear that the claim is true of proximate matter; contrast Hicks, 306.

11. I am unsure whether 1042a32–b8 refers (*a*) to proximate, or (*b*) to remote matter. If the *hupokeimenon hôs kata sterêsin* of 1042b3 is the matter that precedes the existence of a natural organism, (*b*) is required—and that would be the normal use of *kata sterêsin*. But (*a*) is tenable if this subject is the subject that comes into being and passes away; in that case *kata sterêsin* will refer to the subject as a potential this as opposed to the actual this that is the form.

12. On the relation between form, matter, and compound see further § 152. The particular formal sensible compound, as such, is separable unconditionally, whereas the particular sensible form, as such, is separable in account; for the form states the definition, and since the definition must be true of a formal compound, and the formal compound is separable, the form will also turn out to be unconditionally separable. (Aristotle does not exclude unconditional separability from form; contrast the way he excludes being actually a this from matter as such, 1042a27–8.) In a31 Aristotle reminds us that not all forms have to be sensible formal compounds; those that do not include sensible proximate matter are not subject to becoming and destruction—the ones that are subject to them are formal compounds.

The formal compound (and therefore the form qua formal compound) is separable unconditionally (and therefore meets the condition in 1028a33–4; see § 108) in so far as it depends on no particular bit of remote matter; separability is consistent with dependence on some bit of remote matter or other.

13. 1034a5–8 does not imply either (*a*) that Aristotle takes Socrates and Callias to be identical to the species form Man (as Woods argues, [1974], 177); or (*b*) that 'the formal component of a hylomorphic composite is general' (Code [1984], 16). Against (*a*): to say they are the same in respect of their species form is not to say they are identical to it. Against (*b*): if Aristotle recognizes particular forms, the *eidos* mentioned here will be the species

form. The claim that the species form is *atomon* need not preclude further determination; it may simply preclude further division into species. See n17.

14. Claims about the difference between conspecific particulars raise questions about the role of form and matter in individuation; see Owens, 394n77, Cousin [1935], 176, Cherniss [1944], 506, Anscombe [1953], Lloyd [1970], Charlton [1972], Marc Cohen [1984], Whiting [1986]. A particular form seems to provide both a principle of unity (what makes something a single thing rather than a collection) and a principle of distinctness (what makes two things two rather than one). (For these two principles see Lloyd, 519, Popper [1953], 100f, Whiting, 362.) Two particular forms of penny are needed to explain why there are two pennies rather than four (as there would be if we were counting penny-halves). 1040a28ff and *DC* i 9 (cited by Cohen on behalf of matter; see § 141) show that Aristotle takes matter to be necessary for a particular (since it provides the non-qualitative feature that makes it not logically repeatable); but they do not refute the claim that form is also necessary for distinguishing one particular from another.

15. This argument is rather abbreviated. For it is not essential to Socrates that he should be distinct from Callias in particular, if that is taken to imply the existence of Callias—Socrates could have existed even if Callias had not. But it is essential to him that he should have some features distinguishing him from other conspecific particulars, whatever they are.

16. This question about identity and difference is about what the difference between two conspecific individuals consists in, not about how we can recognize the difference when it is present (see further Woods [1965]). An answer to it should show (i) what is essential to each subject; (ii) how they differ from each other at the same time (the synchronic question); (iii) what constitutes the persistence of one, as opposed to the persistence of the other (the diachronic question). Difference in remote matter, e.g., seems to answer the synchronic question; the two coins, or Socrates and Callias, are two in so far as they now occupy two bits of remote matter. But it does not answer the diachronic question very well.

17. Aristotle would have to believe that particular forms differ only numerically (as, e.g., two coins made from the same die, from bronze of just the same composition, with the very same shape and so on, will be distinct simply in so far as they are constituted by two bits of bronze), if he believed that every qualitative difference between them would imply a difference in species; for he insists that particular compounds differ not in species but because of their matter, 1058a37–b12. He believes, however, that females and males in a species differ qualitatively without differing in species, 1058a29–36; analogously, there is no reason why qualitative differences between particular forms should imply distinct species. This point removes the objections to qualitatively distinct particular forms raised by Lloyd [1970], 521f (though cf. [1981] 27), Hartman [1977], 63f, Albritton [1957], 700. Neglect of the point infects Aquinas's discussion of angels, *ST* 1a, q.50, a4, *in corp.*

18. Hence we do not explain the identity of the particular form if we simply

appeal to the proximate matter; for the identity of the proximate matter is not explicable independently of the identity of the particular form.

19. Alternatively, we might suggest that Socrates and Callias differ simply in so far as they have different histories, and that no qualitative (i.e. not purely historical) distinguishing properties are essential to their particular forms. On this view, however, Socrates requires only the persistence of human functions in a bit of proximate matter, and no qualitative changes could cause Socrates to perish if human functions continue. Such a view does not provide clear conditions for the persistence of the proximate matter. If Socrates and Callias exchange most of their remote matter, which bit is Socrates' proximate matter? Socrates' previous qualities cannot distinguish them, since (on this view) these are inessential to the form. But the remote matter cannot distinguish them either, since it is not the same as the proximate matter. If persistence of (not merely historical) qualities is required, then, even if human functions are continuous, Socrates' functions may not persist; if they do not, then Socrates has perished and this particular bit of proximate matter has perished too.

20. 1070a9–14, taken by itself, does not rule out the view that the compound is a particular, and the form is a this but not a particular. But 1071a19–24 implies that thises (e.g. this letter B) are particulars as opposed to universals, and so implies that if a form is a this it is a particular.

21. In 767b34 I read *kai gar to ginomenon*, with the OCT; Peck [1953] omits the *gar*.

22. I use 'parent' rather than 'father', since the claim is defensible even if Aristotle is wrong to believe that only the male transmits form.

23. See 5n9.

24. On GC 321b25–8 see Anscombe [1961], 55f, Hartman [1977], 60 (who rightly takes it to be evidence for particular forms), Marc Cohen [1984], 63f. Cohen suggests that Aristotle may be considering the persistence of a kind. But only a persisting particular can grow (as opposed to being replaced by a larger conspecific particular), and Aristotle thinks the form grows.

25. A particular form must be more than a set of repeatable properties, since Aristotle rejects that conception of a particular (see § 141). The spatio-temporal characteristics that make the particular unique and unrepeatable must also be part of the particular form. We have argued not that the qualitative characteristics of the particular form are all it is, but only that they are essential to it, and especially to the explanatory role of form as actuality. See §§ 193, 212.

26. Aristotle cannot intend separability and thisness to rule out matter as substance. (*a*) He mentions form, matter, and compound as three types of substance, 1029a30–3. (*b*) He continues to maintain that matter is substance, 1035a1–2, 1038b4–6, 1042a26–b3, b9–11, 1049a34–6, DA 412a6–7. (*c*) He also claims that matter is not a this, 1042a27–8, 1049a24–36, or not in itself a this, DA 412a7–8, though it is potentially a this.

It follows that thisness and separability cannot simply be necessary conditions for substance; matter fails them and yet counts as a substance.

Nor can they be merely sufficient, since that would not make form and compound substance more than matter is. See 10n24.

27. Since the water from the same well is one only in kind, not in number, *Top.* 103a14–23, Aristotle implies that a particular pool of water is only a collection, not a numerically one individual. Similarly, logs and bodies will also be mere collections, not numerical unities, unless they are something more than their similar parts. On collections see further Cartwright [1970].

28. Book x adds this condition to the account of unity in 1015b36–1016a9 (1016a7–9 comes closest to it).

29. On numerical unity and indivisibility see 3n19, 4nn32–4.

30. Even if heaps of matter cannot be thises, might their constituents be thises? (*a*) If some non-compositional property determines the identity and persistence of the constituents, each of them will then be a formal unity, undermining the claim that matter is the only substance. (*b*) But if each constituent is itself a heap, its identity and persistence will depend on some more basic constituents. If this regress cannot be stopped, matter cannot be a this, and therefore cannot be a primary subject.

    Democritean atomism, as Aristotle understands it, claims that the atom is a substance and a this. See Simp. *in DC* 295.5 (reading *tô(i) tô(i)de*, following Bekker [1831], 1514b12), 1039a8–11, *GC* 325a32–6 (on unity), *DC* 303a5–10, with Stocks in OT ad loc. Since points cannot constitute an extended body, *GC* 316a23–9, the atom must be physically indivisible, and essentially constituted of these parts, but logically divisible. Since the parts depend on the whole, the atom avoids objection (*b*). But for the same reason, the account of the parts seems to depend on their relation to the whole, and the whole cannot, therefore, be defined simply by reference to its parts. It therefore seems to be open to objection (*a*).

    This argument implies that even elementary stuffs have some sort of form (as 1042b11–1043a7 suggests—though 1043a4–7 insists that this sort of form does not make a genuine substance, and the demand for genuine unities explains why not). A molecule of water, e.g., must have not only a definite type of matter—hydrogen and oxygen—but also these constituents in the ratio 2 : 1. If something's identity depends on any formal conditions, we can distinguish these conditions from the subject of which they are predicated, and therefore we still have not found a subject that is predicated of nothing else, in the sense required by the broad predication-formula. Aristotle assures us that nothing except matter could satisfy the broad formula. His later argument shows that in fact that matter does not satisfy it. See 10n25.

31. Different views on why matter is not a this:
    (1) My account is closest to Sellars's suggestion, [1957], 134, and [1963], that primary 'thing kind expressions' are confined to 'direct purpose servers', to teleologically ordered things; and I agree with Kung's appeal, [1978], 156f, to the degree of unity found in living organisms. Both Sellars and Kung provide an incomplete explanation, however, until we show how Aristotle's general views about thises justify the preferences for unity and for teleologically ordered things; these

preferences do not follow trivially from the sense of 'this' (no such preference, e.g., seems to underlie the contrast between this and such).

(2) Sokolowski [1970], 282f, Hartman [1977], 31f, rely on the alleged arbitrary and conventional character of the application of 'lump of bronze', 'bucketful of water', and so on, and their conditions for individuation and reidentification. I doubt if the relevant sort of arbitrariness is special to bits of matter. For it is not arbitrary that this is a bucketful of water etc., and there may be good reason for counting bucketfuls rather than drops; useful conditions for identity need not give a definite answer in every conceivable case.

(3) Owen [1978], 288, argues from vii 3 and vii 16 (citing 1033a2, 1034a6, 1041b5–7) that only prime matter fails to be a this (though he adds reservations about non-prime matter). His view conflicts with the examples in vii 16, and with 1042a27, where matter is recognized as a substance but as only potentially a this.

(4) Chappell [1970] and [1973] (effectively criticized by Cartwright [1972] and by Kung [1978], 146f), suggests that Aristotle refers to the distinction between stuff (referred to as e.g. 'bronze') and things (referred to as e.g. 'this lump of bronze'). But vii 16 makes it clear that lumps are not (primary) substances, and therefore implies that they are not thises.

32. This view explains the claim that no substance is composed of substances, 1041a4–5 (cf. 1039a3–14). Aristotle does not mean to deny that (in one sense) Socrates is composed of his remote matter, or that bits of it are substances of some sort. He means to deny that the remote matter or any bit of it is a more basic substance that determines the identity of Socrates. On the other hand, the parts of Socrates' proximate matter are not substances. The distinction between remote and proximate matter solves the puzzle of 1039a14–23.

33. In 1038b5 *tode ti* might be the form (Cousin [1933], 327) or the compound (Ross, ii.164, Owens, 334). I take it to be the form (which is also the formal compound), and take the matter to be the proximate matter (since the form is identified with the actuality, and the grounds for the identification are partly anticipated in 1035b16–22, 1036b28–32, which attribute the potentiality to the proximate matter).

34. The 'F is G-en' test is familiar from *Phys.* 245b9–246a1; cf. 1033a16–22. But only ix 7 explains it by reference to potentiality. On Brunschwig's discussion see 10n36.

35. Woods [1967], 229 (criticized by Lesher [1971], Driscoll [1981], 134) argues that Aristotle attacks things spoken of universally, *katholou legomena*, and that he counts species as universals, but not spoken of universally, so that the attack is confined to genera. The distinction Woods relies on is dubious. (1) 1035b27–31 denies that universals are substances. (2) Woods renders 1038b11 not as I have (agreeing with Code [1978], 66), but as 'for what is spoken of universally is what is of a nature to belong to a plurality'. But even with this translation 'for. . .' seems to cover man, horse, etc. (3)

Hence Aristotle reverts to 'universal', 1038b11, 16, not confining himself to 'spoken of universally'.

36. 'Each thing', *hekaston*, in 1038b10 probably includes particulars such as Socrates and Callias, since 1029b14, 1032a8, 1039b25 refer to particular essences, and 1040b17 (in admitting the possibility that the substance of something is numerically one) refers to them again. If Socrates and Callias are the bearers of essences, the species form is a universal, and therefore not a substance; for it belongs to many things of the same species.

On 1038b12–15 I generally agree with Code [1978]. Unlike Ross, I take what follows *pantôn d' ouch hoion te*, b13, to support it (and hence would prefer *henos dê* suggested in one ms., to *henos d'ei*). Aristotle argues: if it is the substance of all, it is the substance of each one; but if you take any one you like (see Woods [1967], 218f), all the others will be identical to that one. (Hence *hôn gar. . .*, b14, gives a reason for *pantôn . . . .* I render b14–15: 'If the substance of things is one (comma after *ousia*), then their essence is also one (no comma after *hen*) and the things themselves are one.')

Albritton's view ([1957], 706: if the substance of x and y has a given type of unity, then x and y have the same kind; hence if their substance is one in species so are they) makes it hard to see why Aristotle should conclude that no universal (or nothing spoken of universally) is a substance, since both species and genera satisfy Albritton's condition. (See Woods [1967], 221–4.) Heinaman [1980] argues in detail that vii 13 regards particulars rather than universals as substances.

37. At 1040b23–7 Aristotle assumes that what is common is what is found in many places at once, and that this fact explains the inseparability of universals. He must assume, then, that if, e.g., man is in many places at once it is a universal and not numerically one (see 3n20). Since a species-form is not numerically one, it is a universal, and therefore within the range of Aristotle's objections to universal substances.

38. *Catg.* 2b7–14 claims that the second substance shows what the first substance is; but it probably means only that the second substance, e.g. man, shows what it is to be a particular man (i.e. some man or other), not that it shows what it is to be this man (e.g. Socrates) in particular. In the *Metaphysics* Aristotle considers the question overlooked in the *Categories*. He can therefore still agree with his claim in the *Categories*, distinguishing it from the false claim that the universal reveals the essence of Socrates.

39. On 1038b16–22 see Woods [1967], 231–4. The argument assumes that the universal is only present in the essence, as animal is present in the essence of man and horse. Aristotle replies that the genus is some account of at least part of the species (b18–19, taking *estai* in 19 and *esti* in 20 as predicative); it will therefore be the substance of that part; and (by the previous argument) the different species of animal will have an identical part and (if this is supposed to apply to the relation of man to particular men) particular men will have a numerically identical part. (In b23 *eidei* should probably be deleted, following Brandis, as an over-restrictive gloss; see Ascl. 431.11.)

40. On 1038b35–1039a3 Driscoll [1981], 151, argues: (i) a universal is predicated of countable particulars (*pleiosin*, 1038b11); (ii) the species-form

is predicated of matter, not of particular compounds; (iii) matter without form is not countable; and hence (iv) the species-form is not a universal and may still be a this. (Modrak [1979], 379, gives a less plausible argument for denying that a species-form is a universal.)

Driscoll's (iv) does not follow from (i)–(iii). If we make four statues from four countable lumps of bronze, then, by (iii), the lumps have some form; but they do not need the form of statue (but only the form of lump of bronze). Hence the species-form of statue is predicable, consistently with (iii), of these four lumps, and so satisfies (i), and is not a this. See also Code [1978], 72n13.

41. In vii 13 Aristotle concentrates on genera, to answer those who believe that substantiality increases with generality (as 1028b34–5 suggested; cf. 998a20–b14, and § 89). For Plato, the specific Forms belonging to the generic Form Animal are parts of a whole (*Tim.* 30c), and, like Aristotle, Plato thinks the whole is more substantial than its parts. By discussing genera Aristotle attacks his opponents' most favoured candidates; but his arguments work equally against species. He takes the treatment of universals as thises and particulars to be a basic error in the Theory of Forms. The Platonists rightly thought universal substances must be Forms, because that would make each of them numerically one and separable, which are necessary conditions for being a substance, 1040b27–30. But they did not see that only a particular, not a universal, meets these conditions.

42. Plato thinks of proper names as abbreviations for descriptions, and so is ready to allow that something qualitatively indistinguishable from Cratylus would be a second Cratylus, *Cra.* 432b4–c5. Similarly, an account of Theaetetus' snubness requires only qualitative features, *Tht.* 209c. Aristotle believes that on this point Plato has misrepresented the nature of particularity.

43. Popper [1953], 112f, defends Aristotle.

44. 1040b25–6 (cf. *PA* 644a27–8, *APo* 87b30–3) seems to imply that actual, not only possible, plural instantiation is necessary for a universal. 1038b11–12 ('The universal is common; for what is called universal is what is of a nature to belong to many things') is ambiguous. See further § 41.

45. *DC* 277b32–3 distinguishes the form 'by itself' from the particular form that is combined with matter (cf. 278a8–18), but does not say if the form without matter is in every case a universal. Even if all the suitable matter available for noses has been used to make one particular nose, being a nose would still not be the same as being this nose; and if all the available matter is used to make one world, even so being a world is not the same as being this world, 278b3–8. Though this world is a particular, 278b3, it is not clear if being a world is a particular when it has only one instance. Aristotle is free to claim that it is a particular, since it is in just one place at a time, and is therefore one in number.

46. A particular (universal) can be defined either (*a*) as what exists in only one place (in many places) at one time, or (*b*) as what cannot exist (can exist) in many places at once. Both (*a*) and (*b*) make the divisions exhaustive. (*a*) implies that properties such as being a man will be particulars if they have

only one instance, that a universal comes into existence if another man does, and that the property may be either a particular or a universal at different times. (*b*) also makes the division exhaustive, but implies that the property is a universal even if it has only one instance. The priority of particulars requires (*a*); see 4n17.

Alexander, *Quaest.* i 11 (p. 23.25–24.1, 24.8–11; see Lloyd [1981], 54), attributes (*a*) to Aristotle. He seems to refer to *Met.* vii 15, and seems not to take 'being a world' in *DC* i 9 to be a universal. Simplicius, *in Catg.* 85.5–9 (see Lloyd, 75), uses (*b*) against Alexander's suggestion that the sun, the moon, and the world are particulars with no universal.

47. The Stoic 'peculiar quality' is this sort of repeatable determinate property, lacking the essentially indexical aspects of Aristotelian particulars (since the Stoics do not hold an essentially indexical account of place or time either). See Simp. *in DA* 217.32–218.2, Lloyd [1981], 67f.

48. Our account of properties suggests a possible defence of Owens's claim, 390–5, 399 (cf. 14) that Aristotle recognizes things that are neither universal nor particular. But, contrary to Owens, I doubt if the property could be the substantial form that is Aristotle's primary substance. (See also Owens [1960], 18f.) For even if Socrates is the only man, the property of being a man will not be his essence; hence it will be open to the arguments of vii 13. Owens's view is sympathetically discussed and effectively criticized by Gewirth [1953], 588f.

49. 1032b14 describes the essence as the 'substance without matter' and apparently regards the 'form in the soul' (probably a particular; see n36 above) that explains craft-production as such an essence. This immaterial essence cannot be a this, and so cannot be a primary substance. It will be a secondary substance, in so far as it specifies the essence that will be a substance when it includes proximate matter. A similar argument will show why the universal is a substance to some degree.

50. Sachs [1948], 223, Owens, 369, Harter [1975], 19, argue that the *Met.* does not accept the *Catg.* doctrine of second substances. (Owens's argument that the two doctrines are consistent rests on a distinction between the order of logic and the order of being, which does not seem to me to protect Aristotle's consistency; see 3n5.) Lesher [1971] and Sykes [1975] deny that Aristotle has a consistent view about rival candidates for substance.

51. Lacey [1965], Lloyd [1981], 2, Harter [1975], 17, attribute nominalist or conceptualist anti-realism to Aristotle. Lloyd's evidence (1040a4–5, *APo* ii 19, *DA* 417b19–24 (Lloyd, 9; and see below, § 169), 1039a33–b2 (Lloyd, 20; cf. Plato, *Parm.* 131a–c)) does not show that Aristotle rejects realism, but only that he rejects some realist theories (e.g. the view that a universal is numerically one in all its instances; for a good discussion see Heinaman [1982], 47). Harter's version of conceptualism is not evidently consistent with Aristotle's conception of the objects of science.

52. Instead of accepting nominalism, Aristotle might claim that (1) universals belong to some non-substance category, or that (2) they exist, but do not belong to any category. (1) is unattractive, since universals corresponding to primary substances will not fit into any non-substance category. 1039a1

does not show (contrast Heinaman [1982], 46) that they belong in the category of quality, as the category is defined in 1020b8 –13, on which see 3n32. But (2) will require all universals to be outside the categories (why should only substance universals be outside?), which will then lose their primary classifying function, since the classifying universals will be outside the category of the items they classify.

53. I have not discussed the defence of particulars in xiii 10, on which see Leszl [1972], Heinaman [1981a], Lear [1987]. Though it is certainly relevant to this issue, I do not think it undermines these points in favour of the universal. (I do not agree with Lear's attempt to show that thises are not particulars; see n3.) The extent to which particulars are knowable does not show that reference to universals is dispensable for knowledge.

54. On this passage see § 2.

55. On this issue about priority see §§ 52, 65.

56. This claim does not necessarily remain true if we take account of some of Aristotle's theology.

57. On the non-empirical character of dialectic see § 24.

58. See § 162.

CHAPTER 13

1. The theory should account for different types of appearances: (1) It must fit the empirical appearances 'proper', *oikeia*, to this area of study, 402b16–403a2 (on the appropriate *sumbebêkota*; see 2n17). (2) It should fit common beliefs, and in particular the views of previous theorists about the soul. Many of these are much more general and abstract, and less direct products of observation, than the proper appearances.

2. Rodier [1900], 8, takes *zô(i)ôn*, 402a7, as = 'living being'; but cf. 402a10, 403b18, 413b14.

3. I take (a) *poteron* . . ., 402b5, and (b) *ê kath'hekastên* . . ., b6, to express two views that Aristotle eventually rejects (and I take *estin*, b8, to express a counterfactual consequence, not Aristotle's actual view about the genus animal; see Rodier [1900], 17, and contrast Hicks [1907], 185–7). If (b) is right, we should follow those who concentrate on the human soul, and add further accounts of similarly narrow scope for other animals. If, however, (a) is right, we should look for a single universal account that will apply to all animals. Being men is a genuine common property of men, while being horses is not a genuine property of equine horses and clothes-horses. Though Aristotle does not accept (a), he thinks there is some truth in it, and his own account of the soul rejects (b).

4. I take *hôs eipein* with *trisin* rather than with *pantes*. See Philop. 90.27–30; contrast Hicks [1907], 234.

5. If, e.g., we find that the heart is the cause of pumping blood and the lungs are the cause of respiration, we might define an organ called a 'hung', as the cause of pumping blood or of respiration or of both. But we will discover

nothing new about hearts and lungs, and we will have defined no genuine kind of organ. Aristotle wants to avoid the analogous result with 'soul'.

6. Democritus, e.g., assumes that the soul can be the cause of movement only if it is some sort of stuff that is itself easily moved and so can agitate the rest of the body, 406b15–22. Those (e.g. Empedocles) who explain perception by appeal to the soul assume that perception must be the contact of like with like, of similar stuff in the object and in the perceiver's body, 409b26–9.

7. Aristotle assumes that plants have souls, 409a9–10, 411b27–8, and rather unfairly criticizes other people for not mentioning plant souls, 410b22–4. Plato admits plant souls, but infers that they must have perceptions and desires too, *Tim.* 77b. (Cf. *De Plantis* 815a18 on Empedocles and Anaxagoras.) Aristotle, however, agrees with the general view that plants do not have perceptions and movements, but insists that because they have life they have soul.

　　On the unintuitive character of Aristotle's attribution of soul to plants see Hardie [1976], 394f, [1980], 369–71. On related questions see Matthews [1977].

8. Incorporeality: see 405a5–7, b12, 409b20–1. In Aristotle's view, those who identify soul with a fine-textured body implicitly recognize that it is not really an ordinary body. See Them. 14.4–8 (quoted but rejected by Hicks ad 405b11). Contrast Phil. 90.24–5, accepted by Hicks and by Rodier ad 405a6, b12.

9. In 411b25–7 I follow Hicks's text, with *homoeideis . . . allêlais* (= the souls in each of the insects formed from the division of the first one, as opposed to the 'whole' in the original insect) and *dihairetês*, without the *ou* in OCT (i.e. we cannot split the original whole soul into many independently existing faculties, since these faculties are inseparable from each other (*allêlôn men hôs ou chôrista onta*), and the whole soul is divisible only into complete souls).

10. In *DA* i Aristotle does not actually mention the connexion between Socrates and Socrates' soul, assumed by Plato in the *Phd.* But it is clearly relevant; for the Pythagoreans and Plato affirm the immortality of the person by affirming the immortality of the soul.

11. Aristotle refers to Pythagorean myths, 407b22, and so not necessarily to an explicitly immaterialist conception of the soul. But his criticism applies equally to an immaterialist Platonic conception.

12. The attunement theory (cf. Plato, *Phd.* 92a6–95a2) seems to anticipate Aristotle's own conception of the soul as the form of the body, 407b23–4. But his objections, 407b32–408a5, suggest that he thinks it misses the essential point. An attunement or proportion of elements depends on the existence of just these elements, and cannot cause movement in them. But in attributing perception or the origin of movement to the soul we treat it as a subject in its own right, not as a quality or coincident of a subject.

13. See § 139.

14. The argument is this: (1) The living body is a compound of form and matter, 412a15–16. (2) It is a compound of body and soul. (3) Since it is a

living body, it is a body of a certain kind, a16–17. (4) Hence the body is subject and matter, not said of a subject, a17–19. (5) Hence the soul is not body, a17. (6) Hence the soul is not matter. (7) Hence the soul is form, a19–21.

Here (1) and (2) rest on assumptions about life and soul that are made clearer only in 414a12–14, discussed in the text. Similar assumptions are needed to support the claim in (4), that the body must be matter (so that 'is a living body' does not predicate a quality of a substance).

15. Empedocles on nutrition; see 5n23.

16. In 412b25–6 we must understand *to sôma* (cf. *toiondi sôma*, b27) with *to apobeblêkos tên psuchên* and with *to echon*. Aristotle therefore commits himself to the continued existence of a body that once had a soul and has lost it. (Cf. Them. 43.6–8, *tou nekrou sômatos*, and Hicks's translation.) 'Potentially alive' here must mean 'potentially having the life of the type of organism in question'; a seed has some sort of life potentially, since it is actually alive, and Aristotle's point is simply that the seed or embryo of a dog does not have a dog's life potentially. See § 126.

17. The form is taken to be something that has matter, in *to hou hê hulê*, 412b8. Hicks, 315, sees this and thinks Aristotle must be expressing himself incautiously, since, strictly speaking (in Hicks's view) only the compound, and not the form, has matter. If we identify the form with the formal compound (and understand it in Wiggins's way, rather than Ackrill's; see 11n24), there is nothing incautious or inexact in Aristotle's expression.

A mere reference to unity would not show that Aristotle has identity in mind; but to say that something and its actuality are *kuriôs hen*, 412b9 (understanding *hen* with *kuriôs hê entelecheia estin*), is exaggerated unless identity is intended. Charles [1984], 222n takes the passage to refer to constitution without identity; but this view will seem less plausible once we distinguish proximate from remote matter. A similar question arises about Hartman's suggestion, [1977], 99, that Aristotle has something other than strict identity in mind; see 11n34.

18. See § 127.

19. See *Met.* 1049a13–16, § 126. The claim that the body is potentially alive is explicable in the light of Aristotle's conditions for potentiality. The states that constitute being alive depend on bodily organs; at the same time they explain why the body has these organs and these movements—the body has the potentiality for *these* states. For discussion of Aristotle's claims about potentiality and actuality in his account of the soul see Charlton [1980].

20. 412a17 must be about the proximate body, since the discussion is about the body that is potentially alive.

21. We might compare other cases where the F and the G are the same but being F is not being G: (*a*) The musical man is the white man, but their being is different (i.e. the definition of musical man is not the same as the definition of white man). This is a case of coincidental identity between particulars (see *Met.* 1037b6, 11n37). (*b*) Universal justice is complete virtue, but their being is different, *EN* 1130a12 (cf. 1141b23; the same state of character, but the being is different). Qua one thing the state of character

is justice, qua another thing it is virtue; the identity holds between the universal states, not merely between some of their particular instances, and it is not merely coincidental (see § 228). (*c*) The Athens-Thebes road and the Thebes-Athens road are the same, but their being is different, *Phys.* 202a18–20, b11–16. Here also the relation is not merely coincidental identity. I do not think Aristotle means to deny identity (the relation satisfying Leibniz's Law) here, but the issue is disputed. See White [1971], 179f, Miller [1973], Charles [1984], 10–15, Irwin [1986], 72.)

22. 408b1–18 need not deny that the soul is a substance, even though Aristotle instructs us not to say that the soul is afraid or angry, any more than that it builds or weaves; in all these cases we should say that the human being does these things 'with' or 'in respect of' the soul, *tê(i) psuchê(i)*, 408b15. In so far as these psychic states require some movement, they require proximate matter, and in attributing them to the human being we make this fact clear. It does not follow that the soul is not identical to the human being, or that it would be false to attribute these processes to the soul.

23. Plato is right, then, to suppose that, e.g., we explain an action by referring to psychic states we are not explaining it by reference to bodily constituents. He is wrong, however, to infer that the soul must be some further non-bodily component added to the bodily components (the view rejected in *Met.* vii 17). In a way he is even wrong to infer that the soul is not identical to the body, since it is identical to the proximate body; he is right only about the remote body, and then only with qualifications.

24. Alex. *Quaest.* ii 26 (p. 76.25–33; cf. Rodier [1900], 186) argues from the dependence of the proximate matter on the form to the conclusion that the soul is not in the body as 'in' a subject (i.e. in the *Catg.* sense of 'in'). The same argument works against the attunement theory.

25. If Socrates, as we might say, becomes a vegetable, and only the nutritive functions survive, then, in Aristotle's view, Socrates must have ceased to exist and his soul must have been replaced by a nutritive soul that is continuous with part of Socrates' soul. Socrates does not have three souls— nutritive, perceptive, and rational—though he certainly has these three psychic activities, which are all parts of his rational soul. See also n45, 16n38.

26. We might conceive continuous human functions in fairly continuous remote matter, but functions that change so radically as to persuade us that Socrates has been replaced by Callias in this remote matter. Aristotle can say that in this case Socrates' soul has been replaced by Callias' soul only if he recognizes qualitatively different particular forms and particular souls. On this issue see § 136.

27. My views are indebted to Taylor [1967], Boyd [1980], Sorabji [1974], Hartman [1977], chs.3–4, Nussbaum [1984], and especially to Shields's careful argument for regarding Aristotle as a dualist, [1986], ch.3, [1988].

28. This passage is quoted and discussed in § 133.

29. Aristotle presents this as an objection to Pythagorean stories about reincarnation; but it seems to apply equally well to the Platonic account. The same sort of objection may underlie 408b1–18.

30. See § 150.

31. Some readers have interpreted remarks about the formal aspect of psychological processes as evidence that Aristotle takes them to have some non-physical aspect; see Barnes [1971], 36–8, well answered by Sorabji [1974], 47f. For other dualist inferences see Hardie [1964], [1980], 77f, 370, Robinson [1978], [1983].

32. The argument against dualism relies rather heavily on some understanding of 'component', 'element', and 'part'; Aristotle sees some of the complexity in these notions, 1034b32–1035a4. He has to rely, e.g. in *Met.* vii 17, on a distinction between the claims (a) that the syllable is to be identified with the letters plus another component, and (b) that it is the letters plus something else; for he denies (a) and accepts (b).

33. On the importance of the heart see Block [1961], Hardie [1964], Hartman [1977], 106–9, Tracy [1983]. In saying that the heart is *kurion*, Aristotle does not claim that the heart is any more essential to the creature than its spleen is (since this is also called *kurion tês ousias* at 1024a23–8, noticed by Hartman; for this role cf. 1013a5, GA 771a13, 773a8–13; for *en* cf. *Phys.* 210a18–21). The same creature will have the same proximate heart (which may be constituted of different remote matter), whose persistence therefore depends on the persistence of the same form (of the whole creature); hence the persistence of the heart does not provide an independent criterion for the persistence of the creature (pace Hartman, 108).

It is not so clear, however, that Aristotle is entitled to claim that the soul is the sort of thing that could be in one part rather than in the whole body (and yet MA 703a29–b2 suggests that the soul is localized in some one part of the body). If he identifies the soul with the whole organism, conceived as its form, it is not natural to maintain at the same time that the soul is in some part of the body, as though the organism were located in some part of itself.

If Aristotle changes his mind here, an explanation is not hard to find. In other discussions of the soul Aristotle does not identify it with actuality; but this is the crucial claim in the DA, showing how the soul can be identical to the organism whose soul it is. Only the *Metaphysics* reaches a conception of form and substance that allows the identification. Before Aristotle has reached this position, he does not have this reason for resisting a conception of soul that makes it a quality or potentiality of some part of the body; and that is the conception that is most easily associated with the biological works.

For some purposes, and especially for the detailed content of the biological works, it makes rather little difference which conception of the soul we accept. The actuality theory never excludes an important role for the heart, or implies the unimportance of physiology. But we saw earlier that the Platonic claim that Socrates is identical to his soul fits very well with the doctrine of the *Metaphysics*; and it fits less well with a doctrine that makes the soul a quality or potentiality of the heart.

I have accepted the view that Aristotle's views about the relation of soul and body change, and that his claims about the heart are a partial index of the change. This developmental view is expounded in an extreme form by

Nuyens [1948] (discussed by Lefèvre [1972], and partly supported by Ross [1955], [1961]. Block [1961], Hardie [1964], and Kahn [1966] have encouraged scepticism about development. The scepticism is justified, to the extent that an important role for the heart is quite consistent with the hylomorphic theory of the *DA*; but I do not think this point undermines the whole developmental account.

34. This form of immaterialism is characterized as 'Minimal Dualism' by Shoemaker [1977], 141–53, who explores its correspondences with materialism. A similar view is described in less detail by Putnam [1975], 291–5.

35. See Descartes, Letter of 23 Nov. 1646 (= Kenny, 208); Wilson [1978], 183–5.

36. Aristotle himself claims that thinking has no bodily organ, 429a15–27 (see 14n45 below), and that intellect, or part of it, is capable of existing without a body, 430a22–3. Recognition of spiritual components is consistent with his general hylomorphic view. Hence Robinson's argument from such evidence to the conclusion that Aristotle is a dualist is unwarranted; see [1983], 123–8.

37. In 413a8–9 Aristotle suggests that it is unclear whether the soul is the actuality of the body in the way a sailor is of a ship. A sailor (i.e. passenger; cf. 406a6) on a ship is no longer a sailor once he is out of the ship, but the man who was the sailor still exists. Similarly, if something has a soul if and only if it has a spiritual component, the spiritual component may be separable from the body. This degree of quasi-dualism is quite consistent with Aristotle's general conception of soul. (Contrast Blumenthal [1976], 85f.) It does not imply Platonism (as Aquinas thinks, *in DA* 243, *SG* ii.57 (1327)) or that soul and body do not make a genuine unity (as Descartes thinks, *Med.* vi (=AT vii.81). Aristotle identifies a component of the soul, not the soul itself, with the spiritual component. It is therefore unnecessary to alter the text as OCT does (by adding *ê* before *hôsper* in 413a8).

Among those who use this passage as evidence of Aristotelian dualism see Robinson [1983], 128–31. See also Alex. *DA* 15.9–26 (perhaps influenced by *Phys.* 254b30–3); Hicks [1907], 321; Easterling [1966], 159–62.

38. An eliminative view is presented by Rorty [1970], Churchland [1984], Stich [1983], chs.10–11. For a reductive view see Armstrong [1968] (questions about its reductive aspect are raised sharply by Nagel [1970], 203). 'Non-reductive' materialism includes the views of those who think token mental events are identical to token physical events, but no such identity holds at the level of types (see Davidson [1970]), and those who hold that the relation is composition rather than identity (see Boyd [1980]).

39. For arguments against reductive materialism see Davidson [1970], Putnam [1975], Taylor [1967].

40. Charles [1984], 217–27, attributes to Aristotle a general argument for materialism, but I do not think the attribution is warranted. See Irwin [1986], 74–6. Sorabji's view, [1974], 55f, on whether Aristotle is a non-reductive materialist is not completely clear. Nussbaum's argument, [1984], 202f, to show that Aristotle is a non-reductive materialist holding

that material states constitute psychic states, fails to distinguish claims about proximate and about remote matter. The version of materialism that Slakey [1961] attributes to Aristotle is still less warranted.

41. Hence the distinction between quasi–dualism and compositional materialism will be as clear as the boundaries of a reasonable conception of matter.

42. On different appearances see § 19.

43. On the empirical aspects of Aristotle's views on formal and final causation see § 148.

44. On materiate forms see § 132. If Aristotle is thinking of them, the reading *logoi enhuloi* in 403a25 (as in OCT) is plausible, despite the fact that *enhulos* is a *hapax legomenon* in the Corpus. The most suitable sense is 'having matter in them'. Hicks appropriately cites *Met.* 1033a4–5. The variant reading *logoi en hulê(i)* makes sense, but its point is less exact.

45. I accept Förster's [1912] transposition of *hôste . . . thêriou*, 414bb32–3, to b28, after *toiouton*. I take *aphentas ton toiouton*, 414b27–8, to mean that a common definition of souls ought not to be pursued *to the exclusion of* an account of each specific type (so that *ton toiouton* = the specific accounts). See Hicks, and contrast Rodier. Aristotle is not saying that the common definition is either impossible or useless, only that it is insufficient. Hicks's comment, 'the study of soul in the abstract leads to no discoveries', 337, is therefore exaggerated.

   In speaking of different types of soul, Aristotle does not mean that a perceptive creature that nourishes itself has both a nutritive and a perceptive soul. The lower soul is only present potentially in the higher, 414b28–32; to reduce a dog to something with a purely nutritive soul we have to deprive the dog of his perceptive capacities, just as we have to remove a side from a quadrilateral to make a triangle. (Hicks's and Ross's explanation of the parallel is inexact.)

46. On the argument about nutrition see § 58.

47. On the form of teleological explanation see § 57.

48. What tends to promote a creature's survival need not always actually promote its survival; e.g. plants may begin to grow in an early spring and then get killed by a late frost. But they have not been deceived about the spring.

49. This description need not be accurate—'description of' indicates a causal relation, not a resemblance. It is possible for an appearance to be an appearance of a rock that describes a rock as a hedgehog, because of the subject's previous appearances.

50. We might challenge this appeal to 'content' here. Something has the relevant sort of content if it is related appropriately to subjects who intend it or take it to have content. Hence to explain content we must apparently appeal to some understanding of intending and taking. And so we must apparently concede that Aristotle's account of a mental state cannot explain what a mental state is to someone who cannot recognize any mental states. This concession, however, does not undermine Aristotle's account as a whole. We could have some notion of some mental states without being able to give a general account of what makes a state mental; and Aristotle offers the general account.

CHAPTER 14

1. In Aristotle's repeated formula, *hê phusis outhen poiei matên*, we should understand *matên* to refer to pointless activity, aiming at no end, rather than unsuccessful activity—Aristotle does not claim that nature is always successful in achieving the ends it tends towards. In most contexts nature's way is contrasted with something done pointlessly, or for no reason, or superfluously (*periergon*). See 415b16–17, 434a30–b8, *DC* 271a30–3, 290a27–35, 291b11–15, *PN* 469a27–8, *PA* 641b12–15, 658a8–10, 661b3–5, 691b1–4, 694a13–15, 695b17–19, *GA* 739b19–20, 741b2–6, 744a36–b1, *Pol.* 1252b1–3, 1253a9–18. When Aristotle claims that nature does nothing inadequate, he distinguishes this from the claim that nature does nothing pointless, *GA* 788b20–7, *Pol.* 1256b20–6; and the claim about adequacy has exceptions, *DA* 432b21–3. On benefit see further 15n9.
2. For benefits from the senses see 434a30–b8, b9–29, 435b19–25, 411b22–4, 420b16–22, *PN* 436b12–437a3. A capacity may benefit both the individual creature and its species, since nature tends to reproduce creatures of the same species, and thereby to confer a degree of immortality on the individual, 415a25–b7, 416b23–5. The function of a sense or a sense-organ explains some of its properties, 420a9–11, 421a9–13 (where the function of the sense explains a difficulty in identifying the object), and distinguishes it from other senses, ˙421b21–3; and the analogy of organs in different creatures is determined by their similarity of function, 412b1–3, 416a3–5.

   Aristotle's case is easiest with locomotive animals, 434a31–b8; but he also recognizes stationary animals that have perception, 410b18–21, 413b2–4, 415a6–7, 432b19–21, *HA* 588b10–30, 621b2–5, *PA* 681b31–682a1. Even though they do not move from place to place, they move parts of themselves; a sea-anemone or a shellfish, e.g., may close up and protect itself if it is poked, *HA* 487b7–11.
3. In arguing that perception and appearance are not the same Aristotle claims that some perceivers, insects with a low level of awareness, do not have appearance, 428a9–11. (As Hicks notices, following Torstrik [1862], the inclusion of bees raises a difficulty in the light of *Met.* 980b21–7.) But later he agrees that if incomplete animals with only the sense of touch have perception, then they also have appetite; and he concedes that they have an indefinite form of appearance, corresponding to their indefinite form of motion, 433b31–434a7. These later thoughts seem to be the best. See also 15n1.
4. On processes and actualities see 11n19. A process is directed entirely at some end distinct from it, and is completed only when it is over, and has ceased to exist. Perception is different, since it does not aim only at some end outside itself, and it need not cease to exist when an end has been achieved. For this reason it is not appropriate to speak of perception as a process.

   In *Phys.* vii 3 Aristotle argues that states of the soul in general are completions, 246a10–b2, that cannot come about without alterations, but are not mere alterations, 246b10–20. He applies the distinction to the virtues and to states of the understanding, 247b1–2, apparently allowing alteration in the perceptive part of the soul, 248a6–9. In the *DA*, however, he seems to apply the same distinction to perception as well.

5. The passage is quoted and discussed at § 124.
6. On necessary conditions for change see § 37. Change between contraries requires the potentiality for losing one contrary and gaining another.
7. The passage is quoted at § 124.
8. On Presocratic views see 13n6.
9. On truth as correspondence see § 2.
10. As Themistius explains, when a vegetable is affected by something with a taste (e.g. a pickle by brine), it is not affected by it qua having the taste, but qua the sort of thing it is (i.e. by the causal properties of brine as brine; *hê(i) toiadi poiotês*, 79.19–20).
11. Aristotle might deny that this example satisfies F2, and claim that my body realizes its natural potentiality to nourish itself from the environment (which in this case coincidentally involves getting wetter), not a natural potentiality to become like the environment. But some conceivable potentialities to become like the object still seem to count against Aristotle; we can imagine either plants or animals being able to camouflage themselves without perception of the environment.
12. Aristotle sees that F1 and F2 by themselves might still seem no better than the Presocratic 'like to like' principle, 409b26–8. He replies that when I see a stone I do not get a stone in my soul, 431b28–432a3, but only the form without the matter. To be affected 'together with the matter' is to have my matter affected by the matter of the object affecting me in the usual way, so that if I become like the object I acquire the same power of material interaction with other objects; if, e.g., the paint is spilt on me I can whiten other objects too and if I become wetter by absorbing moisture some moisture can be extracted from me. Williams [1965] discusses F3 sympathetically; Hirst [1965] presents some non-fatal criticisms.
13. F3 cannot understand 'form' in Aristotle's usual way. For the form he recognizes in the *Metaphysics* cannot exist (if it is the form of a sensible object) without matter, and apparently the form is identical to the subject whose form it is; but Aristotle assumes that we can absorb a form of a sensible object without its matter; we do not absorb the material subject or state that has the form. We have a clearer conception of this form if we recall the claim that the builder (or other craftsman) has the form of the house (etc.) in his soul when he begins to build the house and that he uses this form to guide his process of building, *Met.* 1032b1, 11–14 (see 11n22). In natural generation the preexistent form is the form of the parent, and so is the sort of form that is a substance; but in the production of an artifact, no preexistent substantial form has a similar role. The builder has no actual house in his soul, since an actual house includes the matter; but he has the form without the matter.
14. Sceptical questions about similarity are raised by Goodman, [1968], 1–10, [1970]. I do not mean to be committing Aristotle to the claim that a clay model of Austria is more like Austria than a map is, or that in general degree of resemblance distinguishes pictures from (e.g.) diagrams, or that

degree of similarity explains degree of accuracy or provides some independent test of it.

15. Such 'sensitivity' falls short of 'registration' as Bennett describes it, [1976], 46–59; his account of registration includes the aspect of content that is essential to Aristotelian perception (see esp. 48, 54 on the non-accidental relation between P and 'a registers that P').

16. Perhaps some complex machines, e.g. computers and robots, might meet F3; but they do not necessarily raise an objection to F3. If a machine is complicated enough to justify us in explaining its behaviour by the content of its states, and not merely by their physical interactions (as we might 'deceive' a plant by heating it), then we may legitimately wonder whether it is not aware of the features that are the content of these states.

17. In the *DA* Aristotle treats perception as a potentiality of the soul. He recognizes that functions of the soul belong to the animal, 402a9–10, and to the body, 403a3–25; but he declines to discuss functions common to soul and body, i.e. the physiological aspects of perception and desire, 433b19–21; cf. *PA* 643a35–b1. The *PN*, however, takes perception to be a function common to the soul and the body, 436a6–10, b1–8, because it supplies the empirical and physiological detail omitted in the *DA*.

18. The formal character of Aristotle's account makes it reasonable that he normally distinguishes senses by their objects, 422b1–7, 23, 423b27–424a2. When he refers to a temptation to distinguish senses by their organs, 423a17–21, he does not endorse it. (Contrast Sorabji [1971], 85–92.) Some of Grice's objections to individuation by objects [1962], 136–8, raise questions about the tenability of Aristotle's claims about the coincidental perception by one sense of the objects of another. Grice adds introspectible difference to Aristotle's criteria. His argument is challenged by Coady [1974], who also adds some functional criteria, 121–5, that are not Aristotle's, but fit Aristotle's teleology well.

19. Aristotle sometimes speaks of 'the perceptive', *to aisthêtikon*, as one of the parts of the soul. The parts of the soul are its different faculties or potentialities; see 413a4, 413b14, 414a31, 432a18. The perceptive faculty is intended to satisfy F1 (418a5–6), F2 (422a7, b15–16), and F3 (424a17–19). This faculty is distinguished from the organ of perception, the *aisthêtêrion*; the organ is the primary bearer of the faculty (424a24–5), since that is where the faculty belongs (423b30–1, 426b9). Hence Aristotle applies the formulae of perception to the organ as well as to the faculty, 423b30–1, 425b23–4.

20. Since the organ is composed of remote matter that has ordinary perceptible qualities, it will itself have these qualities; and if we can guess the sorts of qualities that are needed for absorbing the immaterial form, we can guess that the organ has these qualities. Knowledge of the proximate matter may allow us to infer some of the properties (at least disjunctively) of the remote matter. (Cf. *Phys.* 200a30–b8, and § 59.) But Aristotle does not imply that if the object literally has a perceptible quality, it follows from that fact alone that the organ has the same perceptible quality. We need not treat the formulae of perception as extravagant a priori physiology.

Aristotle argues that to perceive an object as hot or cold I must have an organ that is either cooler or warmer than the object—otherwise I would perceive no contrast. Similarly I would be unaware of an object as hard or soft if it were no harder or softer than my organ of touch, 424a2–5. Though the argument is dubious, it is strictly limited. Aristotle shows no sign of claiming that I become harder or softer when I perceive hardness or softness.

The claims about taste, smell, and hearing allow the same sort of limited explanation, 422a6–7, a34–b5, 420a3–7. The remarks about the organ of touch immediately follow the application of F2 to touch, 423b30–424a2; cf. 435a24–b3. My sense-faculty and sense-organ become 'formally' sharp when I touch something that pierces my skin; but this formal similarity does not imply that formally similar things share their causal properties. For similar reasons, the eye need not become coloured when it sees colour, any more than the builder's soul needs to acquire all the properties of a house when it acquires the immaterial form of a house. Contrast Sorabji [1971], 49n22. The evidence apparently committing him to such a claim about sight consists of general remarks about the faculty, 417a20, 418a3, 424a7, 18, b2, 425b22–4, 429a15, *PA* 653b24, or applications, such as we have seen, of the formulae of perception to the organ, e.g. 435a20–4, or of the much more restricted claims about the physical features of the organs of taste, smell, and touch, 423a7, 13–17, b30, *HA* 491b21.

21. The *DA* does not state the doctrine of the *PN*, that the heart is the central organ of perception, or that he thinks all the perceptive faculties are united there, *PN* 467b13–468a1, 468a20–5, 469a2–b1. See Ross [1955], 8–12. In the *DA* references to the heart are incidental and unimportant, 403a21, 408b8, 420b26, 432b31. Aristotle recognizes that the organ of touch must be internal and cannot be the skin, 423b1–26; but only the *PN* connects touch with the heart, 438b30–439a5. He recognizes that the senses are unified and that there is a single 'mean', the intermediate condition required for perception, *DA* 431a19, but does not say that it must be a single organ. (The *eschaton* in 431a19 need not be a single organ, i.e. some single bit of remote matter.) The *PN*, however, finds the unified sense-organ in the heart, 459b6–8, 469a10.

Silence about the heart in the *DA* does not imply any conflict with the *PN*. (Contrast Block [1961]. See Hardie [1964], 66f; but see also 13n33 above.) The formal account of the faculty of perception does not imply that the material basis for the unity of the faculty must be found in a single material organ.

22. Aristotle tries to show how one physically plausible account might meet the a priori causal conditions for perception; if no physically plausible account seemed possible, we would have some reason to believe that perception is not possible either. If we reject Aristotle's empirical physiology, we will reasonably believe that some more plausible physiology will satisfy the causal component of perception better. But if this is our view, we are accepting Aristotle's formal account, not rejecting it.

23. Malcolm [1968], 62–73, offers this sort of argument as an objection to the 'conceivability of mechanism'. It seems to offer no objection, however, to

any mechanistic theory that does not seek to eliminate mental states (contrast Malcolm, 53–5; but see also 72). It is a far more serious objection to some eliminative accounts. Churchland [1984], 48, briefly dismisses a less plausible argument somewhat similar to Malcolm's (he argues against the view that an eliminative materialist claim cannot be meaningful or true; he does not reply to the argument that even if it is true, we cannot justifiably believe that it is).

24. Aristotle describes perceptible objects in realist terms at 418a3, 31, 419a8, 19, 421a26, 422a10, 16, b15, 423b27, 424a22, 425b22. He uses 'white' etc. (as in other works; see 4n5, 10n5, 45) for the perceptible quality and for the subject that is perceptible qua white (see 418a21–3, 425a24–7, reading *alla to leukon* in a26, perhaps supported by Themistius 82.10).

   On coincidental objects see Cashdollar [1973] (who claims on Aristotle's behalf that coincidental perception involves the senses alone, but does not show that Aristotle is entitled to the claim). See also Block [1969].

25. Aristotle takes the qualities of bodies rather than the bodies themselves to be the objects of perception, because he wants to isolate the explanatory role of perceptible objects. We often say that we perceive bodies themselves, but on further analysis this turns out not to be the full explanation. I may say I see the tree over there; but I can be asked for a further explanation: 'How do you see the tree?' I will answer that I see the tree by seeing a green shape. Each of the initial perceptual judgments turns out to rest on an inference from a more immediate judgment together with further information (that this shape belongs to a tree, that tea produces this sort of stain, etc.), and the more immediate judgment partly explains the inferential judgment. Aristotle wants to find the qualities in which this sequence of explanations ends—some qualities that we simply perceive and do not perceive because we more directly perceive some other qualities.

26. The appeal to explanatory asymmetry may help to answer Hussey's objection [1983], 65, that if one simply considers which subject the *kinêsis* is the actuality of, one has no reason to prefer the patient over the agent.

27. On the teleological conception of potentiality see § 123.

28. My perceiving the rock is not simply my being affected by the rock; see § 160.

29. Aristotle argues as follows, 425b26–426a1: (1) The actuality of the object is the actuality of the perceiver. (2) In perception the perceiver becomes actually red (e.g.). (3) Hence in perception the object becomes actually red. (4) Therefore the object is actually red only when it is perceived. The previous claims about perception and actualities support (1) and (2), and Aristotle thinks (2) implies (3). Once (3) is conceded, and we agree that the change is really in the patient, the perceiver, we seem to have to agree that the object's being actually red is an event that happens only when it is perceived, and that it is primarily a state of the perceiver; the object's being actually red consists in its being perceived as red.

   425b26–426a1 suggests that actual sound happens only when it is perceived; contrast 419b4–11, 420a7–9. In iii 2 Aristotle generalizes the account to all sensibles, so that, e.g., only seen colour is actual colour, and unseen objects are merely potentially coloured, 426a8–19; contrast 419a1–8.

30. If Aristotle uses 'actually red' in a rather eccentric way, simply to mean 'being perceived as red', without wanting to deny that in the ordinary sense the object was red before it was perceived, then it is hard to understand his answer to sceptics in 426a20–6—if he is using 'actually red' in his eccentric sense, he misunderstands their claim. Kosman [1975], 513f, and Lear [1987], 157–60, seem to me to underestimate the difficulties raised by Aristotle's claim.

31. In *Met.* 1010b30–1011a2 Aristotle agrees that without perceivers there would be neither perceptibles, *aisthêta*, nor perceptions, *aisthêmata*, since these are an affection of the perceiver, but insists that the subjects that produce perception would still exist without it. In 1047a6–8 he urges that the Megarians must agree with Protagoras, and say that nothing has any perceptible quality when it is not being perceived. In the *DA* Aristotle distinguishes two claims: (1) Nothing is potentially white (etc.) without potential perception. (2) Nothing is actually white without actual perception. Apparently he agrees with the Megarians and Protagoras about (2) and disagrees with them over (1). But in *Met.* iv he seems to agree about (1) also. He gives an odd reason for accepting (1), that perceptibles and perceptions are an affection of the perceiver, 1010b33. Even Aristotle's most stringent account of potentiality, requiring the existence of breathers if air is breathable, *Top.* 138b3–5, does not imply that being perceptible is simply an affection of a perceiver. The concession in *Met.* iv seems to bring Aristotle closer to Protagoras than he wants to be in *Met.* ix.

32. Aristotle might claim: (1) if I see, I am always right in thinking I see colour; (2) if I see red, there is some actual red object that I see; (3) if I think I see colour, I am right; (4) if I think I see (e.g.) red, I am always right. While (1) might be defensible at 418a11–16, it does not fit 427b8–16 (since (1) does not distinguish perception from the corresponding 'infallibility' of appearance and thought). Neither (1) nor (2) fits 428b18–30 (the qualification at b19 would be inappropriate if (2) were meant), and here Aristotle seems to endorse (4), not merely (3); cf. 430b29–30, *PN* 442b8, *Met.* 1010b14–25.

   For different accounts of Aristotle's doctrine see Hamlyn [1959], Kenny [1967], 190–3, criticized by Scholar [1971]. Block's discussion, [1961a], makes the difficulties especially clear, but underestimates Aristotle's commitment to subjectivism.

33. Perhaps we might say (with Epicurus; see Taylor [1980]), that the wall is brown now, whenever it looks brown, and reject the assumption that it will continue to have this colour in normal daylight. But Aristotle cannot accept it; for he does not think something loses its colour in the dark, 419a1–8, and he has no better reason to say that it changes its colour in different light.

34. Aristotle confines his claims to the special senses, perhaps because the common sense depends on the special senses and on inference from them; the right combination, e.g., of sight and touch produces the awareness of movement. On Aristotle's view the reports of sight and touch are infallible, but inferences from them may not be. Hence the reports of the common

sense result from fallible inferences based on infallible reports by the special senses.

35. Aristotle cannot remove sceptical doubts about the external object, the *hupokeimenon*, as opposed to the perceiver's condition, *pathos*. See 9n22.

36. See § 17, 7n5.

37. In 428b19–22 'x perceives the F' must create an opaque context, involving belief *that* this is the son of Cleon, since otherwise the question of error would not arise. 425a24–7 also suggests an opaque reading, while 418a20–2 allows a transparent reading.

38. Aristotle rejects three views: (1) The common sense is a special sense on its own. (2) Common sensibles are simply objects of the five recognized senses. (3) They are simply coincidental objects of perception.

    He agrees that each of the five senses perceives the common sensibles only coincidentally, 425a14–15. But he rejects any special sense for them, 425a20–7. A sixth special sense would be inconsistent with the role of the five senses. If (1) were true, then the role of sight in perception of motion would be similar to its role in the perception of sweetness; sight is dispensable for the recognition of sweetness, in a way that the special senses are not dispensable for the recognition of motion, 425a20–7. (2) under-estimates the role of the senses working together, 425a27–30. (3) makes the common sensibles coincidental objects of sense only in the way the son of Cleon is, 425a24–7. Aristotle assumes that we perceive movement, not just some sensible quality from which we infer the movement.

    In 425a21 *idian* = a special sixth sense. In a28 *idia* = objects of the recognized five senses. Torstrik's [1862] deletion in a29–30 (followed in OCT) is reasonable. On the common sense see further Block [1964], [1965].

39. Aristotle distinguishes (as Hamlyn [1968], 128, and [1968a], stresses, and indeed overstresses; see Modrak [1981]), but also closely connects, two functions of sense: (1) Common sense allows us to perceive the common sensibles. (2) Unified sense allows each sense to perceive coincidentally the proper objects of the other senses, 425a30–b4, 426b17–427a14. He does not show why the unifying faculty might not be appearance rather than sense.

40. Aristotle asks whether second-order perception of sight belongs to sight or to some other sense. He offers two answers: (1) We can say that we perceive by sight in more than one way, e.g. we perceive that it is dark because we cannot see anything, 425b20–2. (2) What sees is indeed coloured, in so far as the sense-organ receives the form without the matter, and to that extent acquires the colour of the object.

    (2) implies that the faculty of sight acquires a new condition, 'immaterial coloration', when it and the organ receive the form without the matter; in second-order perception and in appearance this is the condition we are aware of. We are aware of the state the faculty is in when it receives form without matter. And we are aware of this 'by sight' in the way suggested by the first solution; for it is the exercise of sight that makes us aware of the condition we are in. The two solutions complement each other, and do not compete. On second-order perception see further Kosman [1975].

41. I take *phantasia* to be present whenever perception is part of a teleological explanation of an action. Schofield's attempt to confine it to non-paradigmatic sensory experience, [1978], 106, 109n20, appeals especially to 428a12–15 (see 114), which does not seem to me to exclude the presence of *phantasia* in accurate perception. On the other hand, I hesitate to speak, as Nussbaum does, [1978], 258–60, 268f, of *phantasia* as active or interpretative, since it is difficult to attribute these characteristics to the appearances of non-rational perceivers (indeed, this difficulty partly explains why *phantasia*, rather than anything more explicitly active or interpretative, is ascribed to such perceivers). *Phantasia* is also discussed by Rees [1971].

42. I retain *eti . . .d'ou*, 428a22–4 (deleted by OCT); it makes clear the dependence of *doxa* on *logos*. I take *akolouthein* in a logical rather than a temporal sense. On belief and evidence see Bennett [1964], 52–8.

43. Aristotle recognizes that there are significant combinations that lack a truth-value, and mentions a prayer as a significant utterance (*logos*) that is neither true nor false, *DI* 17a2–4. When we pray 'Thy will be done' and when we assert 'Thy will is done', we entertain the same proposition 'Thy will is done', but only in the second case do we believe and assert it.

44. Aristotle's remarks do not commit him to anti-realism. He remarks that perception depends on external objects, while it is up to us to think when we choose, since knowledge is of universals and these are 'in a way' in the soul, 417b19–26. The attitude to realism depends on 'in a way'. It would be true to say that since thinking is of universals and does not depend on causal confrontation on a particular occasion, universals must in some way be available to be thought about by the soul. If this is all Aristotle means by speaking of them being in the soul in a way, then his claim may be accepted.

    Aristotle applies the formulae of perception to thought, claiming that when we think the faculty in a way becomes the object, 431b20–432a3; if I acquire the form, the object is in me to the extent that a state of mine expresses a quality of the object. Such a claim does not imply the rejection of realism about perceptible qualities or about universals. On claims that do conflict with realism see § 164.

45. To this extent Aristotle can fairly claim that intellect has no bodily organ, 429a24–7. If he infers that the operation of intellect requires no bodily process at all, or that it requires non-bodily processes, he is not justified in this anti-materialist claim (discussed by Hartman [1977], ch.6, who is perhaps too quick to see evidence of anti-materialism).

46. The thoughts that are not combinations of thoughts, but the simple elements from which the combinations are formed, 430a26–8, need not be acquired before we are able to combine thoughts.

47. See Kant, *KrV* A100–3. Kant allows that non-conceptual creatures can associate perceptions (Kant's 'intuitions') without the capacities that he ascribes to creatures aware of the temporal character of their experience.

48. Davidson [1975], 163f, argues from the indeterminacy of the alleged beliefs of non-rational subjects to a sceptical conclusion about their having beliefs. Reasons for hesitation in attributing very precise propositional structure to

beliefs are given by Stalnaker [1984], ch.4, who uses some arguments similar to Davidson's to argue that indeterminacy of content may be more widespread than Davidson suggests.

Perhaps the distinction between content and structure partly explains Malcolm's distinction between thinking that p (taken to be possible for animals) and having the thought that p (possible only for rational subjects); see [1972], 49–53. The non-propositional (in the structural sense) character of animal feelings is discussed by Vendler [1972], 152–63.

49. Abstraction is discussed by Mueller [1970], Lear [1982], 162–75. (Cf. 8n43.) The parallel between the mathematical and the psychological cases is not exact. In the psychological case, as opposed to the mathematical case, the 'poorer' objects with 'fewer' properties (i.e. the animal psychological states) really exist in separation from the 'richer' objects. In the mathematical case the poorer objects are used to describe the richer, and in the psychological case the richer are used to describe the poorer.

50. Aristotle insists, against Plato, *Rep.* 602cd, *Sph.* 264ab, that appearance need not involve belief. See Lycos [1964], Chisholm [1957], 43–54. But we still need to distinguish a non-rational perceiver's merely being aware of something from the state that Aristotle himself regards as analogous to assertion, 431a8–17. The problem about truth and falsity of appearances is discussed by Engmann [1976], whose solution does not seem to me to cope with Aristotle's reasons for attributing something analogous to propositional truth and falsity to non-rational perceivers.

51. The Stoics recognize different uses of '*aisthêsis*' (*SVF* ii.71); but if it is used in its veridical sense they take it to involve assent (ii.74, 75, 78).

52. See § 25.

CHAPTER 15

1. 432b19–26 suggests that some animals are (1) stationary, and (2) without desire. But 432a15–18 challenges (1), and 414b1–6 challenges (2) (see 14n3). Since stationary animals can move and change different parts of themselves in response to their perceptions, Aristotle, quite reasonably, thinks they must have desire. His broader conception of the extent of desire seems more reasonable.

2. Aristotle challenges the division of the soul into rational, emotional, and appetitive parts, and the division into rational and non-rational parts—if bipartition or tripartition is taken to divide the soul into separable parts, 432a20, b2. He argues that the difference relied on by his opponents multiplies separable parts beyond their intentions; if we look for the sorts of differences that justify these divisions we find many more separable parts, even an indefinitely large number, 432a24–31. Aristotle does not reject either of the two Platonic divisions; he simply argues that the parts cannot be separable.

He therefore says nothing in the *DA* against his acceptance of the

Platonic divisions in his ethical works, and says nothing in the ethical works to provoke the criticisms in the *DA*. Contrast Gauthier [1970], ii.56 on 1098a3–4 (who takes the bipartition asserted there to conflict with the *DA*); Rees [1957], 118, [1960], 197f (who takes the *DA* to attack the division of the soul accepted in the *Ethics*, though he appeals (and is fairly criticized by Gauthier ii.92f) to 1102a23–6 to reject chronological inferences); Fortenbaugh [1975], 26–8 (distinguishing Aristotle's biological psychology (*DA*) from his political and ethical psychology).

3. On the connexions of belief and desire see Geach [1957], 8f, Chisholm [1957], 181–5, Davidson [1970], 221f.

4. 433a1–8 suggests, by appeal to continence and incontinence, that thought and desire seem to be movers, i.e. (1) sometimes thought, sometimes desire, seems to be sufficient for movement. But a9–26 suggests that (2) both (if 'thought' is taken to cover both reasoning and appearance) are always necessary for movement. 433a13–21 gives the argument (similar to that in *EN* 1139a31-b4) for accepting (2) rather than (1). The role of thought and desire in the *DA* is discussed further by Hudson [1981].

5. We might, for instance, say that sometimes watering the plants makes them grow, and sometimes fertilizing them makes them grow, but sometimes each treatment is insufficient to make them grow. We discover that neither watering nor fertilizing is the real explanation of growth. The real explanation will refer to all the relevant conditions of soil and atmosphere; sometimes we produce these by adding water, sometimes by adding fertilizer. If this is a fair parallel, then we would need an account of the conditions in which sometimes thought and sometimes desire seems to be the mover. (It is important to state this claim so that it does not commit Aristotle to the belief that a cause must be a sufficient condition; see § 57.)

6. We often say 'I thought I should do it though I didn't want to', and someone who claims that if we did it we must really have wanted to after all is extending the ordinary use of 'want'. Such an extended use of 'want' is defended by Goldman [1970], 53–5, Brandt and Kim [1963], 426–32, Davidson [1963], 4 (who speaks of pro-attitudes). Nagel [1970a], 27–33, argues that the extended use is trivial and theoretically useless; but see Charles [1984], 88.

7. 433a21–2 raises the counterfactual possibility that intellect and desire might both be movers (i.e. independently of each other). Aristotle replies that in this case they would be two species of a genus (so Themistius 119.9–12, Philoponus 585.18–21), and we would need some account of the generic mover responsible for goal-directed movement.

8. In claiming that *nous* is always correct while desire and appearance are not, 433a26–7, Aristotle presumably intends *nous* more narrowly than *logismos*, since he does not say that *logismos* is always correct. Correct reasoning = *nous* (cf. Philoponus 585.25, *ho alêthinos nous*; Themistius 119.17, *ho ge kuriôs*) presumably finds the actual good, and incorrect reasoning or appearance finds only the apparent good.

9. On the relation of the appearance to the actual good of the creature see 16n42, Dennett [1969], 177–9, Davidson [1970], 221–3.

10. On 433b8–9 see n20.
11. On this contrast between human beings and other animals see also § 215.
12. At *Treatise* ii.3.3, 415f, Hume makes clear the purely technical character of reason, by denying that reason can be an 'original influence'; it is far less clear that Aristotle denies this. The limited and less-than-Aristotelian scope of practical reason in Hume is explained by Falk [1975], 14–17 (who describes Hume's account as a modified Aristotelian account). A much fuller and fairer discussion of Hume than mine is Sturgeon [HRP].
13. In Hume's view, we know whether or not we have passions, and what passions we have, directly, by introspection; and no limits can be assumed for their contents or objects or mutual relations. See *Treatise* ii.1.2, 277: 'The passions of pride and humility being simple and uniform impressions, 'tis impossible, we can ever, by a multitude of words, give a just definition of them, or indeed of any of the passions.' In understanding passions we look for ideas 'presented to the mind', 278. Hume is influenced by a Cartesian conception of mental states, and so does not consider any restriction of their content that might result from their role in the explanation of action. Davidson [1976], 278, argues that this is an over-simplification of Hume's view; but it is one aspect that fits well with Hume's general conception of mental states.
14. On dialectic, common beliefs, and first philosophy see § 95.
15. On the limitations of animals see § 171.
16. Action requires a so-called 'practical syllogism'— a universal belief about the kind of thing that is good or pleasant, a particular belief that this particular thing is that kind of thing, and the resulting belief that this particular thing is good or pleasant, *EN* 1147a25–31, *DA* 434a16–21. On the assumption that we desire what is good or pleasant, this concluding belief results in action. (I agree with Charles [1984], 91, in distinguishing the conclusion of a practical syllogism from action on the conclusion.) This account of the relation of beliefs to action cannot apply directly to non-rational animals without beliefs. In them appetite says only 'I should drink'; and when perception or appearance says 'this is drink', they drink at once, *MA* 701a32–3. Though past experience of sweet things affects an animal's present awareness of this thing as sweet, Aristotle does not agree that the effect results from inference.
17. In speaking of 'measuring by a single standard' Aristotle commits himself to some form of commensurability referring to the good. Charles [1984], 134, argues convincingly, against Burnyeat [1980], 91, that Aristotle consistently accepts a version of commensurability.
18. When Aristotle suggests that if there is only one apparent means, we consider the means to that, *EN* 1112b17–20, he omits cases where deliberation might show that the cost is morally or prudentially prohibitive (unless he includes these under impossibility, 1112b24–8).
19. See Hume, *Treatise* ii.3.3, 416.
20. I take a parenthesis to begin at *phainetai*, 433b8, not at *ho men*, b7. Probably Aristotle means not that appetite always makes something appear good *haplôs*, but that this is another effect of not foreseeing the future (as Hicks,

561, says, a second mistake). See further Irwin [1986], 81, commenting on Charles [1984] 145.

21. Themistius 120.10–17 tries to restrict the point to human agents, by interpreting 'perception of time' very narrowly, so as to deny it to non-rational perceivers.

22. A desire based on deliberation about the satisfaction of an appetite is not a decision; an incontinent person may deliberate about the satisfaction of his incontinent desire, and act on the resulting deliberative desire, but he still fails to act on his decision, *EN* 1111b13–15, 1142b18–20. Aristotle distinguishes wish from the other types of desire by placing it in the rational part, 432b5, and describing its object as the good rather than the pleasant; that is why decision is not concerned with the pleasant, 1111b16–18, but with the good.

I follow Anscombe [1965], 148, against Charles [1984], 151–3, in taking an agent's *boulêsis* to express her conception of happiness as a whole; that is the best explanation of why the incontinent person does not act on a *boulêsis*, and therefore does not act on a *prohairesis*. (The connexion between *prohairesis* and *boulêsis* is still clearer if we follow the authorities that read *kata tên boulêsin* in 1113a12.) Charles's objections do not clearly explain what makes a desire a *boulêsis* rather than a non-rational desire.

23. See § 191.

24. Following most critics (see e.g. Cooper [1975], 64n), I take *telos*, 1142b33, to be the antecedent of *hou*. The passage should not be taken to exclude the possibility that correct deliberation about what conduces to the end will also form the correct grasp of the end.

25. For fuller explanation and defence see § 191–3.

26. See § 215.

27. The *energeia* referred to in 1100a1 is fine action proceeding from a virtuous character, 1099b31–2. Since a virtuous character requires the right *prohairesis*, and a rational soul (cf. Aspasius 27.11–13), and this requires a conception of one's life and one's good (see n22), animals and children cannot have it.

28. *Met.* 1046a36–b13 contrasts non-rational potentialities of inanimate things with the potentialities involving reason in animate things. 1047b31–1048a11 contrasts the congenital potentialities, e.g. perception, with the potentialities acquired 'by habit and reason', 1047b34. Aristotle has no clear place for potentialities that are acquired by training in non-rational subjects (or by non-rational training in rational subjects). If he recognizes the possibility of such training, but refuses to call it *ethismos*, then *ethismos* includes some rational component. (On this point see Sorabji [1973], and Burnyeat [1980].)

29. *EE* 1224a28–30 denies *prattein* (i.e. rational action) to animals, but neither denies nor affirms that their movements are voluntary. It is not clear which condition for voluntariness they would fail (perhaps *eph' heautô(i) on*, 1225b8).

30. Aristotle suggests that we praise the good person and his virtue for his actions and achievements, and that we praise the strong person or the good

runner for being well equipped for something good and excellent, *EN* 1101b12–18. This remark does not show whether the good runner must have made himself good by his own efforts; when Aristotle says we praise him 'because of his (i) being of a certain sort by nature, *pephukenai*, and (ii) being in some state in relation to something good and excellent', 1101b16–18, he might be taken to suggest that someone's natural, non-voluntary condition is a ground for praise. But such natural talent would be a capacity, and Aristotle seems to distinguish capacities from the conditions that are praised, 1101b12; cf. 1105b28–1106a10. If this is right, we must not take clause (i) to imply a condition wholly antecedent to the agent's efforts, or else we must take (i) and (ii) to state two distinct components of the condition that is praised (perhaps suggested by Aspasius 32.30–1).

31. Hume, *Inquiry*, 98. See Irwin [1980], 134f.

32. If 1111a22–4 means that an action is voluntary and I am responsible for it if it is caused neither by force nor by ignorance, the account cannot be quite right. For I may know I am digesting my food without digesting it voluntarily; my knowledge makes no difference. Even if it makes some difference, even if it causes my action, the action does not thereby become voluntary. My knowledge that I have eaten something poisoned may make me so anxious that my digestion is upset, but I need not have upset my digestion voluntarily. Aristotle needs to say that my knowledge is not only a cause, but also a cause because it is a reason for my action. See further Irwin [1980], 122f.

33. If I am pushed into you and knock you over when I wanted to knock you over in any case, we might say that I contribute a desire capable of causing the action, even though in fact my contribution was unused (I may contribute money towards the erection of a building even if my contribution is not needed). This sort of contribution explains why forced action is always painful (1110b11–13; cf. *EE* 1224b8–16). Sauvé's persuasive discussion in [1987], ch.4, reaches a different conclusion.

34. We are to imagine, e.g., that Oedipus killed the old man because he did not know it was his father, but when he finds out he does not mind; though he would have wanted to avoid killing his father, he would have wanted this for the wrong reason, since he does not mind that his father is dead. The result is not contrary to his desire, though it should be.

35. If the internal origin is sufficient for voluntariness, then actions caused by ignorance cannot have their origin in the agent himself. The event that was Oedipus' ignorant slaying of his father was also a voluntary action of Oedipus'—in so far as it was killing the old man; and so the event had its origin in Oedipus. However, in so far as it is killing his father, it does not have its origin in Oedipus—for his choice was not to kill his father, but to kill the old man. Aristotle is justified in claiming that the origin of the event, in so far as it was the killing of his father, was Oedipus' ignorance, and not Oedipus himself. (For such 'negative' causes cf. *Phys.* 195a11–14.)

36. The demand for an internal origin should cover actions that are just like forced actions except that they are what the agent wants to do. In such a case, Aristotle must claim, the agent makes a causal contribution that just

happens to go unused in this case, so that he acts voluntarily. If this is right, then 'origin' must be taken to include not only the actual efficient cause, but also the sufficient causal contribution that is made but not used. Hence, despite first appearances, the origin of the willing prisoner's imprisonment is in himself and not entirely external. The two apparently distinct conditions, external causation and non-contribution by the agent, are really parts of a single condition for forced action.

37. If capacity for decision is a condition for responsible agency, the condition can be modified to provide a condition of responsibility for an action. Just as it will be pointless to treat an agent incapable of decision as a responsible agent, it will be pointless to treat him as responsible for actions he cannot affect by decision. See further Irwin [1980].

38. On this passage see 16n23.

CHAPTER 16

1. The text in 1214b34–1215a3 is dubious. Aristotle imposes some restriction on indiscriminate consideration of the views of the many. But I do not agree with the emendations (accepted by Rackham [1935], and Woods [1982]) that require him to restrict his attention to the views of the wise—a restriction unparalleled in any other work. On *exetazein* see 2n38.

2. Teichmüller [1879], iii.12–35 (see also Ando [1958], 169–73), argues that ethics (the discipline practised in the *Ethics*) is the same as *phronêsis*, and is therefore practical and deliberative. I agree, but I do not follow Teichmüller (see n20) in inferring that ethics must therefore exclude the appeal to other areas of philosophy that I take to be characteristic of strong dialectic.

3. At 1094b19–27 (no *EE* parallel, as Devereux [1986], 498f, points out) Aristotle disclaims any ambition of 'exact' demonstration in ethics, because ethical premisses have to be 'usual', not necessary. The implications of this remark are not clear. (1) While practically useful moral rules may have exceptions (1103b34–1104a11, 1164b22–1165a4), it is not clear why, e.g., 'It is always finer to be brave than to be cowardly' should have exceptions. (2) Usual premisses do not always exclude demonstration (see *APo* i 30; cf. 5n30).

   This passage, then, does not itself rule out ethical demonstration. On the other hand, Aristotle never contemplates demonstration of ethical conclusions, and never suggests that *nous* grasps first principles. (See further Irwin [1981a], 197n, and Allan [1961].)

4. On 1172b36 see 2n71.

5. My account of Aristotle's theory is mainly derived from the *EN* rather than the *MM* or *EE* (which I take to represent, in that order, earlier stages of Aristotle's ethical thought). At some points (e.g. the function argument, the defence of friendship) the *EN* relies more clearly on metaphysical premisses; but I have not tried to compare the works in detail on this point. The remarks on dialectic are somewhat fuller in the *EE* (including the

'Common Books', *EN* v–vii, which I take to originate in the *EE*) than in the *EN*, but I see no doctrinal difference about it. I am less sure that the method of the *EE* is the same as that of the *EN* at every point, partly for some of the reasons suggested by Allan [1961], but I am not sure how deep the differences are. I think both *Ethics* share the aim of finding *archai*; contrast Kullmann [1974], 227f. On some questions about the ethical works see further Irwin [1980a], Cooper [1981], commenting on Kenny [1978], [1979].

6. On the dialectical character of Aristotle's ethics see Burnet [1900], pp. v, xxxix–xlii (who assigns an important role to intuition, since he has a limited view of dialectic), Cooper [1975], 58–71 (who, like Teichmüller (see n2) overestimates the difference between dialectical and deliberative reasoning), Hardie [1980], 35–45, 366–8 (who underestimates the difficulty of finding demonstrations in ethics). The difficulty about dialectical arguments claiming to reach objectively true conclusions is sharply raised, with special reference to Rawls [1971], by Dworkin [1973], 27–36. A similar point is made by Barker [1906]; see n20.

7. On scepticism see Burnyeat [1980a], esp. 41f, and on moral scepticism Annas [1986a].

8. Burnyeat [1980], 81, 90 (n15) argues from 1179b4–31 that Aristotle does not intend the *Ethics* to persuade anyone who lacks a good upbringing that the virtuous life is worth while; the function argument, e.g. 'is not an argument that would appeal to anyone who really doubted or denied that he should practice the virtues' (90). Whether or not this is true (contrast *Pol.* 1332b1–8), we should not infer that Aristotle does not intend his argument to prove to any rational person's satisfaction that a critic of the virtues is mistaken, and that it is bad for a person to be vicious (cf. ix 4, esp. 1166b26–8). If we are too corrupt to be persuaded by a proof that ought to persuade us, that is a fault in us, not in the proof. There is no good reason to think that Aristotle believes that only people with a good upbringing ought to be persuaded by his arguments.

9. On the *kalon* see further Engberg-Pederson [1983], ch.2, Irwin [1985a], and § 237 below.

10. On Plato's correction of common beliefs see Irwin [1977a], 208f.

11. See § 148.

12. Plato, *Rep.* 353b–d, *MM* 1184b22–7, *EE* 1218b37–1219a28, appeal to x's function primarily to explain x's goodness, i.e. x's virtue, rather than x's good, i.e. x's welfare; and then they have difficulty in connecting goodness with welfare. (The difficulty is stressed and discussed by Wilkes [1978], 354–6.) 1097b22–1098a7, by contrast, connects x's function directly with x's good, i.e. welfare.

13. The prospectus at *EN* 1181b2–23 sets out these tasks. We should, first, discuss any suggestions by our predecessors; second, consider from the collected constitutions the means of preserving and destroying cities and constitutions, and why some cities conduct their political affairs finely and others do not; and, third, find the best state, its constitution, laws, and habits.

The three parts of the prospectus correspond roughly to Books ii, v–vi, and vii–viii. Nothing explicitly corresponds to i, iii, and iv. But this will not matter much if the three unmentioned books clearly forward the plan described for the work. This point undermines Newman's arguments, [1887] i.3, to show that the *Pol.* does not follow the plan of the prospectus.

The aim of finding the best state and constitution is mentioned at the beginning of Book ii, 1260b27–36, and of Book vii, 1323a14–16, but is not introduced to justify the discussion in Book i, or in Books iii–vi. Book i is introduced without any explanation at all. Book iii is addressed to someone 'reasoning about the constitution, what and what sort each is', 1274b32 (cf. 1260b12, 1272b27, 1288b3, 35, 1293b29, 1329a40). Its discussion is a basis for the account both of the best state and of the more generally practicable states (Newman, i.226, iii.130f). In Book iv Aristotle elaborately justifies his discussion of actual as well as ideal constitutions, 1288b10–1289a7, by arguing that the science studying the best constitution should also study the best that is suitable for most people and the best that is possible if certain restrictions are taken for granted, 1289b11–26. This general aim provides the justification for the inquiry into political changes, begun in v, 1301a19–25. The prospectus in the *EN* gave a reason for studying actual constitutions—that this would prepare us for the study of the best constitution. But *Pol.* iv suggests that actual constitutions should be studied for their own sake, as an appropriate part of political science. The transition from the inquiry into the ideal, recalled at the end of iii, 1288b2–4, to the study of the actual at the beginning of iv is especially harsh. Not surprisingly, it has encouraged the suggestion that Aristotle intended Books vii–viii to follow iii. (Zeller [1897], ii.502–4 summarizes the arguments for this view.) But if we transposed the books we would break the order prescribed in the prospectus, which makes a study of actual states a necessary preliminary to the study of the best state. I agree with Ross [1957], 5–7, in preferring the ms. order for this reason. Contrast Brandt [1974], 196–200, who argues unconvincingly that the *EN* does not refer to the extant *Pol.*

Four different aims, then, are stated in the *Pol.*: (1) The study of the best constitution. (2) The technical and therapeutic aim of repairing actual constitutions. (3) Finding the best constitution, given certain assumptions about the circumstances. (4) Understanding the parts, growth, varieties, and functions of the city (biological analogies: 1252a17–26, 1290b25–38, *PA* 644a29–32). On the relation between these aims see further 21n38, Rowe [1977].

14. See 8n4.
15. On assumptions see 20n16.
16. Sometimes Aristotle argues from common beliefs, and tries to solve puzzles that they raise. Much of the argument in *Pol.* i and iii proceeds by raising and solving puzzles, conforming to the advice of *EE* 1235b13–18; see *Pol.* 1253b14–23, 1255a3–4, 1258a19, 1259b22, 1275b34, 39, 1276a22, 1277b33 (showing that the previous questions have also been *aporiai*), 1281a11, b22, 1282a23, 32. In the empirical books, iv–vi, the characteristically dialectical method of raising and solving puzzles is much less frequent

than in i and iii. (On the different roles of aporetic argument see Newman [1887], i.352, 480, 490, ii.133, 387, iii.498.) While Books i and iii proceed largely by raising puzzles and by offering Aristotle's characteristic 'determination' or 'definition', *dihorismos*, to solve them, this method with its associated vocabulary largely drops out of iv–vii, though it reappears in vii with the discussion of education; see 1336b24–6, 1340b33–4. Book vii does not use puzzles in its ethical argument, since it is applying and summarizing principles that have already been worked out. (But see 1324a25, 1327a13; for *amphisbêtêsis* cf. 1274b34.) Puzzles are also out of place in the empirical books, since Aristotle is there applying the principles he has worked out by solving puzzles, and illustrating their application with detailed examples.

The *Pol.* never seems to use 'puzzle' in the way characteristic of, e.g., the *GA*, referring to cases where we just lack empirical information that is needed to answer a question. On this point the *Pol.* is closer to the philosophical than to the empirical works. See § 20.

17. Some of Aristotle's arguments might be accused of reliance on partisan assumptions that the other side have been given no reason to accept; see e.g. § 36.

18. See 1253b14–23, 1255a1–5, b4–5, 1257b5–30, 1259b21–1260a2, 1274b34–6, 1277a20–5. For the arbitrator see *Met.* 995b2–4, *DC* 279b3–12. The middle class plays this political role, 1297a5–6; see § 249.

19. Wood and Wood [1978] present an especially clear and crude attack on the conservative character of Aristotle's political theory. They claim that 'Aristotle's social and political ideas are fundamentally ideological, forged as weapons to be used in the political struggles of his age' (209). See the criticisms by Vlastos [1980], 345f. Some of their less unconvincing arguments rest on an exaggerated account of Aristotle's respect for received opinion in his philosophical method (216f). A much more just (indeed over-charitable) and accurate account of Aristotle from a Marxist point of view is presented by De Ste Croix [1981]; see 21n37.

20. Newman [1887], i.5, exaggerates the purely dialectical aspects of Aristotle's ethical and political method (appealing to 1097a28, 30, 34), though he also modifies his exaggerated claim (11–14). Teichmüller [1879], iii.352–7, argues more strongly that Aristotle has no right, within his own conception of practical inquiry, to rely as he does on his conclusions in metaphysics and natural philosophy, 356. See n2 above. Teichmüller takes an equally limited view of the capacities of dialectic.

Barker's account of Aristotle's method also makes it seem close to pure dialectic, [1906], 231: 'It is actual Greek practice, and contemporary Greek opinion, which form Aristotle's starting-point. . . . What he does is to generalize and to rationalize all these data in the light of a doctrine of Final Causes; and in the light of that doctrine he occasionally corrects or modifies the opinions and practices on which his theory is based.' Barker greatly underestimates the extent to which Aristotle corrects common beliefs.

Later Barker explains why he thinks pure dialectic is the special method appropriate to practical as opposed to theoretical science: '. . . its subject is political institutions moulded, worked and directed by men's minds—

alterable by human thinking, and by human thinking made what they are. And thus while a theoretical science like physics, dealing with things eternal, need not so much be treated—though by Aristotle it *is* treated—with reference to previous research or opinions, a practical science like politics must always be discussed with regard to opinions, because it is constituted by them', 252. Barker acknowledges that Aristotle does not mark the distinction of method to which Barker refers; and the reason Barker gives is not a good one in any case. (Practical science studies the tendency of human institutions to promote the human good; and it is not clear how human beliefs constitute the subject-matter of this study.)

Barker also recognizes (as the reference to final causes in the first passage above suggests) another side of Aristotle's method: 'And here the second, or a priori, element of discussion enters. For Aristotle applies to opinion metaphysical principles of his own, principles elsewhere established, to elicit the deeper meaning of opinion, or to correct its errors', 253. Barker is quite right to emphasize this aspect of Aristotle's method (though 'a priori' is a rather disputable description of it); but he does not explain why it is reasonable for Aristotle to apply it to a subject that is allegedly constituted by people's opinions. The second passage from Barker reflects a view similar to those who think the pursuit of 'reflective equilibrium' in moral theory conflicts with a realist conception of its subject-matter (see n6 above). But he also recognizes the aspects of Aristotle that go beyond pure dialectic.

21. See, e.g., 1254a17–20 on unnatural slavery, 1254b27–34 on 'natural' distinctions that are often absent, 1258a6–10, a35–b8 on unnatural accumulation of possessions. Aristotle is criticized for combining descriptive and prescriptive elements in his claims about nature, by Robinson [1962], p. xx.

22. Following Hardie [1980], 16f (among others), against Ackrill [1974], 25f, I take 1094a19–21 (*kai mê . . . orexin*) to state a necessary, not a sufficient, condition for the existence of a final good. 1094a24–b7 argues for the existence of such a good.

23. *EE* 1214b6–11 claims that everyone capable of living by his own *prohairesis* actually does set up some ultimate end. For *epistêsantas* = 'having noticed, attended to' cf. *GC* 315a34, b18, *PN* 459b25, *DC* 300b21, *Pol.* 1335b3. Contrast Woods [1982], 200. Rackham [1935] is therefore probably wrong to translate by 'should set before him'—though the parenthesis *hôs to ge mê . . . sêmeion estin*, b9–11, makes this translation more attractive. The OT less plausibly takes *epistêsantas* as 'enjoin'. The account of rational agency shows how the psychological claim (cf. 1101b35–1102a4) might be defended. For discussion of the psychological claim and the *EE* passage see McDowell [1980], 263f, Cooper [1975], 94.

24. On deliberative appearance see §§ 178–80.

25. Political science might discover that we need shoemakers to mend sails instead of making shoes, and that we should manage with fewer shoes than the unregulated shoemakers would have produced. The end of political science, therefore, includes the end of shoemaking to the extent that the

subordinate end is really good for us; and we find whether or not it is good for us by considering its end against the ends of all other sciences and pursuits—if we leave some out we may be wrong in our estimate of shoemaking. Hence if political science is to regulate the pursuit of different ends correctly, its end must include the ends of all the other sciences.

Aristotle is right, then, to confine his claims about pursuit of the good to a proper subset of voluntary actions. He mentions crafts and disciplines (*methodoi*) and actions and decisions, 1094a1–2, 1097a16–22. All these involve rational, deliberate actions. They are all ultimately actions on decision (*prohairesis*), since Aristotle thinks that practical intellect provides the end that guides productive intellect, 1139a35–b4. These actions do not include actions on non-rational desires, which do not aim at any good. Hence Aristotle does not agree entirely with the Eudoxan account of the good as what all things aim at, 1094a2–3, if that implies that we aim at the good in all our voluntary actions.

26. This sort of Kantian argument is discussed by Beck [1960], 166–75.
27. See further 2n65.
28. See § 151.
29. On formal conditions see Ackrill [1974], 21 (who goes further than I would in taking them to be analytically or conceptually true), White [1981], 231–3.
30. I render *teleion* as 'complete', rather than 'final' or 'perfect'. (Ackrill [1974] uses 'final' and (27f) 'complete'; Cooper [1975], 100n, favours 'final'; all three renderings appear in the OT.) 'Complete' is needed at 1098a18 for the *bios teleios*; and this is so closely connected with *teleiotatên*, immediately proceeding, that we should try to render the term uniformly throughout the argument of i 7. This initial argument about the *EN* might be supplemented, though more disputably, by appeal to *MM* 1184a8–14, *EE* 1219a35–9.

Aristotle argues: 'If only one thing is complete, this will be the good we seek; if more things are complete, the good we seek will be the completest of these', 1097a28–30. In his support he describes three degrees of completeness: (1) x is completer than y if and only if x is pursued for its own sake and y is pursued for the sake of something else. (2) x is completer than y if and only if x is pursued for its own sake and never for the sake of something else, whereas y is pursued both for its own sake and for the sake of x. (3) x is unconditionally complete if and only if x is always chosen for itself and never for the sake of something else, 1097a30–4.

In (1) we must take y to be pursued *only* for the sake of something else (for if both x and y were pursued for both reasons, each would be completer than the other). We might say that relative to shoemaking the comfort of our feet is the completer end; for when we achieve that, we completely achieve the end that is relevant to shoemaking.

The difference between (2) and (3) depends on the force of 'always', which might mean (3a) whenever we choose it' or (3b) 'in all our choices'. Aristotle probably intends (3b); if he did not, he would unaccountably overlook one feature of the good described in i 2—it must be that for the sake of which we choose all other things (cf. 1097a18–19).

We might argue that, e.g., pleasure or a good conscience satisfies (3b), in that (i) we choose it in every choice we make, and (ii) we choose it only for itself, not for the sake of anything else; and yet perhaps (iii) it is not the whole ultimate good, since there are several different things that we also choose for themselves and not for the sake of anything else. Aristotle replies that such goods in fact fail (ii), because we choose them also for the sake of happiness, supposing that through them we will be happy, 1097b1–6. All the partial intrinsic goods, such as virtue, honour, and pleasure, are chosen as parts of the whole that they constitute. For further discussion of this argument see Engberg-Pederson [1983], ch.1.

31. See § 138.

32. Psychological egoism is sometimes defended by consideration of desires one at a time, or by reflexion on what makes any desire at all intelligible. Hume and Mill, e.g., suggest that inspection of each particular desire and its ultimate object will always discover pleasure. Aristotle's argument for psychological egoism, by contrast, is essentially global and structural. Our comparison of different objects of desire reveals our pursuit of a final good; and this structural feature of desires is not visible in a single desire considered in isolation. Cf. § 176.

33. The account of a person's good in Rawls [1971], 408–24, involves deliberative rationality applied to a person's wants, and hence results in a conative theory, given Rawls's conception of deliberative rationality. Though the 'Aristotelian principle', introduced at 424, leads to some views similar to those connected with self-realization, 431, it relies on claims about what people want that remain within a conative theory. A conative conception is applied to *EN* i 7 by Engberg-Pederson [1983], ch.1; it especially influences his account of self-sufficiency (which does not explain the reference to a human being's political nature).

34. The contrast between conative and normative conceptions is related, though not identical, to Kraut's contrast between subjective and objective conceptions; see [1979a].

35. I might concede that I need the instrumental benefits of support and cooperation—to help me gather my harvest, dig sewers, use public transport, and so on—without agreeing that the good of others is to be chosen for its own sake as a part of my own good. However, Aristotle assumes that my good includes the good of these other people, since the self-sufficient good is to be *sufficient* both for myself and for others—sufficient, that is, for their good. See § 215.

36. Aristotle claims that the final good is the most choiceworthy of all, not counted with other goods. If it could be counted with others it would be one of a number of goods; hence the addition of another good would create a greater good; but if another good is greater than our alleged final good, our alleged final good is not final after all, 1097b16–20. This is probably a further explanation of self-sufficiency, and hence of completeness. If the final good really makes life lack nothing, then life cannot be made better by the addition of some further good; otherwise the lack of that good would be a failure to achieve self-sufficiency.

I follow Ackrill's interpretation of this passage, [1974], 23f, and the further discussion by Cooper [1981], 384f. Though some of *MM* 1184a15–38 is obscure, its main tendency is parallel to that of 1097b16–20.

37. Aristotle begins to explain the notion of function by one of his normal expository devices, an appeal to crafts, 1097b24–30. The good for a craftsman consists in his function, in his doing what a craftsman does. In so far as we understand something as an F, what is good for it will be doing what F does; that is what is good for it *as* F. Since we know what craftsmen qua craftsmen do, we can easily say that the good of a tailor qua tailor consists in cutting and stitching.

The usefulness of this appeal to function, however, depends on the character of the description under which the function is ascribed to the subject; if Socrates is a tailor, an idler, and a gourmand, we can find what is good for him qua each of these, and be none the wiser about what is good for Socrates. If the description identifies an essential property of the subject, then the description of the function will be useful; for if Socrates is essentially a human being, then what is good for Socrates must be good for him as what he essentially is, as a human being; and it must consist in performing human functions in some way.

The parts of animals (1097b30–3; cf. *DA* 412b17–25) provide essential descriptions, and so are better examples than craftsmen were. But they are still not perfectly adequate examples, since they are not substances, but have functions instrumental to the wholes of which they are parts. Craftsmen perform their functions well when they perform the right actions for some end external to them; and organs perform their functions well in subordination to the whole that is partly external to them. But unless natural substances are purely instrumental to something else, this will not be a sufficient account of their function; and if they were purely instrumental, they would not be substances.

Having illustrated his concept of function from artifacts and organs Aristotle asks if a human being has a function in the same way. But 'in the same way' does not imply that he retains the disputable features of the previous examples. 1097b28–33 does not involve a fallacy of composition; it is an analogical exposition, to show what Aristotle has in mind, but is not in itself an argument to show that a human being has a function. The function that Aristotle seeks for the whole organism is a pattern of goal-directed activity that is essential to the organism in the way its relation to the whole is essential to the part; but the function of the whole organism is not purely subordinate to anything else. These issues are clearly discussed in Whiting [AFA].

38. A dog does not have a nutritive soul and a perceptive soul; it has a perceptive soul that is potentially nutritive—a soul that would perish and turn into a nutritive soul if the dog turned into a vegetable that was alive but unable to perceive. See 13n25.

39. The genuineness of 1098a3–4 (suspected by Rassow [1874], 72, followed by Stewart [1892] and Gauthier [1970], ad loc., because of *epipeithes*, a *hapax legomenon* in Aristotle) is supported by *kai tautês*, a5, suggesting that

something else has just been mentioned as *dittôs legomenon*. (Rassow admits this, since he suggests the deletion of *kai* as yet another gloss.)

    If Aristotle identified the human function with activities performed by nothing else, he would have to exclude nutrition, perception, desire, and action because these are not peculiar to human beings. On that criterion, however, plants and animals would not have peculiar functions (since human beings are capable of nutrition and perception). More probably, the peculiar human function is meant to be the *life* guided by practical reason. Aristotle does not claim that just any peculiarity of human beings is their peculiar function; pleasure in purposeless killing, e.g., will not count. For further discussion see Nagel [1972], 9–11.

40. If peculiarity is understood this way, we need not follow Kraut [1979] in looking for a type of peculiarity that will make contemplation, *theôria*, peculiar to human beings. I do not think the function argument is meant to isolate contemplation as the peculiar function. Nor do I believe that in *EN* i or x Aristotle means to identify happiness with contemplation; I take him to mean that contemplation is the most valuable single component of happiness. If I am wrong about this, and if Book x does identify happiness with contemplation alone, then it is better to conclude that the *EN* is inconsistent (as Cooper does, [1975], 155–77) than to try to make Books i–ix consistent with a purely contemplative view. That is why I have discussed the rest of the *EN* without reference to the questions about happiness in Book x; though they are clearly relevant, I do not think that in fact they ought to change our minds about the interpretation of the rest of the treatise. For the most plausible views on this controversial issue see Keyt [1983], Whiting [1986a]. See also 18n24.

41. A good carpenter does his work well when he does it effectively for the result to which his performance is an instrumental means; and this is his good qua carpenter. But since the function of a human being is not instrumental, his good is not success at performing some instrumental task; hence his goodness will not consist in efficiency in performing it, but in the best way of performing his characteristic activities. If we apply Aristotle's distinction, we can say that the human virtue will be a virtue in action (*praxis*) rather than production (*poiêsis*).

    The OCT unjustifiably deletes 1098a12 *anthrôpou . . . houtô* a16. In fact a15 makes a crucial move, if *eu . . . apoteleitai* refers to good = welfare as the result of good = virtuous action.

42. On the role of the agent's good in teleological explanation see 15n9, Wallace [1978], ch.1.

43. Future-directed desires are not sufficient for rational agency. I need not merely desires focused on the future, but concern for *my* future and concern for my future desires.

44. This sort of problem about deliberation is raised by the case of the Russian noble in Parfit [1984], 327, Williams [1976], 9f.

45. His argument is this: (1) Being is choiceworthy and beloved for all. (2) We are by being in actuality, since we are by living and acting ⟨which are actualities⟩. (3) The product is in a way the producer in actuality. (4) Hence we love the product because we love being, 1168a5–8.

The argument combines conative and normative features. In saying that life is 'choiceworthy' and 'beloved' Aristotle means to imply at least that it is actually loved—otherwise (4) would not follow. But (2) and (3) are not about what we desire or love, but about what our being really consists in. It consists in our realizing our capacities; and the more we realize our capacities the more we fulfil our desire for being. If 'choiceworthy' in (1) implies 'deserving to be chosen', Aristotle assumes that what is good for x must be good for x as F if F is what x essentially is, and hence must be good for x doing what Fs essentially do, hence for x as F in actuality.

46. See § 160.

47. What is distinctive of a dachshund may be bad for these particular dachshunds in so far as they are dogs; hence, if different essential properties require conflicting goods, then appeal to the essence will not be enough to settle on one beneficial course of action. But we might hope to show that a human being's good as a human being does not conflict with his good as an animal; since his essence as a human being is the rational direction of his activities, we need not assume in advance (though we cannot exclude the possibility without further examination) that his activities as an animal will be harmed by the exercise of reason.

48. See § 125.

CHAPTER 17

1. See § 181.

2. Aristotle needs to claim, and does implicitly claim, that virtue is always the dominant component of happiness, always to be preferred over any other component or combination of components. If Aristotle can show this, he can maintain the common-sense belief that virtue involves genuine sacrifices and still maintain his own view that the best policy for happiness is to be virtuous. See § 241.

3. On types of potentiality see § 125.

4. In human beings, as opposed to animals, the non-rational desires are responsive to reason, and these are parts of the human function, 1098a3–5. Hence they are elements of human virtue in a way that purely vegetative functions are not, 1102a32–b12. The task of moral education is not merely to subject this part of the soul to practical reason. We could achieve that result by leaving the non-rational desires as strong as they naturally are and learning to frustrate them (as the continent person does), or (cf. 1146a9–16) by weakening of the non-rational appetites until they do not bother us when we rationally choose not to satisfy them. Neither of these results will satisfy Aristotle. For each may involve the suppression of one essential aspect of human nature in the service of another; and in that case virtue will not complete human nature as a whole.

5. Though Aristotle does not use Plato's political analogy here, he seems to have in mind the sort of view that Plato expresses through his account of psychic justice. The rational agent will properly consider his plan from the

point of view of his non-rational impulses. In forming impulses so that they agree with reason, we also educate reason so that it agrees with impulse. This education is necessary if a virtue of character is to complete the whole of human nature in the way Aristotle claims.

McDowell [1980], 369f, and [1978], 27–9, suggests that if a virtuous person has to give up, e.g., some appetitive satisfaction, he does not regard himself as having any reason (even prima facie) to pursue the satisfaction, and therefore suffers no loss by giving it up. To attribute such a view to Aristotle seems to me to assimilate him too closely to the insensible person's view. A person would not be more virtuous if she performed mixed actions without regret (since the regret might indicate that she owes apology or compensation); it is not clear why 'silencing' is any more appropriate in McDowell's case.

6. When Aristotle says that good deliberation is correctness about what promotes the end correctly grasped by wisdom (1142b32–3; see 15n24), we should not assume that deliberation contributes nothing to the correct grasp of the end. On the contrary; the wise person's correct grasp must say more than that the end is happiness (everyone agrees about that), and his correct grasp must result from deliberation (since that is what the wise person does). His task is therefore very similar to the task that Aristotle sets himself in the *Ethics*; that is why Aristotle claims to be practising political science, which is the same state of character as wisdom.

7. The relation between virtue and self-love is helpfully discussed by Homiak [1981], relying on a more conative conception of happiness than the one I have ascribed to Aristotle.

8. 'In himself', *kath'hauton*; cf. 1156a10–11. Cf. 'because of himself', *di'hauton*, 1156b10, and 'in so far as he is who he is', 1156a17–18.

9. If Ann became a god, the god would be her replacement, not her continuation, and hence Al does not wish this further good to Ann, 1159a5–11. Aristotle suggests further that I must remain not only a human being rather than a god, but also the particular human being I am, 1166a19–22 (retaining *ekeino to genomenon*, a21, deleted in OCT, and taking *genomenos d'allos*, a20, to refer to becoming another person, not simply to becoming a god).

10. See §§ 137, 183.

11. If this is Aristotle's view of a particular self and essence, we will expect him to claim that if Ann's character could change and she could lose her virtue, then Al's friendship for her would cease. We can see that Aristotle believes this when he discusses the actual cases that are most closely analogous— those in which we believe a friend is virtuous and he turns out not to be. If we suppose someone is good, and he turns out vicious and seems so, then we cannot keep on loving him in the same way; 'for it was not to that sort of person that he was a friend', 1165b21–2. In these conditions the friend who breaks off the friendship 'would seem to be doing nothing absurd', 1165b21. In one way we might think the same person evidently persists, and so the same person persists to be loved for her own sake. But this is not the individual self Ann whom Al loved for herself in the first place.

I speak of 'persistence' so as to avoid the implications of identity (so that, e.g., if identity cannot be a matter of degree, it will not follow that persistence cannot be). This is one of Parfit's reasons for distinguishing survival from identity, [1984], 298f.

12. He may be sorry for what happened, since things may not turn out as he expected them to, and to that extent he may be sorry for not having done something other than what he did. But he will not wish that, believing what he believed at the time, he had made some different decision.

13. In 1166b12 I read *pepraktai dia* (*kai dia*, OCT) and *misousi te kai* (*misountai kai*, OCT).

14. Incontinents are contrasted with both virtuous and vicious people at 1102b14–28, 1146b22–4, 1150b29–1151a10, 1152a4–6. Annas [1977], 541, 553f, suggests that ix 4 violates the usual contrast.

15. For similar reasons, the case of the half-bad, but not irreparably bad, person shows that mere preservation of the present self is not overridingly important. For if such a person is to become better, he must change quite radically, and so lose much of his present self. This does not mean he ought not to change in his own interest. For he will not really manage to preserve himself if he refuses to reform. If he is concerned with external goods above all, he will have to adapt himself to changing conditions; he will have no stable character if he keeps on as he is or if he becomes thoroughly intemperate. The fact that a half-bad person must change and partly destroy himself is part of the reason why he is in a bad condition; being who he is is not good for him, so that aiming at what is good for him is a self-contradictory aim. One of the bad features of his condition is his inability both to be a good person and to achieve *his* good to the extent that a virtuous person achieves it. Aristotle sometimes says that what is good without qualification is good for the good person but not good for everyone, *EE* 1248b26–7. The bad person cannot fully achieve his own good; he must first become someone else.

16. Exclusive attachment to rational agency might be attributed to Socrates, the Cynics, and (on some views) the Stoics. Fixed attachments seem typical of a tragic character such as Ajax. See Irwin [1985].

17. On the fine, *kalon*, see § 237.

18. Hence Aristotle claims that the intemperate person thinks 'he must always seek the pleasant thing in front of him', 1146b22–3. This feature of the intemperate person makes him slavish, *andrapodôdês*; see §§ 220, 246. The natural slave lacks the capacity to deliberate about his life as a whole, and can only live for the satisfaction of immediate desires; hence he is incapable of happiness, *EN* 1177a6–9. The intemperate person is capable of this deliberation, but decides not to rely on it in the conduct of his life. He differs from the natural slave in that his reason assents to the neglect of reason in his life.

19. This description of prudent vice is derived from Plato, *Phd.* 68d–69c, *Rep.* 365c, 554a–555a, *Phdr.* 256e.

20. This account of virtue allows us to understand more of Aristotle's views on incontinence. (The brief suggestions here are developed slightly in Irwin

[1986].) An imperfectly trained person will be incontinent, or at best continent. The incontinent tends to lapse from acceptance of the virtuous person's outlook to acceptance of the intemperate person's. He agrees that it is worth pursuing goals beyond the goals of appetite, and makes the right decisions. But when his appetites are especially strong he is no longer convinced that he has reason to act on his conception of his happiness. He relapses into doing what he has the strongest impulse for, not because he accepts the intemperate person's conception of happiness, but because he is not convinced that he has good reason to rely on his own conception of happiness. When he abandons his policy of acting on his conception of happiness, he acts incontinently. The temperate person is better off than the incontinent in so far as his rational desire controls his actions. It controls him because he sees more clearly the reasons for following his conception of his final good against the inducements of his appetites; and because he sees this clearly he has been able to train his appetites so that they do not conflict with his rational desires as they do in the incontinent person.

21. On 1098a18–20 see Irwin [1985], 104f. 1101a11–17 shows that a lifetime is neither necessary nor sufficient for a complete life, and that a complete life must include the right sorts of virtuous activities.

22. On the vulgar and the menial see § 22.

23. 'Nameless' states are discussed at 1107b1–2, 1107b30–1108a1, 1108a16–19, 1125b17–29, 1127a11–17. Aristotle shows that namelessness is not accidental. Sometimes a state has no standard name because it rarely or never occurs; but sometimes people simply have not seen the possibility of a mean state in relation to a particular emotion or external good.

24. In explaining the doctrine of the mean with reference to types of rational control I try to meet some of the challenge presented by Hursthouse [1980] to Urmson [1973].

CHAPTER 18

1. In the *Republic* Plato admits that justice is the hardest of the commonly recognized virtues to defend within a theory that tries to relate all the virtues to happiness. It is unfortunate that Aristotle does not say how he intends to answer Plato's problem. But unless he can answer it, his theory will have failed one reasonable test of adequacy.

2. The initial claim about friendship in 1155b31–4 suggests that each of the three types of friendship, for the good, the advantageous, and the pleasant, should involve active goodwill, 1156a3–5. But this appearance may be misleading, since it conflicts with Aristotle's later remark that goodwill is not found in the lower friendships, 1167a10–14. We can remove the conflict if we attend to Aristotle's claims about the place of goodwill in each type of friendship. Friends wish good to the other in the respect in which they love him; hence friends for advantage love the other 'not in accordance with himself ⟨i.e. not in so far as he is who he is in himself⟩, but in so far as they

will get some good from him. Similarly also for those who love because of pleasure; for they like a witty person not because he is the sort of person he is ⟨or: has the character he has⟩, but because he is pleasant to themselves', 1156a10–16. Aristotle tries to explain why full altruistic concern is confined to the best type of friendship by explaining (*a*) 'for his own sake' or (*b*) 'because of himself' as (*c*) 'because he is the person he is', 1156a16 (where I agree with Gauthier ad loc. in following Bonitz's suggestion, *hê(i) ho philoumenos estin ⟨hosper estin⟩*), a17–18, and (*d*) 'because he is who he essentially is'. He then explains 'the person he is' as (*e*) 'the sort of person he is' and (*f*) 'the sort of character he has'. This account of altruistic concern and of the virtuous people's friendship explains why such friendship fully embodies altruistic concern and the others do not, 1156b7–12.

Cooper [1977], 629–43, relies on the initial remarks about goodwill to argue that all three types of friendship display intrinsic concern for the other. I think he underestimates the restrictions implied by the later remarks. A position between Cooper's and mine is well defended by Alpern [1983], 307–10.

3. Aristotle sees no special difficulty in the degree of goodwill that he associates with friendships for pleasure and advantage. Since these friendships have goodwill limited by the prospects of pleasure and advantage, the goodwill has a clear instrumental justification. Such goodwill may extend to other aspects of the person beyond those directly involved in the pleasure or advantage. Someone will be a better friend for advantage or pleasure to the extent that he is a better person, hence more capable of the best kind of friendship. See n28. The self-confined egoist, concerned with no one for his own sake besides himself, may therefore discover that an altruist, whose concerns are not confined to himself, is better at securing his own advantage. It does not follow that the self-confined egoist who sees this can at once make himself altruistic. For while he might like to believe that other people matter for their own sakes, he may still see no good reason to believe this, and awareness of the good consequences of the belief may not be enough to make him hold it. We still need to know why anyone has good reason to be concerned for others in the way characteristic of the best sort of friendship.

4. It is important that the attitude to be justified is metaphysical, not simple, altruism. Common sense assumes that we have the right sentiments for simple altruism, but it does not explain why we should have them, or justify them to someone who doubts that they are a necessary part of the human good. A critic can still raise these doubts even if simple altruism is a natural psychological tendency of ours; he can still fairly ask whether its satisfaction is a prominent part of our good.

Simple altruism requires us to count the other person's desire for some good as a reason for giving him that good; but we still want to know how strong a reason his desire should be for us, and how far we should cultivate this tendency to take other people's desires to give us reasons for our own actions. The critic might argue that we ought to weaken, not to cultivate, this tendency, because it interferes with the rational pursuit of our good;

perhaps we will satisfy some of our other desires more fully if we inhibit our altruistic desires. Common sense has no answer if it accepts a conative account of our good. If we reject a conative account, the critic's question returns. Even if we have strong altruistic desires, and their satisfaction does not seriously interfere with the satisfaction of our other strong desires, how do we know that satisfaction of these desires achieves our good? Since he accepts a normative conception of the good as realization of human capacities, Aristotle needs to justify altruism on metaphysical grounds that do not simply appeal to the psychological naturalness of simple altruism. On self-love and the love of others see Engberg-Pederson [1983], ch.2.

5. In ix 7 Aristotle examines the popular view that the benefits of friendship all consist in receiving the benefits—benefits of the sort that a self-confined egoist will appreciate. The disadvantages of friendship are the services that I have to do to get the benefits. Hence the rational person, it seems, has to calculate the relation of the recipient's benefits to the benefactor's burdens. Aristotle rejects this popular view, and argues that the more important benefits of friendship consist in giving rather than receiving, so that the popular method of calculation rests on a false assumption.

6. *MM* 1213a10–26 and *EE* 1245a29–37 appeal to the friend as a mirror in whom I can contemplate myself better; and Cooper [1980], 320–4, takes this to be one of Aristotle's two best defences of friendship (and he also finds it in *EN* 1169b28–1170a4). But this heuristic function of a friend does not seem to be enough. For would another virtuous person sufficiently like me not do just as well, even if I lacked the causal connexions with his thoughts and actions that are essential for friendship? It is not clear why I would have to be concerned for the friend's good if I wanted him to be a mirror for me. He might be another self in one sense (someone sufficiently similar to me), but not in the sense relevant to altruistic concern (one whom I care about in the way I care about myself).

The argument of 1170a13ff is partly anticipated in *EE* 1244b21–1245a26. But Aristotle now entirely removes the claims about the mirror, and so radically changes the role of the other self. He is no longer simply a means for me to contemplate my own actions better. He is a further source of actions that I can enjoy contemplating for themselves in the same way as I contemplate my own. The other self is an extension of my own activity, not simply a means for me to see my own unextended activity.

7. See § 205.

8. See § 141.

9. In Kahn's view, [1981a], 34–40, the 'self' that is involved is the *nous* shared by all human beings. This view makes it hard to see how a distinct individual (cf. 'another Heracles', *MM* 1213a10–13, *EE* 1245a29–35), as opposed to some feature that all human individuals share, could be the object of love.

10. On political friendship see *EE* 1242b25–37, *Pol.* 1295b21–5, Cooper [1977], 645–8. Barker [1906], 236, notices that the conception of a friend as another self is important for the theory of the state: 'Now friendship means that a man regards his friend as "another self", for whom, exactly as if he *were*

himself, he wishes and does all that is good for his own sake . . . The conception of a common good, the conception that the good of another is one's own good, these things are thus the essence of friendship, as they are of the State. If the State is to have political fellowship, it must possess the virtue of friendship.' Barker quite reasonably assumes some connexion between the 'other self' (characteristic of the best sort of friendship) and the political friendship in a state; but he does not explain how the connexion is to be demonstrated.

11. The child is the parent's other self because he is scarcely separate from the parent, and for this reason the parent finds the child's actions very closely related to the parent's thoughts and deliberations. Isaac loves Jacob not just because he is another person but because Jacob is specially related to Isaac himself, and therefore Isaac comes to regard Jacob's good as part of his own, as something 'of his own' or 'akin', *oikeion*. Aristotle explains that the product is 'made akin' to the producer, that the producer regards it as his own, 1161b19–24. Isaac is aware of Jacob as his product, continuing some of Isaac's characteristics; Isaac is interested in the success of his plans and designs and the results of his own causal agency. This is what makes craftsmen fond of their products, 1120b13–14, 1167b33–1168a9. Aristotle implies that the more of Isaac's efforts and rational agency are associated with Jacob the more Isaac will be concerned with Jacob. If Isaac wanted a child and intended to have a child, and having the child is related to Isaac's other plans, we expect Isaac to have a stronger concern for Jacob than otherwise. And we expect the concern to be strengthened the more Isaac sees of Jacob and the more he finds Jacob dependent on him. Aristotle is aware of these sources of concern; he mentions them to explain why mothers love children more than fathers do (despite his striking and objectionable tendency to speak of paternal love as the paradigm of parental love), and how love grows between brothers, 1161b26, 1161b33–1162a1, 1168a24–6.

The child is less of *another* self than the virtuous friend is; he does not share the parent's aims because he has freely and rationally accepted them, but because, at this stage, he has no developed aims and goals that are independent of the parent's. He is perhaps more like an extension of the parent than a genuinely other self. Moreover, familial friendship results from a relation that is independent of and prior to the friendship. A father's natural and social relations to his child make it reasonable for him to regard the child's interest as part of his own, and hence to care about the child for the child's own sake. The best kind of friendship needs a special explanation just because it requires disinterested goodwill with no antecedent natural or social relation that make it reasonable. In the best friendship the character of the other in himself, not his antecedent relation to me, has to be the ground of the friendship.

12. If the city is self-sufficient and complete, it includes within itself all the activities that constitute happiness and the necessary means for them, including the right number of people, 1261b11–15. (These will be necessary conditions rather than parts; see 1278a2–6, 1291a23–33, 1326a16–21,

1328a21–b4, 1329a34–9, *EE* 1214b14–27.) Once it has reached this stage it need not grow any further, but has reached its proper natural limit; see n15.

13. The demand for similarity in 1295b21–7 is consistent with the demand for dissimilarity in 1261a22–b15, 1277a5–12, if Aristotle is right in supposing that the second demand is met by citizens of similar virtue who are willing to occupy different roles at different times.

14. See 1276a27–30, 1324b9–11, 1325a7–10, 1326b3–5, on the nation, *ethnos*.

15. On the proper limit see *Pol.* 1256b31–9, 1326a35–b11, *PA* 646b7–10, *GA* 745a4–9, 760a33–5, 776a3–6, 777b26–30, *DC* 268a21–2, *EN* 1170b31–3. On limit and completeness see *DC* 286b18–23.

16. He could consistently agree that a larger community (e.g. a nation or alliance of cities) is needed to secure some necessary conditions for the parts of happiness. His claim about the completeness of the city rests on deeper grounds than the lack of distinct Greek words for city and state (mentioned by Newman [1887], i.40).

17. *HA* 488a7–10 (cf. 588b30–589a2) makes a common function sufficient for being a political animal—a weaker condition than the one assumed in the *Ethics* and *Politics* (for which cf. 488b24–5). Mulgan [1974] discusses 488a7–10, but not 488b24–5, which makes clear the limited degree to which the other animals are political (and if we allow this, we need not speak of 'two senses' of *politikon*, as Mulgan does). For further discussion see Brandt [1974], 191–6, Kullmann [1980].

18. On voice, pleasure, and pain in animals see *DA* 420b32, *PA* 660a35–b2, *HA* 588b27–30, 608a17–21.

19. The passage is quoted in § 210.

20. I take 'for every day' in 1252b13 to be parallel to 'for more than a day', b16, and so to indicate (cf. *EN* 1162a20–2) the permanence of the household. Newman, ii.112, takes the two phrases to mark a contrast.

21. See 16n35.

22. I take *tauta* in 1280b40 to refer to the smaller communities. Newman, iii.209, on b38 underestimates the role of friendship in the argument, by suggesting that its end is simply to be contrasted with the end of the city; b39–40 implies that it also helps to identify the end of the city.

23. See n12.

24. In *Pol.* vii Aristotle adds something to his remarks in the *EN* (see 16n40) about theoretical study. He considers the claims of (*a*) the citizen's life and (*b*) the life of theoretical study, to achieve happiness, 1324a13–35. But he also discusses two conflicting accounts of the political life: (b1) the despotic life, ruling over fellow-citizens or foreigners alike, with or without their consent; (b2) the non-aggressive life, sharing in the ruling offices but not grabbing them, and not seeking despotic rule over others.

   Aristotle first rejects (b1) in favour of (b2), 1324b32–1325a15, 1325a34–b14. He does not want us to decide in favour of the theoretical over the political life because we confuse the political with the despotic life. He explains that the good achieved in the political life does not depend on the power and security that results from ruling others, 1325a7–10, b3–14, 1328a35–7.

In returning to (*a*) and (*b2*), the relative claims of the theoretical and the political life, Aristotle suggests his own settlement of the dispute. (1) The critics of the political life would be right if it were the despotic life; but it is not. And they are wrong to suggest that inactivity is better than activity, 1325a31–4. (2) The critics of the theoretical life are wrong to suppose that it requires inactivity. For someone can be active without acting in relation to others, and the theorist's thoughts are active in any sense that is required when we speak of happiness as a good activity, 1325b16–21.

We cannot have a complete life if it excludes intrinsic goods; and Aristotle allows that just and temperate people achieve intrinsic goods in their actions, 1325a32–4. Since the theorist does not achieve these goods by theoretical study alone, he does not achieve a complete and self-sufficient good. Equally, the active citizen does not achieve in his political activities the good that the theorist achieves, and hence does not achieve the complete good either. It is reasonable to conclude that the best life includes both theoretical study and the actions characteristic of the moral virtues. I believe that this is Aristotle's conclusion in the *EE* and *EN* as well. On leisure see 19n13.

25. This is the case of necessity mentioned in *Met.* 1015a22–6.

26. The organic aspects of Aristotle's conception of the state are discussed by Barker [1906], 225f, 276–81 (including some justified criticism). Barker's discussion would be clearer if he distinguished the claims about the organic character of the state that follow from Aristotle's teleological doctrines from those that do not. See further Mulgan [1977], 32.

27. To simplify things so far, we have assumed that citizens know a little about each other, and in particular know that all of them are virtuous. These conditions may be relaxed further while still allowing some other-regarding concern; but in fact Aristotle is anxious not to dilute the demands for virtue, mutual knowledge, and cooperation too much. He insists on strict limits on the number of citizens, so that they will know something about each other, *Pol.* 1326b12–18. He wants them to be not too disparate in virtue, and for this reason wants artisans to be disqualified from citizenship as far as possible, 1328b34–1329a2. His conception of citizenship is further evidence that he intends something like the justification of extended altruism that we have described.

28. It follows that in a city (or other community resting on altruism) friendship for advantage will be different from what it will be in other conditions. If Al and Dora are friends for advantage, but not friends of the best type, but are concerned with each other's welfare as fellow-citizens, then Al can rely on Dora to be just; she will be guided by her own interests in laying down the terms of the friendship and will not treat Al as she might treat Ed, her friend of the best type; but the extent of her pursuit of her own advantage will be regulated by the concern for fellow-citizens that makes her just. If citizens are just, they will be able to make the sorts of bargains that other people might find risky, in particular the agreements that rest on a person's character (cf. *EN* 1162b21–1163a1). Since they are just people, they have a further reason for fulfilling the terms of the bargain, and for caring about

the other for the other's own sake. In *EN* viii–ix Aristotle describes the secondary types of friendship by themselves, not considering the further motives that just people have for conducting such friendships with some intrinsic concern for the other.

CHAPTER 19

1. The ideal state should not be a fantasy. Since it is supposed to display the political system that achieves the human good, it should not assume impossible external conditions or a fantastic change in human nature. Apart from this restriction, Aristotle is not worried about the immediate feasibility of the best city. He helps himself to all the natural resources we might pray for, 1260b27–9, 1288b22–4, 1325b33–40, and is unmoved by the difficulty of introducing the institutions of the ideal city in any empirically likely situation; only an impossibility is rejected (cf. 1263a30–40). Since the realization of the human good depends on specific and fairly demanding external conditions, these must be assumed in the account of the ideal state.
2. On assumptions see 20n16.
3. See 21n14. In particular cases Aristotle remarks that concern for wealth caused the deviation of the Carthaginian constitution from aristocracy, 1273a31–b1, and the Spartan obsession with military virtue is responsible for the shape of Sparta's political system, 1324b3–12.
4. We might say that 'freedom' is used in two senses: (*a*) for someone whose legal status makes him free, not a slave; (*b*) for lack of restraint over us in living our lives. Aristotle tries to show how they are connected.

   Democrats did not usually argue that everyone should have an equal share of everything; not many of them actually redistributed the lands and wealth of the rich (cf. 1281a14–19, 1318a11–26).
5. On freedom see § 225.
6. See § 214.
7. See the objections to the *Republic*, 1264b15–25, 1329a21–6.
8. See 3n10 on homonymy.
9. At 1275b17–20 Aristotle says that in oligarchies mere eligibility for office is the extent to which citizens hold the 'indefinite rule' that is taken to define citizenship, 1275a31–3. He could have replaced his initial definition with a more obviously comprehensive definition that referred simply to eligibility; but he refuses to do this, since the second definition would not make clear that oligarchies show an inferior degree of citizenship.
10. His account of friends in the *EN* provides a partial parallel. The definition of the best kind of friendship explains why the lower forms are also called friendships; they have some of the features that are combined in the best form, and the presence of these features in the best form explains what is good about the inferior forms, 1156b33–1157a3, 1157a25–33. The hierarchy explains why we call all these people friends, but at the same time

think that the best friendship is a more complete friendship than the other two. The best friendship best displays the place of friendship in happiness, and by doing this displays the good of the other friendships too. See § 209.

11. In non-ideal states the good citizen is not the same as the good man without qualification, 1293b1–6; these states try, justifiably, to make good citizens in relation to a particular political system, 1309a36–9.

12. This is a serious qualification of 1255b12–18. On this point rule over slaves resembles tyranny, 1311a2–4; and this resemblance explains some of what is wrong with tyranny.

13. On leisure see 1326b26–32 (associated with self-sufficiency), 1333a30–b5, 1334a2–40, 1337b28–32; cf. 1269a34–6, 1273a24–5 (leisure requires wealth), 1329a1–2, 1341a28. For the wrong sort of people leisure is not always good, and in some conditions Aristotle agrees with political measures to reduce it, 1292b28, 1293a5, 1313b25, 1318b12. On leisure see Stocks [1936], Solmsen [1964]. Both of them attribute to Aristotle a more radical withdrawal from political activities than he seems to think necessary for the leisured life. (Hence Stocks compares Aristotle's remarks with Plato, *Tht.* 172–7, assuming that Aristotle advocates the same sort of withdrawal; this leads him into some unwarranted speculations about the chronology of the *Pol.*) There is no reason to think that Aristotle takes freedom from 'necessary' occupations to require freedom from, or a bare minimum of, moral and political activity; indeed, such a view makes his conception of the citizen in the ideal state hard to understand.

14. On a Stoic conception of freedom see Epictetus, *Disc.* iv 1.62–75.

15. See § 195.

16. On the menial and the slavish character see § 246, 1277a35, 1334a39, 1336b11–12, 1342a18–28, *EN* 1095b19, 1118a25–6, b20–1, 1126a7–8, 1128a20–2, *EE* 1231b10–26, *Rhet.* 1387b12.

17. On contested goods see § 210.

18. The passage is quoted in § 216.

19. The farmer's life might be all right in itself, but simply takes up too much time, but the other occupations are positively harmful. This is why Aristotle thinks an agricultural lower class is the safest for a democracy, since it lacks leisure but does not have its virtue sapped, 1318b9–16.

The most menial crafts are those that injure the body most, the most servile those that involve most use of the body, and the most ignoble those that have least need of virtue, 1258b37–9. Though these are the most menial, others are menial too if they damage a person's intellect; these include wage-earning activities, since these make the intellect unleisured and humble, 1337b8–15. We call a pursuit menial when it is pursued for the sake of payment by a customer, 1341b10–18. This view of menial occupations explains why Aristotle often associates them with being a hired labourer, *thês,* 1278a12, 17, 21, 1296b29, 1317a25, 1319a27, 1341b13, 1342a20. A hired labourer works for wages paid him by someone else; this in itself is menial, since it leaves him at the beck and call of another, *Rhet.* 1367a32–3. The work he does will usually damage his body, because it is hard physical labour, *Rhet.* 1367a30–2; and since this requires little virtue, it will also be servile and ignoble. On the other hand, someone can be menial without being a hired labourer, if he single-mindedly devotes all his energies to making a profit, or even to securing some other goal besides the life of virtue; hence the Spartans are condemned as menial because they devote themselves single-mindedly to cultivating a militaristic character to secure their city's domination over others, 1338b32–6; cf. 1334a41–b4. (Aristotle's attitude contrasts sharply with that expressed in Plutarch, *Ages.* 26.5, quoted by Newman, iii.342.)

At one point Aristotle suggests that the only difference between menial and slavish functions is that the menial does not belong to a single householder, 1278a11–13. A menial works like a slave for part of his life, though he is not wholly at another's disposal, and hence has a limited slavery, 1260a36–b2, because he performs slavish services, 1277a35–b7. The presence of menial workers is responsible for the poor quality of the lower classes in some states, 1326a16–25, 1319a24–32; Aristotle thinks that in some states the masses are slavish, 1282a15, sometimes practically no better than beasts, 1281b18.

On menial occupations see De Ste Croix [1981], 182–5.

20. To see that this is not a mere optimistic fantasy we might consider a historical example familiar to Aristotle. The increasing political role of the Athenian demos was partly a result of the material security provided by Solonian reforms. Aristotle suggests that menial labour makes someone's mind 'unleisured and abased', 1337b14–15; but abasement hardly seems characteristic of the Athenian demos. Quite the contrary; Aristotle thinks it is safer if the demos are more abased by menial labour, so that they must always struggle for necessities, 1318b9–16. When they have more leisure, the menials start to hold assemblies and to want a role in government, 1319a24–32; cf. 1292b25–9, 1293a1–10. Aristotle does not explain why these slavish, menial, nearly bestial people should take advantage of increased leisure to start holding assemblies, rather than to satisfy their slavish lusts for gain or sensual pleasure. See § 246.

21. If the necessary work is not done by citizens, it might be done by (*a*) machines—only a mythological possibility for Aristotle, 1253b33–1254a1; (*b*) natural slaves; (*c*) other non-citizens; (*d*) citizens. To justify (*b*) Aristotle should show that (i) a natural slave is benefited, or at least not harmed, by working as a slave, or that (ii) a natural slave's interests need not be considered, any more than a machine's, then he can advise the ideal city to employ natural slaves.

Aristotle does not try (ii), since he clearly thinks natural slaves have interests, and he is ready to say that it is in the slave's interest to be ruled by a master with the rational capacities that the slave lacks, 1254b19–20, 1255b4–15. We may agree so far, however, without agreeing with the further claim Aristotle needs—that it is in the slave's interest to do menial work for his master under the conditions that will make him a profitable investment for his master; 1278b36–7 offers the slave rather limited protection.

If Aristotle favours (*b*), 1330a23–8, though, it is puzzling that he suggests that freedom should always be offered to slaves as a prize or reward,

1330a31–3. If these are natural slaves, it is not clear why they should want freedom. But even if they do come to want it, how could it be in their interest?

Sometimes Aristotle supports (*c*), 1328b5–23, 1329a35–7, 1330a28–30; since the labourers are not natural slaves, it is not clear what justifies their serfdom or other inferior status, or why (*c*) is preferable to (*d*).

22. Aristotle criticizes Plato for producing two cities, when the producers lack the appropriate moral education and are left in control of production, 1264a13–40. Will Aristotle's ideal city, with non-citizen producers, not be even more exposed to these criticisms?

23. Aristotle agrees that the single-minded pursuit of a military way of life will make someone menial, slavish, and bestial, 1334a36–b4, 1338b29–36; cf. 1271a40–b10. However, the danger that military life will produce a menial character does not persuade Aristotle to prescribe a specialized military class for the ideal city, even though the contemporary practice of employing mercenaries would make this entirely conceivable for him. His reason for wanting the soldiers to be citizens is clear and plausible; those who control the arms also control the stability of the political system, and it would be foolish to take the risk involved in allowing non-citizens to be soldiers, 1329a7–17. The possible bad effects of the military way of life do not dissuade Aristotle from wanting citizens to be soldiers. He might argue that the dangers are avoidable if the troops are properly educated and properly led. But these arguments for citizen soldiers seem to be quite good arguments for citizen workers too.

24. See §§ 213–14.

25. Aristotle needs to defend one or both of these empirical claims: (1) Manual work is so much more destructive than military service is for virtue that citizens must not be exposed to it. (2) Manual workers are so much less dangerous than soldiers that we need not impose on citizens the burden of menial work even though we must impose the burden of military service on them.

Neither of these empirical claims is very plausible; and (1) without (2) would simply force us into an awkward dilemma. If (2) is false, then Aristotle must admit that his ethical principles require the citizens to share menial labour.

26. Aristotle's views on the function of the state are criticized, on highly disputable liberal grounds, by Robinson [1962], p. xxiii. His argument for moral education is criticized by Mulgan [1977], 26.

27. See 1102a7–13, 1103b2–6, 1109b34–5, 1113b21–6, 1177b12–15, *MM* 1187a14–18, *Pol.* 1263a39–40, 1283b35–1284a3, 1332a28–b11. No similar concern is evident in the *EE*.

28. See 1293b12–14, 1330b32–3, 1280b5–6, contrasting states (e.g. Sparta) that have a conscious programme of public education with those that do not.

29. Nozick [1974], ch.10, esp. 309–12, argues that the minimal state previously justified by appeal to rights and justice is also a framework for utopia, because it offers better prospects than a non-minimal state would offer for its members to achieve their good.

30. Those who suppose that the city should accumulate material wealth

without limit confuse the conditions of mere living with those of living well, 1257b40–1258a1, 1280a31–2, or else they rely on a false conception of happiness, 1258a2–14. Seeing happiness in the sort of gratification that requires the use of material goods, and seeing no limit to the gratification, they set no limit on accumulation either. On this view economic activity will not be designed as a means to the right kind of political activity—providing the citizen with enough leisure for politics; instead political activity will be merely instrumental to accumulation. It will either be a direct source of profit through public office, as in Carthage, 1273a21–b5, or an indirect source, in so far as the laws and constitution make it easier for one class to profit from another; the rich are unrestrained in an oligarchy, and the poor live off the rich in an extreme democracy.

Many cities have been protected from the results of their errors about happiness because they have been less than unanimous or because they have been unsystematic in its pursuit. Indeed, the recognition of a single good and its systematic pursuit will often be a source of conflict; if both the oligarchs and the democrats find happiness in the gratification that requires wealth, their unanimity will force them into further conflict. That is because wealth is a 'contested good' (see 1271b7–9, § 210).

The Spartans have been the most self-conscious and efficient in organizing the city to achieve their shared goals. But the goals have been the usual ones; they have wanted to secure the contested goods, and have decided that military virtue is the way to secure them, 1271a40–b10. Since they have had no true conception of happiness, they have had no true conception of a city's proper tasks, and so they have made their city into a barracks.

31. Aristotle agrees that if there is no deliberate public education, then parents may have to do what they can by themselves, *EN* 1180a24–32. But if private citizens agree with the basic assumption of the political system, then the city will do more efficiently what they do.

The city forms character and habits by its laws or the lack of them. It forms character no less by the honours and rewards offered for and in political activity. When wealth, good birth, military or rhetorical ability, is the qualification for public office, different aims and characters will be formed. In so far as the city has other ways to bestow praise, honour, blame, and disgrace, it encourages the growth of the corresponding characters.

32. Aristotle recognizes a reciprocal relation between the characters of citizens and the nature of the political system, 1337a11–27. But some cities allow their unconscious formation of characters to threaten the system, and this is what we should expect when they are founded on a partly false conception of happiness. A system that extends its inherent defects into defective characters in its citizens will threaten its own stability; hence the one-sided pursuit of the conception of happiness that underlies an oligarchy or a democracy will eventually threaten the oligarchic or democratic system itself, 1310a12–38. To maintain itself, the system needs to form characters that will suit the constitution, since without them it will find survival difficult, 1292b11–21, 1319b1–4. See § 248.

33. See § 220.
34. See § 217.
35. The choice that a citizen makes in maturity is a choice of a common moral education that he has to have begun long before he is able to make a choice about it. Being a virtuous person, he is pleased that the previous generation chose a political and social system that imposed this moral education on him. It is not a restriction of his freedom; for it is the system that he rationally prefers to have imposed on him. Nor does it constrain him more than any other early life would have constrained him. Conscientious refusal to impose moral education seems to Aristotle to rest on a false conception of the alternatives. Someone who grows up untrained is simply exposed to the social pressures resulting from the city's institutions and practices, and has his desires ill-equipped for becoming virtuous.
36. Aristotle does not imply an unthinking endorsement of every political system that tries to perpetuate itself by moral education. In 1310a12–36 he thinks the preferable route to stability is the route that will make a political system better, and that hence the preferable form of education will encourage some degree of genuine virtue. See § 248.
37. On the importance of freedom and initiative for the virtuous person's *prohairesis* see Allan [1965a], 68. On democratic freedom see Mulgan [1970].
38. On arbitration see § 189.

CHAPTER 20

1. To show that general justice is the whole of virtue Aristotle argues:
   (1) Justice is what legislative science prescribes.
   (2) Laws (i.e. the products of legislative science) aim at the common benefit in all they prescribe.
   (3) Hence justice secures the common benefit by promoting happiness and its parts for the community.
   (4) Laws prescribe actions required by all the virtues.
   (5) Hence justice is the whole of virtue in relation to another, 1129b11–27.

   Since legislative science is the same as political science, which is practical wisdom aiming at the good of the community, 1141b23–33 (cf. 1094a27–b10), we can agree with Aristotle's claim that legislative science aims at the good of the community. Hence the commonly recognized connexion between law and justice is intelligible. It is wrong to say that whatever a positive law prescribes is thereby just; bad constitutions and bad laws fail to achieve the common benefit, and hence fail to achieve justice, 1129b24–5. However, it is true to say that what is lawful, *nomimon*, is in a way just, 1129b12. For what is lawful is what is prescribed by legislative science, and this, unlike positive law, will aim at the common good. Positive laws approximate to justice in so far as they coincide with the provisions of legislative science.

If (5) is to follow, (4) must mean that the laws seek to make citizens virtuous, not simply to make them do the actions that a virtuous person would do. Unless I am a virtuous person who sees how the other-regarding aspects of the virtues promote my good, I will be less rationally convinced of the appropriateness of just actions. I will not value just action for its own sake unless I can relate it to my happiness and hence to the other virtues; and if I value it only instrumentally, I cannot be trusted to do the just action in conditions where the just person will gladly do it. The same point applies to the other-regarding aspects of each virtue of character.

Allan [1965a], 62–72, argues for a more restricted view of the functions of law. On the serious issues he raises about compulsion see § 227.

2. On the same state with two different 'beings' see 13n21.
3. A rather over-simplified and one-sided consequentialist account of Aristotle is offered by Miller [1981].
4. The competitive aspects of *pleonexia* are captured in a translation such as 'overreaching', 'outdoing', 'getting the better'. When Aristotle speaks of 'gain', *kerdos*, as characteristic of greed, he needs to restrict it to gain at the expense of another—the sort of gain that is also another's loss.
5. A similar distinction explains why Fred is merely ungenerous, even miserly, if he cares too much about his money, whereas Bert displays special injustice, since he wants to enrich himself by taking advantage of other people. Again, Fred is competitive against Curt to win something that both of them want; but Bert is pleonectic because he wants to get the better of Curt by depriving Curt of something that Curt is justly entitled to.
6. Williams [1980] rejects Aristotle's efforts to connect injustice with *pleonexia*, or any one motive. But Williams's own view, 198f, seems not to distinguish someone who is indifferent to, or insufficiently concerned with, justice from the positively unjust person; this distinction is plausible enough to suggest that Aristotle might be right. On the scope of general justice see Allan [1965a], 65–7.
7. The goods Aristotle has in mind include not only such occasional windfalls as the revenues from the Athenian silver mines, but also the distribution of political power and office, both an intrinsic and an instrumental good. This is suggested by the reference to different political systems, 1131a25–9, and by the parallels in the *Pol.* Contrast Hardie [1980], 191. Joachim [1951], 138f, remarks rightly that such distributive questions are a concern of wisdom, and infers unjustifiably that they cannot be a concern of justice. The same distributive principles will presumably also cover taxation (e.g. Athenian capital levies, *eisphorai*, and liturgies) and questions about the distribution of land and the nature of laws about debt—two important issues for Greek radical democrats.
8. The passage is quoted and discussed further in § 233.
9. Perhaps, however, Aristotle means instead or as well that we should consider someone's political virtue, and hence his *likely* contribution to the common welfare, before we appoint him to public office. This would be a prospective criterion; and we cannot guarantee that its results will coincide

with the results of the retrospective criterion, looking at a person's past services. But Aristotle does not seem concerned with the possible difference between these two criteria.

The possible difference emerges still more clearly in an analogy he uses to support virtue as the criterion. He remarks that in distributing flutes we would not give the best flutes to the handsomest or tallest or richest people if they were no good as flautists; we give the best flutes to the best flautists, 1282b30–1283a3. Evidently the criterion here is prospective. We look at people's likely performance and regard the item to be distributed as a resource or instrument to be used for some purpose, and hence appropriately given to whoever will use it best for the intended purpose. Aristotle sees no potential conflict between this way of looking at distributive justice and the retrospective view of it that focuses on rewards for past services.

10. Aristotle's scheme looks unhelpfully naïve if it is taken to state a sufficient condition for just punishment (see Hardie [1980], 194). It is more reasonable if it states a necessary condition. In punishment we consider general justice and the common interest, and these may lead us to impose a harsher penalty than corrective justice alone would impose. Might it not also allow us to ignore a harm that corrective justice tells us to correct? We need some account of the relation between the rather specific requirements of corrective justice and the requirements of the rest of morality, above all of general justice.

11. Aristotle does not distinguish commercial justice from the first two types, 1130b30–1131a4, and initially might seem to be treating it as a type of corrective justice. This, however, is hard to believe. (See Hardie [1980], 194.) For he remarks that retaliation fits very poorly with corrective justice, and then concedes that it is quite a good account of commercial justice, as long as the retaliation and reciprocity are proportional, not numerically equal, 1132b21–5. Since corrective justice is concerned with numerical equality, it seems to contrast rather sharply with commercial justice; and since Aristotle says a city holds together by proportional reciprocity, 1132b33–4, this form of justice deserves some attention.

Commercial justice is the type that is most relevant to friendships for advantage that are an important part of a political community. When Aristotle says that the political community seems to have come together at the start and to remain in being for the sake of advantage, 1160a8–14, he does not contradict his claim that the city is not merely an association for carrying on transactions for advantage, but for living well, *Pol.* 1278b20, 1328a35–b2. Though these are not distinctive activities of the city, they may still be necessary for the city to exist and survive. If citizens regularly cheated each other, and could not rely on satisfactory bargains, the distinctively political life of the city would not survive either.

When is a transaction genuinely reciprocal, and hence just? Aristotle's initial claim is rather minimal and unhelpful. There must be some way to measure and compare beds with corn, so that a carpenter and a farmer can exchange their products. This sort of measure is provided by money, 1133a5–25, but need is the basic measure, 1133a25–7. If 'need' is to be understood conatively, in relation to someone's desires, then if X is willing to pay the price Y asks, he has no ground for complaint of unfairness or injustice. Such a view of need is assumed, e.g., by Hardie [1980], 198, who moves from talk of needs to talk of the ' "demand" which springs from these needs', without exploring the relation between demand and need, and also takes Aristotle to assume that 'the social value of a producer is measured by the demand for his product', 200.

On this view, even if X is mistaken about his good he has no ground for complaint. Aristotle, however, recognizes some grounds for complaint in such bargains, when he discusses the casuistry of friendship for advantage. Sometimes the beneficiary complains that the benefactor did something easy and wants too much in return, and the benefactor tells the opposite story. Aristotle suggests that in these cases the benefit to the beneficiary rather than the effort of the benefactor should be decisive, 1164b16–20; at the same time he requires the beneficiary to decide how much the service is worth to him before, not after, he obtains it, 1164b20–1. If these remarks can be applied to commercial justice, the just price will apparently correspond to the benefit of the buyer.

This seems to raise some further questions. If Croesus has been able to buy all the corn and will sell it to me only at exorbitant rates that will reduce me nearly to destitution, I may be willing to pay a huge price for corn because I correctly judge that I need it to stay alive; but does that make it a just transaction with Croesus? These problems would be solved if Aristotle could show how degree of need can be determined without reference to the conditions of supply and demand. On the difference between need and 'demand', as conceived in economic theory, see Finley [1970], 146–50. Agreement with Finley on this point does not imply acceptance of his general claim that Aristotle's account is ethical *rather than* part of an economic analysis (on this point Finley is criticized by Meikle [1979]).

12. We might think there are obvious counterexamples, in clearly just transactions that confer unequal benefits. If Croesus is far better off than I am, then apparently he needs nothing from me, and I cannot pay him enough for what he sells me. But Aristotle is not worried by those cases when he discusses unequal friendships; there the inferior party gives honour in return when he can give no other service, 1163b1–3. Nor will Aristotle shrink from the implication that when Croesus becomes so rich that he needs no more money, he should retire and take up transactions in honour instead—that is just what the magnificent person will do. If, however, he needs the profit of his business for his magnificent activities, that is a basis for commercial justice.

Hence Aristotle seems to accept the general principle that commercial justice ensures that someone who pays the just price will not suffer a net loss of happiness by doing it, absolutely or in relation to the other party in the transaction, and that he will not commit *pleonexia* on the other, enhancing his own prospects at the expense of the other.

13. I might also properly be concerned about distribution between different

stages of myself if they benefit to different degrees from my action. See §
195 and 16n44 for analogies between the intra-personal and inter-personal
cases. The stability and concord of virtuous people within themselves and
with each other will be important for both cases.

14. Happiness requires the life of a virtuous active citizen adequately supplied
with external goods. Hence the constitution will prescribe a share in ruling
for all the citizens. It will do this for three reasons: (1) This is part of each
citizen's happy life. (2) It is most likely to reach the correct answers about
what promotes the common interest. The collective intelligence of virtuous
and intelligent people is more likely to reach the right answer than is the
unaided reflexion of one person. (3) It is most likely to produce the
appropriate concord and satisfaction with the constitution. A citizen will
not feel himself slighted and dishonoured, as he would if he were allowed
no role in deliberation about the common interest; that would be the
condition, Aristotle thinks, of a slave and an enemy, 1274a15–18.

Similarly, the requirements of happiness will guide the state in assuring
an adequate level of external goods, offering the citizen no opportunity for
unlimited accumulation, and ensuring the private property needed for
individual initiatives in virtuous action.

15. 1288a32–b2 (cf. 1325b3–14) suggests that each correct constitution will be
correct only in the conditions appropriate for it, not in every condition.
Monarchy is not correct when there is no one of preeminent virtue; and
restricted aristocracy, not including all the citizens, is not correct if all the
citizens are of roughly equal virtue. Since the best conditions are those in
which all the citizens are virtuous, the best of the three correct constitutions
in the best conditions will be the one that gives all the citizens a share in
ruling; but this will not be correct in less than ideal conditions. And if the
conditions deviate too far from the ideal, a correct constitution may be
difficult or impossible (cf. 1286b20–2, 1293a1–9, 1297b22–8).

Only the correct systems rule with a view to the common interest, and
the deviant ones rule with a view to the interest of one group within the
state, 1279a17–21. A true conception of general justice is the standard for
judgments about the correctness or deviance of a political system. Every
political system, Aristotle assumes, will claim to some degree that it is
concerned with the common interest of its citizens; this is part of the status
of a citizen as opposed to a slave, 1279a30–2. However, not all systems are
in fact designed to do what they say they are doing. Aristotle's division is
like a division between accurate and inaccurate thermometers. We may use
inaccurate ones with the intention of measuring the temperature accurately,
and say that this is what we are doing, but we still will not be able to do it.
On the other hand, a correct constitution might fail to promote the
common interest because of unforeseeable circumstances; but it is still a
correct constitution if the design of its institutions and laws tends to
promote the common interest, and avoids the bias that is characteristic of
the deviant forms. A true conception of general justice is needed for a
correct system, and hence for a correct conception of special justice and of
equality.

16. Assumptions, *hupotheseis*, are an important part of constitutions as Aristotle analyses them. He identifies and criticizes the assumption of the Spartan legislator, 1271a41–b3, and describes the democratic assumption and aim as freedom, 1317a40–b2; cf. *telos*, *Rhet.* 1366a2–6. The best constitution rests on the best assumption, 1329a21–4; cf. 1334b11; since it is the best, however, it can also be described as 'best without qualification', not 'best on an assumption', 1278a4, 1293b1–7, 1328b38, 1332a7–10. In some cases a false assumption is taken for granted without argument, as it is in deviant constitutions.

   Sometimes a regime may proceed on a false assumption that should be rejected even for the sake of that regime. The tyrant proceeds on false assumptions about how to preserve his position, and these must be rejected, 1314a25–9; but still the politician's advice must proceed from the assumption that the tyranny is to be preserved, 1314a33–40. Again, Plato's assumption about the unification of the ideal state is to be rejected as false, because it is inconsistent with the nature of a state altogether, 1261a16–22. The tyrant's assumptions would presumably have the same effect, of making the city into a collection of slaves and masters.

17. Aristotle thinks the crucial division in political systems is between democracy and oligarchy, between the rule of the poor and the rule of the rich, 1290a13–b20. See 1280a7–11, 1296a22–3, 1301b39–1302a2, 1303b15–17, 1307a5–27, 1309b35–1310a2. Aristotle's description of the different systems raises some further questions about their relation to the two basic principles.

   'Aristocracy' is the name not only for the rule of genuinely virtuous people, in the ideal state, 1293b1–7, but also for a restricted form of government that modifies oligarchy by paying some attention to virtue as such, 1293b7–21. Such attention is reflected in concern for good birth and nobility, since good birth is simply long-established wealth and virtue, 1294a20–2. Hence aristocracy appeals to the oligarchic conception of justice, allowing for virtue as well as (or instead of) wealth. It rightly supposes that virtue is a relevant criterion, but wrongly supposes that this requires a restricted political class. In the ideal state the citizen will be appropriately virtuous, and in actual states there is enough virtue in the lower classes collectively to justify a share in ruling for them.

   It is harder to see why the non-ideal sort of aristocracy counts as a correct constitution. Aristotle recognizes that all the constitutions fall short of the ideal state, 1293b24–6. But still he regards aristocracy as one of the three correct forms, and oligarchy as a deviation from it, 1293b22–7. He assumes that the extent to which a constitution cares about virtue in its rulers will advance its concern for the common interest. He realizes that not all regimes claiming to be aristocracies cultivate anything like genuine virtue, 1293b42–1294a9; the ones that fall short of proper virtue thereby fall short of being aristocracies. But even those that are non-ideal constitutions may be concerned for the common interest in so far as they cultivate virtue.

   Sidgwick [1892] and Newman [1892], [1887], iii.p. xxxvi, iv.p. ix, discuss the treatment of aristocracy in *Pol.* iii and vii. I am sceptical of claims about inconsistency or development in Aristotle's view. In iii he relies, reasonably, on the *endoxa* about aristocracy and (as Sidgwick emphasizes) ordinary putative examples of aristocracies; in vii he presents his own example, based on a theory that only partly coincides with ordinary views.

A monarchy follows the same conception of justice as an aristocracy, claiming sufficient superiority in virtue for a single person. Hence it also reflects a variation in the oligarchic principle.

Tyranny is apparently another variation on the oligarchic principle, though its exact claim to justice is not clear, since it is least like a genuine constitution, 1293b27–30; cf. 1289a38–b5, 1310b2–7. Does Aristotle think that a tyrant makes a claim of justice that corresponds to the king's claim in the way an oligarchic claim corresponds to an aristocratic? The oligarch claims that superiority gives him a just claim to rule; here he agrees with the aristocrat, and is right; but he picks the wrong kind of superiority. Similarly, we might think, the tyrant might claim that his supremacy gives him a just claim; here he agrees with the king, and is right; but he picks the wrong kind of superiority, since he has supreme power but not supreme virtue.

However, Aristotle does not seem to examine the tyrant's claim to justice on these terms. He suggests instead a second sort of claim, that the tyrant presents himself as an expedient for the protection of the masses against injustice by the upper classes, 1310b12–14. In that case the tyrant's claim will be the democratic claim plus the claim that he is needed to secure justice in these particular conditions.

This second claim to justice is considerably more plausible than the first. The moderately plausible conception of a state as a business partnership makes the oligarchic claim to superiority seem more plausible; but the tyrannical claim about superiority rests on no equally plausible conception of the state. The claim about temporary expediency is far more plausible. If Aristotle had concentrated more on this, he could have formed a much clearer and more interesting conception of a tyranny, and could explain why it is not a constitution in the same way as the others. Tyranny, he might say, does not have its own conception of justice. Rather, it presents itself as a defender of one of the other conceptions of justice; though Aristotle mentions it only as a defender of the masses, it might equally be a defender of the rich against the masses, as Gelon was in Syracuse.

This defence of tyranny shows why it is relevant to constitutions and cities; for in these cases the tyrant can appeal to the common interest that is the characteristic aim of the city. If the tyrant could make no such appeal, his rule would be the suppression of the constitution because it would be the suppression of the city of which the constitution is the organization, 1274b38. As Aristotle often insists, a mere orderly and stable collection does not constitute a city without the common aim at the common interest, 1280a31–3, 1283a17–20, 1291a8–10, 22–8, 1295b21–5, 1303a25–7, 1328b16–19. But since, as Aristotle recognizes, a tyrant often appeals to the common interest, tyranny has a legitimate place in the discussion of constitutions.

18. For partial grasp of some truth or principle cf. *EE* 1227a1–2, *GC* 324a14–15, *Phys.* 191b35–6.
19. Wood and Wood [1978], 239, suggest without warrant that Aristotle thinks the oligarchic conception of justice less defective than the democratic; they do not consider the points of superiority in the democratic conception.
20. The connexion between democracy and a particular way of life is suggested in Thucydides ii 37.2–3, vii 69.2.
21. See § 23.
22. On preliminary questions see § 90.

CHAPTER 21

1. See § 199.
2. The character sketches may seem quite unlikely to support our general claims about the *Ethics*. (1) Aristotle seems to be sketching some commonly recognized traits of character and the types of people who display them. The canon seems to be taken from common beliefs, not justified from any less conventional basis. (Wood and Wood [1978], 223–6 give a brief and flagrantly one-sided account of the 'aristocratic conservatism' (223) of Aristotle's discussion of the principal moral virtues.) (2) These seem to be described as distinct and separable traits; we find no systematic argument to show how each virtue promotes the common good. (3) The actions and attitudes required by some of the virtues (e.g. magnificence in iv 2, or wit in iv 8) seem to have very little to do with the common good, or indeed with morality as it would normally be conceived. If the virtues fit into our account of Aristotle's ethics, these objections need to be removed.
3. Aristotle takes the fine to be good in itself, 1104b31 (cf. *Top.* 118b27), 1155b18–21, 1169a6, but not identical to what is good in itself; 'best', 'finest', and 'pleasantest' are three different features of the final good, 1099a24, and Aristotle will not agree that every pleasure that is good in itself is thereby fine. His practice in the *Ethics* conforms to his explicit account of the fine as what is both good in itself and praiseworthy, *EE* 1248b18–25.

   We have already seen that praise is awarded for actions that are in the agent's power, and that this is why legislators are concerned with voluntary action, since they are concerned with praise and blame. (See § 81.) But we already know that the sort of action that a legislator will correctly praise is the sort of action that promotes the common good. Here, then, Aristotle marks the connexion he needs between the virtuous person's aims and motives and the legislator's concern for general justice. For more details on the fine see Engberg-Pederson [1983], ch.3, Irwin [1985a].
4. This passage connects three important concepts used in the account of the virtues; what is right and ought to be done (*dein*), what is fine, and what is beneficial to others. Aristotle assumes, as 1120a11–13 shows, that by doing what he ought to the virtuous person does fine actions and actions that

benefit others. Other comments connect what we ought to do with what is correct and what is fine, 1119a11–20, 1120a23–9, 1121a1, b4–5, 1179a3–13, 29. These comments are important because Aristotle refers to what ought to be done in his specification of the doctrine of the mean; we hit the mean when we are angry, e.g., as, when, and towards whom we ought to be. When the action we ought to do is identified with fine action and this in turn is expected to benefit others, the doctrine of the mean acquires more definite content.

5. It would be quite a usual use of 'brave' to say that someone who commits a crime without fear of danger or punishment is brave (cf. Plato, *Rep.* 561a1), but Aristotle refuses to say so, 1115a23–4.

6. Intemperate people are ungenerous to others, so that they can devote their resources to their own pleasures, 1121b7–10. They form the wrong sorts of attachments, because they must always be looking for an adequate return of pleasure or advantage, and so will always be suspicious and ready to quarrel, 1159b7–10, 1166b13–17, 1167b9–16, 1172a8–10. While genuine friendship will be hard for them, they will be easily attracted to flatterers who offer them pleasures, 1121b3–7.

7. See § 205.

8. The magnificent person will want to build himself a grand house, and he will want to fit out his warships and his choruses in a way that does him honour. But he will not seek pointless display that merely advertises his own wealth in a way that benefits no one else; he will not equip his chorus with purple robes simply to show he can afford them, 1123a20–7. Someone whose expenditure is regulated by concern for the common good can benefit both himself and the community; but someone with no concern for the community will be lavish only when it advertises his wealth, not when the community needs some large expenditure, 1123a24–7.

9. On slavishness see § 220.

10. I assume that Aristotle takes some external goods to be intrinsic goods for a good person, not just instrumental to virtuous activities. See Irwin [1985], 93–7, against Cooper [1985a], 187–90, and Nussbaum [1986], 327–36.

11. See § 202.

12. It would be a mistake to suppose that the virtuous person's inflexibility about virtue will simply make him less concerned than other people are about external goods. For he may actually be readier than some people to pursue them. If we think that wealth is, or is a necessary means to, a dominant component of happiness, we may be conservative in taking risks, fearful of poverty, and so inclined to be miserly (cf. 1121b21–31). The virtuous person may actually be a keener investor in worthwhile ventures that are less than absolutely safe. Similarly, the lover of honour will play safe and avoid some competitions, for fear of failure and dishonour. The virtuous person does not mind dishonour so much that he will avoid any risk of it. The person who is afraid of a rebuff in his demands for honour is pusillanimous; the magnanimous person will readily compete for honour, and demand honour even if he is rebuffed. Since honour is not the dominant component of happiness, a virtuous person will not think

dishonour necessarily leaves him with no life worth living; and for this very reason he will not try to cultivate indifference to honour and dishonour. To the extent that the common good and the agent's own good require risky ventures, we have reason to encourage the relative insouciance of the virtuous person over the miserly calculating of the person who overvalues external goods.

13. See §§ 233–4.

14. To explain why there are different types of political systems Aristotle appears to offer different answers: (1) They reflect different views about happiness, and hence about who is capable of it, 1328a37–b2; see § 218. (2) They reflect different conceptions of justice, 1280a7–25, 1301a25–39; cf. 1317b8–9, 1318a11–26, 1337b2–3. (3) They reflect the different kinds of people and their relative numbers and strength in a particular city, 1286b20–2, 1289b27–1290a13, vi 4, 1296b24–34, 1297b16–28, 1317a22–9. See Newman, i.219–23.

   Aristotle does not say which of these explanations is basic; each state of affairs is taken to be the, or a, cause, *aition*, 1289b27, 1328a40; *archê*, 1301a26; *ek*, 1301a29.

15. See § 235.

16. Another traditional principle distinguishes states in which the laws are supreme from those in which they are not. Aristotle thinks this is also a significant principle of division, since he thinks the supremacy of the laws is in the common interest, 1282b1–13. But he thinks this only with an important restriction. The supremacy of the laws is not sufficient for a correct and just constitution, since the character of the laws depends on the character of the constitution, and bad constitutions will have bad laws, 1274b15–18, 1286a3, 1287a3–6, 1289a11–25. Hence it will be good only *ceteris paribus* if the law is supreme. If the laws are bad and the violation of them will promote the common interest, then apparently it would be better to violate them, e.g. in tyrannies that arise in reaction to legally sanctioned oppression of the many by the few. Aristotle does not discuss precisely this case. (Such temporary absolute rulers as Pittacus did not violate the laws, 1285a29–b3, and were not genuine tyrants.) But he seems to be committed to allowing it as a practical possibility; hence he cannot say it is always better to observe the laws than to violate them.

   If, however, a tyrant violates oppressive laws, he should (Aristotle believes) replace them with more just laws; if the conditions require it, these laws might include a legally recognized position for himself, such as Pittacus had, 1285a37–b1, so that he would cease to be a tyrant, 1295a7–24. Aristotle sees no excuse for the continuation of a lawless condition or a condition in which the law is not supreme. A law has to guide and to justify actions for a reasonable length of time, and to provide some publicly known and accepted basis for the action. These features of law will encourage a deviant regime to moderate its claims, and to mitigate the consequences of its false conception of justice. Freedom from legal restraint will remove these mitigating tendencies and display more fully the faults in the regime's conception of justice. Hence Aristotle distinguishes types of oligarchy and democracy by the role they allow to law, and regards the supremacy of law as a count in favour of a regime, 1291b30–4, 1292a1–38, b5–10, 27, 37, 41, 1293a9–10, 12–34.

17. Rawls [1971], 145, 176–8, argues against conceptions of justice that demand a degree of self-sacrifice imposing severe strains of commitment.

18. On Thrasymachus see § 213.

19. Oligarchies allow public offices to be sources of profit, and apply inadequate checks and oversight to public officials, 1308b31–4. Democracies allow popular assemblies and courts to do as they please unrestrained by law, and under the influence of demagogues. Here the conflict is not simply the result of private injustice and greed; it is also the result of the structure of the constitution, which tends to undermine its own conception of justice.

The few commit injustice against the many both in oligarchies and in polities; and by doing this they threaten the stability of each constitution, even in some cases encouraging the growth of tyranny, 1307a7, 24, 1308a9, 1310b13, 1311a25, 1318b37. The proper motive of special injustice, *pleonexia* (see § 229), is especially characteristic of the few, 1301a35, 1307a31, 35; cf. 1311a5, 1333b10. Certainly Aristotle often says or implies that the many commit injustice against the few, 1266b40, 1267a41, 1281a14, 1304b32, 1305a4, 1307a31, 35, 1308a9, 1311a1, 1318a25. He implies that they are also capable of *pleonexia*, 1267b7–8, 1297a11–13. But he does not attribute it to them as a motive for injustice; and he remarks that the greed of the rich is more dangerous than the greed of the many to the stability of the polity, 1297a11–13.

20. Aristotle remarks that if oligarchs had enough virtue to achieve concord among themselves the oligarchy would be hard to destroy from within, 1306a9–12. But often they prefer to commit injustice on each other and destroy concord among themselves; they distrust each other too much to conduct business well, 1306a19–31. Similarly, their injustice to the demos makes the demos ready to listen to aspiring tyrants leading them against the oligarchy, 1305a21–3, 1310b14–16. On injustice and instability see Mulgan [1977], 120, who overemphasizes the importance for Aristotle of the *sense* of injustice, and underemphasizes the role of the *actual* injustice of a state. In attending to the role of injustice, Aristotle is not concerned solely with citizens' *beliefs* that they are being treated unjustly.

21. Aristotle cites the oligarchic oath enjoining malevolence towards the demos, 1310a7–12. He cites no similar example of open anti–oligarchic expression of sentiment in democracies; he simply alleges that the demagogues divide the city into two by fighting the rich, 1310a2–6. Tyranny takes this attitude still further, since the tyrant tries to encourage distrust among all the citizens, so that they will be unwilling to take the risk of combining against him, 1314a15–23.

22. A government has to be especially careful not to insult and provoke lovers of honour, 1302b10–14, 1315a17–24, since, together with love of gain, it is the most prevalent source of injustice, 1271a13–18. But the systems in which honour-loving people grow up are also the most likely to provoke

this. The restricted citizenship in Sparta was partly the result of the Spartiates' competitive conception of honour; but it excluded and humiliated other honour-loving people who were ready to rebel, 1306b22–6. Someone with the appropriate 'manly' character (*andrôdês*, 1306b34, *Rhet.* 1391a22, *EN* 1125b12) is encouraged in an honour-loving system, and easily finds something to provoke him. In a tyranny honour-lovers are a special threat, since the regime requires the humiliation of any citizens who might challenge the tyrant; the tyrant's measures to secure his position may provoke the very reaction he fears, 1315a16–24. These are the people who are liable to attack the tyrant, 1312a21–30 (different motives); cf. 1311a18–20. The honour-lover is easily provoked to anger, associated with love of honour in Aristotle as in Plato; and an angry person is less likely to restrict himself to safe methods, 1315a27–31, 1312b25–34. He has the necessary boldness, *thrasos*, 1312a17–19, 1315a8–14, to do what his honour seems to require.

A competitive attitude to honour characteristically reflects the view that honourable qualities demand competition—success in war, business, politics. And we think of these as honourable qualities because they assure for us the external and contested goods that we need for gratification. Hence a competitive attitude to honour is characteristically associated with some attachment to the life of gratification. The Spartans are professional honour-lovers, but their conception of honour is itself highly competitive; that is why they are so keen to dominate their neighbours. They think they cannot be properly honoured without domination, because they value the contested goods that are needed for a life of gratification (cf. 1271a41–b10, 1324b1–12, 1334a36–b4).

Love of honour is especially dangerous to regimes of the few, in which the rulers tend to struggle against each other, 1308a31–2. Sometimes these struggles cause one group of rulers to inflict humiliating punishments on their opponents, 1306a36–b2. Sometimes they encourage oligarchs to compete against each other for the favour of the many, 1305b22–3; they disturb the constitution in either a democratic or a tyrannical direction.

The many do not completely lack love of honour, and Aristotle thinks it is fairly easily satisfied if they are allowed to elect and to supervise office-holders, 1297b6–8, 1318b21–7. He sees that it is important not to abase and humiliate the masses, 1274a15–17, 1281b28–30. But since they are not concerned so strongly with the competitive aspects of honour, they are not so likely to cause the sort of trouble caused by oligarchs. Oligarchy appeals to competitive motives; but these motives themselves threaten the stability of oligarchy.

23. Hence Aristotle associates aggressiveness especially with wealth, *Rhet.* 1390b32–1391a5; cf. 1385b19–21, 1391a33–b3. The *Pol.* identifies a similar vice characteristic of those who cannot use their leisure and good fortune correctly, 1308b10–16, 1334a25–34. These people turn to luxury, *truphê*, 1291a4, 1295b13–18, 1310a22–3, 1311a11, 1314b28–32, 1326b38–9, *Rhet.* 1391a3, since it is a sign of good fortune, allowing someone to live lavishly

above the margin of necessity. For the same reason such people like to display their position by aggression against others.

24. Aristotle distinguishes greed as a motive for special injustice from the other vices as motives for general injustice. Greed essentially requires the desire to have more, to profit by taking what is justly due to my neighbour. Aristotle admits that the many may have ever-increasing desires for more and more, 1267a39–b9; but this need not be a pleonectic desire, since it need not include the desire to get more than someone else has. The poor may well form pleonectic desires, but they are less characteristically moved by them than the rich are. For the rich tend to seek honour from wealth, since they have more than they need to gratify their appetites; the desire for honour easily makes them competitive; and then greed to have more than someone else at the other's expense becomes intelligible.

Oligarchs are therefore more likely than democrats to quarrel among themselves, since their competitive desires aim at each other even more than at the many. Democracies try to raise the level of the poor to gratify the desires of the poor, but not primarily to impoverish or humiliate the rich. Plato's Callicles sees in democracy the results of jealousy and envy, resulting in a desire to humiliate the better people, *Gorg.* 483b4–484a2; but this is not Aristotle's explanation.

For similar reasons Aristotle sees the injustice of the few expressed in private lawless actions, either violating the law or wrongly permitted by the law. This was the sort of injustice that Solon and Peisistratus tried to curb; it still tends to force oligarchies towards tyrannies, though, ironically, tyrannies allow the most licence for such lawlessness by the tyrant himself. In democracies injustice against the few is normally collective, using the constitutional provisions applying to assembly or courts, directed against the rich as a class, and only secondarily against individual rich people. The reason for the difference is related to the different roles of *pleonexia*. Democrats are not out to display individual superiority over individual oligarchs, but to gratify their appetites; superiority over individual oligarchs is a side-effect, sometimes but not always independently desired.

25. Aggression is a vice of the upper classes. Aristotle never suggests that the many inflict it on the few, though they certainly inflict other sorts of injustice on them. Aggression is characteristic of tyrants, 1311a25–8, 32–6, b18–20, 1314b23–7 and of oligarchs, 1295b9–11, 1297b6–8, 1307a15–20, 1310b40–1311a2. It is such a serious threat to oligarchies that they will be wise to punish aggression by a rich on a poor person more harshly than they punish aggression by one rich person on another, 1309a22–3.

26. Though the honour-loving outlook reflects a basically false conception of happiness, it may encourage people in right actions and restrain them from wrong actions. Some sense of honour encourages particularly energetic people to rebel against tyrants. Still more important, it encourages collective resistance to injustice; it is part of the motive for the poor not to accept unpunished aggression by the rich. For this reason the ideal state will

cultivate some love of honour, 1328a6–16, and tyrants try to suppress it because they see it is dangerous to themselves, 1314a15–25. Since it is a protection against pusillanimity, 1314a15–17, love of honour must not be rejected altogether; someone who has it takes a 'dignified', *semnon*, attitude, 1314a5–10, b18–20, *Rhet.* 1391a20–9, and will not allow himself to do just anything for gain or allow anyone else to abuse or insult him.

27. The upper classes evidently seek gratification, since oligarchs aim at wealth, and tyrants are the most conspicuous advocates of gratification, 1312b23–5, 1314b28–32. However, these people pursue gratification in competition with others, to display their own superiority; hence their pursuit of gratification also aims at honour. The lower classes display the non-competitive pursuit of gratification.

28. Aristotle relies on the old picture of the demos as tyrant and the demagogues as flatterers to suggest the sources of injustice in an extreme democracy. See Plato, *Rep.* 493a–d, and Aristophanes' *Knights*.

29. On living as one pleases see § 223.

30. See 19n23 on military service.

31. See § 225.

32. They may be caused by wars, by foreign influence, 1296a32–8, or by changes in the social and economic conditions or composition of the state, e.g. 1286b20–2, 1302b33–1303a2, 1310b17–18, 1320b17–32, or in the relative status of some part of it, 1297b12–26, 33, 1304a17–33.

33. See 1274a11–15 (excusing Solon), 1293a1–6, 1303a3–10, a25–b3, b7–14 (location of the city), 1306b6–16 (peace increases the number of wealthy people), 1321a5–14. The political scientist needs the appropriate resources, the external goods that partly depend on chance, 1289a32, 1295a28, 1325b40, 1326a5, 1332a1, 1333b17, though success with them requires not only chance but the wise person's correct use of them, 1323b26–31, 1323b40–1324a2, 1332a29–32.

34. Aristotle develops Plato's account of constitutional change in *Republic* viii–ix, and, as usual, criticizes Plato's account for being over-simplified. Plato fails even to consider many changes, and offers too few possible explanations of the changes that are considered, 1316a1–b27; concentrates too heavily on conflict within the ruling class as a cause of change, e.g. 1316a39–b3; and considers only one direction of change, 1316a23–4. The characteristic difference between the *Pol.* and the *Rep.* is displayed in Aristotle's enthusiastic presentation of historical examples that do not fit Plato's account. Still, he follows Plato in one important feature of his explanations; Plato draws attention to the effects of character on constitutional change, and Aristotle develops Plato's general claim into a more precise and complex pattern of explanation.

35. See § 240.

36. Bradley [1927], 196. Here Bradley actually appeals to what he takes to be Aristotle's moral epistemology, to support uncritical acceptance of the moral principles of one's own society. He reaches his conclusion from Aristotle, by ignoring Aristotle's conception of the ideal state, his criticism of deviant states, and his division between the virtue of a man and the virtue

of the citizen. ('My station and its duties', however, is not Bradley's last word on morality either.)

37. Aristotle has no revolutionary strategy or tactics to suggest either, for these reasons: (1) He has no account of how to create the conditions for the ideal state, and hence no advice for those who want to transform actual states in the ideal direction. (2) He does not agree with the competing parties in actual states that their interests necessarily conflict in present conditions. Hence he does not believe that violent action against one class or another is necessary for producing an improvement. (3) He does not think moral principles, especially principles of justice, are relative to a particular political or economic order, or that the true principles can be practised only in the ideal state.

On all these points Aristotle presents a sharp contrast with Marx; it is all the sharper when their views are so close on many other points. Some points of comparison are usefully marked by Wood [1981], 22–4, 126f. They are explored in a helpfully thought-provoking polemical discussion by Meikle [1985], 18–25. An explanation of the contrast is offered by De Ste Croix [1981], who, during a sympathetic comparison of Aristotle's political sociology with Marx, 69–80, comments appropriately: '. . . in the class society for which Aristotle was prescribing the conflicts were indeed inescapable, and no radical transformation of society for the better was then conceivable. In the later Middle Ages the ending of feudal restrictions and the full transition to capitalism offered real hope of betterment to all but a few; and in our own time the prolonged death-throes of capitalism encourage us to look forward to a full socialist society. For Aristotle and his contemporaries there were no prospects of fundamental change that could offer any expectation of a better life for even a citizen of a *polis*, except at the expense of others', 76.

38. Aristotle says it is the task of each craft to find what is best altogether, given the right initial conditions, and what is 'fitting' or 'expedient' in particular conditions, given the external circumstances and the customer's desires, 1288b10–21. It is the doctor's task to advise someone who refuses to give up mountaineering even though it is bad for his health, or someone who refuses to migrate to Arizona to relieve his asthma. The politician is supposed to consider not only (i) the best system in the right external conditions; (ii) the system that best suits these people in these external conditions; (iii) the system that best suits all cities; but also (iv) the system that is best 'on an assumption', 1288b21–38.

Aristotle does not suggest, though, that a craft should allow itself to be misused; he considers only the use of the craft for its proper end. The doctor should advise the patient about how to stay healthy within these restrictions, not about how to ruin his health, even though the doctor might be the best qualified adviser about that also. The sort of advice a political scientist should give depends on the proper end of political science, which is the good of the community. Hence he should give advice about stability only in so far as it fulfils this prior aim. If this is Aristotle's view, then the right technical advice must rest on a true conception of the end.

His aims in reforming constitutions are discussed by Rowe [1977] (who sees more disunity in Aristotle's views than I am inclined to see), and by Mulgan [1977], 130–6.

39. On assumptions see 20n16. Some assumptions underlying deviant systems are neither true nor disastrously false. In these cases we must distinguish what is best without qualification from what is best in relation to a specific assumption, and some of our criticisms and advice must be restricted by the assumption (cf. 1269a39, 1279a36, 1294a7, 1296b9, 1314a38).

40. A tyranny, e.g., that has proceeded on a false assumption may have done so much harm that it cannot improve itself. Nor does Aristotle say it is always better for a politician to offer preservative advice.

41. His advice might actually encourage the right kind of constitutional change, even if it retards the pace of it. If an oligarchy improves itself enough to change into a responsible democracy rather than a tyranny, Aristotle might point to this direction of change as a benefit of political advice.

42. He disdains constitutional 'tricks' (*sophismata*, 1307b39–1308a3), devices intended to conceal the real bias of the constitution, and to give the weaker group the appearance of some power without the reality, 1297a14–38. Aristotle suggests that these will be 'found out', 1308a1, because they will not deceive their intended victims. But some of the harsher measures of tyranny and democracy are more than tricks; though Aristotle rejects them also, he does not say they are ineffective, 1313b32–1314a14, 1319b19–32. See further Mulgan [1977], 132.

43. If the assembly is controlled by the many and the courts by the few, the few will suffer injustice in the assembly and repay it in the courts, and the state will be more unstable. Aristotle criticizes these divided loyalties in a state whose education does not agree with the laws, 1293b11–21, 1310a12–28. Divided loyalties result from the unskilful mixing that Aristotle criticizes in the existing mixed constitutions of Crete, Sparta, and Carthage, e.g. 1270b6–35. Clearly it is not the result he intends when he advocates mixing, e.g. 1307b26–39.

44. Aristotle's main advice concerns the treatment of the losers in the oligarchic or democratic state. The winners should pay special attention to the welfare of the losers, and avoid the sort of injustice against them that is the work of oligarchs unchecked by law or of demagogues who use the forms of legality for unjust exaction, 1298b13, 1303a10, 1309a14, 20, 1310a3, 1311a15, 1316a13, 1320a4, 26. Democracy is on the whole more stable than oligarchy, and the polity is more stable if it tends to democracy, 1296a13, 1307a16, 1308b30, 1309b18. Aristotle allows that the inherent tendency of oligarchy to oppress the poor is stronger and less easily controlled than the inherent tendency of democracy to oppress the rich. For the many are stronger and more content with equal shares, 1307a17–20, while the few are always eager to compete against each other. Hence he recognizes a tendency to greater democracy, and argues that it need not be as seriously unjust as some of its critics suggest, if it takes proper account of the interests of the political losers.

45. Aristotle is especially concerned to avoid extremes of wealth and poverty, since these lead citizens both to have and to notice conflicting aims and interests, 1306b36, 1320a17–b4. This advice is intended to avoid the tendency of a poor demos to demand support from public funds, and so to be eager to commit injustice on the rich. But the same advice seems to commit Aristotle in many conditions to the advocacy and approval of considerable redistribution. Here again he seems to provide for arrangements that in many actual conditions will require more democracy than he actually mentions; for it would surely be hard to carry out the necessary redistribution without democracy or some strong tendencies to it. The constitution that best suits most conditions and cities is polity; and democracy deviates less from this, its corresponding correct constitution, than other deviant constitutions deviate from their correct forms. It is reasonable to expect, then, that in many conditions democracy will be the best deviant system, and in the subset of these cases where a polity is impossible, democracy will be the best available system altogether.

46. See 1266b34–8, 1269a20–4, 1310a12–22, 1319b1–6, 1337a11–18, and 19n32.

47. In non-ideal states the citizens are incapable of a virtuous and happy life. If the ideal state provides a reasonable standard for justice and the common interest, 1296b2–12, a constitution aiming at the degree of happiness possible for the citizens must be the best one, and a virtuous life with an adequate supply of external goods must be preferable to the lives that aim at honour or gratification of appetite, even for people whose nature, training, and environment make them incapable of complete virtue.

48. On Aristotle's misuse of the doctrine of the mean see Robinson [1962], 103 (who endorses a different unwarranted inference from the doctrine), Mulgan [1977], 107–10.

49. This is true provided that there should be private property in the state at all; see § 251.

50. See § 220.

51. Private property is meant for a state in which all the citizens are in a position to live a life of leisure and virtue, so that each has a sufficient supply of externals to free him from concern with them. Aristotle is not thinking of a way to supply the needs of the desperately poor by making them dependent on the charity of the rich; indeed he argues against this, in so far as he stresses the evil of letting the lower classes be impoverished and dependent, e.g. 1309a20–6; and cf. 1329b41–1330a18. The sort of generosity he wants to protect assumes that citizens are in roughly equal conditions and that none is totally dependent on the generosity of others. Since these are Aristotle's assumed background conditions for private property, his view raises the possibility that in conditions where private property encourages the sorts of evils that he wants to avoid, its advantages may be overridden by the greater importance of avoiding these other evils.

52. Aristotle uses these points about self-sacrifice to criticize Plato for going to self-defeating extremes in his efforts to make the whole city promote its common interest. Aristotle supposes (most dubiously) that Plato has deprived the guardians of happiness to secure the happiness of the whole

city, and argues against Plato that the happiness of the whole cannot be secured by forcing one large part to renounce its own self-confined interest for the sake of the other parts, 1264b15–25. On Aristotle's own use of the organic analogy see § 217.

53. On menial workers see 19n19.

54. In an ideal state why should a citizen not exercise generosity without exclusive ownership, through his role in collective actions? Even apart from collective action, the state might loan him some resources to use as he sees fit; and in disposing of these, he apparently exercises generosity without ownership.

55. Similarly, we need not accept without question his rejection of artifacts as substances, and we need not make this a count against his general view of substance, if we see that the general view does not support the specific conclusion about artifacts. See 12n8.

CHAPTER 22

1. See *Phys.* 185a12–20, 192a34–b1, *EN* 1097b30–1, 1102a18–23, *EE* 1216b40–1217a10. See §§ 11, 77.

2. See e.g. *EN* 1094b19–1095a2; cf. 16n3.

3. Aristotle is fond of saying that he has discussed something only 'in outline', *tupô(i)*. See *IA* 779a24–48, Régis [1935], 155f.

4. See the just comments of Bonitz [1848], ii.29: 'Is enim ut est diligentissimus in cognoscendis rebus singularibus, quorum ingentem prorsus et prope incredibilem animo complexus est scientiam, ut est acutus et ingeniosus in redigendis his singulis rebus ad summas, quas distinxit, omnium entium categorias; ita quum de iaciendis altissimis doctrinae fundamentis et de confirmandis interque se conciliandis principiis agitur, plurimum relinquit dubitationis.' Both Eucken [1872], 33, and Le Blond [1939], 122n, have thought Bonitz's remark striking enough to deserve quotation in a book on Aristotle's methods.

5. On *Phys.* 192a34–b2, 194b14–15, *DA* 403b15–16, see 3n52, 8n2.

6. On the lateness of the *DA* see 13n33. On the *DA* and the ethical works see 15n2. On the *EN* see 16n5.

7. Contrast, e.g., *DA* 412a3–13 with *Phys.* 192b33–4, where the claim about substance is both less precise and less similar to the *Met.*

8. See § 95.

9. See § 194.

10. See § 78.

11. Cf. § 6.

12. See § 154.

13. Ross [1923], preface.

14. See § 84. In referring to Aristotle's aims in studying past philosophers, I am not assuming that he succeeds in his aims. The fairest general assessment of his views on the Presocratics is Guthrie [1957], reacting to the unfair,

sometimes uncomprehending, attacks by Cherniss [1935]. Cherniss [1944] attacks Aristotle's criticism of Plato from the same point of view as in his previous book. Fine [1983], [1984], [1987], examines Aristotle's criticism of Plato from a point of view far more sympathetic than Cherniss's, but without simply endorsing Aristotle's criticisms.
15. Green [1890], i.4f.
16. The passage is quoted in § 84.

BIBLIOGRAPHY

Ackrill, J. L., [1963] (tr. and ed.), *Categories and De Interpretatione*, Oxford, 1963.

—— [1965] 'Aristotle's distinction between *energeia* and *kinesis*', in Bambrough [1965], 121–41.

—— [1972] 'Aristotle on "good" and the categories', in *AA* ii, 17–24. From *Islamic Philosophy and the Classical Tradition*, ed. S. M. Stern, V. Brown, and A. Hourani (Oxford, 1972), 17–25.

—— [1972a] 'Aristotle's definitions of *psuche*', in *AA* iv, 65–75. From *PAS* 73 (1972–3), 119–33.

—— [1974] 'Aristotle on *eudaimonia*', in *EAE*, 15–34. From *PBA* 60 (1974), 339–59.

—— [1981] 'Aristotle's theory of definition', in Berti [1981], 359–84.

Albritton, R. G., [1957] 'Forms of particular substances in Aristotle's *Metaphysics*', *JP* 54 (1957), 699–708.

Allan, D. J., [1961] 'Quasi-mathematical method in the *Eudemian Ethics*', in Mansion [1961], 303–18.

—— [1964] 'On Aristotle's metaphysics', *Dialogue* 2 (1964), 454–9.

—— [1965] 'Causality, ancient and modern', *SPAS* 39 (1965), 1–18.

—— [1965a] 'Individual and state in Aristotle's *Ethics* and *Politics*', in *Entretiens sur l'Antiquité Classique* 11 (Geneva, 1965), 53–85.

Allen, R. E., [1969] 'Individual properties in Aristotle's *Categories*', *Phr.* 14 (1969), 31–9.

—— [1973] 'Substance and predication in Aristotle', in Lee [1973], 362–73.

Alpern, K. D., [1983] 'Aristotle on the friendships of utility and pleasure', *JHP* 21 (1983), 305–15.

Ando, T., [1958] *Aristotle's Theory of Practical Cognition*, 3rd edn., The Hague, 1958.

Annas, J., [1974] 'Individuals in Aristotle's *Categories*: two queries', *Phr.* 19 (1974), 146–52.

—— [1977] 'Plato and Aristotle on friendship and altruism', *Mind* 86 (1977), 532–54.

—— [1982], 'Aristotle on inefficient causes', *PQ* 32 (1982), 311–26.

—— [1986a], 'Doing without objective values', in *The Norms of Nature*, ed. M. Schofield and G. Striker (Cambridge, 1986), 3–29.

—— and Barnes, J., [1986] *The Modes of Scepticism*, Cambridge, 1986.

Anscombe, G. E. M., [1953] 'The principle of individuation', in Anscombe [1981], 57–65, and *AA* iii, 88–95. From *SPAS* 27 (1953), 83–96.

—— and Geach, P. T., [1961] *Three Philosophers*, Oxford, 1961.

—— [1965] 'Thought and action in Aristotle', in Anscombe [1981], 66–77, and *AA*, ii 61–71. From Bambrough [1965], 143–58.

—— [1981] *Collected Papers* i, Oxford, 1981

Anton, J. P., and Kustas, G. L., eds., [1971] *Essays in Ancient Greek Philosophy* i, Albany, 1971.
—— and Preus, A., eds., [1983] *Essays in Ancient Greek Philosophy* ii, Albany, 1983.
Apelt, O., [1891] *Beiträge zur Geschichte der griechischen Philosophie*, Leipzig, 1891.
Aquinas, Thomas, *In Aristotelis Metaphysica*, ed. M. R. Cathala and R. M. Spiazzi, Turin, 1950.
—— *In De Anima*, ed. A. M. Pirotta, Turin, 1959.
—— *Summa contra Gentiles*, ed. C. Pera *et al.*, Turin, 1961.
—— *Summa Theologiae*, ed. R. Caramello, Turin, 1952.
Armstrong, D. M., [1968] *A Materialist Theory of the Mind*, London, 1968.
—— [1973] *Belief, Truth, and Knowledge*, Cambridge, 1973.
—— [1978] *Universals and Scientific Realism*, 2 vols., Cambridge, 1978.
—— [1983] *What is a Law of Nature?*, Cambridge, 1983.
Arpe, C., [1938] *Das ti ên einai bei Aristoteles*, Hamburg, 1938.
Aubenque, P., [1961] 'Sur la notion aristotélicienne de l'aporie', in Mansion [1961], 3–19.
—— [1966] *Le problème de l'être chez Aristote*, 2nd edn., Paris, 1966.
Ayers, M. R., [1974] 'Individuals without sortals', *CJP* 4 (1974), 113–48.
Balme, D. M., [1972] (tr. and ed.) *Aristotle: De Partibus Animalium* i, Oxford, 1972.
Bambrough, R., ed., [1965] *New Essays on Plato and Aristotle*, London, 1965.
Barker, E., [1906] *The Political Thought of Plato and Aristotle*, London, 1906.
Barnes, J., [1969] 'Aristotle's theory of demonstration', in *AA* i, 65–87. From *Phr.* 14 (1969), 123–52.
—— [1969a] 'The Law of Contradiction', *PQ* 19 (1969), 302–9.
—— [1970] 'Property in Aristotle's *Topics*', *AGP* 52 (1970), 136–55.
—— [1971] 'Aristotle's concept of mind', in *AA* iv, 32–41. From *PAS* 72 (1971–2), 101–14.
—— [1975] (tr. and ed.) *Aristotle: Posterior Analytics*, Oxford, 1975.
—— [1977] Review of Hintikka [1973], *JHS* 97 (1977), 183–6.
—— [1981] 'Proof and the syllogism', in Berti [1981], 17–59.
—— [1981a] 'Aristotle and the methods of ethics', *Revue Internationale de la Philosophie* 34 (1981), 490–511.
—— ed., [1984] *Complete Works of Aristotle: the Revised Oxford Translation*, 2 vols., Princeton, 1984.
—— Schofield, M., and Sorabji, R., eds., [1975a] *Articles on Aristotle*, 4 vols., London, 1975–9 (cited as '*AA*').
—— Burnyeat, M. F., and Schofield, M., eds., [1980] *Doubt and Dogmatism*, Oxford, 1980.
Beck, L. W., [1960] *A Commentary on Kant's Critique of Practical Reason*, Chicago, 1960.
Bekker, I., [1831] (ed.) *Aristotelis Opera*, 5 vols., Berlin 1831–70.
Bennett, J., [1964] *Rationality*, London, 1964.
—— [1976] *Linguistic Behaviour*, Cambridge, 1976.
Berlin, I., [1973] 'Austin and the early beginnings of Oxford philosophy', in *Essays on J. L. Austin* (Oxford, 1973).

Berti, E., [1965] *L'unità del sapere in Aristotele*, Padua, 1965.
—— ed., [1981] *Aristotle on Science*, Padua, 1981.
Block, I., [1961] 'The order of Aristotle's psychological writings', *American Journal of Philology* 82 (1961), 50–77.
—— [1961a] 'Truth and error in Aristotle's theory of sense perception', *PQ* 11 (1961), 1–9.
—— [1964] 'Three German commentators on the individual senses and the common sense in Aristotle', *Phr.* 9 (1964), 58–63.
—— [1965] 'On the commonness of the common sensibles', *Australasian Journal of Philosophy* 43 (1965), 189–95.
—— [1969] 'Aristotle and the physical object', *Philosophy and Phenomenological Research* 21 (1969), 93–101.
Block, N. J., [1971] 'Are mechanical and teleological explanations of behaviour incompatible?', *PQ* 21 (1971), 109–17.
—— ed., [1980] *Readings in Philosophical Psychology*, vol. 1, Cambridge, Mass., 1980.
Blumenthal, H. J., [1976] 'Neoplatonic elements in the *De Anima* commentaries', *Phr.* 21 (1976), 64–87.
Bolton, R., [1976] 'Essentialism and semantic theory in Aristotle', *PR* 85 (1976), 514–44.
Bonitz, H., [1848] (ed.) *Aristotelis Metaphysica*, 2 vols., Bonn, 1848–9.
—— [1853] 'Ueber die Kategorien des Aristoteles', *Sitzungsberichte der Wiener Akademie* 10 (1853), 591–645 (repr. Darmstadt, 1967).
—— [1870] *Index Aristotelicus*, Berlin, 1870 (vol. 5 of Bekker [1831]; cited as '*IA*').
Boorse, C., [1976] 'Wright on functions', *PR* 85 (1976), 70–86.
Bostock, D., [1982] 'Aristotle on the principles of change in *Physics* i', in Schofield [1982], 179–96.
Bourgey, L., [1955] *Observation et expérience chez Aristote*, Paris, 1955. Chapter 3 reprinted as 'Observation and experiment in Aristotle', in *AA* i, 175–82.
Boyd, R. N., [1980] 'Materialism without reductionism', in Block [1980], 67–106.
Bradley, F. H., [1927] *Ethical Studies*, 2nd edn., Oxford, 1927.
Brandt, R., [1974] 'Untersuchungen zur politischen Philosophie des Aristoteles', *Hermes* 102 (1974), 190–200.
Brandt, R. B., and Kim, J., [1963] 'Wants as explanations of actions', *JP* 60 (1963), 425–35.
Brody, B. A., [1972] 'Towards an Aristotelian theory of scientific explanation', *Philosophy of Science* 39 (1972), 20–31.
Brunschwig, J., [1964] 'Dialectique et ontologie chez Aristote', *Revue Philosophique* 89 (1964), 179–200.
—— [1967] (tr. and ed.) *Aristote: Topiques i–iv*, Paris, 1967.
—— [1979] 'Forme, prédicat de la matière?', in *Etudes sur la Métaphysique d'Aristote*, ed. P. Aubenque (Paris, 1979), 131–58.
Burnet, J., [1900] (ed.) *Aristotle: Ethics*, London, 1900.
Burnyeat, M. F., [1979] 'Conflicting appearances', *PBA* 65 (1979), 69–111.

—— [1980] 'Aristotle on learning to be good', in *EAE*, 69–92.

—— [1980a] 'Can the sceptic live his scepticism?', in Barnes [1980], 20–33.

—— [1981] 'Aristotle on understanding knowledge', in Berti [1981], 97–139.

—— [1982] 'Idealism in Greek philosophy', in *Idealism Past and Present*, ed. G. N. A. Vesey (Cambridge, 1982), 19–50. Also in *PR* 91 (1982), 3–40.

—— et al., [1979] *Notes on Zeta*, Oxford, 1979.

—— et al., [1984] *Notes on Eta and Theta*, Oxford, 1984.

Carnap, R., [1956] *Meaning and Necessity*, enlarged edn., Chicago, 1947.

Cartwright, H. M., [1970] 'Quantities', *PR* 79 (1970), 25–42.

—— [1972] 'Chappell on stuff and things', *Nous* 6 (1972), 369–77.

Cashdollar, S., [1973] 'Aristotle's account of incidental perception', *Phr.* 18 (1973), 156–75.

Chappell, V. C., [1970] 'Stuff and things', *PAS* 71 (1970–1), 61–76.

—— [1973] 'Aristotle on matter', *JP* 70 (1973), 679–96.

Charles, D. O. M., [1984] *Aristotle's Philosophy of Action*, London, 1984.

Charlton, W., [1970] (tr. and ed.) *Aristotle: Physics i–ii*, Oxford, 1970.

—— [1972] 'Aristotle and the principle of individuation', *Phr.* 17 (1972), 239–49.

—— [1980] 'Aristotle's definition of soul', *Phr.* 25 (1980), 170–86.

—— [1983] 'Prime matter—a rejoinder', *Phr.* 28 (1983), 197–211.

Chen, C. H., [1964] 'The universal concrete', *Phr.* 19 (1964), 48–57.

Cherniss, H. F., [1935] *Aristotle's Criticism of Presocratic Philosophy*, Baltimore, 1935.

—— [1944] *Aristotle's Criticism of Plato and the Academy*, i, Baltimore, 1944.

Chisholm, R. M., [1957] *Perceiving*, Ithaca, 1957.

—— [1982] *The Foundations of Knowing*, Minneapolis, 1982.

Churchland, P. M., [1984] *Matter and Consciousness*, Cambridge, Mass., 1984.

Clark, S. R. L., [1975] *Aristotle's Man*, Oxford, 1975.

Clatterbaugh, K. C., [1973] 'Leibniz's doctrine of individual accidents', *Studia Leibnitiana*, Sonderheft 4 (1973).

Coady, C. A. J., [1974] 'The senses of Martians', *PR* 83 (1974), 107–25.

Code, A., [1976] 'Aristotle's response to Quine's objections to modal logic', *Jl. of Phil. Logic* 5 (1976), 159–86.

—— [1976a] 'The persistence of Aristotelian matter', *PS* 29 (1976), 357–67.

—— [1978] 'No universal is a substance', in *Paideia* [1978], 65–74.

—— [1984] 'The aporematic approach to primary being', *CJP* Supp. 10 (1984), 41–65.

—— [1986] 'Aristotle's investigation of a basic logical principle', *CJP* 16 (1986), 341–57.

Cohen, G. A., [1978] *Karl Marx's Theory of History: A Defence*, Oxford, 1978.

Cohen, S. Marc, [1978] 'Individual and essence in Aristotle's *Metaphysics*', in *Paideia* [1978], 75–85.

—— [1984] 'Aristotle and individuation', *CJP* 10 (1984), 41–65.

—— [1986] 'Aristotle on the Principle of Non-Contradiction', *CJP* 16 (1986), 359–70.

Cohen, Sheldon M., [1984] 'Aristotle's doctrine of the material substrate', *PR* 93 (1984), 171–94.

Colle, G., [1924] (tr. and ed.) *Aristote: la Métaphysique, Livres ii–iii*, Louvain, 1924), *Livre iv*, Louvain, 1931.

Cooper, J. M., [1975] *Reason and Human Good in Aristotle*, Cambridge, Mass., 1975.

—— [1977] 'Aristotle on the forms of friendship', *RM* 30 (1977), 619–48.

—— [1980] 'Aristotle on friendship', in *EAE*, 301–40.

—— [1981] Review of Kenny [1978], *Nous* 15 (1981), 381–92.

—— [1982] 'Aristotle on natural teleology', in Schofield [1982], 197–222.

—— [1985] 'Hypothetical necessity' in Gotthelf [1985], 151–67.

—— [1985*a*] 'Aristotle on the goods of fortune', *PR* 94 (1985), 173–96.

Copi, I. M., [1954] 'Essence and accident', in Moravcsik [1967], 149–66. From *JP* 51 (1954), 706–19.

Cousin, D. R., [1933] 'Aristotle's doctrine of substance, Part I', *Mind* 42 (1933), 319–39.

—— [1935] 'Aristotle's doctrine of substance, Part II', *Mind* 44 (1935), 168–85.

Cummins, R., [1975] 'Functional analysis', *JP* 72 (1975), 741–65.

Dancy, R. M., [1975] *Sense and Contradiction*, Dordrecht, 1975.

—— [1975*a*] 'On some of Aristotle's first thoughts about substances', *PR* 84 (1975), 338–73.

—— [1978] 'On some of Aristotle's second thoughts about substances', *PR* 87 (1978), 372–413.

Davidson, D., [1963] 'Actions, reasons, and causes', in Davidson [1980], 3–19. From *JP* 60 (1953), 685–700.

—— [1970] 'Mental events', in Davidson [1980], 207–25. From Foster and Swanson [1970], 79–101.

—— [1975] 'Thought and talk', in Davidson [1984], 155–70. From *Mind and Language*, ed. S. D. Guttenplan (Oxford, 1975), 7–23.

—— [1976] 'Hume's cognitive theory of pride', in Davidson [1980], 277–90. From *JP* 73 (1976), 744–57.

—— [1980] *Essays on Actions and Events*, Oxford, 1980.

—— [1984] *Essays on Truth and Interpretation*, Oxford, 1984.

De Pater, W. A., [1965] *Les Topiques d'Aristote et la dialectique platonicienne*, Fribourg, 1965.

De Blic, J., [1930] 'Un aspect remarquable de la dialectique aristotélicienne', *Gregorianum* 11 (1930), 568–77.

De Ste Croix, G. E. M., [1981] *The Class Struggle in the Ancient Greek World*, London, 1981.

Décarie, V., [1961] *L'objet de la métaphysique selon Aristote*, Montreal, 1961.

Dennett, D. C., [1969] *Content and Consciousness*, London, 1969.

—— [1971] 'Intentional systems', in *Brainstorms* (Cambridge, Mass., 1978), 3–22. From *JP* 68 (1971), 87–106.

Descartes, cited from *Oeuvres de Descartes*, ed. C. Adam and P. Tannery (Paris, rev. edn., 1964–76, cited as 'AT'), usually following *Philosophical Writings of Descartes*, tr. J. Cottingham *et al.*, 2 vols. (Cambridge 1985).

—— *Letters*, tr. A. J. P. Kenny, Oxford, 1970.

Devereux, D. T., [1985] 'The primacy of *ousia*', in *Platonic Investigations*, ed. D. J. O'Meara (Washington, 1985), 219–46.

—— [1986] 'Aristotle's conception of practical knowledge', *RM* 39 (1986), 483–504.

Diels, H., and Kranz, W., [1952] (eds.) *Die Fragmente der Vorsokratiker*. 10th edn., Berlin, 1952.

Driscoll, J., [1981] '*Eidê* in Aristotle's earlier and later theories of susbtance', in O'Meara [1981], 129–59.

Duerlinger, J., [1970] 'Predication and inherence in Aristotle's *Categories*', *Phr.* 15 (1970), 179–203.

Düring, I., [1943] (ed.) *Aristotle: De Partibus Animalium*, Gothenburg, 1943.

—— [1961] 'Aristotle's method in biology', in Mansion [1961], 213–21.

—— and Owen, G. E. L. eds., [1960] *Aristotle and Plato in the Mid-Fourth Century*, Gothenburg, 1960.

Dworkin, R. M., [1973] 'The Original Position', in *Reading Rawls*, ed. N. Daniels (New York, 1975), 16–53. From *Univ. Chicago Law Rev.* 40 (1973), 500–33.

Easterling, H. J., [1966] 'A note on *De Anima* 413a8–9', *Phr.* 11 (1966), 159–62.

Engberg-Pederson, T., [1979] 'More on Aristotelian *epagôgê*', *Phr.* 24 (1979), 301–19.

—— [1983] *Aristotle's Theory of Moral Insight*, Oxford, 1983.

Engmann, J., [1976] 'Imagination and truth in Aristotle', *JHP* 14 (1976), 259–65.

Eucken, R., [1870] *Ueber die Methode und die Grundlagen der aristotelischen Ethik*, Berlin, 1870.

Eucken, R., [1872] *Die Methode der aristotelischen Forschung*, Berlin, 1872.

Evans, J. D. G., [1974] 'Aristotle on relativism', *PQ* 24 (1974), 193–203.

—— [1977] *Aristotle's Concept of Dialectic*, Cambridge, 1977.

Falk, W. D., [1975] 'Hume on practical reason', *PS* 27 (1975), 1–18.

Ferejohn, M., [1980] 'Aristotle on focal meaning and the unity of science', *Phr.* 25 (1980), 117–28.

Fine, G. J., [1979] 'Knowledge and *logos* in the *Theaetetus*', *PR* 88 (1979), 366–97.

—— [1982] 'Owen, Aristotle, and the Third Man', *Phr.* 27 (1982), 13–33.

—— [1983] 'Plato and Aristotle on form and substance', *Proc. Camb. Philol. Soc.* 29 (1983), 23–47.

—— [1984] 'Separation', *OSAP* 2 (1984), 31–87.

—— [1987] 'Forms as causes', in Graeser [1987], 69–112.

—— [KPC] 'Knowledge, perception, and change in the *Theaetetus*', unpublished.

Finley, M. I., [1970] 'Aristotle and economic analysis', in *AA* ii, 140–58. From *Past and Present* 47 (1970), 3–25.

Förster, A., [1912] (ed.) *Aristotelis De Anima*, Budapest, 1912.

Fortenbaugh, W. W., [1975] *Aristotle on Emotion*, London, 1975.

Foster, L., and Swanson, J. W., eds. [1970] *Experience and Theory*, Amherst, 1970.

Frede, D., [1974] Comments on Hintikka [1972], *Synthèse* 28 (1974), 79–89.

Frede, M., [1978] 'Individuals in Aristotle', in Frede [1987a], 49–71. From *Antike und Abendland* 24 (1978), 16–39.

Frede, M., [1981] 'Categories in Aristotle', in Frede [1987a], 29–48. From O'Meara [1981], 1–24.

—— [1985] 'Substance in Aristotle's *Metaphysics*', in Frede [1987a], 72–80. From Gotthelf [1985], 17–26.

—— [1987] 'The unity of special and general metaphysics', in Frede [1987a], 81–95.

—— [1987a] *Essays in Ancient Philosophy*, Oxford, 1987.

Furley, D. J., [1985] 'The rainfall example in *Physics* ii 8', in Gotthelf [1985], 177–82.

Furth, M., [1978] 'Trans-temporal stability in Aristotelian substances', *JP* 75 (1978), 627–32.

—— [1985] (trans.) *Aristotle: Metaphysics vii–x*, Indianapolis, 1985.

—— [1986] 'A note on Aristotle's Principle of Non-Contradiction', *CJP* 16 (1986), 371–81.

Gauthier, R. A., and Jolif, J. Y., [1970] (eds. and trs.) *Aristote: l' Ethique à Nicomaque*, 2nd edn., 4 vols., Louvain, 1970.

Geach, P. T., [1957] *Mental Acts*, London, 1957.

Gewirth, A., [1953] Review of 1st edn. (1951) of Owens [1963], *PR* 62 (1953), 577–89.

Gillespie, C. M., [1925] 'The Aristotelian categories', in *AA* iii, 1–12. From *CQ* 19 (1925), 75–84.

Goldman, A., [1970] *A Theory of Human Action*, Englewood Cliffs, 1970.

Goodman, N., [1968] *Languages of Art*, New York, 1968.

—— [1970] 'Seven strictures on similarity', in *Problems and Projects* (New York, 1972), 437–46. From Foster and Swanson [1970], 19–29.

Gotthelf, A., [1976] 'Aristotle's conception of final causality', *RM* 30 (1976), 226–54.

—— ed., [1985] *Aristotle on Nature and Living Things*, Pittsburgh, 1985.

Graeser, A., ed., [1987] *Mathematik und Metaphysik bei Aristoteles*, Berne, 1987.

Graham, W., [1975] 'Counterpredicability and *per se* accidents', *AGP* 57 (1975), 182–7.

Granger, H., [1981] 'The differentia and the *per se* accident in Aristotle', *AGP* 63 (1981), 118–29.

Green, T. H., [1890] *Philosophical Works*, 3 vols., London, 1890.

Greenwood, L. H. G., [1909] (tr. and ed.) *Aristotle: Nicomachean Ethics vi*, Cambridge, 1909.

Grice, H. P., [1962] 'Some remarks about the senses', in *Analytical Philosophy (First Series)*, ed. R. J. Butler (Oxford, 1962), 133–53.

Grote, G., [1872] *Aristotle*, 2 vols., London, 1872.

Guthrie, W. K. C., [1957] 'Aristotle as historian', in *Studies in Presocratic Philosophy*, ed. D. J. Furley and R. E. Allen (vol. 1, London, 1970), 239–54. From *JHS* 77 (1957), 35–41.

Hadgopoulos, D. J., [1976] 'The definition of the "predicables" in Aristotle', *Phr.* 21 (1976), 59–63.

Hager, F. P., ed., [1969] *Metaphysik und Theologie des Aristoteles*, Darmstadt, 1969.

—— ed., [1972] *Logik und Erkenntnislehre des Aristoteles*, Darmstadt, 1972.

Hamblin, C. L., [1970] *Fallacies*, London, 1970.

Hamelin, O., [1920] *Le système d'Aristote*, Paris, 1920.

Hamlyn, D. W., [1959] 'Aristotle's account of aesthesis in the *De Anima*', *CQ* 9 (1959), 6–16.

—— [1968] (tr. and ed.) *Aristotle: De Anima*, Oxford, 1968.

—— [1968a] 'Koinê aesthêsis', *Monist* 52 (1968), 195–200.

—— [1976] 'Aristotelian *epagôgê*', *Phr.* 21 (1976), 167–84.

—— [1977] 'Focal meaning', *PAS* 78 (1977–8), 1–18.

Happ, H., [1971] *Hyle*, Berlin, 1971.

Hardie, W. F. R., [1964] 'Aristotle's treatment of the relation between the soul and the body', *PQ* 14 (1964), 53–72.

—— [1976] 'Concepts of consciousness in Aristotle', *Mind* 85 (1976), 388–411.

—— [1980] *Aristotle's Ethical Theory*, 2nd edn., Oxford, 1980.

Hare, J. E., [1979] 'Aristotle and the definition of natural things', *Phr.* 24 (1979), 168–79.

Haring, E. S., [1956] 'Substantial form in *Metaphysics* vii', *RM* 10 (1956–7), 308–32, 482–501, 698–713.

Harter, E. D., [1975] 'Aristotle on primary *ousia*', *AGP* 57 (1975), 1–20.

Hartman, E., [1977] *Substance, Body and Soul*, Princeton, 1977.

Heinaman, R. E., [1979] 'Aristotle's tenth aporia', *AGP* 61 (1979), 249–70.

—— [1980] 'An argument in *Metaphysics* Z 13', *CQ* 30 (1980), 72–85.

—— [1981] 'Non-substantial individuals in Aristotle's *Categories*', *Phr.* 26 (1981), 295–307.

—— [1981a] 'Knowledge of substance in Aristotle', *JHS* 101 (1981), 63–77.

—— [1982] Review of Lloyd [1981], *CR* 32 (1982), 44–8.

Hess, W., [1970] 'Erfahrung und Intuition bei Aristoteles', *Phr.* 15 (1970), 48–82.

Hicks, R. D., [1907] (tr. and ed.) *Aristotle: De Anima*, Cambridge, 1907.

Hintikka, K. J. J., [1972] 'On the ingredients of an Aristotelian science', *Nous* 6 (1972), 55–69.

—— [1973] *Time and Necessity*, Oxford, 1973.

—— [1974] Reply to Frede [1974], *Synthèse* 28 (1974), 91–6.

—— [1977] *Aristotle on Modality and Determinism*, Amsterdam, 1977.

Hirst, R. J., [1965] 'Form and sensation', *SPAS* 39 (1965), 155–72.

Hocutt, M., [1974] 'Aristotle's four becauses', *Phil.* 49 (1974), 385–99.

Homiak, M. L., [1981] 'Virtue and self-love in Aristotle's ethics', *CJP* 11 (1981), 633–51.

Hudson, S. D., [1981] 'Reason and motivation in Aristotle', *CJP* 11 (1981), 111–35.

Hume, *Inquiries*, ed. L. A. Selby-Bigge, Oxford, 1902.

Hume, *Treatise of Human Nature*, ed. L. A. Selby-Bigge, Oxford, 1888.

Hursthouse, R., [1980] 'A false doctrine of the mean', *PAS* 81 (1980–1), 57–72.

Husik, I., [1906] 'Aristotle on the law of contradiction and the basis of the syllogism', in Husik [1952a], 87–95. From *Mind* 15 (1906), 215–22.

—— [1952] *Philosophical Essays*, Oxford, 1952.

—— [1952a] 'The *Categories* of Aristotle', in Husik [1952], 96–112.

Hussey, E. L., [1983] (tr. and ed.) *Aristotle: Physics iii–iv*, Oxford, 1983.

Ide, H. A., [1987] 'Potentiality and Possibility', PhD thesis, Cornell University, 1987.

Inwood, B., [1979] 'A note on commensurate universals in the *Posterior Analytics*', *Phr.* 24 (1979), 320–9.

Irwin, T. H., [1977a] *Plato's Moral Theory*, Oxford, 1977.

—— [1980] 'Reason and responsibility in Aristotle', in *EAE*, 117–56.

—— [1980a] Review of Kenny, [1978], [1979], *JP* 77 (1980), 338–54.

—— [1981] 'Homonymy in Aristotle', *RM* 34 (1981), 523–44.

—— [1981a] 'Aristotle's methods of ethics', in O'Meara [1981], 193–223.

—— [1982] 'Aristotle's concept of signification', in Schofield [1982], 241–66.

—— [1985] 'Permanent happiness', *OSAP* 3 (1985), 89–124.

—— [1985a] 'Aristotle's concept of morality', in *Proc. Boston Colloquium in Ancient Phil.*, ed. J. J. Cleary (Washington, 1986), 115–43.

—— [1986] Review of Charles, *Phr.* 31 (1986), 68–89.

Jaeger, W. W., [1912] *Studien zur Entstehungsgeschichte der Metaphysik des Aristoteles*, Berlin, 1912.

—— [1948] *Aristotle: Fundamentals of the History of his Development*, ET, 2nd edn., Oxford, 1948.

Joachim, H. H. (ed.), [1922] *Aristotle on Coming-To-Be and Passing-Away*, Oxford, 1922.

—— [1951] *Aristotle: Nicomachean Ethics*, Oxford, 1951.

Jones, B., [1972] 'Individuals in Aristotle's *Categories*', *Phr.* 17 (1972), 107–23.

—— [1974] 'Aristotle's introduction of matter', *PR* 83 (1974), 474–500.

—— [1975] 'Introduction to the first five chapters of Aristotle's *Categories*', *Phr.* 20 (1975), 146–72.

Jope, J., [1972] 'Subordinate demonstrative science in the sixth book of Aristotle's *Physics*', *CQ* 22 (1972), 279–92.

Joseph, H. W. B., [1906] *An Introduction to Logic*, Oxford, 1906.

Kahn, C. H., [1966] 'Sensation and consciousness in Aristotle's psychology', in *AA* iv, 1–31. From *AGP* 48 (1966), 43–81.

—— [1978] 'Questions and categories', in *Questions*, ed. H. Hiz (Dordrecht, 1978), 227–78.

—— [1981] 'The role of *nous* in the cognition of first principles', in Berti [1981], 385–414.

—— [1981a] 'Aristotle and altruism', *Mind* 90 (1981), 20–40.

Kant, *Critique of Pure Reason* (cited as '*KrV*'), tr. N. Kemp Smith, London, 1929.

—— *Philosophical Correspondence*, ed. A. Zweig, Chicago, 1967.

Kapp, E., [1920] 'Die Kategorienlehre in der aristotelischen Topik', in *Ausgewählte Schriften* (Berlin, 1968), 215–53.

Kenny, A. J. P., [1967] 'The argument from illusion in Aristotle's *Metaphysics*', *Mind* 76 (1967), 184–97.

—— [1978] *The Aristotelian Ethics*, Oxford, 1978.

—— [1979] *Aristotle's Theory of the Will*, London, 1979.

Keyt, D., [1983] 'Intellectualism in Aristotle', in Anton and Preus [1983], 364–87.

King, H. R., [1956] 'Aristotle without *materia prima*', *JHI* 17 (1956), 370–89.

Kirwan, C. A., [1970] 'How strong are the objections to essence?', *PAS* 71 (1970–1), 43–59.

—— [1971] (tr. and ed.) *Aristotle: Metaphysics iv, v, vi*, Oxford, 1971.

—— [1981] 'Truth and universal assent', *CJP* 11 (1981), 377–94.

Kneale, W. C., [1939] 'The notion of a substance', *PAS* 40 (1939–40), 101–34.

—— [1962] 'Modality *de dicto* and *de re*', in *Logic, Methodology, and Philosophy of Science*, ed. E. Nagel *et al.*, (Stanford, 1962), 622–34.

Konstan, D., [1975] 'A note on *Physics* i 1', *AGP* 57 (1975), 241–5.

Kosman, L. A., [1966] 'Aristotle's first predicament', *RM* 20 (1966–7), 483–506.

—— [1969] 'Aristotle's definition of motion', *Phr.* 14 (1969), 40–62.

—— [1973] 'Understanding, explanation, and insight in the *Posterior Analytics*', in Lee [1973], 374–92.

—— [1975] 'Perceiving that we perceive', *PR* 84 (1975), 499–519.

—— [1984] 'Substance, being, and *energeia*', *OSAP* 2 (1984), 121–49.

Kraut, R., [1979] 'The peculiar function of human beings', *CJP* 9 (1979), 467–78.

—— [1979*a*] 'Two conceptions of happiness', *PR* 88 (1979), 167–97.

Kullmann, W., [1974] *Wissenschaft und Methode*, Berlin, 1974.

—— [1980] 'Der Mensch als politisches Lebewesen bei Aristoteles', *Hermes* 109 [1980], 419–43.

Kung, J., [1977] 'Aristotle on essence and explanation', *PS* 31 (1977), 361–83.

—— [1978] 'Can substance be predicated of matter?', *AGP* 60 (1978), 140–59.

—— [1981] 'Aristotle on thises, suches and the Third Man Argument', *Phr.* 26 (1981), 207–47.

Lacey, A. R., [1965] '*Ousia* and form in Aristotle', *Phr.* 10 (1965), 54–69.

Le BLond, J. M., [1939] *Logique et méthode chez Aristote*, Paris, 1939.

—— [1945] (tr. and ed.) *Aristote: philosophe de la vie*, Paris, 1945.

Lear, J., [1980] *Aristotle and Logical Theory*, Cambridge, 1980.

—— [1982] 'Aristotle on mathematics', *PR* 91 (1982), 161–92.

—— [1987] 'Active *epistêmê*', in Graeser [1987], 149–74.

Lee, E. N., Mourelatos, A. P. D., and Rorty, R. M., eds., [1973] *Exegesis and Argument*, Assen, 1973.

Lee, H. D. P., [1935] 'Geometrical method and Aristotle's account of first principles', *CQ* 29 (1935), 113–24.

Lefèvre, C., [1972] *Sur l'évolution d'Aristote en psychologie*, Louvain, 1972.

Leibniz, *The Leibniz-Clarke Correspondence*, tr. H. G. Alexander, Manchester, 1956.

Lennox, J. G., [1985] 'Are Aristotle's species eternal?', in Gotthelf [1985], 67–94.

Lesher, J. H., [1971] 'Substance, form and universal: a dilemma', *Phr.* 16 (1971), 169–78.

—— [1973] 'The meaning of *nous* in the *Posterior Analytics*', *Phr.* 18 (1973), 44–68.

Leszl, W., [1970] *Logic and Metaphysics in Aristotle*, Padua, 1970.

—— [1972] 'Knowledge of the universal and knowledge of the particular in Aristotle', *RM* 26 (1972–3), 278–313.

Leszl, W., [1975] *Aristotle's Conception of Ontology*, Padua, 1975.

Lewis, F. A., [1984] 'What is Aristotle's theory of essence?', *CJP* Supp. 10 (1984), 89–131.

Lloyd, A. C., [1966] 'Aristotle's *Categories* today', *PQ* 16 (1966), 258–67.

—— [1970] 'Aristotle's principle of individuation', *Mind* 79 (1970), 519–29.

—— [1981] *Form and Universal in Aristotle*, Liverpool, 1981.

—— [1981a] 'Necessity and essence in the *Posterior Analytics*', in Berti [1981], 151–71.

Lloyd, G. E. R., and Owen, G. E. L., eds., [1978] *Aristotle on Mind and the Senses*, Cambridge, 1978.

Locke, *Essay concerning Human Understanding*, ed. P. H. Nidditch, Oxford, 1975.

Long, A. A., [1981] 'Aristotle and the history of Greek scepticism', in O'Meara [1981], 79–106.

Loux, M. J., [1973] 'Aristotle on the transcendentals', *Phr.* 18 (1973), 225–39.

—— [1979] 'Form, species, and predication', *Mind* 88 (1979), 1–23.

Lukasiewicz, J., [1910] 'Aristotle on the law of contradiction', in *AA* iii, 50–62. From *Bulletin Internationale de l'Académie des Sciences de Cracovie*, 1910.

Lycos, K., [1964] 'Aristotle and Plato on appearing', *Mind* 73 (1964), 496–514.

McClelland, R. T., [1981] 'Time and modality in Aristotle', *AGP* 63 (1981), 130–49.

McDowell, J. H., [1978] 'Are moral requirements hypothetical imperatives?', *SPAS* 52 (1978), 13–29.

—— [1980] 'The role of *eudaimonia* in Aristotle's ethics', in *EAE*, 359–76. From *Proc. African Class. Assoc.* 15 (1980), 1–15.

Maier, H., [1896] *Die Syllogistik des Aristoteles*, Tübingen, 1896–1900.

Malcolm, J., [1981] 'On the generation and corruption of the categories', *RM* 33 (1981), 662–81.

Malcolm, N., [1968] 'The conceivability of mechanism', *PR* 77 (1968), 45–72. Also in *Free Will*, ed. G. Watson (Oxford, 1982), 127–49.

—— [1972] 'Thoughtless brutes', in *Thought and Knowledge* (Ithaca, 1977), 40–57. From *Proc. Amer. Philos. Ass.* 46 (1972–3), 5–20.

Manicas, P. T., [1965] 'Aristotle, dispositions, and occult powers', *RM* 18 (1965), 678–89.

Mansion, A., [1946] *Introduction à la physique aristotélicienne*, 2nd edn., Louvain, 1946.

—— [1958] 'Philosophie première, philosophie seconde et métaphysique chez Aristote', *Revue Philosophique de Louvain* 56 (1958), 165–221.

Mansion, S., [1955] 'Les apories de la métaphysique aristotélicienne', in *Autour d'Aristote* (Louvain, 1955), 141–79.

—— ed., [1961] *Aristote et les problèmes de méthode*, Louvain, 1961.

Mates, B., [1986] *The Philosophy of Leibniz*, Oxford, 1986.

Matthews, G. B., [1977] 'Consciousness and life', *Phil.* 52 (1977), 13–26.

—— [1982] 'Accidental unities', in Schofield [1982], 223–40.

—— and Cohen, S. M., [1967] 'The one and the many', *RM* 21 (1967–8), 630–55.

Meikle, S., [1979] 'Aristotle and the political economy of the polis', *JHS* 99 (1979), 57–73.

—— [1985] *Essentialism in the Thought of Karl Marx*, London, 1985.

Merlan, P., [1957] 'Metaphysik: Name und Gegenstand', in Merlan [1976], 189–94, and Hager [1969], 251–65. From *JHS* 77 (1957), 87–92.

—— [1960] *From Platonism to Neoplatonism*, 2nd edn., The Hague, 1960.

—— [1968] 'On the terms "Metaphysics" and "Being-*qua*-being"', in Merlan [1976], 238–58. From *Monist* 52 (1968), 174–94.

—— [1976] *Kleine philosophische Schriften*, Hildesheim, 1976.

Mignucci, M., [1981] '*Hôs epi to polu* et nécessaire', in Berti [1981], 173–203.

Miller, F. D., [1973] 'Did Aristotle have a concept of identity?', *PR* 82 (1973), 483–90.

—— and Bradie, M., [1984] 'Teleology and natural necessity in Aristotle', *HPQ* 1 (1984), 133–46.

Miller, R. W., [1981] 'Marx and Aristotle', *CJP* Supp. 7 (1981), 323–52.

Modrak, D. K., [1979] 'Forms, types, and tokens', *JHP* 17 (1979), 371–81.

—— [1981] 'Common sense and the discrimination of sensible differences', *CJP* 11 (1981), 405–23.

Moline, J., [1975] 'Provided nothing external interferes', *Mind* 84 (1975), 244–54.

Moore, F. C. T., [1975] 'Evans off target', *PQ* 25 (1975), 58–9.

Moore, G. E., [1923] 'Are the characteristics of particular things universal or particular?', in *Philosophical Papers* (London, 1959), 17–31. From *SPAS* 3 (1923), 95–113.

Moraux, P., [1961] 'La méthode d'Aristote dans l'étude du ciel', in Mansion [1961], 173–94.

—— [1968] 'La joute dialectique', in Owen [1968*a*], 277–311.

Moravcsik, J. M. E., [1967] 'Aristotle on predication', *PR* 76 (1967), 80–96.

—— [1967*a*] 'Aristotle's theory of categories', in Moravcsik [1967*b*], 125–45.

—— ed., [1967*b*] *Aristotle*, Garden City, 1967.

—— [1974] 'Aristotle on adequate explanation', *Synthèse* 28 (1974), 3–17.

—— [1975] '*Aitia* as generative factor in Aristotle's philosophy', *Dialogue* 14 (1975), 622–38.

Morrison, D. R., [1985] 'Separation in Aristotle's metaphysics', *OSAP* 3 (1985), 125–57.

Mourelatos, A. P. D., [1967] 'Aristotle's "powers" and modern empiricism', *Ratio* 9 (1967), 97–104.

Mueller, I., [1970] 'Aristotle on geometrical objects', *AGP* 52 (1970), 156–71.

Mulgan, R. G., [1970] 'Aristotle and the democratic conception of freedom', in *Auckland Classical Essays*, ed. B. F. Harris (Auckland, 1970), 95–111.

—— [1974] 'Aristotle's doctrine that man is a political animal', *Hermes* 102 (1974), 438–45.

—— [1977] *Aristotle's Political Theory*, Oxford, 1977.

Mure, G. R. G., [1949] 'Aristotle's doctrine of secondary substances', *Mind* 58 (1949), 82–3.

—— [1975] 'Cause and because in Aristotle', *Phil.* 50 (1975), 356–7.

Nagel, T., [1970] 'Armstrong on the mind', in Block [1980], 200–7. From *PR* 79 (1970), 394–403.

—— [1970*a*] *The Possibility of Altruism*, Oxford, 1970.

Nagel, T., [1972] 'Aristotle on *eudaimonia*', in *EAE*, 7–14. From *Phr.* 17 (1972), 252–9.

Newman, W. L., [1887] (ed.) *Aristotle: Politics*, 4 vols., Oxford, 1887–1902.

—— [1892] 'Aristotle's classification of forms of government', *CR* 6 (1892), 289–93.

Noonan, H. W., [1976] 'An argument of Aristotle's on non-contradiction', *Analysis* 37 (1976–7), 163–9.

Nozick, R., [1974] *Anarchy, State, and Utopia*, New York, 1974.

Nussbaum, M. C., [1978] (tr. and ed.) *Aristotle: De Motu Animalium*, Princeton, 1978.

—— [1984] 'Aristotelian dualism', *OSAP* 2 (1984), 197–207.

—— [1986] *The Fragility of Goodness*, Cambridge, 1986.

Nuyens, F., [1948] *L'évolution de la psychologie d'Aristote*, Louvain, 1948.

O'Meara, D. J., ed., [1981] *Studies in Aristotle*, Washington, 1981.

Owen, G. E. L., [1960] 'Logic and metaphysics in some early works of Aristotle', in Owen [1986], 180–9, and *AA* iii, 13–32. From Düring [1960], 163–90.

—— [1961] '*Tithenai ta phainomena*', in Owen [1986], 239–51, and in *AA* i, 113–26. From Mansion [1961], 83–103.

—— [1965] 'The Platonism of Aristotle', in Owen [1986], 200–20, and in *AA* i, 14–34. From *PBA* 51 (1965), 125–50.

—— [1965a] 'Aristotle on the snares of ontology', in Owen [1986], 259–78. From Bambrough [1965], 69–95.

—— [1965b] 'Inherence', in Owen [1986], 252–8. From *Phr.* 10 (1965), 97–105.

—— [1968] 'Dialectic and eristic in the treatment of the Forms', in Owen [1986], 221–38. From Owen [1968a], 103–25.

—— ed., [1968a] *Aristotle on Dialectic*, Oxford, 1968.

—— [1978] 'Particular and general', in Owen [1986], 279–94. From *PAS* 79 (1978–9), 1–21.

—— [1986] *Logic, Science, and Dialectic*, London, 1986.

Owens, J., [1960] 'Aristotle on categories', in *Aristotle: Collected Papers* (Albany, 1981), ch.2. From *RM* 14 (1960), 73–90.

—— [1963] *The Doctrine of Being in the Aristotelian Metaphysics*, 2nd edn., Toronto, 1963 (1st edn., 1951).

Paideia: Special Aristotle Issue, Brockport, 1978.

Parfit, D. A., [1984] *Reasons and Persons*, Oxford, 1984.

Patzig, G., [1960] 'Theology and ontology in Aristotle's *Metaphysics*', in *AA* iii, 33–49. From *KS* 52 (1960–1), 185–205.

Peck, A. L., [1937] (tr.) *Aristotle: Parts of Animals*, London, 1937.

—— [1953] (tr.) *Aristotle: Generation of Animals*, London, rev. edn., 1953.

Penner, T., [1970] 'Verbs and the identity of actions', in *Ryle*, ed. G. Pitcher and O. P. Wood (Garden City, 1970), 393–460.

Popper, K. R., [1953] 'The principle of individuation', *SPAS* 27 (1953), 97–120.

Preisewerk, A., [1939] 'Das Einzelne bei Aristoteles', *Philologus* Supp. 32.1 (1939).

Putnam, H., [1975] 'Philosophy and our mental life', in *Philosophical Papers* ii (Cambridge, 1975), 281–303.

—— [1983] 'Why there isn't a ready-made world', in *Philosophical Papers* iii (Cambridge, 1983), 205–28.

Quine, W. V., [1966] *The Ways of Paradox*, New York, 1966.

Rackham, H., [1935] (tr.) *Aristotle: Eudemian Ethics*, London, 1935.

Raphael, S., [1974] 'Rhetoric, dialectic and syllogistic argument', *Phr.* 19 (1974), 153–67.

Rassow, H., [1874] *Forschungen über die Nikomachische Ethik*, Weimar, 1874.

Rawls, J., [1971] *A Theory of Justice*, Cambridge, Mass., 1971.

Reale, G., [1980] *The Concept of First Philosophy and the Unity of Aristotle's Metaphysics*, ET, Albany, 1980.

Rees, D. A., [1957] 'Bipartition of the soul in the early Academy', *JHS* 77 (1957), 112–18.

—— [1960] 'Theories of the soul in the early Aristotle', in Düring [1960], 191–200.

—— [1971] 'Aristotle's treatment of *phantasia*', in Anton [1971], 491–505.

Régis, L. M., [1935] *L'opinion selon Aristote*, Ottawa, 1935.

Reichenbach, H., [1951] *The Rise of Scientific Philosophy*, Berkeley, 1951.

Reiner, H., [1954] 'Die Entstehung und ursprüngliche Bedeutung des Namens Metaphysik', in Hager [1969], 139–74. From *Zeitschrift für philosophische Forschung* 8 (1954), 210–37.

Robinson, H. M., [1974] 'Prime matter in Aristotle', *Phr.* 19 (1974), 168–88.

—— [1978] 'Mind and body in Aristotle', *CQ* 28 (1978), 105–24.

—— [1983] 'Aristotelian dualism', *OSAP* 1 (1983), 123–44.

Robinson, R., [1962] (tr. and ed.) *Aristotle: Politics iii–iv*, Oxford, 1962.

Rodier, G., [1900] (tr. and ed.) *Aristote: Traité de l'âme*, Paris, 1900.

Rorty, A. O., ed., [1980] *Essays on Aristotle's Ethics*, Berkeley, 1980.

Rorty, R. M., [1970] 'Incorrigibility as the mark of the mental', *JP* 67 (1970), 399–424.

—— [1973] 'Genus as matter: a reading of *Metaphysics* vii–viii', in Lee [1973], 393–420.

Ross, W. D., [1923] *Aristotle*, London, 1923.

—— [1924] (ed.) *Aristotle: Metaphysics*, 2 vols., Oxford, 1924.

—— [1936] (ed.) *Aristotle: Physics*, Oxford, 1936.

—— [1939] 'The discovery of the syllogism', *PR* 48 (1939), 251–72.

—— [1949] (ed.) *Aristotle: Prior and Posterior Analytics*, Oxford, 1949.

—— [1955] (ed.) *Aristotle: Parva Naturalia*, Oxford, 1955.

—— [1957] 'The development of Aristotle's thought', in *AA* i, 1–13, and in Düring [1960], 63–78. From *PBA* 43 (1957), 63–78.

—— [1961] (ed.) *Aristotle: De Anima*, Oxford, 1961.

Routila, L., [1969] *Die aristotelische Idee der ersten Philosophie*, Amsterdam, 1969.

Rowe, C. J., [1977] 'Aims and methods in Aristotle's *Politics*', *CQ* 27 (1977), 159–72.

Ryle, G., [1965] 'Dialectic in the Academy', in Bambrough [1965], 39–68. Another version in Owen [1968a], 69–79.

Sachs, D., [1948] 'Does Aristotle have a doctrine of secondary substances?', *Mind* 57 (1948), 221–5.

Sauvé, S. M., [1987] 'Aristotle's causal discriminations: teleology and responsibility', PhD thesis, Cornell University, 1987.

Schofield, M., [1972] *'Metaphysics* vii 3; some suggestions', *Phr.* 17 (1972), 97–101.

—— [1978] 'Aristotle on the imagination', in *AA* iv, 102–32. From Lloyd [1978], 99–140.

—— and Nussbaum, M. C., eds., [1982] *Language and Logos*, Cambridge, 1982.

Scholar, M. C., [1971] 'Aristotle's *Metaphysics* iv, 1010b1–3', *Mind* 80 (1971), 266–8.

Sellars, W. S., [1957] 'Substance and form in Aristotle', in Sellars [1967a], 125–36. From *JP* 54 (1957), 688–99.

—— [1963] 'Raw materials, subjects, and substrata', in Sellars [1967a], 137–53. From *The Concept of Matter in Greek and Mediaeval Philosophy*, ed. E. McMullin (Notre Dame, 1963), 259–72.

—— [1967] 'Aristotle's *Metaphysics*', in Sellars [1967a], 73–124.

—— [1967a] *Philosophical Perspectives*, Springfield, Ill., 1967.

Sharples, R. W., [1983] (tr. and ed.) *Alexander: De Fato*, London, 1983.

Shields, C. J., [1986] 'Aristotle's philosophy of mind', PhD thesis, Cornell University, 1986.

—— [1988] 'Soul and body in Aristotle', *OSAP* 6 (1988), 103–37.

Shoemaker, S., [1977] 'Immortality and dualism', in *Identity, Cause, and Mind* (Cambridge, 1984), 141–53. From *Reason and Religion*, ed. S. C. Brown (Ithaca, 1977), 259–81.

Sidgwick, H., [1879] 'The establishment of ethical first principles', *Mind* 4 (1879), 106–11.

—— [1892] 'Aristotle's classification of forms of government', *CR* 6 (1892), 141–4.

—— [1907] *The Methods of Ethics*, 7th edn., London, 1907.

Slakey, T. J., [1961] 'Aristotle on sense perception', *PR* 70 (1961), 470–84.

Smith, J. A., [1921] *'Tode ti* in Aristotle', *CR* 35 (1921), 19.

—— and Ross, W. D., [1910] (eds.) *The Works of Aristotle* (cited as 'OT') 12 vols., Oxford, 1910–52.

Sokolowski, R., [1970] 'Matter, elements, and substance in Aristotle', *JHP* 8 (1970), 263–88.

Solmsen, F., [1929] *Die Entwicklung der aristotelischen Logik und Rhetorik*, Berlin, 1929.

—— [1958] 'Aristotle and prime matter', in Solmsen [1968a], i, 397–406. From *JHI* 19 (1958), 243–52.

—— [1961] 'Aristotle's word for matter', in Solmsen [1968a], i, 407–20. From *Didascaliae: Studies in honour of A. M. Albareda* (New York, 1961), 395–408.

—— [1964] 'Leisure and play in Aristotle's ideal state', in Solmsen [1968a], ii, 1–28. From *Rheinische Museum* 107 (1964) 193–220.

—— [1968] 'Dialectic without the Forms', in Owen [1968a], 49–68.

—— [1968a] *Kleine Schriften*, i–ii, Hildesheim, 1968.

Sorabji, R. R. K., [1971] 'Aristotle on demarcating the five senses', in *AA* iv, 76–92. From *PR* 80 (1971), 55–79.

—— [1973] 'Aristotle on the role of the intellect in virtue', in *EAE*, 201–19. From *PAS* 74 (1973–4), 107–29.

—— [1974] 'Body and soul in Aristotle', in *AA* iv, 42–64. From *Phil.* 49 (1974), 63–89.

—— [1980] *Necessity, Cause, and Blame*, London, 1980.

—— [1981] 'Definitions: why necessary and in what way?', in Berti [1981], 205–44.

—— [1985] 'Analyses of matter, ancient and modern', *PAS* 86 (1985–6), 1–22.

Sprague, R. K., [1968] 'The four causes: Aristotle's analysis and ours', *Monist* 52 (1968), 298–300.

Stahl, D., [1981] 'Stripped away', *Phr.* 26 (1981), 177–80.

Stalnaker, R. C., [1984] *Inquiry*, Cambridge, Mass., 1984.

Stebbing, L. S., [1929] 'Concerning substance', *PAS* 30 (1929–30), 285–308.

Stewart, J. A., [1892] *Notes on the Nicomachean Ethics*, 2 vols., Oxford, 1892.

Stich, S. P., [1983] *From Folk Psychology to Cognitive Science*, Cambridge, Mass., 1983.

Stocks, J. L., [1936] '*Scholê*', *CQ* 30 (1936), 177–87.

Stough, C. L., [1972] 'Language and ontology in the *Categories*', *JHP* 10 (1972), 261–72.

Strawson, P. F., [1959] *Individuals*, London, 1959.

Sturgeon, N. L., [HRP] 'Hume on reason and passion', unpublished.

Sykes, R. D., [1975] 'Form in Aristotle', *Phil.* 50 (1975), 311–31.

Taylor, C., [1964] *The Explanation of Behaviour*, London, 1964.

—— [1966] 'Teleological explanation', *Analysis* 27 (1966), 141–3.

—— [1967] 'Mind-body identity, a side issue?', *PR* 76 (1967), 201–13.

—— [1970] 'The explanation of purposive behaviour', in *Explanation in the Behavioural Sciences*, ed. R. Borger and F. Cioffi (Cambridge, 1970), 49–79 (with reply, 89–95).

Taylor, C. C. W., [1980] 'All perceptions are true', in Barnes [1980], 105–24.

Teichmüller, G., [1879] *Neue Studien zur Geschichte der Begriffe*, 3 vols., Gotha, 1879.

Thurot, C., [1860] *Etudes sur Aristote*, Paris, 1860.

Tiles, J. E., [1983] 'Why the triangle has two right angles *kath'hauto*', *Phr.* 28 (1983), 1–16.

Todd, R. B., [1976] 'The four causes; Aristotle's explanation and the ancients'', *JHI* 37 (1976), 319–22.

Torstrik, A., [1862] (ed.) *Aristotelis De Anima*, Berlin, 1862.

—— [1875] '*Peri tuchês kai tou automatou*', *Hermes* 9 (1875), 425–70.

Tracy, T., [1983] 'Heart and soul in Aristotle', in Anton [1983], 321–39.

Trendelenburg, F. A., [1846] *Geschichte der Kategorienlehre*, Berlin, 1846.

Urmson, J. O., [1973] 'Aristotle's doctrine of the mean', in *EAE*, 157–70. From *Amer. Phil. Quart.* 10 (1973), 223–30.

Van Fraassen, B. C., [1980] 'A reexamination of Aristotle's philosophy of science', *Dialogue* 19 (1980), 20–45.

Vendler, Z., [1972] *Res Cogitans*, Ithaca, 1972.

Viano, C. A., [1958] 'La dialettica in Aristotele', *Rivista di Filosofia* 49 (1958), 154–78.

Vlastos, G., [1980] Review of Wood and Wood [1978], *Phoenix* 34 (1980), 347–52.

—— [1983] 'The Socratic elenchus', *OSAP* 1 (1983), 27–58.

Von Arnim, H., [1905] (ed.) *Stoicorum Veterum Fragmenta*, 4 vols., Leipzig, 1905–24.

—— [1928] Review of Jaeger, *Wiener Studien* 46 (1928), 1–48.

Von Wright, G. H., [1971] *Explanation and Understanding*, Ithaca, 1971.

Waitz, T., [1844] (ed.) *Aristotelis Organon*, 2 vols., Leipzig, 1844–6.

Wallace, J. D., [1978] *Virtues and Vices*, Ithaca, 1978.

Waterlow, S., [1982] *Nature, Change, and Agency*, Oxford, 1982.

Wedin, V. E., [1973] 'A remark on *per se* accidents and properties', *AGP* 55 (1973), 30–5.

Weil, E., [1951] 'The place of logic in Aristotle's thought', in *AA* i, 88–112. From *Revue de Métaphysique et Morale* 56 (1951), 283–315.

White, N. P., [1971] 'Aristotle on sameness and oneness', *PR* 80 (1971), 177–97.

—— [1972] 'Origins of Aristotle's essentialism', *RM* 26 (1972–3), 57–85.

—— [1981] 'Goodness and human aims in Aristotle's *Ethics*', in O'Meara [1981], 225–46.

Whiting, J. E., [1984] 'Individual forms in Aristotle', PhD thesis, Cornell University, 1984.

—— [1986] 'Form and individuation in Aristotle', *HPQ* 3 (1986), 359–77.

—— [1986a] 'Human nature and intellectualism in Aristotle', *AGP* 68 (1986), 70–95.

—— [AFA] 'Aristotle's function argument; a defence', *Ancient Philosophy* 8 (1988), 33–48.

Wieland, W., [1960] 'Aristotle's *Physics* and the problem of inquiry into principles', in *AA* i, 127–40. From *KS* 52 (1960–1), 206–19.

—— [1970] *Die aristotelische Physik*, 2nd edn., Göttingen, 1970.

—— [1975] 'The problem of teleology', in *AA* i, 140–60. From Wieland [1970].

Wiggins, D. R. P., [1967] *Identity and Spatio-Temporal Continuity*, Oxford, 1967.

—— [1980] *Sameness and Substance*, Oxford, 1980.

Wilkes, K. V., [1978] 'The good man and the good for man', in *EAE*, 341–57. From *Mind* 87 (1978), 553–71.

Williams, B. A. O., [1976] 'Persons, character, and morality', in *Moral Luck* (Cambridge, 1981), 3–19. From *The Identities of Persons*, ed. A. O. Rorty (Berkeley, 1976), 197–216.

—— [1980] 'Justice as a virtue', in *EAE*, 189–99.

Williams, C. J. F., [1965] 'Form and sensation', *SPAS* 39 (1965), 139–54.

—— [1982] (tr. and ed.) *Aristotle: De Generatione et Corruptione*, Oxford, 1982.

—— [1985] 'Aristotle's theory of descriptions', *PR* 94 (1985), 63–80.

Williams, D. C., [1958] 'Form and matter', *PR* 67 (1958), 291–312, 469–521.

Wilpert, P., [1940] 'Zum aristotelischen Wahrheitsbegriff', in Hager [1972], 106–21. From *Philosophisches Jahrbuch* 53 (1940), 3–16.

—— [1956] 'Aristoteles und die Dialektik', *KS* 48 (1956–7), 247–57.

Wilson, M. D., [1978] *Descartes*, London, 1978.

Wood, A. W., [1981] *Karl Marx*, London, 1981.

Wood, E. M., and Wood, N., [1978] *Class Ideology and Ancient Political Theory*, Oxford, 1978.

Woodfield, A., [1976] *Teleology*, Cambridge, 1976.

Woods, M. J., [1965] 'Identity and individuation', in *Analytical Philosophy (Second Series)*, ed. R. J. Butler (Oxford, 1965), 120–30.

—— [1967] 'Problems in *Metaphysics* vii 13', in Moravcsik [1967], 215–38.
—— [1974] 'Substance and essence in Aristotle', *PAS* 75 (1974–5), 167–80.
—— [1982] (tr. and ed.) *Aristotle: Eudemian Ethics i, ii, viii*, Oxford, 1982.
Wright, L, [1973] 'Functions', *PR* 82 (1973), 139–68.
—— [1976] *Teleological Explanations*, Berkeley, 1976.
Zeller, E., [1897] *Aristotle and the Earlier Peripatetics*, ET, 2 vols., London, 1897.

INDEX LOCORUM

'101' = § 101, '4n1' = Ch. 4 n. 1. The more important references are indicated by an asterisk.

A. ARISTOTLE

B. OTHER ANCIENT AUTHORS

CAG refers to volumes of *Commentaria in Aristotelem Graeca* (Berlin, 1882–1909)

INDEX NOMINUM

This list includes writers on Aristotle (apart from the Greek commentators), and recent philosophers. For other names see the General Index. More important references are indicated by an asterisk.

GENERAL INDEX

a priori argument 257; in ethics 16n20; in first philosophy 147; about soul 157
a priori conditions for perception 14n22
abstraction 171, 14n49, 8n43; and particular 12n4; and universal science 91, 92, 8n42
action; and practical syllogism 15n16; forced 182
activity, *v.* passivity 195
actuality; and activity 195; first 8, 127, 133, 135, 152, 202; and form 8, 121; of perceived object and perceiver 163, 164; prior to potentiality 128; *v.* process 125, 160, 11n20, 14n4; and soul 13n37; and substance 121; and unity 152
adjectives and non-substances 29, 33, 38, 3n29
aggression (*hubris*) 245, 249; and menial character 222; and wealth 21n23, 21n25
agreement, universal 184
akribeia see exactness
alteration *v.* actuality 125, 160
altruism 18n3; in community 18n28; extended 213, 228, 229, 232; and friendship 209; and moral virtues 208; and self-love 210; simple *v.* metaphysical 209, 18n4
always, and necessity 57, 5n17, 5n20
analogy, and common principles 79
analytics, education in 11
Anaxagoras 8n16
anger 239
animals, non-rational: act voluntarily 181; have appearance without belief 158, 168, 171, 177, 14n48; and appearance of good 174; cannot form character 181; desires of, and intemperance 238; incapable of rational action 15n29; lack decision 179; lack rational discourse 215, 18n18; locomotive *v.* stationary 14n2, 15n1; not members of city 180; and perception 159; and perception of time 178; soul 151, 158, 194, 16n38
Antiphon, on nature 53, 54, 55
aporia see puzzle
appearance (*phantasia*): and desire 174; and good 175; and memory 170; and perception 159, 166, 172, 14n3, 14n41; and reason 168, 177, 179–80, 14n50; and

teleological explanation 167, 171; and truth 168, 172; *see also* animals
appearances (*phainomena*): authoritative 13, 16, 23; cannot support universal science 79; conflict with 16, 23, 2n24; conflicting 21, 84, 102, 104, 9n20; correct 105; discovery of new 16; empirical *v.* dialectical 14, 19, 22, 45, 49, 75, 79, 157, 172, 13n1; equipollent 104; in ethics 184; explanation of 23, 2n75; and facts 14, 2n10; and four causes 55, 85; perceptual 15–17, 23, 77, 165, 2n13, 2n16; in progress towards intuition 78; proper (*oikeia*) 88, 2n17; theory should yield 16, 2n24, 2n27; treated as true 13
appetite (*epithumia*): *v.* decision 179; life of 218; *v.* rational desire 174–5; *v.* reason 178
arbitration, in dialectic 189, 16n18
archê see first principle
aristocracy, types of 20n17
Aristophanes 21n28
Aristotle: and Plato 5; silences 254; system 9, 259; works aimed at educated person 11
Aristotle's development 5, 25, 40, 49, 61, 82, 254–6, 1nn19–23, 3n45, 4n9, 7n19, 7n20; on causes 85, 8n10; on dialectic 148, 9n39; ethical works 16n5; on form 148; on justification 106; in *Metaphysics* 8n33; on parts of soul 15n2; on philosophy 83; on substance 65, 109, 144, 255, 10n15, 12n50; on universal science 96, 8n51
artifacts, forms of 156; *v.* organisms 50, 126, 130, 5n26; as substances 12n8
association *see* community
assumption (*hupothesis*) 86, 3n54, 7n14; Plato and Aristotle on 76, 7n11; sceptical attack on 106
assumption, of political system 188, 218, 20n16, 21n39
Athenian democracy 19n20
Atomism, on substance 65, 147, 12n30
attunement and soul 150–2; *see also* soul
autarkeia see self-sufficiency
authoritative (*kurion*) 12, 13, 16; *see also* appearances, common beliefs
automaton see chance
axioms *see* principles, common

oligarchy 243, 20n17; on ruling 234; stereotypes of 21n28; treatment of losers in 21n44; vices of 248, 246

Democritus 7, 44; ontology 96; on scepticism 102, 9n20; on soul 13n6; on substance 121, 12n30

demonstration: circular 68, 69; and common principles 79; and problem of criterion 105; *v.* dialectic 75, 80, 6n1, 7n10; not in ethics 184, 16n3; and experience 12; not for first principles 4, 72; when inappropriate 104–6; *v.* infinite regress 70; and intrinsic coincidents 32, 141; and justification 73; possible in mathematics, not in ethics 11; and natural priority 66; and philosophy 7n14; and preliminary questions 90; premisses of 74, 77; from proper principles 7n15; puzzles about 8n22; by refutation (elenctic) 97, 100, 9n15, 9n18; and science 4, 83, 88; and universal science 93

deontological theories 229

Descartes 2n40, 8n7; on history of philosophy 84, 262; on intuition 84, 7n17; on materialism 13n35; on soul and body 13n37

desire: and action 171; animal 203; and apparent good 175; and appearance 167; deliberative 15n22; and happiness 181; as mover 15n4; non-rational 17n4, 17n5; non-rational, and virtues 200, 204, 238, 17n4; object of 174; and perception 159, 173; and pleasure 173; rational 177, 178, 200; second-order 179; strength of 179; teleological role 158, 173; unity 174–6

desiring part, inseparable 173

determinism 120, 3n62, 5n15, 5n20; assumed 37; and teleology 55

dialectic: aims 49; arbitration 189; Aristotelian and Platonic 7n13; categories 26, 36 79; coherence 25, 165; and common beliefs 4, 34, 148; common places 2n47; and common principles 79, 88; constructive role of 3; counterintuitive theses 19, 21, 23; critical 88; debate 26, 1n15; and definitions 27; *v.* demonstration 75, 80, 6n1, 7n10; development in Aristotle's view 148, 9n39; difficulty in finding truth 172; and discovery 22; and educated person 11; and empirical argument 22, 24, 61, 148, 157, 162; encounter (*enteuxis*) 18; in ethics 9, 184, 192, 16n6; evaluates methods 11, 23; examination (*exetazein*) 18, 184, 2n38; and first philosophy 3n50; and form 54; studies form rather than matter 162; and four causes 50–1; and friendship 209; functions 18, 22, 2nn

35–6, 2n40; has no genus 79; use of grammatical arguments 26, 33; gymnastic function 18, 22, 35, 76, 80, 3n52; and history of philosophy 84, 262; use of homonymy 27; ideological function 189; induction in 22, 2n63; inquiry and justification 172; and intuition 75; role in justification 76, 78, 81; limitations 7, 36, 40, 43, 44, 50, 52, 53, 58, 62, 75, 77, 82, 94, 96; logical 26, 35, 44, 46, 79, 83, 92, 114, 2n48, 7n15, 8n48, 10n32; method 18, 83, 100, 153; in moral and political theory 9; use of multivocity 36, 8n37; and natural kinds 3n13; and new starts 22, 23, 26, 91, 95, 111, 119, 192, 256; non-empirical aspects 24; objections to use of common beliefs 261; and objective principles 7, 35, 255; peirastic 76, 97, 8n56; and philosophy 3, 6, 10, 8n56, 8n59; Platonic and Aristotelian 76, 1n13, 3n12; and PNC 100, 9n13; political implications 9; and positivism 81; and prejudice 9; and principles 3, 12, 18, 36, 46, 58, 62, 73, 75, 76, 83, 7n9, 7n10; questions (*problêmata*) 20, 26, 2n46; redirecting (*metabibazein*) 18, 2n39; *v.* science 8, 62, 71, 82; and science of being 8n59, 8n60; and second-order questions 94; superficial conclusions 39; tactics 100, 2n68; and teleology 154; terms in *Categories* 3n3; and construction of theory 22; theses in 19; and truth 189; and universal science 5, 94–5; universal and particular in 22, 2n62; and universal agreement 2n71; and virtues 248; *see also* common beliefs, puzzle

dialectic, pure 6, 7, 9, 37, 50, 51, 58, 59, 60, 61, 85, 91, 94, 97, 100, 106, 114, 119, 121, 146, 147, 3n50; in ethics 185, 16n20; in politics 189; on substance 109

dialectic, strong *v.* pure 8, 19, 25, 61, 85, 94, 95, 96, 97, 100, 106, 111, 114, 116, 148, 150, 154, 166, 176, 182, 186, 190, 194, 207, 217, 228, 236, 237, 239, 241, 252, 253, 257; and foundationalism 260; and human good 198; in moral and political argument 9, 190, 256 outside *Metaphysics* 9; and PNC 101; premisses of 101; on substance 109; uses of 258

difference: in being 45, 152, 13n21; difference, numerical *v.* qualitative 136–7, 12n17, 13n21, 13n26

differentia 44, 3n18, 3n46; anomaly 33; *v.* necessary property 3n47

disputes: about final good 192; in politics 189

doxa see belief

Printed in the United States
23562LVS00001B/21-24